332.45
G562W
v. 1

P9-DUB-856

Global Development Finance

Financing the Poorest Countries

ANALYSIS AND SUMMARY TABLES   2002

THE WORLD BANK

POINT LOMA NAZARENE UNIVERSITY
WITHDRAWN
RYAN LIBRARY

© 2002 The International Bank
for Reconstruction and Development / The World Bank
1818 H Street, NW
Washington, DC 20433

All rights reserved.

1 2 3 4 04 03 02

The findings, interpretations, and conclusions expressed here do not necessarily reflect the views of the Board of Executive Directors of the World Bank or the governments they represent.

The World Bank cannot guarantee the accuracy of the data included in this work.
The boundaries, colors, denominations, and other information shown on any map in this work do not imply on the part of the World Bank any judgment of the legal status of any territory or the endorsement or acceptance of such boundaries.

Rights and Permissions

The material in this work is copyrighted. No part of this work may be reproduced or transmitted in any form or by any means, electronic or mechanical, including photocopying, recording, or inclusion in any information storage and retrieval system, without the prior written permission of the World Bank. The World Bank encourages dissemination of its work and will normally grant permission promptly.

For permission to photocopy or reprint, please send a request with complete information to the Copyright Clearance Center, Inc., 222 Rosewood Drive, Danvers, MA 01923, USA, telephone 978-750-8400, fax 978-750-4470, www.copyright.com.

All other queries on rights and licenses, including subsidiary rights, should be addressed to the Office of the Publisher, World Bank, 1818 H Street NW, Washington, DC 20433, USA, fax 202-522-2422, e-mail pubrights@worldbank.org.

Cover design by W. Drew Fasick, Serif Design Group
Cover photo: Curt Carnemark, World Bank Photo Library

ISBN 0-8213-5085-4
ISSN 1020-5454

Table of Contents

Summary tables

Tables

Figures

Boxes

The Report Team

THIS REPORT WAS PREPARED BY THE ECOnomic Policy and Prospects Group, and drew on resources throughout the Development Economics Vice-Presidency, the Economic Policy Sector Board, the World Bank operational regions, the International Finance Corporation, and the Multilateral Investment Guarantee Association. The principal author was William Shaw, with direction by Uri Dadush. Chapter 1 was led by Hans Timmer, with contributions by John Baffes, Betty Dow, Caroline Farah, Fernando Martel Garcia, Bernard Hoekman, Robert Keyfitz, Annette I. De Kleine, Robert Lynn, Donald Mitchell, Mick Riordan, Virendra Singh, Shane Streifel, Dominique van der Mensbrugghe, and Bert Wolfe. Chapters 2–4 were largely prepared by the international finance team of the Economic Policy and Prospects Group, including Gholam Azarbayejani, Shweta Bagai, Maria Pia Iannarello, Himmat Kalsi, Eung Ju Kim, Aparna Mathur, Sanket Mohapatra, Shoko Negishi, Bilin Neyapti, Malvina Pollock, Dilip Ratha, and Jeff Ziarko. Additional contributions and background papers were provided by Dilek Aykut, Punam Chuhan, and Barry Eichengreen (chapter 2); Sara Calvo, Stijn Claessens, Susan Collins, Sebastian Edwards, Simon Evenett, Nagesh Kumar, Jeffrey Lewis, Deepak Mishra, Koh Naito, Claudine Ndayikengurutse, Andrew Powell, Jaya Prakash Pradhan, Felix Remy, Tony Thompson, Esen Ulgenerk, Aristomene Varoudakis, and Peter van der Veen (chapter 3); and Paul Collier, David Dollar, Robert Keyfitz, and Dan Morrow (chapter 4). Appendix 1 was prepared by Ibrahim Levent, appendix 2 by Eung Ju Kim, and appendix 3 by Malvina Pollock. Appendix 4 was prepared by Caroline Farah, Robert Keyfitz, Annette I. De Kleine, Robert Lynn,

Mick Riordan, and Virendra Singh, and benefited from the guidance of the Bank's regional chief economists. Appendix 5 was prepared by John Baffes, Betty Dow, Don Mitchell, and Shane Streifel. The financial flow and debt estimates were developed in a collaborative effort by Punam Chuhan, Nevin Fahmy, Shelley Fu, Ibrahim Levent, and Gloria Moreno of the Financial Data Team along with Himmat Kalsi, Eung Ju Kim, and Malvina Pollock of the Economic Policy and Prospects Group. The report was prepared under the general direction of Nicholas Stern.

Many others from inside and outside the Bank provided input, comments, guidance, and support at various stages of the report's publication. Gerard Caprio, Paula Donovan, Guy Pfeffermann, and Sanjivi Rajasingham were discussants at the Bankwide review. Sebastian Edwards, Shahrokh Fardoust, Jan Willem Gunning, Jim Hanson, and Stephen O'Connell provided extensive reviews of individual chapters. Comments were provided by Jehan Arulpragasam, Amarendra Bhattacharya, Jaime Biderman, Gerard Caprio, Haydee Celaya, James Emery, Alan Gelb, Ian Goldin, Charleen Gust, Daniel Kaufman, Jeni Klugman, Stefan Koeberle, Jacob Kolster, Richard Newfarmer, John Page, Enrique Rueda-Sabater, Sudhir Shetty, Philip Suttle, Axel van Trotsenburg, and Ulrich Zachau. Comments were also received from the International Monetary Fund. Mark Feige edited the report to highlight the main messages. Awatif Abuzeid and Katherine Rollins provided assistance to the team. Robert King managed dissemination and production activities by the Economic Policy and Prospects Group. Book design, editing, production, and dissemination were coordinated by the World Bank Publications team.

Preface

GLOBAL DEVELOPMENT FINANCE WAS formerly published as *World Debt Tables*. The new name reflects the report's expanded scope and greater coverage of private financial flows.

Global Development Finance consists of two volumes: *Analysis and Summary Tables* and *Country Tables*. *Analysis and Summary Tables* contains analysis and commentary on recent developments in international finance for developing countries. Summary statistical tables are included for selected regional and analytical groups comprising 148 countries.

Country Tables contains statistical tables on the external debt of the 136 countries that report public and publicly guaranteed debt under the Debtor Reporting System. Also included are tables of selected debt and resource flow statistics for individual reporting countries, as well as summary tables for regional and income groups.

For the convenience of readers, charts on pages x to xii summarize graphically the relation between debt stock and its components; the computation of flows, aggregate net resource flows, and aggregate net transfers; and the relation between net resource flows and the balance of payments. Exact definitions of these and other terms used in *Global Development Finance* are found in the Sources and Definitions section.

The economic aggregates presented in the tables are prepared for the convenience of users; their inclusion is not an endorsement of their value for economic analysis. Although debt indicators can give useful information about developments in debt-servicing capacity, conclusions drawn from them will not be valid unless accompanied by careful economic evaluation. The macroeconomic information provided is from standard sources, but many of them are subject to considerable margins of error, and the usual care must be taken in interpreting the indicators. This is particularly true for the most recent year or two, when figures are preliminary or subject to revision.

Acronyms and Abbreviations

CIS — Commonwealth of Independent States
CPPR — Country Portfolio Performance Review
DAC — Development Assistance Committee (of the OECD)
DCB — debt conversion bond
DDSR — debt and debt service reduction
DRS — Debtor Reporting System (of the World Bank)
EI — eligible interest bond
EMBI — Emerging Market Bond Index
EPZ — export processing zone
EU — European Union
FDI — foreign direct investment
FfD — Financing for Development
FLIRB — front-loaded interest reduction bond
FRN — floating-rate note
G-7 — Group of Seven (Canada, France, Germany, Italy, Japan, United Kingdom, United States)
GATS — General Agreement on Trade in Services
GDP — gross domestic product
GNI — gross national income
HIPC — heavily indebted poor countries
HIV — human immunodeficiency virus
IBRD — International Bank for Reconstruction and Development (of the World Bank Group)
ICT — information and communications technology
IDA — International Development Association (of the World Bank Group)
IFC — International Finance Corporation
IMF — International Monetary Fund
LIBOR — London interbank offered rate
LILIC — less indebted low-income country
LIMIC — less indebted middle-income country
M&A — mergers and acquisitions

Mercosur — Southern Cone Common Market (Argentina, Brazil, Paraguay, Uruguay; Bolivia and Chile are associate members)
MILIC — moderately indebted low-income country
MIMIC — moderately indebted middle-income country
MUV — manufacturing unit value
MYRA — multiyear rescheduling agreement
NAFTA — North American Free Trade Agreement
NBC — National Bank of Commerce (Tanzania)
NGO — nongovernmental organization
NIE — newly industrialized economy
NPV — net present value
OA — official aid
ODA — official development assistance
OECD — Organisation for Economic Co-operation and Development
OPEC — Organization of Petroleum Exporting Countries
PRSC — Poverty Reduction Support Credit
PRSP — Poverty Reduction Strategy Paper
REER — real effective exchange rate
SDR — special drawing right (of the International Monetary Fund)
SILIC — severely indebted low-income country
SIMIC — severely indebted middle-income country
SMEs — small and medium enterprises
U.N. — United Nations
UNCTAD — United Nations Conference on Trade and Development
URR — unremunerated reserve requirement
VAR — vector autoregression
WTO — World Trade Organization
XGS — exports of goods and services

Dollars are current U.S. dollars, unless otherwise specified.

Debt stock and its components

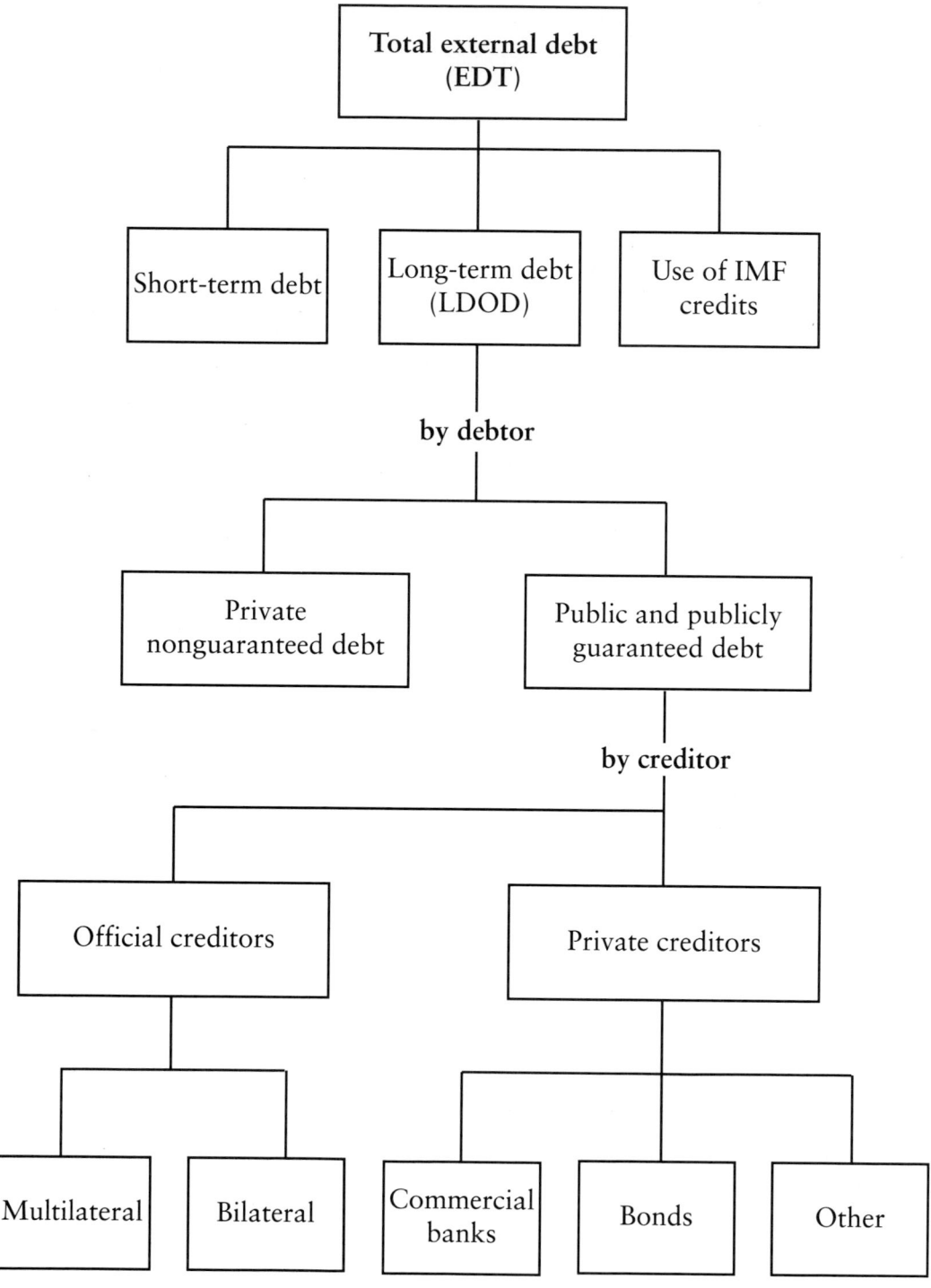

Aggregate net resource flows and net transfers (long-term) to developing countries

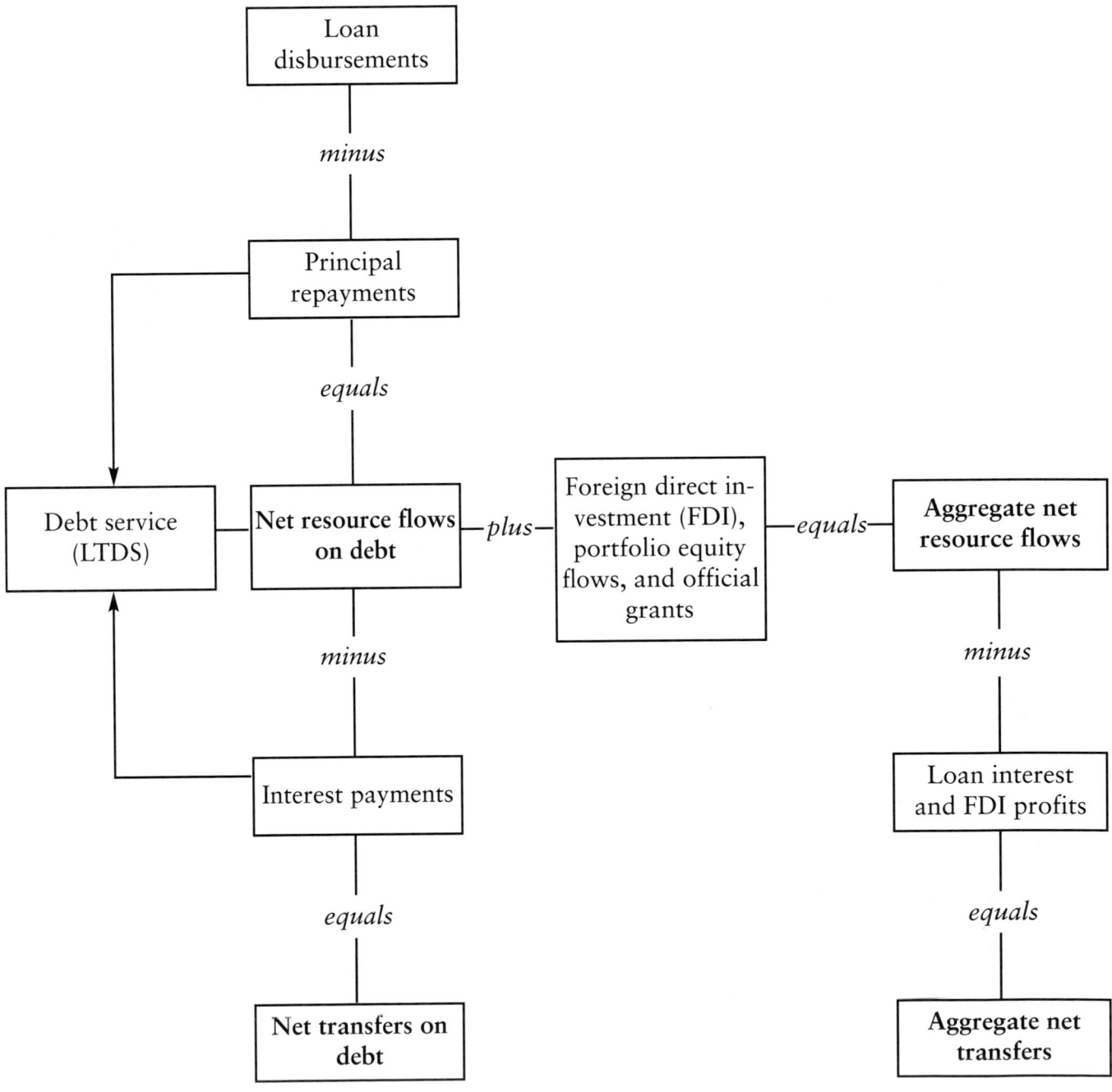

Note: Includes only loans with an original maturity of more than one year (long-term loans). Excludes IMF transactions.

Aggregate net resource flows (long-term) and the balance of payments

	Credits	*Debits*
Current account	• Exports of goods and services • Income received • Current transfers Including workers' remittances and private grants	• Imports of goods and services • Income paid • Current transfers
	• Official unrequited transfers (by foreign governments)	• Official unrequited transfers (by national government)
Capital and financial account	• Official unrequited transfers (by foreign governments) • Foreign direct investment (by nonresidents) (disinvestment shown as negative)	• Official unrequited transfers (by national government) • Foreign direct investment (by residents) (disinvestment shown as negative)
	• Portfolio investment (by nonresidents) (amortizations shown as negative) • Other long-term capital inflows (by nonresidents) (amortizations shown as negative)	• Portfolio investment (abroad by residents) (amortizations shown as negative) • Other long-term capital outflow (by residents) (amortizations shown as negative)
	• Short-term capital inflow	• Short-term capital outflow
Reserve account	Net changes in reserves	

☐ Aggregate net resource flows

▨ Net resource flows on debt (long-term)

Overview: International Finance and the Poorest Developing Countries

THE INTEGRATION OF DEVELOPING COUN-tries into the global economy increased sharply in the 1990s with improvements in their economic policies; the massive expansion of global trade and finance driven by technological innovations in communications, transport, and data management; and the lowering of barriers to trade and financial transactions. Many of the poorest developing countries[1] participated strongly in this process despite their limited access to capital markets. This report analyzes the interaction between the global expansion of finance and improvements in domestic policies in the poor countries over the 1990s, and the implications for growth and poverty reduction. Three main messages are developed: (a) a strong investment climate is critical to attracting foreign capital and using it productively; (b) poor countries' increasing integration in the global economy means that they face similar policy challenges as middle-income countries, including how to deal with capital mobility; and (c) achieving the Millennium Development Goals will require a substantial rise in aid flows, an increased allocation of aid to countries with good policies, and improvements in policies by both developing countries and donors.

A greater integration of poor countries and private capital—

The surge in foreign direct investment (FDI) flows and the decline in aid have transformed external finance to the poor countries. FDI flows to the poor countries rose from 0.4 percent of the gross domestic product (GDP) in the late 1980s to 2.8 percent in the late 1990s in response to the globalization of production and improvements in domestic policies (see pages 59–61). Aid to these countries fell by 20

percent in real terms over the same period. The poor countries now receive about the same level of FDI as middle-income countries, relative to the size of their economies. In addition, the global expansion of international banks coupled with the liberalization of domestic financial systems in the poor countries increased the average share of foreign bank assets to more than 40 percent of total assets, more than double the share of 1995 and comparable to that of many middle-income countries that have recently benefited from increased foreign bank participation (see pages 64–66).

—good policies and governance, along with strong institutions, are critical to using private flows productively

A rise in private flows can have a substantial impact on investment in the poor countries and, if productively used, on growth. However, the policy framework must be right. Improvements in the investment climate (a term that refers to the numerous ways in which government affects the productivity of investment, including policies, governance, and the strength of institutions) have boosted the impact of international financial transactions on productivity in the poor countries. Domestic firms in countries with strong investment climates are more able to absorb the foreign technology and skills that come with FDI (see pages 62–63). Better policies have enabled some poor countries to attract more diversified FDI flows—the share of countries that export natural resources in the poor countries' FDI dropped from half in 1991 to 20 percent toward the end of the decade. Countries that established the competitive conditions required to attract foreign banks experienced an improvement in the efficiency of their domestic banks and thus a decline in the cost of financial intermediation (see pages 66–69).

Poor countries face similar challenges from globalization as middle-income countries

The events of the past year underlined the risks of capital mobility for the middle-income emerging markets. The current global economic slowdown, exacerbated by the bursting of the high-tech bubble at the end of 2000 and the terrorist attacks in September 2001, is exceptionally deep and broad (see pages 7–11). Capital market flows once again proved to be procyclical: the growth slowdown in industrial countries reduced both emerging markets' export revenues and their access to external finance (see pages 32–36). By contrast, the level of FDI in 2001 was virtually unchanged from the previous year despite adverse global conditions, including a drop in global FDI flows (see pages 37–40). The crisis in Argentina illustrates how open capital accounts can compound the effects of unsustainable macroeconomic policies and high public sector debt, thus seriously complicating stabilization efforts (see pages 43–47).

The poor countries are also vulnerable to capital mobility. While most still impose restrictions on capital account transactions, controls have had only limited success in controlling capital outflows in the context of a weak investment climate, where domestic investment opportunities are limited and fears of confiscation or reduction in the value of assets provide considerable incentive to put money abroad (see pages 69–78). Poor countries with better than average policies (as measured by the World Bank) had more success in retaining domestic capital: a rough estimate of the stock of their capital outflows relative to GDP was about one-sixth the size in poor countries with worse than average policies. Capital outflows have been more volatile in the poor countries than in the middle-income countries, while volatility can be more costly (in terms of welfare) in poor countries because more people live close to subsistence and have little private insurance or public safety nets. Thus policymakers in poor countries need to recognize the potential impact of capital mobility on both stabilization policies and long-term development.

Good policies and strong governance are also key to improving aid effectiveness

Earlier empirical studies consistently found a weak relationship between aid and investment, with even less of an impact of aid on growth. However, more recent research shows that aid makes an effective contribution to growth and poverty reduction in countries with good economic policies, sound institutions, and strong governance, but has little effect in countries with poor policies. A doubling of aid flows would help ensure that developing countries achieve the Millennium Development Goals, provided that this aid is allocated to countries with good policies and large numbers of poor people (pages 99–100).

Aid continued to decline in 2001, and the prospects for a substantial rise in the medium term are limited (pages 90–94). Most countries with good policies can continue to absorb additional aid resources without seriously impairing the effectiveness of that aid (see pages 96–99). Aid does not, in general, increase the volatility of government resources, and appropriate policies can ensure that aid does not contribute to inflationary pressures or cause excessive exchange-rate appreciation. It is true that even in many countries with good policies, lack of administrative capacity lowers the marginal productivity of aid as aid levels rise. However, recent research indicates that aid levels to most countries with strong economic programs are well below the threshold where aid becomes ineffective.

Better aid policies by donors also contribute to poverty reduction

There is evidence that donors have made progress in improving their own policies, through increasing resources to debt relief for good performers, easing complex administrative requirements that can strain limited government capacity, and reducing the share of tied aid (see pages 101–104). Modifications of adjustment assistance have helped to preserve the use of conditionality in channeling aid resources to good performers and supporting the credibility of government policies, while ensuring adequate government flexibility and domestic stakeholder commitment to the program. Here also, recipient government policies are key: strong leadership and effective administration by the government can help promote aid coordination and make it easier for donors to adopt more flexible policies.

Note

1. The poor countries are defined to represent developing countries with relatively low per capita income and almost no access to international capital markets. The group includes all IDA-only countries plus a few blend countries that have had few IBRD loans over the past few years. The countries included are Afghanistan, Albania, Angola, Armenia, Bangladesh, Benin, Bhutan, Bolivia, Burkina Faso, Burundi, Cambodia, Cameroon, Cape Verde, Central African Republic, Chad, Comoros, the Democratic Republic of Congo, the Republic of Congo, Côte d'Ivoire, Djibouti, Eritrea, Ethiopia, The Gambia, Georgia, Ghana, Guinea, Guinea-Bissau, Guyana, Haiti, Honduras, Kenya, Kiribati, the Kyrgyz Republic, the Lao People's Democratic Republic, Lesotho, Liberia, Madagascar, Malawi, Maldives, Mali, Mauritania, Moldova, Mongolia, Mozambique, Myanmar, Nepal, Nicaragua, Niger, Nigeria, Pakistan, Rwanda, Samoa, São Tomé and Principe, Senegal, Sierra Leone, Solomon Islands, Somalia, Sri Lanka, Sudan, Tajikistan, Tanzania, Togo, Tonga, Uganda, Vanuatu, Vietnam, Republic of Yemen, Zambia, and Zimbabwe. These countries' average per capita income is under $500 per year compared with $2,900 for other developing countries. And most of them are small; only Pakistan, Bangladesh, Nigeria, Vietnam, Ethiopia, and the Democratic Republic of Congo have more than 50 million people.

Challenges for Developing Countries during the Coming Global Recovery

THE CURRENT GLOBAL ECONOMIC SLOW-down is exceptionally deep and broad. Global growth in 2001, at 1.2 percent, was 2.7 percentage points lower than in 2000 (figure 1.1). In the last 40 years the deceleration in gross domestic product (GDP) was sharper only in 1974, during the first oil crisis. The current slowdown is also broad in that the deceleration is equally rapid for industrial countries and developing countries. The slowdown in economic activity coincides with an unprecedented 14 percentage point deceleration of world trade, from record growth of 13 percent in 2000 to a 1 percent decline in 2001 (table 1.1). However, contrary to many earlier downturns, inflationary pressures remained very subdued and this allowed monetary authorities to loosen their policies substantially.

The bursting of the high-tech bubble at the end of 2000 and the terrorist attacks in September 2001 made the deceleration of the global economy so exceptionally sharp. The unpredictable character of these events made it difficult to anticipate the depth of the downturn. Nevertheless, after the terrorist attacks the expectations—a deeper recession and a delay of the recovery by one or two quarters—appear to be materializing.[1] Several of the strong market reactions to the terrorist attacks have been reversed and signs of a recovery in the United States and the high-tech sectors have started to mount.

Even during this unusually synchronized downturn, the intensity and character of the economic malaise differ across countries, sectors, and income groups. Especially hard hit are countries dependent on commodity exports, with many commodity prices at historical lows; highly indebted emerging economies, because private investors have reduced their exposure in emerging markets in reaction to increased uncertainty, reduced value of portfolios in industrial countries, and increased default provisions; high-tech sectors, with many firms decimated after the high-tech bubble burst; and tourism industries, suffering from the aftermath of the terrorist attacks. As in every severe downturn, poor people pay a high price. Without buffers or safety nets to rely upon, their ability to satisfy basic needs is immediately at stake when incomes decline.

The current sharp deceleration in economic activity largely follows a typical investment and inventory cycle, even if it was triggered by other factors, such as the bursting of the high-tech bubble or the terrorist attacks. Likewise, the standard investment cycle is expected to play a major role in recovery. The steep decline in investment and stock building in recent quarters carries seeds for a forceful cyclical recovery. As capital stocks and inventories are adjusted downward to reflect lower growth expectations, the decline in investment and stock-building tends to become less steep and activity starts to rebound. The rebound will be further fueled by aggressive monetary and fiscal stimulus, especially in the United States. The current synchronism of the cycles in different parts of the world will likely be reflected in a strong global recovery, even if recovery in individual countries is not exceptionally vigorous.

The economic consequences of the terrorist attacks probably delayed this rebound by about two quarters, implying strong growth in the second half of 2002. Weak growth in the second half of 2001 and the first half of 2002 is expected to keep global growth in 2002 at 1.3 percent, slightly above growth rates for 2001. This outlook implies a downward adjustment since the publica-

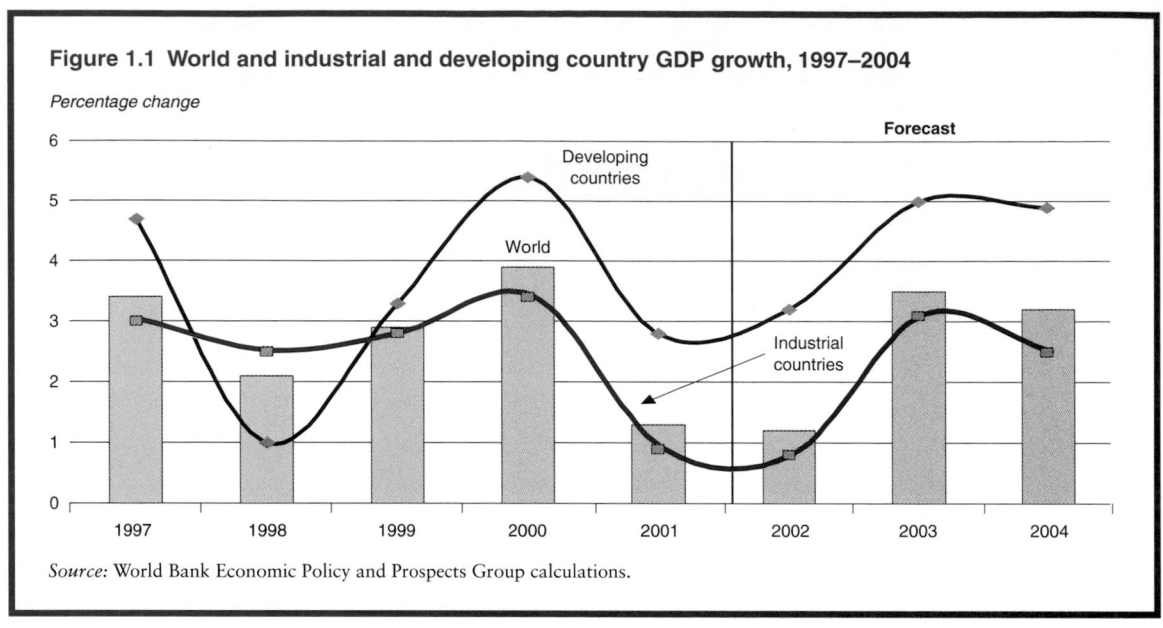

Figure 1.1 World and industrial and developing country GDP growth, 1997–2004

Percentage change

Source: World Bank Economic Policy and Prospects Group calculations.

tion of *Global Economic Prospects 2002* (World Bank 2001), mainly reflecting more pessimistic views on Japan and Latin America. World trade could very well decline in 2002 for a second year in a row. However, an anticipated acceleration in the second half of 2002 will likely result in a strong recovery in annual growth for 2003. Although global GDP growth in 2003 of 3.6 percent would fall short of the strong 3.9 percent performance of 2000, advances in world trade are expected to breach 8 percent.

Not all economies will benefit immediately from the robust global rebound. Argentina's financial strains have resulted in defaults and devaluation, heralding a protracted period of painful adjustment; but there is also hope that a new base can be created for resumption of long-term growth. As financial weakness in Japan has worsened during the global downturn, a recovery of the external environment can probably not avert, but only alleviate, structural adjustments. Commodity exporters, including oil producers, have experienced large terms-of-trade losses that will limit their short-term ability to rebound. The speed of recovery toward normal trends in tourism is uncertain, leaving the prospects cloudy for many of the developing countries that are heavily dependent on this revenue source.

On average, however, developing countries' growth is expected to be robust in 2003 and 2004, reaching 5 percent per year. A strong recovery seems achievable in the absence of additional adverse shocks to the global economy. Such a recovery would be supported by modest inflation—median inflation in the developing world is around 5.5 percent, only half the average rate during the 1990s—relatively low interest rates after the recent easing of U.S. monetary policy, rapidly growing import demand in the industrial countries, and a slight rebound in real commodity prices. Exporters of high-tech products are likely to benefit more than average from this recovery. The main risks to this favorable outlook are to be found in financial markets. The fragile Japanese banking sector may trigger more adverse developments than is currently assumed, and the full complement of ramifications stemming from financial crises in Argentina and Turkey remains uncertain.

Many developing countries, even those that currently do not have large financial imbalances, face difficult challenges. The global downturn and country-based policy responses to slowing growth have reversed the trend of declining fiscal deficits in many countries, and deterioration of deficits tend to persist well after economic growth has returned to normal levels. Some oil exporters—such as Nigeria, the República Bolivariana de Venezuela, and Indonesia—are particularly vulnerable, as oil prices are expected to continue their downward trend. Furthermore, the global downturn implies a deterioration of the current account for

Table 1.1 Global conditions affecting growth in developing countries and world GDP growth
(percentage change from previous year, except interest rates and oil prices)

	2000	Current Estimate 2001	Current Forecasts 2002	2003	2004	GEP 2002 forecasts 2001	2002	2003
Global conditions								
World trade (volume)	13.1	−0.8	1.8	8.3	7.3	1.0	4.0	10.2
Inflation (consumer prices)								
G-7 OECD countries[a][b]	1.9	1.7	0.9	1.6	1.8	1.8	1.4	1.5
United States	3.4	2.8	1.5	2.4	2.6	2.8	2.2	2.3
Commodity prices (nominal dollars)								
Commodity prices, except oil (dollars)	−1.3	−9.1	1.3	7.3	6.4	−8.9	1.6	8.1
Oil price (dollars, weighted average),								
dollars a barrel	28.2	24.4	20.0	21.0	19.0	25.0	21.0	20.0
Oil price, percent change	56.2	−13.7	−17.9	5.0	−9.5	−11.3	−16.0	−4.8
Manufactures export unit value (dollars)[c]	−2.0	−1.4	−0.5	3.6	3.7	−4.6	4.0	4.4
Interest rates								
LIBOR, 6 months (dollars, percent)[c]	6.7	3.3	2.3	4.0	4.6	3.6	2.8	3.0
EURIBOR, 6 months (euro, percent)[d]	4.5	4.0	3.0	4.0	4.2	4.1	3.3	3.3
World GDP (growth)	3.9	1.2	1.3	3.6	3.1	1.3	1.6	3.9
High-income countries	3.5	0.8	0.8	3.2	2.6	0.9	1.1	3.5
OECD countries	3.4	0.9	0.8	3.1	2.5	0.9	1.0	3.4
United States	4.1	1.1	1.3	3.7	3.1	1.1	1.0	3.9
Japan	2.2	−0.8	−1.5	1.7	1.1	−0.8	0.1	2.4
Euro Area	3.5	1.4	1.2	3.3	2.7	1.5	1.3	3.6
Non-OECD countries	6.6	−1.0	1.7	4.4	4.0	0.6	3.2	5.7
Developing countries	5.4	2.8	3.2	5.0	4.9	2.9	3.7	5.2
East Asia and Pacific	7.4	4.6	5.2	6.9	6.5	4.6	4.9	6.8
Europe and Central Asia	6.4	2.2	3.2	4.3	4.0	2.1	3.0	4.2
Latin America and the Caribbean	3.8	0.6	0.5	3.8	3.8	0.9	2.5	4.5
Middle East and North Africa	4.2	3.1	2.7	3.3	3.3	3.4	2.9	3.6
South Asia	4.0	4.3	4.9	5.3	5.2	4.5	5.3	5.5
Sub-Saharan Africa	3.1	2.6	2.6	3.6	3.6	2.7	2.7	3.9
Memorandum items								
East Asian crisis–affected countries[e]	7.1	2.3	3.5	5.9	5.5	2.3	3.4	5.4
Transition countries of ECA	6.2	4.4	3.4	4.0	4.0	4.0	3.1	3.8
Developing countries,								
Excluding the transition countries,	5.3	2.6	3.2	5.2	5.0	3.1	3.8	5.5
Excluding China and India	5.1	1.8	2.2	4.4	4.2	1.9	2.9	4.5

a. The G-7 countries are Canada, France, Germany, Italy, Japan, the United Kingdom, and the United States.
b. Unit value index of manufactures exports for G-5 countries (G-7 minus Canada and Italy) to developing countries, expressed in dollars.
c. London interbank offered for dollars.
d. Interbank offered rate for euros.
e. Indonesia, the Republic of Korea, Malaysia, the Philippines, and Thailand.
Source: World Bank Economic Policy and Prospects Group, February 2002 forecast; *Global Economic Prospects (GEP) 2002* projections of October 2001.

many developing countries. Together with limited availability of international private capital, this could generate new financial strains, which could impede further recovery.

Recession and recovery in the industrial world

The United States, Japan, Germany, and several smaller industrial countries in Europe entered into—or came close to—recession in the course of 2001. Aggregate annual growth in the industrial world decelerated from 3.4 percent in 2000 to 0.9 percent in 2001. With almost all recessions having started in the second half of 2001, it is unlikely that aggregate annual growth in 2002 will exceed 2001 growth, even with a solid rebound in the second half of the year. Indeed, measured growth is likely to decline further, to only 0.8 percent. The advance in output in 2003, in contrast, is expected to return to 3.1 percent, assuming that no major crisis evolves from the fragilities in the Japanese banking system or other sources of tension in the forecast. Growth in 2004 is assumed to fall back to near its long-term trend of 2.5 percent.

In the fall of 2000 the downturn still had characteristics of a soft landing, with cyclical corrections that did not suggest one of the most severe decelerations in economic activity in decades. However, in two steps—the first initiated by the burst of the high-tech bubble at the end of 2000, and the second by terrorist attacks in September 2001—the global economy decelerated further.

A three-phase slowdown—

At the root of the simultaneous economic downturn in all major industrial countries was a severe slowdown in manufacturing sectors (figure 1.2). That slowdown went through three phases. The *first phase* began in the middle of 2000 with the slowdown in the United States, which was partly a reaction to the tightening of monetary policy by the Federal Reserve Board, a move designed to slow an economy that had been growing well above capacity. Production of traditional durables declined, and production in high-tech sectors started to slow. The latter was partly a reaction to the high-tech investment bubble that had been swelling since 1998, especially in the United States, and then burst. Japan and the European economies clearly lagged in the downturn.

The *second phase* began at the end of 2000 when the recession in durable goods had begun to bottom out, but the high-tech bubble burst yet further, forcing stock markets into sharp decline while high-tech production started to fall at dramatic rates (figure 1.3). Japanese output, highly dependent on high-tech exports, declined precipitously. The fall in exports and the accompanying drop in equity prices exacerbated the bad-loan problems in the Japanese banking sector, which could not escape the spiral of defaults and thin margins in a deflationary environment. In Europe, signals were mixed in the beginning of this phase. Since European growth in 2000 hardly exceeded its long-term capacity trend, the internal cyclical forces were much weaker than in the United States. However, the slowdown in world trade affected the manufacturing sectors, while the European telecommunications industry shared the fate of the global high-tech sectors as future profitability was suddenly reassessed. The European Central Bank hesitated to ease monetary policy in the face of inflationary pressures originating from temporary increases in food prices due to livestock diseases, high oil prices, and a weak euro. The slowdown, first apparent in Germany, gradually spread to several other European countries.

The terrorist attacks in September 2001 marked the start of the *third phase*. At that time the recessions in manufacturing production had more

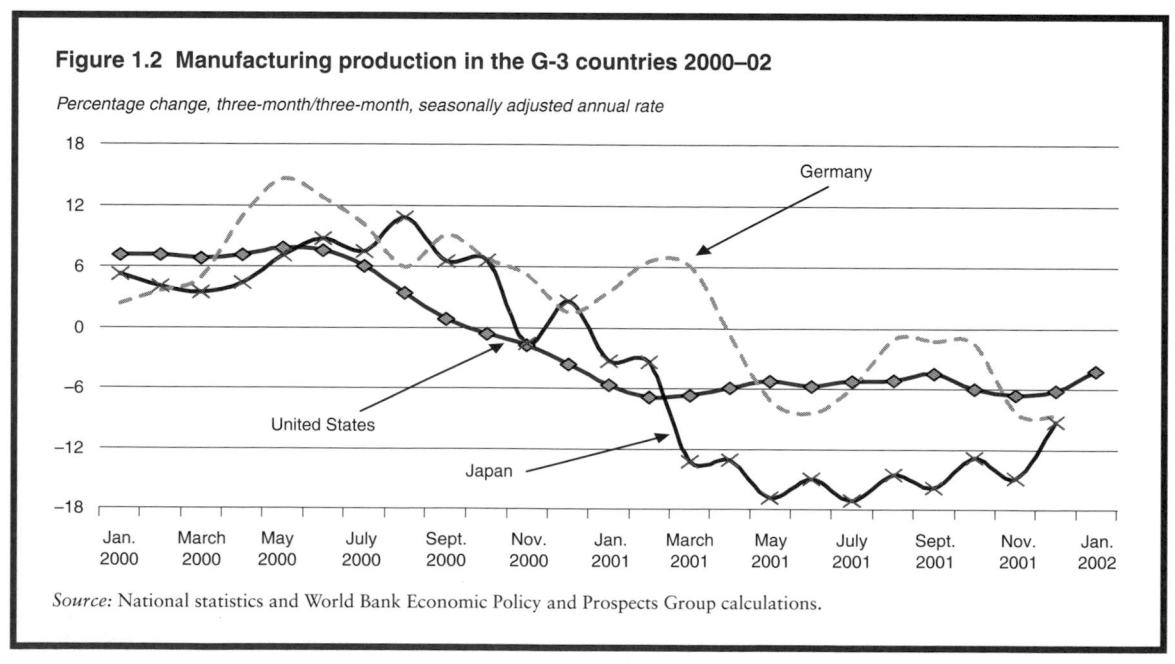

Figure 1.2 Manufacturing production in the G-3 countries 2000–02

Percentage change, three-month/three-month, seasonally adjusted annual rate

Source: National statistics and World Bank Economic Policy and Prospects Group calculations.

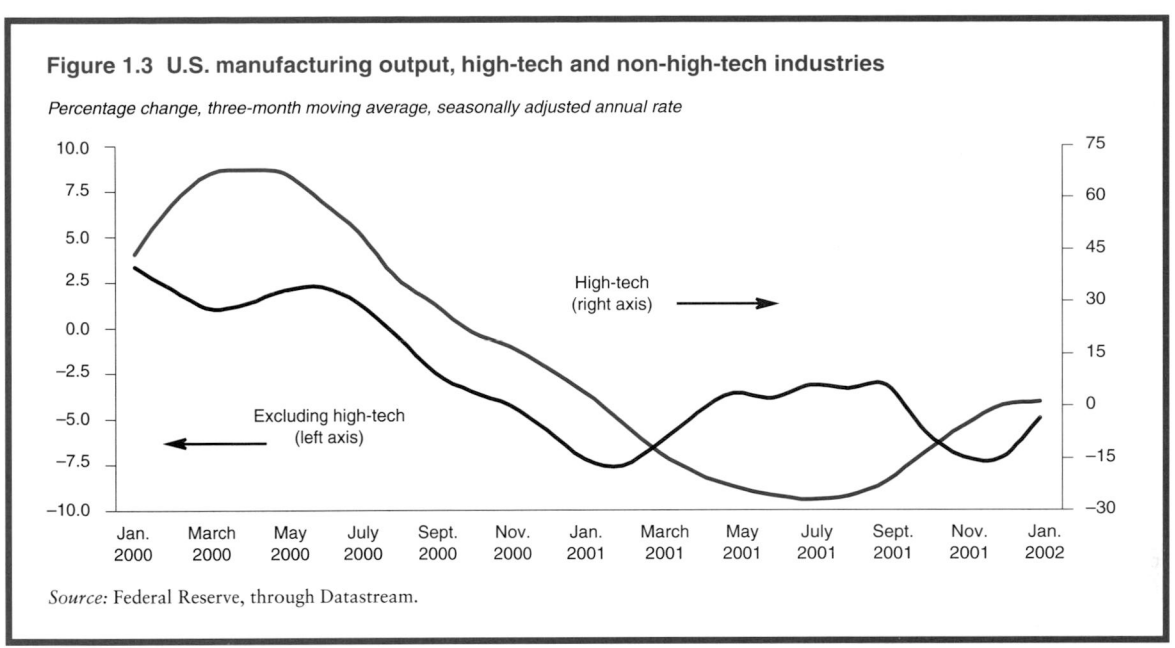

Figure 1.3 U.S. manufacturing output, high-tech and non-high-tech industries

Percentage change, three-month moving average, seasonally adjusted annual rate

Source: Federal Reserve, through Datastream.

or less bottomed out, albeit for Japan and the United States at still large declining rates. The period immediately after the terrorist attacks was characterized by an extraordinary, but temporary, loss of consumer confidence and deterioration of business sentiment (figure 1.4). Equity prices plummeted 15 percent immediately after the attacks, spreads on junk bonds jumped 200 basis points within weeks, and commodities prices fell 7 percent within one month. Industrial production dipped once again, although it seemed that the high-tech cycle was less affected (figure 1.3). While these first market reactions were reversed within one quarter, economic recovery will probably be delayed by about two quarters as a result of supply disruptions and shaken confidence.

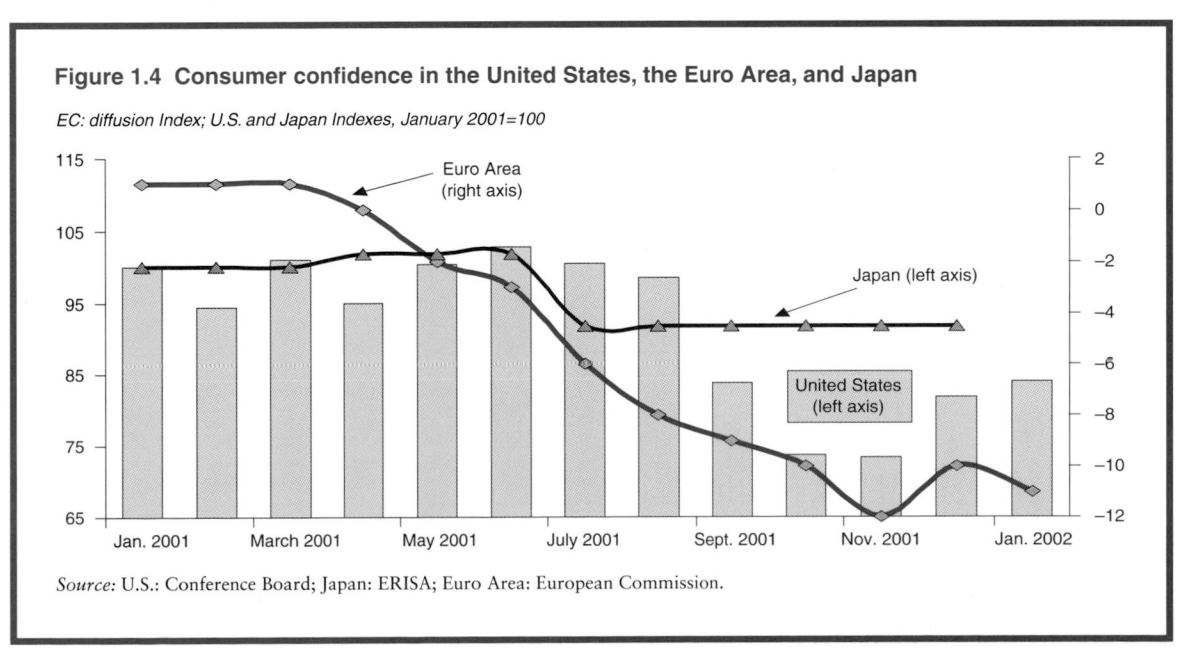

Figure 1.4 Consumer confidence in the United States, the Euro Area, and Japan

EC: diffusion Index; U.S. and Japan Indexes, January 2001=100

Source: U.S.: Conference Board; Japan: ERISA; Euro Area: European Commission.

The prolongation and deepening of the downturn in the aftermath of the terrorist attacks made this recession comparable in intensity to the recessions of the early 1980s and 1990s, at least for industrial countries. Although the downturn in individual countries has not necessarily been as deep as during those two severe recessions, its simultaneous character made the current slowdown especially sharp for the industrial world as a whole. Experience during the last decades suggests that the turning point to positive growth will probably be triggered by the investment cycle, and that recessions of this magnitude tend to result in a deterioration of fiscal balances that typically lasts for three or more years. The sharp fall in private spending implies an improvement of the current account in the short run, despite increased fiscal deficits. The mirror image of the industrial countries' reduced current account deficit is the tendency of current account surpluses to narrow and deficits to widen in the developing world. The remainder of this section will discuss triggers of turning points in economic activity and the behavior of government balances in the industrial world. Increased trade linkages have made developing countries more dependent on these turning points in the industrial countries' business cycles, and as the current account surpluses of developing countries start to decline, a deterioration of government balances could increase tensions in global capital markets.

—largely driven by investment cycles
The deep recessions and subsequent recoveries in the United States during the last three decades were primarily the reflection of inventory and investment cycles.[2] Table 1.2 summarizes the main sources of change in GDP growth at the beginning and end of recessions. In the majority of U.S. recessions since the 1970s, changes in investment or inventories were the main source of changes in GDP growth, both at the start and close of each recession. With the structural decline in inventories through the use of new technologies and just-in-time supply systems, the inventory cycle, still dominant in the 1970s and 1980s, has become less important. The investment cycle was the main contributing factor in the current recession, and investment will likely be the force that brings GDP growth out of negative territory. As capital stocks adjust downward, the decline in investment rates will soften, reversing the downward spiral.

Table 1.2 highlights the fact that net exports have been a relatively more important factor determining the dynamics of recessions in Europe

Table 1.2 Initiating factors: turning points to downturn and recovery in OECD recessions
(changes in contribution to growth, at seasonally adjusted annualized rates)

	Downturn		Contributions	Recovery		Contributions	
	Starting quarter	Change in GDP growth	Principal sources	Ending quarter	Change in GDP growth	Principal sources	
United States							
Mid-1970s	Q1, 1974	−6.4	S: −4.6 C: −1.6	Q2, 1975	6.0	S: 3.6	I: 1.9
Early 1980s	Q4, 1981	−9.5	S: −4.8 C: −3.2	Q4, 1982	3.8	I: 1.4	C: 1.3
Early 1990s	Q4, 1990	−2.8	C: −1.5 I: −1.0	Q1, 1991	2.8	C: 2.1	S: 0.9
Current	Q3, 2001	−1.3	I: −1.1 C: −0.7	—	—	—	—
Japan							
Mid-1970s	Q3, 1973	−6.1	S: −3.3 I: −3.3	Q1, 1975	5.5	C: 2.4	I: 2.3
Early 1990s	Q2, 1993	−3.5	G: −1.7 S: −0.8	Q3, 1992	1.0	S: 0.9	G: 0.6
Asia crisis–present	Q2, 1997	−7.3	C: −7.1 I: −1.5	—	—	—	—
Europe							
Mid-1970s	Q4, 1974	−3.6	S: −3.8 C: −1.6	Q3, 1975	3.4	I: 1.4	S: 1.4
Early 1980s	Q2, 1980	−3.5	C: −2.1 I: −1.4	Q3, 1980	1.2	X: 0.8	I: 0.5
Mid-1990s	Q2, 1992	−2.4	I: −1.0 C: −0.9	Q2, 1993	2.0	C: 2.1	I: 0.7
Current	Q2, 2001	−1.7	X: −1.9 C: −0.6	—	—	—	—

— Not available.
Notes: GDP growth and contributions by expenditure component are expressed as the *change* in GDP growth and contributions to growth, measured (1) for "downturn": average of one or two quarters prior to the turning point, and (2) for "recovery": turning point to the average of two quarters following. Principal sources: C=private consumption, G=government expenditures, I=gross fixed investment, S=change in stocks, X=net exports of goods and services.
Source: World Bank Economic Policy and Prospects Group calculations.

than in the United States. The inventory cycle has never been as important in Europe as in the United States. This could reflect the less pronounced domestic business cycles in Europe, which has more automatic stabilizers in place, as well as greater regional diversity in monetary and fiscal policies. Note that the recent downturn in Europe was triggered mainly by swings in international trade, rather than by changes in domestic consumption, investment, or inventories. It is thus likely that the international trade cycle will also be an important ingredient of the recovery, in which case Europe will lag behind the United States in the rebound.

Japan is the odd one out in this picture. Recessions were avoided during the 1980s due to strong, continuous growth in investment and productivity. However, investment growth has been declining since the early 1990s, when structural growth rates fell, financial bubbles burst, and problems in the banking sector began to mount. This trend was so strong that it overwhelmed the tendency for investment to experience sharp cyclical changes. As a result, investment failed to play the standard role of initiating a turning point in economic activity. This is one reason why Japan staggered from one recession into another during the 1990s, and why it is not easy to identify a source that could reverse the current downturn.

Policy is supportive, but will operate with some delay—

Policies will play an important role in the recovery of the industrial countries. Monetary policy has now turned highly expansionary in the United States, and with some delay, has eased in the Euro Area. In Japan the economy remains in a state of deflation (consumer prices have declined for the past two years), and interest rates can hardly fall any further. Given the lack of headroom for alternative action, the Bank of Japan initiated a program of liquidity injections—potentially weakening the yen as a way to combat deflation and stimulate exports.

The effects of monetary easing are likely to be felt with some lag, and should provide a needed fillip to demand for consumer durables and housing across the Organisation for Economic Cooperation and Development (OECD) countries. But there is concern that the eventual impact of lower interest rates on business investment may be limited. In particular, investor risk aversion has

risen significantly, depressing investment in high-risk assets, especially in the United States. In Japan, financial markets are burdened by the accumulated debt of failed businesses, which has reached ¥50 trillion ($420 billion) since 1999, of which ¥16 trillion accrued during 2001. This has exacerbated the "bad loan" problems of the commercial banking system, adding new nonperforming assets almost as quickly as "old" nonperforming loans are written off. Under these circumstances, additional Bank of Japan liquidity is unlikely to greatly increase the willingness of Japanese commercial banks to lend, and signs of a credit crunch for the small-business sector may be emerging.

Fiscal policy also offers promise for boosting growth, especially in the United States. The U.S. Congress approved more than $40 billion in emergency and industry-support funds in the immediate aftermath of September 11. Moreover, tax reductions enacted earlier in 2001 will continue to be implemented over the next few years. In the Euro Area, automatic stabilizers will tend to increase public deficits, but the constraints inherent in the Stability and Growth Pact of the European Union could limit government support for slowing economies.[3] In Japan debate continues regarding the degree and nature of supplemental budget programs, against the background of Prime Minister Junichiro Koizumi's stated limits to bond-market funding of such efforts. On balance, fiscal stimulus is likely to be a significant additional driving force for recovery in the major industrial economies, particularly for the United States.

However useful and needed the fiscal stimulus may be in the short term, increased deficits could become a burden in the medium run. Historically, deficits that originated in severe downturns tend to last well beyond the recovery in economic activity (figure 1.5). After the brief and steep recession following the first oil crisis in the mid-1970s, the average fiscal deficit (as a share of GDP) in the OECD turned from positive to negative, never again to return to positive territory. After the second oil crisis, it took a decade for the deficits to come back close to precrisis levels, and after the Gulf War this took five years. The stubbornness of deficits is partly due to the vicious circle of higher debt and increasing debt service, and partly due to the temptation to see recessions as unique, temporary phenomena and a subsequent recovery as a permanent improvement. While the deterioration of government

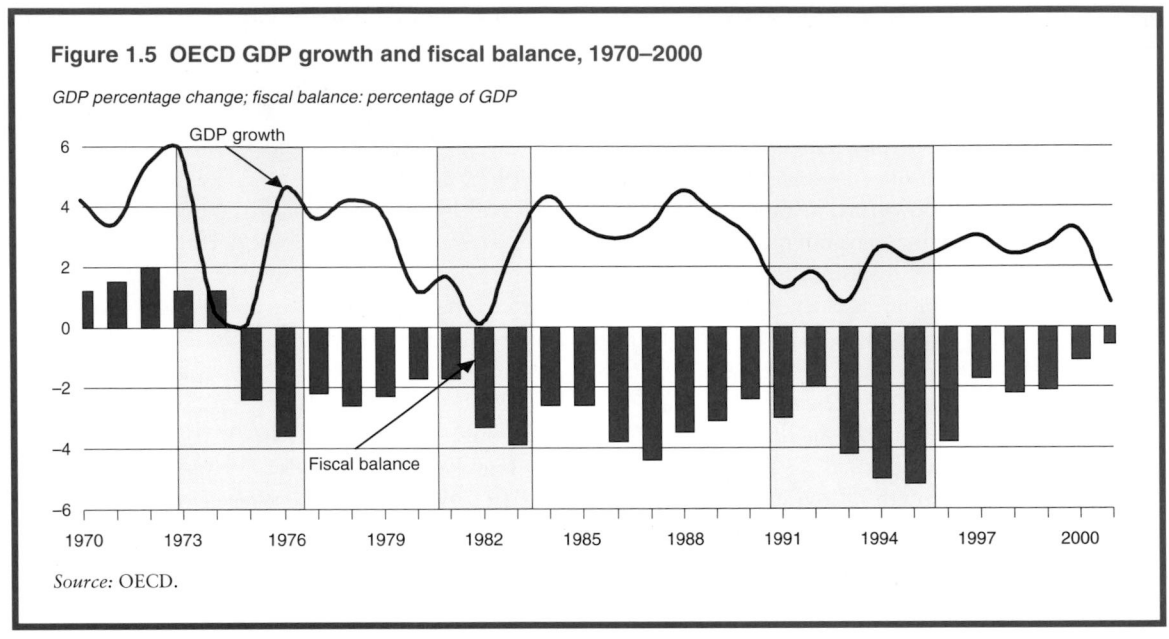

Figure 1.5 OECD GDP growth and fiscal balance, 1970–2000

GDP percentage change; fiscal balance: percentage of GDP

Source: OECD.

deficits is often abrupt, the restoration tends to be smoothed out over time. Of course, many regional differences and different policy decisions determined the trend in the average deficit. Nevertheless, the historical pattern of persistent deficits is clear, and the main challenge in the current recession is to keep the necessary stimulus confined to the short run. In the medium run, improvement in the industrial countries' fiscal deficits will facilitate a resumption of capital flows toward developing countries.

—auguring a strong recovery in 2003

Taking into account the likely impact of the inventory and investment cycles, and the policy responses, we anticipate that the United States will come out of the recession in the beginning of 2002 and European countries will follow one or two quarters later, but Japan will hardly reach positive growth during the year—resulting in annual 2002 growth rates of 1.3, 1.2, and –1.5 percent respectively for these countries (figure 1.6). As industrial production, investment, and global trade pick up rapidly over the course of the year, 2003 is expected to provide a much rosier picture, with GDP growth climbing to 3.7, 3.3, and 1.7 percent in the three industrial centers. If banking problems in Japan remain unsolved, a relapse into low or negative growth after a temporary export-led recovery in that country cannot be excluded.

The U.S. current account deficit, which already diminished to $420 billion in 2001 from $445 billion in 2000, as a result of recession and falling oil prices, is expected to deteriorate only modestly over the next two years. The adjustment in 2002 and coming years is expected to be accompanied by a gradual weakening of the dollar and a widening of current account deficits in some Euro-

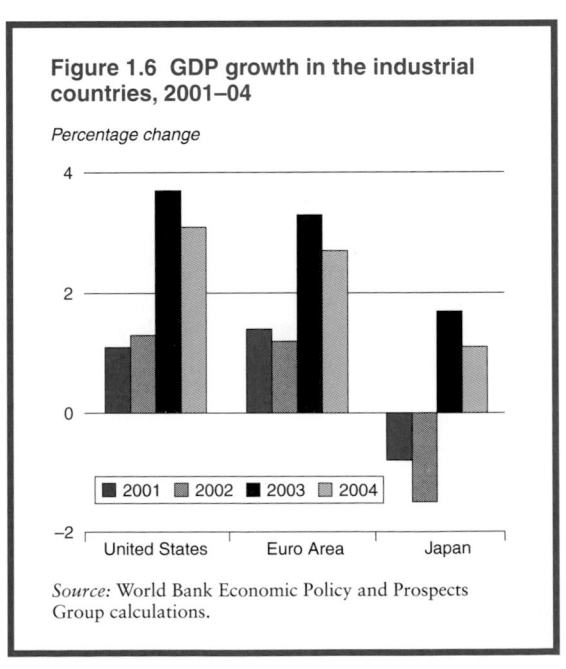

Figure 1.6 GDP growth in the industrial countries, 2001–04

Percentage change

Source: World Bank Economic Policy and Prospects Group calculations.

pean countries. The Japanese current account surplus declined substantially in 2001 because the latest recession in Japan was driven mainly by a decline in exports instead of a deceleration in investment. Because Japanese investment is also not likely to recover strongly in the near future, the current account surplus is expected to widen again when world trade, and Japanese exports, rebound. The current account deficit for the industrial countries as a whole is expected to decline from $280 billion in 2000 to $240 billion by 2004, most of the improvement being realized in the near term. The mirror image of this development is a reduced current account surplus in the developing countries, partly reflecting declining oil prices and partly reflecting reduced export opportunities.

Bust and boom in world trade

World trade, already undergoing the sharpest deceleration on record, suffered additional setbacks following the terrorist attacks of September 11. These events delayed the expected recovery in output, which will in turn delay the rebound in merchandise trade for one or two quarters. Moreover, security concerns disrupted trade flows, as did increased shipping and insurance costs, although medium-term effects arising from these developments are more uncertain. The attacks also reduced developing countries' revenues from international tourism. However, longer-run prospects for global trade have improved after a first important step toward a new round of trade negotiations was made at the World Trade Organization (WTO) ministerial conference in Doha, Qatar, in November 2001.

The record deceleration of merchandise trade growth in 2001 was due to a collapse in high-tech markets and recessions in the manufacturing sectors of the industrial countries. Import demand declined sharply in the United States and Japan during the first half of 2001, while European import demand fell in the second half. High-tech-intensive merchandise exports from the East Asian newly industrialized economies (NIEs—Hong Kong (China); Singapore; and Taiwan (China) declined much more rapidly than merchandise exports from the rest of the world (figure 1.7).[4] Trade flows also slowed in the developing world, although not as sharply as in the NIEs. By the third quarter of 2001, developing-country export volumes were near levels

of a year ago, and this deterioration intensified into the fourth quarter.

The regions most affected by the fall-off in trade were East Asia—from depressed world demand for high-tech goods and associated slippage in intraregional trade—and Latin America, due to the extensive trade relations between Mexico and the United States. Central European economies continued to witness robust (although slowing) trade growth, while Sub-Saharan African countries were more affected by falling commodity prices than by declines in volume. Merchandise imports are now expected to rebound strongly in the second half of 2002, together with a recovery of world industrial production (figure 1.8). By 2003 growth rates could approach double-digit levels again, of which 3 percentage points will be positive carryover from 2002.[5] North American exports are expected to return to 9 percent growth in 2003, European exports to 7.5 percent, while Japanese trade flows are expected to achieve growth of 6.5 percent. The high-tech exporters are likely to experience the most rapid recovery, with particularly fast export growth expected for East Asia (near 10 percent), boosted by China's accession to the WTO.

Trade logistics disrupted . . . air transport continues to suffer—
The disruption of the global transportation system resulting from the terrorist attacks appears

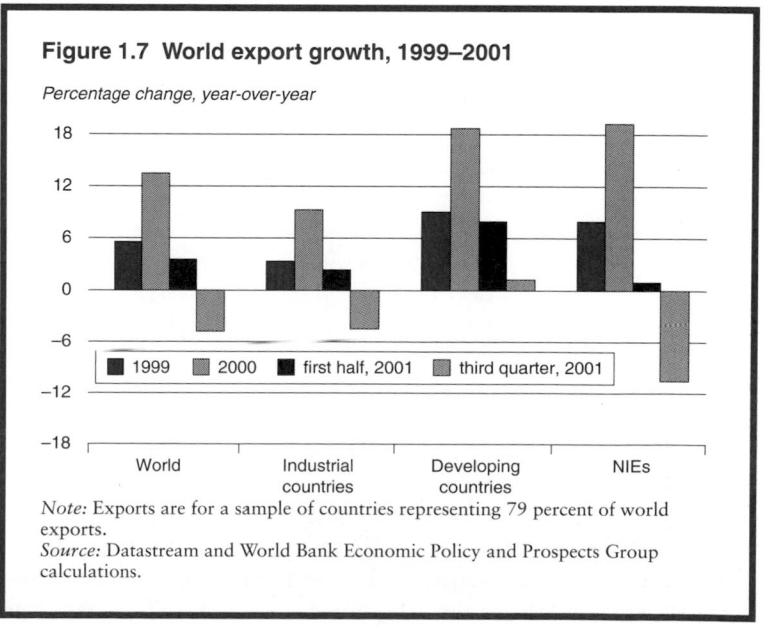

Figure 1.7 World export growth, 1999–2001

Percentage change, year-over-year

■ 1999 ■ 2000 ■ first half, 2001 ■ third quarter, 2001

Note: Exports are for a sample of countries representing 79 percent of world exports.
Source: Datastream and World Bank Economic Policy and Prospects Group calculations.

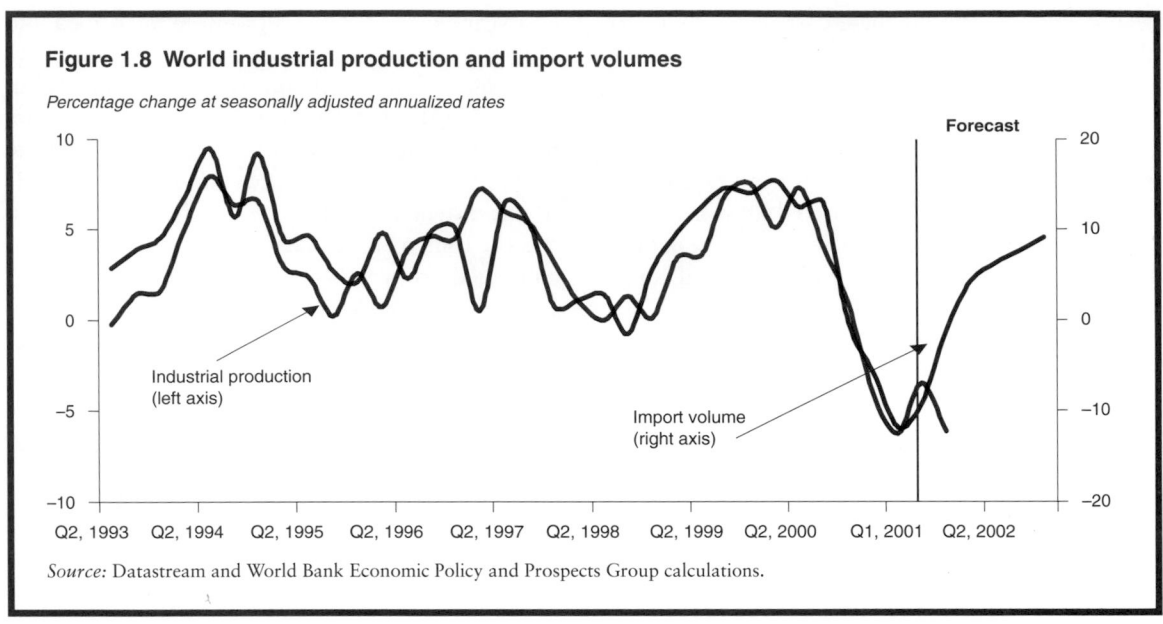

Figure 1.8 World industrial production and import volumes

Percentage change at seasonally adjusted annualized rates

Source: Datastream and World Bank Economic Policy and Prospects Group calculations.

to have had only temporary adverse impacts on trade growth, but uncertainties continue to loom. Air cargo has suffered more than other transport modes. After September 11, U.S. airspace was completely shut down for several days to domestic and international passenger and cargo traffic, and capacity utilization and revenues in air transport remained significantly below preattack levels for several months. Other parts of the world, especially South Asia and the Middle East, also suffered interruptions in transportation, albeit less severe than those in the United States. There is evidence to suggest, however, that the physical constraints on trade from the security response to the attacks are abating.

The attacks had the immediate effect of increasing insurance and security costs. Maritime shipping costs rose for 10 to 15 days in the aftermath of September 11, rising on average 7 percent according to the most widely available shipping cost indexes. One of these indexes, the Baltic Dry Index, shows a price spike shortly after September 11 (figure 1.9). However, costs declined quickly thereafter. The Baltic Dry Index resumed its sharp downward trend in a matter of days, continuing to track the decline in world trade volumes over the last year. Furthermore, the available data on seaborne shipping costs generally cover the major trade routes—for example, those between Asia and North Amer-

ica, and between North America and Europe. There is anecdotal evidence suggesting that costs have risen substantially more on less-traveled routes, particularly those close to the conflict zone around the Middle East and South Asia. For example, insurance rates on traffic through the Suez Canal increased dramatically after September 11.

Security concerns following the terrorist attacks had a more pronounced impact on the cost of air transport. In September, the air cargo index for transportation across major routes increased by an average of 17 percent, with cargo costs from the United States increasing by 22 percent. By October, the global index had declined by only 2 percent, with costs still nearly 15 percent higher than before September 11. It is likely that a significant portion of the rise in air cargo rates may be longer lasting.

Developing countries' exports will be more affected by rising transportation costs than will exports from industrial countries, because developing countries tend to specialize in exports of primary goods and labor-intensive manufactures, which have higher trade margins (international transport costs) than the high-tech exports from industrial countries.[6] One estimate of the effects of a sustained increase in the cost of trade on world trade flows suggests that, if the terrorist attacks caused a 10 percent increase in the port-to-port costs of merchandise trade, world trade could decline by

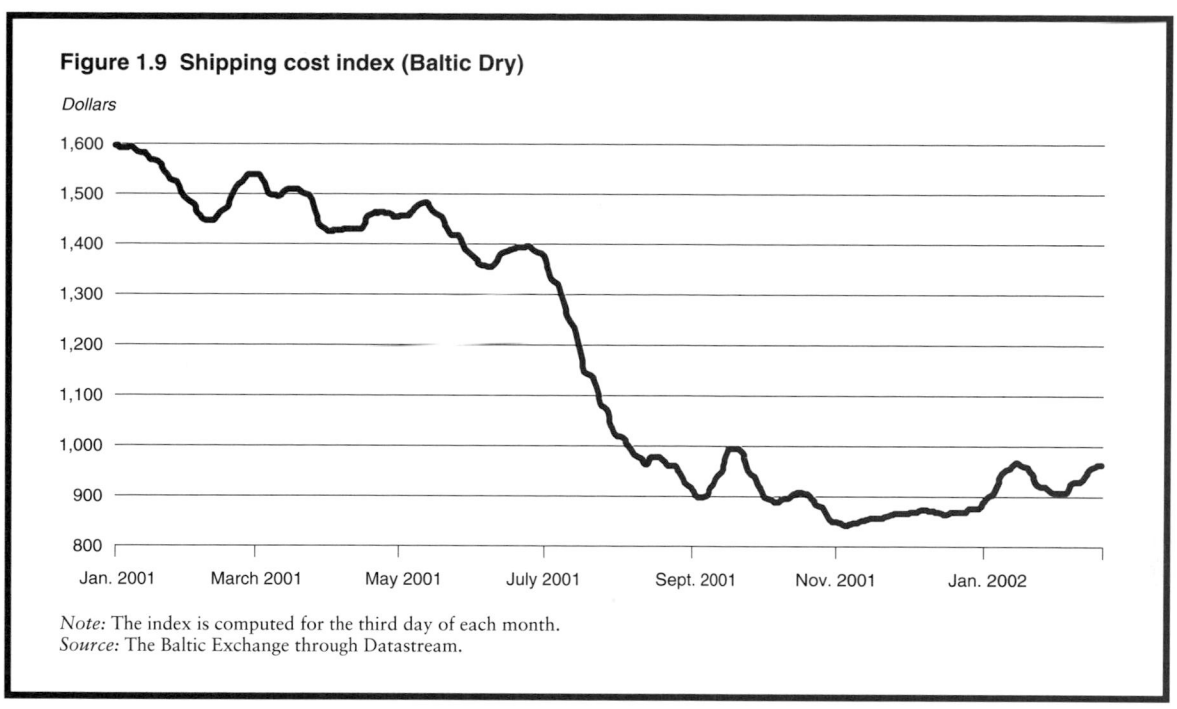

Figure 1.9 Shipping cost index (Baltic Dry)

Note: The index is computed for the third day of each month.
Source: The Baltic Exchange through Datastream.

about 1 percent, approximately $60 billion (relative to a projection where the terrorist attacks have no lasting impact on costs).[7] Developing countries' trade would fall by 1.6 percent, and industrial countries' exports would fall by 0.8 percent.

—and world tourism arrivals and revenues approach record lows

The terrorist attacks also reduced developing countries' foreign exchange revenues from international tourism, which amount to 7 percent of total exports of goods and services, about equivalent to revenues from high-tech exports or exports of agricultural and food products. The World Tourism Organization reports that travel reservations worldwide in November 2001 stood 12 to 15 percent below the levels of a year earlier.[8] Anecdotal evidence suggests that the fall in tourism revenues may well have reached double-digit rates, as both tourist arrivals and expenditures collapsed. Directly after September 11, 40 percent of booked vacation trips with Caribbean countries as the destination were canceled. Airlines have substantially trimmed their schedules to other destinations as well. Several mid-size carriers in Europe have failed in the last few months, and some carriers in the United States are threatened with bankruptcy despite the

$15 billion support package quickly enacted in the aftermath of September 11. Aside from declines in volume, price effects may also be important as resorts and hotels drop their prices in order to entice visitors.

In the first eight months of 2001 world tourism was on track for an increase of 2.5 to 3 percent for the year as a whole, but after September 11 expectations were adjusted to only 1 percent growth, implying a decline of more than 20 percent (annualized) in fourth quarter momentum.[9] Assuming a 20 percent drop in tourism revenues during a period of six months, the loss in export revenues for developing countries could amount to $14 billion. The impact on employment could be particularly severe, because tourism services tend to be highly labor intensive. Short-term impacts probably far exceed the longer-term consequences, since past trends indicate that demand for travel and tourism services recovers relatively rapidly from setbacks. Even so, countries near the conflict zone in South Asia and the Middle East may suffer a more sustained reduction of revenues. The impact of any decline in tourism revenues will vary enormously among developing countries. For example, tourism can constitute as much as 70 percent of goods and services exports in some small island economies, and also has become a key export sector in many Sub-Saharan African countries. Revenues from tourism for the 14 Sub-Saharan African countries with the highest dependency on tourism revenues average 22 percent of total export revenues.[10] In absolute terms, Turkey is the largest recipient of tourism revenues, and the sharp fall in these receipts since September 11 has complicated efforts to overcome the financial crisis.

Improved prospects for a development round of multilateral trade negotiations

The Doha Development Agenda—which emerged from the WTO Ministerial Conference held in Doha, Qatar, in November 2001—demonstrates the increased prominence of development concerns in WTO deliberations, in turn reflecting increased participation by developing countries in the international trading system. Doha launched negotiations on market access for manufactures, dispute settlement, WTO rules, environmental policies, and intellectual property protection. These negotiations will complement ongoing talks on market access in agriculture and services, which are mandated by the Uruguay Round agreements. Negotiations will be launched on four so-called Singapore issues—competition, investment, trade facilitation, and transparency in government procurement—at the next WTO ministerial meeting in 2003, if consensus can be reached on the modalities of such negotiations at that time. Completing negotiations by January 1, 2005, as envisaged in the Doha Ministerial Declaration, represents a major challenge (box 1.1), but success in doing so would imply large welfare gains for both developing and industrial countries.

Secular declines and cyclical swings in commodities prices

Non-oil commodities. The global economic slowdown, a strong dollar, and large supplies of most commodities reduced the average dollar price of developing countries' non-oil primary commodity exports by 9 percent in 2001. Demand for metals was most affected by the economic slowdown, while agricultural commodities continued to face large supply increases despite falling prices. Non-oil commodity prices are now one-third below their cyclical high of 1997. Currency depreciation in major commodity exporters in East Asia and Latin America resulted in sharp price declines for

coffee, oilseeds, sugar, and raw materials such as rubber. Continued rapid technological progress contributed to supply increases in a number of commodities,[11] and improved policies in some developing countries contributed to large increases in exports.[12] Coffee prices were especially hard hit (down 30 percent in 2001 compared with 2000) due to a 20 percent increase in global production over the past three years with little increase in consumption. Cotton prices declined 20 percent in 2001 due to large production increases in China and the United States, and rice prices fell 15 percent due to the large exports from Thailand and Vietnam. Copper prices fell by 12 percent in 2001, and prices would have declined even further if major producers had not cut production by about 5 percent in an effort to prevent additional price declines.

The price declines have been especially hard for exporters in Africa, where non-oil commodities often account for 70 percent or more of export revenues. Ethiopia, for example, derives nearly two-thirds of total export revenues from coffee, and Mali derives about 40 percent of total exports from cotton. Moreover, the prices of commodities that account for a large share of Sub-Saharan exports (such as cocoa, coffee, and copper) have fallen by more than the prices of commodities exported by other developing countries (figure 1.10). Since 1980, the index of real non-oil commodity export prices of Sub-Saharan African countries has declined by 10 percent relative to the index of all developing countries. On top of that, the African index tends to be more volatile over the price cycle, implying a sharper fall during a downturn. African producers have been unable to make up for the decline in prices through higher volumes, since African agricultural production has been flat over the past two decades, while agricultural production increased rapidly in developing countries as a whole (figure 1.11). Sub-Saharan Africa's non-oil commodity export revenues dropped at least $3 billion between 1997 and 2001—equal to 3.6 percent of non-oil export revenues in 1997 and 25 percent of total official development aid to these countries in 1999.

We expect a recovery of only 15 percent in non-oil commodity prices from current cyclical lows over the interval through 2004. This will leave non-oil commodity prices 22 percent below their 1997 level. The short-term recovery will be driven

Box 1.1   The Doha Development Agenda

The Doha agenda has great potential to be beneficial from a development perspective. A great deal of research has documented that there is still a large market-access agenda and that dealing with this agenda will significantly increase real incomes and reduce poverty in developing countries (World Bank 2001). Research also suggests that care is required to determine the development relevance and payoffs of extending the WTO into regulatory areas (Hertel, Hoekman, and Martin 2002). The key areas of concern for developing countries in the new trade round will be market access, regulatory issues, and the magnitude and effectiveness of the technical assistance that was promised in Doha.

Improving *market access* remains a key goal of multilateral trade negotiations. Industrial countries will need to mobilize the political will to reduce remaining pockets of protection in key sectors such as agriculture, labor-based services, and labor-intensive manufactures. Developing countries also need to be willing to liberalize access to their markets for goods and services. The relatively high barriers to trade in goods *and* services that continue to prevail in many developing countries implies that they have a lot to bring to the table in a mercantilist sense. Identifying a set of "concessions" that are of interest to politically powerful groups in OECD countries and that are beneficial to developing countries is the major challenge confronting policymakers in the coming years. The research and development communities need to help identify what such issues might be and assist in mobilizing the affected constituencies.[13]

As far as multilateral rule-making on *regulatory issues* is concerned, better understanding of the issues in developing countries is required, not just by government officials but also by the private sector and civil society. Despite five years of studying trade and investment-competition linkages in WTO working groups set up for that purpose, many low-income countries were fearful in Doha of launching negotiations in these areas. There is clearly a need to provide greater assistance to build capacity and undertake analysis in developing countries to determine the merits and implications of multilateral disciplines.

Whether it makes sense to rely on negotiation and binding dispute settlement to address behind-the-border policies in the WTO is a question that developing countries need to answer for themselves. The Doha ministerial meeting revealed that many countries had an answer to that question, but that many others did not.

The Doha declaration contains numerous commitments by high-income WTO members to provide *technical assistance*. However, there is no mention of the magnitude of assistance that will be offered, nor is there discussion of any mechanism to determine what the needs are and how they should be addressed (that is, what the delivery mechanism might be). Embedding technical assistance in a broader development framework is critical in ensuring that the assistance focuses on the priority needs of each country and is consistent with its development strategy. The separate section in the Doha declaration on technical cooperation and capacity building provides scope to move in this direction: Ministers "instruct the Secretariat, in coordination with other relevant agencies, to support domestic efforts for mainstreaming trade into national plans for economic development and strategies for poverty reduction" (paragraph 38). A concerted effort will be needed to ensure aid is targeted at national priorities, and to ensure that assistance is provided in an effective manner by agencies with a comparative advantage in an area.

Ensuring that the new round of trade negotiations achieves a pro-development negotiating outcome is a major challenge. Resistance to liberalization of agriculture and textiles is very strong. Conversely, many low-income countries are unwilling to extend the reach of the WTO to cover issues such as competition and investment policies. A major question confronting WTO members is whether a deal should be constructed that involves linking old market access issues to disciplines on new issues such as investment and competition. The feasibility of any such linkage will depend greatly on what is done in the coming years to address developing-country concerns regarding implementation of Uruguay Round agreements and the magnitude and effectiveness of the technical assistance that was promised in Doha.

---

by a rebound in global economic activity, reduced supplies and stocks in response to current low prices, and some weakening of the dollar. There is uncertainty associated with the factors that underlie the recovery of commodities prices, but the impacts of the uncertainties on prices differ markedly. While the timing of the rebound of demand is uncertain, a recovery that is further delayed will have only a limited negative impact on prices. The potential for unexpected supply increases may be a greater risk. During the 1990s rapid technological progress, combined with improved policies, led to the emergence of major producers in a relatively short period of time, resulting in sharp declines in prices (as

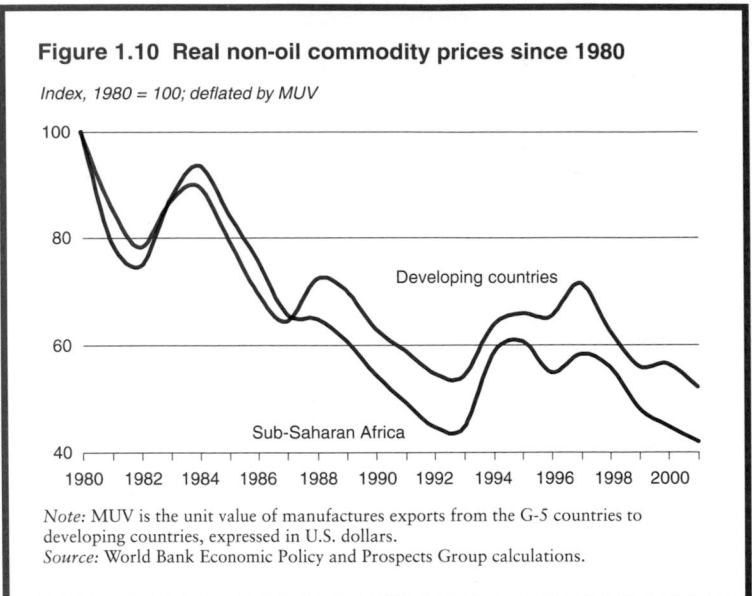

Figure 1.10 Real non-oil commodity prices since 1980

Index, 1980 = 100; deflated by MUV

Note: MUV is the unit value of manufactures exports from the G-5 countries to developing countries, expressed in U.S. dollars.
Source: World Bank Economic Policy and Prospects Group calculations.

in the case of coffee). While such supply increases are difficult to predict, they remain an important risk to the forecast. Conversely, abnormal weather conditions are more likely to lead to higher prices, since bad harvests tend to result in much larger falls in production than would be the case when good weather conditions boost production.

Oil prices. The global economic slowdown contributed to a reduction of oil prices from $28.2 a barrel in 2000 to $24.4 in 2001.[14] Oil prices

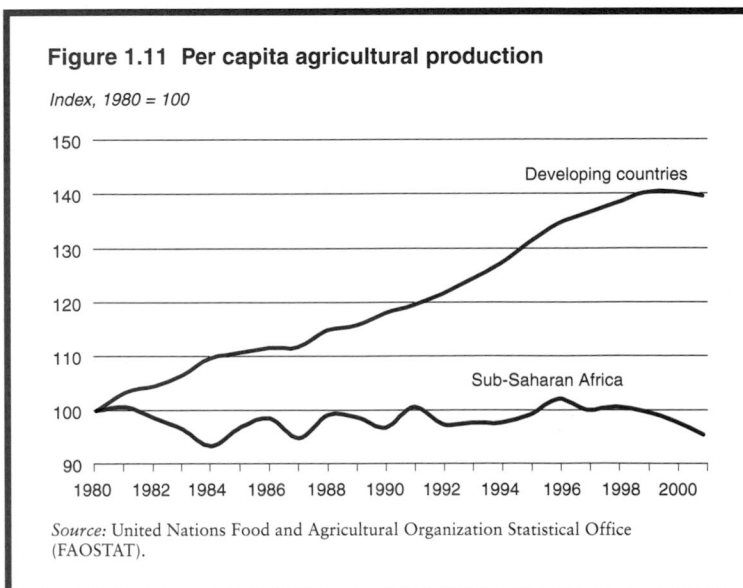

Figure 1.11 Per capita agricultural production

Index, 1980 = 100

Source: United Nations Food and Agricultural Organization Statistical Office (FAOSTAT).

spiked briefly to $31 a barrel immediately following September 11, but when it became apparent that there were no immediate threats to oil supplies, prices quickly fell, ending the year at $18.5. World oil demand grew little in 2001, and actually fell by 1 percent year-on-year in the second half of the year as a result of the after-effects of the attacks (such as reduced jet travel, for example), the deepening economic slowdown, and mild weather. With non-OPEC (Organization of Petroleum Exporting Countries) production growing moderately overall (increases occurred mainly in the Commonwealth of Independent States, or CIS), oil inventories have risen back to a more comfortable range compared with the low levels of 2000 (figure 1.12).

OPEC reduced production three times prior to September 11 to keep the price of its crude basket within its target range of $22 to $28 a barrel. But, with the changed political environment after September 11 and as the economic slowdown worsened, OPEC chose not to activate its "automatic mechanism" that reduces output when the price of oil falls below $22 for 10 consecutive days. Instead, OPEC countries relied on reducing their production above quota (estimated at 0.54 million barrels a day in November) to help support prices.

With oil prices well below $20 a barrel in November, OPEC agreed to reduce quotas by 6.5 percent or 1.5 million barrels per day (mb/d) beginning January 1, 2002—but only if non-OPEC producers firmly committed to reducing production by 0.5 mb/d. OPEC threatened a price war if a deal could not be reached. Non-OPEC producers responded in part, with major producers Norway and the Russian Federation each agreeing to cut production by 0.15 mb/d. While non-OPEC cuts fell short of the 0.5 mb/d demanded, they were large enough for OPEC to follow through on its proposed cuts, which will last "as long as necessary" according to OPEC's secretary general.

We expect oil prices to average $20 a barrel in 2002, somewhat above current levels but well below the 2001 average. It will be difficult to lift prices to 2000 levels, mainly because of the underlying weakness in demand and because non-OPEC capacity has been increased during the recent period of high prices. But with an economic recovery in the second half of 2002, oil demand is expected to increase marginally, following sharp declines in the prior year. Non-OPEC supplies are expected to rise by 1 mb/d, excluding any temporary, volun-

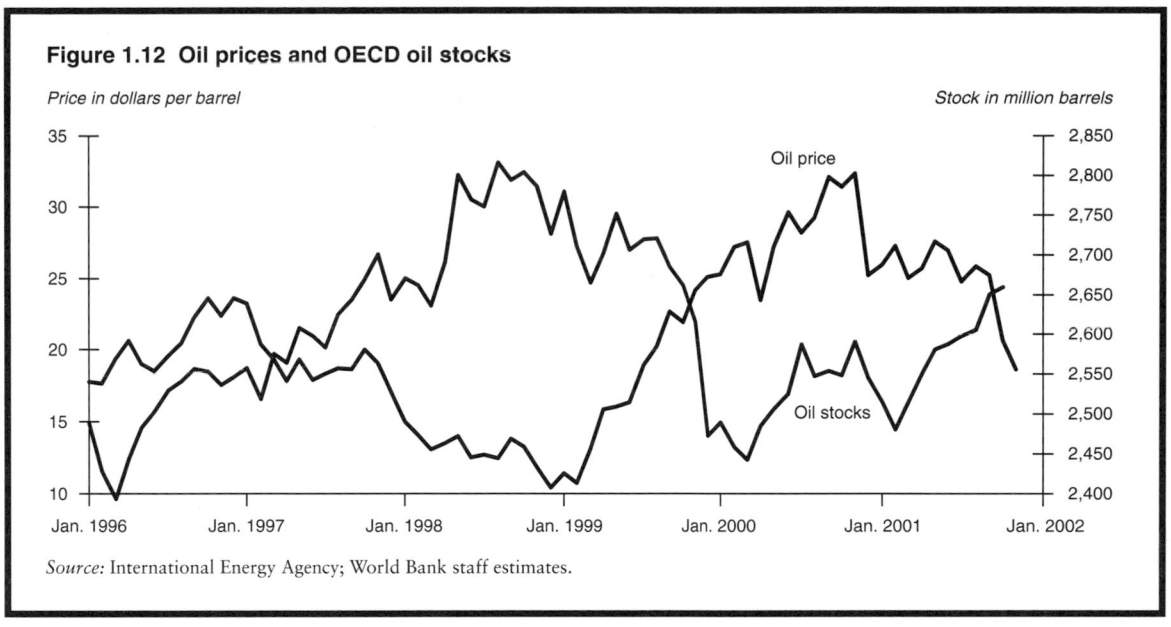

Figure 1.12 Oil prices and OECD oil stocks

Price in dollars per barrel   *Stock in million barrels*

Source: International Energy Agency; World Bank staff estimates.

tary reductions. Consequently, OPEC will be required to produce less oil in 2002. If oil producers maintain low levels of output throughout the year, oil inventories could begin to tighten; that would help firm prices later in 2002 and into 2003, to average $21 for the latter year. In 2004 non-OPEC supplies are expected to capture much of the expected growth in demand, and oil prices are expected to weaken, to $19 a barrel, as OPEC members continue to lose market share. The increase in non-OPEC supply is expected to exceed the rise in demand when global economic growth solidifies.

The risks to the price forecast are mainly on the downside, since the agreement between OPEC and non-OPEC producers is likely to be fragile under expected weak demand conditions. However, while the potential for supply disruptions is thought to be small, disruptions could have a large impact if they do occur. The major uncertainties include the prospects for exports from Iraq, which will depend on that country's reactions to changes in the sanctions regime, and any military conflict in the Middle East due to the war on terrorism. The impact of the latter could be extremely significant. For example, the loss of 5 mb/d of Iranian production in 1980 caused a 150 percent rise in prices within several months, and the similar-size loss of Iraq and Kuwait production in 1990 caused a temporary doubling of prices within three months.

Regional developments

Severe recession in the rich countries, unprecedented deceleration in world trade, weak commodity prices, and heightened risk perceptions and increased selectiveness in financial markets affected all developing regions during 2001.[15] GDP growth for the aggregate of developing and transition countries fell from a record 5.4 percent in 2000 to 2.8 percent in the year, and per capita growth declined to 1.4 percent, both rates well below the averages of the 1990s (table 1.3). The intensity of the international effects differed across countries and regions, tied to—among other factors—market orientation and product specialization in patterns of trade; initial conditions in domestic financial markets, and different policy measures adopted in response to the slowdown. Country-specific conditions are likely to shape the recovery onto differing paths of growth by region following the expected rebound in industrial-country activity and trade.

The movement from boom to bust in the external environment is reflected distinctly in the fall of export market growth from 13 percent to 1.1 percent, and the concomitant decline in developing-country export performance from 15 percent to 4 percent—although this movement still implies a pick-up in market share for the group. Terms of trade, expressed as a proportion to GDP, dropped

Table 1.3 Developing-country forecast summary, 1991–2004

(percent per year)

Growth rates/ratios	1991–2000	1999	2000	Estimate 2001	Forecast 2002	Forecast 2003	Forecast 2004
Real GDP growth	3.2	3.3	5.4	2.8	3.2	5.0	4.9
Consumption per capita	0.9	1.0	3.2	1.5	1.8	3.0	3.1
GDP per capita	1.6	1.8	3.9	1.4	1.8	3.7	3.5
Population	1.6	1.5	1.5	1.4	1.4	1.3	1.3
Gross domestic investment/GDP[a]	23.5	23.2	24.0	24.2	24.6	24.8	25.0
Inflation[b]	11.7	5.4	6.4	5.3	4.4	4.2	4.1
Central government budget balance/GDP	–3.6	–4.0	–3.2	–3.2	–3.5	–3.5	–3.1
Export market growth[c]	7.6	5.3	12.9	1.1	2.5	7.7	7.4
Export volume[d]	7.1	4.9	14.6	3.7	6.1	9.6	9.4
Terms of trade/GDP[e]	–0.2	0.6	0.4	–0.1	–1.1	–0.2	–0.3
Current account/GDP	–1.2	0.4	1.2	0.4	–0.2	–0.4	–0.7
Memorandum items							
GDP growth: developing excluding							
the transition countries	4.8	3.3	5.3	2.6	3.2	5.2	5.0
Excluding China and India	2.1	2.3	5.1	1.8	2.2	4.4	4.2
Excluding transition, China, India	3.7	2.1	4.8	1.3	2.0	4.4	4.3

a. Fixed investment, measured in real terms.
b. Local currency GDP deflator, median.
c. Weighted average growth of import demand in export markets.
d. Goods and nonfactor services.
e. Change in terms of trade, measured as a proportion to GDP (percent).
Source: World Bank baseline forecast, February 2002.

by 0.1 percent. These developments pushed export revenues into negative territory (a decline of 1.3 percent), and contributed to a narrowing of the aggregate current account surplus to 0.4 percent of GDP in the year. At the same time, however, underlying inflation trends have continued on a path of deceleration, central government budget balances have narrowed from the averages of the 1990s, and a general improvement in the investment climate in many countries, including new emphases on governance and institutional reforms, have helped maintain the flow of FDI into selected developing and transition economies at high levels. These factors have opened the door—for those countries with a favorable climate—to pursue countercyclical policy options to help mitigate the full brunt of the external shocks of 2001. For example, large levels of reserves, low inflation, and manageable government debt enabled many countries in East Asia to reduce interest rates and to implement fiscal stimuli. Other countries, with weaker initial conditions (including, for example, Indonesia), several countries in Latin America, and Turkey, were forced to persist in fiscal consolidation, or even to tighten further,

and many did not see lower international interest rates reflected in reductions in domestic rates.

An important challenge for most developing countries during the current downturn has been coping with much-reduced export revenues, at the same time that access to international capital has grown more limited. Decline in export receipts ($26 billion or 1.3 percent of regional GDP), was largest for East Asia, the origin of some 80 percent of developing countries' high-tech exports. And oil exporters throughout the developing world have seen their export revenues fall more than $100 billion as the price of oil fell sharply. For these countries, though, financing difficulties are not as pressing, since most East Asian and oil-exporting countries accumulated substantial current account surpluses and reserves over the last several years. More vulnerable are countries that depend largely on non-oil commodities exports, or on tourism, other services receipts, and transfers; these countries usually have less-than-creditworthy borrowing status. Most pressing are the financing problems for countries such as Turkey and Argentina that had amassed very large financial imbalances.

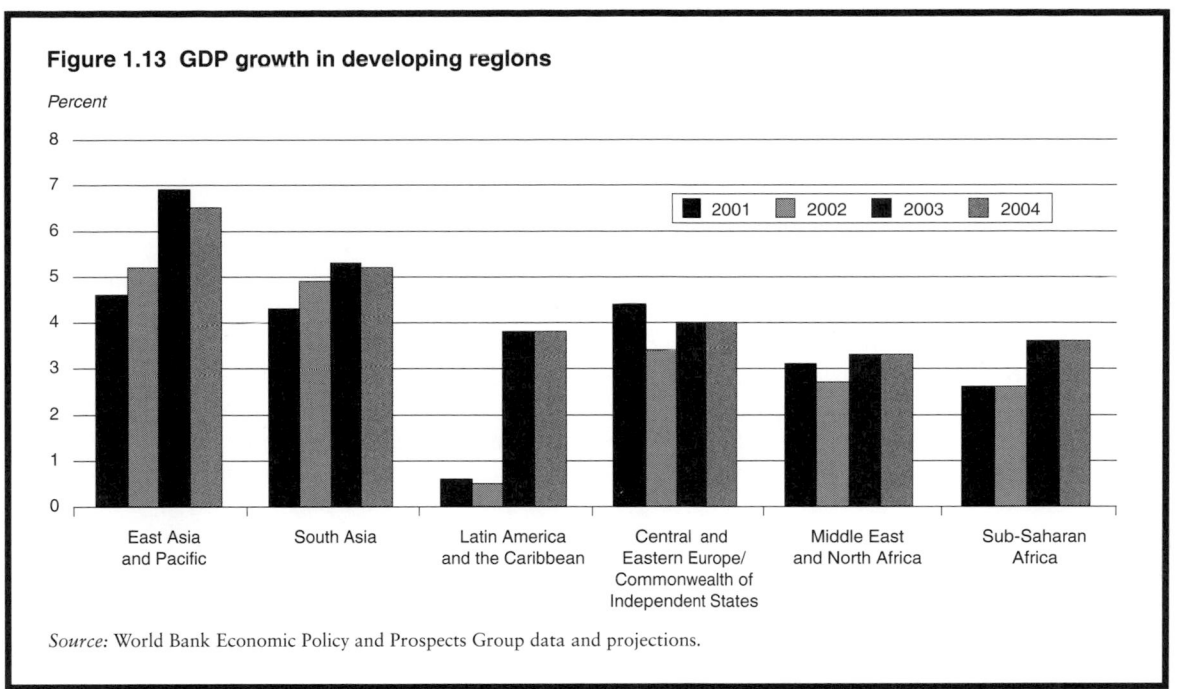

Figure 1.13 GDP growth in developing regions

Source: World Bank Economic Policy and Prospects Group data and projections.

For developing and transition countries as a group, recovery is anticipated to build momentum over the course of 2002. Growth is expected to reach 3.2 percent in 2002, and rise to 5 percent during 2003–04 (table 1.3). A rebound in export market growth to rates near 8 percent by 2003 would suggest a return of export performance toward double-digit gains. Terms of trade for the aggregate of developing countries is likely to worsen in the short to medium term, since it is tied in part to the large weight of oil exporters in the group, as well as to anticipated increases in the dollar cost of manufactures imports from the industrial countries.[16] Nonetheless, strong export volume growth should underpin domestic investment, with positive multiplier effects, and falling inflation should boost real incomes and consumption. A gradual return of private capital to emerging markets will accentuate these developments, so that by 2003 growth will be returning toward 5 percent. Moreover, recent developments, including the Doha Round, China's accession to the WTO (and the Russian Federation's expressed interest in the organization), offer promise of a broader scope for fuller participation in global trade, which will benefit the new members and their trading partners alike.

Recovery in the developing world is likely to begin, and to be strongest, in East Asia, where countries have benefited from domestic stimuli, and where strong dynamics in the high-tech sectors could once again work in their favor (figure 1.13). In contrast, little recovery for the aggregate of Latin American countries is anticipated, given their much less favorable starting points, since financial strains remain elevated and commodity prices are expected to rebound only modestly. Subdued commodity prices will also continue to restrain economic growth in Sub-Saharan Africa. The war on terrorism could hamper growth in South Asia and the Middle East and North Africa in the short run as trade and tourism flows remain disrupted, while at the same time financial flows to frontline states should ease current account tensions. In the medium run, necessary fiscal austerity in South Asia is expected to dampen growth rates in the region somewhat. Recovery in Central and Eastern Europe will hinge critically upon developments in the European Union (EU), suggesting somewhat delayed recovery relative to East Asia, while the Russian Federation and other countries of the CIS are likely to see recent stronger rates of growth—linked in large measure to the price of oil—fade gradually over the next years.

East Asia and Pacific

Growth in East Asian developing countries slowed to 4.6 percent in 2001 from the 7.4 percent registered during the 2000 boom. The growth slowdown in the region, excluding China, was more dramatic—from 7 percent in 2000 to 2.3 percent. Chinese growth remained above 7 percent, boosted by large-scale fiscal stimulus.

The collapse of global demand for high-tech products, compounded by progressively weaker economic conditions in the United States and Japan, hit exports, industrial production, and investment in most countries quite hard and raised unemployment rates. Regional export volume growth slowed sharply to 3 percent—in contrast to the robust 22 percent advance of 2000—with the largest growth decline occurring in the five countries most affected by the 1997–98 Asian crisis. Manufacturing output in the larger countries, excluding China, dropped by some 7.5 percent, fixed investment slowed by 4 percentage points, and liquidation of unwanted inventories played a substantial role in the downturn, subtracting more than 1 percentage point from the regions' output in the year. The high-income, high-tech-dependent *entrepôt* centers of the NIEs were battered into recession despite strong monetary and fiscal stimuli; this led to a sharp compression of East Asia's intricate network of intraregion trade. The events of September 11 only exacerbated the difficult external environment facing the region, especially for tourism revenues, as tourist arrivals in the five leading Association of Southeast Asian nations countries are thought to have fallen by 10 to 15 percent in October (year-over-year).

Low and declining inflation rates allowed most countries to use fiscal and monetary stimuli to mitigate the downturn. For example, the Republic of Korea lowered interest rates by 140 basis points, stepped up fiscal outlays—with the central government balance deteriorating from a surplus of 1.3 percent of GDP in 2000 to a small deficit in 2001—and tapped international capital markets for gross flows of some $21 billion in the year. These measures provided cushion for domestic demand while increasing reserve levels. Similar policy measures by several other economies in the region (with the exception of Indonesia) yielded a widening of the average fiscal deficit to 3 percent of GDP from 2.5 percent in 2000, while the current account surplus position diminished by 1.5 percent of GDP. Finan-

cial difficulties in Indonesia—and to a lesser degree, in the Philippines—were being addressed through agreements with the International Monetary Fund and multilateral development banks.

East Asia may be the first developing region to emerge from the current global downturn, and growth there is expected to pick up to 5.2 percent in 2002—reflecting the positive impact of looser monetary and fiscal positions and improvement in external conditions. But the strength of recovery will hinge upon the revival of world trade and rise in global demand for technology-based products. There are some early signs of encouragement in the information and communications technology (ICT) sector, as world semiconductor sales appear to have reached a trough. Industrial production is now rising across key ICT-producing economies of the region—notably Korea, but also Malaysia, the Philippines, Thailand, and the NIEs. As demand is unlikely to gain substantial momentum until the second half of 2002, however, a more robust export-led recovery in East Asia is not likely until 2003, with GDP growth expected to reach about 7 percent, before moderating toward potential growth of 6.5 percent in 2004. Challenges will remain during recovery, especially the potential widening of fiscal balances and the need to re-address fragile banking systems in several countries. China's recent accession to the WTO offers the broader region both substantial opportunities, in an opening of the large Chinese market to the region, and potential competitive pressures in third markets, because these open wider to Chinese products.

Latin America and the Caribbean

Regional GDP grew 0.6 percent in 2001 in Latin America and the Caribbean, a substantial slowdown from the 3.8 percent advance registered in 2000. The weak growth performance reflects adverse external conditions alongside a progressive worsening of the political and economic situation in Argentina. Output in Latin America, excluding Argentina, increased by 1.3 percent in the year. Following September 11, economic conditions worsened for the region as Argentina's crisis deepened, commodity prices fell, secondary market spreads rose, and capital flows fell from already subdued levels in July and August. The Caribbean region witnessed a steep decline in tourist bookings, while weakening labor markets in North America led to a slackening of remittances to Central American and

Caribbean countries. Few countries (among them, Chile and the República Bolivariana de Venezuela) were able to pursue countercyclical fiscal policy or monetary expansion to mitigate the growth slowdown, due to generally high public debt and relatively large external financing requirements. These developments translated into a rise in regional unemployment, with falling inflation rates in most countries, but little change in real interest rates or fiscal balances.

International developments were a major constraint on external revenues in 2001. The regional trade balance moved from a deficit of $35 billion in 1998 to a surplus of almost $10 billion in 2000 on the back of rising surpluses for major oil exporters. During 2001, however, aggregate dollar exports declined 1.5 percent and imports fell 1 percent, narrowing the trade surplus by about $3.6 billion. Oil exporters saw their surpluses diminish while Argentina and Brazil raised their surpluses significantly. In combination with these trends, a softening of receipts from tourism and remittances contributed to a widening of the region's current account deficit by $5 billion. With declines in financing from international capital markets, the current account deficit was balanced by a drawdown of reserves and increased support from the international financial institutions.

The outlook for 2002 has dimmed, with GDP now expected to rise by 0.5 percent—assuming that the repercussions of the Argentine default and devaluation have been discounted by financial markets, and that regional contagion remains limited. The forecast revision is also due to a much weaker fourth quarter 2001 outturn for most countries—implying delay to the recovery, the growth-eroding effects of crisis for Argentina itself, and a decidedly weaker outlook for private-capital market and business-related foreign direct investment (FDI) inflows. Fiscal deficits were deteriorating sharply at the end of 2001 for a number of countries due to slowing growth and continued declines in the prices of commodity exports, and government debt levels have risen. Hence fiscal consolidation may be required in 2002 to avoid excessive debt burdens, and this may constrain governments' ability to support growth through increased spending. Growth is expected to recover to 3.8 percent in 2003—yet with considerable downside risks, should Argentina's output decline become more protracted—maintaining growth at that rate during 2004, as the

industrial world eases. By that time private capital flows will have increased again, and earlier recovery in industrial countries should boost the price of the region's primary commodities and the volume of manufactured exports.

Europe and Central Asia

Europe and Central Asia grew by 2.2 percent in 2001, contrasted with 6.4 percent growth in 2000. The sharp deceleration was due to a 7.5 percent contraction in Turkish output, the fall in Russian growth to 4.8 percent following robust 8.3 percent performance in 2000, and a 0.9 percentage point deceleration in Central and Eastern European output. Growth for the region, excluding Turkey, amounted to 4.4 percent, down from 6.2 percent in 2000. Most transition economies witnessed declining inflation and interest rates, reflecting lower import prices and falling international interest rates. However, adoption of accommodative fiscal and monetary policies in the face of slowing growth led to a slight deterioration of fiscal deficits in several Central European countries.

Developments during the year served to narrow current account surpluses for those countries recently attaining positive balances (for example, Kazakhstan, the Russian Federation, and Ukraine) and widened deficits for countries whose external balances have remained persistently negative (such as Bulgaria, Croatia, Romania, and the Slovak Republic). This reflects delayed spending of oil revenues (as in the Russian Federation and Kazakhstan), and a deterioration in the external environment, particularly weaker external demand from the EU area. There are exceptions. In Turkey, the current account deficit shifted into a $3 billion surplus in 2001, as net external finance plummeted and the February 2001 crisis resulted in drastic measures to reduce domestic demand, and to switch expenditure, including a 56 percent depreciation of the lire. In Poland compressed domestic demand (linked to previously tight monetary policy, easing as of late 2001) has contained imports, translating into a narrowing of the current deficit, from $10 billion to $7 billion in 2001.

Growth in the region is expected to pick up modestly in 2002, to 3.2 percent from 2.2, but largely based on the assumed strength of recovery in Turkey. In contrast, among the transition economies, growth in the CIS is anticipated to decline to 3.8 percent in 2002, driven principally by a sharp decline in Russian oil revenues. Growth may ease moderately in Central and Eastern Europe from 2.9 percent to 2.8, while recovery in the Euro Area develops only gradually and fiscal consolidation may be necessary for potential accession countries to the EU. The region as a whole should see an acceleration of growth to between 4 and 4.5 percent in 2003–04, as the eventual pickup in Europe increases demand for the region's exports, although continued sluggish oil markets will partially constrain growth in the CIS.

South Asia

Although South Asia is relatively less integrated into the global economy than most developing regions, trends in the external environment served to restrain the pace of growth during 2001. Growth rose from a 4 percent advance in 2000 to 4.3 percent in 2001, as a decline in manufacturing output offset general improvement in agricultural performance (agriculture accounts for 50 percent or more of output for all countries of the region). Export market growth declined abruptly and sharply, leading to a fall in regional export growth to 1.1 percent from the strong 12.3 percent outturn of 2000. Indian exports, for example, dropped by 2 percent over the period from April to September compared with the levels from a year earlier. Manufacturing output in that country showed no growth in the first half of the calendar year. Pakistan will clearly pay a toll in economic activity for the duration of the military activities in Afghanistan, but it will also receive adequate financial support from the international community to reduce debt-servicing requirements, possibly establishing a foundation for renewed growth.

Given the size and relative self-sufficiency of the Indian economy, tepid domestic demand is the main culprit behind the current sluggishness of growth, although external factors have played a greater role than was typical in the past. Investment is slowing, in part due to the slackening of export growth, and capital goods output dropped 8 percent during the first half of fiscal 2001. However, positive developments on the inflation front, with the consumer price index moving below 3 percent, provided some headroom for easing of monetary policy in response to increasingly weak conditions. The recent fall in oil prices, continued growth of software exports (albeit at reduced 30–percent rates),

and slower import growth are expected to keep India's current account deficit well below 2 percent of GDP. FDI inflows ballooned to $4.5 billion in the year, twice the level of any previous fiscal year. Given a comfortable foreign reserve position, India is unlikely to face tight constraints in external finance. But increasing direct government spending and subsidies, in India as well as in Bangladesh and Pakistan, will tend to widen central government fiscal deficits—to 5.3 percent, 6.3 percent, and 5.3 percent respectively—and these deficits are likely to remain impediments to a more robust acceleration of growth in the medium term.

Output in the region is expected to gain momentum over 2002–03, partly on the strength of global trade recovery, although political and military tensions in the region create large uncertainties. Removal of sanctions by the United States on India and Pakistan and a potential pick-up in textile and clothing exports linked to eventual opening of rich-country markets are additional favorable factors that could support the medium-term outlook. And hoped-for progress in addressing structural reforms across countries of the region should support gains in productivity. Regional output is expected to register growth of 4.9 percent in 2002, before rising somewhat faster over 2003–04 at a pace above 5 percent.

Middle East and North Africa

Middle East and North Africa region GDP slowed to 3.1 percent in 2001, following above-average growth performance of 4.2 percent during 2000. Cutbacks in oil production by OPEC members of the region to support oil prices within a target band, coupled with volatility—and recent sharp declines—in the oil price, depressed growth among the major hydrocarbon producers. For example, following a rise of some 4.5 percent in 2000, GDP in Saudi Arabia advanced by slightly less than 2 percent in 2001. At the same time, progressive weakening of conditions in continental Europe (the dominant export market for countries of the Maghreb and several countries of the Mashreq) dampened export performance substantially—Moroccan export growth dropped into negative territory during the first half of the year. These trends were exacerbated by declines in revenues from tourism and remittances due to heightened security concerns after September 11. Against this background output growth for the oil exporters of the region dropped from 3.6 percent in 2000 to 2.5 percent in 2001; and with the exception of Morocco, which was recovering from severe drought conditions, growth among the diversified exporters of the region slowed to 3.2 percent from 4.7 percent in 2000.

An important consequence of these developments has been a substantial waning of external surpluses across the region. This is most evident among the oil-exporting countries, where current account balances that ballooned to some $59 billion (13 percent of GDP) with the jump in oil prices in 2000, dropped quickly to less than $40 billion on the back of slumping prices and curtailment of exports. Although public spending levels were adjusted in many countries, fiscal deficits increased. In the case of Saudi Arabia, despite public sector wage restraint, the 2002 budget foresees a deficit of some $6 to $7 billion, contrasted with a surplus of similar magnitude in 2000. Similar adverse fiscal trends are affecting countries such as the Arab Republic of Egypt, Morocco, and Tunisia, and may broaden across the diversified exporters as external revenue shortfalls become more acute in the near term.

Some countercyclical policy actions have been possible. Improved inflation performance in Egypt has allowed a full percentage point reduction in the central bank discount rate; and exchange rates have been falling relative to the dollar as well as the euro over the second half of 2001 in Egypt, Morocco, Tunisia, and the Republic of Yemen. These measures may help to mitigate the effects of the global slowdown to a modest degree; but given the importance of the EU as an export market and a principal source of remittance and tourism income, recovery there will be necessary for a return of more buoyant external conditions in the Middle East and North Africa.

Given difficult conditions in the external environment, near-term prospects appear muted: growth recovery in the EU is likely to lag behind that of North America and East Asia; underlying demand for hydrocarbons will require some time to reach 1999–2000 levels, and uncertainty associated with the war on terrorism will likely remain a dampening factor for regional dynamism. GDP growth is anticipated to fall to 2.7 percent in 2002, while recovery over the following years may be protracted relative to other developing regions, rising by 3.3 percent over 2003 and 2004.

Sub-Saharan Africa

Growth in Sub-Saharan Africa eased to 2.6 percent in 2001 from 3.1 percent in 2000, as the global slowdown exacted a toll on commodity prices and growth in the region's export markets. The slowing of Sub-Saharan Africa's aggregate growth was moderate because oil exporters enjoyed relatively high oil prices for much of the year, and favorable weather conditions boosted agricultural production in several countries (for example, cocoa production in West Africa increased sharply). But terms-of-trade losses as a proportion to GDP were 1 percent, the worst performance outside of the Middle East and North Africa region, and export market growth fell from 11 percent in 2000 to 1 percent. These fundamental conditions were reflected in African high-frequency data covering production, trade, and financial markets, which indicate that, as elsewhere, economic conditions deteriorated sharply over the course of the year. Growth of regional export volumes dropped by 5.4 percentage points, to 2.1 percent, and revenues by 24 percentage points, to –4.3 percent from 2000 outturns. Moreover, weak tourism demand in the critical year-end period—and in the wake of September 11—further affected a number of countries dependent on tourism, especially Kenya and Tanzania. In South Africa GDP registered growth of 1.2 percent (seasonally adjusted annual rate) in the third quarter, down from a recent peak of 3.4 percent in the fourth quarter of 2000. A deterioration in the country's trade balance coupled with a decline in equity capital flows precipitated a sharp fall in the value of the rand, which lost nearly a third of its value over the fourth quarter.

Looking to 2002, the projected decline in oil prices will adversely affect fiscal and external balances of hydrocarbon exporters, but at the same time it will provide a degree of relief to the large number of oil-importing countries of Sub-Saharan Africa. Oil contributes 70–80 percent of export revenues for Angola, the Republic of Congo, Gabon, and Sudan, and more than 90 percent for Nigeria and Equatorial Guinea. It is also the source of a majority of government revenues, pointing to a difficult period of fiscal consolidation. At the same time lower oil prices, if sustained, reduce the attractiveness of FDI flows into new production facilities in southern and western Africa. Elsewhere, revenues from tourism are also likely to remain depressed pending a resumption of faster growth in the industrial countries (even without concerns over security in the wake of the September 11 attacks), and the recovery in non-oil commodity prices is expected to be relatively muted. This balance of factors suggests that regional output should only maintain growth of 2.6 percent in the year.

Both export revenues and the terms of trade may decline slightly in 2002, requiring a further 3 percentage point reduction in import growth. However, for the 19 Sub-Saharan Africa countries that have fulfilled the conditions for debt relief under the Heavily Indebted Poor Countries Initiative, a reduction in debt service payments by $656 million compared to the average of recent years will provide some offset to reduced export revenues. Conditions in export markets (particularly in Europe) are expected to improve progressively through the year, setting the stage for 3.6 percent GDP growth over 2003–04, when oil prices may stabilize and non-oil commodity prices rise by a cumulative 15 percent.

Risks to the forecast

Uncertainties involved in macroeconomic forecasts are sizeable, and substantial forecast errors are virtually impossible to avoid. Errors in GDP growth forecasts made one year ahead tend to average around 1.5 percentage points.[17] Once leading indicators or partial data are available, the accuracy of forecasts improves dramatically. Current-year forecasts of GDP growth typically have errors substantially below 1 percentage point. It is extremely difficult to predict cyclical developments well in advance, partly because the timing of turning points is highly uncertain.

The prediction of recessions or severe downturns is particularly difficult, since they are often triggered by the burst of a speculative bubble or other unforeseeable events. Even if some tensions were observable in advance, the timing of their unwinding is close to random. The U.S. recession in the early 1990s provided an example of how forecasters can fail to anticipate recessions. The contraction of the U.S. economy (that started in the third quarter of 1990 and ended in the first quarter

of 1991) resulted in a 0.5 percent annual decline of GDP in 1991 over 1990. From Spring until late Fall of 1990 international organizations forecast an increase of around 2 percent,[18] implying an average forecast error of 2.5 percentage points. In 1991 the forecast errors were reduced to on average 0.3 percentage points. The recent U.S. recession—reflected in the 1.1 percent GDP growth in 2001, compared to the more than 4 percent growth in 2000—provided an almost identical picture. The average forecast error in 2000 (for growth in 2001) was 2 percentage points, and it dropped to 0.3 percentage points in 2001 (figure 1.14).

This experience implies that uncertainty may be relatively small for the 2002 growth rate forecasts, but substantially larger concerning the strength of the recovery in 2003. Figure 1.15 shows that the current cycle, including the baseline forecast, is expected to have a recovery pattern similar to the 1990–91 cycle. Although the recent recession seems more shallow, the deceleration in growth was actually quite similar, as could be the acceleration. With the larger share of high-tech production in the current cycle, and possible further stimulus packages, the recovery could even turn out to be sharper. However, there are also significant downside risks to this prediction. The prospects for high-tech industries depend, to a large extent, on the sentiment in financial markets, which is notoriously difficult to predict. Continued nervousness about future profitability could make the recovery more fragile than is currently forecast.

The prospects after the coming recovery are even more uncertain, particularly given that earlier recessions were often followed by a second dip. For example, in the beginning of 1993 U.S. GDP growth again fell below zero following the European recession. Since the current regional cycles are much more synchronized than a decade ago, such a strong double dip is not foreseen in the baseline. However, the cumulated financial imbalances in the U.S. economy could set off another reversal in market sentiment, leading to a sharper slowdown after the current recovery than is anticipated in the baseline forecast. In other words, a major risk is that the cyclical pattern could be more pronounced than is assumed in the baseline, with a stronger recovery, but a substantial reversal in the medium run.

Although the recovery may be stronger than currently anticipated, possible downside risks de-

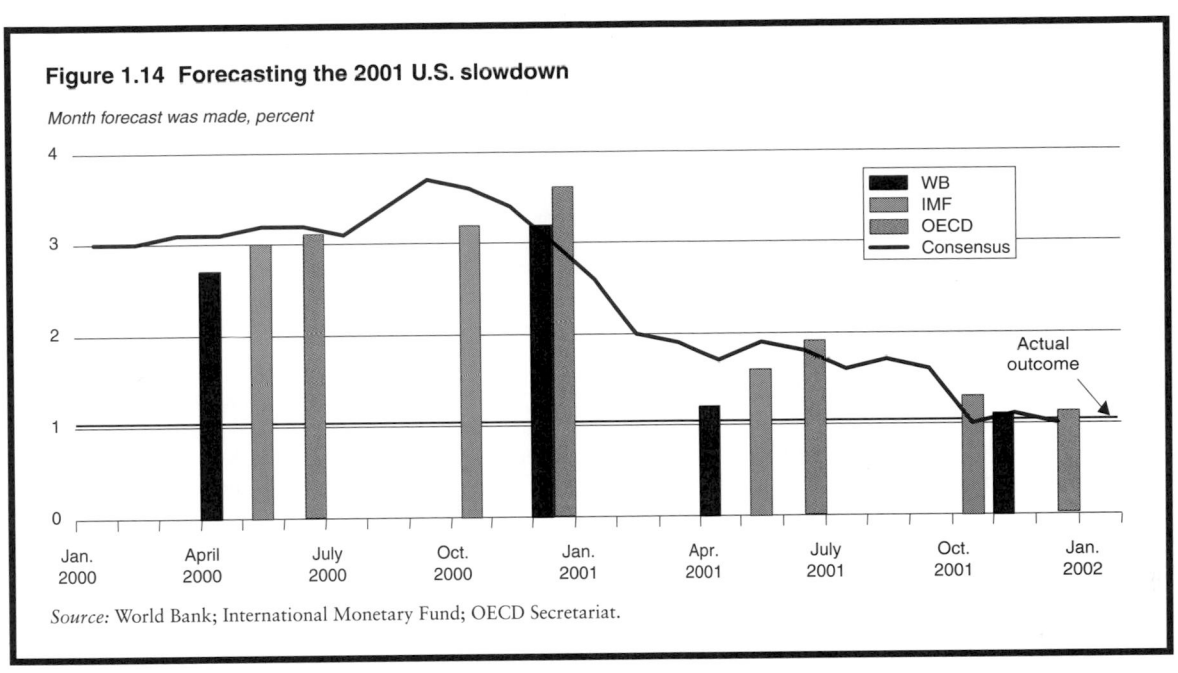

Figure 1.14 Forecasting the 2001 U.S. slowdown

Month forecast was made, percent

Source: World Bank; International Monetary Fund; OECD Secretariat.

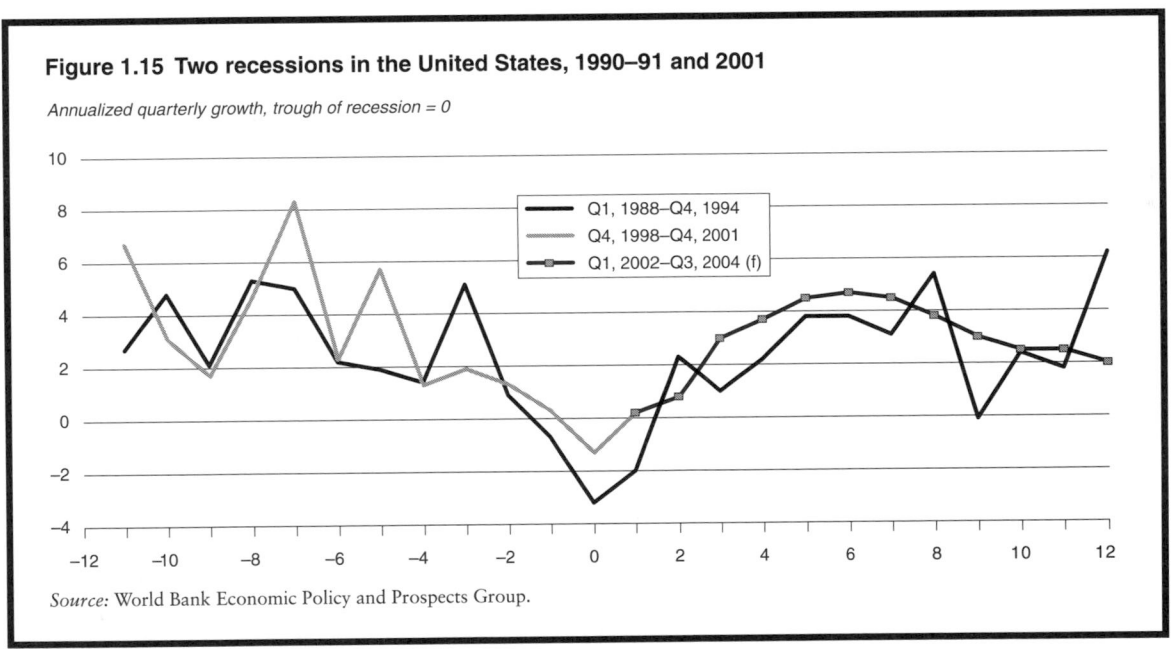

Figure 1.15 Two recessions in the United States, 1990–91 and 2001

Annualized quarterly growth, trough of recession = 0

Source: World Bank Economic Policy and Prospects Group.

serve more attention, since they often pose more serious challenges than do upside risks. Because the baseline forecast does not anticipate new major adverse shocks to the global economy, assumes only limited contagion from the breakdown of the Argentine economy, foresees an uninterrupted recovery of Turkey's economy, and excludes an out-

right Japanese banking crisis in the short run, the downside risks are significant.

Japan is mired in deep recession and deflation, with corporate profits declining sharply and bankruptcies mounting, and is beset by heightening concerns about credit availability and the soundness of the banking system. Commercial banks have become hesitant to lend, while the banks' capital base is being eroded by falling equity prices—commercial bank stocks dropped 45 percent during 2001. Credit availability for smaller companies is tight, a flight to quality into Japanese government bonds has ensued, and Japanese sovereign debt has been downgraded by Moody's and other credit rating agencies.

However serious these problems are, the probability of a full-blown crisis seems to be relatively low in the near term because the economy will benefit from the recovery of export demand, possibly fueled by a weakening of the yen. Such a depreciation could help to fight deflation through an increase in exports and a rise in import prices. This could have a negative impact on emerging countries in Asia who compete with Japanese exporters, depend on Japanese imports, or are recipients of Japanese FDI. However the adverse impacts are likely to be limited in the case of a modest depreciation, since the yen has appreciated in recent years, most countries in the region have adopted flexible exchange rate systems, and a gradual real depreciation of the yen seems warranted from a structural perspective.

Whatever happens in the current rebound of the global economy, the challenges are formidable in the medium term. The escalation of Japan's fiscal deficit has limited the scope for large injections of public funds for re-capitalization or closure of institutions. The major risk of a severe credit crunch is growing rather than shrinking. A sharp fall in Japanese domestic demand would be a major setback for developing economies in East Asia, with, for example, 15 percent of Chinese exports and 11 percent of Korean exports going to Japan.

Notes

1. See *Global Economic Prospects 2002* (World Bank 2001).

2. The so-called accelerator mechanism makes inventory and investment cycles much more pronounced than cyclical developments in other components of aggregate demand. Firms generally attempt to keep the *stock* of inventories and capital goods at a desired ratio to GDP. This implies that the *flows* of inventory accumulation and investment are linked to *changes* in GDP. Thus as stocks reach desired levels, the change in inventory accumulation and investment from the previous period can be quite large, generating sharp changes and turning points in GDP growth.

3. The Stability and Growth Pact, setting out the rules for budgetary behavior in stage three of the European Union's (EU's) Economic and Monetary Union, provides for

a degree of budgetary flexibility during severe recessions. While the projected downturn in European economic activity could not be described as a severe recession, the September 11 attacks would certainly qualify as unusual events outside the control of member states. And some flexibility in fiscal positions may be witnessed in the short run.

4. On a momentum basis (quarter-over-quarter), these economies experienced the deceleration earlier, with a decline of 9 percent (seasonally adjusted annualized rate) in the last quarter of 2000 and the first quarter of 2001, before reaching 25 percent decline at the trough in the second quarter.

5. Almost 40 percent of each year's annual growth rate is determined by the quarterly growth pattern in the previous year. The contribution of the previous year's quarterly growth to the current year's annual growth is called "carryover."

6. The average trade margin for total exports from industrial countries toward developing countries is 3.8 percent, but is 5.5 percent for developing-country exports toward industrial countries.

7. The impacts of higher international trade margins were evaluated using the World Bank's global computable general equilibrium model of world trade (van der Mensbrugghe 2001).

8. World Tourism Organization, Tourism Industry Takes Action to End Crisis, November 12, 2001. www. world-tourism.org.

9. World Tourism Organization third quarter 2001 news release. Other information confirms the sharp drop in tourism: two months after September 11 worldwide travel reservations were 12 to 15 percent below levels of the previous year.

10. Not all of the countries highly dependent on travel services are tourist destinations. A few countries affected by conflict (for example Sierra Leone and Rwanda) are dependent on revenues from travel services, probably due to the presence of staff from international organizations and nongovernmental organizations, as well as the presence of peacekeepers. The data from IMF's Balance of Payments database lack sufficient detail to separate out the different purchasers of travel services for these countries.

11. An interesting example of the impact of technology on commodity production is the new technique for cutting two-by-fours from logs. In the past a curved log could not be used to produce a straight board without huge wastage. However, lasers and computers are now used to scan a log and cut with the curve of the log. The two-by-fours are then pressed and dried to produce a straight board from a crooked log.

12. Vietnam reformed coffee marketing, which resulted in a large increase in the producer's share of international prices and led to a significant increase in exports.

13. To some extent this has already begun. A noteworthy difference between Doha and previous ministerials was the active involvement of representatives of development ministries on national delegations. National development communities and stakeholders represent a potentially powerful constituency in many European countries.

14. The price used to represent oil market conditions is the average of West Texas Intermediate and Brent and Dubai crudes, and is roughly equivalent to the Brent price.

15. See appendix 4 for a fuller treatment of recent macroeconomic and financial developments and prospects for the developing regions.

16. The manufacturing unit value (MUV) of exports in *dollar terms* from the G-5 countries to developing countries is anticipated to rise by 3.6 and 3.7 percent respectively in 2003–04, reflecting market expectations for a likely weakening of the dollar against the euro over the next years, counterbalanced by a trend of strength relative to the yen. For non-oil developing-country exporters, such development is likely to offset part of the firming of non-oil commodity prices, while mitigating gains from lower fuel import prices. For hydrocarbons exporters, the up-trend in MUV will serve to pressure terms of trade yet further.

17. See, for example, Batchelor 2001 and Loungani 2000.

18. IMF 1990a and 1990b. The World Bank did not produce annual forecasts at that time.

References

The word *processed* describes informally reproduced works that may not be commonly available through libraries.

Batchelor, R. A. 2001. "How Useful Are Forecasts of Intergovernmental Agencies? The IMF and OECD versus the Consensus." *Applied Economics* 33 (2): 225–35.

Hertel, Thomas W., Bernard M. Hoekman, and Will Martin. 2000. "Developing Countries and a New Round of WTO Negotiations." World Bank, Washington, D.C. Processed.

IMF (International Monetary Fund). 1990a. *World Economic Outlook*. Washington, D.C.

———. 1990b. *World Economic Outlook*. Washington, D.C.

Loungani, Prakash. 2000. "How Accurate Are Private Sector Forecasts? Cross-Country Evidence from Consensus Forecasts of Output Growth." IMF Working Paper WP/00/77. IMF, Washington, D.C.

OECD (Organisation for Economic Co-operation and Development). 1990a. *OECD Economic Outlook* 47 (June).

———. 1990b. *OECD Economic Outlook* 48 (December).

van der Mensbrugghe, Dominique. 2001. "Linkage Technical Reference Document." World Bank, Washington, D.C.

World Bank 2001. *Global Economic Prospects* 2002. Washington, D.C.

World Tourism Organization. 2001: "Tourism Industry Takes Action to End Crisis." November 12. www. world-tourism.org

———. News bulletin. Third quarter 2001 news release.

2

Private Capital Flows to Emerging Markets

The global slowdown reduced capital market flows to developing countries

The global economic slowdown in 2001 translated into reduced private capital flows to developing countries. The reevaluation of prospective returns in technology investments severely reduced demand for developing countries' technology stocks. Further, the global slowdown and collapse of equities prices increased the riskiness of the debt of highly leveraged corporations, reduced investors' appetite for risk, and increased economic uncertainty. All of these had the effect of tightening bank lending criteria and reducing access by speculative-grade borrowers, which sharply depressed bank lending to developing countries. By contrast, bond issues by developing countries remained stable, because the share of developing-country investment-grade borrowers is greater among bond issuers than bank borrowers. The level of foreign direct investment (FDI) in 2001 was virtually unchanged from the previous year, with changes in flows largely driven by changes in the domestic economic environment, by large privatization transactions, or by a few major private sector acquisitions.

Financial crises highlighted the problems of rescue packages

The crisis in Argentina highlighted the challenges facing the international community in assisting countries in crisis. Fixed exchange rate regimes are vulnerable to asymmetric shocks. There are severe costs associated with hanging on to a pegged, overvalued exchange rate. The success of multilateral rescue packages depends critically on strong adjustment by recipient countries. Contagion can be contained through prudent external financial management, including flexible exchange rates, disci-

plined domestic monetary polices, and lower short-term debt. Finally, there is more work to be done on private sector involvement in crisis prevention and resolution. Recent experience has underlined the importance of a clear definition of the limits on official resources and of the role and responsibilities of the official sector, debtor countries, and their private creditors. This challenge points to the need to consider more ambitious proposals for facilitating orderly workouts of problematic private sector debts, and the recent proposal by the International Monetary Fund (IMF) to provide for a standstill of debt payments to allow time for an orderly restructuring will, no doubt, be debated in the year ahead.

No significant recovery in capital flows until 2003

Capital market flows are forecast to decline further in 2002. Investors are likely to remain cautious about emerging markets, because low growth and recession in industrial countries limits demand for developing countries' exports, financing constraints on banks and other investors remain tight, and the appetite for risk remains low. The recovery anticipated to begin in the second half of 2002, coupled with low interest rates, should spark a rise in capital market flows in 2003–04. Nevertheless, the increase in flows will remain modest, since commodity exports will continue to experience low export revenues, investors will remain concerned after the string of emerging market crises since the mid-1990s, and low rates of capacity utilization will reduce the need for capital in some of the more creditworthy developing countries. FDI flows should remain high, and perhaps rise somewhat, over the next few years, while growth in developing countries accelerates and they continue to enjoy the benefits from sustained improvements in policies over the past 10 years. FDI flows are likely to remain the largest source of external finance for developing countries.

Net resource flows

The global slowdown has depressed capital flows to developing countries

Developing countries' net long-term flows (gross inflows of capital less amortization) fell to an estimated $196 billion in 2001, $65 billion below the previous year's level and $145 billion less than the peak in 1997 (see table 2.1, and see annex 2.2 for a definition of the measurement of capital flows used). Expressed as a share of gross domestic product (GDP), net long-term flows have fallen from 5.3 percent in 1997 to 3.1 percent in 2001. Deteriorating prospects for developing countries, the collapse in the price of technology stocks, the crises in Argentina and Turkey, and increased concern over risk have reduced demand for developing-country debt. Speculative-grade borrowers saw a sharp fall in access, with much higher spreads and sharply reduced flows. By contrast, investment-grade borrowers enjoyed improved terms from the decline in interest rates.[1] The decline in access to capital markets exacerbated the impact of the global growth slowdown on developing countries. This experience contrasts sharply with the early 1990s, when

lower interest rates and increased access by developing countries helped to cushion the impact of the global recession. FDI, which is less sensitive to cyclical changes in output than capital market flows, was little changed from the previous year, and remained only $16 billion below the peak level of 1999.

Capital market flows

Developing countries' access to capital markets deteriorated substantially in 2001. Total capital market commitments (bank loans, bond issues, and portfolio equity) declined to an estimated $171 billion, about one-quarter less than the level in 2000 (see table 2.2). External factors played the predominant role in reducing external finance. The slowdown in industrial countries led to a decline in developing countries' export revenues, the impact of which was only in part mitigated by the drop in international interest rates. Because most developing-country borrowers are speculative grade, they were hurt by a widespread retreat from speculative-grade investments. Slower growth and the collapse of technology stock prices increased uncertainty and sharply reduced the wealth of investors in high-risk assets, and thus reduced their appetite for risk. Private flows failed to compensate for adverse cyclical conditions; the fall in developing countries' market access exacerbated the impact on growth of reduced demand for their exports.

Table 2.1 Net long-term resource flows to developing countries, 1991–2001
(billions of dollars)

	1991	1992	1993	1994	1995	1996	1997	1998	1999	2000[a]	2001[b]
Net long-term resource flows	124.2	153.7	220.9	222.4	260.2	306.6	341.4	336.7	271.8	261.1	196.5
Official flows	62.2	54.3	53.4	46.0	54.1	30.3	40.7	53.4	47.4	35.3	36.5
Private flows	62.0	99.4	167.6	176.4	206.1	276.2	300.7	283.3	224.4	225.8	160.0
Capital markets	26.4	52.2	101.0	86.3	99.3	145.5	128.2	105.0	40.1	59.1	–8.3
Debt flows	18.8	38.2	50.0	51.2	63.3	96.5	98.1	89.4	5.6	8.2	–26.8
Bank lending	5.0	16.3	4.1	9.3	30.9	32.2	45.6	51.9	–23.3	–6.1	–32.3
Bond financing	11.0	11.1	36.7	38.1	30.7	62.3	49.6	40.9	29.5	16.9	9.5
Other	2.9	10.8	9.2	3.7	1.7	2.1	2.9	–3.4	–0.5	–2.5	–4.0
Equity flows	7.6	14.1	51.0	35.2	36.1	48.9	30.1	15.6	34.5	50.9	18.5
FDI	35.7	47.1	66.6	90.0	106.8	130.8	172.5	178.3	184.4	166.7	168.2

a. Preliminary.
b. Estimate.
Source: World Bank.

Table 2.2 Capital market commitments to developing countries, 1991–2001
(billions of dollars)

	1991	1992	1993	1994	1995	1996	1997	1998	1999	2000	2001[a]
Total	77	80	116	135	173	236	316	189	178	228	171
Bond issuance	11	20	50	46	53	98	114	73	68	68	68
Bank lending	61	54	57	73	113	125	179	108	90	125	93
Equity Placement	5	6	8	17	8	14	22	9	20	35	10

Note: The data in this table are gross commitments, and thus differ significantly from the data in table 2.1 which are gross disbursements minus amortization. The data on equity placements refer only to initial offerings of equity transactions marketed across borders, and do not include net purchases of securities by foreigners in domestic stock markets (which are included in the line "equity flows" in table 2.1).
a. Estimate.

Slowdown in world trade partially offset by lower interest rates

The growth slowdown in industrial countries reduced developing countries' export revenues, but the direct impact on borrowing capacity, at least for investment-grade borrowers, was softened by the fall in interest rates. The drop in world trade growth coupled with the continued fall in commodity prices (see chapter 1) reduced developing countries' export revenues by almost 1 percent in dollar terms in 2001.[2] The export revenues of the East Asian and Latin American regions, which accounted for almost three-fourths of developing countries' private-source debt in 2000, fell by 2 percent in 2001 (compared with a rise of 20 percent in the previous year). This decline would have increased the aggregate debt to exports ratio of the two regions by 3 percentage points (from 123 to 126 percent), if there had been no net borrowing in 2001. However, slower growth in industrial countries also resulted in a significant fall in short-term interest rates, because the demand for funds declined and central banks in the United States and Europe cut policy rates. The fall in interest rates resulted in improved terms on new lending for many developing countries. For example, in 2001 the interest rate on new bond issues by investment-grade sovereign borrowers among developing countries fell by 130 basis points, compared with the previous year. At unchanged debt levels, the two regions would have seen a decline in the ratio of interest payments to exports from 7.6 percent in 2000 to 7 percent in 2001.[3] Thus, the direct impact of the growth slowdown on borrowing capacity was relatively modest, particularly in comparison with the sharp deterioration in debt ratios during the recession of the mid-1970s and early 1980s (although debt ratios improved in the early 1990s recession—see table 2.3).

The impact of the technology crash

The reevaluation of prospective returns in technology sectors also had a role in reducing flows to developing countries. By the middle of 2000, markets perceived that the investment boom in telecommunications had created massive overcapacity, and that many of the newly formed Internet companies would be unlikely to generate the profits required to justify the investments made. This reevaluation of the likely profits from technology investments led to a general drop in technology stocks, while the slowdown depressed equities prices in general. The technology-heavy Nasdaq index fell 21 percent in 2001, and an index of global information technology and telecommunications stocks (the Morgan Stanley Global Industry Indices) fell 28 percent. By contrast, the more broad-based Dow Jones industrial index fell 7 percent.

Just as the boom in global stock markets in 1995–99 encouraged greater equity placements from developing countries, it appears that the sharp fall in stock markets is now associated with a decline in placements. Developing-country average stock market prices, after falling by 33 percent in 2000, dropped another 5 percent in 2001. The

Table 2.3 Debt ratios during recessions, East Asia and Latin America
(percent)

	1973	1975	1980	1982	1991	1993
Debt to export	123	135	124	169	140	127
Interest to export	6.6	8.7	11.7	17.9	7.5	6.4

Source: World Bank.

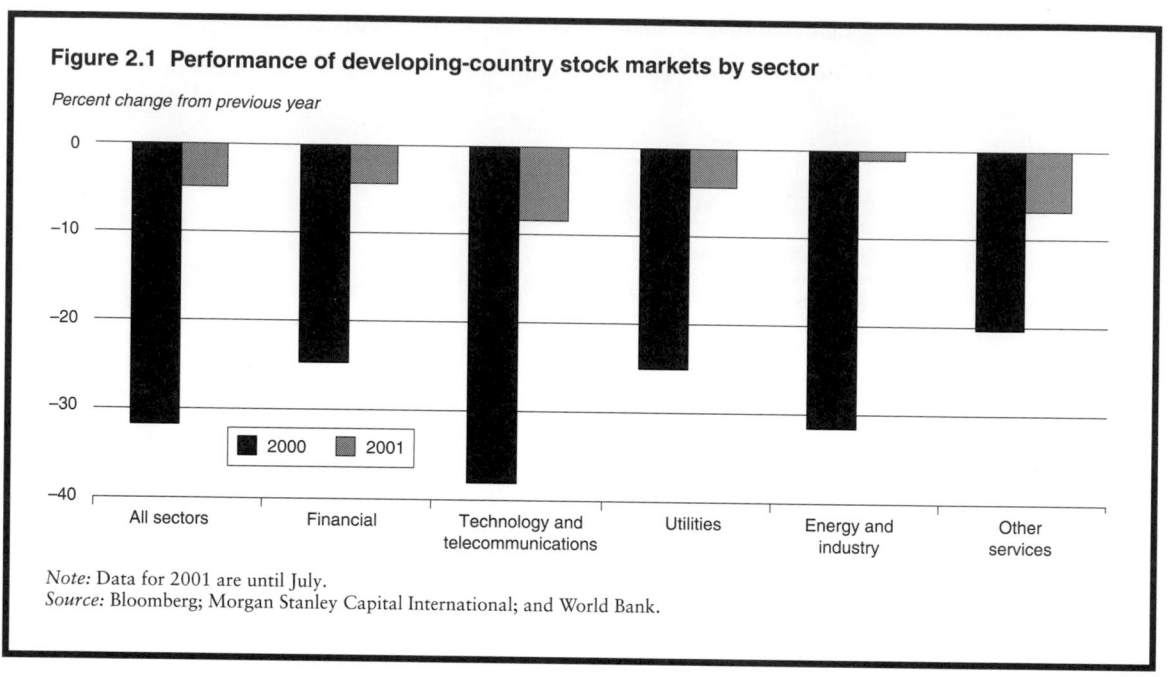

Figure 2.1 Performance of developing-country stock markets by sector

Percent change from previous year

Note: Data for 2001 are until July.
Source: Bloomberg; Morgan Stanley Capital International; and World Bank.

technology sector, which accounts for about one-third of Morgan Stanley's emerging stock market index, suffered the largest price declines (figure 2.1). Capital market flows were pro-cyclical in response to booms and busts in equities prices. International equity placements by developing countries fell by 72 percent in 2001, to only $10 billion. All developing-country regions experienced a decline in equity placements, but China alone accounted for some three-fourths of the total fall (table 2.4). China had received over 60 percent of developing countries' equity placements in 2000, largely in technology sectors.

A retreat from speculative-grade investments—
The growth slowdown and collapse of technology prices also reduced capital market flows by reducing the demand for speculative assets in general. Spreads on global high-yield debt in 2001 were 203 basis points higher than the average in 2000, and shot up by about 400 basis points in the aftermath of the September 11th terrorist attacks (figure 2.3).[4] Since about two-thirds of developing-country sovereign borrowers (and a much larger share of private borrowers) are speculative grade, this implied a general decline in flows to developing countries. The retreat from speculative-grade assets reflected an increase in the riskiness of

Table 2.4 International equity placement and performance of stock markets

	2000	2001
Developing country equity placement *(billions of dollars)*	35.1	9.8
China	21.9	2.9
Other countries	13.2	6.9
Performance of stock markets *(percent change over previous year)*		
All developing countries	−33.1	−1.0
Asia	−44.8	11.9
China	−9.8	−19.5
Nasdaq	−39.3	−21.1

Source: Bloomberg; Capital DATA; Standard & Poor's/IFC.

highly leveraged corporations, a fall in investors' appetite for risk, and increased uncertainty about economic prospects:

1. Speculative-grade corporations tend to be more highly leveraged, and thus more likely to default during recessions (they have less access to loans to support operations, but need to allocate a growing share of declining revenues to meet fixed debt service payments). The global default rate of corporations with speculative-grade credit ratings reached 9.8 percent in 2001, the highest level since 1992 (Moody's

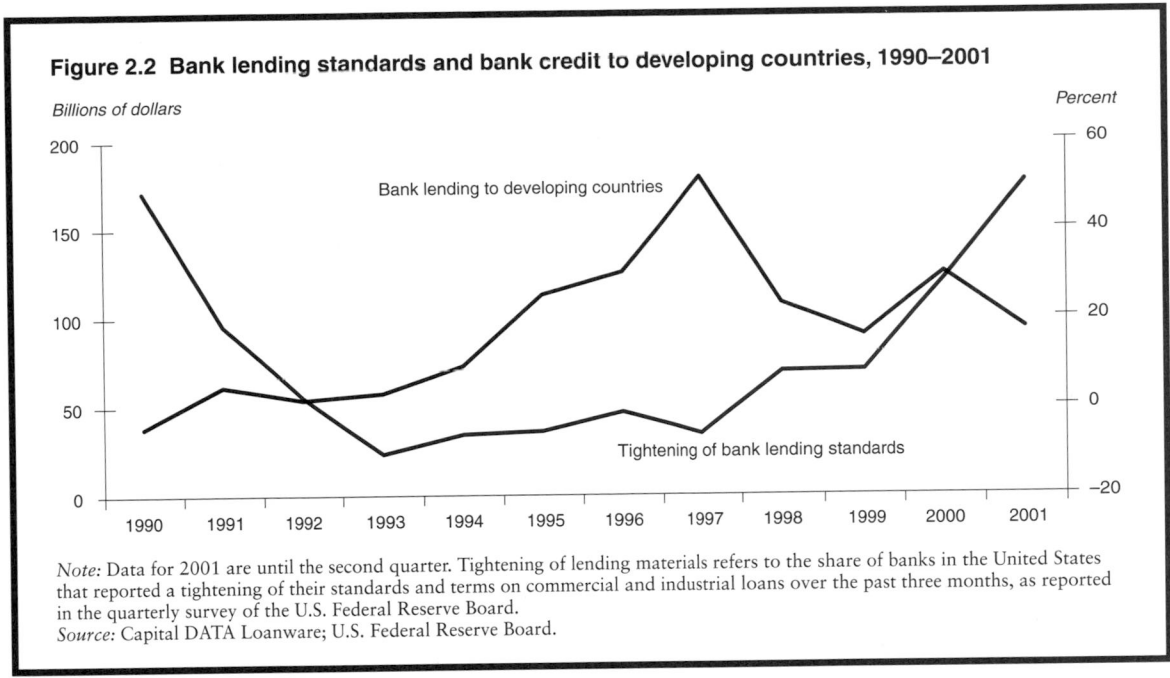

Figure 2.2 Bank lending standards and bank credit to developing countries, 1990–2001

Billions of dollars

Percent

Bank lending to developing countries

Tightening of bank lending standards

Note: Data for 2001 are until the second quarter. Tightening of lending materials refers to the share of banks in the United States that reported a tightening of their standards and terms on commercial and industrial loans over the past three months, as reported in the quarterly survey of the U.S. Federal Reserve Board.
Source: Capital DATA Loanware; U.S. Federal Reserve Board.

Investor Service). Therefore, when growth slows banks tend to tighten their credit standards to restrict loans to speculative-grade borrowers, both in reaction to the deterioration in the banks' portfolios while default rates increase and in anticipation of the impact of recession on highly leveraged corporations. The percentage of U.S. banks tightening their lending conditions exceeded that of the recession of the early 1990s (figure 2.2), and the volume of global cross-border bank lending commitments fell by 13 percent in 2001. While bank credit contracted in all categories of credit risk, the most severe pull back was from the high-risk borrowers.[5]

2. Reduced demand for speculative-grade assets also may have reflected investors' reduced appetite for risk after their wealth declined (see box 2.1), exacerbated by the events of September 11. Investors in high-risk assets have experienced a sharp fall in wealth: since its peak in early 2000, the market capitalization of the Nasdaq stock index has fallen by over $3 trillion.

3. Reduced demand for speculative assets may also reflect increased uncertainty about economic prospects. The collapse of technology stocks and the industrial countries' plunge from 3.4 percent growth in 2000 to 1 percent in

2001 may have increased the range of outcomes that investors feel they should consider. Increased uncertainty can cause risk-averse investors to reduce the share of high-risk assets in their portfolios.

For all of these reasons, the past year has seen a widespread retreat from speculative-grade borrowers. Because their share in total developing-country borrowers is three times that of industrial-country borrowers, the decline in loan commitments to developing countries was relatively large. Bank lending to developing countries dropped to $93 billion in 2001, or less than 75 percent of the 2000 figure—the second-lowest annual level since 1994. The decline in commitments was biased against new entrants to the market: the share of bank credit attributed to refinancing rose from 26 percent in 2000 to 34 percent in 2001. The cost of refinancing for investment-grade borrowers rose minimally. By contrast, the cost of refinancing for borrowers rated below-investment-grade rose sharply and loan maturities fell. Unlike the case for bonds (see next paragraph), the decline in bank lending affected most developing countries. Even excluding Argentina and Turkey, which are suffering severe domestic crises, and Brazil, which had been greatly affected by developments in Argentina during most of 2001, the decline in bank lending

Box 2.1 Evidence of changes in the appetite for risk and capital market flows

Changes in investors' appetite for risk are often associated with changes in developing-country access to private capital flows. The appetite for risk under conditions of uncertainty in part depends on the level of wealth (Guay 1999 shows this in a theoretical model of managers' behavior). Because each dollar of income becomes more important as wealth declines, risk-averse investors are less willing to undertake greater risks at lower levels of wealth. Clark (1998) finds that one reason for capital flows from rich to poor countries is that the higher wealth of rich countries' investors makes them more willing to undertake risky investments. The converse of this effect was important during the Russian devaluation of 1998, when huge losses suffered by investors in Russian securities reduced the appetite for risk (Kumar and Persaud 2001; Institute of International Finance 1998), and capital flows to developing countries collapsed.

However, apart from crises that are clearly related to changes in investors' wealth, it is difficult to determine whether changes in the appetite for risk have had an important impact on market access. The appetite for risk is extremely difficult to measure. Market sources, including Chase Securities, J. P. Morgan, and Credit Suisse–First Boston, do provide statistical approaches to measuring investors' appetite for risk. These indices generally include measures of market liquidity: for example, spreads between recently issued and off-the-run Treasury securities;[6]

and measures of credit risk, including spreads between risk-free and high-risk assets, differences between the riskier small-cap stocks and the S&P 500, foreign exchange volatility, and changes in the price of options relative to their value if exercised (referred to as implied volatility). In general these indices do record reductions in the appetite for risk during periods when it is likely that such declines occurred, for example the Russian devaluation of August 1998. In addition, the J.P. Morgan index registers a substantial rise in risk aversion during July 2001 when the Argentine crisis deteriorated, and then immediately following the September 11th attacks.

However, these indicators face difficulties in distinguishing between changes in risk appetite and changes in the riskiness of assets. For example, deterioration in growth could harm credit quality and thus raise high-risk spreads in general. While risk appetite may also decline, the change in spreads would be a combination of the two rather than predominantly a measure of the appetite for risk. Similarly, greater willingness to hedge against risk (measured by increases in the implied volatility of options contracts) may represent reduced appetite for risk or the perception that the environment has become more risky (Kumar and Persaud 2001). Thus, the indicators have value in alerting market observers to changes in the demand for risky assets, but are less effective in determining the cause.

was about 25 percent. Bank lending is less tolerant of changes in risk than are bond markets, reflecting banks' high leverage and the greater concentration of their loan portfolio compared to investors in bonds.

—might benefit developing-country bonds

Perhaps surprisingly, the reduced demand for high-risk assets may have helped support developing countries' bond issues, which remained stable in 2001, at $68 billion. Developing-country bond issuers have higher credit ratings, on average, than developing-country bank borrowers. Thus bond issues were less affected by increased uncertainty and reduced appetite for risk. Moreover, the decline in interest rates and a slight reduction in investment-grade spreads implied a significant reduction in interest rates for investment-grade borrowers, thus encouraging more of them to come to the market.

The stability in bond volume in 2001 was supported by increased borrowing by higher quality borrowers (rated either investment grade or just below), including China, Hungary, Malaysia, Mexico, and Poland, as well as smaller borrowers, such as Colombia, Latvia, Panama, and Uruguay.

Reduced capital flows partially reflect a fall in demand

Declines in the demand for capital played a modest role in determining the volume of capital market commitments in 2001. Most developing countries' access to foreign capital is constrained by the willingness of foreign investors and lenders to supply funds. However, a few countries could borrow more even at the current interest rate, but do not because their demand for capital is low. For example, during 1998–99 the demand for funds from the East Asian crisis countries collapsed with the

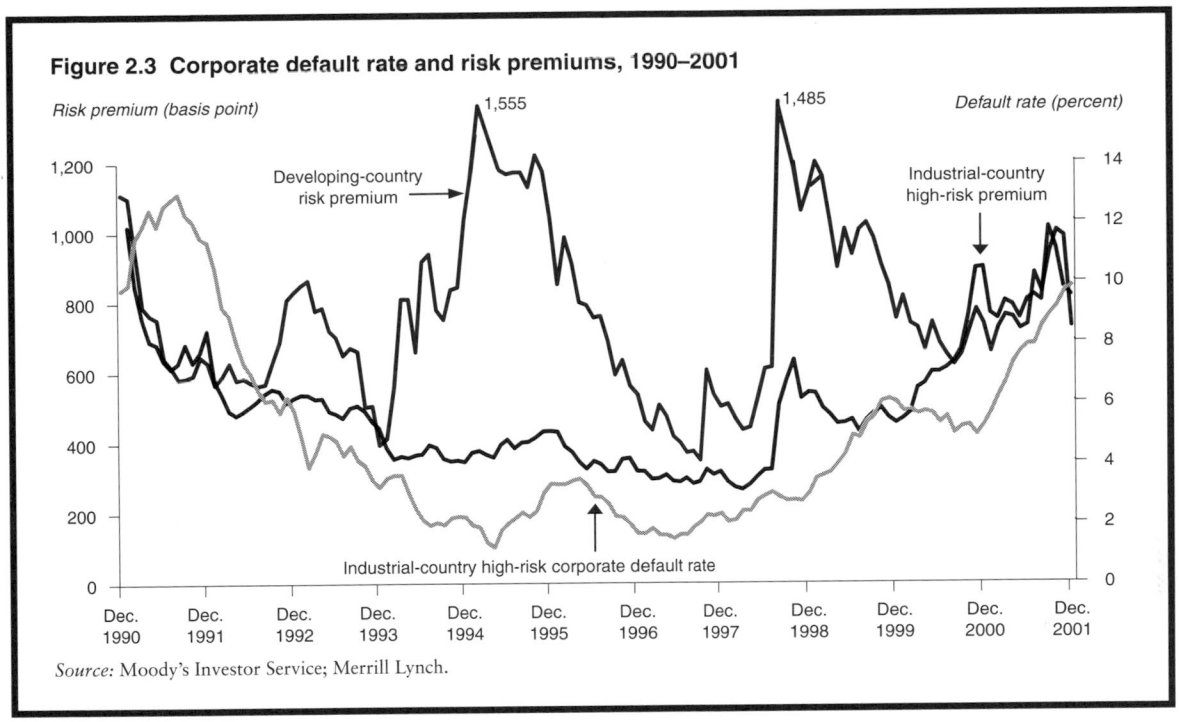

Figure 2.3 Corporate default rate and risk premiums, 1990–2001

Risk premium (basis point) ... *Default rate (percent)*

Developing-country risk premium → 1,555

Industrial-country high-risk premium 1,485

Industrial-country high-risk corporate default rate

Source: Moody's Investor Service; Merrill Lynch.

30 percent fall in investment, and they ran large current account surpluses. Capital market commitments to the crisis countries fell to about $30 billion per year during this period, compared with $74 billion in 1997. It appears that demand also remained low in the five crisis countries in 2001, since investment fell slightly and the government deficit improved by almost 1 percent of GDP. Capital market commitments fell to $34 billion. Thus low demand from the crisis countries most likely reduced the level of capital market commitments compared with what would have happened with a robust recovery. Nevertheless, there was no repeat of the experience of the 1998–99 period, when the drop in capital market commitments in the crisis countries had a noticeable impact on the total for developing countries. A few of the richer oil-exporting developing countries also reduced their capital market commitments in 2001, presumably choosing to increase saving in response to continued high oil prices.

Capital market commitments declined until late in the year

The overall decline in capital market commitments accelerated in 2001 while the global slowdown deepened. Capital market commitments fell to about $16 billion per month during the first half of 2001 (compared with $19 billion per month in 2000), and then dropped to only $9 billion per month following the September 11 terrorist attacks (table 2.5). Spreads on developing countries shot up to 924 basis points in the aftermath of the attacks, compared with 716 basis points in the first half of 2001, although the rise in spreads (excluding Argentina and Turkey, the two major countries most affected by domestic economic crises) was modest. Commitments recovered during the last quarter, but remained well below the 2000 level. The average spread excluding Argentina and Turkey fell to 400 basis points (100 basis points below the average of the previous year) while interest rates fell and optimism about an early recovery increased.

Trends in FDI

Net FDI to developing countries is estimated at $168 billion in 2001, almost unchanged from the previous year, and just 8 percent below the peak reached in 1999. The stability of FDI flows was achieved in the face of a significant fall in global FDI flows. Changes in FDI flows to developing countries in 2001 were driven more by

Table 2.5 Capital market commitments and spreads for developing countries

	2000	2001			
		January–June	July–August	September–October	November–December
(monthly average, billions of dollars)					
Capital market commitments	19.3	15.8	12.7	9.3	16.6
Bonds	5.7	6.9	4.1	2.5	6.8
Banks	10.6	7.7	7.9	6.7	9.1
Equity	3.0	1.2	0.6	0.2	0.7
(basis points)					
Developing-country spreads	707	716	844	924	865
without Argentina and Turkey	507	440	416	447	404

Note: Developing-country spreads refer to J. P. Morgan Chase's Emerging Market Bond Index Global, which uses country weights based on market capitalization of outstanding debt.
Source: Dealogic; J. P. Morgan Chase; World Bank staff calculations.

domestic economic developments (for example decisions over privatization transactions and policy improvements) in a few of the large FDI recipients than by changes in the global economy.

Global FDI in downturn—

Preliminary estimates from the United Nations Conference on Trade and Development (UNCTAD) indicate that global FDI flows fell massively in 2001, to $760 billion from about $1.3 trillion in the previous year. Global mergers and acquisitions (M&A) activity show a 45 percent drop in 2001. Slow growth or recession is often associated with a decline in FDI outflows (paralleling the decline in domestic investment) since multinational corporations face stringent financing constraints with the

decline in profits and tightening of bank credit standards. For example, FDI outflows from the United States dropped from $19 billion in 1980 to only $1 billion during the 1982 recession year, and then recovered to $13 billion in 1984.

—but developing countries were less affected

The past years have seen considerable stability in FDI flows to developing countries, although their share of global FDI flows was cut in half in the wake of the Asian crisis. Essentially, the trends observed since FDI flows plateaued in the late 1990s have remained constant. Developing countries' share of global FDI flows turned up with the drop in global flows, but remained well below the 36 percent level reached in 1997 (see figure 2.4). FDI

Figure 2.4 FDI and M&A in developing countries, 1991–2001

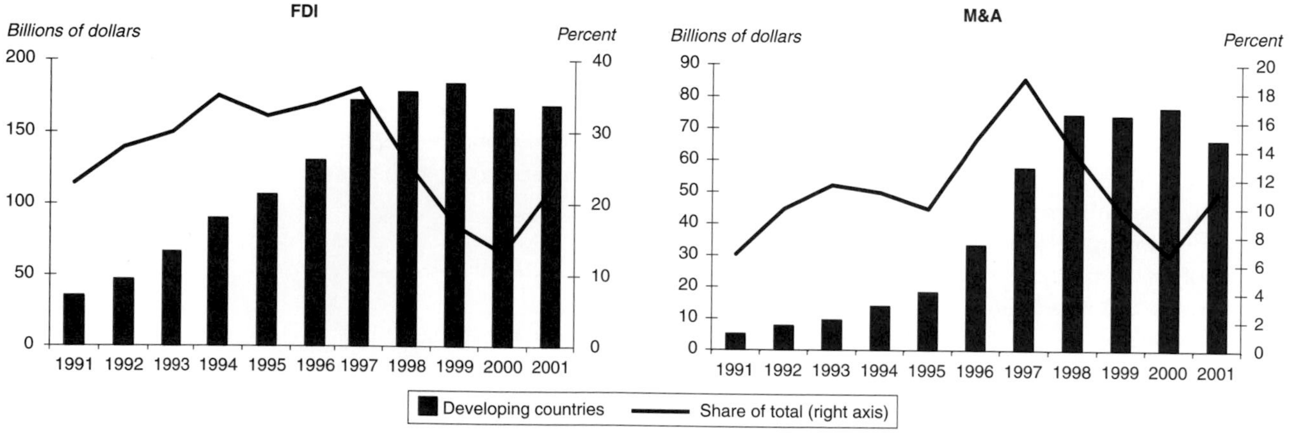

Source: World Bank, *Global Development Finance: Country Tables* and sources cited therein, various years; UNCTAD, *World Investment Report 2001*; World Bank staff estimates for 2001.

flows continue to decline relative to developing countries' GDP, down to 2.3 percent in 2001 from 3 percent in 1998. FDI flows remain highly concentrated: as has been true for the past few years, the top 10 recipients of FDI received over 70 percent of total FDI to developing countries (box 2.2).

The stability of FDI flows in 2001 largely reflects offsetting changes in a few large countries rather than the impact of the economic slowdown or other global factors. Eight out of the top ten recipients saw changes (either increases or decreases) in FDI flows of 20 percent or more from the previous year. These changes were driven largely by internal factors, often privatization, private sector M&A transactions, or general domestic economic conditions. In Mexico the sale of Banamex-Accival

Box 2.2   The concentration of FDI flows

Most FDI flows have remained concentrated in just a few developing countries throughout the 1990s, when the share of the top 10 has never fallen below 64 percent.[7] Market size appears to be a major explanation of concentration: of the top 10 developing-country FDI recipients, 6 are also among the top 10 countries in terms of GDP, but market size is not the only factor. The average ratio of FDI to GDP in the top 10 recipients is almost a full percentage point higher than in developing countries as a group (figure 2.5). While Brazil, China, and Mexico alone account for about half of developing countries' FDI, they make up only a little more than one-third of developing countries' GDP. While FDI flows to India—the fourth largest developing country—have increased over the 1990s, the country remains 14th on the list of developing-country FDI recipients.

FDI is also concentrated in relation to other indicators of economic activity. Of the 10 largest FDI recipients, 7 are also the developing countries with the largest exports. UNCTAD (2001) developed a more comprehensive index that measures FDI inflows relative to economic size, as represented by an unweighted average of three ratios—a country's share in world FDI inflows to its share in world GDP, employment, and exports. By this measure, FDI is mildly concentrated; only 30 out of 102 developing countries had shares of FDI that equaled or exceeded their average shares of world GDP, employment, and exports. Only half the top 10 FDI recipients received more FDI than expected, based on their shares of global economic activity. The concentration of FDI flows does not mean that FDI only benefits the larger countries; all of the 10 developing countries with the highest ratio of FDI to GDP are relatively small-scale economics.

FDI to some of the larger recipients has been boosted by good policies. The largest FDI recipients have an average World Bank policy rating of 4.1, compared with 3.3 for other developing countries. Perhaps more important for determining FDI *flows*, however, is the change in policies. Countries that have undergone an improvement in the investment climate may see a large inflow of FDI until the stock reaches the levels desired by foreign investors. The huge surge in FDI to China with the introduction of market reforms is perhaps the most spectacular example of this phenomenon. Similarly, FDI flows to Mexico were boosted by Mexico's entrance into the North American Free Trade Agreement. FDI also has increased to countries with strong economic programs that liberalize the rules governing FDI; for example, FDI to the Republic of Korea rose from about $2 billion before the East Asian crisis to an average of $7 billion following the easing of rules against foreign investment (see World Bank 2000a). Finally, FDI has responded to government decisions on privatization programs; 7 of the 10 largest FDI recipients received more than $1 billion in foreign funds to finance privatization activities in 1999 (World Bank 2001).

The concentration of other flows is similar to that of FDI. The 10 developing countries with the largest domestic investment levels accounted for 70 percent of all investment in developing countries. This is unsurprising, because foreign and domestic investors are likely to respond to the same factors—market size and investment climate. Moreover, FDI inflows tend to crowd in domestic investment (World Bank 2001, chapter 3; Bosworth and Collins 1999). The concentration of capital market flows is somewhat higher than FDI; the top 10 recipients accounted for 75 percent of total flows. Access to capital market flows depends on the presence of relatively well-developed financial markets (Hausmann and Fernandez-Arias 2000). Thus while the poorest developing countries receive significant amounts of FDI, they receive almost no portfolio flows (see chapter 3). A concentration of FDI flows is often observed within countries as well. For example, nearly 90 percent of China's FDI stock is in the coastal regions, almost all FDI flows to Mexico were absorbed in central states and those bordering the United States (UNCTAD 2001), while in India the top five recipient states (Maharashtra, Tamil Nadu, Karnataka, Andhra Pradesh, and Delhi) accounted for 75 percent of total FDI approvals in 2000. Again, the quality of policies appears to be a major determinant of the distribution of FDI flows in India (Dollar, Iarossi, and Mengistae 2001).

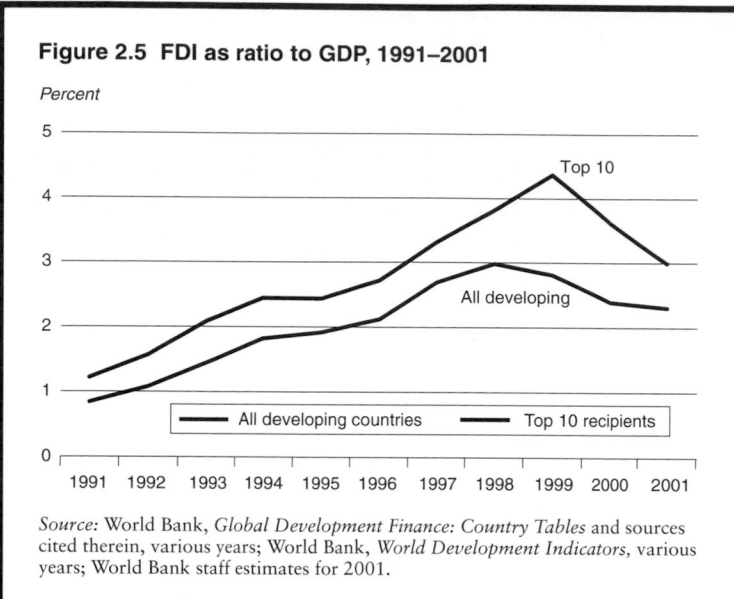

Figure 2.5 FDI as ratio to GDP, 1991–2001

Percent

Top 10

All developing

Legend: All developing countries — Top 10 recipients

x-axis: 1991 1992 1993 1994 1995 1996 1997 1998 1999 2000 2001

Source: World Bank, *Global Development Finance: Country Tables* and sources cited therein, various years; World Bank, *World Development Indicators,* various years; World Bank staff estimates for 2001.

financial group to Citigroup for $12.5 billion boosted FDI flows, and in South Africa, a foreign firm took over De Beers mining company by acquiring shares worth $20 billion. In Poland lower FDI flows signaled the completion of major privatization transactions. In other countries changes in FDI flows reflected changes in the overall economic environment rather than the impact of a few transactions. Examples include Brazil, where economic uncertainty restrained greenfield FDI; Argentina, where lower FDI flows reflected a slowdown in private sector M&A transactions with the increasing economic difficulties; Korea, where the process of corporate and financial restructuring has slowed;[8] and China, where FDI boomed with the anticipation of accession to the World Trade Organization. The extent to which FDI inflows in China represent additional resources to the country remains open to question, because a significant portion of registered FDI to China may have originated in the country (box 2.3).

These major changes largely determined the regional trends. FDI continued to fall in Latin America, the largest recipient region, because cross-border M&A activity in the region dropped by around 5 percent. Several privatization plans have been postponed or delayed (examples include Copel, Brazil's electricity generation and transmission company, and Cintra, the holding company

of Mexico's major airlines), whereas some foreign investors have withdrawn large-scale offers to acquire stakes in private companies (including two Brazilian telecommunications companies). FDI flows to Eastern Europe remained stable; while large-scale privatization programs in banking and telecommunications neared completion, the region received an increase in greenfield investment. Net FDI flows to Middle East and North Africa remained at about the level of the past few years. The De Beers sale boosted flows to Sub-Saharan Africa. FDI to East Asia and Pacific declined despite higher FDI to China, because of slow growth in several regional economies, low demand for funds in the high-tech industries, and reduced M&A transactions in the East Asian crisis countries (figure 2.6).

Developing countries may also be a growing source of FDI

While the data are incomplete, it appears that developing countries have become a major source of FDI flows to other developing countries. Out of $185 billion FDI inflows to developing countries in 1999, only $72 billion are identified by the Organisation for Economic Co-operation and Development (OECD) as coming from the industrial countries. Developing countries also receive about $40 billion in FDI flows from other high-income countries.[9] If these statistics are accurate, the remainder of developing countries' FDI inflows (about one-third or $70 billion) would have to be from other developing countries (figure 2.7). South-South FDI may also have contributed to the resiliency of FDI flows during the financial crisis. By these calculations, South-South FDI flows continued to rise in 1998 and 1999 despite the financial crises, during which total FDI flows from high-income OECD countries declined.

South-South FDI has increased at the same time as South-South trade was rising (intra-developing countries imports rose from 30 percent of their total imports in 1990 to 36 percent in 1999). Thus, the production and ownership structures of developing countries seem to have become more integrated through FDI, not only with the industrial countries, but also with other developing countries. In addition, major developing-country exporters who face quota restrictions in industrial countries may have invested abroad in order to export from countries that are less affected by such trade barriers.

Box 2.3   Round-tripping of capital flows between China and Hong Kong

FDI inflows to China surged in the 1990s, boosted by the acceleration of market reforms and the introduction of incentives for FDI, including concessions on tax, leasing of land and property, government guarantees for investments, and special arrangements regarding retention and repatriation of foreign exchange. Preferences for foreign capital are believed to have encouraged Chinese investors to move money offshore and then bring it back to China disguised as foreign investment (Sicular 1998). Another motivation for "round-tripping," or "recycling," is the concern that the government may impose exchange restrictions on residents, as occurred in July 1993 (Adams 1993; Gunter 1996). Some early studies estimated that round-tripping accounted for nearly a quarter of foreign inflows to China in 1992 (Lardy 1995, p. 1067; Harrold and Lall 1993, p. 24). The extent of recycling may have increased in recent years (box figure).

Throughout the 1990s, FDI inflows to China originated mostly outside the industrial countries, notably from Hong Kong (China). For example, FDI inflows from Hong Kong constituted nearly half of total FDI flows to China in 1996. Hong Kong's share has declined since 1997, to below 40 percent by 2000 (see table below). This decline has been offset by a comparable increase in FDI inflows reported from the Virgin Islands, however, which suggests

that there is round-tripping through this offshore financial center. The FDI inflows from Hong Kong (and the Virgin Islands) appear to be highly correlated with outflows from China in the form of "other investment assets" (mostly bank deposits) held abroad by Chinese residents, and errors and omissions in China's balance of payments (see figure below). Hong Kong, in its turn, reports large amounts of FDI inflows from mainland China, and from offshore financial centers such as Bermuda and the Virgin Islands.

China's FDI by source
(percent)

	1996	1998	1999	2000
Hong Kong (China)	50	42	40	38
Virgin Islands (U.K.)	0	9	7	9
United States	8	9	10	11
Singapore	0	8	7	5
Japan	9	8	7	7
Taiwan (China)	8	7	6	6
Korea, Democratic People's Republic of	0	4	3	4
Germany	0	2	3	3
Netherlands	0	2	1	2
France	1	2	2	2
Others	24	7	14	13

Round-tripping of capital flows: China and Hong Kong (China), 1986–1999

Billions of dollars

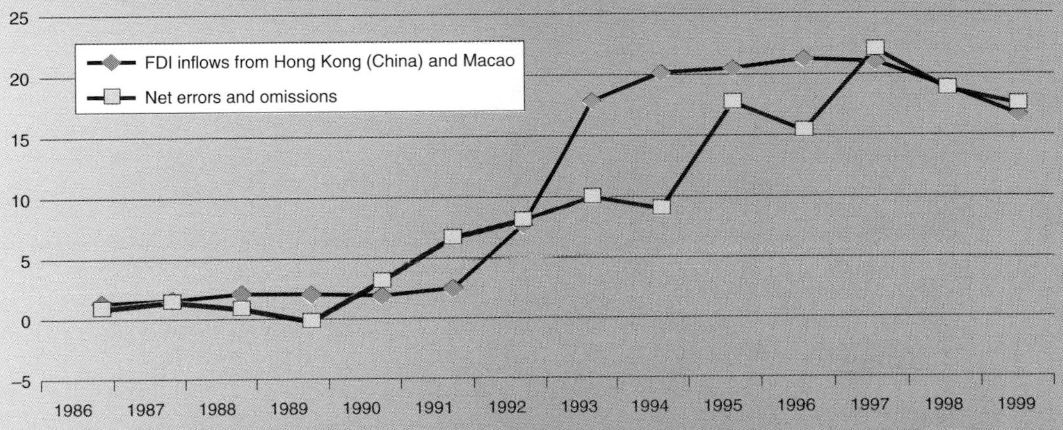

Source: World Bank staff estimates.

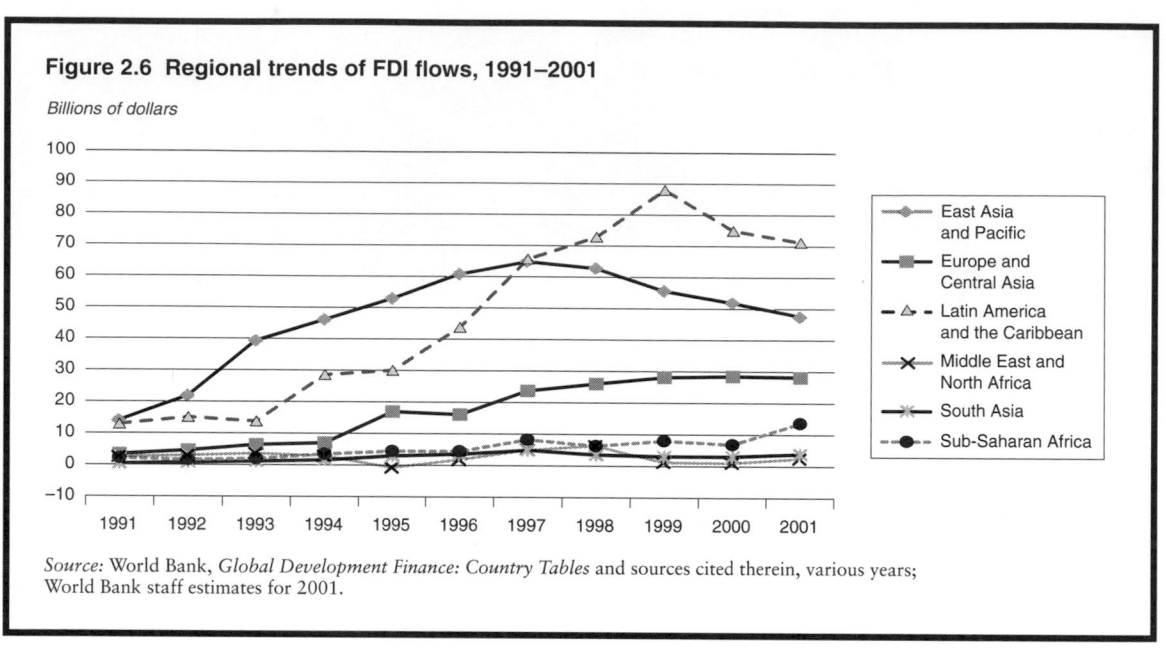

Figure 2.6 Regional trends of FDI flows, 1991–2001

Billions of dollars

Legend:
- East Asia and Pacific
- Europe and Central Asia
- Latin America and the Caribbean
- Middle East and North Africa
- South Asia
- Sub-Saharan Africa

Source: World Bank, *Global Development Finance: Country Tables* and sources cited therein, various years; World Bank staff estimates for 2001.

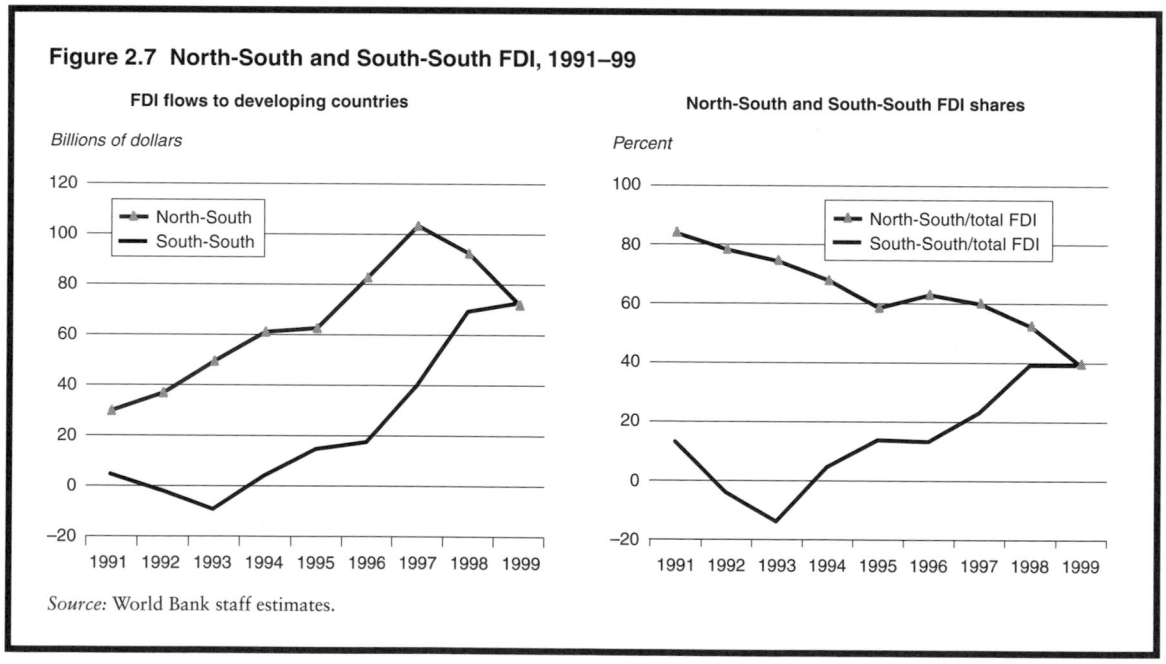

Figure 2.7 North-South and South-South FDI, 1991–99

FDI flows to developing countries

Billions of dollars

Legend:
- North-South
- South-South

North-South and South-South FDI shares

Percent

Legend:
- North-South/total FDI
- South-South/total FDI

Source: World Bank staff estimates.

The data given above calculate South-South FDI by comparing developing countries' FDI inflows with recorded outflows from other regions. This is probably more reliable than basing the calculation on identified outflows from developing countries. The problem of under-reporting FDI outflows is acute in the developing countries, many of which have capital controls, exchange controls, and high taxes on investment incomes, combined with weak accounting rules and tax administration. Nevertheless, the trend of increasing outflows of FDI from developing countries is also evident from the data on identified outflows reported in the country pages of the IMF balance of payments statistics. However, reported outflows from developing countries, which reached only $12 billion by 1998, are much smaller than the estimate given above, due to under-reporting of outflows by source countries.

Emerging market financial crises in 2001

The past year has seen a continuation of the severe economic crises of the 1990s that afflicted major middle-income emerging markets (Mexico in 1994–95, East Asia in 1997–98, the Russian Federation in 1998, and Brazil in 1998–99). The causes of each crisis differed in important respects, but in all of them shortcomings in external financial management and defects in corporate and financial sector governance played an important role. The past year's problems in Argentina and Turkey shared many features with these earlier crises.

A critical difference, however, is that contagion effects to other emerging markets, and other debt markets, have been limited (box 2.4). This is especially noteworthy since Argentina's crisis developed into a full-blown sovereign default. The only recent instance of such an extreme outcome by a major debtor was the Russian Federation in August 1998; that situation produced severe dislocation across global financial markets.

The crisis in *Argentina* has its roots in the buildup of vulnerabilities after the highly successful exchange rate-based stabilization of the early 1990s. After a long history of inflation (including a period of hyperinflation) and failed efforts to stabilize, the adoption of a dollar-based currency board in 1991 stopped the country's inflation in its tracks.[10] The country experienced a post-stabilization boom on the order of 7 percent growth in GDP, while the reduction in interest rates toward world levels stimulated domestic demand.

However, substantial vulnerabilities remained, and were increasingly exposed during the second half of the 1990s. Despite strong export growth, foreign exchange revenues were insufficient to finance buoyant import demands, rendering the country dependent on capital inflows. Fiscal policy was not only too loose on average, but was also unhelpfully procyclical—too expansionary in the recovery phase of 1996–97, leaving the authorities with no scope but to tighten policy into the down-

turn after 1998.[11] As a result, public sector debt remained high (at 50 percent of GDP in mid-2001), and maturities shortened.

The steady appreciation of the dollar in the second half of the 1990s and the sharp Brazilian devaluation led to a 15 percent real exchange rate appreciation between January 1997 and mid-2001, further constraining growth. Most importantly of all, deflation persisted throughout the economy (consumer prices have fallen by a cumulative 3 percent over the past three years), and the real economy remained stuck in recession, leading to a further rise in an already intolerably high unemployment rate. With nominal incomes across the economy falling sharply during 2001, there was little realistic chance for the authorities to meet the tax revenue projections that were the backbone to a planned "zero deficit" budget strategy. Market awareness of the sizeable dollar liabilities of both the public and private sectors completed a picture that made creditors leery of maintaining, let alone adding to, exposures as the end of the year approached.

Public disturbances—in part a reaction to limits imposed on cash withdrawals from the banks—led to the resignation of the Argentine president in December 2001. Soon after, the government formally defaulted on its debts and the currency was devalued. A floating exchange rate system was introduced in mid-February. It remains to be seen who will bear the considerable losses from the devaluation, but given all these dislocations, a phase of renewed output declines and rising unemployment seems inevitable. The only issue now is how long this situation will persist.

Turkey also faced a severe crisis in 2001, which was marked by efforts to control a large public sector deficit (12 percent of gross national product [GNP] in 2000), high levels of public sector debt (in the range of 90 percent of GNP by end-2001), and difficulties in rolling over short-term debt (100 percent of reserves). Adoption of a crawling peg in 1999 was aimed at reducing high levels of inflation. Fixing the exchange rate encouraged large capital inflows with a substantial buildup of foreign exchange liabilities of the banking system. In February 2001, the government was compelled to abandon the crawling peg, which led to a 26 percent real devaluation (year-on-year) by the end of 2001 and large losses in the banking sector that the government is now cleaning up. There are a number of reasons, however, why

Box 2.4   Financial market contagion from the Argentine crisis

There is little evidence that investors have retreated from most other emerging markets because of the crisis in Argentina. The correlation between secondary markets bond spreads between Argentina and 15 emerging markets rose from 0.27 in the months before the exacerbation of Argentina's difficulties in October 2000 to 0.47 from October 2000 to August 2001.[12] However, this period coincided with the global growth slowdown that was associated with a general rise in spreads and in the volatility of spreads (and measured correlations tend to rise with increases in volatility), so it is difficult to isolate the impact of the two crises. Brazil does appear to have been affected by the crisis in its neighbor to the south, perhaps because they compete in the same markets.[13] The correlation between Brazilian and Argentine spreads increased from 0.6 in mid-2000 to between 0.8 and 0.9 in each of the three-month periods from October 2000 to August 2001. However, late in the year market sentiment toward Brazil improved, and spreads narrowed despite the increasing problems in Argentina.

Looking at specific crisis episodes (October 2000, March/April 2001, July 2001, and December 2001), we can see some rise in the spreads on other emerging market bonds. However, the rise in spreads during the crisis periods varied, and spreads tended to return to former levels relatively quickly. The index of emerging market spreads was at almost the same level in December 2001 as in October 2000. Overall, spreads in emerging markets excluding the two crisis countries appear to have been little affected by the crisis in Argentina, and were stable until the September 11 terrorist attacks.[14]

There are various reasons why the Argentine crisis has generated such limited contagion effects so far, in marked contrast to the East Asian crisis and the Russian

Change in spreads during crisis periods, 2000–01
(basis points)

	October 2000	April 2001	July 2001	December 2001
Argentina	317	363	874	3,806
Developing countries (excluding Argentina and Turkey)	64	–1	68	–46

Note: Each crisis period is defined as the previous low point of spreads to the peak. The weights used for developing countries excluding Argentina and Turkey in December 2001 differ slightly from the previous periods.

devaluation. Unlike these earlier crises, which were considerable surprises, investors have been aware of the problems in Argentina for some time. Thus most investors may already have taken whatever steps they felt necessary in absorbing the losses on Argentine bonds. Moreover, many investors are less leveraged this time around than during the Asian crisis (particularly after the debacle that highly leveraged speculators suffered with the Russian devaluation), which means that there is a reduced need to liquidate across-the-board to meet margin calls. At the same time, developing countries are less vulnerable than they were a few years ago. Currently, very few major emerging markets have pegged exchange rates, which proved to be particularly vulnerable to contagion from the collapse of other pegged exchange rates. Levels of reserves have risen while short-term debt levels have fallen, improving a key indicator of vulnerability. Several of the Asian countries are presently running current account surpluses, and so are less dependent on international capital markets. Finally, low international interest rates eased external financing pressures on heavily indebted emerging markets.

Turkey's difficulties have been less severe than Argentina's:

- Despite the crisis, Turkey is making significant progress in improving the fiscal accounts: the primary balance of the consolidated public sector shifted from a deficit equivalent to 2 percent of GNP in 1999 to (an estimated) surplus of 5.7 percent of GNP in 2001.
- The exchange rate regime was less rigid and thus provided for an easier (albeit still very messy) exit mechanism.

- Turkey's debt is higher than Argentina's (relative to output), but a greater share is owed to domestic residents, which helped facilitate efforts at restructuring.
- A larger and more diversified export sector means that exchange rate depreciation can have a greater and more rapid impact on production.
- Turkey's strong ties to Europe and its importance as a front-line state following the September 11 attacks have helped to facilitate substantial financial support. However, the attacks also severely damaged Turkey's foreign

exchange receipts, due to the drop in revenues from tourism and slower export growth. A new IMF standby arrangement to help Turkey absorb this additional external shock and sustain its reform program is expected to be in place in February 2002.

Lessons of the turmoil in Argentina

The situation in Argentina is difficult, and the role of clear-sighted economic policy is critical. The challenge for the Argentine authorities now is to adopt appropriate measures to allow the economy to take advantage of the newfound flexibility of a floating exchange rate, while also addressing some the key structural problems that have been exposed and worsened by recent developments. It is worth noting that—in the cases of Mexico in early 1995, Thailand and Korea in the winter of 1997–98, the Russian Federation in the fall of 1998, and Brazil in early 1999—the early stages in the move to a free float were very difficult and it took time for signs of successful stabilization to be visible. The Argentine crisis is especially complex, since it combines large private sector foreign exchange exposure and public sector default.

It is not too early to draw important lessons from the developments in Argentina. Most of these lessons reinforce those that became evident during the East Asian and Russian crises of 1997–98. Five stand out:

- *Fixed exchange rate regimes are vulnerable to asymmetric shocks.* The success of fixed exchange rate regimes requires that the countries involved are affected similarly by shocks. Events of the past few years, including the decline in commodity prices and the Brazilian devaluation, required a devaluation in Argentina to restore external balance. But at the same time the dollar was appreciating, responding to a very different set of economic factors. The resulting appreciation of the peso depressed output, particularly given rigidity in labor markets which impeded real wage adjustment. The resulting recession in turn undermined support for the program.

- *There are severe costs associated with hanging on to a pegged, overvalued exchange rate.* In Mexico (December 1994) and Thailand (third quarter of 1997), failed defenses of currency pegs led to country credit crises. The Argen-

tine authorities structured their economic system around the inviolability of the one-for-one exchange rate peg against the dollar. However, this structure encouraged investors to incur mounting dollar liabilities, in the belief that the government would maintain the peg. The size of dollar-denominated debt then greatly increased the economic costs when the peso was devalued.

- *The success of multilateral rescue packages depends critically on strong adjustment by recipient countries.* Crises can be successfully resolved only when policy implementation is strong; government commitment to taking difficult adjustment measures is critical. Multilateral financing is designed to support, not substitute for, adjustment. The size of potential outflows dwarfs the resources available to the multilaterals. Moreover, greatly increasing the size of rescue packages could encourage excessive risk taking by private investors, although so far the evidence that rescue packages have generally contributed to risk taking is inconclusive (box 2.5).

- *There is more work to be done on private sector involvement in crisis prevention and resolution. Recent experience has underscored the importance of clearer definition of the limits on official resources and of the rules and responsibilities of the official sector, debtor countries, and their private creditors.* Contingent credit lines can provide for new money in case of crisis. But the government's counter-parties can avoid increasing their exposure during a crisis by selling other holdings of government bonds, thus undermining confidence. In the case of Argentina voluntary debt exchanges were relatively easy to organize, but they did little to ease the country's financing difficulties. These challenges point to the need to consider more ambitious proposals for facilitating orderly workouts of problematic private sector debts, and the recent proposal by the IMF to provide for a standstill of debt payments in order to allow time for an orderly restructuring will, no doubt, be debated in the year ahead.

- *Contagion can be contained through prudent external financial management.* Most countries in Latin America and Asia that are dependent on private capital flows have strengthened their ability to withstand shocks through

Box 2.5   Moral hazard and rescue packages

Considerable concern has been raised that the expectation of multilateral support for crisis-hit countries may encourage excessive risk taking by investors in emerging market debt (Meltzer 2000; Calomiris 2000).[15] It is difficult to evaluate what might have happened in the absence of rescue packages, and so far the evidence that rescue packages have encouraged excessive risk taking is inconclusive. Zhang (1999) finds that spreads on emerging market bonds in the seven quarters following recovery from the Mexican crisis were no lower than precrisis levels, after controlling for other determinants of spreads. Lane and Phillips (2000) find no evidence that IMF-related news and announcements of rescue packages had an immediate impact on spreads. By contrast, Eichengreen and Mody (1998) find that, by 1996, spreads on emerging market bonds had fallen to levels that failed to adequately compensate for the risk of lending, and spreads fell further in 1997.

Concern that some investors have escaped the losses associated with financial crises has boosted concern over moral hazard. It is difficult to estimate creditor losses from recent emerging market crises, although losses are less than they would have been in the absence of official support. International equity investors may have lost $166 billion during the Asian crisis (International Council of Securities Agencies 1999) and international banks $60 billion (UNCTAD 2001). Losses during the Asian and Russian crises may have totaled $350 billion (Institute of International Finance, various years). Nevertheless, the provision of multilateral funds undoubtedly facilitated the repayment of international banks during the Mexican and Asian crises. Authorities had to balance the erosion of market discipline with the consequences of a complete collapse, which could have had severe effects on many emerging markets.

While the evidence of moral hazard–induced excessive lending is inconclusive, given the uncertainties involved it is prudent to explore means of reducing the potential impact of multilateral support on moral hazard. Of the 15 largest emerging market borrowers in 1997 (which together account for 80 percent of capital market flows to developing countries), 8 had been the subject of rescue packages by 2001. Some of them received several individual loans. Some proposals have focused on limiting the flexibility of multilateral institutions by allowing rescue packages only for solvent borrowers who prequalify for loans (Meltzer 2000). Other proposals have emphasized prior actions that force private creditors to recognize losses or provide resources during a crisis. For example, eligibility for multinational assistance during a future crisis could be conditioned on the government's obtaining prior commitment by the private sector to roll over maturing claims or to provide new money. Still other proposals have focused on ex ante

provisions that would facilitate the private sector absorbing losses. A modification to collective action clauses could permit the restructuring of bond instruments by majority vote of the creditors rather than unanimity. This would reduce the ability of small creditors to force repayment of their debts as the price of agreement to restructure and greatly ease the complexity involved in restructuring bonds. The implications of such modifications to collective action clauses are difficult to determine. Eichengreen and Mody (2000) found that collective action clauses with this provision tend to reduce the borrowing costs of more creditworthy borrowers and raise them for less creditworthy ones, which would strengthen market discipline. However, Becker and others (2001) found no evidence that such collective action clauses increase yields for either higher- or lower-rated issuers.

Another, complementary, approach is to provide for officially sanctioned standstills that would impose a cooling-off period to avoid investor panic (Eichengreen and Mody 2001); still another approach under some conditions is to use IMF facilities to continue lending to countries when borrowers are in arrears (Goldstein 1998; Fischer and Citrin 2000). The Bank of Canada and Bank of England (2001) have recommended adoption of an officially sanctioned standstill to provide a "time-out" during which governments can demonstrate their commitment to reform, and hence encourage investors to return. Kaufman and Litan (1998)[16] propose that multilateral support be contingent on changes in borrowing country laws that implement automatic write-downs on foreign currency denominated interbank loans.

All of these proposals face difficulties. Prequalification requirements could precipitate crises for countries that fail. Banks' prior commitments to rollover loans during a crisis can come at the cost of a sell-off of other assets, because banks attempt to limit their total exposure to the crisis country. It is difficult to define before the crisis what particular institutional arrangements would be most desirable to "bail in" private investors. This may depend, in part, on whether a liquidity or solvency crisis is involved. Standstills and write-down requirements could have a chilling effect on the provision of finance to emerging markets (although majority-based collective action clauses could support market discipline). Nevertheless, there is a growing recognition that greater attention to private sector participation in resolving crises is warranted. For example, the recent IMF loan to Argentina provided that the disbursement of some committed resources could be brought forward to support a voluntary and market-based operation to increase the viability of Argentina's debt profile. A review of international arrangements for crisis support that provided for greater private sector recognition of losses could help limit the potential for moral hazard in future lending.

flexible exchange rate regimes, disciplined domestic monetary policies and, most important of all, limited short-term external liabilities and near-term refinancing needs. These measures have helped limit the spread of problems from Argentina to other emerging markets over the past year.

The prospects for capital market flows and FDI

Capital market flows are expected to contract further in 2002—

Capital market commitments, after dropping from $228 billion in 2000 to only $171 billion in 2001, may moderate further to some $160 billion in 2002 (see table 2.6), which is the lowest level since 1994. Investors are likely to remain cautious about emerging markets in early 2002, because the synchronized economic slowdown in all major industrial countries limits demand for developing countries' exports, affecting the latter's ability to service external debt. Risk appetite remains low and financing constraints on banks and other investors remain tight in the industrial countries, so the demand for developing-country assets (especially subsovereign assets) is likely to remain low during the first half of 2002, at least. These influences are likely to outweigh the reduction in interest rates and increase in liquidity with the easing of monetary policy in the United States (and, to a lesser extent, in Europe) over the past year.[17]

—but a rebound is anticipated for 2003

The recovery in industrial countries that is anticipated to begin in the second half of 2002 should set the stage for a rise in capital market commitments, to $179 billion in 2003 and $216 billion in 2004. Capital flows should recover because economic growth in most of the major emerging market economies is expected to improve and international interest rates are expected to remain low. The recovery in flows will also be supported by the low levels of short-term debt and high levels of reserves in many emerging markets after the experience of the financial crises in the late 1990s. For 25 major emerging markets, the ratio of short-term debt to reserves fell from about one in 1997 to two-thirds by June 2001. Bond and bank lend-

Table 2.6 Projected capital market flows to developing countries
(billions of dollars)

	2001	2002	2003	2004
Total	171	160	179	216
Bonds	68	55	66	76
Equity	10	32	24	30
Loans	93	73	89	110
East Asia and Pacific	41	54	59	82
Latin America and the Caribbean	75	60	68	77
Other	55	46	53	57

Note: These projections for 2002–04 are based on 53 separate vector autoregression (VAR) models (see annex 2.1 for a description) for bond, equity and bank lending flows to 21 emerging market economies (ranked according to the size of gross flows in 2001 starting with the top recipient country): Brazil, Mexico, Korea, Turkey, South Africa, Argentina, China, Poland, Malaysia, the República Bolivariana de Venezuela, Colombia, the Philippines, Russia, Lebanon, Hungary, Egypt, India, Thailand, Indonesia, Lithuania, Morocco. The flows covered in these models accounted for 81 percent of gross capital market flows to developing countries in 2001. The projected flows were then scaled up using 2001 actual flow numbers, to arrive at the total for all developing countries.

ing flows are expected to rise by nearly a third by 2004, compared to the level in 2002, while equity flows are expected to recover rapidly from the extremely low level of 2001.

The pace of recovery in gross flows will also vary depending on creditworthiness and demand conditions in recipient countries. The trends in the forecast are driven by East Asia and Latin America, which accounted for over two-thirds of total capital market commitments in 2001. Flows to East Asia will increase relatively rapidly, largely because of China's forecast strong growth, low level of short-term debt, and high level of international reserves. By contrast, the recovery in flows to some of the East Asian crisis countries may be slower, because excess capacity continues to depress the demand for finance. In Latin America and the Caribbean flows will recover more slowly, in part because Argentina is likely to see impaired access to the capital markets in the wake of its restructuring of outstanding debt. Also, commodity exporters in the region will see only a limited rise in export revenues (and thus market access), because non-oil commodity prices are expected to rise by only 8 percent in 2003, and remain 25 percent below the level of 1997, and oil prices are expected to fall through 2003. By contrast, Mexico is expected to benefit from the recovery in the United States, and is likely to see a sharp rise in flows due to improved economic conditions. Flows to the other regions will also rise, and they generally maintain their share of total capital flows during the forecast period.

Any rebound depends on developments in Argentina

The crisis in Argentina is a major risk to this forecast. Before the events of the past year Argentina accounted for 16 percent of emerging markets' bonds outstanding on the international capital markets. Proposals to restructure Argentina's bonds could reduce investors' willingness to take on emerging market assets, particularly if negotiations are lengthy and marked by confrontation.[18] However, there are several reasons why the contagion effects of the crisis could be limited. Over the past year the Argentine crisis has had only a limited and fleeting impact on the demand for the debt of other emerging markets (see box 2.4). The crisis in Argentina has been long anticipated, which has tended to mute the impact on investors in comparison with the crises in East Asia and the Russian Federation, which were major surprises. Secondary market prices on Argentine bonds have already fallen substantially, and reflect relatively low recovery rates. Many current bondholders are likely to have bought the bonds at low prices, or to already have adjusted their portfolios to account for losses, so they may not react significantly to a debt restructuring. In fact, a speedy settlement with creditors that involves a debt restructuring sufficient to enable Argentina to make regular repayments could improve market sentiment and increase secondary market prices of Argentine debt. The forecasts assume that any debt renegotiation will be settled quickly; although Argentina (and Turkey) receive little in the way of new commitments over the forecast period, these crises have a relatively limited impact on investors' willingness to lend to other emerging markets.

FDI is expected to rise steadily

FDI flows to developing countries are expected to be much less sensitive to cyclical developments than capital market flows.[19] In 2002 FDI to developing countries is forecast at $160 billion, a slight decline from the estimated $168 billion in 2001, consistent with slow growth in global output and little increase in world trade. The same resiliency of FDI flows was seen in 2001, when the recession in industrial countries, near stagnation in world trade,

and a decline in global FDI flows were accompanied by rough stability of FDI flows to developing countries. This resiliency of FDI to developing countries in the face of adverse global economic conditions reflects the importance of domestic determinants of FDI flows (see section above on FDI trends in 2001). In addition, some of the major recipients of FDI flows, in particular China, are expected to continue to achieve robust growth despite the global slowdown.

While FDI flows are expected to remain resilient, the projected 4 percent per year increase from 2001–04 (2 percent in real terms) is less than half the rate experienced over the 1990s. We anticipate that the same forces that drove FDI in the 1990s—globalization in production due to technological innovations in communications and transport, coupled with better policies in developing countries—will continue over the next few years. However, the stock of FDI in developing countries is much larger now than 10 years ago, and exports, an important driver of FDI, are expected to grow at a much lower pace over the next few years (less than 3 percent more rapidly than GDP, compared with 6 percent during the 1990s). Moreover, M&A activity by multinationals, an important source of FDI flows, is declining after its peak in 2000. Although recent surveys indicate that multinationals' investment plans were relatively unaffected by the September 11th terrorist attacks, the full impact of the economic slowdown on multinationals' investments remains uncertain.[20] Thus it is unlikely that FDI flows would rise as rapidly over the next few years as they did over the last decade. Nevertheless, by 2004 FDI flows would remain the largest source of finance for developing countries.

The bulk of FDI inflows are forecast to continue to go to countries with relatively large market size and reasonably good policies. Brazil, China, and Mexico attract more than half of flows to the sample countries. The growth rate of FDI is high to countries with good policies and rapid expansion of trade. FDI in East Asian economies is expected to rise by over 10 percent per year, due to robust increases in flows to China, where the new commitments are already rising significantly, as well as to Korea and Thailand, where strong recovery in GDP and exports is expected. The anticipated economic growth is likely to boost FDI flows in South Asia, largely driven by India. On the other hand, Latin America's share of FDI to developing countries will decline, because privatization transactions (which made up a substantial share of FDI to Latin America in the 1990s—see World Bank, *GDF,* 2001: appendix 4) is likely to play a less significant role in attracting FDI.

Annex 2.1: Forecasts of Private Flows to Developing Countries

Capital market flows

The econometric framework used for generating the forecasts for capital market flows to developing countries follows Taylor and Sarno 1997, which extended the framework developed by Fernandez-Arias and Montiel 1996. In this framework equilibrium, or "desired" level, of capital flows to a developing country is affected by both global factors and country-specific factors. Changes in current capital flows are then determined partly by the difference between desired and actual capital flows in the previous period and partly by the changes in the factors determining the desired level of capital flows.

Global factors include growth in the industrial countries (proxied by the U.S. GDP), global liquidity (indicated by the U.S. interest rates), risk aversion on the part of international investors (proxied by U.S. high-yield spread and Emerging Market Bond Index [EMBI] spread), and the prices of oil and non-oil commodities. Developing country–specific variables include domestic economic growth (proxied by the index of industrial production), domestic consumer price index, domestic credit, domestic interest rates, the level of international reserves relative to short-term debt, and (separately) relative to imports, and the stock price index.[21] The global variables are assumed to evolve exogenously, without being influenced by developing-country variables. The latter variables, however, are jointly determined along with capital flows, since they affect and are in turn affected by capital flows. The econometric framework uses the vector autoregression (VAR) technique that determines country-specific variables endogenously on the basis of their lagged values, taking the global variables as exogenous.

The model is estimated separately for bonds, equity, and loans for each of the 21 major developing countries, using monthly data for the period from January 1990 to December 2001.[22] The flow forecasts are then summed up, and a scaling factor (equal to actual flows to all developing countries divided by the model-generated flows in 2001) is used to compute flows for all developing countries as a group.

The 21 countries included in this round accounted for 81 percent of gross capital market flows in 2001 (85 percent of bond flows, 96 percent of equity flows, and 75 percent of bank lending). The coverage of these countries in various types of flows as well as in different regions is summarized in table 2A.1. Also in 2001, the countries covered in these forecasting exercise accounted for 99 percent of all flows to East Asia, 81 percent of flows to Latin America, 73 percent for Europe and Central Asia, 83 percent for South Asia, 57 percent for Sub-Saharan Africa, and 58 percent for the Middle East and North Africa.

Forecasts generated by these VAR models indicate that industrial-country growth had a positive impact on the supply of capital flows to developing countries. Increases in interest rates reduced capital flows, while increases in U.S. high-yield spreads were positively associated with increases in EMBI spreads, which in turn had a negative effect on capital flows. In simulations with the model for last year's *Global Development Finance* (World Bank 2001) changes in industrial-country growth had a significantly larger impact on capital flows than changes in interest rates. Indeed, changes in U.S. interest rates and the U.S. high-yield spread caused only a slight deviation in capital flows from their original trends, and flows soon began to revert to their original values (Mody and others 2001). The effects of oil and non-oil commodity prices varied depending on whether a country was

Table 2A.1 How representative is the forecasting model?

	Flows to 15 countries as percent of 2001 actual flows
Bond total	85
Equity total	96
Loan total	75
East Asia and Pacific	99
Latin America and the Caribbean	81
Europe and Central Asia	73
South Asia	83
Sub-Saharan Africa	57
Middle East and North Africa	58
Total	81

Table 2A.2   Comparison of forecasts with actual capital market flows to developing countries
(billions of dollars)

Year	Forecast	Actual
1990	42	38
1991	63	68
1992	76	80
1993	127	114
1994	140	133
1995	169	172
1996	253	233
1997	320	315
1998	206	188
1999	187	179
2000	240	238

a net exporter or importer of oil and non-oil commodities in a given year.

Domestic economic factors also played a critical role in determining capital flows to developing countries. However, these domestic factors are also treated as endogenous in the model, so that they both affect, and are affected by, capital flows. A decline in capital flows was generally associated with decreases in the level of domestic credit, domestic industrial production, and stock prices. Increases in reserves were associated with higher capital inflows, while increases in short-term debt reduced flows. A moderate increase in the price level was positively associated with capital inflows, whereas a strong upsurge in prices tended to discourage capital flows (Mody and others 2001).

Table 2A.2 compares the flows estimated using the methodology outlined above with their historical trend. Evidently, the model performs fairly well.

FDI

The forecast of FDI included in the text is based on an econometric model of the determinants of FDI, expressed as a share of developing countries' GDP. Large and growing markets can accommodate more suppliers and help them achieve scale and scope economies (UNCTAD 1998), and the size of the recipient country's internal market as measured by GDP is one of the most frequently applied variables in the past research on determinants of FDI.[23] The determinants of FDI include:

1. The average growth rate of GDP over three years prior to the current period is a proxy for investors' view of future economic perfor-

mance. GDP growth has been found to be associated with larger FDI inflows in several studies (Root and Ahmed 1979; Nigh 1985).

2. The ratio of exports to GDP represents export-orientation, which should increase a country's attractiveness to multinationals by providing greater access to export markets (Caves, Porter, and Spence 1980; Saunders 1982). A third of world trade is accounted for by intrafirm transactions by multinationals, who also provide the bulk of FDI flows.

3. The GDP growth rate of the top seven industrial countries is used to account for a change in the relative attractiveness of emerging markets to international investors. Thus higher industrial-country growth is associated with lower FDI inflows to developing countries.

4. A better investment climate, in terms of sound macroeconomic policies, open regimes toward FDI, and nondiscriminatory frameworks for business facilitation, is likely to induce FDI inflows to the recipient economy (see chapter 3; UNCTAD 1998).

The model is estimated for the panel data from 1981–2000, which covers 30 developing countries that account for more than 80 percent of FDI flows to developing countries.[24] GDP growth in developing countries, GDP growth in industrial countries, and exports are lagged under the assumption that FDI is determined largely on the basis of long-term commitments by multinationals (World Bank 1999). Note that this approach to estimating FDI flows does not take into account cyclical effects, as was done with the forecasts of capital market flows. Such effects are probably of less importance to FDI, which typically is based on the prospects for growth over a longer time horizon than for capital market flows.

The constant variable $\{\hat{\alpha}_i\}$ $(i=1,..,30)$ and coefficients $\{\hat{\beta}_k\}$ $(k=1,..,5)$ are estimated from the equation below, and applied to the set of expected values for the independent variables to forecast FDI flows for 2001–04.[25]

$$FDI_i = \hat{\alpha}_i + \hat{\beta}_1 (GGDP_i) + \hat{\beta}_2 (EX_i) + \hat{\beta}_3 (G7_i) + \hat{\beta}_4 (IC) + \hat{\beta}_5 (T)$$

FDI, GGDP, EX, IC, G7, and *T* represent, respectively, FDI as ratio to GDP, average growth rate of

Table 2A.3 Statistics for the forecast of FDI

Independent variable	
GDP growth rate	0.047[a]
Exports	0.043[a]
G-7[b] GDP	−0.046[c]
Investment climate	1.093[a]
Time	0.079[a]
Adjusted R^2	0.50

a. Denotes significance at the 1 percent level.
b. Group of Seven: Canada, France, Germany, Italy, Japan, the United Kingdom, and the United States.
c. Denotes significance at the 5 percent level.
Source: World Bank, *Global Development Finance: Country Tables* and sources cited therein, various years; *World Bank, World Development Indicators,* various years; and World Bank staff estimates.

GDP over three years, export volume as ratio to GDP, investment climate index, annual growth rate of GDP of the G-7 countries, and time trend.

Annex 2.2: Measuring resource flows to developing countries

International organizations that collect and report data on international financial transactions use different approaches to measuring the movement of financial resources to and from developing countries. The IMF's *World Economic Outlook* reports flows in a balance of payments framework. An alternative approach is to aggregate from more specialized systems that independently compile statistics for different types of flows: the World Bank takes a recipient country or debtor perspective and operates the Debtor Reporting System. The OECD takes a donor or creditor country perspective: its data are derived from information on aid activities reported to the Development Assistance Committee and on export credits reported through the Creditor Reporting System. The Bank for International Settlements also takes a creditor perspective and compiles information on a quarterly and on a semi-annual basis on the claims of its reporting banks on developing countries.

In *Global Development Finance* (*GDF*) the World Bank uses a broad concept of net aggregate resource flows: equal to net disbursements on long-term loans, direct investment, portfolio equity flows, and official and private grants. These data are presented in the text and summary tables of volume I of *GDF*. The World Bank also presents a narrow measure of net flows on debt for individual countries in volume II of *GDF*.

The data on net aggregate resource flows presented in *GDF* reflect liability transactions only (gross disbursements minus repayments). Capital outflows (such as net lending by developing-country residents abroad), short-term flows, and net use of IMF credit are not included. This results in a substantial difference between net long-term flows as shown in *GDF* and net external finance as shown in the balance of payments.

These data are available only on an annual basis. However, data on certain components (for example loan commitments and bond issues) are available at higher frequency. The analysis of capital flows in this chapter depends heavily on this higher-frequency data. The quality of the most recent year estimates varies depending on the lending category. Reasonably accurate information is available from market sources on gross disbursements from bond markets and commercial banks. Debt repayments are calculated from information on terms, although actual payments may vary. Data on portfolio equity flows are particularly difficult to estimate: while data on international equity issues are readily available, estimates of direct foreign purchases in developing-country stock markets are based on reports from exchanges that differ in accuracy and coverage.

Notes

1. Moody's Investors Service classifies Barbados, Botswana, Chile, China, Croatia, the Czech Republic, El Salvador, Estonia, Hungary, the Republic of Korea, Lithuania, Malaysia, Mexico, Mauritius, Oman, Poland, Saudi Arabia, the Slovak Republic, Thailand, Trinidad and Tobago, Tunisia, Uruguay, and South Africa as investment-grade countries.

2. In part, this reflects dollar appreciation. In Special Drawing Rights (SDRs), developing countries' export revenues increased by 2.6 percent.

3. This calculation reflects the fall in European and U.S. interest rates, the share of floating rate debt, and the share of euro- and dollar-denominated debt. It is a lower bound of the impact of lower interest rates, since countries could switch to dollar-denominated debt to take advantage of the larger decline in U.S. interest rates.

4. The largest rise in speculative-grade spreads reflected, in part, the problems of telecommunications and other technology firms. However, the increase was wide-

spread (only 5 out of 15 high-yield sectors saw a decline in spreads in 2001).

5. The global volume of credit to investment-grade borrowers rose by 4 percent in 2001, while credit to speculative-grade borrowers fell by 23 percent.

6. The most recently issued Treasury securities tend to be more frequently traded, and hence more liquid, than securities that were issued earlier. Since both recently issued and off-the-run Treasury securities have the same risk-free return, the spread between the two is used by some observers as an indicator of liquidity preference. However, this spread may also reflect technical market factors (Duffie 1996).

7. The top 10 developing country FDI recipients (in order of the size of flows) are China, Brazil, Mexico, Argentina, Poland, Chile, Malaysia, Korea, Thailand, and the República Bolivariana de Venezuela.

8. A number of planned sales of domestic firms have been delayed or called off, including a long-standing acquisition plan of Daewoo Motors by General Motors and the cancellation of a plan by Deutsche Bank's subsidiary to purchase Seoul Bank.

9. About $25 billion of this amount represents flows through Hong Kong (China) that may have originated in China.

10. In the face of capital mobility, fixing the exchange rate limits the ability of the central bank to print money. The exchange rate–induced stabilization of import prices also enhances credibility by showing evidence that inflation is coming down. Agreement to forgo further wage and price increases requires a metric against which mark-ups and contracts can be gauged; a pegged exchange rate provides just such a measure. In contrast, other approaches to stabilization—keying on reductions in the rate of money growth or on the central bank's inflation target—are harder to verify and therefore less credibility-enhancing. Fischer (2001a) observes that few if any countries have successfully brought down high inflations without first stabilizing the exchange rate.

11. Fiscal policy was tightened by 1.7 percent of GDP in 1999, 1 percent in 2000, and 1.3 percent in 2001, according to J. P. Morgan estimates (Werling 2001).

12. Similarly, the correlation of spreads on Turkish bonds with other emerging markets rose from 0.12 before the crisis to 0.39 afterwards.

13. Twenty-six percent of Argentine exports go to Brazil and 11 percent of Brazilian exports are to Argentina. Moreover, each country's top 10 markets (which for Argentina and Brazil cover 57 percent and 64 percent of exports, respectively) are also the top 10 for the other country, with the exception of Mexico (for Argentina) and Uruguay (for Brazil).

14. The evidence of contagion effects is even weaker if we look at stock market prices. There is almost no evidence from stock market prices that the Argentine or Turkish crises affected other emerging markets, again with the exception of the impact on Brazil.

15. There is also concern that rescue packages may encourage borrowers to pursue unsustainable policies in anticipation of being bailed out. This is unlikely, considering the economic costs to countries hit by the crises and the loss of power of politicians who governed in the run-up to crises.

16. Cited in Helfer 1998.

17. This forecast for capital market flows is based on an econometric model that takes into account global macroeconomic developments (such as industrial-country growth and interest rates) that are largely exogenous to individual developing countries, as well as domestic macroeconomic developments in individual countries (see annex 2.1).

18. The debt workout process may be difficult. Some recent events have made it more attractive for holdout investors (that is, those who do not agree to a bond restructuring). See the case of the Elliott Associates vs. Peru as discussed in World Bank 2001.

19. This forecast is based on an econometric model (estimated from panel data for a sample of 30 countries that account for 80 percent of FDI flows to developing countries), where the major determinants of FDI are the level of GDP, the past growth rate of GDP, growth in industrial countries, the share of exports in GDP, and the policy environment (see annex).

20. A. T. Kearney 2001; UNCTAD 2002.

21. See World Bank 2001, chapter 2, for more on the explanation of the choice of variables.

22. We did not estimate a VAR model for an individual type of commitment (bank lending, bond issues, or portfolio equity flow) if it constituted less than 5 percent of total flows received by the country.

23. Literature includes Root and Ahmed 1979; Schneider and Frey 1985; Papanastassiou and Pearce 1990; and Wheeler and Mody 1992. See also UNCTAD 1998 for detailed discussions.

24. Some adjustments were made to FDI data for select countries where a small number of large-scale privatization transactions distorted the trend, or the major privatization programs have reached completion, or both.

25. The set of constant variables represents fixed effects across countries.

References

The word *processed* describes informally reproduced works that may not be commonly available through libraries.

Adams, A. H. 1993. "Hong Kong's Charms." *The China Business Review* (November–December).

A. T Kearney. 2001. "FDI Confidence Index—Flash Survey." Presented at OECD Global Forum on International Investment—New Horizons and Policy Challenges for Foreign Direct Investment in the 21st Century, November 26–27, Mexico City.

Bank of Canada and Bank of England. 2001. "Resolution of International Financial Crises." February. Processed.

Becker, Torbjorn, Anthony Richards, and Yungyong Thaicharoen. 2001. "Bond Restructuring and Moral Hazard: Are Collective Action Clauses Costly?" IMF Working Paper *01/92*. International Monetary Fund, Washington, D.C.

Bosworth and Collins. 1999. "Capital Flows to Developing Economies: Implications for Saving and Investment." IMF Seminar Series. No. 1999-21, pp. 1–44.

Calomiris, Charles. 2000. "When Will Economics Guide IMF and World Bank Reforms?" *Cato Journal* 20 Spring/Summer.

Caves, R. E., M. E. Porter, and A. M. Spence. 1980. "Competition in the Open Economy." Harvard University Press, Cambridge.

Clark, E. 1998. "Risk Aversion, Wealth and International Capital Flows." *Review of International Economics* (U.K.) 6: 507–15.

Dollar, David, Giuseppe Iarossi, and Taye Mengistae. 2001. "Investment Climate and Economic Performance: Some Firm Level Evidence from India." Prepared for Economists Forum, May. World Bank, Washington, D.C.

Duffie, Darrell. 1996. "Special Repo Rates." *Journal of Finance.* June.

Eichengreen, Barry, and Ashoka Mody. 1998. "What Explains Changing Spreads on Emerging Market Debt: Fundamentals or Market Sentiment?" NBER Working Paper W6408, Cambridge, Mass. February.

———. 2000. "Would Collective Action Clauses Raise Borrowing Costs?" World Bank Policy Research Working Paper 2363. May. Washington, D.C.

Fernandez-Arias, Eduardo, and Peter J. Montiel. 1996. "The Surge in Capital Inflows to Developing Countries: An Analytical Overview." *World Bank Economic Review* 10: 51–77.

Fischer, Stanley. 2001a. "Exchange Rate Regimes: Is the Bipolar View Correct?" *Finance and Development* June.

Fischer, Stanley, and D. Citrin. 2000. "Strengthening the International Financial System: Key Issues." *World Development:* 1133–42.

Goldstein, Morris. 1998. *The Asian Financial Crisis: Causes, Cures, and Systemic Implications.* Institute for International Economics: Washington, D.C.

Guay, W. 1999. "The Sensitivity of CEO Wealth to Equity Risk: An Analysis of the Magnitude and Determinants." *Journal of Financial Economics* (Netherlands) 53 (1): 43–71.

Gunter, Frank R. 1996. "Capital Flight from The People's Republic of China: 1984–94." *China Economic Review* 7 (1): 77–96.

Harrold, P., and R. Lall. 1993. "China, Reform and Development in 1992–93." World Bank Discussion Papers 215, Washington, D.C.

Hausmann, Ricardo, and Eduarto Fernandez-Arias. 2000. "What's Wrong with International Financial Markets?" Inter-American Development Bank, Research Department Working Paper 429, Washington, D.C.

Helfer, R. 1998. "Rethinking IMF Rescues." Brookings Institution Conference Report #1. http://www.brookings.org/pa/conferencereport/cr1/cr1.htm.

IMF (International Monetary Fund). Various years. *World Economic Outlook.* Washington, D.C.

International Council of Securities Agencies. 1999. "Private Burden Sharing: A Voluntary Approach." http://www.sia.com/international/html/burden.html.

Institute of International Finance. Various years. "Capital Flows to Emerging Market Economies."

Kumar, Manmohan S., and Avinash Persaud. 2001. "Pure Contagion and Investors' Shifting Risk Appetite: Analytical Issues and Empirical Evidence." IMF Working Paper 01/134, Washington, D.C.

Lane, T., and S. Phillips. 2000. "Does IMF Financing Result in Moral Hazard?" IMF Working Paper 00/168.

Lardy, N. 1995. "The Role of Foreign Trade and Investment in China's Economic Transformation." *China Quarterly* (U.K.) 144: 1065–82.

Meltzer, A. 2000. "Report of the International Financial Institutions Advisory Commission." U.S. Congress, Washington, D. C.

Mody, Ashoka, Mark P. Taylor, and Jung Yeon Kim. 2001. "Modeling Economic Fundamentals for Forecasting Capital Flows to Emerging Markets." World Bank, Washington, D.C. Processed.

Nigh, D. 1985. "The Effect of Political Events on U.S. Direct Foreign Investment: A Pooled Time-Series Cross-Sectional Analysis." *Journal of International Business Studies* 16: 1–17.

Papanastassiou, M., and R. D. Pearce. 1990. "Host Country Characteristics and the Sourcing Behaviour of U.K. Manufacturing Industry." Discussion Papers in International Investment and Business Studies, Series B, Vol. 2 (140), Department of Economics, University of Reading. United Kingdom.

Root, F. R., and A. A. Ahmed. 1979. "Empirical Determinants of Manufacturing Direct Foreign Investment in Developing Countries." *Economic Development and Cultural Change* 27: 751–67.

Saunders, R. S. 1982. "The Determinants of Inter-Industry Variation of Foreign Ownership in Canadian Manufacturing." *Canadian Journal of Economics* 15: 77–84.

Schneider, F., and B. S. Frey. 1985. "Economic and Political Determinants of Foreign Direct Investment." *World Development* 13 (2): 161–75.

Sicular, T. 1998 "Capital Flight and Foreign Investment: Two Tales from China and Russia." *World Economy* (U.K.) 21: 589–602.

Taylor, Mark P., and Lucio Sarno. 1997. "Capital Flows to Developing Countries: Long- and Short-Term Determinants." *World Bank Economic Review* 11.

UNCTAD (United Nations Conference on Trade and Development). 1998. *World Investment Report: Trends and Determinants.* Geneva.

———. 2001. *World Investment Report 2001: Promoting Linkages.* Geneva.

———. 2002. "FDI Downturn in 2001 Touches Almost All Regions." Press Release TAD/INF/PR36, January 21, Geneva.

Werling, Vladimir. 2001. "Argentine Confidence Crisis: Facing a Policy Dilemma." *Economic Research,* Morgan Guaranty Trust Company. August 10.

Wheeler, David, and Ashoka Mody. 1992. "International Investment Location Decisions: The Case of U.S. Firms." *Journal of International Economics* 33: 57–76.

World Bank. 1999. *Global Development Finance.* Washington, D.C.: World Bank.

———. 2000a. *Global Economic Prospects.* Washington, D.C.: World Bank.

———. 2000b. *Global Development Finance.* Washington, D.C.: World Bank.

———. 2001. *Global Development Finance.* Washington, D.C.: World Bank.

Zhang, Xiaoming Alan. 1999. "Testing of Moral Hazard in Emerging Market Lending." Institute of International Finance Research Papers, 99–1. August. Washington, D.C.

3

The Poor Countries' International Financial Transactions

Poor countries have benefited from the growth of global capital flows

The globalization of production and financial services has provided the opportunity for poor countries to increase their reliance on private sector international financial transactions.[1] Poor countries lack access to capital markets and official flows have fallen, while total aid has declined along with the share of the poor countries. However, foreign direct investment (FDI) flows have risen substantially: while the poor countries remain dependent on official external finance, they now receive the same amount of FDI as other developing countries, in relation to the size of their economies (table 3.1). FDI flows to the poor countries have become more diversified: the share of the mineral- and oil-exporting countries in total FDI to the poor countries fell from almost half in 1991 to 20 percent in 1997. Poor countries have participated in the global expansion of commercial banks: foreign banks' assets now account for 40 percent of total bank assets in the poor countries, twice as high as in 1995. Despite capital controls, poor countries' residents have placed significant amounts of capital abroad: the stock of capital outflows from the poor countries were larger relative to cumulated domestic savings and the stock of reserves, and only slightly smaller relative to gross domestic product (GDP), than outflows from other developing countries.

As in middle-income countries, the quality of the investment climate determines the extent of poor countries' access to capital and the extent to which foreign capital benefits the domestic economy. Countries with sound investment climates tend to attract more FDI, limit capital outflows, and enjoy greater productivity of both foreign and domestic capital than countries with weak invest-

ment climates. Those countries that established the stable macroeconomic policies and effective regulatory regimes necessary to attract foreign bank participation increased the access of domestic banks to trained personnel and technological advances, while rising competition from foreign banks helped reduce the costs of financial intermediation. Poor countries' greater openness to capital flows means that they have to cope with the macroeconomic effects of capital mobility. Sustainable macroeconomic policies marked by low inflation and debt levels are essential to limit capital outflows, and sharp changes in outflows (or capital repatriation) can complicate efforts at stabilization.

Financial integration in the poor countries

Financial integration has increased since the 1980s

The poor countries' private international financial transactions increased substantially during the 1990s. Official flows have fallen with the decline in total aid and the fall in the poor countries' share of aid (see chapter 4), while capital market flows (bank lending, bond issues, and portfolio equity) have remained relatively small. By contrast, FDI has risen seven-fold, and now represents over 40 percent of all long-term resource flows (table 3.2).[2] Nevertheless, the poor countries' reliance on private flows remains somewhat below that of other developing countries, where private flows averaged about 4 percent of GDP in the late 1990s.

One indicator of the extent of integration with the rest of the world is the correlation be-

Table 3.1 Net external financial flows to developing countries, 1999
(percent of GDP)

	FDI	Capital market flows[a]	ODA[b]	Capital outflows
Poor countries	2.8	−0.6	5.6	1.6
Other developing countries	2.8	0.7	0.4	3.2

a. Includes bonds, portfolio equity, and bank lending.
b. Official development assistance.
Source: World Bank Debtor Reporting System (DRS) and staff estimates.

tween investment and savings.[3] Countries that are tightly integrated into global financial markets should exhibit a low correlation between domestic savings and gross investment. For example, if a natural disaster reduces domestic savings but does not affect the return on new investment, firms in well-integrated economies can rely on international capital markets to maintain investment levels. At the extremes, in an autarkic economy savings and investment are identical (the correlation is one), while in a perfectly integrated economy the correlation would in theory be zero.[4] In the poor countries, the correlation between savings and investment declined sharply in 1995–99, after a steep rise from the late 1980s to the mid-1990s (figure 3.1). The variability in the series over time makes it difficult to say whether the recent decline will be sustained over the medium term. Again, the correlation in the poor countries remains above that of other developing countries, although the difference has narrowed since the mid-1980s.[5]

The preference for FDI reflects high risks—
While FDI to the poor countries has surged since the mid-1980s, net capital market flows to the poor countries has remained near zero. In other developing countries these resources represent an average

of 1.4 percent of GDP. Albuquerque (2001) has noted that countries with worse international credit ratings tend to have greater difficulties in attracting capital market flows than in attracting FDI. This dependence on FDI rather than capital market flows reflects a range of higher risks associated with investing in poor countries, notably less stable macroeconomic conditions, weaker institutions, and a less favorable environment for private sector activity. Moreover, the economies of most poor countries are relatively undiversified. For example, primary commodities account for 70 percent of exports from Sub-Saharan Africa. The poor countries are thus more prone to exogenous shocks, such as changes in the terms of trade and, in the case of agricultural products, adverse weather conditions. Higher risk leads to a bias toward equity finance, in part because FDI typically includes management expertise and branding, which help to compensate for greater risk. Perhaps more important, banks face difficulties in raising interest rates sufficiently to compensate for risk, owing to adverse selection. Different entrepreneurs have different (and unobservable) probability of repaying loans. The more risky entrepreneurs are willing to pay a higher interest rate, so banks limit risk by rationing credit through quantity limits, rather than through changes in interest rates.

—including asymmetric information
International investors often have little information on poor-country borrowers. Most poor countries often have relatively small markets, little coverage in the international media, and significant geographic and cultural distance from high-income countries. Thus external investors are particularly subject to asymmetric information with respect to opportunities in poor countries: that is, the owners of firms tend to have much more information on the firms' profitability than lenders or

Table 3.2 Net long-term capital flows to poor countries, 1986–99

	Billions of dollars			Percent of GDP		
	1986–88	1991–93	1997–99	1986–88	1991–93	1997–99
Total	15.7	20.9	22.2	6.1	7.8	6.6
Official flows	13.9	17.4	13.0	5.4	6.5	3.9
Private flows	1.8	3.5	9.2	0.7	1.3	2.8
Capital markets	0.7	0.5	−0.3	0.3	0.2	−0.1
Foreign direct investment	1.1	2.9	9.5	0.4	1.1	2.7

Source: World Bank DRS.

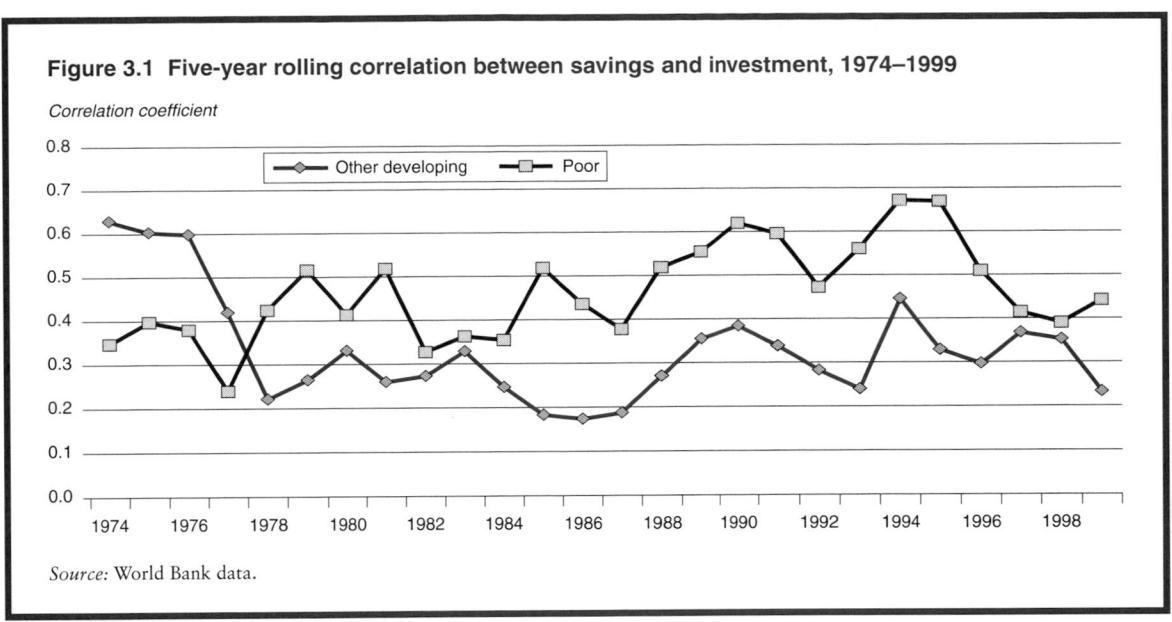

Figure 3.1 Five-year rolling correlation between savings and investment, 1974–1999

Correlation coefficient

Source: World Bank data.

outside investors, particularly foreign ones. High risk in the presence of asymmetric information leads to quantity constraints on loans (Stiglitz and Weiss 1981), and debt contracting may not be feasible or desirable (Trester 1998). Lending to poor countries is thus severely constrained, and much of the bank lending that occurs must be guaranteed (see chapter 4). By contrast, when foreign firms take an ownership stake through FDI they can exert more control over local managers, and thus obtain better access to information (compared with banks) about a project's current and potential profitability (Razin, Sadka, and Yuen 1997).

The preference for FDI also reflects institutional weakness in debt and capital markets

The institutional and legal structures required to reliably enforce contracts in the debt and capital markets are often lacking in poor countries. Protection of minority shareholders is often limited, disclosure standards are inadequate, and the administrative processes necessary to buy and sell shares impose high costs and delays, so issuance on the capital markets is discouraged. Stock markets tend to be very small in the poor countries. For example, of the 19 African stock markets, almost half have market capitalization of less than $1 billion, compared to the $220 billion capitalization of the Johannesburg exchange (Oxford Analytica

2001). On the debt side, the laws and infrastructure necessary to collect on collateral in the case of loan defaults are often inadequate, so that banks are often unwilling to lend.[6] While increased securitization of loans is a potential approach to improving access to debt flows, the cost and complexity of arranging such deals, and the risks involved in reducing the flexibility of foreign exchange management and taking on large debts at market rates, limit the use of securitization by the poor countries (box 3.1).

Trade credit is often an attractive financing option

Another means of increasing credit to risky countries in the presence of asymmetric information is to borrow from suppliers rather than banks. Trade credit, a financial agreement under which an exporter (or supplier) extends credit to finance the purchase by an importing firm, offers a good alternative for firms that lack access to banks. Suppliers are often better placed than banks to lend to firms in developing countries because suppliers have considerable information on the firm and its markets, and thus are less affected by asymmetric information. Suppliers can impose greater sanctions in the case of default by cutting off access to supplies and repossessing goods against which credit has been granted. Suppliers have an advantage over financial intermediaries in selling repos-

Box 3.1   Improving market access through future-flow securitization

Securitization—the conversion into tradable securities—of future hard-currency receivables is a potential means of improving the access of poor countries to international capital markets. At the same time, securitization in the poor countries must be handled cautiously, due to the limits imposed on government's access to foreign exchange and the risks of incurring debt at market rates.

In a typical future-flow transaction, the borrower pledges the future revenues from sales of a product (for example, oil) as collateral. By a legal arrangement between the borrower and major international customers, payments for the future product are directly deposited in an offshore collection account managed by a trustee. The debt is serviced from this account, and excess collections are forwarded to the borrowing entity in the developing country. This transaction structure reduces the ability of the government to interfere with debt servicing, while the market risk arising from price and volume volatility is mitigated by setting the amount of collateral higher than the debt service liability. So far, there have been no debt defaults on rated future-flow asset-backed securities issued by developing-country borrowers, even during crises. For example, in the telecommunications transaction mentioned below, Pakistan continued to service this debt even in the face of selective default on its sovereign debt.

Future-flow securitization in developing countries. Since the first important future-flow securitized transaction in a developing country (by Mexico's Telmex in 1987), 150 future-flow securitizations (that were rated by major rating agencies) have raised more than $36 billion. The issuance of future-flow receivable-backed securities increased especially after the Mexican crisis in 1994–95 (see figure). About 45 percent of rated future-flow transactions in U.S. dollar terms (and one-sixth in terms of number of deals) are backed by oil and gas export receivables. Hard-currency future receivables such as credit card and telephone receivables, and workers' remittances, and even export receivables to be generated in the future by new investment projects have also been securitized. In Argentina, some provinces have securitized portions of their future tax receivables from the federal government.

Future-flow securitization. Future-flow securitization has been used rarely in the poor countries. One example is the 1997 transaction in which Pakistan Telecommunications Company Limited, a state-owned company, raised $250 million in bonds backed by future telephone settlement receivables from international telephone companies. This issue was rated investment grade, four notches higher than the sovereign rating. Given their revenues from commodities, tourism, and remittances, poor countries could potentially raise as much as $11 billion by securitizing exports (using a conservative 5:1 overcollateralization ratio on 1998 receivables),[7] in addition to the potential for securitization of telephone receivables.

Securitized lending may be useful at the margin to increase access to finance and to gain entry to capital markets. There may also be positive externalities associated with securitization: the close scrutiny of the legal and institutional en-

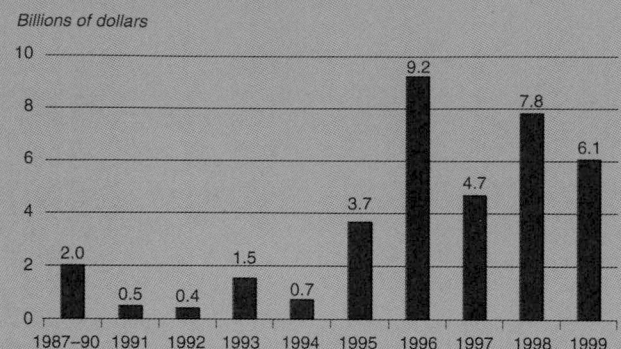

Future-flow securitization, 1987–99

Billions of dollars

Year	Value
1987–90	2.0
1991	0.5
1992	0.4
1993	1.5
1994	0.7
1995	3.7
1996	9.2
1997	4.7
1998	7.8
1999	6.1

Source: Fitch, Moody's, Standard & Poor's.

vironment involved in these transactions may identify priorities for reform. Public policy to facilitate future-flow-backed securitizations could focus on clarifying bankruptcy laws, reducing transaction costs by facilitating the pooling of receivables generated by several issuers, and educating policymakers and potential issuers about the benefits and risks involved. A number of factors, however, constrain the growth of future-flow transactions in the poor countries, including the high preparation costs and long lead times involved, and the lack of legal clarity on bankruptcy procedures in many countries.

Securitized lending also presents some risks to poor-country governments. Securitized arrangements that commit a substantial share of a country's foreign exchange resources may also reduce the attractiveness of nonsecuritized debt. A country's securitizations may violate negative pledge commitments to multilateral lenders. Escrow accounts reduce the authorities' flexibility in mobilizing and managing foreign exchange. For example, escrow account arrangements made by a public sector company may make it impossible for a government to draw on the company's foreign exchange receipts to support imports during a temporary decline in the terms of trade, thus imposing a costly and perhaps unnecessary adjustment. Committing a large share of the public sector's foreign exchange receipts to securitized arrangements can significantly increase the economic contraction required due to a withdrawal of flight capital. There is also a danger of proliferation: governments that agree frequently to the use of such arrangements may see creditors insist on them in most cases. This concern may be more muted in the case of a private company, although even here governments with foreign exchange surrender requirements may see their access to foreign exchange decline. The major issue is that poor-country governments, and in particular heavily indebted governments, must remain cautious about contracting debt at market rates. Securitized arrangements may facilitate access to capital markets, but they do not necessarily make it prudent for poor countries to borrow on hard terms.

sessed goods, since usually the supplier already has a network for selling its goods, especially if they have not been transformed by the buyer. By contrast, a bank's threat to cut off future finance may have little influence on the buyer's immediate operations (Petersen and Rajan 1994). Moreover, the prospect of a close and continuing trade relationship with the supplier reduces the likelihood that a solvent buyer would default, as the cost of obtaining goods from a single firm can be lower than purchasing them through separate transactions (Mian and Smith 1994).

FDI to the poor countries

Poor countries benefit from a global surge in FDI flows—

The surge in FDI reflects both the increase in global FDI flows and improvements in the investment climate in the poor countries. Global FDI flows increased by 24 percent per year during 1991–2000 as reduced trade barriers and technological innovations encouraged the growth of globally integrated supply networks (World Bank 2001a). Developing countries as a group saw FDI flows rise 20 percent at constant prices, and the rise in FDI as a share of GDP during the 1990s was virtually identical in the poor and other developing countries (figure 3.2), although the share of the poor countries in total FDI to developing countries declined during the 1990s. FDI flows to the poor countries increased to almost 3 percent of GDP and 15 percent of domestic investment, about the same ratios as in other developing countries.

—and improvements in their investment climates

The rise in FDI flows to the poor countries over the 1990s in part reflects significant progress in improving the investment climate, a term which refers to the numerous ways in which government policies affect the productivity of investment by fostering openness to trade and FDI, macroeconomic stability, fair and efficient public sector administration, low corruption and effective law enforcement, strong financial institutions, the provision of effective infrastructure, sound regulation, and measures to ensure the health and education of the work force. Several empirical studies have

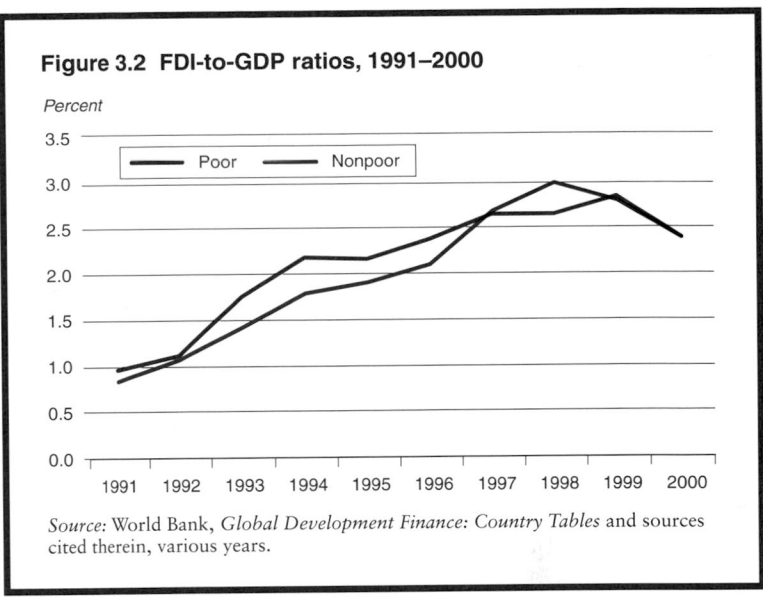

Figure 3.2 FDI-to-GDP ratios, 1991–2000

Percent

Legend: Poor, Nonpoor

Source: World Bank, *Global Development Finance: Country Tables* and sources cited therein, various years.

confirmed the importance of the investment climate in determining the level and efficiency of domestic investment (box 3.2).

The poor countries have made significant progress in improving the investment climate. The median inflation rate in the poor countries fell to under 5 percent by the late 1990s, compared with almost 8 percent early in the decade. The poor countries' average fiscal deficit fell from 7 percent of GDP in the early 1990s to 4 percent in the late 1990s. Almost half of a sample of 44 poor countries (the choice of countries was based on data availability) reduced their fiscal deficit by more than 2 percent of GDP, and only 12 saw a deterioration in the fiscal deficit. Some countries achieved broader reforms to encourage private sector activity. Restrictions on foreign entry and ownership were either eased or removed, and export processing zones (EPZs) and various tax and duty reductions were introduced. Twenty-two out of a sample of 24 poor countries either introduced EPZs or provided other forms of tax- or duty-exemption for imports, or reduced taxes on imports over the 1990s. Several countries eased rules on foreign currency transactions, at least as far as the current account is concerned (see below). The poor countries also have made some progress in health and education indicators that reflect improvements in human capital, a critical component of a strong investment climate. For example, the adult illiteracy rate declined from 45 percent in 1990 to 37 percent in

Box 3.2 The investment climate and domestic investment

The economic literature provides considerable empirical evidence regarding the impact of the investment climate on the level and productivity of private investment. The elements of the investment climate covered in empirical studies include macroeconomic policy, the legal framework, political instability, infrastructure, and health and education services. Both the policy framework and uncertainty concerning its administration are important.

Poor *macroeconomic policies* have a negative impact on the level of investment. Pfeffermann and Kisunko (1999) list inflation among the major deterrents to investment worldwide. Ndikumana (2000) shows that inflation has had a negative effect on investment in Sub-Saharan Africa, while Oshikoya (1994) gets the same results for a sample of low-income countries. Other authors have found that uncertainty about macroeconomic policies reduces investment (Alesina and Tabellini 1989). Several authors have shown that real exchange rate volatility, a proxy for uncertainty, is negatively related to private investment (Aizenman and Marion 1995; Servén 1996 and 1998; Servén and Solimano 1993; Brunetti and Weder 1998; Hausmann and Gavin 1996).

An *appropriate legal framework* and its fair enforcement have an important impact on investment. Uncertainty in property rights enforcement (Knack and Keefer 1995) and corruption (Mauro 1995) have significant negative effects on investment.[8] Brunetti and Weder (1998), in a cross-sectional study of 60 countries, find that the lack of rule of law and a high level of corruption are especially detrimental to investment. Analyses based on surveys (Pfeffermann and Kisunko 1999) and panel data (Bubnova 2000) emphasize corruption, crime, and unpredictable public administration as deterrents to investment. Individual country studies also provide evidence of the impact of the policy environment on investment in Africa. For example, Devarajan, Easterly, and Pack (2001) find that inappropriate public policies severely reduced the productivity of the Tanzanian manufacturing sector.

Empirical studies also have found that *political instability* has a significant negative effect on investment (see studies of large cross-country data sets by Barro [1991] and Alesina and Perotti [1996]). A survey of foreign-owned firms in 24 African countries found political and policy stability to be the most important factors affecting their investment decisions (Sievers 2001). Gyimah-Brempong and Traynor (1999) also provide evidence on the negative effect of political instability on investment for a cross-section of 39 Sub-Saharan African countries during 1975–88. Studies on individual countries in Africa have provided similar evidence (Thomas 1994 for Tanzania, and Jenkins 1998 for Zimbabwe). In a study of 18 Latin American countries over the period 1970 to 1981, Gyimah-Brempong and Muñoz de Camacho (1998) show that political instability reduces investment in both human and physical capital. Using a sample of 40 countries, Bubnova (2000) points out that political disorder aggravates risk and therefore reduces private infrastructure investment.

The lack of adequate *infrastructure and human capital* has been found to reduce private investment. Pfeffermann and Kisunko (1999) report that inadequate infrastructure constitutes one of the major obstacles to doing business. Reinikka and Sevensson (1999) identify the role of unreliable and inadequate power supply in reducing investment in Uganda, despite considerable progress in establishing macroeconomic stability and structural reform. Oshikoya (1994) finds a positive relationship between the infrastructure component of public sector investment and private investment in low-income countries. A study on Pakistan shows the complementary effect of public infrastructure investment on private sector investment (Sakr 1993). Likewise, a study of the Caribbean region (Clements and Levy 1994) shows that public education investment have significant effects on private investment.

Analyses of subnational impediments to investment have also emphasized the importance of the investment climate. In a study of Indian states Dollar, Iarossi, and Mengistae (2001) find that after controlling for establishment size and industry type, the variation in factor productivity across the states can in part be attributed to the variation in regulatory burden. The study also shows that the average annual fixed capital formation is four times higher in states with better investment climates (based on business managers' rankings) than in others. A survey of perceptions of business environment in five regions of Russia identified inflation, lack of access to financing, poorly functioning judiciary systems, and administrative barriers to investment (that is, high tax rates, tax regulations, and corruption in the public sector) as the most serious obstacles to investment (Coolidge, Kisunko, and Rahman 2001).

1999, and the infant mortality rate dropped from 85 per 1,000 live births in 1990 to 73 in 1999.

Nevertheless, the investment climate in most poor countries remains less attractive than in many middle-income countries. The average fiscal deficit is one percentage point of GDP higher in the poor countries than in the other developing countries. Health sector indicators are worse, despite the progress outlined above. For example, life expectancy at birth remains 13 years below the level in other developing counties, and the adult illiteracy rate is more than twice as high. Growth in the poor countries has been slower: per capita GDP rose by only 0.3 percent per year in the 1990s, compared with 1.9 percent in other developing countries.[9]

Improved investment climate is associated with rapid growth of FDI

Poor countries that made progress in improving the investment climate during the 1990s attracted large FDI increases. In the countries where policy and institutional performance improved most, FDI as a ratio to GDP increased by 25 percent per year, while in the countries whose policies improved least, the FDI-to-GDP ratio increased by less than 6 percent annually (table 3.3). The countries that showed relatively good policy and institutional performance in 1995 received more FDI as a ratio to GDP during 1996–99 (table 3.4).

The relationship between improvements in the investment climate and increases in FDI flows can also be seen in the experience of individual poor countries. Uganda, Tanzania, and Mozambique

Table 3.3 Annual change in policy performance and FDI as ratio to GDP, 1991–99

(percent)

	Highest group	Lowest group
Improvement in policy performance index	6.6	–3.2
Increase in FDI as ratio to GDP	25.5	5.7

Note: Highest and lowest groups of countries are based on the order of improvement in the policy performance index during the period of 1991–99. Policy performance is measured by the Bank's Country Policy Performance Rating.
Source: World Bank, *Global Development Finance: Country Tables* and sources cited therein, various years; World Bank, *World Development Indicators*, various years; World Bank staff estimates.

Table 3.4 FDI as ratio to GDP and policy performance index in poor countries

	FDI-to-GDP ratio	Policy performance index
High	8.9	3.4
Middle	4.6	3.0
Low	0.5	2.5

Note: This excludes oil and mineral exporters. The policy performance index is measured in 1995. FDI as ratio to GDP is an average during the 1996–99 period. The sample for this figure consists of 30 countries.
Source: World Bank, *Global Development Finance: Country Tables* and sources cited therein, various years; World Bank, *World Development Indicators*, various years; and World Bank staff estimates.

achieved the greatest improvement in the investment climate for a sample of 23 African countries during 1992–97 (World Economic Forum 1998), and the ratio of FDI to GDP rose by 81 percent in Uganda, 35 percent in Tanzania, and 33 percent in Mozambique.[10] Armenia pushed ahead with opening sectors to foreign investors and promoting privatization, which led to an 80 percent upsurge in FDI as ratio to GDP over the past decade. Privatization transactions accounted for a significant share of FDI inflows in some of these countries (15 percent in Uganda from 1992–97, and 25 percent in Bolivia from 1995–99).

Policy measures that attract FDI—

In addition to overall improvements in the investment climate, policy measures that are specifically designed to ensure equal treatment of foreign and domestic investors have been important in attracting FDI to the poor countries. New laws on foreign investment have been formed to permit profit repatriation since the early 1990s, while accessions to international agreements and institutions as well as conclusions of bilateral investment treaties and double taxation treaties have accelerated (UNCTAD 2001a). According to a survey conducted by UNCTAD in 1997, 26 of the 32 least developed countries in Africa in the survey had a liberal or relatively liberal regime toward the repatriation of capital.

—and factors that discourage it

Some of the poor countries have not achieved the improvements in the investment climate necessary to encourage higher FDI flows. Civil strife, which affected 13 poor countries during the 1990s, can depress foreign investment (although some of the countries affected by conflict have continued to receive foreign investment in protected natural resource projects). Some countries continue to impose restrictions on foreign entry and ownership and foreign exchange transactions, as well as discriminatory tax provisions. In Kenya, where foreign investors face multiple licensing requirements and high withholding taxes on royalties, FDI remained less than 0.2 percent of GDP during 1991–99 (Pigato 2001). Similarly, in Yemen, where sizable outflows of FDI have been recorded since the mid-1990s, licensing requirements discouraged new investments, despite incentives such as tax holidays and customs exemptions. Pakistan has seen a steady decline in FDI inflows since 1996 due to investor concerns over political developments.

FDI can boost investment and productivity—

Recent empirical work indicates a strong link between the volume of FDI and domestic investment. Bosworth and Collins (1999) and Mody and Murshid (2001) find that a dollar of FDI results in an almost one-dollar increase in investment. By contrast, international portfolio flows and bank loans have a much smaller impact on investment. In addition to the impact of FDI on the volume of investment, the presence of foreign firms can generate important benefits for domestic firms by increasing their knowledge of—and access to—advanced technology, by improving the overall skills of the work force, and by increasing demand for domestic firms' products and the supply of inputs.[11] These "spillover" benefits of FDI are greatest in countries with sound investment climates marked by well-developed human capital, efficient infrastructure services, sound governance, and strong institutions.[12]

The presence of foreign firms also can be important in the poor countries by improving local firms' access to international markets. The role of foreign firms as export catalysts has been examined for some 2000 Mexican manufacturing plants for the period 1986–90. Controlling for factor costs, output prices, and other variables, Aitken, Hanson, and Harrison (1994) found that the presence of foreign affiliates significantly increases the probability that domestic firms export. To the extent that growth in Sub-Saharan Africa is reduced by foreign investors' lack of information (Collier and Gunning 1999), exposure to foreign firms may help

eliminate an important constraint on the market access of African firms.

—but only if the investment climate is sound

Nevertheless, estimates of the average impact of FDI on growth in poor countries are mixed, in contrast to comparable estimates for developing countries as a group, which often show a positive impact of FDI on growth.[13] Kumar and Pradhan (2001) find that a 1 percent rise in the ratio of FDI to GDP in the poor countries is associated with an increase in GDP growth of about 0.18 percent, compared with a rise of 0.12 percent in the case of domestic investment.[14] By contrast, Blomström, Lipsey, and Zejan (1994) found the impact of FDI on growth of the lower-income countries to be positive but not statistically significant.

These mixed results reflect weak investment climates in some countries. Even if FDI is strongly linked to higher investment, increased investment may generate limited benefits for growth if the investment climate is poor. Devarajan, Rajkumar, and Swaroop (1999) present some cross-country evidence for Africa in which neither public nor private investment is correlated with growth due to low capacity utilization and a distorted policy environment.[15] Bhagwati (1978) and Balasubramanyam, Salisu, and Sapsford (1996) find that the effect of FDI on growth is stronger in countries that pursue export-oriented trade policies than in those adopting inward-oriented policies. Even in poor countries with sound macroeconomic policies and limited public sector interventions in competitive markets, low levels of education and skills may limit the benefits of FDI. Borensztein, De Gregorio, and Lee (1995) and UNCTAD (1999b) find that the interaction between FDI and an indicator of human capital in cross-country regressions has a significant impact on growth in developing countries, but that FDI alone does not.[16]

The size of the technological gap between domestic and foreign firms may limit the benefits of FDI to poor countries. FDI can be highly growth-enhancing when FDI and domestic investment are closer substitutes, which is more likely in technologically advanced countries than in developing countries (de Mello 1999). If local firms have insufficient capacity to absorb technology and skills from foreign affiliates, then the poor-country firms might lose out in the face of competition from foreign firms (Kokko 1994; Kokko, Tansini, and

Zejan 1996; Kathuria 1998; Fry 1992; Agosin and Mayer 2000). In addition, resource- or labor-seeking FDI—which is the most common form of FDI in the poor countries—is likely to generate fewer backward or forward linkages for domestic enterprises compared to FDI in intermediate or capital goods industries—the type more common in middle-income countries (Ozawa 1992; Porter 1990).

Even when the short-term impact of FDI is limited by a poor investment climate, the medium-term impact on growth may be positive. Initially domestic firms may see an erosion of their market share due to the entry of foreign firms with superior technology. Subsequently, however, domestic firms may regain market share as they absorb spillovers of technology and skills through vertical—backward and forward—linkages of foreign firms with domestic enterprises (Marksun and Venables 1997). In a study of 55 poor countries for the 1980–99 period, a 1 percent increase in FDI as ratio to GDP in the current period reduces domestic investment as ratio to GDP by 0.8 percent. However, a 1 percent increase in the FDI-to-GDP ratio in the previous period results in 0.7 per cent increase in the domestic investment ratio of the current period (Kumar and Pradhan 2001).

Effective competition policies are critical

In the absence of effective competition policies, FDI also can have a negative impact on the domestic economy by establishing a local monopoly and reducing production to maintain high prices, thus generating rents for foreign investors. There are two types of situations where firms might be able to keep prices higher than competitive levels over a considerable length of time. The first is in competitive markets in small economies where the government maintains barriers to entry, for example through high trade barriers or by limiting foreign entry to particular firms. Here the obvious remedy is to reduce trade barriers and establish an open regime for FDI. As many of the poor countries have small markets that could be dominated by a few firms, ensuring low barriers to entry is a high priority. Opening the economy to import competition tends to lower domestic market concentration and reduce price differentials between the local

and international markets (Harrison 1994; Levinsohn 1993; Tybout 2000; and Hoekman, Kee, and Olarreaga 2001). Economies with more active policies toward fighting monopoly power tend to grow faster, even after controlling for the height of trade barriers (Hayri and Dutz 1999).

Research on the impact of foreign entry on market concentration in competitive markets is limited. Several studies have found little evidence of anticompetitive practices, including studies in the Republic of Korea after the opening to FDI in 1998 (Yun 2000), in Mexico on the competitive effects of foreign acquisitions of domestic firms (Mexico Federal Commission on Competition 1997), and in the Czech Republic on the impact of sales of domestic firms to foreigners on market concentration in manufacturing (Zemplinerova and Jarolim 2000).

The second area where foreign entry may act to stifle competition is in natural monopolies that are subject to economies of scale and have limited potential for cross-border provision of services (such as telecommunications and power). For example, the privatization of state-owned monopolies, without either removing barriers to entry or establishing an effective regulatory framework to maintain competitive prices, can lead to a private monopoly. Here efforts to maintain efficient markets are more difficult than in competitive markets such as manufacturing, as poor countries often lack the institutional capacity required to effectively regulate natural monopolies. Thus building adequate rules and institutions to regulate natural monopolies may be necessary before privatization. However, once the decision is made to privatize, fear of natural monopolies is not a reason to bar foreign participation in bidding for privatized firms.

FDI in the mining sector has risen with policy reform

The investment climate is not the only determinant of the allocation of FDI among the poor countries. Some countries receive significant levels of FDI simply because they have natural resources that are not widely available. The rents associated with the exploitation of these resources may be so high as to compensate for weaknesses in the overall investment climate. In some cases, investment in natural resource sectors can be isolated by imposing special regulations, building dedicated infrastructure, or even providing special security in regions affected by conflict. Nevertheless, with improvements in the investment climate in non–natural-resource-exporting countries and the increase in privatization programs, the share of oil- and mineral-exporting countries in the poor countries' FDI flows fell from almost 50 percent in 1991 to 20 percent in 1997.

Even in mineral-exporting countries, the quality of the investment climate is an important determinant of access to FDI. Global surveys indicate that efficient and stable policies, liberal and transparent mining legislation, and accountable and nondiscriminatory tax regimes play a key role in the international mining companies' investment decision making, second only to geological conditions (Naito and others 1998; Clark and Naito 1997; Otto 1992; Johnson 1990). According to a 1997 survey of 35 countries, long-term success in attracting FDI in mining exploration depends on the quality of the legal, fiscal, and institutional framework, in addition to the existence of mining resources and a favorable geographic location. Eight of the 10 countries that received the highest FDI in exploration in 1997 had better-than-average policies, as measured by an index of reforms in the mining sector (Naito and Remy 2001).[17] One major obstacle facing the poor countries in increasing minerals production is the poor quality of policies in many countries. Of the 13 poor countries in the survey, 10 scored less than 0.4 on the reform index (indicating worse-than-average policies) and only three scored more than 0.7. In middle-income countries, by contrast, 8 scored below 0.5 and 13 above (figure 3.3).

Nevertheless, some poor countries have undertaken significant reforms of their mining sectors during the 1990s in order to attract foreign investment in mineral resource development (World Bank 1992 and 1996; Otto 1995; Smith and Naito 1998; Naito, Remy, and Williams 2001). According to recent forecasts by World Bank staff, some countries that have launched substantial reform programs are expected to achieve significant increases in exploration investment and—subsequently—increases in the value of the minerals produced and exported (table 3.5).[18] For example, Mali had historically attracted very little foreign investment in mining. In the 1990s the country undertook a reform of the rules governing mining and strengthened government oversight and service institutions. As a result, new investment started to flow in, leading to two new operating mines, and gold has become the largest contributor to Mali's export earnings, ac-

Figure 3.3 Foreign direct investment in mining exploration and government policies

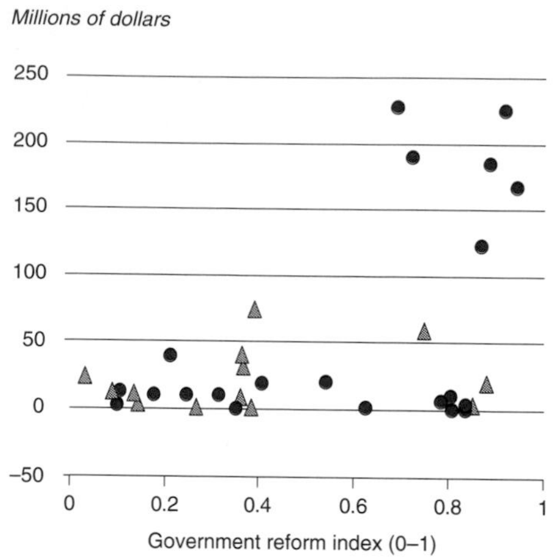

Millions of dollars

Note: Triangles represent poor countries, while circles represent other developing countries.
Source: Naito, Remy, and van der Veen 2001.

counting for over 40 percent of total exports in 1999. Mining sector reform has typically addressed the establishment of an appropriate legal framework for private sector activities, including the fiscal regime; modernization of government institutional arrangements in the mining sector; public enterprise reform and privatization; and establishment of a sound environmental management system.

The participation of foreign banks in poor countries' financial systems

Foreign bank presence in the poor countries increased in the 1990s—

In addition to capital flows, poor countries are tied to the international financial system through foreign banks. During the 1990s, the liberalization of financial markets in combination with rapid trade growth (which increased banks' ties with exporters from developing countries) spurred the global expansion of banks. Cross-border mergers and takeovers of banks rose from 320 over the course of the 1980s to about 2,000 in the 1990s. The middle-income countries of Latin America and East Asia and the transition economies experienced

Table 3.5 Mining sector performance in three countries, before and after reforms

(millions of dollars)

	Exploration		Production		Exports	
	Before	After	Before	After	Before	After
Ghana	<1	n.a.	125	700	125	650
Mali	<1	30	<1	242	<1	230
Tanzania	<1	35	53	350	53	350

n.a. Not applicable.
Sources: Naito, Remy, and van der Veen 2001 and sources cited therein. Staff projections based on ongoing projects and price forecasts.

a rapid increase in the number of foreign banks.[19] These recipients accounted for the biggest share of banks going to the developing world. However, the poor countries have also seen a substantial rise in foreign bank entry, as the failure of state-directed financial systems led to the privatization of many financial institutions and the removal of obstacles to the establishment of new banks in many countries. For example, in Africa cross-border mergers between financial institutions in the 1990s surged to 96, up from only seven in the 1980s (Buch and Delong 2001).[20] In 2000 only 15 of the 58 low-income countries had no reported foreign

bank activity, down from almost half in 1995. Foreign banks represent 38 percent of the total number of banks in the poor countries, up from 13 percent in 1995 (figure 3.4). Foreign banks' assets account for more than 40 percent of total bank assets in the poor countries, twice as high as in 1995. It is possible, however, that the sizeable losses incurred by foreign banks in the Argentine crisis may discourage a continued expansion of foreign banks in developing countries, at least in the near term.[21]

Some poor countries have had significant foreign bank presence for a long time (beginning with colonial domination of local banking systems), and colonial ties remain an important determinant of the home country of foreign banks. U.K. banks account for about one-third of all foreign bank capital in English-speaking Africa, and French banks enjoy a similar presence in French-speaking Africa. In low-income transition economies, the home countries of the foreign banks are more diverse, reflecting weaker cultural or colonial ties, although geographic proximity is an important determinant of foreign bank presence. For example, Turkish banks are important in a number of Central Asian countries, Arab banks are present in the Republic of Yemen and Pakistan, and banks

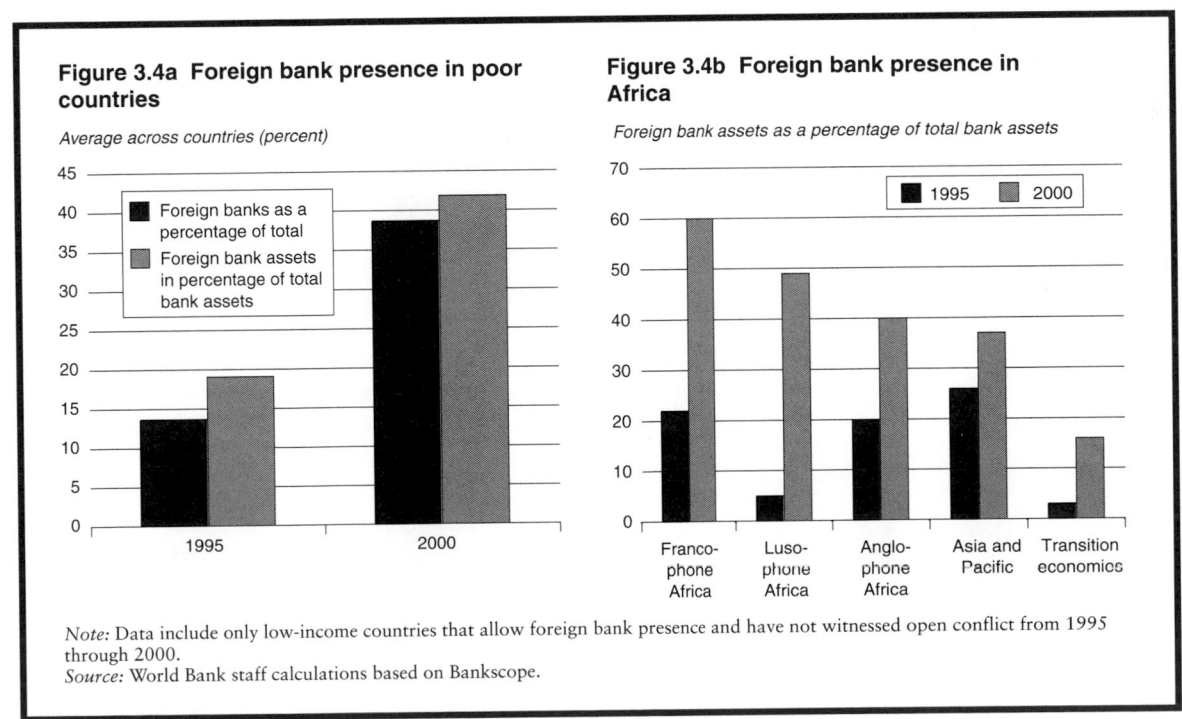

Figure 3.4a Foreign bank presence in poor countries

Average across countries (percent)

Legend: Foreign banks as a percentage of total; Foreign bank assets in percentage of total bank assets

Figure 3.4b Foreign bank presence in Africa

Foreign bank assets as a percentage of total bank assets

Legend: 1995, 2000

Categories: Francophone Africa, Lusophone Africa, Anglophone Africa, Asia and Pacific, Transition economies

Note: Data include only low-income countries that allow foreign bank presence and have not witnessed open conflict from 1995 through 2000.
Source: World Bank staff calculations based on Bankscope.

from middle-income East Asian countries have established subsidiaries in low-income East Asia.

—but regulatory barriers limit opportunities

Despite the rise in the presence of foreign banks in many poor countries, regulatory barriers and the limited opportunities in poor countries' financial systems continue to constrain foreign bank participation. Regulatory barriers are higher in poor countries than in other developing countries. On an index that ranges from 0 (closed) to 1 (fully open), middle- and high-income countries scored, on average, 0.77—well above the average (0.54) for all countries.[22] The main determinants of differences in commitments made to the World Trade Organization concerning the liberalization of financial services were found to be income level, openness to trade, and the depth and competitiveness of the financial sector (Qian 2000; Sorsa 1997). On these indicators, poor countries generally score worse than middle-income countries. Many poor countries also have limited scope for the provision of financial services, owing to the small scale of trading, the low level of savings, and competition from traditional and informal methods of savings collection (such as rotating savings and credit associations). The high cost of doing business—despite low wages—is an additional obstacle, reflecting poor business infrastructure, and greater difficulties in evaluating loans in low-income countries. Finally,

the weak regulatory framework and the frequent policy reversals in the financial sector—including nationalizations of foreign banks—increase the regulatory risk perceived by investors, while the effective subsidy to loss-making state banks distorts competition and creates an additional entry barrier.

Foreign bank presence is associated with higher efficiency of banking systems in the poor countries

The presence of foreign banks is associated with improvements in the efficiency of banking systems in the poor countries. Increased competition from foreign banks may reduce intermediation costs by eroding excess profits that domestic banks can enjoy due to the small size of the financial systems of many poor countries (see World Bank 2001b). In poor countries where foreign bank presence is greater than average, financial intermediation costs tend to be lower, as reflected in domestic banks' lower net margins and noninterest income. At the same time, domestic banks' overhead costs are lower in countries with substantial foreign bank presence, perhaps indicating improved practices learned from the foreign banks. On balance, domestic banks' pretax profitability in high-foreign-entry markets is much lower than in markets with low foreign bank presence (figure 3.5).

Differences in domestic bank performance across markets with varying levels of foreign bank entry are also likely to reflect other factors, apart from the presence of foreign banks—for example, differences in macroeconomic conditions that affect bank profitability. Taking into account differences in country circumstances and the financial characteristics of individual banks, econometric results confirm that stronger foreign bank presence is associated with significantly lower domestic bank net interest margins, noninterest income, and overhead costs (see annex 3.1). The net impact of higher foreign bank presence is a decrease in domestic bank profitability, after controlling for the influence of other factors.[23] This decline is a *partial* influence, which may be offset in the long term to the extent that foreign bank entry is associated with lower financial intermediation costs, which could improve credit provision to the private sector and thus foster higher growth and bank profitability (Levine 1996).

Foreign bank entry can help improve the quality of domestic bank staff by training staff that

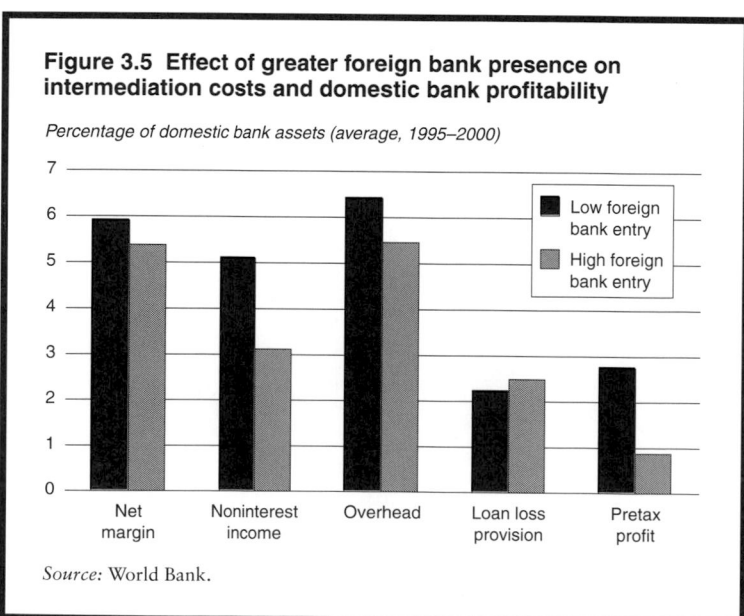

Figure 3.5 Effect of greater foreign bank presence on intermediation costs and domestic bank profitability

Percentage of domestic bank assets (average, 1995–2000)

Legend: Low foreign bank entry; High foreign bank entry

Categories: Net margin, Noninterest income, Overhead, Loan loss provision, Pretax profit

Source: World Bank.

then move to domestic banks. For example, Citibank is said to have trained an estimated 5,000 bankers in developing countries. In Pakistan, the government hired personnel from Citibank, Bank of America, Société Générale, and ABN-AMRO to help rehabilitate its national commercial banks, starting in 1997. French and British banks that have long been active in Africa have also contributed to training of banking personnel there. Foreign banks also can facilitate the provision of certain financial services, such as international syndications, letters of credit confirmations for exports to third countries, treasury products for commodity hedgers, depositary receipts, and international mergers and acquisitions possibilities for local corporate customers.

Foreign banks have also contributed to the soundness of domestic banking systems by participating in the privatization of failed state banks. For example, the sale of Tanzania's National Bank of Commerce (NBC) to ABSA, a South African bank, led to a sharp acceleration in the pace of restructuring and in loan recovery efforts. When ABSA took over NBC in March 2001 it launched an aggressive loan recovery effort that generated immediate results. Whereas previously NBC had been continually thwarted in its collection efforts by court injunctions and other avoidance tactics, ABSA successfully overcame many of these obstacles, thereby establishing its credibility and eliciting more constructive behavior from borrowers.[24]

Despite the improvements in efficiency brought about by greater foreign bank penetration, policymakers in developing countries are often concerned that access to credit may be impaired for some sectors of the economy—in particular small and medium enterprises (SMEs)—because foreign banks tend to serve primarily large customers compared with domestic banks. However, evidence from a survey of over 4,000 enterprises in 38 developing and transition economies—including 8 poor countries—suggests that, though large enterprises seem to take better advantage of foreign bank presence, benefits appear to also accrue to SMEs (Clarke, Cull, and Soledad Martinez Peria 2001). In countries with high foreign bank penetration, SMEs tended to rate interest rate costs and access to long-term loans as lesser constraints than in countries with low foreign bank entry. Medium-size enterprises also appear to finance a larger share of investment through commercial bank loans in

countries with higher foreign bank presence. The benefits perceived by SMEs may reflect, first, the lower interest margins spurred by foreign bank entry, which may help expand the *amount* of lending to SMEs even if the share of lending to them declines. Second, foreign bank competition for large customers may displace some domestic banks, forcing them to more actively seek new market niches. This could potentially improve credit access for small borrowers in the medium term. On the whole, based on a sample of 59 countries, Barth, Caprio, and Levine (2001b) concluded that limitations on foreign bank entry (captured by a cross-country comparable survey of national regulatory agencies) tend to be associated with a smaller share of bank credit to the private sector in GDP.

Greater foreign bank presence may also help attract foreign bank lending to poor countries, although the evidence is limited. Increased foreign bank presence can facilitate project selection and screening of borrowers, thus improving foreign banks' access to information, a critical input to lending decisions. Poor countries with high foreign bank presence attracted nearly 50 percent more international bank lending as a share of their GDP than countries with no foreign banks (figure 3.6).

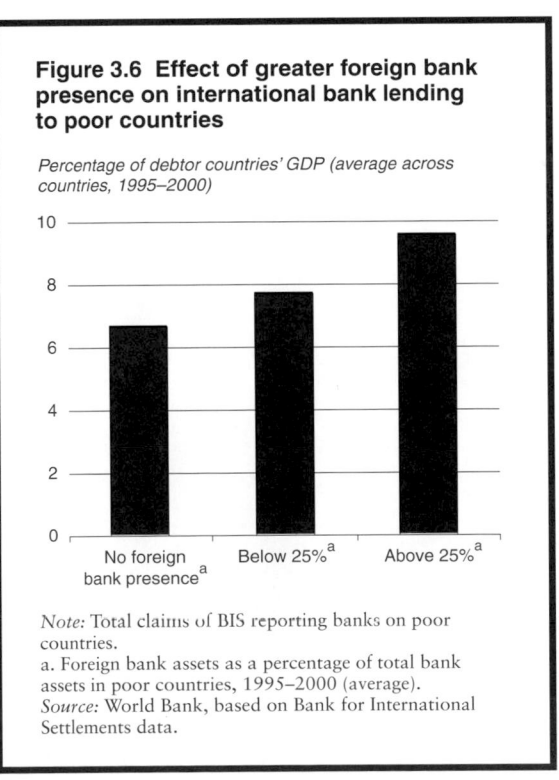

Figure 3.6 Effect of greater foreign bank presence on international bank lending to poor countries

Percentage of debtor countries' GDP (average across countries, 1995–2000)

Note: Total claims of BIS reporting banks on poor countries.
a. Foreign bank assets as a percentage of total bank assets in poor countries, 1995–2000 (average).
Source: World Bank, based on Bank for International Settlements data.

Of course, this relationship may be due to other factors. For example, countries with high foreign bank presence may also have better investment climates, which would explain the higher level of foreign loans. Countries with low foreign bank presence may also restrict private borrowing from abroad, thus limiting the amount of outstanding international bank claims.

Foreign bank entry does not appear to be associated with greater risk taking by domestic banks—

While the fall in domestic bank profitability that is associated with foreign bank entry may signal reduced financial intermediation costs for bank clients, it may also engender instability: banks that see a decline in their franchise value may have an incentive to take on greater risks (Hellmann, Murdock, and Stiglitz 2000). Pressure on domestic banks may also increase if foreign banks capture the most lucrative segments of the market (such as loans to export-oriented manufacturing), thus leaving domestic banks more exposed to the low-end, less profitable segments. This problem could be particularly severe in many poor countries, where domestic banks may lack the expertise to compete effectively with foreign banks and domestic banks may already be weakened by poor super-

vision, a history of high nonperforming loans, and government pressure for unprofitable lending to loss-making state enterprises. On the other hand, foreign bank presence may have a positive impact on financial stability, because it helps introduce better risk management practices, while foreign banks are likely to be better supervised by home country regulators.

One approach to investigating the impact of foreign banks on stability is to examine whether the domestic banks' portfolio and performance characteristics that have been shown to affect the chances of a financial crisis differ significantly in "low" and "high" foreign bank entry environments (Demirgüç-Kunt and Detragiache 2000; Goldstein, Kaminsky, and Reinhart 2000).[25] Analysis suggests that poor-country banking systems with high foreign bank presence had, on average, a smaller share of nonperforming loans in the late 1990s (figure 3.7). Provisions for nonperforming loans are also higher in countries with large foreign bank presence. While domestic banks in low-entry countries provision less than 100 percent for each nonperforming loan, banks in high-entry markets provision, on average, 150 percent. To be sure, lower nonperforming loans and better provisioning may partly reflect better prudential requirements and supervision in countries that are more attractive to foreign banks. On balance, domestic banks in poor countries with high foreign bank presence do not appear to have taken on particularly high risk.

—but a banking system that is more competitive and open to foreign entry can increase risks

While on average foreign bank presence is not associated with collateral damage to domestic banks, on occasion foreign banks have increased domestic financial instability by pulling out of host countries or by contagion from problems in the home country. A foreign bank affiliate may be forced to cut back on its local asset portfolio, in response to a deterioration of the parent bank's balance sheet. The impact of a decline in lending by a foreign bank may be particularly great in poor countries, where the number of banks is limited and foreign banks are often major players. For example, Kentbank of Turkey, which had purchased the National Commercial Bank of Albania in 1999 (with 60 percent market share in deposits and loans), had to be taken over by the Turkish Deposit Insurance

Figure 3.7 Effect of greater foreign bank presence on nonperforming loans

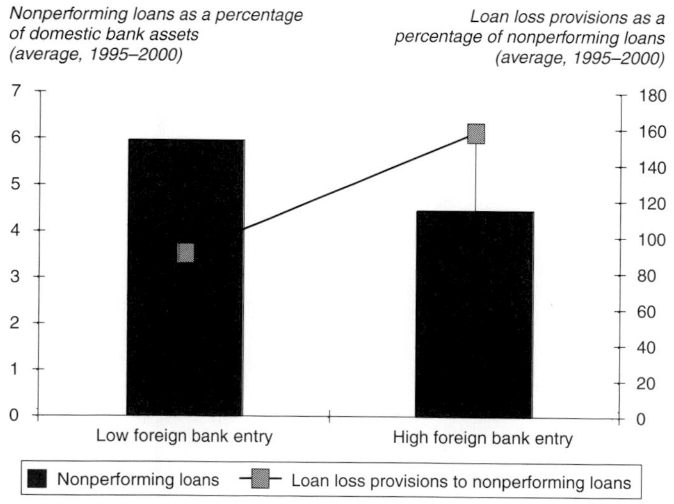

Nonperforming loans as a percentage of domestic bank assets (average, 1995–2000)

Loan loss provisions as a percentage of nonperforming loans (average, 1995–2000)

■ Nonperforming loans   ▬■▬ Loan loss provisions to nonperforming loans

Low foreign bank entry   High foreign bank entry

Source: World Bank; Claessens and Lee 2001.

Fund. Fears over instability were calmed, however, when the Turkish Fund lent $10 million to the Albanian bank. In Romania, rumors that the Turkish shareholder in Banco Turco (24 percent market share) was directing the funds of Banco Turco Romano back to Turkey led to a run on the bank in 2000. The run was stopped when the Turkish government persuaded Vakifbank of Turkey, a bank partially owned by the government, to support the bank. The sale of Uganda Commercial bank, the main state bank, to a Malaysian industrial and real estate company had to be cancelled when the parent bank got into difficulties.

These events point to the potential transmission of instability from foreign banks, particularly those from countries subject to substantial instability and without strong regulation and supervision. Diversification of the home countries of foreign banks is particularly important to reduce exposure to financial contagion. However, to minimize risks of contagion, the host country regulators also should be careful in screening entrants on the basis of two criteria: the quality of the foreign bank's domestic supervisory framework and the foreign bank's reputational risk exposure (to protect its reputation, a large international banking group is more likely to recapitalize a subsidiary than to let it fail).

With increased presence of foreign banks, maintaining effective cross-border supervision has become important to reduce the risk of contagion.[26] However, enforcing effective cross-border supervision raises difficult policy challenges for poor countries, as it requires a regular exchange of high-quality financial information between the home and host country regulators. The host supervisors should also be ready to permit on-site inspections by the home country supervisors. Many poor countries lack the resources and capabilities to effectively align their prudential regulation with best practice and comply with cross-border supervision guidelines. Moreover, almost all poor countries have relatively small financial systems, so that the fixed cost of establishing effective supervision can be high. Regional cooperation among poor countries could help, by upgrading and harmonizing standards of prudential regulation in financial services, pooling resources and expertise, and intensifying information exchange. For example, despite the need to further reinforce the regulatory framework, the West African Banking Commission established in 1990 has been an important step toward ensuring uniform and more efficient supervision of financial institutions in the eight member countries of the West African Economic and Monetary Union (IMF 2001a).

Capital outflows

Most poor countries have de facto open financial systems, in the sense that residents are able to place assets abroad—although these transactions, referred to as capital outflows, are not always legal. Since most capital outflows are not recorded, they are measured by inference, as the difference between recorded capital inflows and the sum of the current account deficit and increases in international reserves. This measurement is inevitably imprecise.[27] Despite these difficulties, there is no doubt that outflows are large relative to economic activity in many, if not most, of the poor countries, which has important implications for the volume of domestic investment and the conduct of macroeconomic policy. This section discusses the determinants of capital outflows and their implications for the domestic economies of the poor countries.

Capital outflows are high relative to domestic savings for the poor countries

The poor countries have experienced substantial capital outflows over the past two decades. Nevertheless, capital outflows remain smaller than inflows, and in most poor countries net external finance makes a positive contribution to domestic investment. Cumulated outflows totaled $62 billion, equivalent to 17 percent of GDP, almost 12 percent of cumulated savings for 1980–99, nearly a fifth of cumulated official flows during 1980–99, and nearly two-and-a-half times international reserves in 1999 (table 3.6).[28] Capital outflows from the poor countries were larger relative to domestic savings and reserves, and only slightly smaller relative to GDP, than outflows from other developing countries (which generally are viewed as more financially integrated with the rest of the world).

Capital outflows are extremely volatile, however, and these aggregate data conceal considerable variation over time and across countries. Since 1985, capital outflows from the poor countries have varied from less than 3 percent of GDP to just

Table 3.6 Cumulated outflows during 1980–99

	Cumulated outflows (billions of dollars)	As share of 1999 GDP (percent)	As share of cumulated domestic savings (percent)	As share of cumulated domestic capital formation (percent)	As share of cumulated official inflows (percent)	As share of net international reserves in 1999 (percent)
Poor countries	62	17	11.5	8.1	19	242
Other developing countries	1,182	20	6.5	6.6	278[a]	175

a. This ratio is high because aid flows to middle-income countries are very small.
Sources: IMF Balance of Payments; World Bank staff estimates.

over zero (meaning capital repatriation) (figure 3.8). Moreover, the cross-sectional standard deviation of the ratio of capital outflows to GDP is greater than the average over the period. Another way of gauging cross-sectional variability is that capital outflows averaged $8 billion a year during 1995–99, but 20 countries have outflows that total over $10 billion, while 6 countries account for more than $2 billion of reverse outflows (repatriation of residents' capital).

Indeed, capital outflows from the poor countries are more volatile than outflows from the middle-income countries, while inflows are less volatile (presumably because the poor countries receive little of the more volatile capital market flows) (table 3.7). This highlights an important point: many poor countries face the same issues surrounding capital flows volatility and the implications for

Table 3.7 Volatility of capital flows, 1990–99

	Inflows as share of GDP (coefficient of variation)	Outflows as share of GDP (coefficient of variation)
Poor countries	0.12	3.6
Other developing countries	0.30	2.1

Note: For each country group, the mean is estimated by dividing the sum of flows by the sum of GDP for each year, and then taking the mean over the decade. Standard deviation is computed using the annual averages for the decade. Coefficient of variation is the ratio of standard deviation to the mean. Resource flows include short-term debt flows and are taken from GDF. Outflows are estimated using IMF BOP.
Source: World Bank staff estimates.

macroeconomic stabilization as the middle-income countries. Moreover, at lower levels of income, volatility is likely to be more costly in terms of welfare (a decline in income can push more people to subsistence levels or below). Poor countries typically lack the range of instruments (for example, an efficient government bond market) available to middle-income countries to deal with macroeconomic volatility, and they are also more subject to volatility from the external sector due to their dependence on primary commodities. The average volatility of the poor countries' terms of trade (as measured by the coefficient of variation) in 1990–99 was about 40 percent higher than in other developing countries. Thus the poor countries face higher levels of volatility, volatility is more costly for them, and they are less equipped to deal with it, compared with middle-income countries.

A poor investment climate encourages capital outflows

The quality of the investment climate in the poor countries is the main determinant of the level of capital outflows. War and civil conflict, corruption, macroeconomic instability, uncertainty over property rights, high tax rates, weak governmental

Figure 3.8 Capital outflows from developing countries, 1985–99

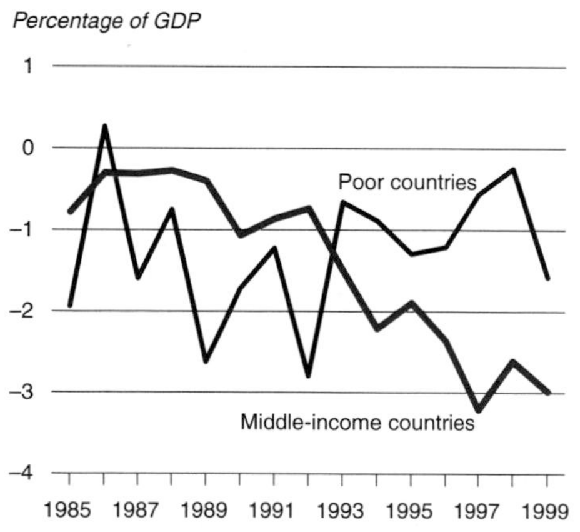

Percentage of GDP

Source: IMF Balance of Payments (BOP); World Bank staff estimates.

institutions, financial sector repression, and unnecessary constraints on private sector economic activity encourage outflows by limiting the opportunities for profitable domestic investment (box 3.2) and increasing the risk of confiscation or capital losses on funds held domestically (Tornell and Velasco 1992).[29] Several authors have mentioned that capital flight is driven by the desire to safeguard incomes derived from corruption and crime (see Varman-Schneider 1995 in the case of India, and Loungani and Mauro 2000 in the case of the Russian Federation). In poor countries with better than average economic policies (as measured by the Bank's Country Policy Performance Rating), the stock of capital outflows totaled only 6 percent of GDP, compared with 30 percent of GDP in countries with worse than average policies (table 3.8). Sheets (1996) found that inflation, budget deficits, and low interest rates were associated with increased capital flight. Schineller (1997, 1999) also found that the fiscal deficit was an important determinant of capital outflows, and re-

versals of outflows were associated with macroeconomic stabilization and structural adjustment programs. A high debt-to-GDP ratio raises the risk of future taxation, and also the risk of default on sovereign liabilities to residents. Cumulative capital outflows averaged 39 percent of GDP in poor countries with higher than average debt-to-GDP ratios, but only 5 percent of GDP in countries with lower than average debt ratios.

In some countries, preferential treatment of foreign capital versus domestic capital also boosted outflows in the form of round tripping (see example of round-tripping in China in chapter 2). Preferential treatment for foreigners may include tax breaks, preferential access to prime land and other inputs, and exemption from exchange controls faced by residents (Dooley 1986; Khan and Ul-Haque 1985; Eaton 1987; Ize and Ortiz 1987).[30] Such discriminatory treatment of resident capital relative to nonresident capital may encourage investors to deposit their wealth in a foreign bank, and then raise debt financing from the same bank for their domestic investments (Lessard and Williamson 1987).

Just as a poor investment climate encourages outflows, improvements in the investment climate can encourage capital repatriation. Ajayi (1997) describes how improvements in macroeconomic stability and better governance encouraged the reversal of capital flight in Côte d'Ivoire, Central African Republic, Uganda, Ghana, and Kenya during the 1980s and 1990s. Olopoenia (2000) estimated that capital flight from Uganda rose during periods of political instability (1971–74, 1976–79, and 1981–87), but there was a "reflow" of flight capital following a return to peace and economic liberalization (including exchange rate unification and lifting of exchange controls) during the 1990s. In Kenya, Tanzania, and Uganda, high Treasury bill rates offered by governments have attracted funds from returning emigrants (Bhinda, Griffith-Jones, and Martin 1999). Tax amnesty programs have been used as another means of attracting inflows (see Ng'eno 2000 for the example of Kenya). However, such programs can only provide one-off, short-term effects (Das-Gupta and Mookherjee 1995), and are effective only if accompanied by measures to reduce the distortions that encouraged outflows in the first place. If repeated, tax amnesty programs increase incentives for evasion, as taxpayers wait for the next amnesty.

Table 3.8 Cumulated outflows as a share of GDP, 1999

(percent)

		Poor countries	Other developing countries
Investment climate			
Policy environment[a]	High	−5.9	−19.8
	Low	−30.3	−20.1
GDP growth	High	−16.4	−17.3
	Low	−19.7	−28.7
Debt/GDP	High	−39.2	−23.9
	Low	−5.1	−19
M2/GDP	High	−6.3	−20.5
	Low	−37.7	−20.2
Trade/GDP	High	−40.7	−28.2
	Low	−7.6	−16.8
Income effects			
Per capita income	High	−6.1	−20.8
	Low	−21.2	−19.4
Gini	High	−49.7	−22.1
	Low	−6.7	−14.2
Discrimination of resident capital			
Exchange premium	Positive	−21.6	−23.4
	Zero	−7.6	−17.5

Note: Outflows cumulated over the 1980–99 period. High and low usually refer to above and below median of the concerned variable. The numbers reported are sum of cumulated outflows for countries above median (say) divided by sum of GDP of the same countries.
a. Policy environment is measured by World Bank's country policy performance rating.
Source: World Bank staff estimates.

Outflows are also associated with increased wealth and globalization

Capital outflows do not always signal a poor investment climate. In many middle-income countries, the rise in capital outflows before the East Asian crisis appeared to be tied to increases in

wealth that increased the demand for international portfolio diversification (box 3.3). By contrast, the poor countries with higher than average per capita incomes (for the poor-country group) experienced smaller outflows (table 3.8), perhaps because wealth levels, while higher than those of the aver-

Box 3.3   Capital outflows from the middle-income countries

Capital outflows from the middle-income countries have a different composition than outflows from the poor countries, and the predominant motivations are different as well. Many middle-income countries became more integrated into the global economy over the course of the 1990s. In the first half of the decade, the official data showed a sharp rise in private capital inflows, but this was substantially offset by an increase in capital outflows, as increased wealth and trade transactions boosted the desire for portfolio diversification (Gordon and Levine 1988). About one-quarter of capital outflows from middle-income countries took the form of foreign direct or portfolio investment (see figures). Thus, in the early 1990s, growing capital outflows from many middle-income countries were consistent with economic progress, while in the poor countries capital outflows often reflected a poor climate for investment and slow growth. In the second half of the 1990s, capital outflows by residents increased from countries affected by crises, for example Mexico in 1995, Indonesia, Korea, and Thailand in

1997–98,[31] and the Russian Federation in 1998. A significant portion of capital outflows may also represent round-tripping. For example, the experience of the crises may also have encouraged domestic investors to try to benefit from explicit and implicit guarantees on foreign debt.

The different motivations of capital outflows from the middle-income countries have meant that some of the relationships outlined in the main text concerning poor countries do not hold. For example, middle-income countries with better policies and with higher per capita income have experienced almost the same level of cumulative capital outflows as middle-income countries with poor policies and low income. Thus, good policy environments in some of the more successful middle-income countries have facilitated growth while still allowing residents to diversify their portfolios internationally. On the other hand, middle-income countries with high debt-to-GDP levels, greater openness to trade, and greater inequality have had relatively high levels of capital outflows, as in the poor countries.

Composition of cumulated outflows from middle-income countries during 1980–99

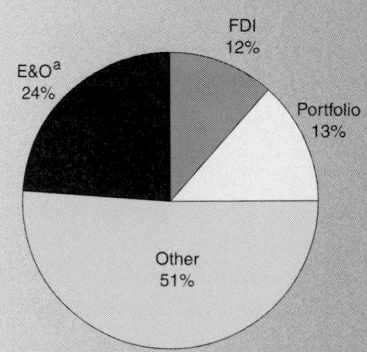

Composition of cumulated outflows from poor countries during 1980–99

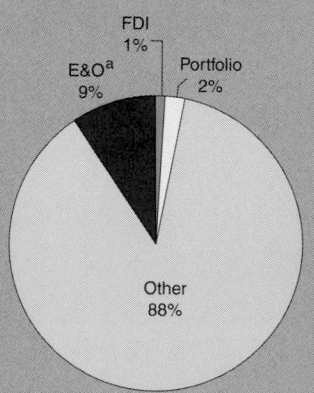

Note: Other includes trade credit, bank deposits, and currency holdings.
a. Errors and omissions.

age poor country, had not reached levels where substantial international diversification was necessary. Higher trade openness may also encourage outflows as residents have more contact with international markets, there is a rising incentive to hold foreign exchange as a hedge against changes in the exchange rate, and the scope for misinvoicing of exports and imports increases. Capital outflows from poor countries with higher than average ratios of trade to GDP equaled 41 percent of GDP, compared with 8 percent in countries with lower than average trade-to-GDP ratios.[32]

Income inequality also can have an important impact on outflows. Cumulated outflows from poor countries with high inequality, as measured by the Gini coefficient, averaged 50 percent of GDP, compared with 7 percent for poor countries with low inequality. A high concentration of wealth may mean that some residents have large individual portfolios that make them more likely to diversify their assets and more able to pay the implicit and explicit transaction costs associated with capital outflows. High income inequality may also be associated with greater sociopolitical risks, which would in turn encourage outflows. The size of outflows is positively related to large mineral resources (such as oil, gold, and diamonds [figure 3.9]), and countries with large natural resource endowments also tend to have higher income inequality (Goreux 2001). For example, the largest source of capital outflows from Sub-Saharan Africa is Nigeria, where outflows seem to be highly correlated with oil exports (Ajayi 2000).

It is difficult to determine whether simple comparisons of the investment climate and capital outflows, as shown in table 3.8, reflect causality (and in which direction) or the influence of some third factor that determines both indicators. For example, large capital outflows may be associated with high debt ratios because residents place funds abroad in order to escape the potential for higher taxes to service the debt. Alternatively, high capital outflows may reduce growth, thus increasing debt-to-GDP ratios. Or, high levels of corruption may mean that large inflows of official finance end up in private hands and are then transferred abroad—thus increasing both external public debt and private outflows. An analysis of the relationship between capital outflows and other macroeconomic variables that takes into account the mutual interactions among endogenous variables (such as

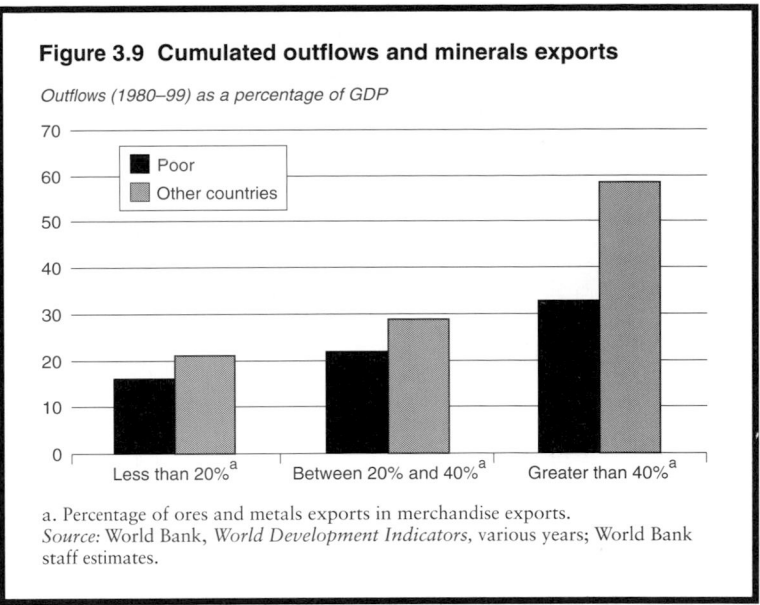

Figure 3.9 Cumulated outflows and minerals exports

Outflows (1980–99) as a percentage of GDP

a. Percentage of ores and metals exports in merchandise exports.
Source: World Bank, *World Development Indicators*, various years; World Bank staff estimates.

growth, capital outflows, capital inflows, the real exchange rate, and fiscal deficits) and controls for the role of other influences (such as degree of inequality and structure of trade) can improve our understanding of the forces at work. This analysis uses panel vector autoregression (explained in more detail in annex 3.1), in which each of the endogenous variables is related to lagged values of the other endogenous variables.

The results for all developing countries indicate a two-way relationship between capital outflows and the government's track record in fostering growth and maintaining economic stability. Higher growth rates are associated with reduced capital outflows in the next period, while higher capital outflows appear to contribute to reduced growth rates in the next period. Similarly, a higher fiscal surplus is associated with smaller capital outflows in the next period. Capital outflows are also significantly related to capital inflows, which may either reflect round-tripping or the tendency for financially integrated economies to engage in both external borrowing and lending. Thus there is strong support for the existence of virtuous (and vicious) cycles, in which, for example, a fall in capital outflows increases the domestic resources available for growth, which in turn lowers outflows. The qualitative results for poor countries follow a similar pattern, although the statistical significance of the coefficients is found to be weaker than the results for all developing countries.[33]

Most poor countries have controls on capital account transactions—

While many poor countries have achieved a significant reduction in restrictions on current account transactions since the 1980s, most continue to impose restrictions on capital account transactions. Four indicators that have often been used to measure trends in foreign exchange restrictions over time are: (a) existence of multiple exchange rates, (b) export earnings surrender requirements, (c) controls on current account transactions, and (d) controls on capital account transactions.[34] The first two of these indicators are available over a long time series through the most recent year, while the latter two are available on a comparable basis only through 1995.[35]

The poor countries have made progress in reducing current account restrictions. The share of reporting poor countries that imposed current account restrictions fell from 75 percent in 1985 to 44 percent in 1995. It appears that the trend toward liberalization of current account restrictions continued in the second half of the 1990s: the share of reporting poor countries that require exporters to surrender foreign exchange earnings to the government dropped from 64 percent in 1995 to 52 percent in 2000. Moreover, the share of reporting poor countries with multiple exchange rates fell from 29 percent in 1995 to only 10 percent in 2000.[36]

By contrast, the share of poor countries reporting capital account restrictions has remained at about 90 percent since the mid-1970s, with a slight rise during the mid-1980s and a slight decline in the mid-1990s when a few countries liberalized capital account transactions (figure 3.10). In addition, there has been almost no change in the share of poor countries reporting various capital account restrictions in the more detailed format used since 1995. While it is impossible to make a precise comparison of the late 1990s with earlier years, the broad conclusion is that most poor countries have maintained capital account restrictions over the course of the last 30 years. The share of other developing countries reporting capital account restrictions also has changed little since the early 1970s, but it remains well below the share of poor countries imposing capital account restrictions.

—but capital controls are porous

Controls often have only a limited impact on capital outflows in the context of a weak investment climate, where domestic investment opportunities are limited and fears of confiscation or reduction in the value of assets give residents considerable incentive to put their money abroad. Controls have had some success in the middle-income countries when they are limited in time or in purpose (see box 3.4). But they have had particularly lim-

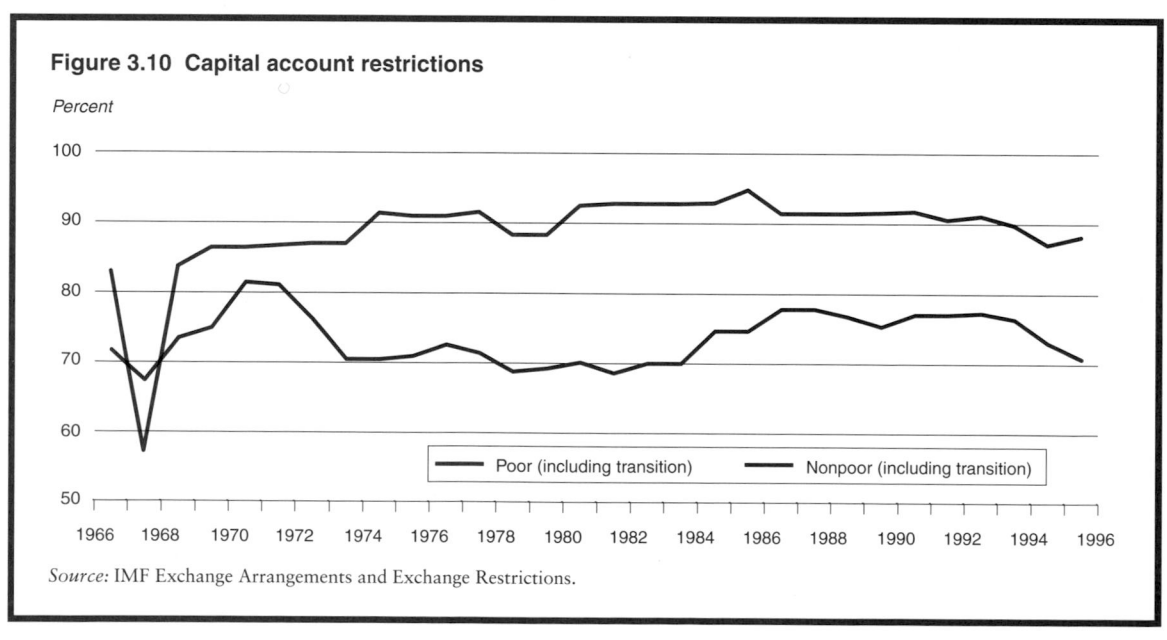

Figure 3.10 Capital account restrictions

Percent

Source: IMF Exchange Arrangements and Exchange Restrictions.

Box 3.4   Narrowly focused capital controls in emerging markets

Thailand's and Malaysia's experiences with capital controls on outflows, and Chile's experience with capital controls on inflows, provide some evidence that controls can be effective if narrowly focused and adjusted in response to attempts at circumvention.

In 1991 the Chilean government imposed controls on inflows to lengthen the maturity of inflows and increase the capacity of the central bank to conduct an independent monetary policy. The controls consisted of unremunerated reserve requirements (URRs) that (initially) mandated that 20 percent of the deposit remain in a non–interest-paying account for the duration of the credit. "Minimum stay" requirements of three years were placed on FDI and portfolio flows. While subsequent changes were made in the specifics of the controls (changes in the URR percentage, reductions in the minimum stay, extensions or exemptions from coverage), the underlying restrictions remained in place until 1998. The controls elicited a tug-of-war between the authorities and the private sector, in which periodic success by the private sector in diluting the effectiveness of the controls led to efforts by government to close the loopholes. Evidence suggests that there was some lengthening of the maturity of inflows with little impact on the aggregate value of inflows. In addition, domestic interest rates were marginally "delinked" from international markets, providing the authorities with an increased space for policy maneuver (De Gregorio, Edwards, and Valdes 2000). The benefits must be balanced off against the costs, though, which included raising the cost of borrowing for domestic firms (especially those without access to international markets).

Both Thailand and Malaysia resorted to controls on capital outflows as part of their response to the Asian crisis. In *Thailand*, the controls were first adopted early in the crisis, in an effort to limit offshore speculation against the baht. The controls were intended to be narrow, and did not apply to legitimate commercial and financial transactions (including trade flows, FDI, and portfolio flows). The initial controls were modified on several occasions, including both loosening in response to changing economic conditions as well as tightening to close loopholes that the private sector had begun to exploit. Measured against the objective of "punishing" speculation by limiting offshore liquidity, the controls were at least partially successful, as they contributed to a wide and persistent gap between onshore and offshore swap rates (IMF 2000a).

Capital controls were adopted in *Malaysia* in September 1998, when the exchange rate had already depreciated sharply, making sizable further outflows unlikely. Moreover, as in Thailand, the Malaysian controls were selective in nature, designed to curtail (if not eliminate) the possibility of speculation against the ringgit while leaving ordinary trade and FDI flows unaffected. The controls were immediately effective. The prohibition on interaccount transactions virtually halted offshore ringgit trading, while the mandatory 12-month holding period on portfolio repatriation shut down outflows. But in retrospect it is also clear that the Malaysian controls were imposed after the worst of the crisis had passed, so that their major contribution was one of safeguarding against further turbulence rather than limiting the direct impact of the crisis itself (see also Dornbusch 2001; and Kaplan and Rodrik 2001). The control system relied heavily on comprehensive regulation and bureaucratic intervention, and active adjustment and fine-tuning of the controls by the authorities occurred in response to private sector efforts to evade the impact (Hood 2001).

What lessons can be drawn from these experiences of capital controls? First, the success of controls depends in part on defining a sufficiently narrow objective. Both Malaysia and Thailand had some success in limiting speculation through offshore markets. Second, the control system must remain dynamic: the private sector will inevitably strive to minimize or avoid the impact of controls, necessitating administrative responses to fine-tune the regulations.

---

ited success in the poor countries, where controls are typically imposed over an extended period, so that individuals and firms have ample opportunity to find means of getting around them.

Means of circumventing capital controls include:

- Trade misinvoicing. A portion of the export earnings may not be reported to the authorities

in an effort to bypass foreign exchange surrender requirements. Similarly, imports may be overinvoiced to gain access to larger amounts of foreign exchange. Residents also may falsify import letters of credit and customs declarations to bypass exchange controls.

- Smuggling. Goods may be smuggled and the proceeds deposited in banks. Sometimes, barter may be arranged for trading contraband (for example, diamonds for arms in Sierra Leone [see Goreux 2001]).

- Changes in transfer prices and leading and lagging of intracompany transfers are used for shifting funds abroad (Mathieson and Rojas-Suarez 1993).

A common method of effecting fund transfers in the presence of exchange controls is *hawala* (meaning "trust" in Hindi), also known as *hundi* in Pakistan, or *fei ch'ien* (literally "flying money") in China. In a *hawala* transaction, a developing-country resident who wants to transfer funds to a transferee abroad deposits local currency with an agent and obtains a "chit." The agent instructs his colleague in a foreign country to pay an equivalent amount of foreign currency to the transferee upon presentation of the chit (or simply a code). It is believed that the net amount outstanding at the end of a long period of time is settled through smuggling. Thus *hawala* is not a distinct means of evading capital controls, but rather a means of effecting international payments transactions when desired, with ultimate settlement done by the means of capital outflows outlined above. This method (believed to have originated in China during the T'ang dynasty) is fairly common in South Asia, the Middle East, Sub-Saharan Africa, and Southeast Asia.[37]

Controls on capital outflows not only have limited success over the medium term, they may also discourage capital inflows. Foreigners will be unwilling to invest where there is significant uncertainty regarding their legal ability to repatriate profits and ultimately liquidate the investment. The presence of capital controls, even if they are widely evaded, will create such uncertainty, because foreigners are typically less knowledgeable about the feasibility and risks involved in committing technical violations of the law. Also, multinationals are usually unwilling to undertake illegal transactions because of the harm to their reputations and the likelihood of being made an example if enforcement of controls is tightened in the future. Conversely, removing capital controls can encourage inflows (Laban and Larrain 1997). Several countries have eased controls on outflows when faced with large inflows (to limit currency appreciation and loss of export competitiveness, see Calvo, Leiderman, and Reinhart 1993), but the liberalization actually resulted in increased inflows.

Examples include Chile, Colombia, and Egypt in the early 1990s (Schadler and others 1993).

As one motivation for capital outflows is to guard against a real devaluation of the domestic currency, several middle-income countries have allowed local deposits denominated in foreign currencies to reduce capital flight and induce nonresident inflows (for example, India, Mexico, Uruguay, and Turkey [see Rojas-Suarez 1990]). Moves toward capital account liberalization such as allowing foreign currency deposits may reduce distortions and corruption that studies find to be associated with capital controls (Edwards 1999; Loungani and Mauro 2000), and can increase the supply of capital to help governments manage difficult times. In Turkey, for example, worker remittances doubled between 1988 and 1989 in response to such a policy. Remittances also doubled between 1992 and 1994 in India when nonresident workers were allowed to hold foreign currency deposits onshore.

Some of the poor countries have also moved toward liberalizing controls on inflows. In the 1990s liberalization of exchange regulations led to rapid growth of foreign currency accounts in a few countries in Sub-Saharan Africa (for example, Ghana, Tanzania, and Uganda), and a significant part of these funds reflected the return of flight capital (Bhinda, Griffith-Jones, and Martin 1999). According to Stryker (1997), foreign currency deposits held by residents onshore in Ghana increased significantly over the early 1990s, to make up a third of total deposits by the end of 1996. Private transfers to Uganda increased from $80 million in 1991 to $415 million in 1996, following capital account liberalization that permitted residents to open foreign exchange denominated accounts; deposits in such accounts accounted for one-quarter of broad money in Uganda in April 2000 (Kasekende 2000). In Kenya, the legalization of foreign currency deposits in the early 1990s in the context of high real interest rates attracted large short-term flows: the level of international reserves rose from $81 million at the beginning of the second quarter of 1993 to $685 million a year later.

Liberalization of the capital account, however, can prove costly, especially when combined with interest rate liberalization in the context of a weak macroeconomic policy environment and underdeveloped financial markets. Capital account liberalization (including allowing local foreign currency accounts) has to be complemented by sound macroeconomic policy and prudential banking regulations, but poor-country governments often lack the resources to obtain the information required for effective supervision, and corporate governance and accountability can be weak. If liberalization induces a large repatriation of flight capital by residents, or attracts significant nonresident inflows, the currency may appreciate and, at the same time, domestic liquidity may expand, generating inflationary pressures. Liquidity management in such a situation may not be easy, especially since many poor countries do not have sufficient instruments of monetary policy to conduct sterilization. (Sterilization may also prove to be very expensive, as in the case of Indonesia before the crisis in 1997.) Increased dollarization of domestic liabilities through allowing foreign currency accounts may also complicate monetary and exchange rate management.[38]

Moreover, allowing unrestricted capital flows can increase the risks assumed by domestic banks and corporations, as happened in East Asia before the 1997 crisis (Corsetti, Pesenti, and Roubini 1998; Krugman 1998). In the presence of a pegged exchange rate and relatively high domestic interest rates, capital account liberalization can encourage residents to take unhedged foreign currency exposure (if the pegged exchange rate is expected to be maintained, borrowers can take low interest rate foreign loans and place the funds in high-yielding domestic accounts). This can result in significant currency mismatches on banks' balance sheets, which in turn can lead to huge losses if a fall in confidence triggers capital outflows (or if devaluation of the currency is required for any reason) (Eichengreen and others 1999; World Bank 1999a). Even with a floating exchange rate (so that the incentive for unhedged exposures is reduced), sharp changes in the exchange rate can introduce considerable volatility in the balance sheets of banks with large foreign currency exposure. Middle-income countries have suffered very severe consequences from capital account liberalization combined with weak financial institutions and insufficient supervision. Poor countries with even greater financial sector weaknesses could confront serious difficulties with open capital accounts.

There is some evidence that the liberalization of capital inflows in Sub-Saharan African countries was associated with both macroeconomic and financial sector difficulties. Bhinda, Griffith-Jones, and Martin (1999) found that increased private capital inflows contributed to real effective exchange rate (REER) appreciation in Tanzania, Uganda, Zambia, and Zimbabwe during 1990–97.[39] The domestic liquidity expansion that resulted from capital inflows may also have been a factor behind the imprudent lending and borrowing behavior by banks in these countries. In Uganda, despite prudent fiscal policy and attempts to supervise banks and regulate corporate borrowings (the Financial Institutions Statute of 1993), two banks had to be taken over for restructuring in 1995. The accumulation of short-term foreign liabilities was a source of distress in these problem banks (Kasekende 2000). In Kenya, nonperforming loans as a share of total loans rose from 20 percent in 1994 to over 30 percent in 1997 (Ngugi 2000; Brownbridge 1998)—the resulting banking crisis may have been related to the surge in repatriated outflows (from $177 million in 1994 to $682 million in 1997).

Moreover, most of the poor countries are small economies with heavy dependence on primary commodities (and are thus subject to severe terms-of-trade shocks, as noted above), and they have relatively shallow capital markets. A completely open capital account could magnify the impact of external shocks. For example, a sharp fall in the price of a major export commodity could lead to large capital outflows in anticipation of a devaluation, potentially leading to overshooting of the exchange rate. The same process would occur with capital controls, but to a lesser degree. In addition, short-term controls that exempt FDI transactions may be an attractive option for poor countries that lack market access and hence do not have to take into account the impact of controls in discouraging portfolio inflows.

Thus the poor countries need to move cautiously toward liberalizing capital account transactions. Countries that have already opened the capital account, established sustainable macroeconomic policies, and made the difficult adjustments required to maintain stability in the face of capital inflows (particularly establishment of strong corporate and financial sector institutions and effective supervision) should not backtrack by imposing controls. Many poor countries continue to confront weak financial sector institutions and difficult challenges in achieving strong governance and sustainable macroeconomic policies. Liberalizing capital inflows under such conditions can lead to excessive risk taking and exacerbate macroeconomic instability. Poor countries need to take into account the degree of volatility of their economies, and be confident in the quality of their policies and institutions, before undertaking the risks involved in capital account liberalization.

Annex 3.1: Econometric analysis of foreign bank participation

The effects of foreign bank presence on the operation of domestic banks can be more completely examined by formal econometric evidence. The regressions in table 3A.1 investigate how foreign bank presence affects five performance indicators of domestic banks: (a) net margin, (b) noninterest income, (c) before-tax profits, (d) overhead expenses, and (e) loan loss provisions. All of these

variables are measured as a share of total domestic bank assets.

Apart from foreign bank presence, the regressions relate the domestic banks' performance indicators to the financial characteristics of individual banks (such as equity capital and other earning assets) and their apparent cost-efficiency (as measured by the overhead expense ratio). The regressions also control for the impact of the macroeconomic environment on bank performance. Macroeconomic factors that may affect interest margins, profitability, and provisioning for bad loans include the rate of GDP growth, inflation, and the real interest rate. In addition to the observed share of foreign banks, an attempt is made to capture the contestability of the domestic market, as measured by the country commitments on commercial presence in banking under the General Agreement on Trade in Services (GATS) financial services agreement of 1997. Re-

Table 3A.1 Foreign bank presence and domestic bank performance

	(1) Net margin/ta	(2) Nonint. income/ta	(3) Before tax profits/ta	(4) Overhead/ta	(5) Loan loss prov./ta
Foreign bank share	−0.076[a] (0.026)	−0.128[a] (0.021)	−0.320[a] (0.063)	−0.124[a] (0.020)	0.166[b] (0.065)
Index on degree of entry	0.150 (0.010)	−0.046[a] (0.010)	0.008 (0.023)	−0.097[a] (0.010)	−0.037[c] (0.020)
Equity/ta	0.129[a] (0.031)	0.037[a] (0.011)	0.365[a] (0.100)	−0.025[c] (0.014)	−0.210[a] (0.079)
Other earning. assets/ta	0.010 (0.010)	0.013[b] (0.007)	0.096[a] (0.022)	−0.012[b] (0.006)	−0.081[a] (0.021)
Cust. & short-term funding/ta	0.040[b] (0.020)	0.001 (0.012)	0.020 (0.058)	0.004 (0.009)	0.010 (0.048)
Overhead/ta	0.508[a] (0.084)	0.444[a] (0.059)	−0.168 (0.247)		0.222 (0.273)
Growth rate of GDP/cap	0.063 (0.059)	−0.049 (0.035)	0.670[a] (0.155)	−0.150[a] (0.029)	−0.690[a] (0.142)
Inflation rate	0.027[a] (0.009)	0.007 (0.007)	0.060[a] (0.011)	0.008 (0.008)	−0.031[a] (0.009)
Real interest rate	0.069[a] (0.017)	0.010 (0.012)	0.131[a] (0.032)	0.029[b] (0.012)	−0.073[a] (0.025)
Constant	−0.030 (0.023)	0.045[a] (0.011)	−0.075 (0.060)	0.137[a] (0.009)	0.084[c] (0.050)
Adjusted R[2]	0.368	0.429	0.503	0.233	0.423
No. of obs.	1349	1349	1342	1362	1213

Note: Regressions are estimated using weighted least squares pooling bank level data across 36 countries for the 1994–2000 period. Only domestic bank observations were used. The number of domestic banks in each period is used to weight the observations. Heteroskedasticity-corrected standard errors are given in parentheses.
a. Significance level of 1 percent.
b. Significance level of 5 percent.
c. Significance level of 10 percent.
Source: Claessens and Lee 2001.

gressions thus also include a "liberalization index"—first created by Sorsa (1997) for the 1995 financial services negotiations, and adapted by Qian (2000) for the 1997 GATS negotiations. The index runs from 0 to 1.

The estimated regression is as follows:

$$I_{ijt} = \alpha_o + \beta\, FS_{jt} + \beta_i\, B_{ijt} + \beta_j\, X_{jt} + \beta_4\, S_{jt} + \varepsilon_{ijt}$$

I_{ijt} is the dependent variable (for example, before-tax profits/total assets) for domestic bank i in country j at time t. FS_{jt} is the number of foreign banks in country j at time t as a share of the total number of banks. B_{ijt} are financial variables for domestic bank i in country j at time t. X_{jt} are country variables for country j at time t, and S_{jt} is the "liberalization index." Further, α_o is a constant, and β, β_i, β_j and β_4, are coefficients, while ε_{ijt} is an error term.

Estimating a regression in levels—as opposed to differences—can be a correct approach provided it is the presence, rather than entry, that causes the local banking systems to behave differently. Moreover, the foreign bank presence at time t should be determined by entry incentives as of period $t–1$. If the foreign bank share is only endogenous to lagged bank variables, the regression can be estimated separately using cross-country time-series data (see further Claessens and others 1998).[40]

Variable definitions and sources

Net margin/ta = Interest income minus interest expense over total assets.

Noninterest income/ta = Other operating income such as trading costs, advisory fees, and so on over total assets.

Before-tax profits/ta = Before-tax profits over total assets.

Overhead/ta = Personnel expenses and other non-interest expenses over total assets.

Other expenses/ta = Nonoverhead, noninterest, other expenses over total assets.

Equity/ta = Book value of equity (assets minus liabilities) over total assets.

Other earning assets/ta = Assets other than loans and non-interest-earning assets such as cash and non-interest-earning deposits at other banks, over total assets.

Customer and short-term funding/ta = All short-term and long-term deposits plus other nondeposit short-term funding over total assets.

Foreign bank share = Number of foreign banks to total number of banks. A bank is defined as a foreign bank if it has at least 50 percent foreign ownership.

GDP/cap = Real GDP per capita in thousands of U.S. dollars.

Inflation = Annual increase of the GDP deflator.

Liberalization Index = Degree of commercial presence in banking as allowed in the financial services negotiations of 1997 and as reported in Qian 2000.

All individual bank-level variables are obtained from the Bankscope database of IBCA; additional data are obtained from various sources. All macro data are from the World Bank.

Econometric analysis of capital outflows

Capital outflows can be both the cause and the effect of macroeconomic variables. While a macroeconomic variable (such as growth or fiscal deficit) may cause outflows, it may also be affected by outflows. This relationship would, of course, depend on the extent to which capital outflows are offset by capital inflows. In turn, inflows may cause outflows and vice versa.[41]

The presence of such interactions among variables would violate the standard ordinary least squares assumption that the explanatory variables are exogenous (that is, not correlated with the error term). This endogeneity problem can be partially addressed by using instrumental variable regressors, but single-equation models cannot fully capture the dynamic interactions among several endogenous variables. A popular method that can capture such interactions is the vector-autoregression (VAR) technique. For our purpose, we applied the dynamic panel-VAR technique that combines the advantages of the VAR model with the advantages of panel data analysis that can admit observable and unobservable country fixed effects. Such fixed effects would include variables that vary a great deal across countries but remain relatively "fixed" over time for each country—for example, financial development, or demographic patterns.

We estimate a panel-VAR model with five variables in the following order: capital inflows; capital outflows (negative = capital repatriation); the REER (an increase implies erosion of export competitiveness); growth; and the fiscal balance (positive = surplus, negative = deficit). This ordering implies that the capital flow variables can affect the macroeconomic variables without restriction (contemporaneously or lagged as the data dictate) but that the macroeconomic variables are restricted to affecting the capital flows variables only through a lag.

Results

We ran a panel-VAR regression for all (137) developing countries for 1980–99 (546 observations), and a separate regression for the poor countries (142 observations) for the same period. The regression coefficients of the five equations are summarized in table 3A.2 for all developing countries and in table 3A.4 for the poor countries. The impulse response functions are summarized in table 3A.3 for all developing countries and in table 3A.5 for the poor countries. (The impulse responses illustrate the effect of a one standard deviation shock to each variable on all the other variables, taking into account the knock-on effects through the system over time.) This summary details any significant effect over several years at the 5 percent level and the sign of that effect.

Table 3A.2 Panel-VAR results for all developing countries

| | Dependent variables | | | | |
	Inflows	Outflows	REER	Growth	Fiscal balance
Inflows	0.509	–0.049	–0.079	0.073*	–0.092
Outflows	–0.029	0.202*	0.086	–0.043*	–0.028
REER	–0.027*	–0.051*	0.555*	–0.003	–0.033*
Growth	0.010	–0.259*	0.600*	0.320*	0.024
Fiscal balance	0.127	–0.119*	–0.388	0.036*	0.115

Note: An asterisk indicates significance at 5 percent level or higher.
Source: World Bank staff estimates.

Table 3A.3 Summary of impulse response functions, all developing countries

| | Dependent variables | | | | |
	Inflows	Outflows	REER	Growth	Fiscal balance
Inflows	+	+			+
Outflows		+	–	–	+
REER	–	–	+		–
Growth		–	+	+	+
Fiscal balance	+	–		+	+

Source: World Bank staff estimates.

Table 3A.4 Results of panel-VAR regression for poor countries

| | Dependent variables | | | | |
	Inflows	Outflows	REER	Growth	Fiscal balance
Inflows	0.503	–0.042	–0.362*	0.056	–0.146
Outflows	–0.046	0.137	0.195*	–0.013	–0.001
REER	–0.016	–0.040	0.487*	0.001	–0.026
Growth	–0.070	–0.319	1.094*	0.371*	0.176
Fiscal balance	0.141	–0.112*	–0.414	0.028*	0.056

Note: An asterisk indicates significance at 5 percent level or higher.
Source: World Bank staff estimates.

Table 3A.5 Summary of impulse response functions, poor countries

| | Dependent variables | | | | |
	Inflows	Outflows	REER	Growth	Fiscal balance
Inflows	+	+	–		+
Outflows		+			
REER	–		+		–
Growth			+	+	+
Fiscal balance	+	–		+	+

Source: World Bank staff estimates.

The results for all developing countries provide support for the existence of virtuous (and vicious) cycles among the five variables under consideration (for example, outflows lead to lower growth which in turn causes further outflows). The qualitative results for poor countries follow a similar pattern, although the statistical significance of the regression coefficients and impulse responses is found to be weaker than in the case of all developing countries.[42]

However, these results from the panel-VAR exercise tend to be sensitive to the choice of time period or the presence of outliers. The data on macroeconomic variables and, in particular, on capital flows, display considerable volatility over time and also suffer from substantial cross-sectional variation. The volatility is even worse in the case of poor countries.

Measuring capital outflows from developing countries

Measuring capital outflows is inherently difficult and imprecise. Typically, outflows are measured indirectly, as the residual of "sources of funds" over the "uses of funds" from the balance of payments (World Bank 1985; Morgan Guaranty 1986; Cline 1985). This is the procedure adopted here. The sources of funds include all identified inflows and credit items in the capital account of the balance of payments, while uses of funds are the current account deficit and increase in international reserves. By the balance of payments identity, this residual estimate yields identical estimates to capital outflows calculated directly as the sum of FDI outflows, debt outflows, portfolio equity outflows, other outflows, and debit items on the capital account. All data are taken from the International Monetary Fund Balance of Payments Statistics database.

One of the shortcomings of the residual measure is that it treats all errors and omissions in the balance of payments as capital outflows. In reality, errors and omissions may reflect unrecorded current account transactions as well (Chang, Claessens, and Cumby 1997), and also measurement and recording errors and lagged registration (Eggerstedt, Hall, and van Wijnbergen 1995). Another shortcoming is that this measure ignores outflows taking place through export underinvoicing or import overinvoicing (Chang, Claessens, and Cumby 1997). It is hard to estimate capital flight through trade misinvoicing. Even if estimates of over- and underinvoicing were accurate, not all misinvoicing represents funds used for capital flight. For example, exports may be overinvoiced to take advantage of export subsidies, and imports may be underinvoiced to reduce import tariffs (Eggerstedt, Hall, and van Wijnbergen 1995; Ajayi 1997).

The residual approach is less restrictive than other measures that are defined according to the motives behind capital flight. For example, the "hot money measure" suggested by Cuddington (1986) attempts to separate the "speculative" or short-term components of capital outflows from "normal" outflows. Dooley's method measures only that part of capital outflows that does not generate a corresponding investment income reported to the domestic authorities (Dooley 1986). Interestingly, Claessens and Naudé (1993) show that the World Bank residual and Dooley methods actually produce similar estimates of capital flight. We have not attempted to measure the magnitude of capital outflows according to motives (for example, speculative reasons, tax evasion, or simply portfolio diversification) given that motives are highly subjective and difficult to distinguish on the

basis of available data (Lessard and Williamson 1987; Collier and others 2001; Varman-Schneider 1991).

Finally, estimates of the *stock* of outflows used in this chapter are calculated simply by cumulating annual flows over time. This is the lower bound for an estimate of the stock of outflows, as the calculation ignores interest earnings. Some authors assume that all interest earnings on flight capital are reinvested abroad, and use the U.S. Treasury bill rates for estimating interest earnings (Collier, Hoeffler, and Pattillo 2001). This may provide some further information on the stock of outstanding assets. However, for the purposes of this chapter we prefer to emphasize the size of flows leaving the economy over time (rather than residents' current holdings), and therefore do not adjust the cumulative stock for any estimate of earnings.

Notes

1. See the overview for a definition of poor countries.

2. Even so, private capital flows remain well below the average of 5 percent of GDP achieved during the late 1970s.

3. Calculated as correlation between savings/GDP and investment/GDP across countries, in each year.

4. In reality even in the highly integrated industrial economies the correlation between investment and saving is far from zero (see Feldstein and Horioka 1980).

5. Data weaknesses (particularly on savings in developing countries) mean that these figures can provide only a general indication of trends in integration. Also, note that the correlation between savings and investment in the middle-income countries does not decline over the 1990s, despite the massive rise in capital inflows. In part this is due to the fact that a large portion of these inflows were used to increase reserves or capital outflows, and thus had only a limited role in supporting domestic investment.

6. Fleisig (1996) outlines how lack of appropriate laws and institutions constrains bank lending in developing countries. Weak institutions likely make these problems most severe in the poor countries.

7. The overcollateralization ratio of 5:1 is taken from Ketkar and Ratha 2000.

8. Knack and Keefer (1995) use a large cross-country time-series dataset; and Mauro's (1995) cross-country dataset covers 58 countries.

9. Slow growth in the poor countries results in part from declines in output in countries affected by conflict. However, even excluding the conflict countries, the poor countries' per capita output rose by only 0.6 percent per year in the 1990s.

10. UNCTAD (1999a) confirms that the three African countries that were most successful in attracting FDI flows (Ghana, Mozambique, and Uganda) achieved significant reductions in inflation rates and the government deficit (as a ratio to GDP).

11. See World Bank 1999b, chapter 3; and UNCTAD 2001b, chapter 4 for detailed discussions of spillover effects in developing countries.

12. See World Bank 2001a.

13. The positive impact on growth in developing countries in general is discussed in World Bank 2001a.

14. This result is based on a study of 55 poor countries during 1980–99 based on a Solow-type production that makes output a function of stocks of capital, labor, human capital, and productivity (see Mankiw, Romer, and Weil 1992; Benhabib and Spiegel 1994).

15. Private investment is only correlated with growth if Botswana is included in the sample.

16. Borensztein, De Gregorio, and Lee (1995) include 69 developing countries for 1970–89. UNCTAD (1999b) analyzes the lagged impact of FDI inflows on the average growth rates of about 100 developing countries for five 5-year periods over 1970–95.

17. Underachievers in attracting FDI among the countries with a high reform index can be explained by limited availability of geological and technical information, inadequate supporting services and infrastructure, and inconvenient geographical location of major mines.

18. Mineral resources are finite, so an accurate measurement of the benefit of minerals exploitation would subtract from these production data the change in asset values associated with the depletion of the stock of minerals in the ground (see estimates of "genuine savings" in World Bank 2001d, p. 183). Thus the data on production overstate the true benefits to the economy of minerals exploitation.

19. The share of bank assets controlled by foreign banks in the Czech Republic, Poland, and Hungary rose from 12 percent in 1994 to 57 percent in 1999. Similarly, in Latin America, by the end of the decade, foreign banks controlled more than half of the banking systems of several countries (Argentina, Chile, Mexico, and the República Bolivariana de Venezuela), up from between 10 and 20 percent in 1994 (Mathieson and Roldos 2001).

20. These numbers refer to mergers where at least one partner is a commercial bank, and thus include cases where a foreign bank acquires a nonbank financial institution. The data cover only those banks reporting to Bankscope, which includes only locally incorporated foreign-owned banks, not the branches of foreign banks.

21. To cushion domestic debtors from the currency devaluation, the government originally sought to convert dollar debts under $100,000 into pesos, while pledging to refund dollar-denominated deposits in dollars. According to estimates, the cost of the currency mismatch for banks could well exceed their total equity—coming on top of losses due to borrowers defaulting. Most of these losses are being incurred by Spanish banks, which had gained a prominent position in Argentina since the liberalization of the country's banking system in the early 1990s.

22. The index is calculated by: (a) assigning a number to a qualitative judgment of the nature of World Trade Organization commitments in three areas (cross-border supply, consumption abroad, and commercial presence); and (b) taking the average of these numbers (Qian 2000).

23. Among other control variables, overhead costs tend to be passed on to customers, in the form of higher margins and fees. In terms of country characteristics, GDP growth improves bank profitability, but also makes banks less conservative in their provisioning policies. Inflation is associated with higher net interest margins, profitability, and overheads, consistent with the notion that high inflation requires higher bank margins and profitability to maintain real bank capital, and that the cost of operating in those environments is also higher.

24. World Bank staff.

25. Levine (1999)—building on earlier work by Demirgüç-Kunt and Detragiache (1998) that controls for the effects of other factors that are likely to produce banking crises—has found that the probability that a crisis would occur is lower in countries with a higher share of foreign bank participation. Moreover, Barth, Caprio, and Levine (2001a) have estimated that the likelihood of a major banking crisis is higher in countries with greater limitations on foreign bank presence.

26. The Basel Committee on Banking Supervision (1996) has elaborated guidelines for supervision of cross-border banking that make the solvency of foreign subsidiaries the joint responsibility of home and host supervisory authorities (see also IMF 2000b). Under these guidelines, the home country supervisor is responsible for the consolidated supervision of the bank on a global basis, while the host countries are responsible for maintaining the liquidity of foreign branches and subsidiaries, based on their better knowledge of local market conditions.

27. The problems involved with this and other approaches to measuring capital outflows are discussed in annex 3.1.

28. This calculation underestimates the stock of residents' assets held abroad. The stock is calculated by cumulating over the 1980–99 period, which ignores the stock of capital outflows as of 1980 because of lack of data. The calculation also excludes interest earned on outflows held abroad as well as any outflows through underinvoicing of exports and overinvoicing of imports (see annex 3.1).

29. See Collier, Hoeffler, and Pattillo 2000; Cuddington 1986; Dornbusch 1985; Dooley 1988; Rojas-Suarez 1990; Meyer and Bastos-Marquez 1990; Sheets 1996; Lessard and Williamson 1987.

30. If foreigners are exempt from exchange controls, then residents may have an incentive, for example, to place receipts from trade flows abroad by under- or overinvoicing, and to then use a foreign front to invest these funds domestically. In this way the resident investor gains greater control over the use of profits without forgoing domestic investment opportunities.

31. Indonesia does not record a net outflow in 1998, but net inflows were strongly negative.

32. This is despite the fact that trade misinvoicing is not included in these estimates of outflows (see annex 3.1).

33. The results from the panel-VAR exercise should be treated with some caution, as the data display considerable volatility over time and also suffer from substantial cross-sectional variation. As a result, the results tend to be sensitive to the choice of time period or the presence of outliers.

34. See IMF 2001b. Examples of controls on current account transactions include restrictions on the repatriation of capital and limits to the amount of foreign exchange that can be obtained for travel.

35. Beginning in 1996, the classification system used to characterize current and capital account restrictions was changed, with the single "yes/no" variable replaced by a more disaggregated assessment that is not comparable to the earlier measures.

36. Multiple exchange rates are typically used either to impose different prices for current versus capital account transactions, or to discriminate among different types of current transactions.

37. For more information on this and other "alternative remittance systems," see Financial Action Task Force 2000; and United Nations 1998.

38. Indeed, the presence of extensive dollarization of liabilities has been advanced as a principal reason why some countries that on paper have exchange rate flexibility appear not to use that flexibility in practice (the "fear of floating" in the language of Calvo and Reinhart 2000). Baliño, Bennett, and Borensztein (1999) review the additional complications of monetary management in dollarized economies.

39. In Tanzania, after controlling for the effects of terms of trade, a 1 percent increase in net capital inflows is estimated to lead to an appreciation of 4 percent in the REER (Kimei and others 1997).

40. Should these assumptions be false, two equations should be estimated simultaneously—one explaining the entry decision, and the other explaining the impact of entry on contemporaneous local banking profits (Claessens and Lee 2001).

41. For example, the proceeds from the sale of a company to nonresidents may be deposited offshore by the resident seller; or residents may indulge in round-tripping of flows, so that outflows are brought back as inflows.

42. The coefficient of the real exchange rate in the outflows equation has a negative sign, implying that an appreciation of the currency reduces outflows with a lag. This result is counter-intuitive, and may reflect the use of the official exchange rate, rather than a market rate, to calculate the real exchange rate. Many of the countries in the sample had exchange controls and substantial differences between market and official rates, especially during the 1980s.

References

The word *processed* describes informally reproduced works that may not be commonly available through libraries.

Agosin, M. R., and Ricardo Mayer. 2000. "Foreign Investment in Developing Countries: Does It Crowd in Domestic Investment?" Discussion Paper 146. United Nations Conference on Trade and Development, Geneva.

Aitken, Brian, Gordon H. Hanson, and Ann E. Harrison. 1994. "Spillovers, Foreign Investment, and Export Behavior." Working Paper 4967. National Bureau of Economic Research, Cambridge, Mass.

Aizenman, Joshua, and Nancy Marion. 1995. "Volatility, Investment and Disappointment Aversion." Working Paper 5386. National Bureau of Economic Research, Cambridge, Mass.

Ajayi, Ibi. 1997. "An Analysis of External Debt and Capital Flight in the Severely Indebted Low Income Countries of Sub-Saharan Africa." Working Paper 97/68. International Monetary Fund, Washington, D.C.

———. 2000. "Capital Flight and External Debt in Nigeria." In S. Ibi Ajayi and Mohsin S. Khan, eds., *External Debt and Capital Flight in Sub-Saharan Africa*. Washington, D.C.: International Monetary Fund.

Albuquerque, Rui. 2001. "The Composition of International Capital Flows: Risk-Sharing through Foreign Direct Investment." University of Rochester. Processed.

Alesina, Alberto, and Roberto Perotti. 1996. "Income Distribution, Political Instability, and Investment." *European Economic Review* 40(6): 1203–28.

Alesina, Alberto, and Guido Tabellini. 1989. "External Debt, Capital Flight and Political Risk." *Journal of International Economics* 27(3/4): 199–220.

Balasubramanyam, V. N., M. Salisu, and D. Sapsford. 1996. "Foreign Direct Investment and Growth in EP and IS Countries." *The Economic Journal*, 106(434): 92–105.

Baliño, Tomás, Adam Bennett, and Eduardo Borensztein. 1999. "Monetary Policy in Dollarized Economies." Occasional Paper 171. International Monetary Fund, Washington, D.C.

Barro, Robert. 1991. "World Interest Rates and Investment." Working Paper Series (U.S.). No. 3849. National Bureau of Economic Research, Cambridge, Mass.

Barth, James, Gerard Caprio Jr., and Ross Levine. 2001a. "Banking System around the Globe: Do Regulations and Ownership Affect Performance and Stability?" In Frederic S. Mishkin, ed. *Prudential Supervision: What Works and What Doesn't*. Chicago. University of Chicago.

———. 2001b. "Bank Regulation and Supervision: What Works Best?" Policy Research Working Paper 2725, The World Bank, Washington, D.C. November.

Basel Committee on Banking Supervision. 1996. "Report on International Developments in Banking Supervision." Report number 10. Basel.

Benhabib, Jess, and Mark M. Spiegel. 1994. "The Role of Human Capital in Economic Development: Evidence from Aggregate Cross-country Data." *Journal of Monetary Economics* 34 (October): 143–73.

Bhagwati, J. N. 1978. *Anatomy and Consequences of Exchange Control Regimes*. Vol. 1. Studies in International Economic Relations, No. 11. Cambridge, Mass.: National Bureau of Economic Research.

Bhinda Nils, Stephany Griffith-Jones, and Matthew Martin. 1999. "Perception and the Causes of Flows." In Nils Bhinda Leape, Matthew Martin, and Stephany Griffith-Jones, eds. *Private Capital Flows to Africa: Perception and Reality*. The Hague: Forum on Debt and Development.

Blomström, Magnus, Robert E. Lipsey, and Mario Zejan. 1994. "What Explains the Growth of Developing Countries?" In William J. Baumol, Richard R. Nelson, and Edward N. Wolff, eds. *Convergence of Productivity*. New York: Oxford University Press.

Borensztein, Eduardo, José De Gregorio, and Jong-Wha Lee. 1995. "How Does Foreign Direct Investment Affect Economic Growth?" Working Paper 5057. National Bureau of Economic Research, Cambridge, Mass.

Bosworth Barry, and Susan Collins. 1999. "Capital Flows to Developing Economies: Implications for Saving and Investment." Brookings Papers on Economic Activity. The Brookings Institute, Washington, D.C.

Brownbridge, M. 1998. "The Causes of Financial Distress in Local Banks in Africa and Implications for Prudential Policy." United Nations Conference on Trade and Development. Development Discussion Papers (International). No. 132:1–24.

Brunetti, A., and B. Weder. 1998. "Investment and Institutional Uncertainty: A Comparative Study of Different Uncertainty Measures." Weltwirtschaftliches Archiv 134(3): 513–33.

Bubnova, N. B. 2000. "Governance Impact on Private Investment: Evidence from the International Patterns of Infrastructure Bond Risk Pricing." Technical Paper 488. World Bank, Washington, D.C.

Buch, Claudia, and Gayle Delong. 2001. "Cross-Border Bank Mergers: What Lures the Rare Animal?" Baruch College, New York. Processed.

Calvo, Guillermo, and Carmen Reinhart. 2000. "Fear of Floating." Working Paper Series (U.S.) 7993. National Bureau of Economic Research, Cambridge, Mass.

Calvo G., L. Leiderman, and C. Reinhart. 1993. "Capital Inflows and Real Exchange Rate Appreciation in Latin America: The Role of External Factors." IMF Staff Papers 40:108–51. Washington, D.C.

Chang, K. S. Claessens, and R. Cumby. 1997. "Conceptual and methodological issues in the measurement of capital flight." International Journal of Finance and Economics (U.K.) 2: 101–19.

Claessens, Stijn, and Jong Kun Lee. 2001. "Foreign Banks in Low-Income Countries: Recent Developments and Impacts." University of Amsterdam, and World Bank, Washington, D.C.

Claessens, S., and D. Naudé. 1993. "Recent Estimates of Capital Flight." World Bank Policy Research Working Paper 1186. Washington, D.C.

Claessens, Stijn, Asli Demirgüç-Kunt and Harry Huizinga. 1998. "How Does Foreign Entry Affect the Domestic Banking Market?" Policy Research Paper 1918. World Bank, Washington, D.C.

Clark, A. and K. Naito. 1997. "Structural Reform of the Mining Industry in Asia and the Pacific Region." Asian Journal of Mining July/August: 28–42.

Clarke, George R., Robert Cull, and Maria Soledad Martinez Peria. 2001. "Does Foreign Bank Penetration Reduce Access to Credit in Developing Countries? Evidence from Asking Borrowers." Policy Research Working Paper 2716. World Bank, Washington, D.C. November.

Clements, B., and J. V. Levy. 1994. "Public Education and Other Determinants of Private Investment in the Caribbean." Working Paper 94/122. International Monetary Fund, Washington, D.C.

Cline, William R., ed. 1995. International Debt Reexamined. Washington, D.C.: Institute for International Economics.

Collier, Paul and Jan Willem Gunning. 1999. "Why Has Africa Grown Slowly?" Journal of Economic Perspectives 13(3): 3–22.

Collier, Paul, Anke Hoeffler, and Catherine Pattillo. 2000. "Flight Capital as a Portfolio Choice." World Bank Economic Review 15 (1): 55–80.

Coolidge, Jacqueline, Gregory Kisunko, and Aminur Rahman. 2001. "Administrative Barriers to Investment in the Russian Federation: Inter-Regional Comparisons." Prepared for Economists' Forum 2001. World Bank, Washington, D.C.

Corsetti, Giancarlo, Paolo Pesenti, and Nouriel Roubini. 1998. "Fundamental Determinants of the Asian Crisis: A Preliminary Empirical Assessment." Paper prepared for the conference on Perspectives on the Financial Crisis in Asia, sponsored by Journal of International Money and Finance and Fordham University, New York.

Cuddington, John T. 1986. Capital Flight: Estimates, Issues and Explanations." Princeton Studies in International Finance 58. Princeton University, Princeton, N.J.

Das-Gupta, Arindam, and Dilip Mookherjee. 1995. "Tax Amnesties in India: An Empirical Evaluation." Discussion Paper 53. Boston University, Institute for Economic Development, Boston, Mass.

De Gregorio, José, Sebastian Edwards, and Rodrigo O. Valdes. 2000. "Controls on Capital Inflows: Do they Work?" Working Paper 7645. National Bureau of Economic Research, Cambridge, Mass

de Mello, Luiz R. Jr. 1999. "Foreign Direct Investment–Led Growth: Evidence From Time Series and Panel Data." Oxford Economic Papers 51(1): 133–54.

Demirgüç-Kunt, A., and E. Detragiache. 1998. "The Determinants of Banking Crises in Developing and Developed Countries." IMF Staff Papers, 45 March: 81–109. Washington, D.C.

———. 2000. "Monitoring Banking Sector Fragility: A Multivariate Logit Approach." World Bank Economic Review 14(2): 287–307.

Devarajan, S., W. R. Easterly, and H. Pack. 2001. " Is Investment in Africa Too Low or Too High? Macro and Micro Evidence." Policy Research Working Paper 2519. World Bank, Washington, D.C.

Devarajan, S., Andrew Sunil Rajkumar, and Vinaya Swaroop. 1999. "What Does Aid to Africa Finance?" World Bank Policy Research Working Paper 2092. Washington, D.C.

Dollar, David, Giuseppe Iarossi, and Taye Mengistae. 2001. "Investment Climate and Economic Performance: Some Firm Level Evidence from India." Prepared for Economists' Forum 2001. World Bank, Washington, D.C.

Dooley, M. 1986. "Country Specific Risk Premiums, Capital Flight and Net Investment Income Payments in Selected Developing Countries." International Monetary Fund, Research Department, Washington, D.C.

———. 1988. "Capital Flight: A Response to Differences in Financial Risks." IMF Staff Papers 35 (September): 422–36. Washington, D.C.

Dornbusch, Rudiger. 1985. "External Debt, Budget deficits and Disequilibrium Exchange Rates." In Gordon W. Smith and John T. Cuddington, eds., International Debt and the Developing Countries. Washington, D.C.: World Bank.

———. 2001. "Malaysia's Crisis: Was it Different?" Prepared for conference on Preventing Currency Crises in

Emerging Markets, National Bureau of Economic Research, January 11–13. Forthcoming in Sebastian Edwards and Jeffrey Frankel, eds. *Preventing Currency Crises in Emerging Markets*. Chicago: University of Chicago Press.

Eaton. 1987. "Public Debt Guarantees and Private Capital Flight." Working Paper Series. (U.S.) 2172 (March): 1–33. National Bureau of Economic Research, Cambridge, Mass.

Edwards, Sebastian. 1999. "How Effective Are Capital Controls?" *Journal of Economic Perspectives* 13(4): 65–84.

Eggerstedt, H., R. Brideau Hall, and S. van Wijnbergen. 1995. "Measuring Capital Flight: A Case Study of Mexico." Policy Research Working Paper 1121. World Bank, Washington, D.C.

Eichengreen, Barry, Michael Mussa, Giovanni Dell'Ariccia, Enrica Detragiache, Gian Maria Milesi-Ferrettir, and Andrew Tweeedie. 1999. "Liberalizing Capital Movements: Some Analytical Issues." *Economic Issues* 17. International Monetary Fund, Washington, D.C.

Feldstein, Martin, and Charles Horioka. 1980. "Domestic Savings and International Capital Flows." Working Paper 0310 (NBER Reprints 0085). National Bureau of Economic Research, Cambridge, Mass.

Financial Action Task Force on Money Laundering. 2000. "Report on Money Laundering Typologies, 1999–2000." (Available at www.oecd.org/fatf).

Fleisig, Heywood. 1996. "Secured Transactions: the Power of Collateral." *Finance and Development* 33 (June). International Monetary Fund, Washington, D.C.

Fry, Maxwell J. 1992. "Foreign Direct Investment in a Macroeconomic Framework: Finance, Efficiency, Incentives and Distortions." PRE Working Paper. World Bank, Washington, D.C.

Goldstein, M., G. Kaminsky, C. Reinhart. 2000. *Assessing Financial Vulnerability: An Early Warning System for Emerging Market*. Washington, D.C.: Institute for International Economics.

Gordon, David, and Ross Levine. 1988. "The Capital Flight Problem." International Finance Discussion Paper 320. U.S. Federal Reserve Board, Washington, D.C.

Goreux, Louis. 2001. "Conflict Diamonds." Africa Region Working Paper 13. World Bank, Washington, D.C.

Gyimah-Brempong, K., and S. Muñoz de Camacho. 1998. "Political Instability, Human Capital and Economic Growth in Latin America." *Journal of Developing Areas* 32(4): 449–65.

Gyimah-Brempong, K., and T. L. Traynor. 1999. "Political Instability, Investment and Economic Growth in Sub-Saharan Africa." *Journal of African Economies* 8 (1): 52–86.

Harrison, Ann. 1993. "Are there Positive Spillovers from Foreign Direct Investment? Evidence from Panel Data for Morocco." *Journal of Development Economics*. (Netherlands) 42 (October): 51–74.

———. 1994. "Productivity, Imperfect Competition, and Trade Reform: Theory and Evidence." *Journal of International Economics* 36: 53–73.

Hausmann, R., and M. Gavin. 1996. "Securing Stability and Growth in a Shock-Prone Region: The Policy Challenge for Latin America." In R. Hausmann and H. Reisen, eds., *Securing Stability and Growth in Latin America: Policy Issues and Prospects*. Paris: Organisation for Economic Co-operation and Development.

Hayri, Aydin, and Mark Dutz. 1999. "Does More Intense Competition Lead to Higher Growth?" Discussion paper 2249. Centre for Economic Policy Research, London.

Hellmann, Thomas F., Kevin C. Murdock, and Joseph E. Stiglitz. 2000. "Liberalization, Moral Hazard in Banking, and Prudential Regulation: Are Capital Requirements Enough?" *American Economic Review* 90(1): 147–65.

Hoekman, Bernard, Hiau Looi Kee, and Marcelo Olarreaga. 2001. "Markups, Entry Regulation and Trade: Does Country Size Matter?" World Bank. Washington, D.C. Processed.

Hood, Ron. 2001. "Malaysian Capital Controls." Policy Research Working Paper 2536. World Bank, Washington, D.C.

IMF (International Monetary Fund). 2000a. "Country Experiences with the Use and Liberalization of Capital Controls." Washington, D.C.

———. 2000b. The Role of Foreign Banks in Emerging Markets." In *International Capital Markets: Development, Prospects, and Key Policy Issues*. Washington, D.C.

———. 2001a. "West African Economic and Monetary Union: Recent Economic Developments and Regional Policy Issues in 2000." IMF Country Report. Washington, D.C.

———. 2001b. "Annual Report on Exchange Arrangements and Exchange Restrictions." Washington, D.C.

Ize, Alain, and Guillermo Ortiz. 1987. "Fiscal Rigidities, Public Debt and Capital Flight." *IMF Staff Papers* 34 (June): 311–32.

Jenkins, Carolyn. 1998. "Determinants of private investment in Zimbabwe." *Journal of African Economies* 7 (March):34–61.

Johnson, C. 1990. "Ranking countries for mineral exploration." *Natural Resources Forum* 14 (3): 178–86.

Kaplan, Ethan, and Dani Rodrik. 2001. "Did the Malaysian Capital Controls Work?" Prepared for conference on Preventing Currency Crises in Emerging Markets, National Bureau of Economic Research, January 11–13. Forthcoming in Sebastian Edwards and Jeffrey Frankel, eds. *Preventing Currency Crises in Emerging Markets*. Chicago: University of Chicago Press.

Kasekende, Louis A. 2000. "Capital Account Liberalization: The Ugandan Experience." Paper presented at the Overseas Development Institute, London, June 21.

Kathuria, V. 1998. "Technology Transfer and Spillovers for Indian Manufacturing Firms." *Development Policy Review* 16 (1): 73–91.

Ketkar, Suihas, and Dilip Ratha. 2000. "Development Financing During a Crisis: Securitization of Future Receivables." Policy Research Working Paper 2582. World Bank, Washington, D.C.

Khan, Mohsin, and Nadeem Ul-Haque. 1985. "Foreign Borrowing and Capital Flight: A Formal Analysis." *Finance and Development* 32(4): 606–28.

Kimei, C., G. D. Mjerna, B. Tarimo, and A. Msutze (with M. Martin and N. Bhinda). 1997. "Tanzania: Capital Flows Study." Paper presented to EFA workshop on

Private Capital Flows and Macroeconomic Policy in Sub-Saharan Africa, Cape Town, July 1997.

Knack, S., and P. Keefer. 1995. "Institutions and Economic Performance: Cross-Country Tests Using Alternative Institutional Measures." *Economics and Politics* 7 (November): 207–27.

Kokko, A. 1994. "Technology, Market Characteristics, and Spillovers." *Journal of Development Economics* 43 (2): 279–93.

Kokko, A., Ruben Tansini, and Mario C. Zejan. 1996. "Local Technological Capability and Productivity Spillovers from FDI in the Uruguayan Manufacturing Sector." *Journal of Development Studies* 32 (4): 602–11.

Krugman, Paul. 1998. *What Happened to Asia?* (available at http://web.mit.edu/krugman/www/disinter.html).

Kumar, Nagesh, and Jaya Prakash Pradhan. 2001. "Foreign Direct Investment, Externalities and Economic Growth: Some Empirical Explorations for the Poor Countries." A background paper for *GDF 2002.* World Bank, Washington, D.C.

Laban, Raul, and Felipe Larrain. 1997. "Can a Liberalization of Capital Outflows Increase Net Capital Inflows?" *Journal of International Money and Finance* 16(3): 415–31.

Lessard, Donald, and John Williamson. 1987. *Capital Flight and Third World Debt.* Washington, D.C.: Institute for International Economics.

Levine, Ross. 1996. "Foreign Banks, Financial Development and Economic Growth." In Claude E. Barfield, ed. *International Financial Markets: Harmonization versus Competition.* Washington, D.C.: AEI Press.

———. 1999. "Foreign Bank Entry and Capital Control Liberalization: Effects on Growth and Stability." University of Minnesota. Processed.

Levinsohn, James. 1993. "Testing the Imports-as-Market-Discipline Hypothesis." *Journal of International Economics* 35(1/2): 1–22.

Loungani, Prakash, and Paolo Mauro. 2000. "Capital Flight from Russia." IMF Policy Discussion Paper 00/6. International Monetary Fund, Washington, D.C.

Mankiw, N. Gregory, David Romer, and David N. Weil. 1992. "A Contribution to the Empirics of Economic Growth." *Quarterly Journal of Economics* 107(2): 407–37

Marksun, J. R., and Anthony J. Venables. 1997. "Foreign Direct Investment as a Catalyst For Industrial Development." Working Paper 624. National Bureau of Economic Research, Cambridge, Mass.

Mathieson, Donald J., and Liliana Rojas-Suarez. 1993. "Liberalization of the Capital Account: Experiences and Issues." Occasional Paper 103. International Monetary Fund, Washington D.C.

Mathieson, Donald J., and Jorge Roldos. 2001. "The Role of Foreign Banks in Emerging Markets." Paper prepared for the IMF–World Bank–Brookings Institution conference on Financial Markets and Development, Washington, D.C.

Mauro, P. 1995. "Corruption and Growth." *Quarterly Journal of Economics* 110(April): 681–712.

Mexico Federal Commission on Competition. 1997. *Annual Economic Competition Report.* Mexico City.

Meyer and Bastos-Marquez. 1990. "A fuga de capital no Brasil: 1975/88." *Pesquisa e Planejamento Economico* (Brazil) 0:49–85.

Mian, S., and C. Smith. 1994. "Getting Help with Credit Administration." *Corporate Finance* 11.

Mody, Ashoka, and Antu Panini Murshid. 2001. "Growing up with Capital Flows." International Monetary Fund, Washington, D.C. Processed.

Morgan Guaranty Trust Company. 1986. "LDC Capital Flight." *World Financial Markets.* March, 13–15.

Naito, Koh, Felix Remy, and Peter van der Veen. 2001. "Mining Sector Reform and FDI." World Bank, Washington, D.C. Processed.

Naito, K., Felix Remy, and J. P. Williams. 2001. "A Comparative Review of Legal and Fiscal Frameworks for Exploration and Mining: Best Practices." *Mining Journal Limited,* p. 177.

Naito, K., H. Myoi, J. Otto, D. Smith, and M. Kamitani, 1998. "Mineral Projects in Asian Countries: Geology, Regulations, Fiscal Regimes and the Environment." *Resources Policy* 24 (2): 87–93.

Ndikumana, L. 2000. "Financial Determinants of Domestic Investment in Sub-Saharan Africa: Evidence from Panel Data." *World Development* 28 (2): 381–400.

Ng'eno, N.K. 2000. "Capital Flight in Kenya." In S. Ibi Ajayi and Mohsin S. Khan, eds., *External Debt and Capial Flight in Sub-Saharan Africa.* Washington, D.C.: International Monetary Fund.

Ngugi, R. 2000. "Financial Reform Process in Kenya." *African Development Review* 12(1): 52–77. African Development Bank (International).

OECD (Organisation for Economic Co-operation and Development). 2001. Cited in figure 4.1.

Olopoenia, Razaq A. 2000. "Capital Flight from Uganda." in Ajoyi and Kahn, eds. *External Debt and Capital Flight in Sub-Saharan Africa.* Washington, D.C.: International Monetary Fund.

Oshikoya, T. 1994. "Macroeconomic Determinants of Domestic Private Investment in Africa: An Empirical Analysis." *Economic Development and Cultural Change* 42(3): 573–96.

Otto, J. 1992. "A Global Survey of Mineral Company Investment Preferences." In J. Otto and T. Waelde, eds., *Mineral Investment Conditions in Selected Countries of the Asia-Pacific Region.* Publication ST/ESCAP/ 1197. New York: United Nations.

———. 1995. "Legal Risk Analysis for Mining Projects." Mineral Industry International No. 1025. Institute for Mining and Metallurgy, London.

Oxford Analytica. 2001. "Africa: Regional Stock Markets." September 4.

Ozawa, Terutomo. 1992. "Foreign Direct Investment and Economic Development." *Transnational Corporations* 1(1): 27–54.

Petersen, M. A., and R. G. Rajan. 1994. "The Benefits of Lending Relationships: Evidence from Small Business Data." *Journal of Monetary Economics* (1): 3–38.

———. 1997. "Trade Credit: Theories and Evidence." *Review of Financial Studies.* U.S. (10): 661–91.

Pfeffermann, G., and G. Kisunko. 1999. "Perceived Obstacles to Doing Business: Worldwide Survey Results." International Finance Corporation, Washington, D.C. Processed.

———. 2001. "The Foreign Direct Investment Environment in Africa." Africa Region Working Paper 15. World Bank, Washington, D.C.

Porter, M. E. 1990. *The Competitive Advantage of Nations*. New York: Free Press.

Qian, Ying. 2000. "The Process of China's Market Transition, 1978–1998: The Evolutionary, Historical, and Comparative Perspectives." *Journal of Institutional and Theoretical Economics* (Germany). 156(1): 151–79.

Razin, Asaf, Efraim Sadka, and Chi-Wa Yuen. 1997. "Channeling Domestic Savings into Productive Investment under Asymmetric Information: the Essential Role of Foreign Direct Investment." Working Paper 6338. National Bureau of Economic Research, Cambridge, Mass.

Reinikka, R., and J. Sevensson. 1999. "How Inadequate Provision of Public Infrastructure and Services Affects Private Investment." Policy Research Working Papers 2262, World Bank, Washington, D.C.

Rojas-Suarez, Liliana. 1990. "Risk and Capital Flight in Developing Countries." Working Paper 90/64. International Monetary Fund, Washington, D.C.

Sakr, K. 1993. "Determinants of Private Investment in Pakistan." Working Paper 93/30. International Monetary Fund, Washington, D.C.

Schadler, S., M. Carkovic, A. Bennett, and R. Kahn. 1993. "Recent Experiences with Surges in Capital Inflows." Occasional Paper 108. International Monetary Fund, Washington, D.C.

Schineller, Lisa M. 1997. An Econometric Model of Capital Flight from Developing Countries. International Finance Discussion Paper 579. U.S. Federal Reserve Board, Washington, D.C.

———. 1999. A Nonlinear Econometric Analysis of Capital Flight." International Finance Discussion Paper 594. U.S. Federal Reserve Board, Washington, D.C.

Servén, L. 1996. "Does Public Capital Crowd out Private Capital?: Evidence from India." Policy Research Working Papers 1613. World Bank, Washington, D.C.

———. 1998. "Macroeconomic Uncertainty and Private Investment in Developing Countries: An Empirical Investigation." Policy Research Working Papers 2035. World Bank, Washington, D.C.

Servén, L., and A. Solimano. 1993. "Debt Crises, Adjustment Policies and Capital Formation in Developing Countries: Where Do We Stand?" *World Development* 21: 127–40.

Sheets, Nathan. 1996. "Capital Flight from the Countries in Transition: Some Theory and Empirical Evidence." International Finance Discussion Paper 514. U.S. Federal Reserve Board, Washington, D.C.

Sievers, Sarah E. 2001. "Competitiveness and Foreign Direct Investment in Africa." In Augustin Kwasi Fosu, Saleh M. Nsouli, and Aristomene Varoudakis, eds., *Policies to Promote Competitiveness in Manufacturing in Sub-Saharan Africa*. Organisation for Economic Co-operation and Development.

Smith, D., and K. Naito. 1998. "Asian Mining Legislation: Policy Issues and Recent Developments." *Resources Policy* 24: 125–32.

Sorsa, Piritta. 1997. "The GATS Agreement on Financial Services: A Modest Start to Multilateral Liberalization." Working Paper 97/55. International Monetary Fund, Washington, D.C.

Stiglitz, Joseph E., and Andrew Weiss. 1981. "Credit Rationing in Markets with Imperfect Information." *American Economic Review* 71: 393–410.

Stryker, Dirck. 1997. "Dollarization and its Implications for Ghana." Associates for International Resources and Development, Cambridge, Mass.

Thomas, R. H. 1994. "Trading and Investing in Tanzania: The Legal Framework." *Development South Africa* 11(3).

Tornell, Aaron, and Andres Velasco. 1992. "The Tragedy of the Commons and Economic Growth: Why Does Capital Flow from Poor to Rich Countries?" *Journal of Political Economy* 100(6): 1208–31.

Trester, Jeffrey. 1998. "Venture Capital Contracting under Asymmetric Information." *Journal of Banking and Finance* 22 (August): 675–99.

Tybout, James. 2000. "Manufacturing Firms in Developing Countries: How Well Do They Do, and Why?" *Journal of Economic Literature* 38(1): 11–44.

United Nations. 1998. U.N. General Assembly Special Session on the World Drug Problem. 8–10 June. www.un.org

UNCTAD (United Nations Conference on Trade and Development). 1999a. "Foreign Direct Investment in Africa: Performance and Potential." Geneva.

———. 1999b. *World Investment Report*. Geneva.

———. 2001a. "Foreign Direct Investment in Least Developed Countries at a Glance." Geneva.

———. 2001b. *World Investment Report 2001*. Cited figure 2.4.

Varman-Schneider, Benu. 1991. *Capital Flight from Developing Countries*. Boulder: Westview Press.

World Bank. 1985. *World Development Report: International Capital and Economic Development*. New York: Oxford University Press.

———. 1992. "Strategy for African Mining." Technical Paper 181. World Bank, Washington, D.C.

———. 1996. "A Mining Strategy for Latin America and the Caribbean." Technical Paper 345. World Bank, Washington, D.C.

———. 1999a. *Global Economic Prospects*. Washington, D.C.

———. 1999b. *Global Development Finance 1999*. Washington, D.C.

———. 2001a. *Global Development Finance 2001*. Washington, D.C.

———. 2001b. "Finance for Growth: Policy Choices in a Volatile World." Washington, D.C.

———. 2001d. *World Development Indicators 2001*. Washington, D.C.

World Economic Forum. 1998. "The Africa Competitiveness Report 1998." Geneva.

Yun, Mikyung. 2000. "Cross-Border M&As and their Impact on the Korean Economy." Paper presented at the UNCTAD Seminar on Cross-border M&As and Sustained Competitiveness in Asia: Trends, Impacts and Policy Implications, Bangkok, March 9–10. Processed.

Zemplinerova, A., and M. Jarolim. 2000. "FDI through M&A vs. Greenfield FDI: The Case of the Czech Republic." Paper presented at the UNCTAD and OeNB Seminar on FDI and Privatization in Central and Eastern Europe, Vienna, March 2–3. Processed.

4

Strengthening Official Financial Support for Developing Countries

Mixed results from aid have led to a fall in aid

Slow progress in poverty reduction during the 1990s outside Asia increased concerns about the effectiveness of aid.[1] Many countries have achieved impressive growth rates with the support of aid flows, and since 1990 the share of people living in extreme poverty in developing countries has dropped from 29 percent to 23 percent, led by rapid progress in China and India. Nevertheless, growth has been slow in many of the poorest aid recipients (see chapter 3), and in Sub-Saharan Africa the share of the population living on less than a dollar a day stagnated during the 1990s, contributing to a growing perception that aid flows have failed to support development. This perception, in conjunction with fiscal pressures in donor countries and the declining strategic value of aid (from the perspective of donors) with the end of the Cold War, led to a sharp fall in aid over the 1990s.

Mixed progress in poverty reduction also led to a reevaluation of aid policies, and to a growing consensus on donor policies required to increase aid effectiveness. Perhaps most importantly, the allocation of aid is increasing to those countries with good policies. Despite high levels of aid, most countries with good policies can continue to absorb additional aid resources without seriously impairing the effectiveness of that aid. High aid levels to countries with good policies should not raise fears of excessive dependence. Over time, strong growth should generate the increase in tax revenues required for a decline in aid. Aid does not, in general, increase the volatility of government resources, and appropriate policies can ensure that aid does not contribute to inflationary pressures or cause excessive exchange rate appreciation. It is true that even in many countries with good policies, lack of administrative capacity lowers the marginal productivity of aid as aid levels rise. However, recent research indicates that aid levels to most countries with strong economic programs are well below the threshold where aid becomes ineffective. This analysis supports the view that a doubling of aid could make an effective contribution toward reaching the Millennium Development Goals, provided that the aid is allocated wisely.

Donors also have made progress in improving the design and administration of aid programs, although much more remains to be done. Greater efforts are directed at ensuring that policy conditions in adjustment assistance reflect a program that has the full support of the government and other domestic stakeholders. This new emphasis involves greater selectivity in aid disbursements. The administrative burden of aid is less because the share of tied aid is reduced, and the government is assuming more leadership in promoting aid coordination.

The policy framework

Providing a policy environment conducive to growth and development—

The growing consensus on how to improve donor policies has its roots in the mixed success of efforts to help developing countries recover from the failure of many economic policies of the 1970s and 1980s. Growth in many developing countries was depressed by unsustainable macroeconomic policies, financial repression, high trade barriers, pervasive state interventions in competitive markets, and complex administrative constraints on entrepreneurial activity. Donor programs during the late 1980s and throughout the 1990s thus increasingly focused on supporting efforts at providing an economic policy environment conducive to growth and development. Improvements in economic policies during the 1990s did help many developing countries to achieve substantial increases in growth rates over the "lost decade" of the 1980s. However, many of the poorest countries continued to be left behind, and it became clear that weak institutions and poor governance were at least as significant constraints on development as inflation and price controls.

—with a reform of donor policies—

At the same time, some instruments that donors used to support developing countries' economic programs proved inadequate. Compliance with conditionality under adjustment lending was mixed. Official lending and guarantees coupled with poor policies contributed to debt burdens. Aid programs increased the administrative burden in many countries where capacity was a principal constraint on growth. Recognition of these problems catalyzed efforts to strengthen the framework for adjustment assistance, provide debt relief, and reduce the administrative burden of aid by improving donor coordination. These efforts do not represent an entirely new departure: aid coordination, capacity constraints, and adjustment assistance have been a focus of analysis for some time. Nevertheless, in the past few years concerted efforts have been made to adjust donor policies in the context of recent experience. At the Bretton Woods institutions, this shift in assistance to low-income countries is being implemented through the Poverty Reduction Strategy Paper (PRSP) approach (see box 4.1).

—to increase the effectiveness of aid

These two debates over development policy—that a deepening of reform programs must address critical institutional and governance issues that constrain growth, and that donor policies must support country ownership, reduce the administrative demands of aid programs, and focus on development results—are intricately related. A greater focus on development outcomes may be useful in determining the overall allocation of funds by donors and as a basis for monitoring and evaluation of reform programs. The recognition that institutional capacity is a major constraint on growth underlines the importance of easing the administrative burden of aid.

Recognition of the failure of aid to boost growth in many heavily indebted poor countries (HIPCs)—increases the legitimacy of focusing resources on debt relief. Ultimately, improved policies in developing countries and a more effective approach to aid should strengthen donor support for increasing aid resources. These messages underscore the important themes emerging from the United Nations (U.N.)'s Financing for Development (FfD) process (see box 4.2). Unfortunately, recent aid trends have been disappointing, and there appears to be little likelihood that a rise in aid will be significant and sustained.

Trends in aid

A widening gap between the availability of aid and the needs of recipients—

Aid flows dropped sharply over the last decade in real terms, and by 2000 stood more than 10 percent below the 1990 level. Expressed as a share of donors' gross national product (GNP), aid fell from 0.33 percent in 1990 to 0.22 percent in 2000. Only five donor countries reached (or surpassed) the U.N.'s target of 0.7 percent of GNP which was endorsed by Group of Seven (G-7) countries at the Earth Summit in Rio in 1992. At the same time, the need for aid continues to grow. Developing countries' population rose by 17 percent during the 1990s, and the number of people (outside China) living on less than $1 a day has remained roughly the same. Some 60 million people in developing countries are infected with the human immunodeficiency virus. The Millennium Development Goals cannot be met without increased aid. For example, preliminary calculations indicate that a doubling of aid, appropriately allocated, will be necessary to halve poverty by 2015. Estimates of the aid (above current levels) required to meet the goals for education, health, and the environment (see box 4.2) range from $35 billion to $76 billion.[2] Vigorous steps to increase the availability of aid resources, in conjunction with improved donor policies to support increased aid effectiveness, should be the top priorities for the international community.

—particularly over the last two years—

After a modest recovery in aid flows beginning in 1998, the past two years have seen a further decline. Concessional aid flows are measured in two

Box 4.1   The PRSPs

In December 1999 the Boards of the International Monetary Fund (IMF) and the World Bank approved a new approach to the challenge of reducing poverty in low-income countries based on country-owned poverty reduction strategies that would serve as a framework for development assistance. Much has been accomplished during the past two years—nine countries have completed their first full PRSP and three countries have completed their first annual PRSP implementation progress reports. Some 41 countries have also completed their interim poverty reduction strategies (I-PRSPs) and eight countries have subsequently submitted their PRSP preparation status reports for consideration by the Boards.[3]

The central message of the forthcoming Review of the PRSP Approach[4] is a substantial affirmation by low-income countries as well as development partners and civil society organizations of the value of the PRSP approach, and the importance of country ownership as a guiding principle, and a corresponding recognition of the need for flexibility to allow for different country starting points.

It is widely recognized that aligning donor programs with the PRSP is crucial to sustaining this approach. In part the PRSP approach has been designed to overcome long-standing problems of poor donor coordination, weak country ownership of donor-financed programs, and the fragmentation of governmental programs and institutions caused by multiple, and often inconsistent, donor interventions. Donor alignment is needed at various levels, both substantive (in ensuring that donors respect country priorities) and in terms of processes (to reduce the transaction costs associated with aid).

Key challenges of the PRSP for development partners include:

- *Pursuing new approaches to support government ownership.* Governments prepare their own poverty reduction strategies through a participatory process designed to build broad ownership at the national level. Medium-term reform programs supported by Poverty Reduction Support Credits (PRSCs) will be principally drawn from, or will elaborate on, policy measures contained in the PRSPs.[5]

- *More coherent partnerships and aid coordination.* PRSPs are intended to be instruments by which governments can achieve better aid coordination. It is good practice for the PRSP process to be inclusive of donors, and most countries are in fact doing this, including, for example, through the representation of donors on PRSP working groups.

- *Harmonizing and simplifying donor procedures,* alongside a *greater focus on development results* as opposed to monitoring and efforts to control inputs. Each PRSP is expected to include intermediate and longer-term indicators on poverty outcomes, to enable regular monitoring of progress, upon which governments would annually report. It is hoped that this will encourage governments and their external partners to focus on the same set of targets and indicators over a sufficiently long period, so as to reduce the costs associated with multiple reporting requirements, during which time it would be possible to measure results and to adjust domestic strategies and external assistance accordingly.

In the longer term it is expected that the PRSP will facilitate greater aid allocations to countries with good policy environments. To the extent that PRSPs reveal what a country is truly prepared to do (in terms of policy and institutional reforms and expenditure allocations), they should provide a reliable indicator for donors to allocate funds on the basis of policies. Over time a country's performance with respect to its PRSP objectives (both policy measures and development results) could help improve donors' judgments concerning the allocation of aid.

As reported in the upcoming Review, early evidence about the PRSP process is positive, and substantial investments are being made by low-income countries and development partners in making this approach work. While the quality of the early full PRSPs has varied (for example, in terms of participation, data collection, the realism of long-term goals, and institutional capacity to monitor expenditures and the link to poverty reduction), the process has helped promote ownership, encouraged a better dialogue within countries, broadened the understanding of development issues, and helped improve donor coordination.

ways: aid recorded as received by developing countries and aid recorded as provided by donor countries. The two measures are different because in any given year the concessional funding provided by donors to multilateral institutions is not the same as those institutions' disbursements to developing countries (see the data annex at the end of this chapter). Aid flows *received by developing countries* (excluding technical cooperation grants) fell by 3.8 percent in 2000 to $40.7 billion and they are estimated to have declined by a further 3.4 percent in 2001 (see table 4.1). Much of this decline was due

Box 4.2   The Financing for Development (FfD) process

The analysis presented in this document supports the agenda of the FfD conference that will take place in March 2002, in Monterrey, Mexico. The FfD process emphasizes the importance of a comprehensive approach to the mobilization of resources for development and of the flexibility and partnerships required to ensure that the needs and opportunities of different countries are taken into account in the support provided by the international community. The purpose of FfD is to assure the means to reduce poverty and reach the Millennium Development Goals as well as other internationally agreed-on development targets.

The FfD agenda recognizes that the means of reaching these goals must be defined broadly. Policy reforms in developing countries are required to boost growth and reduce poverty. At the same time, industrial countries need to open their markets to provide sufficient opportunities for developing countries to benefit from the world trading system, to help shape improvements in the international financial architecture, and to boost the aid resources required to help countries meet the development goals. The main messages of *Global Development Finance 2002* can be viewed under this paradigm:

- *Policies.* The discussion of country policies at the FfD conference will focus on improving the investment climate in developing countries. In particular, policies focused on maintaining macroeconomic stability, increasing openness to trade and foreign direct investment (FDI), improving governance, and strengthening financial sector institutions will help developing countries benefit from greater financial integration while reducing the potential costs. This document shows how a strong investment climate in the poor countries can boost the effectiveness of aid, increase domestic investment by limiting capital outflows and attracting more FDI inflows, and improve the productivity of investment. At the same time, this document outlines ongoing improvements in donor policies to strengthen administration of aid programs, increase the effectiveness of policy conditionality as a means of enhancing government credibility and commitment, ensure that debt relief is directed at countries with good policies, and ensure that guaranteed lending does not contribute to unsustainable debt burdens.
- *Opportunity.* All countries need to cooperate in integrating the developing countries into the world trading system. Industrial countries must cooperate through opening their markets (particularly in agriculture and textiles) and providing resources for

capacity building; developing countries must cooperate through strengthening their infrastructure to support trade and lowering their own trade barriers. The launch of a "development round" following the Doha meeting of the World Trade Organization will involve negotiations of market access issues covering agriculture, services, and manufactures, as well as rules governing dispute settlement, disciplines on regional integration, environment, and trade-related intellectual property rights. In addition, negotiations may also take place regarding investment, competition, trade facilitation, and transparency in government procurement. This approach should enable progress to be made in improving market access for developing countries (assuming they are willing to negotiate on the basis of reducing their own barriers to trade), which is the main priority for the trade agenda.

- *Resources.* Poor countries with good policies will need increased assistance to meet the development goals articulated in the U.N.-sponsored Millennium Declaration. These goals include halving extreme poverty, achieving universal primary education, eliminating gender disparity in education, reducing infant and child mortality and maternal mortality, ensuring access to reproductive health services, and implementing a national strategy for sustainable development in every country. Progress since 1990 has been too slow to achieve most of the goals, and a stepped-up effort by developing countries, industrial countries, and multilateral institutions is required to have any chance of meeting them.[6] This effort should include a doubling of aid to achieve the poverty goal, provided that these resources are allocated to countries with good policies (where aid will be most effective) and with many poor people. Some of the funding needs required to meet the health and education goals are the same as those required to halve poverty, but some will require dedicated funding, such as the need to address communicable diseases or to promote "Education for All." A portion of these resources should be used to finance global public goods, such as the creation of new vaccines, and thus would not be channeled through individual developing-country governments.

In countries with poor policies, even very large amounts of aid are likely to achieve only a limited and short-lived impact on poverty. There is, therefore, an inevitable tension between allocating aid to achieve the maximum global progress toward the goals and allocating aid so that each country or region has a chance of meeting

Box 4.2 *(continued)*

those goals. To resolve this issue, priority attention should be focused on improving policies in countries where they are weak.

Finally, the international community faces a dilemma in supporting progress toward the goals in middle-income countries with poor regions. It may not be advisable to provide large amounts of aid to countries that have substantial financial resources but have not made progress in alleviating poverty in some regions. Since money is fungi-

ble, aid would in fact be financing the marginal expenditure by middle-income governments, which may be less productive in terms of reducing poverty than expenditures in very poor countries with good policies. Nevertheless, it is important for donors to consider how to address the severe poverty issues in some middle-income countries; one recommendation would be to fund relatively small projects aimed at demonstrating effective approaches to specific problems.[7]

---

to a drop in Japanese aid to East Asia, because disbursements against the large commitments made at the time of the Asian crisis fell. Preliminary estimates suggest a continued increase in aid to Eastern Europe and Central Asia, both due to stepped-up assistance to the Balkans and support for the efforts of the advanced Eastern European countries to join the European Union (EU). Aid flows have declined to Sub-Saharan Africa due to delays in implementation of reform in some countries; aid flows have declined to a lesser extent to South Asia despite a rise in humanitarian assistance to India following the devastating earthquake in 2001.

The amount of official development assistance (ODA) *provided by donors* fell by 1.6 percent in real terms in 2000 to $53.1 billion, or 0.22 percent of Development Assistance Committee (DAC) members' GNP (data on aid flows from donors for 2001 are not yet available). This decline, which reversed the upward trend that commenced in 1998, was due to two special factors: the above-noted

fall in aid from Japan, and the removal of countries from the list of those eligible to receive ODA because their per capita incomes now exceed the cutoff for flows to be counted as aid.[8] Adjusting for the change in the DAC list, ODA fell by 0.2 percent in real terms in 2000. The decline was due to the fact that in the G-7 countries aid fell by 4.8 percent in real terms; aid from non–G-7 countries increased by 8.3 percent in real terms.

—and little sign of a reversal of this trend in the medium term—

The prospects for a rise in aid over the medium term are mixed. Several donors, in particular the United Kingdom and several of the non–G-7 countries, have been able to set and meet medium-term targets for substantial increases in aid flows. However, there is little sign of substantial increases in aid from the four largest donors—France, Germany, Japan, and the United States—which together account for almost two-thirds of all aid. In

---

Table 4.1 Net official aid to developing countries, by type and source, 1990–2001

(billions of dollars)

Aid	1990	1991	1992	1993	1994	1995	1996	1997	1998	1999	2000	2001
ODA and official aid	45.1	49.5	46.4	41.7	48.1	46.3	39.7	36.1	39.0	42.3	40.7	39.3
Grants (ex tech coop)	30.1	35.1	30.5	28.3	32.7	32.8	28.1	26.6	27.9	30.2	29.9	29.6
Bilateral	26.5	29.5	23.9	22.5	24.6	26.2	21.8	19.8	20.5	22.0	22.6	22.5
Multilateral	3.6	5.6	6.6	5.8	8.1	6.6	6.3	6.8	7.4	8.2	7.3	7.1
Concessional loans	15.0	14.4	15.9	13.4	15.4	13.5	11.6	9.5	11.1	12.1	10.8	9.7
Bilateral	8.3	6.3	8.5	6.7	6.5	4.9	3.0	1.5	2.9	4.6	3.6	3.0
Multilateral	6.7	8.1	7.4	6.7	8.9	8.6	8.6	8.0	8.2	7.5	7.2	6.7
Memo item												
Tech coop grants	14.6	15.6	17.7	18.2	16.9	20.1	18.7	15.7	16.3	16.6	15.5	15.4

Note: Data are based on the OECD DAC definition of aid as measured by donors. These data differ from concessional flows reported in volume 2, which are primarily based on information collected through the World Bank Debtor Reporting System.
Source: OECD DAC; World Bank Debtor Reporting System; staff estimates.

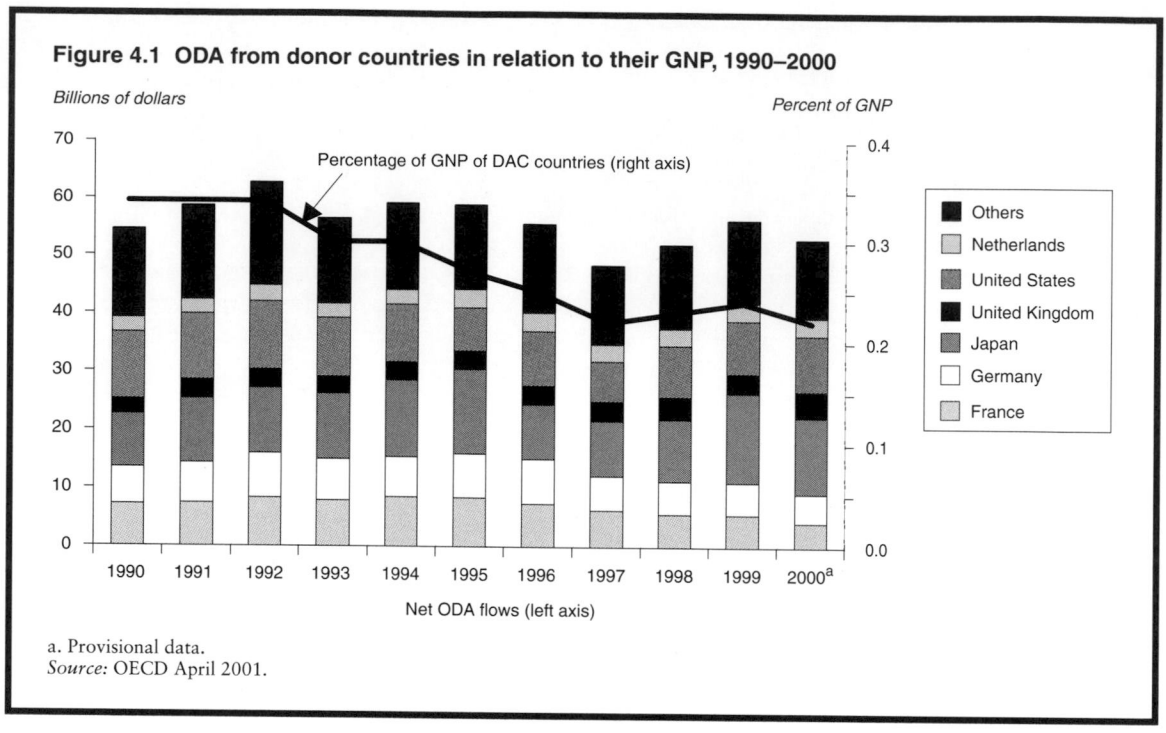

Figure 4.1 ODA from donor countries in relation to their GNP, 1990–2000

a. Provisional data.
Source: OECD April 2001.

part, slow growth or declines in aid flows as recorded by the DAC reflect the removal of a few countries from the list of countries eligible for aid. For example, recorded aid flows from France were affected by the removal of French Polynesia and New Caledonia, the largest beneficiaries of French assistance, from the list of ODA recipients. In the United States the country's largest aid recipient, Israel, was removed from the list of aid recipients in 1997, while the general skepticism about the value of aid has limited the ability to rebuild the U.S. aid program. Germany's aid budget fell by 7.5 percent in 2000, and the integration of the former East Germany continues to put pressure on the German federal budget. Japan, which is running a large fiscal deficit aimed at boosting domestic demand, has announced a 10 percent cut in the aid budget for fiscal 2002.

—although the terrorist attacks on September 11 may translate into a short-term increase
The conflict stemming from the tragic events of September 11 is likely to spur a rise in aid in the near term. Donors typically respond rapidly and generously to disaster—for example in Kosovo

and East Timor following the end of each conflict, in Central America following Cyclone Mitch, and in Turkey and India following earthquakes (in 1999 and 2001, respectively). Aid flows also rise sharply in times of global conflict—for instance, by 20 percent during the Gulf War of 1991. While these flows are an important element in maintaining uninterrupted trade flows and mitigating human suffering, they are temporary in nature and specific in their objectives. As worthy as these objectives are, they are unlikely to have a significant impact on long-term development goals.

The global war on terrorism is also likely to result in a temporary increase in aid as donors move to offset the economic and humanitarian needs in countries at the center of conflict. A total of $5 billion was pledged for Afghanistan in January 2002, although the bulk of this is expected to come from existing aid budgets. Commitments to Afghanistan in 2002 are expected to be almost $2 billion. However, absorptive capacity is limited and the actual inflow to Afghanistan, including the $350 million in emergency assistance already delivered since September 11, is expected to be on the order of $1 billion by the end of 2002.

Aid is not always focused on poverty reduction—

Aid has the greatest impact on poverty reduction when it is provided to countries with good policies and many poor people (World Bank 1998). All donors made a formal commitment to poverty reduction by endorsing the international developmental targets set out in the Organisation for Economic Co-operation and Development (OECD) DAC's *Shaping the 21st Century*. Most donors have policy statements that cite poverty reduction as the, or one of the, overarching goals of their aid programs. Trumbull and Wall (1994) estimate that ODA allocations are responsive to the needs of recipient countries, as represented by high levels of infant mortality (as well as issues surrounding political-civil rights). Nevertheless, donors have several motivations for aid that are not always consistent with allocating aid for the greatest poverty impact. Aid may be used to support countries with which the donor has strong historical connections. For example, Alesina and Dollar (2000) find that aid allocation is greatly influenced by whether a recipient was a former colony. Aid may be directed at solidifying regional ties; Japan's largest aid program is to countries in Asia. Aid also is used to pursue strategic interests: Alesina and Dollar (2000) find that recipients who vote with donors in the U.N. tend to get more aid, Maizels and Nissanke (1984) relate aid to arms transfers from the major donors, and Boschini and Olofsgard (2001) explain the decline in aid during the 1990s as being a byproduct of the end of the Cold War. Thus some of the disaffection with the impact of aid on poverty reduction does not reflect the intrinsic ineffectiveness of aid, but rather the large share of aid that is allocated on the basis of "strategic" criteria, instead of on the basis of the quality of policies and the number of poor. In this context the end of the Cold War may have improved the opportunities for allocating aid according to poverty alleviation, rather than to strategic criteria.

—and the share of aid going to low-income countries is falling—

The multiplicity of motivations for aid is neither surprising nor necessarily unfortunate. The use of aid to further other interests increases popular support for aid in donor countries, and may be entirely consistent with making progress in development. For example, the United States provided substantial aid to the Republic of Korea and Taiwan (China) during the 1950s and 1960s, most likely for strategic reasons. But these countries were spectacularly successful in reducing poverty, as well. However, the many motivations that underlie aid allocations may also have some role in impairing aid allocation from the standpoint of poverty reduction. The share of aid going to low-income countries has fallen from 61 percent in the early 1980s to 56 percent in the late 1990s. Considerable aid still goes to countries that have ready access to private capital flows, and countries that graduate from aid recipients to Part II of the DAC list of recipient countries do not always experience a reduction of aid flows (an estimated $9 billion was given to high-income countries or those on the Part II list in 2000). Moreover, aid to low-income countries with good policies equaled only 1.2 percent of their GDP (see table 4.2), slightly below the average for other low-income countries. This ratio has declined sharply since the early 1990s, which reflects the fall in overall aid and rapid economic growth in countries with good policies (as their share of aid has been stable). Thus substantial progress still is required to ensure that aid is directed to countries with good policies.

Table 4.2 Trends in aid allocation
(percent)

Aid allocation	1981–85	1986–90	1991–95	1996–99
Share of aid to low-income countries (percent of total aid)	61.2	62.1	55.1	55.7
Aid to low income with better than average policies (percent of GDP)	1.1	1.8	1.9	1.2

Note: Policy performance is measured by Country Portfolio Performance Review prepared by the World Bank.
Source: World Bank; OECD.

The macroeconomic impact of aid

Strengthening aid effectiveness will require continued progress in allocating aid to countries with good policies. But will increasing aid levels to countries with good policies in itself erode the effectiveness of aid? In the poor countries aid levels are often large enough to have important macroeconomic repercussions. Will the marginal productivity of aid (in terms of raising growth rates) decline as the share of aid in economic activity increases? Is aid likely to increase inflation, lead to excessive exchange rate appreciation, or erode the efficiency of government administration? And if the answer to any of these questions is yes, then should aid be reduced, or could changes in policy increase a country's ability to absorb aid productively? This section concludes that most poor countries with good policies should be able to maintain aid effectiveness while absorbing further increases in aid. There is no rationale for constraining aid to countries with good policies because they receive "too much" aid.

Aid and the sustainability of fiscal policy in the short term

With appropriate economic management, large amounts of aid do not increase inflation. Understanding the potential impact of aid on inflation requires an appreciation of how aid enters the government budget. Aid is received by the government as foreign exchange. The government then, in effect, sells this foreign exchange to its own central bank, which in turn credits the government's account in domestic currency (sometimes referred to as "counterpart funds"). Thus, the central bank now owns the foreign exchange, which it initially holds in its reserves; at the same time, the government now owns the domestic currency, which it initially holds in its account at the central bank.

Aid is not inflationary with policy coordination—

If decisions by the central bank and the government are not coordinated, it is possible for aid to increase inflationary pressures. For example, if the government spends the domestic currency (thus increasing the demand for goods and services in the economy), but the central bank does not spend the foreign exchange, then the domestic price level rises; in other words, nominal expenditures have

risen, but the real resources being purchased have remained unchanged. In this case aid would be entirely inflationary. At the other extreme, the central bank may sell the foreign exchange, but the government does not spend its domestic currency holding. The extra supply of foreign exchange is an infusion of additional real resources to the economy (as purchasers of foreign exchange use it to buy imports); more goods are available, but nominal demand is unchanged. In this scenario the price level will fall—and aid would be deflationary. Finally, if the two decisions are perfectly coordinated (the central bank sells all the foreign exchange, and the government spends all the domestic currency), the net effect is to slightly reduce the price level. This is because the sale of dollars precisely offsets the initial increase in the nominal money supply, so that the nominal money supply is unaltered. Yet real economic activity is now greater and so the demand for real money balances will have risen. This will be satisfied by a decline in the price level. Usually the only circumstance in which aid becomes inflationary is if there is a coordination failure.[9] However, coordination of the two decisions is simple: expenditures of counterpart funds need to be matched with sales of reserves.

—which is facilitated by an appropriate definition of the government deficit

It is important to the credibility of government policy that the definition of the deficit used in discussions of macroeconomic policy reflect the noninflationary impact of aid. Because grants are essentially equivalent to revenue for the purposes of evaluating the inflationary impact of fiscal policy,[10] the appropriate definition for the fiscal deficit consistent with macroeconomic stability is the deficit after accounting for aid flows. In the case of concessional loans, ideally it is the grant component that should be treated as revenue.[11] In countries with large aid inflows, different treatments of aid in the fiscal accounts can have a significant impact on the reported size of the budget deficit. For example, in the late 1990s, Ethiopia had a deficit of 8 percent of GDP—if aid were treated as a financing item. Recalculated to treat grants and the grant component of concessional loans as part of revenue, the deficit was only 0.8 percent of GDP. By contrast, Zimbabwe in the late 1990s received very little aid and had a deficit of 5 percent of GDP. Using the definition of the deficit that treats aid as a financing item would indicate that Ethiopia's fiscal policy was more inflationary than Zimbabwe's, yet clearly the exact opposite was the case. Much of the framework for public discussion of fiscal policy comes from ideas articulated by economists and policymakers in industrial countries, where the problem of interpreting the impact of aid on the fiscal accounts does not arise. Therefore, the definition of the budget deficit used in aid-recipient countries should be such that a level of deficit deemed to be problematic in OECD countries should be similar to that which signals a policy problem in aid-recipient countries. Regional groupings of African countries are indeed starting to adopt their own norms analogous to the EU's stability pact, and it is essential that these norms be based on a definition of a deficit that corresponds to economic rationality and that produces figures that are well understood by the public.

Volatile aid flows need not translate into volatile government resources

Large amounts of aid to the poor countries with good policies are unlikely to increase the volatility of government resources or lead to excessive reliance on aid flows. Lensink and Morrissey (2000) find that instability of aid resources can have a negative effect on growth. Pallage and Robe (1998) find that aid has been more volatile than recipient countries' output, and aid has been pro-cyclical. However, other empirical work indicates that aid does not generally increase the volatility of government resources. Since the alternative to receiving aid is to finance expenditures through taxation, the appropriate benchmark for the volatility of aid is the volatility of revenues. In a sample of 36 African aid recipients, Collier (1999) found that the coefficient of variation on aid was slightly lower than for revenue. Bulir and Hamann (2001), in a global sample of aid recipients, find that aid is more volatile than tax revenues (with both expressed in U.S. dollars), but the difference was not statistically significant.[12] If aid and tax revenue are almost equally volatile (for example, in U.S. dollars) then unless aid and tax are *perfectly* correlated, aid must reduce overall volatility. Collier (1999) found a slight negative correlation between aid flows and revenues. In that case the addition of aid to revenues actually reduces the volatility of overall resources.

Aid may compensate for other sources of volatility. Guillaumont and Chauvet (2001) find that the effectiveness of aid rises as it is provided to countries that are prone to external shocks. There is some evidence that multilateral flows to poor countries help cushion against external shocks by compensating for withdrawals of private flows (see box 4.3). Collier and Dehn (2001) analyze the effect of aid on growth during periods of negative shocks in the context of the aid-growth model developed by Burnside and Dollar (2000). They find that an additional dollar of aid during an extreme negative shock period raises the growth rate by substantially more than in normal periods. By offsetting the initial income loss, the aid avoids the multiplier contraction in output. The magnitude of these multiplier effects suggests that the rate of return on aid during extreme negative shocks is remarkably high. Aid would be used most effectively in compensating for shocks if care is taken to distinguish between temporary shocks (that should be financed) and permanent declines in income (that should be adjusted to).[13] The international community increasingly recognizes the importance of aid in cushioning external shocks. For example, to offset the impact of external shocks expected in the aftermath of September 11, the estimates of low-income countries' possible resource requirements during the 13th Replenishment of the International Development Association (IDA-13) have been revised upward by about $2 billion.

Though aid does not usually increase the volatility of resources, it is possible that heavy reliance on aid could impose adjustment costs if aid were suddenly to decline. There are three circumstances that may cause aid flows to decrease.[14] First, per capita income in a recipient country can rise sufficiently so that the country is no longer eligible for aid. There is no need to be cautious of dependence on aid while the economy is poor, just because one day it will be sufficiently rich that it will no longer need any aid. Moreover, higher income is associated with a greater ability to finance expenditures from taxes; in 1998 current revenue equaled 14 percent of GDP in low-income countries, 19 percent in middle-income countries, and 29 percent in high-income countries. Second, aid may be cut off because economic policy deteriorates substantially; however, this is not a reason for a country with good policies to refuse aid. Finally, donors may

Box 4.3   The relationship between private and multilateral flows in poor countries

Multilateral flows to poor countries appear to have an inverse relationship to private flows. There are various interpretations in the economic literature of this relationship in the context of all developing countries. Dasgupta and Ratha (2000) argue that multilateral lending plays a stabilizing role during periods of credit rationing. Lerrick (1999) sees this relationship as evidence that multilateral flows crowd out private flows. Easterly (1999) and Svensson (2000) argue that multilateral lending programs create incentives for borrowing governments to delay economic reforms, so that private lenders withdraw in reaction to increased multilateral loans.

The inverse relationship between multilateral and private flows, however, need not imply "crowding-out" of private flows to developing countries. Indeed an inverse relationship in the short term may be consistent with a complementary relationship over the long term. With respect to short-term cyclical variables (for example, an increase in GDP growth or an interest rate hike in the industrial countries), private flows tend to behave procyclically (World Bank 2000a) whereas official flows are expected to react

countercyclically. However, in the long term official flows may lead to an improvement in the structural, policy, and institutional environment of a country, which would encourage greater private flows. Several authors have also found empirical support for the catalytic effects of multilateral flows on private flows. Kharas and Shishido (1991) found that during 1974–85, by alleviating credit rationing and improving creditworthiness (by increasing international reserves, for example), official aid was able to generate spillover effects that attracted private flows. (See also Krueger 1998; Summers 1999; and Checki and Stern 2000.)

This relationship is borne out by statistical tests. Panel data analyses for low-income countries (for the period 1970–98) indicate a negative relationship between multilateral and private flows in the same period, but a positive relationship with a six-year lag. By contrast, bilateral flows (including grants) seem to have a significant and positive effect on private flows in the concurrent period, but a negative effect with a lag. This result may reflect the importance of strategic and noneconomic considerations in aid allocation by bilateral donors (Alesina and Dollar 2000).

---

sharply reduce levels of aid for reasons unrelated to the recipients, for example because donors confront widespread fiscal difficulties. Changes in aid flows tend to be implemented slowly, and it is unlikely that any such reduction in aid would present very sharp adjustment costs to individual developing countries. Nevertheless, this concern does underscore the importance of donors providing for stable aid flows over time.

Aid has a positive impact on growth in countries with good policies—

So far we have shown that there is little reason to worry about the adverse impact of aid on the sustainability of economic policies in countries whose economic policies are sound. We now turn to the question of whether increases in aid are likely to continue to have a positive impact on growth. There is growing evidence that aid has a positive impact on growth in countries with good policies. Earlier empirical studies had consistently found a weak relationship between aid and investment and showed little impact of aid on growth (see, for example, Griffin 1971; Snyder 1990; Boone 1994;

and Reichel 1995).[15] However, Burnside and Dollar (2000), Collier and Dollar (2001a), and Durbarry, Gemmell, and Greenaway (1998) show that aid makes an effective contribution to growth in countries with good economic policies.[16] The extent of the impact on growth can be seen by looking at IDA, which is well targeted on low-income countries with reasonable policies. At the margin, an additional billion dollars of IDA funds raises the growth rate sufficiently to lift around 434,000 people out of poverty.[17] Collier and Dollar (2001b) find that in good policy environments aid raises investment by almost double the value of the aid; Collier and Dollar (2001c) also find that in good policy environments a $1 billion injection of aid raises FDI by $600 million.

—although appropriate policies may be necessary to limit "Dutch disease" effects—

The finding that *on average* aid has had a positive impact on growth in good policy environments does not imply that aid levels can rise forever without a resulting adverse effect on growth. Increasing levels of aid may erode growth by causing

"Dutch disease." Since aid is foreign exchange, it only directly augments the supply of those goods that are internationally tradable. It will thus lower their equilibrium price relative to those goods that can only be traded domestically (nontradables). This relative price change induces a resource shift in the economy from tradables to nontradables. Among the tradables are exports, so that aid will tend, all things being equal, to reduce exports. In fact, other things are not equal. The aid may enable governments to lower taxes on exports, which in the poor countries is typically the most heavily taxed sector. Additionally, aid might finance infrastructure expenditures that facilitate exports, such as roads and ports. However, it seems reasonable to expect that in most circumstances aid will indeed reduce exports. Van Wijnbergen (1986) found that increases in aid were associated with an appreciation of the real exchange rate in African countries. Several empirical studies present evidence of the adverse impact of the Dutch disease on exports (see, for example, Laplagne, Treadgold, and Baldry 2001; Soderling 2000; and Sekkat and Varoudakis 2000). Collier and Hoeffler (2000) show that, controlling for the level of economic policy as measured by the World Bank's Country Portfolio Performance Review, a rise in aid is associated with a decline in the share of primary commodity exports in GDP. Since for Africa these exports still make up around 70 percent of all merchandise exports, it is likely that aid in Africa reduces total exports.[18]

The question remains, is a decline in exports caused by aid-induced real exchange rate appreciation undesirable? It should be recognized that the Dutch disease is more of a problem if the aid flow is short-lived, so that adjustment costs are incurred when aid flows in and when it ceases. But aid to the poor countries is rarely a matter of a few years, and thus the value of aid will be greater than any distortionary effects due to real exchange rate appreciation. The reallocation of resources out of tradables could be undesirable if either exports are initially too low because of taxation, or because exports raise growth through learning and competition effects that enhance productivity; Kraay (1999) finds some evidence of this for China, and Bigsten and others (1999) for Africa. However, a more rational response to these problems would be to use aid to reduce taxation or to finance infrastructure facilities that help exporters.

—and access to large nontax resources may erode government accountability

The productivity of aid may decline due to reasons other than the Dutch disease. It may be possible for governments to have more resources than are good for their societies. Access to very large nontax resources can erode the accountability of government. Indeed, the history of accountable governments in the now-developed societies dates from the need for governments to raise tax revenue (see, for example, Hoffman and Norberg 1994). Similarly, Sachs and Warner (2000) establish that governance is worse in countries where the government has access to large rents from natural resources. Consistent with this theory, Knack (2000) finds that aid tends to be associated with increased corruption. On the other hand, Burnside and Dollar (2000) and Dollar and Svensson (2000) found that aid neither improved nor worsened policies. This is disappointing because it implies that aid may not induce reform; on the other hand, it indicates that aid does not appear to cause a generalized deterioration in economic policies.

A more likely reason for diminishing returns to aid is administrative and managerial congestion. If the really scarce resource in the public sector is competent and motivated civil servants, then each additional aid project, in competing for the same limited pool of skills, inflicts negative externalities on other projects. Beyond a point, these congestion effects can fully offset the direct benefits of the project. Similarly, Taslim and Weliwita (2000) argue that both public and private investments in developing countries are limited by the stock of entrepreneurial skills, so that increased aid is reflected in reduced saving.

The marginal productivity of aid depends upon the quality of policies—

Aid is likely to be subject to diminishing returns.[19] The Collier and Dollar (2001a) results indicate, however, that the level of aid where the marginal productivity is zero depends on the quality of policies, and this level is quite high for countries with good policies. Countries with the highest score on the World Bank's Country Portfolio Performance Review (CPPR) continue to enjoy aid's positive impact on growth at levels of aid up to 30 percent of gross domestic product (GDP). Durbarry, Gemmell, and Greenaway (1998) find that aid continues to make a significant contribution to growth up to 40 percent of GDP in countries with a stable macroeconomic policy environment.[20] The median CPPR among poor countries is 3.2, at which level (by the Collier and Dollar estimations) the impact of aid on growth would remain positive up to 19 percent of GDP, while aid averages 8 percent of GDP for poor countries with better than average ratings. By these calculations, 28 out of the 34 poor countries with better than average policies could continue to absorb increasing amounts of aid before the marginal productivity of aid drops to zero.[21]

Recent calculations indicate that a doubling of aid will be necessary to reach the goal of halving the share of the developing-country population that lives on less than $1 a day by 2015 (World Bank 2001b). But improvements in the allocation of aid are also critical to achieving the poverty goal. Collier and Dollar (2001a) develop a model for allocating aid that reflects the view that the impact of aid on poverty depends on the quality of policies.

A doubling of aid that is distributed according to quality of policies and the level of poverty implies significant changes in aid allocation. South Asia would receive an increase in the share of total aid from 11 percent in 1999 to 45 percent.[22] The largely middle-income regions of Europe and Central Asia, Latin America and the Caribbean, and the Middle East and North Africa would together receive only 4 percent of total aid, compared with about a third in 1999. The share of East Asia and Pacific would decline slightly, because the middle-income countries receive much less aid, but aid would expand sharply to Vietnam and the Philippines due to their relative poverty and good policies. Finally, the share of aid going to Sub-Saharan Africa would change very little, because some of the better performers would receive significant increases but other countries with very poor policies would experience an actual decline in aid flows. The increases in aid-to-GDP levels are modest for most countries, and for all of the countries with good policies aid remains well below the level where the marginal productivity of aid falls to zero. In Sub-Saharan Africa, the region with the highest level of aid relative to GDP, the average ratio of aid to GDP would rise only slightly. Finally, the doubling of aid would lift an estimated 15 million people permanently out of poverty each year, for a total decline of 225 million people in

poverty by 2015 (20 percent of the population in poverty in 1999).

These estimates of the impact of aid are conservative. They assume that donors have no impact on the quality of policies or the elasticity of poverty reduction with respect to growth. It may be true that donors have had only a limited impact on policies, and that aid is often fungible (so that the kind of projects financed would not affect the poverty elasticity). However, a recent study of aid and reform in Africa concludes that donors could have a more systematic impact on policy if they increased aid as policies improved (World Bank 2001c), which is the allocation rule used in this simulation. Further, if the improvement in policies is reflected in better provision of public services that benefit the poor, then countries with good policies will have higher elasticities of poverty reduction with respect to growth. Thus the impact on poverty of a doubling of aid, allocated according to policies and the extent of poverty, is likely to be larger than assumed in this simulation.

—so aid efficiency can be improved

Thus recent econometric evidence indeed suggests that countries can receive too much aid. The most likely explanation for this is neither the Dutch disease, nor the deterioration of governance, but the high congestion costs incurred by attempting to implement many aid projects through a bureaucracy with limited capacity. If this analysis is correct, it has five important implications: First, in countries with good policies, actual aid inflows are unlikely to be near the point where the marginal productivity of aid is zero (the saturation point). Second, in those poor countries that currently are close to or beyond their saturation points, the key task is to raise the saturation point by improving policy. Third, aid programs should aim to reduce congestion costs. Switching more aid from projects to programs would almost certainly raise absorptive capacity. Fourth, to the extent that the capacity constraint is due to a lack of competent and motivated civil servants, incentive systems in the public sector may need revision. Fifth, if the public sector faces real constraints upon its capacity to spend marginal resources effectively, it should reduce tax receipts relative to aid. While aid augments the resources available to the economy, taxation reduces them by introducing distortions (for example, increased income taxes may reduce the incentive to work). A sensible growth strategy for a very low-income economy with a dysfunctional civil service would be for rising aid inflows to be used partly for reducing the share of tax revenue in GDP.

Conditionality and adjustment lending

Strengthening the use of policy conditionality in adjustment lending is an important element in efforts to improve the effectiveness of aid (see World Bank 2001d). Policy conditionality refers to the practice of basing the disbursement of donor funds on the implementation of specific policies. Policy conditionality can support the effectiveness of adjustment assistance by helping to avoid disbursements to governments with inappropriate policies. For recipients, agreement on specific conditions for disbursement (as opposed to basing disbursement on a general evaluation of the government's program) can improve the transparency of donor decisions and the reliability of aid disbursements (Mosley 1999). By increasing the cost of backtracking on policies (in terms of worsening relations with donors or losing disbursements), commitments to donors can enhance the government's credibility in sticking to policies that face opposition from special interests or that have short-term costs but long-term benefits. Case studies of the strong reform programs in Ghana and Uganda suggest that conditionality was successful at facilitating clear decisions from political leadership and publicly signaling the government's commitment (World Bank 2001c). In turn, enhancing credibility can encourage more rapid adjustments to new policies by the private sector and hence reduce the short-term employment and output costs of adjustment. Greater compliance with conditionality under World Bank loans was significantly related to improved economic performance (figure 4.2).[23]

Country ownership is key to success—

A country's commitment and capacity to implement the reforms supported by adjustment lending are key to effective adjustment and sustained development. Research on aid effectiveness indicates that when a country's commitment or implementation capacity is weak, conditionality is unlikely to be effective. In other words, conditionality by itself cannot lead to the adoption of better policies when

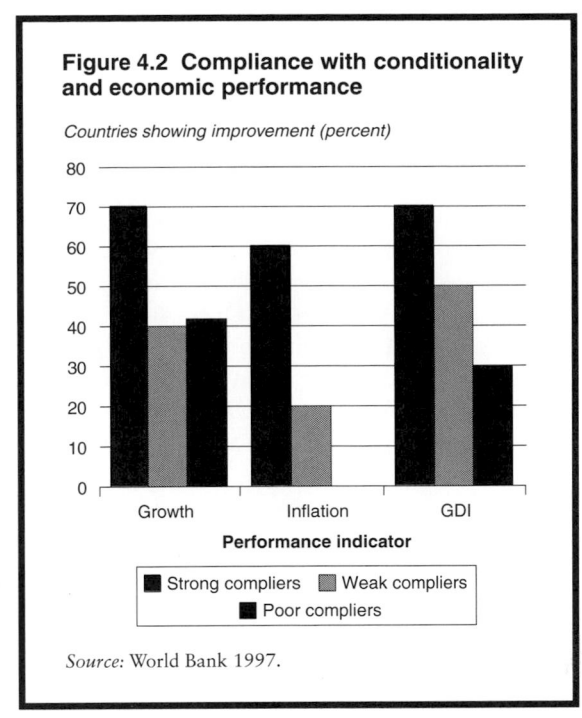

Figure 4.2 Compliance with conditionality and economic performance

Countries showing improvement (percent)

Source: World Bank 1997.

there is no consensus for reform.[24] Conditions attached to adjustment lending may not contribute to successful outcomes in cases where donors lack adequate information (on local conditions, government capacity, and the extent of government commitment) or the interests of donors and recipients diverge. Conditionality is the outcome of a bargaining process that can be subject to failures of coordination and unintended outcomes.[25] To the extent that this process leads to a reform program that is not fully owned by the government, the success of the program can be severely undermined. Domestic political support is critical for the adjustment program (Rodrik 1996; World Bank 1998; Dollar and Easterly 1998; Dollar and Svensson 2000). Both cross-country reviews and individual case studies have confirmed the critical importance of strong country ownership of the adjustment program to the successful use of conditionality in adjustment lending (McClearly 1991; Berg 1991). Johnson and Wasty (1993) find that strong ownership was a major reason for success in 75 percent of adjustment programs with good results. The International Monetary Fund (IMF 1998) attributed poor implementation of IMF programs in Zambia (1978–91) and Uganda (late 1980s) to lack of ownership; these are in contrast to successes in Bolivia,

Uganda in the 1990s, and Côte d'Ivoire, where ownership was strong.

Conditionality and World Bank adjustment lending have evolved—

Conditionality was originally directed largely at achieving macroeconomic stability and reducing market distortions, and adjustment assistance was conceived as a financing vehicle for short-term balance of payments support. Over the years, the policies covered by conditionality and the goals of adjustment lending have evolved in tandem with countries' broader reform agendas, and have become increasingly focused on long-run, structural, social, and institutional issues. The 1980s' narrow focus on short-term stabilization and addressing distortions gave way in the 1990s to greater attention to poverty reduction, institutions, and complex social and structural reforms. This shift included an explicit focus on good governance, with strong support for public sector management reforms.

Reflecting in part the growing long-run structural and institutional focus of countries' reform agendas, Bank-supported adjustment programs have grown more complex, even while the average number of conditions in adjustment loans has fallen significantly, from 61 conditions in the late 1980s to 33 conditions in fiscal 2000. The number of conditions tends to be higher and complexity tends to be a greater challenge in countries with weak performance and capacity, where adjustment lending is less successful (World Bank 2001d). This highlights the ineffectiveness of attempts to address performance deficiencies and capacity limitations through a larger number of more complex and detailed conditions, and confirms the importance of continuing to focus adjustment support in countries with good policy and institutional environments.

—and the quality of Bank adjustment lending has improved

The record of policy conditionality in promoting the objectives of adjustment programs, as reflected in the degree of compliance with agreed-on conditions, has improved in recent years. The problems affecting conditionality in the 1980s have been well documented.[26] Some of these problems may have persisted into the early 1990s. Killick, Gunatilaka, and Marr (1998) find that only 25 percent of World Bank adjustment operations from 1989–90 to 1993–94 were completed on sched-

ule.[27] World Bank (1997) found that out of 35 adjustment operations in Sub-Saharan Africa, compliance was rated as strong in 10 countries, and as weak or poor in 25 countries. Indeed, the performance of World Bank adjustment lending improved sharply throughout the 1990s. Operations Evaluation Department outcome scores increased from 60 percent satisfactory in the 1980s to 68 percent satisfactory in fiscal 1990–94, and to 86 percent satisfactory in fiscal 1999–2000.[28] The World Bank's Quality Assurance Group found that the great majority of a sample of adjustment loans in 1999 were satisfactory or better regarding various dimensions of program design (World Bank 2000b). Bilateral aid evaluations also typically find satisfactory outcomes for a high proportion of adjustment programs (see, for example, USAID 2001; SIDA 1999).

It is of course difficult to attribute improved compliance wholly to improvements in the design of conditionality. There are several reasons why adjustment programs were more successful during the 1990s, including a more favorable international economic environment (at least in some years), greater selectivity on the part of the donors, and greater recognition of the importance of government ownership in crafting an effective adjustment program. It is likely that changes in the process of adjustment lending, including greater selectivity and encouraging ownership through a less intrusive approach to the design of reform programs, was at least as important as the change in the focus of conditionality to address underlying structural, social, and institutional issues. What is clear is that changes in the overall approach to adjustment assistance have contributed to more successful reform programs.

Aid coordination and the administrative burden of aid

The idea that donors could increase the effectiveness of aid by improving the coordination of their activities is not new (Pearson 1969). Donors have made extensive efforts to consult on their aid operations and thus avoid the imposition of conflicting or duplicative administrative requirements, and they have improved the quality and consistency of policy advice, most notably through consultative group meetings, round tables sponsored by the United Nations Development Programme, aid meetings under the auspices of the OECD DAC, the U.N.'s Development Assistance Framework (which harmonizes U.N. agencies' activities) and the Strategic Partnership for Africa. Successive IDA replenishment reports during the 1990s urged greater efforts at coordination. Considerable work remains to strengthen aid coordination, which is particularly important in the poorest aid recipients that receive very significant levels of aid relative to domestic resources.

Reducing administrative burdens—

Aid often imposes a substantial administrative burden on recipient governments (Van Arkadie 1986; Lister and Stevens 1992). Van de Walle and Johnston (1996) report that Kenya had 600 projects from 60 different donors during the mid-1980s, while Zambia had 614 projects from 69 donors. In Tanzania there were even more—over 2,000 projects from 40 donors. Administratively, 600 projects could translate over the course of a year into as many as 2,400 quarterly reports for various oversight agencies and perhaps 1,000 missions requesting meetings with key officials and comments on their reports. Disch (2000, p. 39) describes the multiplicity of import support programs in Mozambique in the late 1980s, each with different procedures and time delays that typically took six to nine months for importers to navigate. The result: skyrocketing import costs. Donors have competed with each other and with the government to recruit scarce local experts for projects, thus undermining the government's capacity (Eisenblatter 1999). Lancaster (1999, p. 501) notes the implications for budget management of uncoordinated donor projects negotiated with individual ministries, each demanding counterpart funding for recurrent costs. In addition to administrative burdens, failures in aid coordination can result in donors pressing inconsistent policy advice on governments. For example, in the mid-1980s the World Bank and the United States Agency for International Development urged the Kenyan government to reduce the role of the National Cereals and Produce Board at the same time as another donor was financing a major expansion of its facilities (Mosley 1986).

—and shifting away from tied aid—

One of the better-known impediments to aid effectiveness is tied aid, which often reflects donors' commercial interests rather than recipients' development needs. Various studies have found that tying requirements limit competition, increase administrative burdens, and lead to countries purchasing goods with an inappropriate technology with greater than desired capital intensity. The additional cost imposed by tying aid has been estimated in the range of 10–30 percent (OECD 2001; Morrissey and White 1994; and Jepma 1991). There are also significant indirect costs, including suspension of standard procurement procedures and higher cost maintenance due to dependence on imported parts that may not be readily available.

Considerable progress has been made to reduce tied aid requirements, and the share of bilateral aid that is tied has dropped from 65 percent in 1990 to 38 percent in 2000, though there is considerable variation across donors. The share of tied aid to the least developed countries is about 50 percent, higher than the average for all developing countries primarily because these countries receive more of the type of aid that is still subject to tying (for example, food aid and technical assistance). The DAC High Level meeting in May 2001 agreed on a recommendation to untie ODA to the least developed countries to the extent that is possible. By January 2002 many important components of ODA to the least developed countries will be untied, including balance of payments support and debt forgiveness. The OECD estimates that this will raise the level of untied aid to the least developed countries to 70 percent.

Changes in process can strengthen aid coordination and reduce administrative burdens

Procedurally, a number of different strategies for improving coordination have been advanced, including sectorwide approaches, greater donor specialization, more support for capacity building, and greater flexibility in some donor requirements. *Sectorwide approaches* can facilitate country ownership by reducing micromanagement by donors and by eliciting longer-term commitments from both sides to help build genuine partnerships. For donors, sectorwide approaches offer a realistic compromise between detailed micromanagement and provision of general budget support, since responsible ministries may be held accountable for results. Sectorwide approaches are most appropriate when both macro and sector reform processes are in place and when governments have a clear vision and ownership of objectives. In Uganda, for example, strong government motivation, active participation by civil society in program monitoring, and a credible medium-term budget process made the Universal Primary Education project a success (Brown and others 2001). However, sector finance is likely to be ineffective if either sector policies or macroeconomic and budget management are weak. In addition, *sectorwide* approaches may limit government's ability to reallocate funds across sectors, compared with disbursing aid through budget support programs.

Greater *donor specialization* is needed. The difficulties of aid coordination increase sharply as more donors become involved in any one area, so specialization along geographic or functional lines according to comparative advantage is desirable. Yet the trend has been toward increasing diffusion of donor activities, and World Bank (1999) found few examples of aid coordination efforts that led to greater specialization (see also World Bank 2001e). Reviewing aid to Ghana in the first half of the 1990s, Eriksson (2001) found a steady increase in the number of sectors for each bilateral donor and a decline in bilateral commitments per sector.

Capacity building is one key to progress. Limited capacity and institutional weakness impede the formulation of country-owned strategies, and undermine the trust donors need to allow countries to take responsibility for detailed financial and project management. Yet capacity building has been one of the least effective areas of donor activity, and in many of the world's poorest countries the quality of public administration has systematically deteriorated (Lancaster 1999). Some donor practices may have even contributed to the problem through insistence on special project management units that draw government officials from their regular duties, and recruitment of expatriate technical assistance personnel whose terms of reference are to substitute for local capacity rather than to build it. Regular civil service staff assigned to projects may be expected to give priority to project work even if there is a conflict with their normal responsibilities (Lancaster 1999; van de Walle and Johnston 1996).

More *flexibility* by some donor agencies is needed to transfer responsibility and accountability to recipients. Incompatible procedures for reporting, accounting for disbursements, and procurement raise transaction costs and inhibit closer coordination among donors, while severely bur-

dening recipient governments. Greater delegation of decisionmaking authority to the field would also facilitate better coordination (World Bank 2001f).

Above all, government leadership is the key

Strong leadership from the recipient government is essential for successful aid coordination (Eisenblatter 1999). For example, Botswana, the fastest-growing country in Africa for some time (and in many years the fastest-growing country in the world) has had the vision and capacity to manage the aid process (Brautigam and Botchwey 1995). In Botswana the government maintains effective control of aid with strong institutions backing up a coherent vision. Donors are encouraged to specialize in specific sectors to build up their expertise and minimize administrative burdens (van de Walle and Johnston 1996). Likewise, the governments of Ghana and Uganda, two of the more successful reformers in Africa, have played an active role in coordinating donor activities.

Aid and debt relief

Strengthening the effectiveness of aid through debt relief—

The increase in concessional debt relief, and efforts to tie debt relief to effective reform programs, have been important components of efforts to strengthen the effectiveness of aid. Debt reduction in the form of concessional rescheduling of guaranteed commercial claims began in 1988 with the introduction of Toronto terms by the Paris Club, which allowed for a reduction of one-third for eligible claims. The level of debt forgiveness has subsequently been raised progressively, to 50 percent reduction (in net present value [NPV] terms) in 1991 (London or enhanced Toronto terms), and 67 percent NPV reduction in 1994 (Naples terms).[29] Donors forgave bilateral ODA claims, financed debt swaps, contributed to the buyback of commercial debt through the IDA debt reduction facility program, and supported programs to help debtor countries meet multilateral debt service obligations. Efforts to deepen debt relief for poor countries suffering from unsustainable debt burdens culminated in the HIPC Initiative. All in all, DAC donors have forgiven about $29 billion in debt over the past 30 years. Of this total, forgive-

Table 4.3   Forgiveness of ODA claims, 1970–2000

(millions of dollars)

	1970–89	1990–95	1996	1997	1998	1999	2000	1970–2000
Total	5,075	11,183	1,026	488	660	600	750	19,783
HIPCs	2,236	6,495	722	260	400	450	480	11,043
Other developing countries	2,840	4,689	304	228	259	150	270	8,740

Source: OECD DAC, national aid agencies, and staff estimates.

ness of ODA loans by DAC donors has amounted to almost $20 billion (see table 4.3), and donors have claimed credit in their aid budgets for the forgiveness of $8.5 billion in non-ODA claims, and have provided almost $400 million in grants in support of the IDA debt reduction facility. However, the figures recorded by the DAC probably underestimate the full extent of the debt relief, because they do not include irrevocable commitments to forgive future ODA claims, while for non-ODA claims the reporting norms are complex and have taken time to be fully integrated into the statistical systems of the export credit agencies.

—as 24 countries have reached the decision point under the HIPC Initiative—

The HIPC Initiative, launched in 1996, aims to increase the effectiveness of aid by helping poor countries achieve sustainable levels of debt while strengthening the link between debt relief and strong policy performance. Forty-two countries, primarily from the Sub-Saharan Africa region, are identified as eligible to receive debt relief under this initiative. In 1999 the scope of the initiative was widened to accelerate and deepen the provision of debt relief. As of December 2001, 24 countries have reached the decision point[30] (the point where debt relief is approved by the Executive Boards of the IMF and the World Bank, and interim relief begins). These countries are now receiving debt service relief which will amount to about $36 billion over time, a $21 billion reduction in the NPV of their outstanding debt stock (see figure 4.3).

—resulting in a halving of the NPV of their external debt—

The 24 countries that have reached their decision points have experienced a halving of their external stock of debt in NPV terms. When combined with other debt reduction mechanisms, this implies a two-thirds reduction in their external indebted-

ness. The pace of delivery of debt relief increased in 2001. All countries that reached their decision points by the end of 2000 are now receiving interim relief, and their aggregate level of debt is forecast to fall from 60 percent of GDP in 1999 to 28 percent after debt relief. Current plans call for a reduction in debt service obligations by one-third ($1.1 billion) during 2001–03,[31] for an average savings of close to $50 million per country per year. Debt service as a percentage of exports for the 24 countries is expected to decrease from 16.8 percent in 1998–99 to 8.2 percent in 2001–03.

—while 4 of these countries have reached the completion point

As of December 2001 four countries (Bolivia, Mozambique, Tanzania, and Uganda) had reached the completion point, where the remainder of the committed debt relief is delivered. For example, Mozambique reached its completion point in Sep-

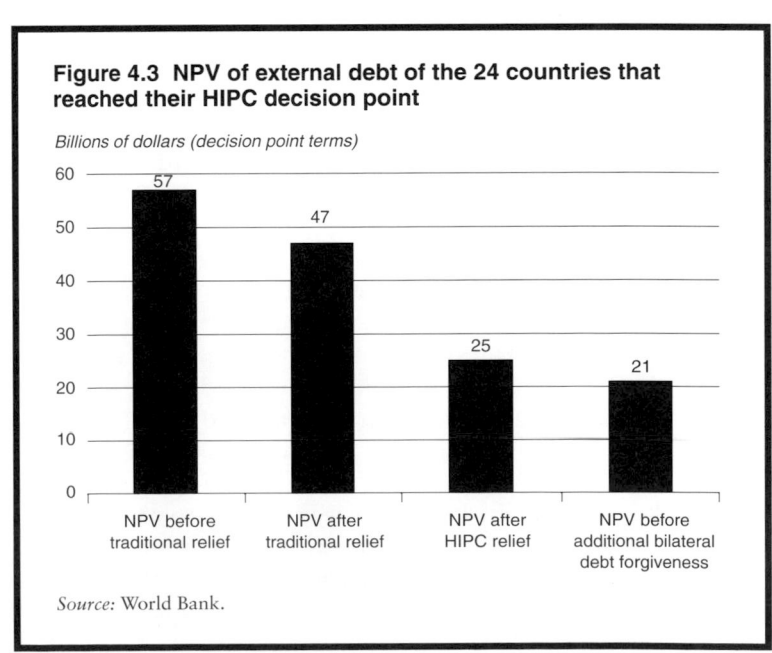

Figure 4.3 NPV of external debt of the 24 countries that reached their HIPC decision point

Billions of dollars (decision point terms)

- NPV before traditional relief: 57
- NPV after traditional relief: 47
- NPV after HIPC relief: 25
- NPV before additional bilateral debt forgiveness: 21

Source: World Bank.

Table 4.4   Impact of HIPC Initiative in 24 decision-point cases

	Before HIPC debt relief (1998–99)	After HIPC debt relief (2001–03)
NPV of total external debt	$57 billion	$25 billion
Debt as a percent of GDP	60%	28
Average debt service as a percent of exports	16.8	8.2
Average debt service as percent of GDP	3.7	2.1
Average debt service as a percent of revenue	27.4	11.9
Average social spending as percent of GDP	5.8	6.9
Average social spending as percent of revenue	35.5	39.9

Source: World Bank.

tember 2001, and will receive debt relief amounting to $4.3 billion, which will cut its debt by 72 percent (in NPV terms). As a result, Mozambique's annual debt service payments will be reduced to an average of 6 percent of export earnings and 10 percent of government revenue over 2000–10, as compared with 20 and 23 percent, respectively, in 1998. Another dozen countries could reach their completion point in 2002.

HIPC has helped provide a more effective environment for aid—

The HIPC Initiative, in addition to increasing resources for debt relief, has helped to support policy improvements and thereby contributed to aid effectiveness. Debt relief under the HIPC Initiative is intended for countries that are pursuing effective poverty reduction strategies, and increased social expenditures is a critical element. For the countries that have reached decision points under the HIPC Initiative, social expenditures are projected to increase about 1.1 percent of GDP compared with 1998–99 (table 4.4).

—which is reflected in ODA flows

There is some evidence that ODA flows to the HIPCs are being allocated to the better performers, a prerequisite for aid effectiveness. Countries that have either reached a decision point (indicating general agreement with donors on the economic program) or have sustainable levels of debt (indicating that their policies were adequate to achieve sustainable debt levels with traditional debt relief mechanisms) observed an increase of 3 percent in gross ODA flows since the initiation of the program in 1996. This is in marked contrast to ODA flows to countries with unsustainable debt levels that have not yet reached a decision point; in those countries, gross ODA has fallen by more than half

since 1996. It should be noted, however, that ODA to the better performers excluding debt relief has declined by 2 percent since 1996. The HIPC Initiative has been essential to place beneficiary countries on a path to long-term debt sustainability[32] and has resulted in increased resources, as shown by the decline in actual debt service payments relative to earlier years. Even countries with significant payments arrears received an important, if more modest, increase in new financial resources, while the HIPC Initiative also will help normalize their relations with creditors. Nevertheless, it is of critical importance that donors maintain their ODA effort in the form of new money as well as debt relief, particularly as the expected supply response to lowering debt levels may take some time to occur.

However, creditors need to continue to deliver on HIPC

Full participation by all creditors is essential to ensure that the 24 countries already at decision points reach sustainable external debt levels and, more broadly, to ensure that the HIPC Initiative achieves its objectives in full. While most bilateral creditors—including all Paris Club creditors—and the majority of multilateral and commercial creditors have already been delivering on their commitments to provide relief to HIPCs, a number of creditors have not. In particular, some of the non–Paris Club official bilateral and commercial creditors (representing about 10 percent of the debt relief to be delivered) along with a few multilateral creditors have not yet agreed to provide relief to the countries that have reached their decision points under the Initiative. Indeed, a small number of creditors have resorted to litigation as a means of recovering assets; of those, there are a few cases where claims of official bilateral or commercial creditors have been bought on the secondary market at a discount in order to maximize recovery through litigation.[33] Given the relatively small number of creditors involved, these problems will not likely undo the achievements of the HIPC Initiative. However, the litigation alone could prove to be very costly for individual HIPCs in terms of legal representation and the implications of adverse judgments.

Postconflict countries present a special challenge

The most important challenge for the HIPC Initiative in the year ahead is to bring the remaining eligible countries to their decision points as quickly as possible, so that these countries can begin to receive debt relief. This challenge presents special difficulties since most of these countries have recently emerged from, or are still engaged in, armed conflict, and many of them are struggling with governance issues. At the same time, these countries have a particularly acute need for debt relief because of their major reconstruction requirements and the urgent need for speedy and effective action to help break the cycle of violence, low growth, and severe poverty.

The framework of the HIPC Initiative has the flexibility to front-load assistance to countries affected by conflict, and a relatively large share of debt relief can be made available at an early stage, taking into account the profile of debt service payments due and the absorptive capacity of the country. To ensure progress toward sustainable growth, the structural and social triggers for the completion point will be customized to reflect the particular set of priorities and needs of the postconflict countries. For example, improvement in fiscal management and demobilization of excombatants were part of the completion point conditions for Guinea-Bissau.

Strengthening the effectiveness of official guarantees

In addition to aid flows, official agencies channel resources to developing countries through guarantees of private sector loans and investments. Export credit agencies' total exposure to developing countries reached an estimated $500 billion at the end of 2000—one-quarter of developing countries' total long-term external debt. Export credit agencies' new commitments to developing countries rose to an average $75 billion a year in the first half of the 1990s (mirroring the steep rise in private flows), and then declined in the wake of the Asian crisis.[34] Nevertheless, new commitments remained at $50 billion in 2000, or 40 percent of all commitments from private creditors, excluding bonds.

Export credit agencies have become increasingly more involved in investment insurance.[35] The Berne Union member agencies extended $13 billion of insurance against FDI projects in developing countries in 2000 (five times more than in 1990), and the total investment under cover by member agencies (the outstanding exposure or stock) rose to $58 billion at end-2000, compared with $9 billion in 1990. This strong growth in investment insurance mirrors the surge in direct investment flows (investment insurance by Berne Union members has covered on average around 12 percent of the FDI flows to developing countries) and has been important in privatization and private sector involvement in the provision of infrastructure services.

Multilateral institutions are expanding their guarantee activities

Multilateral institutions also expanded their guarantee activities during the 1990s. The guarantee programs of the World Bank Group, which are intended to serve as a catalyst for private sector activities in developing countries, supported $18 billion in flows in the second half of the 1990s, double the level of guarantees extended in the period 1990–95. Moreover, the financing leveraged by these guarantees is substantial: International Bank for Reconstruction and Development partial credit and partial risk guarantees of $2 billion helped galvanize almost $20 billion in total project costs. In poor counties, partial risk guarantees from IDA help insure private lenders against country risks that are beyond the control of investors. To date, three countries—Bangladesh, Côte d'Ivoire, and Uganda—have benefited from an IDA partial risk guarantee for a power project. The three guarantees total $206 million, and the aggregate project costs are $1 billion. The Multilateral Investment Guarantee Agency (MIGA) is in the forefront of efforts to facilitate investment in poor countries and to ensure that projects have a significant developmental impact. Since 1988, MIGA has issued 550 guarantees for projects in 79 developing countries. Total coverage issued exceeds $9 billion, bringing the estimated amount of foreign direct investment facilitated since inception to more than $42 billion. Poor countries accounted for over 20 percent of MIGA's gross portfolio on June 20, 2001, spread across 26 countries. The regional development banks, including the Inter-American Development Bank, the Asian Development Bank, the European Bank for Reconstruction and Development, and some of the smaller regional banks, have also developed wide-ranging guarantee programs.

Poor countries rely on guarantees for large external financial commitments—

Official guarantees have supported a limited volume of finance to the poor countries, compared with other developing countries. The export credit agencies' total exposure to the poor countries equals $40 billion at end-2000, or only 8 percent of the agencies' total exposure to developing countries. Most poor countries are not able to support large inflows of guaranteed finance, which is typically provided at nonconcessional terms. Nevertheless, export credit agencies are important for the poor countries: the agencies account for some 16 percent of the poor countries' long-term debt.[36] New commitments to the poor countries from export credit agencies were $2.4 billion in 2000, or 80 percent of gross capital market financing from private sources. Officially supported export credits can provide financing that would not otherwise be available from private sources, or that would be available only at prohibitive terms. In poor countries, official guarantees are nearly always required to access external finance for large projects; every major bank commitment over $20 million over the past five years has had some official guarantee. Official investment insurance also has helped facilitate investment flows to more than one-third of the poor countries, and it provided for about 30 percent of all FDI in poor countries.

Guarantee arrangements have played a particularly important role in facilitating greater private sector participation in infrastructure and in mining projects that require large investors (see box 4.4 on the Mozambique Mozal project). Access to officially supported export credits also may help build a reputation that facilitates access to nonguaranteed finance in the future. For example, in China two-thirds of all private source finance was guaranteed by export credit agencies in 1990, while today only 25 percent is guaranteed. Similar trends are evident for Latin American borrowers such as Chile and Brazil, and for Malaysia and Thailand prior to the 1997 crisis.[37]

—but these facilities have also increased poor countries' debt

While export credit agencies have made an important contribution to boosting the real resources available to poor countries, access to guaranteed finance also has contributed to unsustainable debt burdens. During the past decade, the HIPC countries have received almost $20 billion in loan commitments guaranteed by export credit agencies, and export credit commitments to HIPCs averaged $1.8 billion per year from 1990–96, when the HIPC Initiative began. Since then, steps have been taken to ensure that the debt reduction under the HIPC Initiative is associated with efforts to avoid incurring additional debt on nonconcessional terms. The HIPC Initiative framework provides that new external finance for these countries should be predominantly in the form of grants or loans on highly concessional terms. The injunction on nonconcessional borrowing was reinforced by the communiqué of the Development Committee in April 1999 and more recently by U.S. legislation that governs U.S. contributions to the HIPC Trust Fund.[38] The IMF also agrees with HIPC governments regarding limits on nonconcessional borrowing within the context of the Fund's concessional facility. These limits are established on a case-by-case basis, after an evaluation of the impact of new borrowing on the sustainability of the debt burden.

Some HIPCs are reducing their reliance on guaranteed loans

HIPCs that have reached a decision point, and hence have a policy framework in place that is agreed-on with the international community, have seen a reduction in export credit commitments from $0.9 billion per year in 1990–96 to $0.5 billion from 1997–2000. Moreover, in these countries very little by way of new export credits are going to public sector borrowers, with the bulk of the finance absorbed by the private sector. Countries within the HIPC group that have continued to attract significant export credit financing include those with sustainable debt burdens and important oil producers (for example Angola) or off-

Box 4.4 Official guarantees and the Mozal project

Official guarantees have helped attract external finance for the Mozal aluminum smelter, the single largest private sector investment ever undertaken in Mozambique and one of the largest projects to be developed on a limited recourse basis in Sub-Saharan Africa. The first phase of the project ($2.3 billion for the aluminum smelter) is already completed, and the second phase, which will double capacity, is under construction. Partially as a result of Mozal's success, private sector projects worth another $6.5 billion are in the pipeline.[39] Forty percent of the financing requirements were met by equity provided by the sponsors, the Billiton Group,[40] Mitsubishi Corporation of Japan, the Industrial Development Corporation of South Africa, and by the government of Mozambique. Loan financing was met by officially supported export credits, and loans and guarantees from the European Investment Bank and the International Finance Corporation (IFC) and several development finance agencies, including ones from Germany, South Africa, and France. The perceived political and commercial risks involved in the project were high, and the participation of IFC and official guarantors were an essential catalyst to draw in funding from private creditors.

The success of securing financing was largely due to a well-structured project with leading international sponsors, supported by Mozambique's impressive reform program and rapid recovery from the war. The country's proximity to South Africa and the return to operation of the Cahora Bassa hydroelectric power dam have also enabled Mozambique to become one of the few HIPC countries to have attracted substantial private sector investment from external sources. In addition, the project has been supported by a package of incentives, including exemptions from taxes on imported materials, corporate profits, and the income of foreign workers; allowance of repatriation of all dividends; and a first call on earnings for debt service payments. Such incentives are available to all exporting industries in Mozambique. The cost of energy was an important factor, and favorable rates were negotiated with the South African power utility. The government will receive 1 percent of the gross income from sales.

The Mozal plant, which is already in production, will double the country's total exports and add an estimated 7 percent to GDP, although the contribution to employment is limited (the project added 5,000 temporary workers during the construction phase but only 800 full-time, permanent jobs). As other planned projects develop exports should rise, by nearly 30 percent of GDP in 2010, although this will be partially offset by higher imports of raw materials, debt service on loans, and remittance of profits and wages of foreign workers. The net impact on the balance of payments in 2010 is estimated at less than 3 percent of GDP. Other benefits include infrastructure development, industrialization, and the promotion of regional integration.

These benefits must be balanced against the risk from the project's contribution to higher private sector debt. Borrowing by the private sector has already risen from an average of $36 million between 1990–98 to $340 million in 1999–2000, and it is expected to average well over $400 million over the next four to five years. Private sector debt service is projected to rise to 20 percent of exports over the next five years, assuming all the proposed projects are realized. While the projects promise to generate sufficient returns to cover debt service payments, the expected jump in the private sector's debt and debt service point to the need for vigilant monitoring by the authorities.

shore marine financing centers (Liberia) that can pledge assets as collateral.

Rethinking the costs and benefits of guarantees—

Export credit agencies are also taking steps to ensure that the activities they support (including guarantees and insurance) produce real economic and social benefits that are worth the buildup of debt. Several export credit agencies employ processes that screen projects for their effectiveness and are looking beyond standard issues such as environment and gender screening to include debt sustainability and development impact. In the United Kingdom, for example, the Export Credit Guarantee Department, in collaboration with the Department for International Development, has instituted a productive expenditure screening process that applies to all IDA-only countries. Public sector projects in poor countries are reviewed to ensure that the project supports the borrowing country's public expenditure priorities. For private sector projects the emphasis is on meeting environmental and social standards and examining the risks of the debt being assumed by the public sector or compromising the borrowing country's overall debt management strategy. Export credit agencies are also taking steps to implement common anticorruption measures, to re-

Table 4.5   Export credit commitments to HIPCs, 1990–2000
(annual averages in billions of dollars)

	1990–96	1997–2000
HIPCs at decision point	0.9	0.6
HIPCs with sustainable debt	0.4	0.6
Others	0.5	0.6
Total	1.8	1.7

Source: OECD.

voke insurance cover if corrupt practices are identified, and to blacklist corrupt companies.

—and limiting tied aid

Export credit agencies also are making progress to reduce the practice of attaching tied aid to export credit programs. In the past, export credit agencies have combined their own financing with official aid to create financing packages referred to as "mixed credits" or "parallel financing," where at least some part of the package is tied to the procurement of goods and services from specific countries. The practice of tied aid can impair the effectiveness of donor support for developing countries by increasing project costs, making procurement procedures more complex, and skewing decisions on technology and capital intensity. Under the terms of the OECD Arrangement on Guidelines for Officially Supported Export Credits, projects that are deemed to be financially viable with commercial loans will not receive any tied aid.

Annex 4.1

Aid definition and measurement

Defining aid. The international forum for defining aid is the OECD DAC.[41] There are two categories of aid provided by DAC donors: ODA and official aid (OA). The DAC list of aid recipients is divided into Part I and Part II recipients. Only countries on Part I receive ODA; those on Part II (which includes several countries in Eastern and Central Europe, and Israel) receive OA. Only ODA may be counted by DAC countries as part of their "aid effort."

ODA and OA are defined the same way: both consist of loans or grants to developing countries and territories by donor governments and their agencies that are developmental in intent and designed to promote economic welfare. ODA and OA loans are provided on concessional financial terms, with at least a 25 percent grant element (calculated as the NPV of the future payment stream discounted at 10 percent).

Measuring aid. Aid flows to developing countries can be measured in two ways: when *aid performance by DAC donors* is measured, ODA includes bilateral disbursements of concessional financing to developing countries plus the provision by bilateral donors of concessional financing to multilateral institutions (for example, IDA). When *resource receipts* by developing countries are measured, ODA (and, where relevant, OA) include disbursements of concessional financing from bilateral agencies and multilateral sources. The two measures will not be the same because the concessional funding received from donor sources by multilateral institutions does not match those institutions' disbursements to developing countries in any given year.

Aid and debt forgiveness. The directives for reporting aid statistics are agreed-on within the OECD DAC, and these include specific guidelines on the measurement of debt forgiveness. The impact on aid volumes varies depending on whether the claim being forgiven is an official development loan that was originally disbursed from the aid budget or a commercial loan extended or guaranteed by an official export credit agency. The forgiveness of an ODA loan does not give rise to any new net disbursement of aid. Statistically the benefit is reflected in the fact that because the cancelled or "forgiven" repayments will not take place, net ODA disbursements will not be reduced. The forgiveness of a non-ODA claim has an impact on net ODA. Such forgiveness can be counted by donors as part of their overall aid effort at the time the claim is forgiven. Statistically forgiveness of a non-ODA claim does give rise to a new disbursement of aid and net ODA disbursements will increase.

Official development finance. The concept of official development finance is broader than that of aid. It measures all receipts from official creditors. It includes (a) ODA and OA from bilateral sources, (b) grants and concessional and nonconcessional development lending by multilateral agencies, and (c) other official bilateral flows that are considered to be developmental in intent but for which the grant element is too low to qualify as ODA or OA.

Export credits: data sources and coverage

Data on export credits need to be interpreted with care. Export credit agencies typically provide insurance cover for repayment of both principal and interest; data provided to the Berne Union and to the OECD are based on agencies' exposure, including future interest payments. Also, agencies typically report the full value of contracts, including undisbursed amounts. It is therefore difficult to relate commitment data to actual disbursements. Specific complications arise when nonpayment by the debtor gives rise to arrears and rescheduling. Most agencies include arrears and rescheduled claims, including capitalized interest, in their reports to the Berne Union and the OECD, but interest accrued on arrears is not recorded as an increase in claims by the export credit agency. Similarly when unrecovered claims are regularized through a Paris Club rescheduling agreement, agencies do not record an increase in exposure in their reports to the Berne Union or the OECD despite the fact that the longer repayment periods on rescheduled claims increases the future interest at risk. The recording of rescheduling arrangements on concessional terms (that is with an element of debt reduction) also varies across agencies making the data for debtor countries experiencing debt servicing problems particularly hard to interpret.

The data provided by the export credit agencies are collected by both the Berne Union and the OECD. The Berne Union quarterly survey of member agencies includes data for about 60 developing countries and economies in transition on outstanding commitments, unrecovered claims, outstanding offers, and new commitments. The most attractive element of the Berne Union survey is that data are collected in the way most agencies actually keep their books; the concept commitment encompasses insured principal and, in most cases, interest on undisbursed as well as disbursed credits. This facilitates consistency in reporting and avoids errors that can arise when agencies are asked to make estimates of statistical concepts for which they have no hard numbers. The Berne Union data are available with a substantially shorter time lag than data from other sources. The data also provide a breakdown of total exposure into commitments on outstanding

credits (representing a risk of future claims) and arrears and unrecovered claims (resulting from nonpayment and claims payments by agencies).

A limitation of the Berne Union data is that they are not readily comparable with other types of debt statistics, and they do not accurately reflect trends in new disbursements. Some agencies do not report export credit activity by the government (which may undertake export credit finance separately from the export credit agency). Most agencies include the insurance of certain transactions that are not exports; for example, insurance against exchange rate movements or insurance of preshipment risks, which do not involve export credits. Data presented in the annual reports of some export credit agencies refer to the full value of the exports supported, a measure that includes down payments by the buyer as well as self participation by the exporter in the credit.

The OECD compiles two types of data on export credits. The Statistics on External Indebtedness reports the stock of export credits on a basis broadly consistent with other external debt data: this is covering outstanding disbursed principal only. However, since this does not reflect the way most export credit agencies keep their accounts, estimation by either the reporting country or the staff of the OECD is required. The second set of data from the OECD is compiled by the Secretariat of the Export Credit Group, which records the flow of new commitments of export credits with initial maturities of over one year, and initial maturities of over five years, as well as the stock of officially supported short-term credits.

Notes

1. Aid is defined as grants plus concessional loans.

2. Of course, aid devoted to reducing poverty will also have an impact on education, health, and the environment. Thus these calculations are not entirely additional to the forecast of aid required to halve poverty. See World Bank 2001i.

3. These include Bolivia, Burkina Faso, Honduras, Mauritania, Mozambique, Nicaragua, Tanzania, and Uganda.

4. See http://www.worldbank.org/poverty/strategies/review/index.htm

5. See Interim Guidelines for PRSCs, available at www.worldbank.org.

6. In some cases, progress is not fast enough, while in others there has even been a deterioration (for instance, 14 countries saw increases in child mortality between 1990 and 1999).

7. See World Bank 2001a.

8. Ten countries or territories were removed from the list of ODA recipients on January 1, 2000: Aruba, French Polynesia, Gibraltar, the Republic of Korea, Libya, Macao, the Netherlands Antilles, New Caledonia, Northern Marianas, and the Virgin Islands.

9. In a few high-inflation countries where the domestic retail market is substantially dollarized, foreign exchange sold by the central bank could be used to buy nontradable goods, and thus contribute to inflationary pressures.

10. While aid should be treated as revenue in the fiscal accounts, it is not equivalent to revenue generated by taxes: (a) aid augments the resources available to the economy whereas taxation merely transfers them from the private sector to the government; (b) unlike taxation, aid does not distort relative prices; and (c) aid has radically lower costs of administration than taxes.

11. For example, for the International Development Association (IDA), the grant element is roughly 70 percent. Thus 70 percent of an IDA loan should be viewed as revenue, and 30 percent as a commercial loan. This approach does face some practical difficulties, in part because the ex ante calculation of the grant element depends on expectations regarding future exchange rates and interest rates, and in part because it could introduce inconsistencies between fiscal and external accounts.

12. Appropriately, both studies measured the volatility of aid in constant dollars, which provides an indication of the real value of aid resources available to the economy. Bulir and Hamann (2001) find that aid is significantly more volatile than revenues if both variables are expressed as a share of GDP, or if only the relatively aid-dependent countries are considered.

13. See World Bank 2000c, chapter 4.

14. One major aid program, IDA, has explicit allocation criteria, and the bilateral donors also follow criteria that are well understood (Alesina and Dollar 2000), so it is possible to define the conditions under which aid may fall.

15. A few of the earlier studies did find a positive impact of aid on growth (Dowling and Hiemenz 1983; Levy 1988; and Hadjimichael and others 1995).

16. Hansen and Tarp (2001) criticize the Burnside and Dollar result that policies enhance aid effectiveness as non-robust to choice of sample. However, Collier and Dehn (2001) show that even on the Hansen-Tarp sample the Burnside-Dollar result holds up, once terms-of-trade shocks are included in the specification.

17. A one-off expenditure of $1 billion would result in a *temporary* phase of higher growth, but this temporary growth would take the economy to a *permanently* higher level of income. Thus, the poverty reduction produced even by a one-off injection of IDA funds is permanent.

18. Africa is probably the only region in which the Dutch disease effects of aid need to be considered, since aid as a share of both GDP and exports is much higher than in any other region.

19. With growth as the dependent variable, Collier and Dollar (2001a) find that the coefficient on the square of aid is significant and negative, indicating diminishing returns to aid.

20. However, Lensink and White (1999) found that aid in excess of 40 percent of GDP lowers the growth rate.

21. The Collier and Dollar results are based on GDP valued at purchasing power parity, which provide a standard measure allowing comparison of real price levels between countries (see World Bank 2001j), while this calculation uses GDP valued at dollars. Since the GDP of a developing country valued at purchasing power parity is typically larger than GDP valued in dollars, this calculation understates the number of poor countries where increased levels of aid will continue to have a positive impact on growth.

22. The increase in aid to India, which has about one-third of the world's extreme poor but only gets about 5 percent of total aid, is constrained to $10 billion. Absent this adjustment, the framework would imply massive and unrealistic increases in aid to India.

23. Based on case studies of African countries. See also Mercer-Blackman and Unigovskaya 2000, and Jayarajah and Branson 1995. In some cases, the complexity of conditions contributed to compliance failure.

24. See World Bank 1998 and 2001b.

25. The relationship between donors and recipients has been modeled both as the outcome of a bargaining game (Mosley, Harrigan, and Toye 1991) and in a framework where recipients are viewed as agents, implementing conditions desired by donors (Killick 1997; White and Morrissey 1997; Svensson 2000).

26. See Mosley, Harrigan, and Toye 1991; and Adam 1995.

27. However, measuring the extent of implementation of structural adjustment programs is problematic, because programs are intended to be flexible and are routinely modified or renegotiated during the course of implementation.

28. Weighted by disbursements, the scores for outcomes increased from 73 percent satisfactory in fiscal 1990–94 to 97 percent in fiscal 1999–2000.

29. The NPV refers to the discounted value of future debt service payments, where the discount rate is some market rate. This concept was introduced to measure the impact on the debt burden of different terms on rescheduling. It also provides a comparable measure of the debt burden among countries when a substantial share of outstanding claims is at concessional rates.

30. The 24 countries that have reached a decision point are Benin, Bolivia, Burkina Faso, Cameroon, Chad, Ethiopia, Gambia, Guinea, Guinea-Bissau, Guyana, Honduras, Madagascar, Malawi, Mali, Mauritania, Mozambique, Nicaragua, Niger, Rwanda, Senegal, São Tomé and Principe, Tanzania, Uganda, and Zambia.

31. Compared to actual debt service paid prior to HIPC assistance in 1998–99.

32. See Claessens and others (1996) on the importance of removing the debt overhang facing the HIPCs, and World Bank (2001g) for key aspects of maintaining external debt sustainability.

33. See World Bank (2001h) for a more detailed discussion of the status of creditor participation and for examples of litigation by commercial creditors against HIPCs.

34. New commitments include the value of new business insured, new lending facilities, and guarantees for new FDI (but excluding trade finance with maturities of less than one year).

35. Investment insurance by export credit agencies excludes commercial risks: it is normally limited to coverage of nationalization or expropriation without compensation, losses on investment due to war or civil unrest, and inability to convert and transfer or remit profits and dividends.

36. Differences in the definitions used in data from the export credit agencies and the private markets may distort this comparison.

37. Berne Union statistics.

38. This legislation stipulates that a HIPC country must commit to not borrow on nonconcessional terms for at least two years from any multilateral development bank benefiting from the U.S. contributions.

39. These include a factory to produce iron slabs, a gas pipeline, mining and processing of titaniferous mineral sands, and the expansion of the Mozal smelter.

40. Billiton, formerly a South African company but now listed on the London Stock Exchange, is the major shareholder in Mozal with a 47 percent stake. Billiton has substantial positions in the markets for aluminum, coal, nickel, ferroalloys, and industrial minerals.

41. Aid is also provided by a few countries that are not members of the OECD DAC, including the Republic of Korea, Turkey, and several oil-exporting countries in the Middle East.

References

The word *processed* describes informally reproduced works that may not be commonly available through libraries.

Adam, Christopher. 1995. "Adjustment in Africa: Reforms, Results, and the Road Ahead." *World Economy* (U.K.) 18 (September): 729–35.

Alesina, Alberto, and David Dollar. 2000. "Who Gives Foreign Aid to Whom and Why?" *Journal of Economic Growth* 51(1): 33–63.

Berg, Elliot. 1991. "African Adjustment Programs: False Attacks and True Dilemmas." Paper presented at the Conference on Structural Adjustment: Retrospect and Prospect. The American University, Department of Economics, Washington, D.C.

Bigsten, A., P. Collier, S. Dercon, M. Fafchamps, B. Gauthier, J.W. Gunning, J. Habarurema, A. Oduro, R. Oostendorp, C. Pattillo, M. Söderdom, F. Teal, and A. Zeufack. 1999. "Exports and Firm-level Efficiency in African Manufacturing." Development Research Group, World Bank, Washington, D.C. Processed.

Boone, P. 1994. "The Impact of Foreign Aid on Savings and Growth." London School of Economics. Processed.

Boschini, Anne, and Anders Olofsgard. 2001. "Foreign Aid: an Instrument for Fighting Poverty or Communism?" Processed.

Brautigam, Deborah, and Kwesi Botchwey. 1995. "The Institutional Impact of Aid Dependence on Recipients in Africa." Chr. Michelsen Institute Working Paper, Norway.

Brown, Adrienne, Mick Foster, Andy Norton, and Felix Naschold. 2001. "The Status of Sectorwide Approaches." Working Paper 142. Overseas Development Institute, London.

Bulir, A., and J. Hamann. 2001. "How Volatile and Predictable are Aid Flows: and What Are the Policy Implications." International Monetary Fund, Washington, D.C. Processed.

Burnside, C., and D. Dollar. 2000. "Aid, Policies and Growth." *American Economic Review* 90(4): 846–68.

Checki, Terence J., and Ernest Stern. 2000. "Financial Crises in the Emerging Markets: The Roles of the Public and Private Sectors." *Economics and Finance* 6 (13).

Claessens, Stijn, Enrica Detragiache, Ravi Kanbur, and Peter Wickham. 1996. "Analytical Aspects of the Debt Problems of Heavily Indebted Poor Countries." World Bank Policy Research Working Paper 1618. World Bank, Washington, D.C.

Collier, P. 1999. "Aid 'Dependency': A Critique." *Journal of African Economies* 9 (4): 528–45.

Collier, P., and J. Dehn. 2001. "Aid, Shocks and Growth." Policy Research Working Paper 2688, World Bank, Washington, D.C.

Collier, P., and D. Dollar. 2001a. "Aid Allocation and Poverty Reduction." Policy Research Working Paper 2041. The World Bank, Washington, D.C.

———. 2001b. "Development Effectiveness: What Have We Learnt?" Development Research Group, World Bank, Washington, D.C. Processed.

———. 2001c. "Aid, Risk, and the Special Concerns of Small States." In *Small States in the Global Economy*, D. Peretz. Economic Paper 44, Commonwealth Secretariat.

Collier, P., and A. Hoeffler. 2000. "Aid, Policy and Peace: Reducing the Risks of Civil Conflict." World Bank, Washington, D.C. Processed.

Dasgupta, Dipak, and Dilip Ratha. 2000. "What Factors Appear to Drive Private Capital Flows to Developing Countries? And How Does Official Lending Respond?" Policy Research Working Paper 2392. World Bank, Washington, D.C. July.

Disch, Arne. 2000. "Aid Coordination and Aid Effectiveness." Report to the Norwegian Ministry of Foreign Affairs. Processed. http://odin.dep.no/archive/udbilder/01/01/Rappo015.pdf.

Dollar, David, and William Easterly. 1998. "The Search for the Key: Aid, Investment, and Policies in Africa." World Bank, Development Research Group, Washington D.C.

Dollar, David, and J. Svensson. 2000. "What Explains the Success or Failure of Structural Adjustment Programs." *Economic Journal* 110(466): 894–917.

Dowling, J. M., and U. Hiemenz. 1983. "Aid, Savings and Growth in the Asian Region." *The Developing Economies* 21 (1): 1–13.

Durbarry, Ramesh, Normal Gemmell, and David Greenaway. 1998. *New Evidence on the Impact of Foreign Aid on Economic Growth*. Centre for Research in Economic Development and International Trade Research Paper 1998/8. University of Nottingham, United Kingdom.

Easterly, William. 1999. "How Did Highly Indebted Poor Countries Become Highly Indebted? Reviewing Two

Decades of Debt Relief." Working Paper No. 2225, World Bank, Washington, D.C.

Eisenblatter, Bernd. 1999. "Globalization and aid policies. New Forms of Donor Cooperation and Coordination—Effects and Experiences." *Quarterly Journal of International Agriculture* 38 (4): 375–394.

Eriksson, John. 2001. "The Drive to Partnership: Aid Coordination and the World Bank." World Bank, Washington, D.C.

Griffin, K. 1971. "Foreign Capital: A Reply to Some Critics." *Bulletin of the Oxford University Institute of Economics and Statistics* 32 (2): 156–61.

Guillaumont, P., and L. Chauvet. 2001. "Aid and Performance: A Reassessment." *Journal of Development Studies* 37 (6).

Hadjimichael, M. T., D. Ghura, M. Muhleisen, R. Nord, and E. M. Ucer. 1995. "Sub-Saharan Africa Growth, Savings, and Investment, 1986–93." International Monetary Fund Occasional Paper no. 118. Washington, D.C.

Hansen, H., and F. Tarp. 2001. "Aid and Growth Regressions." *Journal of Developing Economies* 64 (2): 547–70.

Hoffman, P. T., and K. Norberg, eds. 1994. *Fiscal Crises, Liberty, and Representative Government, 1450–1789.* Stanford, Calif.: Stanford University Press.

IMF (International Monetary Fund). 1998. "External Evaluation of the ESAF: Report by a Group of Independent Experts." Washington, D.C.

Jayarajah, C., and W. Branson. 1995. "Structural and Sectoral Adjustment: World Bank Experience, 1980–92." Operations Evaluation Department, World Bank, Washington, D.C.

Jepma, Catrinus. 1991. *The Tying of Aid.* Paris: Development Center of the OECD.

Johnson, J., and S. Wasty. 1993. "Borrower Ownership of Adjustment Programs and the Political Economy of Reform." Discussion Paper 199. World Bank, Washington, D.C.

Kharas, Homi, and Hisanobu Shishido. 1991. "The Transition from Aid to Private Capital Flows." In Uma Lele and Ijaz Nabi, eds., *Transitions in Development: The Role of Aid and Commercial Flows.* San Francisco: ICS Press.

Killick, Tony. 1997, "Principals, Agents, and the Failings of Conditionality." *Journal of International Development* 9: 483–95.

Killick, Tony, with Ramani Gunatilaka, and Ana Marr. 1998. *Aid and the Political Economy of Policy Change.* London: Routledge.

Knack, Stephen. 2000. "Aid Dependence and the Quality of Governance: Cross-Country Empirical Tests." Policy Research Working Paper 2396. World Bank, Washington, D.C.

Kraay, Art. 1999. "Exportations et performances economiques : etude d'un panel de enterprises chinoises." *Revue d'Economie du Developpement* (France) 7 (1–2): 183–207.

Krueger, Anne O. 1998. "Whither the World Bank and the IMF?" *Journal of Economic Literature* 36: 1983–2020.

Lancaster, Carol. 1999. *Aid to Africa.* University of Chicago Press.

Laplagne, Patrick, Malcolm Treadgold, and Jonathan Baldry. 2001. "A Model of Aid Impact in some South Pacific Microstates." *World Development* 29 (2): 365–383.

Lensink, Robert, and Oliver Morrissey. 2000. "Aid instability as a measure of uncertainty and the positive impact of aid on growth." *Journal of Development Studies* February. London.

Lensink, Robert, and Howard White. 1999. "Is There an Aid Laffer Curve?" University of Nottingham (U.K.), Centre for Research in Economic Development and International Trade. Credit Research Paper 99/6.

Lerrick, Adam. 1999. "Has the World Bank Lost Its Way?" *Euromoney* December.

Levy, V. 1988. "Aid and Growth in Sub-Saharan Africa: The Recent Experience." *European Economic Review* 32: 1777–1795.

Lister, Stephen, and Mike Stevens. 1992. *Aid Coordination and Management.* Washington, D.C.: World Bank. Processed.

Maizels, A., and M. K. Nissanke. 1984. "Motivations for Aid to Developing Countries." *World Development* 12 (9).

McCleary, William. 1991. "The Design and Implementation of Conditionality." In Thomas, Vinod, Ajay Chhibber, Mansoor Dailami, and Jaime de Melo, eds. *Restructuring Economies in Distress: Policy Reform and the World Bank.* New York: Oxford University Press, pp. 197–215.

Mercer-Blackman, Valerie, and Anna Unigovskaya. 2000. "Compliance with IMF program indicators and growth in transition economies." IMF Working Paper WP/00/47, Washington, D.C.

Morrissey, Oliver, and Howard White. 1994. "Evaluating the Concessionality of Tied Aid." Institute of Social Studies Working Paper: Subseries on Money, Finance, and Development (Netherlands) No. 53/January: 1–18.

Mosley, Paul. 1986. "Politics of Economic Liberalization: USAID and the World Bank in Kenya 1980–84." *African Affairs* (U.K.) 85 (January): 107–19.

———. 1999. "Recent changes in aid technology: is the White Paper an adequate response?" *Public Administration and Development* 19 (29).

Mosley, Paul, J. Harrigan, and J. Toye. 1991. *Aid and Power: The World Bank and Policy Lending*, Vol. 1. London: Routledge.

OECD (Organisation for Economic Co-operation and Development). 2001. "Untying Aid to the Least Developed Countries." OECD Observer Policy Brief, Paris.

Pallage, Stephane, and Michel Robe. 1998. *Foreign Aid and the Business Cycle.* Center for Research on Economic Fluctuations and Employment Working Paper no. 63. University of Quebec at Montreal.

Pearson, Lester B. 1969. "Partners in Development: Report of the Commission on International Development." New York: Praeger.

Reichel, Richard. 1995. "Development Aid, Savings and Growth in the 1980s—A Cross-Section Analysis." *Savings and Development* 19 (3): 279–96.

Rodrik, Dani. 1996. "Understanding economic policy reform." *Journal of Economic Literature* 34 (March): 9–41.

Sachs, J., and M. Warner. 2000. "Natural Resource Abundance and Economic Growth'. In *Leading Issues in Economic Development*, 7th ed. G.M. Meier and J.E. Rauch, Oxford University Press.

Sekkat, Khalid, and Aristomene Varoudakis. 2000. "Exchange Rate Management and Manufactured Exports in Sub-Saharan Africa." *Journal of Development Economics* 61: 237–253.

SIDA (Swedish International Development Agency). 1999. "Dollars, Dialogue and Development" An Evaluation of Swedish Programme Aid http://www.sida.se/Sida/jsp/Crosslink.jsp?d=410

Snyder, Donald. 1990. "Foreign Aid and Domestic Savings: A Spurious Correlation?" *Economic Development and Cultural Change* 39 (October): 175–81.

Soderling, Ludvig. 2000. "Dynamics of Export Performance, Productivity and Real Effective Exchange Rate in Manufacturing: the Case of Cameroon." *Journal of African Economies* 9 (4): 411–29.

Summers, Lawrence. 1999. "A New Framework for Multilateral Development Policy." Remarks to the Council on Foreign Relations, New York, March 20, www.treas.gov/press/releases/ps477.htm. See also his testimony before the House Banking Committee on March 20, 1999, www.treas.gov/press/releases/ps480.htm.

Svensson, Jakob. 2000. "When Is Foreign Aid Policy Credible? Aid Dependence and Conditionality." *Journal of Development Economics* 61: 61–84.

Taslim, M. A., and A. Weliwita. 2000. "The Inverse Relationship between Saving and Aid: An Alternative Explanation." *Journal of Economic Development* 25 (1/June).

Trumbull, William, and Howard Wall. 1994. "Estimating Aid-Allocation Criteria with Panel Data." *The Economic Journal* 104 (July).

USAID (United States Agency for International Development). 2001. "FY 2000 performance overview." Washington, D.C. http://www.dec.org/partners/2000_po/pdf_docs/fy2000po.pdf

van Arkadie, Brian. 1986. "Some Realities of Adjustment: An Introduction," *Development and Change* 0012–155X 17(3): 371–86. London.

van de Walle, Nicolas, and Timothy Johnston. 1996. "Improving aid to Africa." Policy Essay No. 21. Overseas Development Council, Washington, D.C.

van Wijnbergen, Sweder. 1986. "Macroeconomic Aspects of Effectiveness of Foreign Aid: On the Two-Gap Model, Home-Goods, Disequilibrium, and Real Exchange Rate Misalignment." *Journal of International Economics* 21: 82–116.

White, Howard, and Oliver Morrissey. 1997 "Conditionality When Donor and Recipient Preferences Vary." *Journal of International Development* 9: 497–505.

World Bank. 1997. "Adjustment lending in Sub-Saharan Africa: an update." Operations Evaluation Division, Washington, D.C.

———. 1998. "Assessing Aid: What Works, What Doesn't, and Why?" World Bank Policy Research Report, Washington, D.C. www.worldbank.org/research/aid/

———. 1999. "The Drive to Partnership: Aid Coordination and the World Bank." Operations Evaluation Department, Washington, D.C.

———. 2000a. *Global Development Finance*. Washington, D.C.

———. 2000b. "Quality at Entry in CY99: A QAG assessment." Quality Assurance Group, Washington, D.C.

———. 2000c. *Global Economic Prospects*. Washington, D.C.

———. 2001a. "Report of the Task Force on the World Bank Group and the Middle-Income Countries." (SecM2001-0204). March 27.

———. 2001b. "Financing for Development." (SecM2001). August 28.

———. 2001c. *Aid and Reform in Africa*. Washington, D.C.

———. 2001d. *Adjustment Lending Retrospective*. Operations Policy and Country Services Department. Washington, D.C.

———. 2001e. *Global Development Finance*. Washington, D.C.

———. 2001f. "Review of Aid Coordination in an Era of Poverty Reduction Strategies. IDA 10–12." Operations Evaluation Department, Washington, D.C.

———. 2001g. *The Challenge of Maintaining Long-Term External Debt Sustainability*. (http://www.worldbank.org/hipc/hipc-review/hipc-review.html)

———. 2001h. Heavily Indebted Poor Countries (HIPC) Initiative: Status of Implementation. (IDA/SecM2001-0543/1)

———. 2001i. "Goals for Development: History, Prospects, and Costs." A background paper for the September 2001 Development Committee Meeting. Washington, D.C.

———. 2001j. *World Development Indicators*. Washington, D.C.

Appendixes

Appendix 1

Debt Burden Indicators and Country Classifications

Country classifications for 2002

GLOBAL DEVELOPMENT FINANCE CLASSI-fies indebtedness based on two ratios: the ratio of the present value of total debt service to gross national income (GNI) and the ratio of the present value of total debt service to exports. These ratios cast a country's indebtedness in terms of two important aspects of its potential capacity to service the debt: exports (because they provide foreign exchange to service debt) and GNI (because it is the broadest measure of income generation in an economy). For the 136 countries that report to the World Bank's Debtor Reporting System (DRS) the debt data are drawn from this source. GNI and export data are from World Bank files, as shown in the *Country Tables* volume of *Global Development Finance*. Export figures are earnings from goods and services, including worker remittances. Data on official grants are not included, although they may be a stable source of foreign exchange in some countries.

The two indebtedness ratios in *Global Development Finance 2002* are calculated as follows:

- The ratio of the present value of total debt service in 2000 to average GNI in 1998, 1999, and 2000.
- The ratio of the present value of total debt service in 2000 to average exports (including worker remittances) in 1998, 1999, and 2000.

If either ratio exceeds a critical value—80 percent for the debt service to GNI ratio and 220 percent for the debt service to exports ratio—the country is classified as severely indebted. If the critical value is not exceeded but either ratio is three-fifths or more of the critical value (that is, 48 percent for

the present value of debt service to GNI and 132 percent for the present value of debt service to exports), the country is classified as moderately indebted. If both ratios are less than three-fifths of the critical value, the country is classified as less indebted. Countries are further classified as low-income if 2000 GNI per capita was $755 or less and as middle-income if 2000 GNI per capita was $756 or more but less than $9,265. Combining these criteria leads to the identification of severely indebted low-income countries (SILICs), severely indebted middle-income countries (SIMICs), moderately indebted low-income countries (MILICs), moderately indebted middle-income countries (MIMICs), less indebted low-income countries (LILICs), and less indebted middle-income countries (LIMICs; table A1.1).

The use of critical values to define the boundaries between indebtedness categories implies that changes in country classifications should be interpreted with caution. If a country has an indicator that is close to the critical value, a small change in the indicator may trigger a change in indebtedness classification even if economic fundamentals have not changed significantly.

Moreover, these indicators do not represent an exhaustive set of useful indicators of external debt. They may not, for example, adequately capture the debt servicing capacity of countries in which government budget constraints are key to debt service difficulties. Countries (such as the franc zone countries in Africa) that allow the use or free conversion of a foreign currency can face government budget difficulties that are related to servicing external public debt, but that are not necessarily reflected in balance of payments data. In other countries, the servicing of domestic public debt may be

Table A1.1 Income and indebtedness classification criteria

Income classification	Indebtedness classification		
	PV/XGS higher than 220 percent or PV/GNI higher than 80 percent	PV/XGS less than 220 percent but higher than 132 percent or PV/GNI less than 80 percent but higher than 48 percent	PV/XGS less than 132 percent and PV/GNI less than 48 percent
Low-income: GNI per capita less than $755	Severely indebted low-income countries	Moderately indebted low-income countries	Less-indebted low-income countries
Middle-income: GNI per capita between $756 and $9,265	Severely indebted middle-income countries	Moderately indebted middle-income countries	Less-indebted middle-income countries

Note: PV/XGS is present value of debt service to exports of goods and services. PV/GNI is present value of debt service to GNI.
Source: World Bank.

a source of fiscal strain that is not reflected in balance of payments data. Moreover, rising external debt may not necessarily imply payment difficulties, especially if there is a commensurate increase in the country's debt servicing capacity. Thus, these indicators should be used in the broader context of a country-specific analysis of debt sustainability.

In the context of the Heavily Indebted Poor Countries (HIPC) Initiative, countries are classified based on the ratio of the present value of public and publicly guaranteed debt to exports of goods and services, excluding worker remittances. For those countries for which a joint debt sustainability analysis has been undertaken, the indicators are calculated on this basis and shown in italics in tables A1.4 and A1.5.

The discount rates used to calculate present value are interest rates charged by the Organisation for Economic Co-operation and Development (OECD) countries for officially supported export credits. They represent, on average, the most favorable terms for fixed-rate nonconcessional debt that countries are able to contract in international loan markets. The rates are specified for 19 currencies, including Group-of-Seven currencies—British pounds, Canadian dollars, French francs, German marks, Italian lire, Japanese yen, and U.S. dollars. International Bank for Reconstruction and Development currency-pool loans, International Development Association credits, and International Monetary Fund loans are discounted at the special drawing rights lending rate. For debt denominated in other currencies, discount rates are the average of interest rates on export credits charged by other OECD countries.

In present value calculations, debt service on fixed-rate loans is determined and each payment is discounted to compute its present value. For variable-rate loans, for which the future debt service payment cannot be precisely determined, debt service is calculated using the rate at the end of 2000 for the base specified for the loan.

Classification of low-income countries

Thirty-three countries are classified as SILICs, 16 as MILICs, and 12 as LILICs (table A1.2). The debt indicators for Chad and Tajikistan have worsened, and they joined the severely indebted group of low-income countries. The ratios for Mali and Uganda have improved, and they are now classified in the moderately indebted group of low-income countries. Debt indicators for Armenia, Bangladesh, Georgia, and Vietnam have also improved, and they are now classified in the less indebted group of low-income countries.

Classification of middle-income countries

In the middle-income group, 8 countries are classified as SIMICs, 27 as MIMICs, and 40 as LIMICs. The debt indicators for Ecuador have declined, and it has moved into the group of severely indebted middle-income countries. Also, Croatia has joined the moderately indebted middle-income countries. By contrast, debt indicators for Bolivia, Bosnia and Herzegovina, and Bulgaria have improved, and they have now joined the moderately indebted group of middle-income countries. Morocco's debt indicator has also improved, and it is now classified in the less indebted group of middle-income countries.

Table A1.2 Classification of DRS economies

Severely indebted low-income	Severely indebted middle-income	Moderately indebted low-income	Moderately indebted middle-income	Less indebted low-income	Less indebted middle-income
Angola	Argentina	Burkina Faso	Algeria	**Armenia**[b]	Albania
Benin	Brazil	Cambodia	Belize	Azerbaijan	Belarus
Burundi	**Ecuador**[a]	Gambia, The	**Bolivia**[b]	**Bangladesh**[b]	Botswana
Cameroon	Gabon	Ghana	Bosnia and	Bhutan	Cape Verde
Central African Republic	Guyana	Haiti	Herzegovina[b]	Eritrea	China
Chad[a]	Jordan	Kenya	**Bulgaria**[b]	**Georgia**[b]	Costa Rica
Comoros	Peru	**Mali**[b]	Chile	India	Czech Republic
Congo, Dem. Rep. of	Syrian Arab Republic	Moldova	Colombia	Lesotho	Djibouti
Congo, Rep. of		Mongolia	**Croatia**[a]	Nepal	Dominica
Côte d'Ivoire		Mozambique	Estonia	Solomon Islands	Dominican Republic
Ethiopia		Senegal	Honduras	Ukraine	Egypt, Arab Rep. of
Guinea		Togo	Hungary	**Vietnam**[b]	El Salvador
Guinea-Bissau		**Uganda**[b]	Jamaica		Equatorial Guinea
Indonesia		Uzbekistan	Lebanon		Fiji
Kyrgyz Republic		Yemen, Rep. of	Malaysia		Grenada
Lao PDR		Zimbabwe	Mauritius		Guatemala
Liberia			Panama		Iran, Islamic Rep. of
Madagascar			Papua New Guinea		Kazakhstan
Malawi			Philippines		Korea, Rep. of
Mauritania			Russian Federation		Latvia
Myanmar			Samoa		Lithuania
Nicaragua			St. Vincent and		Macedonia, FYR of
Niger			the Grenadines		Maldives
Nigeria			Thailand		Mexico
Pakistan			Tunisia		**Morocco**[b]
Rwanda			Turkey		Oman
São Tomé and Principe			**Turkmenistan**[c]		Paraguay
Sierra Leone			Uruguay		Poland
Somalia			Venezuela, R.B. de		Romania
Sudan					Seychelles
Tajikistan[a]					Slovak Republic
Tanzania					South Africa
Zambia					Sri Lanka
					St. Kitts and Nevis
					St. Lucia
					Swaziland
					Tonga
					Trinidad and Tobago
					Vanuatu
					Yugoslavia, Fed. Rep. of
33	8	16	27	12	40

Notes: Tables A1.2 and A1.3 classify all DRS and 12 non-DRS economies.

Economies are divided among income groups according to 2000 GNI per capita, calculated using the World Bank Atlas method.

Income groups are low-income, $755 or less; lower-middle-income, $756–$2,995; upper-middle-income, $2,996–$9,265; and high-income, $9,266 or more.

a. Countries whose indebtedness classification has worsened.

b. Countries whose indebtedness classification has improved.

c. Countries whose income classification has changed.

Source: World Bank.

Table A1.3 Classification of non-DRS economies

Severely indebted low-income	Severely indebted middle-income	Moderately indebted middle-income	Less indebted low-income	Less indebted middle-income
Afghanistan	Cuba Iraq	Gibraltar	Korea, Dem. Rep. of	Antigua and Barbuda Bahrain Kiribati Libya Namibia Saudi Arabia Suriname

Table A1.4 Major economic indicators, 2000

(millions of dollars)

Country	EDT	PV	TDS	INT	XGS	GNI
Albania	784	485	27	11	1,350	3,859
Algeria	25,002	25,374	4,467	1,655	22,757	50,606
Angola	10,146	9,653	1,205	163	7,965	4,750
Argentina	146,172	154,961	27,345	11,613	38,342	277,735
Armenia	898	598	43	14	564	1,931
Azerbaijan	1,184	991	181	58	2,252	4,921
Bangladesh	15,609	9,574	790	192	8,657	46,885
Belarus	851	804	232	47	8,107	29,960
Belize	499	484	66	26	411	767
Benin	*1,411*	976	77	19	607	2,150
Bhutan	198	163	7	2	157	498
Bolivia[a]	*4,447*	2,747	662	188	1,694	8,056
Bosnia and Herzegovina	2,828	2,286	334	134	1,510	4,619
Botswana	413	339	68	17	3,779	5,278
Brazil	237,953	223,841	62,788	15,065	69,202	569,770
Bulgaria	10,026	9,617	1,189	529	7,323	11,674
Burkina Faso	*1,432*	663	55	16	316	2,172
Burundi	1,100	644	21	8	58	674
Cambodia	2,357	1,965	31	18	1,546	3,173
Cameroon	*7,343*	6,252	562	289	2,738	8,284
Cape Verde	327	260	16	5	215	547
Central African Republic	872	543	14	6	157	952
Chad	*1,067*	587	26	10	283	1,398
Chile	36,978	34,859	6,163	2,230	23,699	68,141
China	149,800	133,236	21,728	7,594	292,668	1,065,283
Colombia	34,081	33,485	5,171	2,252	18,081	78,855
Comoros	219	157	3	1	54	202
Congo, Dem. Rep. of	11,645	10,947	25	25	1,112	10,586
Congo, Rep. of	4,887	4,595	43	38	2,720	2,232
Costa Rica	4,466	4,483	650	261	7,964	14,624
Côte d'Ivoire	12,138	11,538	1,020	539	4,549	8,615
Croatia	12,120	12,114	2,437	684	9,551	18,721
Czech Republic	21,299	21,419	4,774	1,397	37,561	50,013
Djibouti	262	173	14	3	245	568
Dominica	108	81	10	4	151	240
Dominican Republic	4,598	4,341	521	263	10,953	18,628
Ecuador	13,281	13,143	1,276	611	7,237	12,380
Egypt, Arab Rep. of	28,957	22,965	1,813	726	21,555	99,657
El Salvador	4,023	3,761	374	221	5,538	12,965
Equatorial Guinea	248	197	5	1	2,363	498
Eritrea	311	188	3	3	299	695
Estonia	3,280	3,054	428	123	4,908	4,610

Table A1.4 Major economic indicators, 2000 (continued)

(millions of dollars)

Country	EDT	PV	TDS	INT	XGS	GNI
Ethiopia	5,614	3,264	139	53	1,000	6,331
Fiji	136	129	30	7	1,186	1,435
Gabon	3,995	3,879	468	216	3,113	4,240
Gambia, The	438	265	19	7	267	415
Georgia	1,633	1,271	117	49	1,224	3,042
Ghana	5,918	3,921	472	157	2,451	5,037
Grenada	207	166	12	4	259	377
Guatemala	4,622	4,326	438	245	4,637	18,743
Guinea	3,251	2,341	133	57	870	2,931
Guinea-Bissau	937	700	6	3	72	203
Guyana	1,415	842	116	48	740	660
Haiti	1,169	691	42	20	521	4,064
Honduras	4,068	3,110	578	192	2,991	5,794
Hungary	29,415	27,841	7,946	1,502	32,613	44,061
India	100,367	70,886	9,921	3,902	77,716	470,480
Indonesia	141,803	134,996	18,772	7,476	74,265	142,657
Iran, Islamic Rep. of	7,953	7,421	3,438	604	30,131	105,286
Jamaica	4,287	4,341	643	246	4,563	6,993
Jordan	8,226	7,623	669	301	5,867	8,313
Kazakhstan	6,664	6,689	1,840	448	10,953	17,052
Kenya	6,295	4,680	481	131	2,786	10,223
Korea, Rep. of	134,417	128,445	23,205	5,802	212,083	455,019
Kyrgyz Republic	1,829	1,405	173	76	592	1,223
Lao PDR	2,499	1,208	42	10	516	1,670
Latvia	3,379	3,332	562	183	3,547	7,176
Lebanon	10,311	10,547	1,821	650	5,462	17,420
Lesotho	716	515	66	24	543	1,132
Liberia	2,032	2,053	1	0	—	—
Lithuania	4,855	4,772	906	277	5,297	11,120
Macedonia, FYR of	1,465	1,252	161	53	1,743	3,524
Madagascar	4,461	2,986	93	38	1,210	3,804
Malawi	2,533	1,487	59	20	500	1,660
Malaysia	41,797	42,872	5,967	2,289	113,221	82,392
Maldives	207	145	20	6	468	526
Mali	2,956	1,340	97	28	804	2,260
Mauritania	1,939	1,218	100	33	388	909
Mauritius	2,374	2,358	553	149	2,666	4,349
Mexico	150,288	157,038	58,259	13,722	192,831	559,765
Moldova	1,233	1,138	135	55	811	1,357
Mongolia	859	566	29	11	625	954
Morocco	17,944	15,987	3,333	955	12,890	32,457
Mozambique	5,125	1,162	88	31	769	3,603
Myanmar	6,046	4,341	87	16	1,846	7,337
Nepal	2,823	1,558	100	29	1,529	5,687
Nicaragua	6,660	5,545	300	109	1,304	2,110
Niger	1,539	1,041	28	11	306	1,842
Nigeria	34,134	27,207	1,009	429	23,258	36,726
Oman	6,267	5,958	864	385	11,893	19,853
Pakistan	32,091	26,607	2,857	985	10,675	59,620
Panama	7,056	7,285	928	456	9,154	9,368
Papua New Guinea	2,604	2,195	305	90	2,252	3,651
Paraguay	3,091	2,950	330	131	3,188	7,554
Peru	28,560	28,411	4,305	1,681	10,055	51,925
Philippines	50,063	50,766	6,737	2,724	49,395	79,317
Poland	63,561	58,144	10,290	2,573	49,181	156,819
Romania	10,224	10,006	2,341	588	12,460	36,381
Russian Federation	160,300	148,076	11,671	5,601	115,815	239,952
Rwanda	1,230	722	35	11	142	1,775
Samoa	197	129	9	4	79	236
São Tomé and Principe	304	196	4	2	14	44
Senegal	3,534	2,416	228	74	1,580	4,286

(Table continues on next page)

Table A1.4 Major economic indicators, 2000 (continued)
(millions of dollars)

Country	EDT	PV	TDS	INT	XGS	GNI
Seychelles	163	154	17	6	506	579
Sierra Leone	1,190	792	43	10	89	616
Slovak Republic	9,462	9,071	2,590	557	14,405	18,767
Solomon Islands	155	99	9	3	135	285
Somalia	2,562	2,274	0	0	—	—
South Africa	24,861	23,774	3,860	1,251	38,705	122,643
Sri Lanka	9,066	6,981	738	218	7,670	16,368
St. Kitts and Nevis	140	116	20	7	160	275
St. Lucia	237	221	40	19	420	669
St. Vincent and the Grenadines	192	159	15	7	196	312
Sudan	15,741	14,824	61	3	1,897	9,754
Swaziland	262	218	24	10	1,015	1,515
Syrian Arab Republic	21,657	20,842	344	222	7,191	15,965
Tajikistan	1,170	940	88	31	800	936
Tanzania	6,175	4,487	217	61	1,340	8,984
Thailand	79,675	76,555	14,017	4,850	86,052	120,544
Togo	1,435	1,018	30	10	487	1,195
Tonga	58	35	4	1	35	155
Trinidad and Tobago	2,467	2,553	500	168	4,849	6,701
Tunisia	10,610	10,522	1,900	553	9,402	18,572
Turkey	116,209	114,603	21,136	6,857	58,544	201,517
Turkmenistan	—	—	—	—	2,932	4,227
Uganda	2,261	984	169	47	674	6,156
Ukraine	12,166	11,500	3,661	709	19,665	30,849
Uruguay	8,196	8,204	1,313	637	4,494	19,383
Uzbekistan	4,340	4,245	899	280	3,383	—
Vanuatu	69	35	2	1	162	224
Venezuela, R.B. de	38,196	38,744	5,846	2,553	38,318	119,321
Vietnam	12,787	11,137	1,303	350	17,299	31,344
Yemen, Republic of	5,616	4,238	221	96	5,870	7,386
Yugoslavia, Fed. Rep. of	11,960	12,007	177	104	—	8,448
Zambia	6,226	5,002	186	88	991	2,791
Zimbabwe	4,002	3,599	471	165	2,132	7,142

— Not available.

Note: For definition of indicators, see Sources and Definitions section. Numbers in italics are from debt sustainability analyses undertaken in the context of the HIPC Initiative. Present value estimates for these countries are for public and publicly guaranteed debt only, and export figures exclude worker remittances.

a. Debt numbers do not include foreign currency private sector (nonguaranteed) external debt.

Source: World Bank DRS; staff estimates.

Table A1.5 Key indebtedness ratios, 1998–2000

(percent)

Country	EDT/XGS	PV/XGS	EDT/GNI	PV/GNI	TDS/XGS	INT/XGS
Albania	74	46	22	14	3	1
Algeria	153	156	53	54	27	7
Angola	179	170	283	270	21	2
Argentina	401	425	52	55	75	30
Armenia	176	117	47	31	8	3
Azerbaijan	77	64	26	21	12	3
Bangladesh	195	120	34	21	10	2
Belarus	12	11	3	3	3	1
Belize	129	125	71	69	17	6
Benin	*366*	*253*	*59*	*41*	*20*	*3*
Bhutan	135	111	44	36	4	1
Bolivia[a]	*324*	*200*	*52*	*32*	*48*	*11*
Bosnia and Herzegovina	179	145	61	49	21	9
Botswana	12	10	8	7	2	0
Brazil	368	346	39	36	97	22
Bulgaria	153	147	84	80	18	7
Burkina Faso	*455*	*210*	*55*	*25*	*17*	*5*
Burundi	1,684	985	147	86	33	14
Cambodia	190	158	79	66	3	1
Cameroon	*302*	*257*	*82*	*70*	*23*	*11*
Cape Verde	161	128	59	47	8	2
Central African Republic	571	356	87	54	9	4
Chad	*404*	*222*	*72*	*40*	*10*	*4*
Chile	173	163	54	51	29	9
China	61	54	15	13	9	3
Colombia	209	206	40	39	32	12
Comoros	414	296	103	74	5	2
Congo, Dem. Rep. of	848	797	136	128	2	2
Congo, Rep. of	250	235	270	254	2	1
Costa Rica	57	57	32	32	8	3
Côte d'Ivoire	237	226	123	117	20	12
Croatia	131	130	61	61	26	7
Czech Republic	59	60	40	40	13	4
Djibouti	107	71	48	32	6	1
Dominica	70	53	45	34	7	2
Dominican Republic	47	44	28	26	5	2
Ecuador	204	202	83	82	20	8
Egypt, Arab Rep. of	145	115	32	25	9	3
El Salvador	82	77	33	31	8	4
Equatorial Guinea	16	13	54	43	0	0
Eritrea	124	75	41	25	1	1
Estonia	74	69	67	62	10	3
Ethiopia	*590*	*343*	*88*	*51*	*15*	*5*
Fiji	12	12	9	8	3	1
Gabon	147	142	99	96	17	7
Gambia, The	*359*	*217*	*103*	*62*	*15*	*2*
Georgia	159	124	50	39	11	4
Ghana	*236*	*157*	*89*	*59*	*19*	*6*
Grenada	86	69	59	48	5	1
Guatemala	109	102	25	23	10	5
Guinea	*397*	*286*	*96*	*69*	*16*	*7*
Guinea-Bissau	*1,768*	*1,321*	*430*	*321*	*12*	*4*
Guyana	*203*	*121*	*201*	*120*	*17*	*7*
Haiti	224	132	29	17	8	4
Honduras	*165*	*126*	*76*	*58*	*23*	*6*
Hungary	99	94	65	62	27	5
India	149	105	23	16	15	5
Indonesia	223	212	117	111	30	10
Iran, Islamic Rep. of	35	33	8	7	15	2
Jamaica	98	99	62	63	15	5
Jordan	147	136	103	95	12	5

(Table continues on next page)

Table A1.5 Key indebtedness ratios, 1998–2000 *(continued)*
(percent)

Country	EDT/XGS	PV/XGS	EDT/GNI	PV/GNI	TDS/XGS	INT/XGS
Kazakhstan	80	81	36	36	22	4
Kenya	225	167	59	44	17	5
Korea, Rep. of	74	70	35	33	13	3
Kyrgyz Republic	315	242	138	106	30	13
Lao PDR	504	243	173	83	8	2
Latvia	102	100	51	50	17	5
Lebanon	186	190	60	61	33	12
Lesotho	127	91	61	44	12	4
Liberia	—	—	—	—	—	—
Lithuania	98	96	48	47	18	5
Macedonia, FYR of	92	78	41	35	10	3
Madagascar	*498*	*333*	*118*	*79*	10	3
Malawi	*536*	*314*	*144*	*84*	12	4
Malaysia	42	43	55	57	6	2
Maldives	46	32	45	32	4	1
Mali	*462*	*209*	*110*	*50*	15	3
Mauritania	*508*	*319*	*201*	*126*	26	8
Mauritius	89	89	57	56	21	6
Mexico	92	96	32	33	36	7
Moldova	149	138	86	79	16	7
Mongolia	149	99	91	60	5	2
Morocco	142	127	53	47	26	7
Mozambique	*825*	*187*	*129*	*29*	14	4
Myanmar	345	248	97	69	5	1
Nepal	204	113	54	30	7	2
Nicaragua	*768*	*640*	*340*	*283*	35	8
Niger	*510*	*345*	*77*	*52*	9	3
Nigeria	203	162	105	84	6	2
Oman	73	69	38	36	10	3
Pakistan	298	247	55	45	27	9
Panama	77	79	78	80	10	5
Papua New Guinea	119	100	73	61	14	4
Paraguay	80	77	39	37	9	4
Peru	306	304	54	54	46	17
Philippines	107	109	66	67	14	6
Poland	140	128	41	37	23	5
Romania	95	93	27	27	22	5
Russian Federation	166	154	70	64	12	5
Rwanda	*1,070*	*628*	*65*	*38*	30	8
Samoa	177	115	85	55	8	5
São Tomé and Principe	*2,027*	*1,307*	*647*	*417*	29	15
Senegal	*221*	*151*	*73*	*50*	14	5
Seychelles	35	33	28	26	4	1
Sierra Leone	*1,202*	*800*	*181*	*121*	43	11
Slovak Republic	71	68	48	46	19	4
Solomon Islands	83	53	50	32	5	2
Somalia	—	—	—	—	—	—
South Africa	68	65	20	19	11	3
Sri Lanka	127	98	58	44	10	3
St. Kitts and Nevis	93	77	52	43	13	4
St. Lucia	58	54	38	35	10	5
St. Vincent and the Grenadines	110	91	63	52	9	4
Sudan	1,400	1,319	171	161	5	0
Swaziland	23	19	19	15	2	1
Syrian Arab Republic	357	344	141	136	6	3
Tajikistan	169	136	109	88	13	4
Tanzania	*544*	*395*	*70*	*51*	19	5
Thailand	104	100	69	66	18	6
Togo	281	199	108	77	6	2
Tonga	140	84	37	22	10	2
Trinidad and Tobago	65	67	39	41	13	3
Tunisia	112	111	55	55	20	6

Table A1.5 Key indebtedness ratios, 1998–2000 *(continued)*

(percent)

Country	EDT/XGS	PV/XGS	EDT/GNI	PV/GNI	TDS/XGS	INT/XGS
Turkey	201	198	59	58	37	12
Turkmenistan	—	—	—	—	—	—
Uganda	*317*	*138*	*35*	*15*	*24*	*7*
Ukraine	67	63	36	34	20	4
Uruguay	182	182	40	40	29	14
Uzbekistan	132	129	—	—	27	8
Vanuatu	39	20	30	15	1	1
Venezuela, R.B. de	137	139	36	37	21	7
Vietnam	88	77	44	38	9	2
Yemen, Republic of	131	99	85	64	5	2
Yugoslavia, Fed. Rep. of	—	—	113	113	—	—
Zambia	*668*	*537*	*191*	*153*	*20*	*9*
Zimbabwe	170	153	66	59	20	8

— Not available.

Note: For definition of indicators, see Sources and Definitions section. In the estimated ratios, the numerator refers to the 2000 data and the denominator is an average of 1998 to 2000 data. Numbers in italics are from debt sustainability analyses undertaken in the context of the HIPC Initiative. Present value estimates for these countries are for public and publicly guaranteed debt only, and export figures exclude worker remittances.

a. Debt numbers do not include foreign currency private sector (nonguaranteed) external debt.

Sources: World Bank DRS; staff estimates.

Table A1.6 Classification of economies by income group and region, January 2002

Income group	Subgroup	Sub-Saharan Africa		Asia		Europe and Central Asia		Middle East and North Africa		Americas
		East and Southern Africa	West Africa	East Asia and Pacific	South Asia	Eastern Europe and Central Asia	Rest of Europe	Middle East	North Africa	
Low-income		Angola Burundi Comoros Congo, Dem. Rep. of Eritrea Ethiopia Kenya Lesotho Madagascar Malawi Mozambique Rwanda Somalia Sudan Tanzania Uganda Zambia Zimbabwe	Benin Burkina Faso Cameroon Central African Republic Chad Congo, Rep. of Côte d'Ivoire Gambia, The Ghana Guinea Guinea-Bissau Liberia Mali Mauritania Niger Nigeria São Tomé and Principe Senegal Sierra Leone Togo	Cambodia Indonesia Korea, Dem. People's Republic of Lao PDR Mongolia Myanmar Solomon Islands Vietnam	Afghanistan Bangladesh Bhutan India Nepal Pakistan	Armenia Azerbaijan Georgia Kyrgyz Republic Moldova Tajikistan Ukraine Uzbekistan		Yemen, Republic of		Haiti Nicaragua
Middle-income	Lower	Namibia Swaziland	Cape Verde Equatorial Guinea	China Fiji Kiribati Marshall Islands Micronesia, Federated States of Papua New Guinea Philippines Samoa Thailand Tonga Vanuatu	Maldives Sri Lanka	Albania Belarus Bosnia and Herzegovina Bulgaria Kazakhstan Latvia Lithuania Macedonia, FYR of [a] Romania Russian Federation Turkmenistan Yugoslavia, Fed. Rep. of		Iran, Islamic Rep. of Iraq Jordan Syrian Arab Republic West Bank and Gaza	Algeria Djibouti Egypt, Arab Rep. of Morocco Tunisia	Belize Bolivia Colombia Cuba Dominican Republic Ecuador El Salvador Guatemala Guyana Honduras Jamaica Paraguay Peru St. Vincent and the Grenadines Suriname
	Upper	Botswana Mauritius Mayotte Seychelles South Africa	Gabon	American Samoa Korea, Rep. of Malaysia Palau		Croatia Czech Republic Estonia Hungary Poland Slovak Republic	Gibralter Isle of Man Turkey	Bahrain Lebanon Oman Saudi Arabia	Libya	Antigua and Barbuda Argentina Brazil Chile Costa Rica Dominica Grenada Mexico Panama Puerto Rico St. Kitts and Nevis St. Lucia Trinidad and Tobago Uruguay Venezuela, R.B. de
Subtotal: 156		25	23	23	8	26	3	10	6	32

Table A1.6 Classification of economies by income group and region, January 2002 *(continued)*

Income group	Subgroup	Sub-Saharan Africa		Asia		Europe and Central Asia		Middle East and North Africa		Americas
		East and Southern Africa	West Africa	East Asia and Pacific	South Asia	Eastern Europe and Central Asia	Rest of Europe	Middle East	North Africa	
High-income	OECD			Australia Japan New Zealand			Austria Belgium Denmark Finland France[b] Germany Greece Iceland Ireland Italy Luxembourg Netherlands Norway Portugal Spain Sweden Switzerland United Kingdom			Canada United States
	Non-OECD			Brunei French Polynesia Guam Hong Kong, China[c] Macao, China[d] New Caledonia N. Mariana Islands Singapore Taiwan, China		Slovenia	Andorra Channel Islands Cyprus Faeroe Islands Greenland Liechtenstein Monaco San Marino	Israel Kuwait Qatar United Arab Emirates	Malta	Aruba Bahamas, The Barbados Bermuda Cayman Islands Netherlands Antilles Virgin Islands (U.S.)
Total:	209	25	23	35	8	27	29	14	7	41

For operational and analytical purposes, the World Bank's main criterion for classifying economies is GNI per capita. Every economy is classified as low income, middle income (subdivided into lower middle and upper middle), or high income. Other analytical groups, based on geographic regions and levels of external debt, are also used.

Low-income and middle-income economies are sometimes referred to as developing economies. The use of the term is convenient; it is not intended to imply that all economies in the group are experiencing similar development or that other economies have reached a preferred or final stage of development. Classification by income does not necessarily reflect development status.

This table classifies all World Bank member economies, and all other economies with populations of more than 30,000. Economies are divided among income groups according to 2000 GNI per capita, calculated using the World Bank Atlas method. The groups are low-income, $755 or less; lower-middle-income, $756–$2,995; upper-middle-income, $2,996–$9,265; and high-income, $9,266 or more.

a. Former Yugoslav Republic of Macedonia.
b. The French overseas departments French Guiana, Guadeloupe, Martinique, and Réunion are included in France.
c. On July 1, 1997, China resumed its exercise of sovereignty over Hong Kong.
d. On December 20, 1999, China resumed its exercise of sovereignty over Macao.

Source: World Bank data.

Table A1.7 Classification of economies by income group and indebtedness, January 2002

Income group	Subgroup	Severely indebted		Moderately indebted	Less indebted		Not classified by indebtedness

Low-income		Afghanistan
		Angola
		Benin
		Burundi
		Cameroon
		Central African
		  Republic
		Chad
		Comoros
		Congo, Dem.
		  Republic
		Congo, Rep. of
		Côte d'Ivoire
		Ethiopia
		Guinea
		Guinea-Bissau
		Indonesia
		Kyrgyz Republic
		Lao PDR
		Liberia
			Madagascar
			Malawi
			Mauritania
			Myanmar
			Nicaragua
			Niger
			Nigeria
			Pakistan
			Rwanda
			São Tomé
			  and Principe
			Sierra Leone
			Somalia
			Sudan
			Tajikistan
			Tanzania
			Zambia
				Burkina Faso
				Cambodia
				Gambia, The
				Ghana
				Haiti
				Kenya
				Mali
				Moldova
				Mongolia
				Mozambique
				Senegal
				Togo
				Uganda
				Uzbekistan
				Yemen, Republic
				Zimbabwe
					Armenia
					Azerbaijan
					Bangladesh
					Bhutan
					Eritrea
					Georgia
					India
					Korea, Democratic Pople's
					  Republic of
					Lesotho
					Nepal
					Solomon
					  Islands
					Ukraine
					Vietnam		

Middle-income	*Lower*	Cuba
		Ecuador
		Guyana
		Iraq
		Jordan
		Peru
		Syrian Arab
		  Republic
				Algeria
				Belize
				Bolivia
				Bosnia and
				  Herzegovina
				Bulgaria
				Colombia
				Honduras
				Jamaica
				Papua New Guinea
				Philippines
				Russian Federation
				Samoa
				St. Vincent and
				  the Grenadines
				Thailand
				Tunisia
				Turkmenistan
					Albania
					Belarus
					Cape Verde
					China
					Djibouti
					Dominican
					  Republic
					Egypt, Arab
					  Rep. of
					El Salvador
					Equatorial
					  Guinea
					Fiji
					Guatemala
					Iran, Islamic
					  Rep. of
					Kazakhstan
					Kiribati
					Latvia
					Lithuania
						Macedonia,
						  FYR of[a]
						Maldives
						Morocco
						Namibia
						Paraguay
						Romania
						Sri Lanka
						Suriname
						Swaziland
						Tonga
						Vanuatu
						Yugoslavia,
						  Fed. Rep. of
							Marshall Islands
							Micronesia, Fed. Sts.
							West Bank and Gaza

	Upper	Argentina
		Brazil
		Gabon
				Chile
				Croatia
				Estonia
				Gibraltar
				Hungary
				Lebanon
				Malaysia
				Mauritius
				Panama
				Turkey
				Uruguay
				Venezuela, R.B. de
					Antigua and
					  Barbuda
					Bahrain
					Botswana
					Costa Rica
					Czech Republic
					Dominica
					Grenada
					Korea, Rep. of
					Libya
					Mexico
					Oman
					Poland
					Saudi Arabia
						Seychelles
						Slovak Republic
						South Africa
						St. Kitts and
						  Nevis
						St. Lucia
						Trinidad and
						  Tobago
							American Samoa
							Isle of Man
							Mayotte
							Palau
							Puerto Rico

Table A1.7 Classification of economies by income group and indebtedness, January 2002 *(continued)*

Income group	Subgroup	Severely indebted	Moderately indebted	Less indebted	Not classified by indebtedness	
High-income	*OECD*				Australia	Japan
					Austria	Luxembourg
					Belgium	Netherlands
					Canada	New Zealand
					Denmark	Norway
					Finland	Portugal
					France[b]	Spain
					Germany	Sweden
					Greece	Switzerland
					Iceland	United
					Ireland	Kingdom
					Italy	United States
	Non-OECD				Andorra	Kuwait
					Aruba	Liechtenstein
					Bahamas, The	Macao, China[c]
					Barbados	Malta
					Bermuda	Monaco
					Brunei	Netherlands
					Cayman	Antilles
					Islands	New Caledonia
					Channel	N. Mariana
					Islands	Islands
					Cyprus	Qatar
					Faeroe Islands	San Marino
					French	Singapore
					Polynesia	Slovenia
					Greenland	Taiwan, China
					Guam	United Arab
					Hong Kong,	Emirates
					China[d]	Virgin
					Israel	Islands (U.S.)
Total:	209	44	44	60	61	

This table classifies all World Bank member economies, and all other economies with populations of more than 30,000. Economies are divided among income groups according to 2000 GNI per capita, calculated using the World Bank Atlas method. The groups are low-income, $755 or less; lower-middle-income, $756–$2,995; upper-middle-income, $2,996–$9,265; and high-income, $9,266 or more.

Standard World Bank definitions of severe and moderate indebtedness are used to classify economies in this table. Severely indebted means either present value of debt service to GNI exceeds 80 percent or present value of debt service to exports exceeds 220 percent. Moderately indebted means either of the two key ratios exceeds 60 percent of, but does not reach, the critical levels. For economies that do not report detailed debt statistics to the World Bank DRS, present-value calculation is not possible. Instead, the following methodology is used to classify the non-DRS economies. Severely indebted means three of four key ratios (averaged over 1998–2000) are above critical levels: debt to GNI (50 percent); debt to exports (275 percent); debt service to exports (30 percent); and interest to exports (20 percent). Moderately indebted means three of the four key ratios exceed 60 percent of, but do not reach, the critical levels. All other classified low- and middle-income economies are listed as less indebted.

a. Former Yugoslav Republic of Macedonia.
b. The French overseas departments French Guiana, Guadeloupe, Martinique, and Réunion are included in France.
c. On December 20, 1999, China resumed its exercise of sovereignty over Macao.
d. On July 1, 1997, China resumed its exercise of sovereignty over Hong Kong.

Source: World Bank data.

Appendix 2
Commercial Debt Restructuring

Developments in 2001

In 2001, 26 debt-restructuring agreements between debtor countries and their commercial creditors were completed, restructuring about $104.9 billion of outstanding debt.[1] Among low-income countries, Honduras, Tanzania, and the Republic of Yemen bought back $452 million of principal debt through the International Development Association (IDA) Debt Reduction Facility (see table A2.1).[2] Ukraine exchanged $21.5 million of its external debt to retire the remaining amount outstanding from last year's bond exchange operation. Among middle-income countries, Argentina restructured $85.7 billion of domestic and external debts through a series of debt exchange operations to manage the near-term debt-service profile. Brazil, Jordan, and Mexico retired about $8.6 billion of their collateralized Brady bonds through Brady-Eurobond exchange and straight-buyback operations. Colombia and Turkey restructured $10.5 billion of domestic debt through Treasury notes exchange and an auction process. Also, Panama bought back $160 million of a global bond with cash payment and warrants.

IDA-sponsored debt buybacks in low-income countries

Honduras. In August, Honduras completed the first phase of a debt buyback operation, which was funded by the IDA Debt Reduction Facility and co-financed by the governments of the Netherlands, Norway, and Switzerland. This operation extinguished $13 million (principal only) of the total $14.5 million of eligible debt. The purchase price was 18 cents per dollar of the principal amount. The total operation cost came to about $2.4 million, of which $0.4 million was disbursed from IDA and $2 million was financed by participating bilateral donors. The acceptance rate of the creditors in the operation was 90 percent and thus exceeded the required minimum threshold level of 75 percent.

Tanzania. Sponsored by the IDA Debt Reduction Facility and the governments of Germany and Switzerland, Tanzania completed the first phase of a debt buyback operation in April. The operation extinguished $76.6 million of eligible principal debt and about $79.2 million of associated interest. The debt was bought back at a price of 12 cents to a dollar of principal with a 5 percent foreign exchange risk margin. About $10.1 million was paid to the eligible creditors, and the creditors contributed about $65 thousand to Tanzanian nongovernmental organizations under the Debt for Development Clause.

The Republic of Yemen. Funded by the IDA Debt Reduction Facility and the government of Norway, Switzerland, and the Netherlands, in June the Republic of Yemen completed a debt buyback operation to retire $362 million of principal and $245 million of associated interest. This operation included debt owed to about 50 creditors—suppliers' credit was about 85 percent of the principal debt, and commercial debt amounted to about 15 percent. The buyback price for the operation was set at 2.94 cents per dollar of the principal debt.[3] Total operation cost amounted to about $11.4 million, of which $7.6 million came from IDA and $3.8 million came from participating bilateral donors. The acceptance rate of the creditors in the operation was about 91 percent.

Table A2.1 Completed operations financed by the IDA Debt Reduction Facility as of December 2001
(millions of dollars)

Country	Date completed	Principal extinguished	Price (cents per dollar)[a]	Percentage of eligible principal extinguished	Total resources[b]
Albania	July 1995	371.3	26.0	99.0	97.4
Bolivia	May 1993	170.0	16.0	94.0	27.3
Côte d'Ivoire	March 1998	724.5	24.0	100.0	173.9
Ethiopia	January 1996	226.0	8.0	80.0	18.8
Guinea	April 2000	62.2	13.0	75.0	9.1
Guyana	November 1992	69.2	14.0	100.0	10.2
Guyana	August 1999	34.4	9.0	62.0	3.4
Honduras	August 2001	13.0	18.0	89.8	2.4
Mauritania	August 1996	53.0	10.0	98.0	5.9
Mozambique	December 1991	123.8	10.0	64.0	13.4
Nicaragua	December 1995	1,099.4	8.0	81.0	89.2
Niger	March 1991	107.0	18.0	99.0	19.4
São Tomé and Principe	August 1994	10.1	10.0	87.0	1.3
Senegal	December 1996	71.0	20.0[c]	96.0	15.0
Sierra Leone	September 1995	234.7	13.0	73.0	31.5
Tanzania	April 2001	76.6	12.0	71.8	10.1
Togo	December 1997	44.9	12.5	99.0	6.1
Uganda	February 1993	153.0	12.0	89.0	22.6
Vietnam	March 1998	20.4	44.0	6.6	1.0
Yemen, Republic of	February 2001	362.4[d]	2.9[e]	91.4	11.4
Zambia	September 1994	199.7	11.0	78.0	24.9

a. Of original face value of principal.
b. Includes technical assistance grants.
c. 16 cents for cash buyback and 20 cents for long-term bonds.
d. Excludes $40.7 million of debt owed to the Czech Republic and the Slovak Republic.
e. The effective buyback price reflecting a previous debt reduction of 80 percent on the Russian debt.
Source: World Bank staff estimates.

Other debt restructuring in low-income countries

Ukraine. In March, following the successful completion of last year's bond exchange, the Ukrainian government conducted a new bond exchange operation with the objective of swapping the remaining bonds from a minuscule 0.8 percent of investors who did not take part in the last year's exchange. Under this operation, about $21.5 million of the external commercial debt was exchanged with the remaining amount of the nonexchanged eligible debt at approximately $540 thousand (less than 0.075 percent of total eligible debt). Participating investors received a six-year Eurobond, denominated in either euro at an interest rate of 10 percent or U.S. dollar at an interest rate of 11 percent. Bonds eligible for the swap were a deutsche mark 16 percent Eurobond due in February, euro 10 percent amortizing notes due in March 2007, U.S. dollar 11 percent amortizing notes due in March 2007, and U.S. dollar 11 percent amortizing notes due in March 2007.

Debt buyback and swaps in middle-income countries

Argentina. The government of Argentina successfully completed the first debt swap for the year in February, swapping $4.8 billion of its short- and medium-term peso and dollar-denominated debt for a new $2.6 billion Bonte (Bonos del Tesoro, or Treasury bond) due 2006 and a new $1.6 billion global bond due 2012. This transaction converted $2.9 billion of bonds into a new 5-year Bonte and $1.9 billion of bonds into a new 11-year global bond. The new global bond was priced at par with a coupon of 12.375 percent while the new Bonte came at par with a coupon of 11.75 percent. Of the 17 bonds eligible for the exchange, 12 bonds were exchanged at a discount, and 5 bonds were swapped at a premium. The net present value saving of about $18.5 billion resulted from a net reduction in interest payments.

In June 2002, Argentina carried out one of the largest debt swap operations ever conducted by a developing country, including almost a quarter of its outstanding peso- and dollar-denominated bonds. This operation replaced about $29.5 billion of domestic and external bonds with five new securities with a face value of $30.4 billion. Foreign investors exchanged between $8 billion and $9 billion in this deal. Local banks and pension funds swapped the remainder of tender. The swap extended the average maturity of the government's debt by 2.78 years and the average yield of the new bonds was close to 15 percent. The deal reduced the debt servicing cost by $16.5 billion through the end of 2005 on account of the 5-year grace period. However, it increased Argentina's overall debt by about $2.25 billion.

In August the government arranged a voluntary swap of Treasury securities maturing the second half of 2001 with major private domestic banks for a total of $1.4 billion. Participating banks were given the option of choosing between new 1-year and 3-year bonds. In December, Argentina successfully completed a massive local debt swap with domestic banks and pension funds. This operation aimed to extend bond maturities and reduce near-term interest and amortization payments on local bonds. About $50 billion of domestic bonds—$41 billion in federal debt and $9 billion in provincial debt—was exchanged for new lower coupon loans guaranteed by tax collection[4] (see table A2.2). The new loans extended maturities of all debt due before 2010 by three years and lowered the interest rates by at least 30 percent compared with the original bond, with a cap of 7 percent for fixed rate bonds and Libor+ 300 basis points for floating bonds. This operation allowed the federal government to reduce amortization payments by $2.5 billion in 2002, $3 billion in 2003, and $2.4 million in 2004. It also saved $3.6 billion of interest payments in 2002, $2.4 billion for the federal government and $1.2 billion for the provinces.

Brazil.[5] In March, Brazil completed a par-for-par exchange of Brady bonds for a new global bond due 2024. The new $2.15 billion global issue carried a relatively low coupon of 8.875 percent and was priced at a deep discount, around 72 cents on the dollar. Unlike the typical debt swap where the old bonds are exchanged for a smaller number of new instruments, this operation traded old bonds for new bonds at par value but with a low coupon. In order to compensate for the low coupon, the government offered participating investors a cash premium to make up any difference in the market value of Brady bonds and the new global bond. The cash payment

was funded out of the collateral liberated from swapped Brady bonds. Brady bonds exchanged for the new global bond included $682 million of par bonds, $1.16 billion of discount bonds, $212 million of C-bonds, and $47 million debt conversion bonds (DCBs).[6]

Colombia. Colombia completed a massive $2.5 billion (Ps5.6 trillion) swap of domestic debts in June 2001 to reduce financing needs for next year. The government split the swap into three transactions through which participating investors could exchange their old bonds for 3-year, 5-year, and 10-year Titulos de Tesoreria notes (Treasury notes). About 54 percent of the old debt was exchanged for a 10-year note with a 7.8 percent coupon (Ps3 trillion). A further 32 percent of debt was swapped for 3-year notes with a 15 percent coupon (Ps1.8 trillion) and the remaining 14 percent was placed in 5-year notes (Ps0.8 trillion). The swap lengthened the average maturity of government bonds to 4.5 years from 3.4 years, and reduced the amortization costs by an average of 32 percent through to 2003.[7]

Mexico. In 2001, the Mexican government carried out three swap operations to buy back $4.74 billion of Brady bonds, and conducted five straight buybacks to retire about $1.025 billion of Brady bonds through open market repurchase.[8] In the first exchange, in March, Mexico issued a $3.3 billion 18-year global bond with a yield of 9.3 percent in exchange for Brady bonds (pars and discounts) with the same nominal value. The deal achieved roughly $115 million of net present value savings and freed up about $1.5 billion in collateral. In May Mexico swapped $1.05 billion of outstanding Brady bonds for $1 billion of a 10-year global bond through a reopening of its 10-year, $1.5 billion bond issued in January 2001. The reopening was priced to yield 8.426 percent to maturity, the lowest ever for a 10-year global issue by Mexico. This transaction released $475 million of underlying collateral and realized net present value savings of around $60 million. In August, Mexico completed a $1.5 billion, 30-year global bond issuance involving a $1.06 billion cash sale and a $440 million exchange for outstanding Brady bonds. The new issue was priced at a deeply discounted $92.58, yielding 9.02 percent and a spread of 335 basis points over U.S. Treasuries with an 8.3 percent coupon. By retiring the swapped Brady bonds, Mexico realized about $10 million of net present value savings and liberated $200 million of collateral.

Between April and November 2001, Mexico carried out five buyback operations to fully extinguish about $1.03 billion of its outstanding Brady debts by exercising call options and private buybacks. By exercising the embedded call options, Brazil fully retired around $10 million (NLG31.3 million) of Dutch guilder–denominated discount bonds in April; $15 million (JPY1.73 billion) of Japanese yen–denominated discount bonds in May; $300 million of U.S. dollar–denominated discount bonds in October and $400 million (FRF3 billion) of French franc–denominated par bonds in December. In October 2001, Mexico also bought back around $100 million (CAD162 million) of Canadian dollar–denominated discount bonds through private open-market repurchase.

Jordan. In 2001, according to the Jordanian Ministry of Finance, Jordan conducted six buyback operations to retire $44 million of its outstanding Brady bonds. Under these operations, Jordan bought back its Brady par bonds at an average price of 78.8 cents per dollar of face value. Total operation cost, including the arrangement fees of $100.5 thousand, came to about $36.2 million. These repurchase operations were financed by the proceeds from privatization and the sale of the released collateral.

Panama. In July 2001, Panama bought back $160 million of its global bond due in 2002 using the proceeds from a reopening of a $750 million global bond issued in February 2001. This operation represented the new approach to management of the country's debt service profile. The government offered bondholders a cash payment of $1,039 per $1,000 of face value to compensate for the loss of a coupon payment, as well as two warrants allowing investors to exercise an option to buy new 10-year global bonds with a 9.625 percent coupon to be issued in January 2002 for $990 in cash. The buyback generated estimated savings of $9.6 million in terms of debt-service cost.

Turkey. In June, the Turkish government conducted a voluntary debt swap of short-term lira-denominated debts into longer-term dollar-linked and floating-rate lira paper through a Dutch style auction. About $7.3 billion of debt was swapped in the initial auction and $730 million was exchanged in the following supplementary auction. Participating debt holders received $2.45 billion of three-year U.S. dollar-indexed bond yielding 14.89 percent for debt due 2001 and 14.45 per-

cent for debt due in 2002[9], as well as $2.45 billion of five-year U.S. dollar-indexed bond priced to yield a 50 basis points premium to the three-year dollar indexed bond[10]. They also received $1.5 billion of one-year FRNs (floating-rate notes) and $1.1 billion of two-year FRNs. This operation extended the average maturity of domestic debt from 5.3 months to 37.2 months. Debt service costs were estimated to be reduced by around $1.6 billion.

Notes

1. Transaction information was based on World Bank staff research and Goldman Sachs' debt swap data, which was provided by David Cohen.

2. About $324 million of associated interest was also extinguished.

3. The buyback price reflects an initial debt reduction of the former Soviet Union commercial debt at zero cost. Excluding a previous debt reduction, the buyback price was set at 10 cents of eligible principal debt.

4. The central bank is planning to use the financial transaction tax to fulfill guarantees.

5. There were six other Brady bond exchanges by the Brazilian government in 2001, swapping about $3 billion of outstanding Bradys, including $106.8 million of par bonds in June, $371 million and $108 million of EIs(eligible interest bonds) in June and July, $2.29 billion and $220 million of discount bonds in June and July, $7.5 million of new money bonds in June, and $18.6 million of FLIRBs (front-loaded interest reduction bond) in June. The ministry of finance exchanged its Brady bonds for the domestic securities with the central bank and some other domestic banks, turning dollar-denominated debt into real-denominated debt. These transactions were not included in the total debt restructured, since they were between the government agencies.

6. Brady bonds eligible for the exchange included U.S. dollar par series Z-L bonds due 2024 (par bonds), U.S. dollar discount series Z-L bonds due 2024 (discount bonds), U.S. dollar front-loaded interest reduction with capitalization series L bonds due 2014 (C bonds) and U.S. dollar debt conversion series L bonds due 2012.

7. Amortization payments were cut by 22.5 percent for 2001 to Ps41 trillion from Ps3.2 trillion, 34.1 percent for 2002 to Ps5.4 trillion from Ps8.2 trillion, and 40 percent for 2003 to Ps1.8 trillion from Ps3trillion.

8. Mexico has also likely bought back some other debts through open market purchase, but in undisclosed amounts.

9. At the supplemental auction, three-year dollar-indexed bond was priced to yield 14.39 percent for debt maturing in 2001 and 13.95 percent for debt maturing in 2002.

10. The yield of five-year dollar-indexed bond is calculated by using the interest rate, which is determined by the acceptance rate for 3-year dollar-indexed bond plus 50 basis points spreads.

Table A2.2 Multilateral debt relief agreements with commercial banks, January 1980–December 2001

	Consolidation period		Amount restructured (*millions of U.S. dollars*)		Other assistance (*millions of U.S. dollars*)		Repayment terms (*consolidation portion only*)		
Country and date of agreement	Start date	Length (*months*)	Deferment	Rescheduling	New long-term money	Short-term credit maintenance	Maturity (*years/ months*)	Grace (*years/ months*)	Interest (*margin*)
Albania									
July 1995	Debt buyback (see notes)								
Algeria									
February 1992	See notes			1,500			5–8/0	3/0	1½/1⅜
June 1995	March 1994			3,200			12/6–16	6/6	13/16
Argentina									
January 1983	1 January 1983	12			1,300		1/2	0/7	1¼
August 1983					500		4/6	3/0	2¼
August 1985	1 January 1982	48		9,777	3,593	3,100	10/0	3/0	1⅜
August 1987	See notes			24,286	1,253	3,500	19/0	7/0	13/16
April 1993	DDSR agreement (see notes)								
September 1997	Voluntary debt swap (see notes)								
Mar./Sept. 1998	Debt buyback (see notes)								
March 1999	Voluntary debt swap and debt buyback (see notes)								
Feb./June 2000	Voluntary debt swap (see notes)								
Feb./June/Aug. 2001	Voluntary debt swap (see notes)								
December 2001	Voluntary local debt swap (see notes)								
Bolivia									
December 1980	1 August 1980	8	200				1/0	1/0	1¾
April 1981	1 April 1981	24		411			6/0	3/0	2¼
July 1988	Buyback arrangement (see notes)								
July 1992	DDSR agreement (see notes)								
May 1993	Debt buyback (see notes)								
Bosnia and Hezegovina									
December 1997	Debt rescheduling (see notes)			1,300					
Brazil									
February 1983	1 January 1983	12		4,800	4,195	15,675	8/0	2/6	2¼
January 1984	1 January 1984	12		5,900	6,510	15,100	9/0	5/0	2
July 1986	1 January 1985	12	9,600	6,552		14,750	6/3	4/3	1¼
November 1988	1 January 1987	84		61,482	5,200	14,833	20/0	8/0	13/16
July 1992	Interest arrears end-1990 (see notes)								
April 1994	DDSR agreement (see notes)								
June 1997	Voluntary debt swap (see notes)								
Apr./Oct. 1999	Voluntary debt swap (see notes)								
Mar./July/Aug. 2000	Voluntary debt swap (see notes)								
March 2001	Voluntary local debt swap (see notes)								
Bulgaria									
July 1994	DDSR agreement (see notes)								
Chile									
July 1983	1 January 1983	24		2,151	1,294	1,700	8/0	4/0	2¼
January 1984	Short-term debt only			1,204			8/0	4/0	2¼
June 1984					785		9/0	5/0	1¾
November 1984						1,700	0/6	0/6	
November 1985	1 January 1985	36		3,891	1,037	1,700	12/0	6/0	1⅜
June 1987	1 January 1988	48		9,732		1,700	15/6	5/0	1
August 1988	Modification of terms (see notes)								13/16
December 1990	1 January 1991	48		4,173	320		8–12/0	4/0	13/16

(Table continues on next page)

Table A2.2 Multilateral debt relief agreements with commercial banks, January 1980–December 2000 *(continued)*

	Consolidation period		Amount restructured *(millions of U.S. dollars)*		Other assistance *(millions of U.S. dollars)*		Repayment terms *(consolidation portion only)*		
Country and date of agreement	Start date	Length *(months)*	Deferment	Rescheduling	New long-term money	Short-term credit maintenance	Maturity *(years/ months)*	Grace *(years/ months)*	Interest *(margin)*
Colombia									
December 1985					1,000		8/6	3/0	1½
June 1989					1,640		11/0	5/6	⅞
April 1991							12/6	7/6	1
June 2001	Voluntary debt swap (see notes)								
Congo, Rep. of									
October 1986*	See notes								
Costa Rica									
September 1983	1 January 1983	24		706	202	202	8/0	4/0	2¼
May 1985	1 January 1985	24		470	75		10/0	3/0	1⅝
May 1990	DDSR agreement (see notes)				1,457				
Côte d'Ivoire									
March 1985	1 December 1983	25		485	104		8/0	3/0	1⅞
November 1986	1 January 1986	48		851			9/0	3/0	1⅝
April 1988*	See notes								
May 1997	DDSR agreement (see notes)								
Cuba									
December 1983	1 September 1982	28		130		490	5/6	2/0	2¼
December 1984	1 January 1984	12		103		490	7/0	2/6	1⅞
July 1985	1 January 1985	12		90		490	10/0	6/0	1½
Dominican Republic									
December 1983	1 December 1982	13		500			5/0	1/0	2¼
February 1986	1 January 1985	60		787			13/0	3/0	1⅜
August 1994	DDSR agreement (see notes)								
Ecuador									
October 1983	1 November 1982	14		2,770	433	700	7/0	1/0	2¼
December 1985	1 January 1985	60		4,219	200	700	12/0	3/0	1⅜
November 1987*	See notes								
February 1995*	DDSR agreement (see notes)								
April 1997	Voluntary debt swap (see notes)								
August 2000	Debt rescheduling (see notes)								
Ethiopia									
January 1996	Debt buyback (see notes)								
Gabon									
December 1987	1 September 1986	16		27			10/0	4/6	1⅜
December 1991	1 January 1989	36		75			13/0	3/0	⅞
May 1994	10 July 1994	6		187			10/0	2/6	⅞
Gambia, The									
February 1988	Balance as of 18 December 1986				19		8/0	3/6	1¼
Guinea									
April 1988	Short-term debt only			28			3/0	0/6	1¾
December 1998	Debt buyback (see notes)								
Guyana									
August 1982	11 March 1982	13	14						2½
June 1983	1 July 1983	7	12						2½
July 1984	1 August 1984	12	11						2½
July 1985	1 August 1985	18	15						2½
July 1988			8						
November 1992	Debt buyback (see notes)								
December 1999	Debt buyback (see notes)								

Table A2.2 Multilateral debt relief agreements with commercial banks, January 1980–December 2000 *(continued)*

Country and date of agreement	Consolidation period		Amount restructured *(millions of U.S. dollars)*		Other assistance *(millions of U.S. dollars)*		Repayment terms *(consolidation portion only)*		
	Start date	Length *(months)*	Deferment	Rescheduling	New long-term money	Short-term credit maintenance	Maturity *(years/ months)*	Grace *(years/ months)*	Interest *(margin)*
Honduras									
June 1987*	1 April 1987	33		248			8/0	6/0	1⅛
August 1989	See notes			101					
August 2001	Debt buyback (see notes)								
Indonesia									
June 1998	Debt rescheduling (see notes)								
Iran, Islamic Rep. of									
March 1993	Balance as of March 1993			2,800			1/1	1/0	13/16
December 1994	Balance as of December 1994			10,900			6/0	2/0	13/16
Jamaica									
April 1981	1 April 1979	24		126			5/0	2/0	2
June 1981	1 July 1981	21		89	89		5/0	2/0	2
June 1984	1 July 1983	21		164			5/0	2/0	2½
September 1985	1 April 1985	24		359			10/0	3/0	1⅞
May 1987	1 January 1987	39		366			12/6	9/0	1¼
June 1990	1 January 1990	24		315			14/0	0/6	13/16
Jordan									
September 1989*	1 January 1989	30		580			11/0	5/0	13/16
November 1989*	1 January 1989	18			50	50	10/6	3/0	13/16
December 1993	See notes								
Year 2000	Debt buyback (see notes)								
Year 2001	Debt buyback (see notes)								
Korea, Republic of									
January 1998	Debt rescheduling (see notes)								
Liberia									
December 1982	1 July 1981	24		29			6/0	2/9	1¾
June 1983	See notes			26					
Madagascar									
November 1981	Arrears only			155			3/6	0/0	1½
October 1984	Entire stock of debt			379			8/0	2/6	2
June 1987	See notes						9/0	0/0	1⅝
May 1990*	1 April 1990	69		49			12/0	0/2	⅞
Malawi									
March 1983	1 September 1982	24		59			6/6	3/0	1⅞
October 1988	Balance as of 21 August 1987			36			8/0	4/0	1¼
Mauritania									
August 1996	Debt buyback (see notes)								

(Table continues on next page)

Table A2.2 Multilateral debt relief agreements with commercial banks, January 1980–December 2000 ***(continued)***

	Consolidation period		Amount restructured *(millions of U.S. dollars)*		Other assistance *(millions of U.S. dollars)*		Repayment terms *(consolidation portion only)*		
Country and date of agreement	Start date	Length *(months)*	Deferment	Rescheduling	New long-term money	Short-term credit maintenance	Maturity *(years/ months)*	Grace *(years/ months)*	Interest *(margin)*
Mexico									
August 1983	23 April 1982	28		23,280	5,007		8/0	4/0	1⅞
April 1984					3,873		10/0	5/6	1½
March 1985	1 January 1987	48		28,000			14/0	0/0	1¼
August 1985	1 January 1985	72		20,256			14/0	1/0	1¼
October 1985			950						
March 1987				44,216	7,439		20/0	7/0	13/16
August 1987	1 January 1988	48		9,700			20/0	7/0	13/16
March 1988	Debt exchange (see notes)								
March 1990	DDSR agreement (see notes)			48,231	1,091				
May/Sept. 1996	Voluntary debt swap (see notes)								
Aug./Oct. 1999	Voluntary debt swap (see notes)								
Mar./Sept./Oct./ Nov. 2000	Voluntary debt swap and debt buyback (see notes)								
Mar./May/Aug. 2001	Voluntary debt swap (see notes)								
Apr./May/Oct./Nov. 2001	Debt buyback (see notes)								
Morocco									
February 1986	9 September 1983	16		531		610	7/ 0	3/0	1¼
September 1987	1 January 1985	48		2,415			11/0	4/0	13/16
June 1990	Balance as of 31 December 1989			3,200			18/4	8/10	13/16
Mozambique									
May 1987	Entire stock of debt			253			15/0	8/0	1¼
December 1991	Debt buyback (see notes)								
Nicaragua									
December 1980	Arrears			582			12/0	5/0	¾
December 1981	See notes			192			12/0	5/0	¾
March 1982	See notes			100			12/0	5/0	¾
February 1984	1 July 1983	12		145			8/0	0/0	1¼
December 1995	Debt buyback (see notes)								
Niger									
March 1984	1 October 1983	29		29			7/6	3/6	2
April 1986	1 October 1985	39		36			8/6	4/0	2
March 1991	Debt buyback (see notes)			107					
Nigeria									
November 1987	1 April 1986	21		4,714			9/0	3/0	1¼
March 1989	Short-term debt only			5,671			20/0	3/0	⅞
January 1992	DDSR agreement (see notes)			5,436					
Panama									
September 1983					278	217	6/0	3/0	2¼
October 1985	1 January 1985	24		578	60	190	12/0	3/6	1⅜
May 1996	DDSR agreement (see notes)								
September 1997	Voluntary debt swap (see notes)								
July 2001	Debt buyback (see notes)								
Peru									
January 1980	1 January 1980	12		364			5/0	2/0	1¼
July 1983	7 March 1983	12		432	650	2,000	8/0	3/0	2¼
November 1996	DDSR agreement (see notes)								
Philippines									
January 1986	17 October 1983	38		5,885	925	2,974	10/0	5/0	1⅝
December 1987	1 January 1987	72		9,010		2,965	17/0	7/6	⅞
January 1990	DDSR agreement (see notes)			1,337	715				
December 1992	DDSR agreement (see notes)				135		17/0	5/0	13/16
September 1996	Voluntary debt swap (see notes)								
October 1999	Voluntary debt swap (see notes)								

Table A2.2 Multilateral debt relief agreements with commercial banks, January 1980–December 2000 ***(continued)***

Country and date of agreement	Consolidation period: Start date	Consolidation period: Length (*months*)	Amount restructured (*millions of U.S. dollars*): Deferment	Amount restructured: Rescheduling	Other assistance (*millions of U.S. dollars*): New long-term money	Other assistance: Short-term credit maintenance	Repayment terms (*consolidation portion only*): Maturity (*years/months*)	Repayment terms: Grace (*years/months*)	Repayment terms: Interest (*margin*)
Poland									
April 1982	26 March 1981	9		1,956			7/0	4/0	1¾
November 1982	1 January 1982	12		2,225			7/6	4/0	1¾
November 1983	1 January 1983	12		1,254			10/0	4/6	1⅞
July 1984	1 January 1984	48		1,480		335	10/0	5/0	1¾
September 1986	1 January 1986	24		1,940			5/0	5/0	1¾
July 1988	1 January 1988	72		8,310		1,000	15/0	0/0	15/16
June 1989*	1 May 1989	20	206						
October 1994	DDSR agreement (see notes)		206		138				
October 2000	Debt buyback (see notes)								
Romania									
December 1982	1 January 1982	12		1,598			6/5	3/0	1¾
June 1983	1 January 1983	12		567			6/5	3/6	1¾
September 1986	1 January 1986	24		800			5/6	4/0	1⅜
September 1987*	1 January 1986	24		800			5/6	4/0	13/16
Russian Federation									
December 1991	See notes								
July 1993	See notes								
November 1995	Balance as of 15 November 1995			32,500			25/0	7/0	13/16
November 1998	Debt restructuring (see notes)								
February 2000	Debt restructuring (see notes)								
São Tomé and Principe									
August 1994	Debt buyback (see notes)								
Senegal									
February 1984	1 May 1981	38		96			6/0	3/0	2
May 1985	1 July 1984	24		20			7/0	3/0	2
January 1989				37			9/0	0/0	⅞
December 1996	Debt buyback (see notes)								
Sierra Leone									
January 1984	Arrears (principal)			25			7/0	2/0	1¾
August 1995	Debt buyback (see notes)								
South Africa									
September 1985	28 August 1985	7	13,628						
March 1986	28 August 1985	22		650			1/3		bullet/variable
March 1987	1 July 1987	36		4,500			3/0		bullet/variable
October 1989	1 July 1990	42		7,500					
September 1993	See notes			5,000			8/0	0/6	1⅛
Sudan									
November 1981	1 January 1980	28		593			7/0	3/0	1¾
March 1982	Interest arrears only			3			0/9	0/5	1¾
April 1983	See notes			702			6/0	2/0	1¾
October 1985	See notes			1,037			8/0	3/0	1¼
Tanzania									
April 2001	Debt buyback (see notes)								
Togo									
March 1980	See notes			69			3/6	1/0	
October 1983	See notes			84			7/3	0/0	2
May 1988	See notes			48			8/0	4/0	1⅜
December 1997	Debt buyback (see notes)								
Trinidad and Tobago									
December 1989	1 September 1988	48		473			12/6	4/6	15/16

(Table continues on next page)

Table A2.2 Multilateral debt relief agreements with commercial banks, January 1980–December 2000 ***(continued)***

Country and date of agreement	Consolidation period: Start date	Consolidation period: Length (*months*)	Amount restructured (*millions of U.S. dollars*): Deferment	Amount restructured (*millions of U.S. dollars*): Rescheduling	Other assistance (*millions of U.S. dollars*): New long-term money	Other assistance (*millions of U.S. dollars*): Short-term credit maintenance	Repayment terms (*consolidation portion only*): Maturity (*years/ months*)	Repayment terms (*consolidation portion only*): Grace (*years/ months*)	Repayment terms (*consolidation portion only*): Interest (*margin*)
Turkey									
March 1982	See notes			2,269			10/0	5/0	1¾
June 2001	Voluntary debt swap (see notes)								
Uganda									
February 1993	Debt buyback (see notes)								
Ukraine									
September 1998	Debt restructuring (see notes)								
July 1999	Debt restructuring (see notes)								
February 2000	Debt restructuring (see notes)								
March 2001	Debt restructuring (see notes)								
Uruguay									
July 1983	1 January 1983	24		555	240		6/0	2/0	2¼
July 1986	1 January 1985	60		1,720			12/0	3/0	1⅜
March 1988	1 January 1990	24		1,512			17/0	3/0	⅞
February 1991	DDSR agreement (see notes)			1,284	89				
September 1999	Voluntary debt swap (see notes)								
Venezuela, República Bolivariana de									
February 1986	1 January 1983	72		21,089			12/6	0/0	1⅛
November 1987	See notes				100		14/0	1/0	⅞
September 1988	See notes			20,388			13/0	0/0	⅞
December 1988	See notes								
December 1990	DDSR agreement (see notes)			19,598	1,212				
September 1997	Voluntary debt swap (see notes)								
Vietnam									
December 1997	DDSR agreement (see notes)								
Yemen, Rep. of									
June 2001	Voluntary debt swap (see notes)								
Yugoslavia, Fed. Rep. of									
October 1983	1 January 1983	12		1,300	600	800	6/0	3/0	1⅞
May 1984	1 January 1984	24		1,330			7/0	4/0	1⅝
December 1985	1 January 1985	48		4,004			10/6	4/0	1¼
September 1988	1 January 1988	24		7,000		300	18/0	6/0	13/16
Zaire									
April 1980	See notes			402			10/0	5/0	1⅞
January 1983	1 January 1983	12	58				10/0	0/0	2
June 1984	1 January 1984	16	64				10/0	0/0	2
May 1985	1 May 1985	12	61				10/0	0/0	2
May 1986	1 May 1986	12	65				10/0	0/0	2
May 1987	1 May 1987	12	61				10/0	0/0	2
June 1989	See notes		61						
Zambia									
December 1984	1 January 1985			74					
September 1994	Debt buyback (see notes)								

* Agreement in principle.

Note: Deferment = Short-term rollover of current maturities. *MYRA* = Multiyear rescheduling agreement. *New money* = Loans arranged for budgetary or balance of payments support in conjunction with debt rescheduling, usually in proportion to each creditor bank's exposure; sometimes referred to as concerted lending. *Rescheduling* = Consolidation of debt into new long-term obligations; may include arrears as well as future maturities; interest and short-term debt included only if indicated in country notes. For DDSR agreements, figures include face value of buybacks and of all debt exchanges. *Short-term credit maintenance* = Understanding by banks to maintain the size of existing trade or other short-term credit facilities, arranged in conjunction with debt rescheduling. *Interest (margin)* = percentage points above LIBOR. *DDSR* = Officially supported debt and debt service reduction agreement (Brady initiative).

Country notes

Albania

July 1995: Restructuring of US$501 million due to commercial banks. US$371 million bought back for US$96.5 million funded by grants from IDA debt reduction facility and other donor countries, and US$130 million converted into long-term bonds.

Algeria

Feb. 1992: 1991–93 Financing Facility, designed to refinance maturities falling due from October 1991 through March 1993. Tranche A covers debts with a maturity of two years or more and is repayable in eight years, including three years' grace bearing interest at LIBOR + 1½ percent. Tranche B covers debts with a maturity of more than 360 days and less than two years, and is repayable in five years, including three years' grace.

Argentina

Jan. 1983: Bridge loan.

Aug. 1983: New money, initially US$1.5 billion.

Aug. 1985: Agreed in principle in December 1984.

Aug. 1987: Agreement extended the maturity and lowered the spreads on the 1983 and 1985 agreements. Also includes a noncollateralized debt exchange with interest reduction (US$15 million).

April 1993: DDSR agreement: Outstanding stock of US$19.3 billion exchanged either for 30-year bonds yielding a market interest rate (LIBOR + $^{13}/_{16}$ percent) at a 35 percent discount or for 30-year par front-loaded interest rate reduction bonds. First year interest rate 4 percent, rising to 6 percent in year seven and remaining there until maturity. Both bonds collateralized for principal and contain rolling 12-month guarantees. Agreement also included US$9.3 billion of past-due interest: US$0.7 billion was paid in cash at closing, US$400 million were written off, and the remainder was exchanged for bonds (17-year maturity; 7 years' grace), repayable in rising installments and yielding LIBOR + $^{13}/_{16}$ percent.

Sept. 1997: Argentina swapped $2.4 billion of Brady bonds for $1.8 billion of uncollateralized 30-year bonds at an interest rate of 305 basis points above the U.S. Treasury rate. The offering allowed for direct exchange and cash sales of Brady bonds.

Mar./Sept. 1998: In March, Argentina bought back $760 million of Brady bonds, consisting of $645 million of par bonds and $115 million of discount bonds. In September, Argentina bought back $700 million of Brady bonds at nominal value.

Mar. 1999: Argentina swapped $129 million of Brady bonds, $84.1 million of discount bonds, and $45 million of par bonds for $106 million of Argentine Bonte bonds maturing in 2027 and exchangeable later for 30-year global bonds. Argentina also bought back $539 million of Brady bonds, $104 million of discount bonds, and $435 million of par bonds through open market purchase.

Feb./June 2000: In February, Argentina swapped $1.4 billion of Brady bonds for $3.5 billion of Argentine Bonte bonds maturing in 2003 and 2005 in a local bond exchange. In June, Argentina swapped $3.3 billions of Brady bonds for $2.4 billion of new 15-year global bonds. The new issue carried a coupon of 13.3 percent.

Feb. 2001: Swapping $4.8 billion of peso- and U.S. dollar-denominated debt for a new $2.6 billion Bonte (Treasury bond) due 2006 and a new $1.6 billion Global bond due 2012. $2.9 billion of bonds was converted into new 5-year Bonte, and $1.9 billion of bonds was converted into new 11-year global bond.

June 2001: Argentina exchanged about $29.5 billion of domestic and external bonds with $30.4 billion (face value) of five new bonds including $11.5 billion of 2008 dollar bond, $7.5 billion of 2018 dollar bond, $8.5 billion of 2031 dollar bond, Ps 931 million of 2008 peso bond, and Ps 2.03 billion of promissory note due 2006.

Aug. 2001: About $1.4 billion of Treasury securities were exchanged for a combination of 1-year and 3-year bond.

Dec. 2001: About $50 billion of domestic debts—$41 billion in federal debt and $9 billion in provincial debt—were exchanged for a new lower coupon loans guaranteed by tax collection. The new loans extended maturities of all debt due before 2010 by three years and lowered the interest rates by at least 30 percent lower than original bond.

Bolivia

Dec. 1980: Includes short-term debt.

April 1981: Includes debt deferred in August 1980.

July 1988: Commercial bank debt retired through a buyback (US$272 million) and a local currency bond exchange (US$72 million). An ongoing program. Applies only to previously deferred loans.

July 1992: DDSR term sheet. Cash buyback at 84 percent discount; collateralized interest-free 30-year bullet-maturity par bonds; short-term discount bonds (84 percent) convertible on maturity into local currency assets at a 1:1.5 ratio, exchangeable into investments for special projects. Past-due interest canceled under all options. Value recovery clause based on price of tin.

May 1993: Buyback of US$170 million commercial bank debt, funded by grants from IDA debt reduction facility and other donor countries.

Bosnia and Herzegovina

Dec. 1997: Agreement to restructure $1,300 million of principal and past-due interest owed to commercial banks under the aegis of the London Club. Past-due interest of $700 million was written off. Eligible principal of $600 million was exchanged for $400 million of uncollateralized discount bonds. The tenor of 37.5 percent of the new bonds is 20 years' maturity, including seven years' grace and stepped-up interest rates rising from 2 percent in years one to four to LIBOR + $^{13}/_{16}$ in years 11–20. Servicing on 62.5 percent of the new bonds is linked to economic performance. The country is not required to make principal or interest payments for the first 10 years. After that, the country is required to make debt service payments if per capita income exceeds $2,800 for two consecutive years. Per capita income in 1997 was estimated at $1,079.

Brazil

July 1986: Includes deferment of 1986 maturities.

Nov. 1988: Includes a broad package of creditor options.

July 1992: Interest arrears: December 31, 1990. Cash payment during 1992: US$863 million. When term sheet concludes for long-term debt, the balance was converted into 10-year bonds (three years' grace), bearing market interest rates.

(Notes continue on next page)

Apr. 1994: DDSR agreement: Four components of debt totaling US$48 billion were restructured: (a) debt to foreign banks under the 1988 multiyear deposit facility agreement (US$32.5 billion), (b) debt to Brazilian banks under the MDFA, (c) debt resulting from the 1988 new money facilities (US$8.1 billion), and (d) interest arrears accruing from 1991–94 (US$6 billion). The first category of debt was restructured following a six-choice menu: (1) discount bonds, 35 percent discount, 30-year bullet maturity yielding LIBOR + $^{13}/_{16}$ percent with principal collateral and a 12-month rolling interest guarantee (US$11.2 billion); (2) par bonds with a reduced fixed-rate interest (yielding 4 percent in the first year and gradually rising to 6 percent in year seven), 30-year bullet maturity, also with principal collateral and a 12-month rolling interest guarantee. (US$10.5 billion); (3) front-loaded interest reduction bonds (US$1.7 billion), with interest rising from a fixed rate of 4 percent in year one to 6 percent in years five and six and then reverting to LIBOR + $^{13}/_{16}$ percent from year seven to maturity, 15 years maturity including nine years grace, 12-month rolling interest guarantee; (4) C-bonds, par reduced interest rate bonds with capitalization of interest (US$7.1 billion), with repayment terms of 20 years' maturity including 10 years' grace, interest beginning at 4 percent and the applicable rates in the first six years being capitalized, no collateral; (5) conversion bonds (US$1.9 billion) combined with new money bonds in a 1:5.5 ratio, interest is LIBOR + $^{7}/_{8}$ percent, terms are 18 years' maturity including 10 years' grace for the conversion bonds and 15 years including seven years' grace for the new money bonds, no collateral; (6) interest reduction loan with capitalization, maturity of 20 years including 10 years' grace, interest rising from 4 percent in year one to 5 percent in year six to LIBOR + $^{13}/_{16}$ percent from year seven to maturity.

June 1997: Brazil completed a $3 billion 30-year bond offering involving $0.8 billion cash sale and $2.3 billion exchange for $2.7 billion of Brady bonds. The new issue carries an interest rate of 395 basis points above the U.S. Treasury rate.

Apr./Oct. 1999: In April, Brazil completed a $3 billion, five-year global bond offering involving $2 billion cash sale and $1 billion exchange for $1.5 billion of Brady bonds, consisting of $1,046 million of eligible interest bonds (EIs) and $406 million of interest due and unpaid bonds (IDUs). In October, Brazil issued $2 billion 10-year global bonds in exchange for $2.7 billion of Brady bonds. The new issue carries a coupon of 14.5 percent or 850 basis points over the U.S. Treasury rates.

Mar./July/ Aug. 2000: Buyback of $705 million of Brady bonds using the proceeds from $600 million 30-year global bonds in March. In July, Brazil issued a new $1 billion seven-year global bond involving $612 million cash sales and $388 million exchange for $400 million of Brady bonds. In August, Brazil completed the largest-ever emerging market bond swap with the issue of $5.16 billion 40-year global bonds with a coupon of 11 percent. This swap operation retired $5.22 billion of Brady bonds.

Mar. 2001: Exchange of Brady bonds for a new $2.15 billion of global bond due in 2024. Brady bonds exchanged for the new global bond included $682 million of par bonds, $1.2 billion of discount bonds, $212 million of C-bonds, and $47 million of Debt Conversion bonds (DCBs).

Bulgaria

July 1994: DDSR agreement: Creditors agreed to restructuring of US$8.3 billion in public external debt, including about US$2.1 billion in past-due interest. The menu for the original debt includes: (a) buyback at 0.25 cents per U.S. dollar (US$0.8 billion); (b) discount bond 50 percent discount on face value (30 years' bullet maturity, market rate, US$3.7 billion); the discount bonds are collateralized for principal; and (c) FLIRBs, 18 years' maturity, eight years' grace interest beginning at 2 percent, rising to 3 percent in the seventh year, and thereafter LIBOR + $^{13}/_{16}$ percent (US$1.7 billion). The FLIRBs have one year's interest rolling interest guarantee. Past-due interest includes cash payment of about 3 percent, a buy-back (US$.2 billion), write-off of US$0.2 billion, and past-due interest par bonds (US$1.6 billion) having a 17 years' maturity, including seven years' grace and yield LIBOR + $^{13}/_{16}$ percent.

Chile

Jan. 1984: Short-term debt consolidated.

Nov. 1984: Short-term debt rolled over to June 30, 1985.

Nov. 1985: Short-term trade credit rolled over to 1990.

Aug. 1988: Interest spread reduced to $^{13}/_{16}$ percent. Also cash buybacks (US$439 million).

Dec. 1990: New money bonds not tied to existing banks' exposure. The rescheduling includes previously rescheduled debt.

Colombia

Dec. 1985: New money without restructuring.

June 1989: New money without restructuring.

April 1991: New money without restructuring.

June 2001: Swapping $2.5 billion (Ps5.6 trillion) of domestic debts for 3-year, 5-year, and 10-year Treasury notes. About 54 percent of debt was converted into 10-year note (Ps3 trillion). A further 32 percent of debt was exchanged for 3-year note (Ps1.8 trillion) and the remaining 14 percent was converted into 5-year note (Ps0.8 trillion).

Congo, Republic of

Oct. 1986: Agreement in principle, never concluded. It was to restructure 1986–88 maturities, repayable in nine years, including three years' grace, bearing interest at LIBOR + $^{7}/_{8}$ percent. Approximately US$200 million of debt would have been restructured. In addition there was a new money provision of US$60 million.

Costa Rica

Sept. 1983: Includes principal arrears.

May 1985: Includes deferment of revolving credit (US$2 million).

May 1990: DDSR agreement: cash buyback at 84 percent discount (US$992 million), debt-for-bond exchange (US$579 million), and write-off of US$29 million of past-due interest.

Côte d'Ivoire

Nov. 1986: MYRA.

Apr. 1988: Agreement designed to replace the MYRA. Includes new money to refinance interest. Interest on the new money portion was LIBOR + 1½ percent. Agreement was not put into effect because interest arrears were not cleared, and current interest payments were suspended in April 1988.

May 1997: DDSR agreement restructuring $6.5 billion of principal and past-due interest. For eligible principal of $2,271.5

million, creditors agreed to exchange US$159 million for discount bonds (50 percent discount) subject to stepped-up interest rising from 2.5 percent in years one and two to LIBOR + 13/16 percent in years 11–30; exchange $1,431 million for front-loaded interest reduction bonds (FLIRBs) with a maturity of 20 years, including 10 years' grace, and stepped-up interest rising from 2 percent in years one to seven to LIBOR + 13/16 percent in years 14–20; and buy back $681.5 million at 24 cents per dollar. Principal is collateralized with 30-year U.S. Treasury zero-coupon bonds for the discount bonds, but not for the FLIRBs. A six-month rolling interest guarantee is required for the FLIRBs, but not for the discount bonds. For past-due interest of $4,190.3 million, $30 million was settled in cash at closing, $867 million was exchanged for bonds with a 20-year maturity (half a year of grace period) repayable on a graduated amortization schedule, and $3,293 million was written off.

Dominican Republic
Dec. 1983: Includes short-term debt.
Feb. 1986: MYRA. Includes arrears as of December 31, 1984.
Aug. 1994: DDSR agreement covering principal and past-due interest (US$1.2 billion). The agreement has a menu consisting of (1) buybacks (US$.4 billion); (2) discount exchange bonds (US$.5 billion) 35 percent discount, to be repaid in 30 years, bullet maturity, interest rate LIBOR + 13/16 percent; (3) past-due interest bonds (US$171 million) bearing interest at LIBOR + 13/16 percent, with three years' grace and 15 years' maturity. The accord also included a write-off of US$112 million of past-due interest, and US$52 million paid in cash at closing.

Ecuador
Dec. 1985: MYRA.
Nov. 1987: Replaces the MYRA.
Feb. 1995: DDSR agreement, restructuring US$7.8 billion of principal and past-due interest. For principal, creditors agreed to exchange US$2.6 billion for discount bonds (45 percent discount) yielding LIBOR + 13/16 percent and US$1.9 billion for par reduced-interest rate bonds. Both bonds have a 30-year bullet maturity and are collateralized for principal and have a 12-month rolling interest guarantee. The interest rate on the par bonds is 3 percent for the first year, rising to 5 percent in year 11. US$75 billion on past-due interest is to be settled in cash at closing, US$2.3 billion was exchanged for bonds with a 20-year maturity (no grace period) repayable on a graduated amortization schedule, US$191 million was exchanged for interest equalization bonds, and US$582 million was written off.
Apr. 1997: In April, Ecuador issued $150 million in Eurobonds to buy $214 million of Brady bonds. The principal amount is due at maturity in 2004 and carries an interest rate of 475 basis points above the U.S. Treasury rates. The $50 million saved from the release of collateral was applied toward clearance of debt service arrears with Paris Club creditors.
Aug. 2000: Agreement to exchange about $5.9 billion in defaulted Brady bonds and Eurobonds for $3.95 billion in new 12- and 30-year global bonds. The new 12-year issue was priced to yield 12 percent, and the new 30-year issue carried a multicoupon with the initial coupon rate

of 4 percent. This operation resulted in a 40 percent reduction in principal for the bondholders.

Ethiopia
Jan. 1996: Debt buyback at 8 cents per U.S. dollar of US$226 million owed to commercial banks. Funding for the operation was provided by the IDA debt reduction facility.

Gabon
May 1994: Rescheduled principal due through 1994 on debt contracted prior to September 20, 1986 (debt covered by the 1991 agreement, which had not been implemented). Terms: 10-year maturity including two and a half years' grace. Interest: LIBOR + 7/8 percent. Arrears of interest and arrears of post cut-off maturities as of July 1, 1994, were to be repaid between 1994 and 1996.

Guinea
Dec. 1998: Buyback of US$130 million under the IDA debt reduction facility (DRF) at 13 cents per U.S. dollar, financed by the IDA DRF and other donor countries.

Guyana
Aug. 1982: One-year deferment.
June 1983: Extension of 1982 deferment.
July 1984: Extension of previous deferment.
July 1985: Extension of previous deferment.
Nov. 1992: Buyback of US$69 million under the IDA DRF at 14 cents per U.S. dollar.
Dec. 1999: Buyback of US$55.9 million under the IDA debt reduction facility at 9 cents per U.S. dollar, financed by the IDA DRF and the Swiss government.

Honduras
June 1987: Two agreements, in 1983 and 1984, were not implemented; this agreement incorporated 1981–85 maturities, but it was not signed.
Aug. 1989: Bilateral rescheduling of debt to two commercial banks. The agreement includes interest arrears. The grace period varied from 7 to 10 years. Interest rates were fixed, ranging from 4 to 6.5 percent.
Aug. 2001: Buyback of $13 million under the IDA debt reduction facility. The buyback price was set at 18 cents per dollar of the principal amount. The IDA and the governments of the Netherlands, Norway, and Switzerland provided funding for the operation.

Indonesia
June 1998: Agreement on a framework for restructuring $80.2 billion of the Indonesian private debt. The interbank loans are extended into new government-guaranteed loans with maturities of one to four years, at interest rates of 2.75, 3, 3.25, and 3.5 percent over LIBOR. The corporate debts are to be rescheduled over eight years, including a three-year grace period for repayment of principal. Over an eight-year rescheduling period, the real interest rate was set to be 5.5 percent, but it would decline to 5 percent for debtors who agree to repay in five years. Agreed to pay off trade financing arrears to maintain trade financing from foreign creditor banks.

Jamaica
May 1987: Includes reduced spreads on earlier agreements.

(Notes continue on next page)

June 1990: Agreement also includes a reduction of spreads on earlier agreements to 13/16 percent.

Jordan

Dec. 1993: DDSR agreement restructuring US$736 million of principal and US$153 million of past-due interest (PDI). For restructured principal, a small amount was repurchased at 39 cents per U.S. dollar, US$243 million was exchanged for discount bonds (35 percent discount), and US$493 million was exchanged for par fixed interest bonds. Both bonds have a 30-year bullet maturity with principal collateral and a six-month rolling interest guarantee. The discount bonds yield LIBOR + 13/16 percent interest; the yields on par bonds begin at 4 percent in the first year, rising to 6 percent in year seven. Regarding PDI, US$29 million was paid at closing, US$91 million was exchanged for noncollateralized bonds with a 12-year maturity including three years' grace and yielding LIBOR + 13/16 percent, and US$33 million was written off. Upfront costs totaled US$147 million, all of which was provided from Jordan's own resources.

Year 2000: Jordan bought back $115 million of Brady par bonds at an average price of 70 cents per dollar of face value and $200 million of Brady discount bonds at an average price of 80 cents per dollar of face value. All purchases freed up 30 cents of principal and interest collateral per dollar of face value.

Year 2001: Through six buyback operations, Jordan retired $44 million of its outstanding Brady par bonds. Brady bonds were bought back at an average price of 78.8 cents per dollar of face value.

Korea, Republic of

Jan. 1998: Agreement to restructure the short-term foreign debts owed to foreign commercial banks. Eligible short-term debt of $24 billion is converted into new government-guaranteed loans with maturities of between one and three years and floating interest rates set between 2.25 and 2.75 percentage points over LIBOR. Regarding the government guarantee, the commission to be charged is set between 0.2 and 1.5 percentage points based on the credit rating given by Moody's Investors Service or by Standard & Poor's, and the Bank for International Settlements' capital adequacy ratio. A reserve requirement of 3 percent of the total guaranteed amount in U.S. dollars was set.

Liberia

June 1983: Consolidation of oil facility debt.

Madagascar

Nov. 1981: Arrears on overdrafts consolidated into long-term debt.

Oct. 1984: Restructuring entire stock of debt, including arrears.

June 1987: Modified the terms of the October 1984 agreement.

Malawi

Oct. 1988: Rescheduled balances as of August 21, 1987.

Mauritania

Aug. 1996: Debt buyback of US$53 million, at a 90 percent discount, owed to commercial banks. Funding for the operation was provided by the IDA debt reduction facility.

Mexico

Mar. 1985: MYRA covering previously rescheduled debt.

Aug. 1985: MYRA covering debt not previously rescheduled.

Oct. 1985: Deferment of first payment under the March 1985 agreement.

Mar. 1987: Modification of terms of earlier agreements.

Aug. 1987: Private sector debt restructured.

Mar. 1988: Exchange of debt for 20-year zero-coupon collateralized bonds (US$556 million).

Mar. 1990: DDSR agreement. In addition to new money of US$1 billion, the agreement provided for the exchange of US$20.5 billion of debt for bonds at a 35 percent discount, an exchange of US$22.4 billion of debt at par for reduced interest rate bonds, and conversion bonds totaling US$5.3 billion. The last are not collateralized and have a tenor of 15 years maturity, including seven years' grace, and an interest rate of LIBOR + 13/16 percent. The total base also includes US$693 million not committed to any option.

May/Sept. 1996: On May 7, Mexico swapped $2.4 billion in Brady bonds for a $1.8 billion 30-year uncollateralized bond at an interest rate of 11.5 percent. On September 24, Mexico bought back $1.2 billion of Brady bonds at a cost of 81 cents per dollar. This operation was funded by a $1 billion 20-year bond at an interest rate of 445 basis points above U.S. Treasury rates.

Aug./Oct. 1999: Buyback of $510 million of Brady bonds in exchange for $400 million of new 17-year global bonds at an interest rate of 445 basis points above the U.S. Treasury rate in August. In October, Mexico issued $425 million of 10-year global bonds in exchange for about $525 million face value of Brady bonds, $275 million of par bonds, and $250 million of discount bonds. The new offering carries a coupon of 10.2 percent or 385 basis points over the U.S. Treasury rate.

Mar./Sept./ Oct./Nov. 2000: Two buyback operations to retire $1 billion of Brady bonds in March. Buyback of $150 million of Swiss franc–denominated 30-year Brady bonds at a 22 percent discount plus any accrued and unpaid interest in September. Buyback of $1 billion of Brady bonds denominated in European currencies (Dutch guilders, French francs, Italian lire, and German marks) in October. Buyback of $385 million of Brady bonds by exercising the embedded call options in November.

Mar. 2001: About $3.3 billion of Brady bonds (pars and discounts) were exchanged for new 18-year global bond with a yield of 9.3 percent. This operation generated about $115 million of net present value savings and freed up roughly $1.5 billion in collateral.

April 2001: Buyback of about $10 million (NLG31.3 million) of Dutch guilder–denominated Brady discount bonds.

May 2001: Swapping $1.05 billion of Brady bonds (pars and discounts) for $1 billion of global bond through a reopening of 10-year global bond issued in January 2001. The transaction realized about $60 million of net present value saving and released $475 million of underlying collateral.
The Mexican government also bought back around $15 million (JPY1.73 billion) of Japanese yen–denominated Brady discount bonds by exercising the embedded call options.

Aug. 2001: The new issuance of a $1.5 billion, 30-year global bond involving a $1.06 billion cash sale and a $440 million exchange for outstanding Brady bonds. Brady swap operation realized about $10 million of net present value savings and liberated $200 million of collateral.

Oct. 2001: Buyback of around $300 million of Brady discount bonds and $100 million (CAD162 million) of Canadian dollar–denominated Brady discount bonds.

Dec. 2001: Buyback of about $400 million (FRF3 billion) of French franc–denominated Brady par bonds.

Morocco

Feb. 1986: Agreement in principle initiated August 1983.

Sept. 1990: Phase one of this agreement restructures debt; phase two is a DDSR arrangement that will take effect if Morocco has signed an EFF (extended fund facility) agreement with the IMF by December 31, 1991.

Mozambique

May 1987: Outstanding balance consolidated, including interest arrears.

Dec. 1991: Buyback of US$124 million of outstanding commercial bank debt at a 90 percent discount, funded by grants from the IDA debt reduction facility and from France, the Netherlands, Sweden, and Switzerland.

Nicaragua

Dec. 1980: Covers government debt, all maturities, including arrears.

Dec. 1981: Covers nationalized bank debts, all maturities, including arrears.

Mar. 1982: Covers debts of nonfinancial enterprises, all maturities, including arrears.

Feb. 1984: Deferment of service on rescheduled debt.

Dec. 1995: Buyback of US$1.1 billion of outstanding commercial bank debt at 8 cents per U.S. dollar.

Niger

Mar. 1991: Buyback of all commercial bank debt at 82 percent discount (US$107 million). Resources provided by grants from the debt reduction facility for IDA-only countries (US$10 million), France (US$10 million), and Switzerland (US$3 million).

Nigeria

Nov. 1987: Includes short-term debt.

Mar. 1989: Includes line of credit arrears.

Jan. 1992: DDSR agreement providing for a cash-back at 60 percent discount on US$3.3 billion, and debt exchanges on US$2 billion for collateralized 30-year bullet maturity par bonds with reduced interest rates: 5.5 percent for the first three years, 6.25 percent thereafter. Creditor selections: 62 percent for the buyback; 38 percent for the debt-reduction bond. A third option, new money combined with conversion bonds, was not selected by participating creditor banks.

Panama

May 1996: DDSR agreement: Creditors agreed to restructuring of US$3.9 billion in public external debt, including US$2 billion in past-due interest (PDI). The menu for the principal includes: (a) discount bonds at a 45 percent discount of face value (30 years' bullet maturity, market rate, US$87.8 million); (b) par bonds with reduced interest rates and a 30-year bullet repayment (268 million); and (c) front-loaded interest reduction bonds (FLIRBs) for US$1,612.2 million with a tenor of 18 years' maturity including a five-year grace period. The discount and the par bonds are collateralized with respect to the principal by U.S. Treasury zero-coupon bonds, and with respect to interest in the form of a nine-month rolling interest rate guarantee in the first year rising to 12 months in two to three years. The FLIRBs do not require a guarantee for the capital, but include a six-month rolling interest guarantee. PDI settlement includes progress payments of US$30 million, a payment at closing of US$100 million, a write-off of US$590.4 million arising from the recalculation of penalty interest at a lower interest rate, and PDI par

bonds of US$1,247.6 million with 20 years' maturity, including seven years' grace, and an interest rate of LIBOR + $^{13}\!/_{16}$ percent. Neither principal nor interest is guaranteed. Moreover, Panama may capitalize for the first six years, and the difference is positive between LIBOR + $^{13}\!/_{16}$ and 4.0 percent per year.

Sept. 1997: Panama completed $600 million offering of 30-year uncollateralized bonds for $713 million of Brady bonds. The new issue carries an interest rate of 250 basis points above the U.S. Treasury rate. Nominal savings of about $132 million resulted from the differential between the Brady bonds' par and market values ($112 million) and from the pro rata release of the collateral of the Brady bonds ($20 million).

July 2001: Buyback of $160 million of global bond due 2002 using the proceeds from a reopening of a $750 million global bond issued in February 2001. The government offered participating bondholders a cash payment of $1,039 per $1,000 of face value as well as two warrants allowing investors to exercise an option to buy new 10-year global bonds to be issued in January 2002 for $990 in cash.

Peru

Nov. 1996: DDSR agreement: Creditors agreed to restructuring of US$8 billion in public external debt, including US$3.8 billion in past-due interest (PDI). The menu for the principal includes: (a) discount bonds at a 45 percent discount of face value (30 years' bullet maturity, market rate, US$947 million); (b) par bonds with reduced interest rates and a 30-year bullet repayment (US$189 million); (c) front-loaded interest reduction bonds (FLIRBs) for US$1,779 million with a tenor of 20 years' maturity including an eight-year grace period; and (d) a buyback of US$1,266 million at 38 cents per U.S. dollar. The discount and the par bonds are collateralized with respect to the principal by U.S. Treasury zero-coupon bonds, and with respect to interest in the form of a six-month rolling interest rate guarantee secured by cash or permitted investments. The FLIRBs do not require a guarantee for the capital, but they include a six-month rolling interest guarantee. PDI settlement includes progress payments of US$83 million, a payment at closing of US$225 million—a buyback of US$1,217 million at 38 cents per U.S. dollar, and PDI par bonds of US$2,284 million with 20 years' maturity, including 10 years' grace, and an interest rate of LIBOR + $^{13}\!/_{16}$ percent. Neither principal nor interest is guaranteed. Moreover, Peru may capitalize for the first six years, and the difference is positive between LIBOR + $^{13}\!/_{16}$ percent and 4 percent per year.

Philippines

Jan. 1990: DDSR agreement provided for US$1,337 million of buybacks at a 50 percent discount.

Dec. 1992: DDSR agreement: Following implementation of a cash buyback of US$1.3 billion on May 14, 1992, banks selected debt exchanges from three options: (1) front-loaded interest reduction par bonds; yielding LIBOR + $^{13}\!/_{16}$ percent from year seven to maturity (15 years for series A and 15½ years for series B, both including seven years' grace); (2) collateralized step-down/step-up interest reduction bonds yielding 6.5 percent from year six to maturity (25-year bullet maturity for series A and 25½-year for series B); and (3) new money combined with conversion bonds in a 1:4 ratio, with both bonds

(Notes continue on next page)

attaining 17½- (series A) or 17-year (series B) maturity, including five years' grace and yielding LIBOR + ¹³⁄₁₆ percent. Interest payments on both interest reduction bonds covered by a rolling 14-month guarantee. Creditor choices (total US$4.4 billion, 96 percent total eligible debt): buybacks, US$1.3 billion (27.5 percent): option (a) US$0.8 billion (46.3 percent); option (b) US$1.9 billion (41.1 percent); option (c) US$0.5 billion (11.7 percent).

Sept. 1996: The Philippines issued $0.7 billion in Eurobonds in exchange for Brady bonds originally issued to replace commercial bank debt in 1989. The Eurobond was issued in the form of a 20-year note at an interest rate of 8.75 percent.

Oct. 1999: The Philippines completed a $1,006 million, 25-year global bond offering involving $292 million cash sales and $714 million exchange for $858 million of Brady bonds. The new issue carries a semiannual coupon of 9.5 percent to yield 318 basis points above the U.S. Treasury rate.

Poland

July 1984: Includes some short-term trade credits.

Sept. 1986: Covers debt rescheduled in 1982.

July 1988: MYRA. Also improved the terms of earlier agreements.

June 1989: Principal due May 1989—December 1990 deferred until December 1991; and in October, the interest due in the fourth quarter of 1989, US$145 million, was deferred until the second quarter of 1990.

Oct. 1994: DDSR agreement. Creditors restructured US$14.4 billion. Three categories of debt were affected: (a) long-term debt covered by the 1988 restructuring agreement (US$8.9 billion), (b) debt due under the Revolving Short-Term Arrangement (RSTA) (US$1.2 billion), (c) past-due interest not otherwise restructured (US$4.3 billion). The first category was subject to a menu approach: US$2.1 billion of long-term debt was repurchased at 41 cents per U.S. dollar, and US$0.3 billion of RSTA debt was repurchased at 38 cents per U.S. dollar. For the remaining long-term debt, creditors chose between: (1) discount bonds—45 percent discount (US$5.4 billion), (2) par reduced fixed interest bonds (US$0.9 billion), (3) conversion bonds combined with new money bonds equal to 35 percent of the amount converted (US$0.4 billion). The discount bonds and par bonds have 30-year bullet maturities and feature collateralization of principal only. Interest on the discount bonds is LIBOR + ½ percent. Interest on the par bonds is 2.75 percent for the first year, rising to 5 percent for year 21. The conversion bonds have a 25-year maturity, including a 20-year grace period. Their yield in year one is 4.5 percent, rising to 7.5 percent in year 11. The new money bonds have a 15-year maturity, including a 10-year grace period and yield LIBOR + 1½ percent. The new money and conversion bonds are not collateralized.

The RSTA debt not repurchased (US$0.9 billion) is exchanged for 30-year bullet maturity fixed interest bonds, with similar (but slightly different) step-down/step-up arrangements as the par bonds, starting at 2.75 percent in year one and gradually rising to 5 percent in year 21.

For PDI, US$8 billion was repurchased with related long-term and RSTA principal. A portion is to be settled with cash payments at closing (US$63 million). A portion was written off (US$0.8 billion), and the remainder (US$2.7 billion), was converted into fixed-interest-rate bonds yielding 3.25 percent in year one, rising to 7 per-

cent in year nine. Maturity is 20 years, including seven years of grace. Amortization is graduated.

Oct. 2000: Buyback of $943 million of Brady bonds, $138 million of 15-year new money bonds, and $805 million of discount bonds. This buyback operation was financed by the receipt of hard currency earning from the privatization of telecommunications company TPSA to a consortium led by France Telecom.

Romania

Sept. 1986: Covers previously rescheduled debt only.

Russian Federation

Dec. 1991: Deferment of principal due in December 1991—March 1992 on pre-1991 debt. The deferment was extended for each consecutive quarter until the end of 1993.

July 1993: Reschedule the stock of former Soviet Union debt contracted prior to January 1, 1991 (US$24 billion), to be repaid with 15-year maturity including a five-year grace period. In the fourth quarter of 1993, US$500 million was to be paid on interest accruing during 1993. At the end of 1993, all remaining unpaid interest (estimated at $3 billion) was to then be consolidated and repaid at a 10-year maturity, including five years' grace. The 1993 interest payments were not made; the agreement was not implemented, mainly because Russia refused to accept the bankers' requirement that sovereign immunity be waived. However, an understanding was reached on October 5, 1994, that the banks would drop their insistence on a waiver of sovereign immunity and that the Vneshekonombank (or another public entity) would guarantee the debts. Signing and payment of the US$500 million was expected by the end of 1994.

Nov. 1995: Agreement in principle. Heads of terms were signed for a comprehensive rescheduling of debt of the former Soviet Union in the amount of $25.5 billion of principal outstanding and $7.5 billion in accrued interest due. The eligible principal was to be repaid over 25 years, with seven years of grace, beginning December 15, 1995, in 37 semiannual payments on a graduated schedule at LIBOR + ¹³⁄₁₆ percent per year. It was further agreed that an interest note for $6 billion would be issued with a 20-year maturity and seven years' grace from December 15, 1995, that would be the same interest rate as listed on the Luxembourg Stock Exchange. The remaining $1.5 billion in interest arrears was paid over 1995–96. By September 1996, the minimum subscribership by commercial banks of $20 billion in outstanding principal was reached, and this triggered the Russian agreement to the rescheduling package.

Nov. 1998: The outline agreement to restructure $13.5 billion of defaulted Treasury bills (GKOs and OFZs). Under the restructuring plan, 10 percent of the defaulted bills is to be redeemed in cash rubles, and 20 percents of the debt is to be exchanged for three-year zero-coupon bonds. The remaining 70 percent of the debt is to be restructured into four-year and five-year variable coupon bonds.

Feb. 2000: Agreement to restructure $31.8 billion Soviet-era debts owed to the London Club of commercial banks. The London Club's creditors agreed to write off $11.6 billion of the principal and a seven-year grace period for principal repayments, and swapping the rest of its defaulted debts (principal notes and interest arrears notes) for new 30-year Eurobonds. The interest rate on a new Eurobond was set at 2.25 percent for the first six months, 2.5 percent for the second six months, and 5 percent for years two and seven—yielding 7.5 percent a year.

São Tomé and Principe
Aug. 1994: Buyback under the IDA debt reduction facility at 10 cents per U.S. dollar. US$10.1 million of principal was extinguished (87 percent of eligible debt).

Senegal
Dec. 1996: Debt buyback at 8 cents per U.S. dollar of US$80 million owed to commercial banks. Funding for the operation was provided by the IDA debt reduction facility.

Sierra Leone
Jan. 1984: Covers arrears as of December 31, 1983.
Aug. 1995: Buyback, at 13 cents on average per U.S. dollar, of US$235 million due to commercial banks funded by grants from IDA debt reduction facility and other donor countries.

South Africa
Sept. 1993: Covers arrears of interest.

Sudan
Nov. 1981: Includes arrears of principal and some short-term debt.
Mar. 1982: Covers arrears of interest and modifies the 1981 agreement.
Apr. 1983: Modification of the 1981 agreement.
Oct. 1985: Covers arrears of interest.

Tanzania
Apr. 2001: Buyback of $76.6 million of eligible principal debt and about $79.2 million of associated interest under the IDA debt reduction facility. The buyback price was set at 12 cents per dollar of the principal amount with a 5 percent of foreign exchange risk margin. The IDA and the governments of Germany and Switzerland provided funding for the operation.

Togo
Mar. 1980: Balance of debts to French banks, including arrears of principal. Interest rates vary by currency.
Oct. 1983: Covers all commercial bank debt, including previously rescheduled debt.
May 1988: Restructuring of the 1983 agreement.
Dec. 1997 Debt buyback at 12.5 cents per dollar of $46.1 million owed to commercial banks. Funding for the operation was provided by the IDA debt reduction facility.

Turkey
Mar. 1982: Improved the terms of the August 1979 agreement.
June 2001: Swapping of short-term lira-denominated debts into longer-term dollar linked and floating rate lira paper through Dutch style auction. About $7.3 billion of debt was exchanged in the initial auction and $740 million was swapped in the following supplementary auction.

Uganda
Feb. 1993: Buyback of US$153 million commercial bank debt, funded by grants from the IDA debt reduction facility and other donor countries.

Ukraine
Sept. 1998: As the part of the government's voluntary debt conversion scheme, Ukraine offered to exchange $590 million (principal plus interest) of short-term domestic Treasury bills held by nonresidents for dollar-denominated Eu-

robonds with a maturity of two years and a minimum yield of 22 percent.
July 1999: Agreement to restructure a 10-month $163 million Eurobond (including principal and interest). Under this restructuring scheme, instead of making the $163 million repayment due in June 1999, Ukraine repays 20 percent of bond in cash and swaps the remaining 80 percent into a deutsche mark–denominated Eurobond with a maturity of three years and a coupon yield of 16 percent.
Feb. 2000: Agreement to restructure $2.7 billion of the short-term debt obligations. Under the restructuring terms, no debt forgiveness or reduction in principal was required from bondholders, and all accrued interest on existing eligible bonds would be paid in full and in cash; and all accepting investors would be offered a new seven-year Eurobond, denominated in either euros or U.S. dollars, at an interest rate of 10 percent for euro-denominated bonds and 11 percent for dollar-denominated bonds.
Mar. 2001: About $21.5 million of the external debt was exchanged for a 6-year Eurobond, denominated in either euro at an interest rate of 10 percent or U.S. dollar at an interest rate of 11 percent. Bond eligible for the exchange were deutsche mark 16 percent Eurobond due in February 2001, euro 10 percent amortizing notes due in March 2007, U.S. dollar 11 percent amortizing notes due in March 2007, and U.S. dollar 11 percent amortizing notes due in March 2007.

Uruguay
July 1986: MYRA.
Mar. 1988: Includes improved terms of the July 1986 agreement.
Feb. 1991: DDSR agreement. The agreement provided for cash buyback at a 44 percent discount (US$628 million), collateralized debt reduction bonds (US$535 million), and new money (US$89 million) combined with debt conversion notes (US$447 million). The repayment terms are: 30-year bullet maturity and 6.75 percent fixed interest for the interest reduction bonds, 16-year maturity including seven years' grace with LIBOR + ⅞ percent interest for the conversion notes, and 15-year maturity including seven years' grace with LIBOR + 1 percent interest for the new money notes.
Sept. 1999: In September 1999, Uruguay swapped $96 million of Brady bonds for $85 million of 30-year global bonds.

Venezuela, República Bolivariana de
Feb. 1986: MYRA. Agreed in principle in September 1984.
Nov. 1987: Reduced the spread and extended the maturities of the 1986 agreement.
Sept. 1988: Interest spread reduced on February 1986 agreement.
Dec. 1988: Exchange of debt for bonds outside the framework of the main negotiations.
Dec. 1990: DDSR agreement featuring buybacks in the form of 91-day collateralized short-term notes (US$1,411 million), exchange for bonds at 30 percent discount (US$1,810 million), exchange at par for reduced fixed-rate interest bonds (US$7,457 million), exchange for bonds at par with temporary step-down interest rates (US$3,027 million), and new money combined with debt conversion bonds (US$6,022 million).
Sept. 1997: The República Bolivariana de Venezuela retired $4.4 billion of Brady bonds in exchange for $4 billion of uncollateralized 30-year bonds at an interest rate of 325 basis points above the U.S. Treasury rate. The operation

(Notes continue on next page)

resulted in nominal savings of about $1.8 billion from the differential between the Brady bonds' par and market values ($0.4 billion) and from the pro rata release of the collateral of the Brady bonds ($1.4 billion).

Vietnam

Dec. 1997: DDSR agreement restructuring US$310.9 million of principal and US$486.2 million of past-due interest (PDI). For the restructured principal, $20.4 million repurchased at 44 cents per U.S. dollar, US$51.6 million was exchanged for discount bonds (50 percent discount); and $238.9 million was exchanged for par fixed interest bonds. Both bonds have a 30-year maturity, but the discount bond is repayable in a bullet payment in year 30, while the par bond has a step-up amortization schedule beginning in year 15. Also, 50 percent of the face value due of the par bond is due at maturity. The discount bond is subject to an interest rate of LIBOR + $^{13}/_{16}$ while the par bond is subject to step-up interest rates rising from 3 percent in years one and two to 5.5 percent in years 21–30. One hundred percent of the discount bonds and 50 percent of the par bonds are guaranteed by U.S. Treasury zero-coupon bonds, and the discount bonds have a six-month rolling interest guarantee. Regarding PDI, US$15 million was paid at closing, US$294.8 million was exchanged for noncollateralized bonds with an 18-year maturity including seven years of grace and step-up interest rates, $21.8 million was repurchased at 44 cents per dollar, and US$154.6 million was written off.

Yemen, Republic of

June 2001: Buyback of $362 million of principal and $245 million

of associated interest under the IDA debt reduction facility. The buyback price was set at 2.94 cents per dollar of the principal amount. The IDA and the governments of the Netherlands, Norway, and Switzerland provided funding for the operation.

Yugoslavia, Federal Republic of (Serbia/Montenegro)

Oct. 1983: Includes a one-year rollover of short-term bonds.

Dec. 1985: MYRA.

Zaire

Apr. 1980: Covered stock of debt as of the end of 1979, including arrears.

Jan. 1983: Rescheduling principal due under the April 1980 agreement.

June 1984: Rescheduling principal due under the April 1980 agreement.

May 1985: Rescheduling principal due under the April 1980 agreement.

May 1986: Rescheduling principal due under the April 1980 agreement.

May 1987: Rescheduling principal due under the April 1980 agreement.

June 1989: Finances monthly payments on outstanding claims, mainly interest on arrears.

Zambia

Dec. 1984: Includes arrears as of February 28, 1983.

Sept. 1994: Buyback under the IDA debt reduction facility at 11 cents per U.S. dollar. US$200 million of principal was extinguished (75 percent of eligible debt), using US$10.5 million of IDA resources and US$22.3 million from other donors.

Appendix 3
Official Debt Restructuring

Restructuring with official creditors

This appendix reviews official debt restructuring agreements concluded in 2001. Rescheduling of intergovernmental loans and officially guaranteed private export credits takes place under the aegis of the Paris Club. These agreements are concluded between the debtor country government and representatives of creditor countries with export credit facilities. The terms of Paris Club rescheduling are recorded in an agreed-upon minute. To make the debt relief effective, debtor countries must sign bilateral implementing agreements with each creditor. For a more detailed description of how the Paris Club operates, see *World Debt Tables 1992–93*, volume 1, p. 73, and the Paris Club Web site described below.

Developments in 2001

In the 12-month period from January 1, 2001, to December 31, 2001, the Paris Club concluded multilateral rescheduling agreements with 17 countries covering a total of $25.6 billion (table A3.1). All of these agreements, except the one with the Federal Republic of Yugoslavia, were concluded with low-income countries.

Implementation of the HIPC Initiative

A primary focus of Paris Club creditors over the past two years was delivery of debt relief in the context of the enhanced Heavily Indebted Poor Countries (HIPC) Initiative. In 2001 Paris Club creditors have concluded concessional agreements with 13 HIPC countries covering a total of $6.1 billion (table A3.2). Bolivia and Mozambique

reached the completion point under the enhanced HIPC Initiative and concluded comprehensive stock-of-debt agreements with their Paris Club creditors. These agreements provided 90 percent net present value reduction in the stock of debt, and will allow these countries to exit from the rescheduling process. For seven countries (Cameroon, Chad, Guinea, Guinea-Bissau, Madagascar, Malawi, and Niger) that have reached the decision point under the enhanced HIPC Initiative, Paris Club creditors agreed to provide interim relief that reduces debt service payments due by 90 percent in net present value terms. This interim relief will be extended until each country reaches its completion Point under the enhanced HIPC Initiative. Flow agreements on Naples terms (67 percent net present value reduction) were concluded with Ethiopia, Ghana, and Sierra Leone. It is expected that these agreements will be topped up to 90 percent net present value reduction once these countries reach their decision points. For the Republic of Yemen, Paris Club creditors concluded a stock of debt operation on Naples terms, 67 percent net present value reduction. This agreement brought the debt of this country to a sustainable level and marks an exit from the rescheduling process.

Agreements with other countries

Georgia

In March 2001, the Paris Club concluded an agreement with Georgia covering $58 million in principal and interest falling due from January 1, 2001, to December 31, 2002, on loans contracted prior to November 1, 1999 (the cutoff date). Re-

Table A3.1 Paris Club agreements with HIPC countries, 2000 and 2001

Country	Signature date	Cutoff date	Amount rescheduled (millions of dollars)	Concessionality level (percentage of present value)	Consolidation period start date	Length (months)
Benin	9 Sept. 2000	31 Mar. 1989	7	90	Top-up to Cologne	12
Bolivia	10 July 2001	31 Dec. 1985	685	90	Debt stock rescheduling	n.a.
Burkina Faso	12 Sept. 2000	1 Jan. 1991	..	90	Top-up to Cologne	12
Cameroon	24 Jan. 2001	31 Dec. 1988	1,300	90	1 Jan. 2001	35
Chad	13 June 2001	30 June 1989	15	90	1 May 2001	24
Ethiopia	5 Apr. 2001	31 Dec. 1989	430	67	1 Mar. 2001	36
Ghana	10 Dec. 2001		199	67	1 June 2001	8
Guinea	15 May 2001	1 Jan. 1986	151	90	1 Dec. 2000	40
Guinea-Bissau	26 Jan. 2001	31 Dec. 1986	141	90	1 Dec. 2000	36
Madagascar	12 July 2000	1 July 1983	..	67	Naples	7
Madagascar	7 Mar. 2001	1 July 1983	254	90	1 Dec. 2000	38
Malawi	25 Jan. 2001	I Jan. 1997	68	90	1 Dec. 2000	36
Mali	12 Sept. 2000	1 Jan. 1988	..	90	Top-up to Cologne	9
Mauritania	16 Mar. 2000	31 Dec. 1984	100	90	Cologne	36
Mozambique	20 Nov. 2001	1 Feb. 1984	2,234	90	Debt stock rescheduling	n.a.
Niger	25 Jan. 2001	1 July 1983	115	90	1 Dec. 2000	36
São Tomé and Principe	16 May 2000	1 Apr. 1999	28	67	Naples	37
Senegal	9 Sept. 2000	1 Jan. 1983	..	90	Top-up to Cologne	18
Sierra Leone	16 Oct. 2001	1 July 1983	180	67	1 Oct. 2001	36
Tanzania	14 Apr. 2000	30 June 1986	714	90	Cologne	36.
Uganda	12 Sept. 2000	1 July 1981	145	90	Debt stock rescheduling	n.a
Yemen, Rep. of	14 June 2001	1 Jan. 1993	420	67	Debt stock rescheduling	n.a.

.. Zero or insignificant.
n.a. Not applicable.
Sources: World Bank Development Economics Prospects Group; Paris Club.

payment of the rescheduled maturities will be made over 20 years, including 10 years of grace for official development assistance (ODA) loans, and over 20 years, including 3 years of grace for the guaranteed commercial loans.

Pakistan

Pakistan has the distinction of being the only country to conclude two agreements with Paris Club creditors in the course of one year. The agreement of January 2001 rescheduled $1.8 billion comprising arrears at end November 2000 and 100 percent of principal and interest falling due from December 1, 2000, to September 30, 2001, on loans contracted prior to September 30, 1997 (the cutoff date). The agreement was concluded under Houston terms: repayment of the rescheduled amount will be made over 20 years, including 10 years of grace for ODA loans, and over 18 years, including 3 years of grace, for the guaranteed commercial loans.

The agreement concluded in December 2001 rescheduled $12.5 billion—the entire stock of debt

outstanding on loans contracted prior to the cutoff date (September 30, 1997), including amounts owed under prior rescheduling agreements with Paris Club creditors. Repayment of the rescheduled amount will be over an extended period, and in addition, part of the moratorium interest will be capitalized and debt service due up to June 30, 2002, on debt contracted after the cutoff date, will be deferred. ODA loans will be repaid over 38 years, including 15 years of grace at a concessional interest rate. Guaranteed commercial loans will be repaid over 23 years, including 5 years of grace at market interest rates. The repayment schedule is graduated, rising from an initial payment equivalent to 0.67 percent of the total amount rescheduled to a final payment equivalent to 7.20 percent of the total amount rescheduled.

In recognition of Pakistan's particularly acute balance of payments situation, Paris Club creditors agreed to capitalize 100 percent of moratorium interest accrued from December 1, 2001, to June 30, 2002, and 20 percent of the amount accrued from July 1, 2002, to June 30, 2004, including the rescheduled debt. These amounts will be repaid in four equal semiannual installments beginning May 31, 2005, and ending November 30, 2008. They also deferred 100 percent of principal and interest falling due from December 1, 2001, to June 30, 2002, inclusive of post-cutoff date debt (that is, loans contracted after September 30, 1997). These amounts will be repaid in four equal semiannual installments beginning May 31, 2005, and ending November 30, 2006.

Ukraine

In July 2001 the Paris Club concluded an agreement with Ukraine covering $580 million in principal arrears and maturities due from December 19, 2000, to September 30, 2002, on loans contracted prior to December 31, 1998 (the cutoff date). Repayment of the rescheduled maturities will be made over 12 years, including 3 years of grace.

Federal Republic of Yugoslavia

In November 2001 Paris Club creditors concluded an agreement with the Federal Republic of Yugoslavia to restructure $4.5 billion, of which 98 percent constituted payments arrears. The agreement, which took into account the extraordinary circumstances of the country and the reconstruction needs following almost a decade of conflict, was a concessional one that provides a reduction of 66 percent, in net present value terms, in the total stock of debt outstanding. The agreement has three phases.

Phase one is an immediate deferral of 100 percent of principal and interest (including late interest) due at July 31, 2001, and 100 percent of principal and interest falling due from August 1, 2001, to March 22, 2002. Interest due from July 31, 2001, to March 22, 2002, will be capitalized. The deferred amount will be repaid in 14 equal semiannual installments beginning September 22, 2004, and ending March 22, 2011. *Phase two* will cancel 51 percent in net present value terms of outstanding guaranteed commercial credits. The remaining amounts will be rescheduled over 22 years, with 6 years of grace, at market rates of interest ; 60 percent of the interest charged on the rescheduled debt from March 23, 2002, until March 22, 2005, will be capitalized. *Phase three* will cancel an additional 15 percent in net present

value terms of outstanding commercial credits. This will be implemented on March 23, 2005. Implementation is tied to satisfactory review of the International Monetary Fund program. The debt reduction applies only to guaranteed commercial loans. ODA loans, which constitute only a very small share of the outstanding debt of the Federal Republic of Yugoslavia, will be rescheduled and repaid over 39 years, including 16 years of grace.

Swap arrangements

Houston terms, adopted in September 1990, introduced the possibility of swapping debts covered by Paris Club agreed-on minutes for debt-equity participation, debt-for-development, or other local currency obligations. Swap provisions were incorporated into the Enhanced Toronto terms in September 1991 and have been continued in the subsequent agreements on concessional terms (Lyon, Naples, and, Cologne). They were also included in the special restructuring arrangements for the Arab Republic of Egypt and Poland (see *World Debt Tables 1991–92*, volume 1, pp. 62–64). In 2000 the provision was extended to select middle-income countries, notably Algeria and Bulgaria. Participation in swap arrangements is voluntary for creditor governments.

All ODA debt is eligible for swaps. For non-ODA claims, swaps had been limited to 10 percent of debt covered by relevant Paris Club agreements or $10 million, whichever was larger. Paris Club creditors have now raised the ceiling on the amount of guaranteed commercial credits that may be swapped to 20 percent of the outstanding amount of eligible claims. In exceptional circumstances, this limit may be set as high as 30 percent of the outstanding amount of eligible claims, or SDR40 million (whichever is higher).

Data compiled by the Paris Club Secretariat from participating creditor countries indicate that an estimated $4.2 billion of debt had been swapped for local currency claims by the end of December 2000. Of this, $2.2 billion was in the form of debt-for-equity swaps and $1.6 billion debt-for-nature and debt-for-aid swaps. Other debt swap arrangements accounted for the remaining $0.4 billion. Egypt's debt swaps (debt-equity or other local currency exchanges) have accounted for some 40 percent of the total value of all swaps

($1.7 billion). Morocco and Peru have both swapped approximately $0.5 billion. Among the HIPC countries, Bolivia, Côte d'Ivoire, and Tanzania have undertaken swaps amounting to more than $100 million. France has the largest amount of exchanges ($1.4 billion, followed by Switzerland $0.9 billion, Spain $0.4 billion, and Belgium and Germany $0.3 billion, respectively). The most important swap operation in 2001 was the buyback by Poland of $3.3 billion of its claims on Brazil for a total price of $2.5 billion.

Other developments in 2001

Over the past two years, the Paris Club has increasingly moved toward a policy of openness and transparency. In April 2001, the Paris Club launched its Internet site, www.clubdeparis.org. This site, which represents a key step in the Club's policy toward transparency, provides comprehensive information on the nature of the Paris Club and how it works. It also includes a complete database of all the agreements signed under the auspices of the Paris Club since 1956 and details

the amount rescheduled and the terms of repayment. The Web site is continuously updated, and the outcomes of negotiations with each debtor country are now posted on the Web as soon as they have been completed.

The launch of the Web site coincided with another important event—a meeting with private investors gathered by the Institute of International Finance, the Emerging Markets Creditors Association, and the Emerging Markets Traders Association for an exchange of views on issues related to the restructuring of sovereign external debt. This was the first time in the history of the Club that it has met with private creditors, and the meeting was regarded as a major step toward addressing widespread criticism of the secrecy of the Paris Club. A central topic of discussion was the issue of implementation of the comparability of treatment clause, a principle under which, in resolving a financial crisis, the sovereign's external creditors share the burden on comparable terms. One important outcome was recognition by both groups of creditors of the importance of a regular dialogue and agreement on having similar meetings on a regular (semiannual) basis.

Table A3.2 Multilateral debt relief agreements with official creditors, January 1980–December 2001

Country and date of agreement	Contract cutoff date	Consolidation period for current maturities		Consolidation includes		Share of debt consolidated (percent)	Amount consolidated (millions of dollars)	Repayment terms[a]	
		Start date	Length (months)	Arrears	Previously rescheduled debt			Maturity (years/ months)	Grace (years/ months)
Albania*									
1 Dec. 93	30 Sept. 93	Arrears as of 30 Sept. 93		y		100	109	9/3	2/9
Algeria									
1 June 94	30 Sept. 93	1 June 94	12			100	5,345	14/6	3/0
21 July 95	30 Sept. 93	1 July 95	36			100	7,320	13/0	1/6
Angola									
20 July 89	31 Dec. 86	1 July 89	15	y		100	446	9/6	6/0
Argentina									
16 Jan. 85	10 Dec. 83	1 Jan. 85	12	y		90	2,040	9/6	5/0
20 May 87	10 Dec. 83	1 May 87	14	y		100	1,260	9/5	4/11
21 Dec. 89	10 Dec. 83	1 Jan. 90	15	y	y	100	2,400	9/4	5/10
19 Sept. 91	10 Dec. 83	1 Oct. 91	9	y	y	100	1,476	9/9	6/3
21 July 92	10 Dec. 83	1 July 92	33		y	100	2,700	13/8	1/2
Benin									
22 June 89	31 Mar. 89	1 June 89	13	y		100	193	Menu	Menu
18 Dec. 91	31 Mar. 89	1 Jan. 92	19	y		100	152	Menu	Menu
27 June 93	31 Mar. 89	1 Aug. 93	29		y	100	25	Menu	Menu
24 Oct. 96	31 Mar. 89	24 Oct. 96	Stock		y	100	209	Menu	Menu
24 Oct. 00	31 Mar 89	Interim relief	12		y	100	5	Menu	Menu
Bolivia									
18 July 86	31 Dec. 85	1 July 86	12	y		100	449	9/6	5/0
14 Nov. 88	31 Dec. 85	1 Oct. 88	15	y	y	100	226	9/5	5/1
15 Mar. 90	31 Dec. 85	1 Jan. 90	24		y	100	276	Menu	Menu
24 Jan. 92	31 Dec. 85	1 Jan. 92	18		y	100	65	Menu	Menu
24 Mar. 95[b]	31 Dec. 85	1 Jan. 95	36		y	100	482	Menu	Menu
14 Dec. 95	31 Dec. 85	31 Dec. 95	Stock		y	100	881	Menu	Menu
30 Oct. 98	31 Dec. 85	1 Nov. 98	Stock		y	100	561	Menu	Menu
10 July 01	31 Dec. 85	1 July 01	Stock		y	100	685	Menu	Menu
Bosnia and Herzegovina									
30 Oct. 98	2 Dec. 82	1 July 98	10			100	589	Menu	Menu
7 July 00	2 Dec. 82	12 July 00	12			100	9	Menu	Menu
Brazil									
23 Nov. 83	31 Mar. 83	1 Aug. 83	17	y		85	2,337	9/0	5/0
21 Jan. 87	31 Mar. 83	1 Jan. 85	30			100	4,178	5/6	3/0
29 July 88	31 Mar. 83	1 Aug. 88	20	y		100	4,992	9/6	5/0
26 Feb. 92	31 Mar. 83	1 Jan. 92	20	y		100	10,500	13/4	1/10
Bulgaria									
17 Apr. 91	1 Jan. 91	1 Apr. 91	12	y		100	640	10/0	6/6
14 Dec. 92	1 Jan. 91	1 Dec. 92	5	y		100	251	9/10	6/4
13 Apr. 94	1 Jan. 91	1 Apr. 94	13	y		100	200	9/5	5/11
Burkina Faso									
15 Mar. 91	1 Jan. 91	1 Mar. 91	15	y		100	71	Menu	Menu
7 May 93	1 Jan. 91	1 Apr. 93	33	y		100	36	Menu	Menu
20 June 96	1 Jan. 91	20 June 96	Stock		y	100	64	Menu	Menu
24 Oct. 00	1 Jan. 91	Interim relief	12		y	100	1	Menu	Menu
Cambodia									
26 Jan. 95	31 Dec. 85	1 Jan. 95	30	y	y	100	249	Menu	Menu

(Table continues on next page)

155

Table A3.2 Multilateral debt relief agreements with official creditors, January 1980–December 2001 (continued)

| Country and date of agreement | Contract cutoff date | Consolidation period for current maturities | | Consolidation includes | | Share of debt consolidated (percent) | Amount consolidated (millions of dollars) | Repayment terms[a] | |
		Start date	Length (months)	Arrears	Previously rescheduled debt			Maturity (years/ months)	Grace (years/ months)
Cameroon									
24 May 89	31 Dec. 88	1 Apr. 89	12	y		100	535	9/6	6/0
23 Jan. 92	31 Dec. 88	1 Jan. 92	9	y		100	1,080	19/5, 14/8	9/11, 8/2
24 Mar. 94	31 Dec. 88	1 Apr. 94	18	y	y	100	1,259	Menu	Menu
16 Nov. 95	31 Dec. 88	1 Oct. 95	12		y	100	1,129	Menu	Menu
24 Oct. 97	31 Dec. 88	1 Oct. 97	36	y		100	1,270	Menu	Menu
24 Jan. 01	31 Dec. 88	1 Jan. 01	35	y		100	1,300	Menu	Menu
Central African Republic									
12 June 81	1 Jan. 81	1 Jan. 81	12	y		85	72	8/6	4/0
9 July 83	1 Jan. 83	1 Jan. 83	12	y		90	13	9/6	5/0
22 Nov. 85	1 Jan. 83	1 July 85	18		y	90	14	9/3	4/9
14 Dec. 88	1 Jan. 83	1 Jan. 89	18		y	100	28	Menu	Menu
15 June 90	1 Jan. 83	1 Jan. 90	12	y	y	100	4	Menu	Menu
12 Apr. 94	1 Jan. 83	1 Apr. 94	12	y	y	100	32	Menu	Menu
25 Sept. 98	1 Jan. 83	1 Sept. 98	34	y	y	100	23	Menu	Menu
Chad									
24 Oct. 89	30 June 89	1 Oct. 89	15	y		100	24	Menu	Menu
28 Feb. 95	30 June 89	1 Apr. 95	12	y		100	24	Menu	Menu
14 June 96	30 June 89	1 Jan. 96	32	y	y	100	12	Menu	Menu
13 June 01	30 June 89	1 May 01	24	y	y	100	15	Menu	Menu
Chile									
17 July 85	1 Jan. 85	1 July 85	18			65	146	6/3	2/9
2 Apr. 87	1 Jan. 85	15 Apr. 87	21			85	157	6/2	2/7
Congo, Democratic Republic of									
9 July 81	1 Jan. 79	1 Jan. 81	24			90	500	9/6	4/0
20 Dec. 83	30 June 83	1 Jan. 84	12	y	y	95	1,497	10/6	5/0
18 Sept. 85	30 June 83	1 Jan. 85	15		y	95	408	9/5	4/11
15 May 86	30 June 83	1 Apr. 86	12		y	100	429	9/6	4/0
18 May 87	30 June 83	1 Apr. 87	13	y	y	100	671	14/6	6/0
23 June 89	30 June 83	1 June 89	13	y	y	100	1,530	Menu	Menu
Congo, Republic of									
18 July 86	1 Jan. 86	1 Aug. 86	20	y		95	756	9/2	3/8
13 Sept. 90[c]	1 Jan. 86	1 Sept. 90	21	y	y	100	1,052	14/3	5/9
30 June 94[c]	1 Jan. 86	1 July 94	11	y	y	100	1,175	19/7, 14/7	10/1, 5/1
16 July 96	1 Jan. 86	30 June 96	36	y	y	100	1,758	Menu	Menu
Costa Rica									
11 Jan. 83	1 July 82	1 July 82	18	y		85	136	8/3	3/9
22 Apr. 85	1 July 82	1 Jan. 85	15	y		90	166	9/5	4/11
26 May 89	1 July 82	1 Apr. 89	14	y	y	100	182	9/5	4/11
17 July 91	1 July 82	1 July 91	9	y	y	100	139	9/7	5/1
22 June 93	1 July 82	Arrears as of 31 June 93		y		100	58	6/6	2/0
Côte d'Ivoire									
4 May 84	1 July 83	1 Dec. 83	13			100	230	8/6	4/0
25 June 85	1 July 83	1 Jan. 85	12			100	213	8/6	4/0
27 June 86	1 July 83	1 Jan. 86	36			Variable	370	8/7	4/1
18 Dec. 87	1 July 83	1 Jan. 88	16	y	y	100	567	9/4	5/10
18 Dec. 89	1 July 83	1 Jan. 90	16	y	y	100	934	13/4	5/10
20 Nov. 91	1 July 83	1 Oct. 91	12	y	y	100	806	14/6	8/0
22 Mar. 94	1 July 83	1 Mar. 94	37	y	y	100	1,849	Menu	Menu
24 Apr. 98	1 July 83	1 Apr. 98	36	y	y	100	1,402	Menu	Menu

Table A3.2 Multilateral debt relief agreements with official creditors, January 1980–December 2001 *(continued)*

Country and date of agreement	Contract cutoff date	Consolidation period for current maturities		Consolidation includes		Share of debt consolidated *(percent)*	Amount consolidated *(millions of dollars)*	Repayment terms[a]	
		Start date	Length *(months)*	Arrears	Previously rescheduled debt			Maturity *(years/ months)*	Grace *(years/ months)*
Croatia									
21 Mar. 95	2 Dec. 82	1 Jan. 95	12	y	y	100	861	13/7	2/1
Cuba									
1 Mar. 83	1 Sept. 82	1 Sept. 82	16			100	426		
19 July 84	1 Sept. 82	1 Jan. 84	12			100	204	9/0	5/6
18 July 85	1 Sept. 82	1 Jan. 85	12			100	156	9/0	5/6
16 July 86	1 Sept. 82	1 Jan. 86	12		y	100	..	9/6	5/6
Djibouti									
25 May 00		31 Oct. 99	24	y		100	17	10/0	6/0
Dominican Republic									
21 May 85	30 June 84	1 Jan. 85	15	y		90	290	9/5	4/11
22 Nov. 91	30 June 84	1 Oct. 91	18	y	y	100	850	14/3	7/9
Ecuador									
28 July 83	1 Jan. 83	1 June 83	12			85	142	7/6	3/0
24 Apr. 85	1 Jan. 83	1 Jan. 85	36	y		Variable	450	7/6	3/0
20 Jan. 88	1 Jan. 83	1 Jan. 88	14	y		100	438	9/5	4/11
24 Oct. 89	1 Jan. 83	1 Nov. 89	14	y	y	100	397	9/5	5/11
20 Jan. 92	1 Jan. 83	1 Jan. 92	12	y	y	100	339	19/5, 14/6	9/11, 8/0
27 June 94	1 Jan. 83	1 July 94	6	y	y	100	293	19/9, 14/9	10/3, 8/3
15 Sept. 00	1 Jan. 83	1 May 00	12	y	y	100	887	19/9, 17/9	10/3, 3/3
Egypt, Arab Rep. of									
22 May 87	31 Oct. 86	1 Jan. 87	18	y		100	6,350	9/3	4/9
25 May 91	31 Oct. 86	Balances: 30 June 91		y		100	27,864	Menu	Menu
El Salvador									
17 Sept. 90[c]	1 Sept. 90	1 Sept. 90	13	y		100	135	19/6, 14/6	10/0, 8/0
Equatorial Guinea									
22 July 85	1 July 84	1 Jan. 85	18	y		100	38	9/0	4/6
1 Mar. 89	1 July 84	Arrears as of 31 Dec. 88		y	y	100	10	Menu	Menu
2 Apr. 92*	1 July 84	1 Jan. 92	12	y	y	100	32	Menu	Menu
15 Dec. 94*	1 July 84		21	y	y	100	51	Menu	Menu
Ethiopia									
16 Dec. 92	31 Dec. 89	1 Dec. 92	35	y		100	441	Menu	Menu
24 Jan. 97	31 Dec. 89	1 Jan. 97	34	y		100	184	Menu	Menu
5 Apr. 01	31 Dec. 89	1 Mar. 01	36	y	y	100	430	Menu	Menu
Gabon									
21 Jan. 87	1 July 86	21 Sept. 86	15			100	387	9/5	3/11
21 Mar. 88	1 July 86	1 Jan. 88	12			100	326	9/6	5/0
19 Sept. 89	1 July 86	1 Sept. 89	16	y		100	545	10/0	4/0
24 Oct. 91[d]	1 July 86	1 Oct. 91	15	y	y	100	498	8/0	2/0
15 Apr. 94	1 July 86	1 Apr. 94	12	y	y	100	1,360	14/6	2/0
12 Dec. 95	1 July 86	1 Dec. 95	36	y	y	100	1,030	13/6	1/0
15 Dec. 00	1 July 86	1 Oct. 00	24	y	y	100	687	12/0	3/0
Gambia, The									
19 Sept. 86	1 July 86	1 Oct. 86	12	y		100	17	9/6	5/0
Georgia									
6 Mar. 01	1 Nov. 99	1 Jan. 01	24			100	58	20/0, 20/0	10/0, 3/0

(Table continues on next page)

Table A3.2 Multilateral debt relief agreements with official creditors, January 1980–December 2001 (continued)

Country and date of agreement	Contract cutoff date	Consolidation period for current maturities		Consolidation includes		Share of debt consolidated (percent)	Amount consolidated (millions of dollars)	Repayment terms[a]	
		Start date	Length (months)	Arrears	Previously rescheduled debt			Maturity (years/ months)	Grace (years/ months)
Ghana									
29 Mar. 96	1 Jan. 93	Arrears as of 1 July 95				100	93	4/5	1/0
10 Dec. 01	1 Jan. 93	1 Jun. 01	8	y	y	100	199	Menu	Menu
Guatemala									
25 Mar. 93	1 Jan. 91	Arrears as of 31 Mar. 93				100	440	19/6, 14/6	10/0, 8/0
Guinea									
18 Apr. 86	1 Jan. 86	1 Jan. 86	14	y		95	196	9/4	4/11
12 Apr. 89	1 Jan. 86	1 Jan. 89	12	y	y	100	123	Menu	Menu
18 Nov. 92	1 Jan. 86	Arrears as of 31 Dec. 92		y	y	100	203	Menu	Menu
25 Jan. 95	1 Jan. 86	1 Jan. 95	12	y	y	100	156	Menu	Menu
26 Feb. 97	1 Jan. 86	1 Jan. 97	36	y	y	100	123	Menu	Menu
15 May 01	1 Jan. 86	1 Dec. 00	40	y	y	100	151	Menu	Menu
Guinea-Bissau									
27 Oct. 87	31 Dec. 86	1 July 87	18	y		100	25	19/3	9/9
26 Oct. 89	31 Dec. 86	1 Oct. 89	15	y	y	100	21	Menu	Menu
23 Feb. 95	31 Dec. 86	1 Jan. 95	36	y	y	100	195	Menu	Menu
26 Jan. 01	31 Dec. 86	1 Dec. 00	36	y	y	100	141	Menu	Menu
Guyana									
23 May 89	31 Dec. 88	1 Jan. 89	14	y		100	195	19/5	9/11
12 Sept. 90	31 Dec. 88	1 Sept. 90	35	y	y	100	123	Menu	Menu
6 May 93	31 Dec. 88	1 Aug. 93	17	y	y	100	39	Menu	Menu
23 May 96	31 Dec. 88	23 May 96	Stock	y	y	100	793	Menu	Menu
25 June 99	31 Dec 88	23 May 99	Stock	y	y	100	240	Menu	Menu
Haiti									
30 May 95	1 Oct. 93	31 Mar. 95	12	y		100	117	Menu	Menu
Honduras									
14 Sept. 90[c]	1 June 90	1 Sept. 90	11	y		100	280	19/7, 14/7	8/1, 8/1
26 Oct. 92	1 June 90	1 Oct. 92	34	y	y	100	180	Menu	Menu
29 Feb. 96	1 June 90	30 Jan. 95	12	y	y	100	112	Menu	Menu
13 Apr. 99	1 June 90	1 Apr. 99	36	y	y	100	411	Menu	Menu
Indonesia*									
28 Sept. 98	1 July 97	1 Aug. 98	20			100	4,176	11/0	3/0
13 Apr. 00	1 July 97	1 Apr. 00	24			100	5,440	14/8	3/3
Jamaica									
16 July 84	1 Oct. 83	1 Jan. 84	15	y		100	105	8/5	3/11
19 July 85	1 Oct. 83	1 Apr. 85	12			100	62	9/6	4/0
5 Mar. 87	1 Oct. 83	1 Jan. 87	15	y		100	124	9/5	4/11
24 Oct. 88	1 Oct. 83	1 June 88	18		y	100	147	9/3	4/9
26 Apr. 90	1 Oct. 83	1 Dec. 89	18		y	100	179	9/3	4/9
19 July 91[c]	1 Oct. 83	1 June 91	13		y	100	127	19/6, 14/6	8/9, 6/0
25 Jan. 93[c]	1 Oct. 83	1 Oct. 92	36		y	100	291	18/6, 13/6	9/0, 5/0
Jordan									
19 July 89	1 Jan. 89	1 July 89	18	y		100	587	9/3	4/9
28 Feb. 92	1 Jan. 89	1 Jan. 92	18	y		100	771	19/5, 14/3	9/11, 7/9
28 June 94[c]	1 Jan. 89	1 July 94	35	y	y	100	1,147	18/7, 16/7	9/1, 2/1
23 May 97[c]	1 Jan. 89	1 June 97	21	y	y	100	400	19/2, 14/6	9/8, 2/8
20 May 99	1 Jan. 89	1 Apr. 99	36	y	y	100	821	20/0, 18/0	10/0, 3/0
Kenya									
19 Jan. 94	31 Dec. 91	Arrears as of 31 Dec. 93		y		100	535	7/9	1/3
15 Nov. 00	31 Dec. 91	1 July 00	12	y		100	302	20/0, 14/6	10/0, 3/0

Table A3.2 Multilateral debt relief agreements with official creditors, January 1980–December 2001 *(continued)*

Country and date of agreement	Contract cutoff date	Consolidation period for current maturities		Consolidation includes		Share of debt consolidated *(percent)*	Amount consolidated *(millions of dollars)*	Repayment terms[a]	
		Start date	Length *(months)*	Arrears	Previously rescheduled debt			Maturity *(years/ months)*	Grace *(years/ months)*
Liberia									
19 Dec. 80	1 Jan. 80	1 July 80	18			90	35	7/9	3/3
16 Dec. 81	1 Jan. 80	1 Jan. 82	18			90	25	7/11	3/3
22 Dec. 83	1 Jan. 83	1 July 83	12			90	17	8/6	4/0
17 Dec. 84	1 Jan. 83	1 July 84	12			90	17	9/6	5/0
Macedonia, FYR									
17 July 95	2 Dec. 82	1 July 95	12	y	y	100	288	14/7	3/1
Madagascar									
30 Apr. 81	1 Jan. 81	1 Jan. 81	18	y		85	140	8/3	3/9
13 July 82	1 Jan. 82	1 July 82	12	y		85	107	8/3	3/9
23 Mar. 84	1 July 83	1 July 83	18		y	95	89	10/3	4/9
22 May 85	1 July 83	1 Jan. 85	15		y	100	128	10/5	4/11
23 Oct. 86	1 July 83	1 Apr. 86	21		y	100	212	9/2	4/8
28 Oct. 88	1 July 83	1 Apr. 88	21	y	y	100	254	Menu	Menu
10 July 90	1 July 83	1 June 90	13	y	y	100	139	Menu	Menu
26 Mar. 97	1 July 83	1 Jan. 97	35	y	y	100	1,247	Menu	Menu
4 Sept. 00	1 July 83	1 Jan. 00	12	y	y	100	34	Menu	Menu
7 Mar. 01	1 July 83	1 Dec. 00	38	y	y	100	254	Menu	Menu
Malawi									
22 Sept. 82	1 Jan. 82	1 July 82	12			85	25	8/0	3/6
27 Oct. 83	1 Jan. 82	1 July 83	12			85	26	8/0	3/6
22 Apr. 88	1 Jan. 82	1 Apr. 88	14	y	y	100	27	19/5	9/11
25 Jan. 01	1 Jan. 97	1 Dec. 00	36	y	y	100	68	Menu	Menu
Mali									
27 Oct. 88	1 Jan. 88	1 July 88	16	y		100	63	Menu	Menu
22 Nov. 89	1 Jan. 88	1 Nov. 89	26		y	100	44	Menu	Menu
29 Oct. 92	1 Jan. 88	1 Oct. 92	35	y	y	100	20	Menu	Menu
20 May 96	1 Jan. 88	20 May 96	Stock	y	y	100	33	Menu	Menu
25 Oct. 00	1 Jan. 88	interim relief	12		y	100	4	Menu	Menu
Mauritania									
27 Apr. 85	31 Dec. 84	1 Jan. 85	15	y		90	68	8/3	3/9
16 May 86	31 Dec. 84	1 Apr. 86	12			95	27	8/6	4/0
15 June 87	31 Dec. 84	1 Apr. 87	14			95	90	14/5	5/0
19 June 89	31 Dec. 84	1 June 89	12	y	y	100	52	Menu	Menu
25 Jan. 93	31 Dec. 84	1 Jan. 93	24	y	y	100	218	Menu	Menu
28 June 95	31 Dec. 84	1 Jan. 95	36	y	y	100	66	Menu	Menu
16 Mar. 00	31 Dec. 84	1 July 99	36	y	y	100	100	Menu	Menu
Mexico									
22 June 83*	20 Dec. 82	1 July 83	6	y		90	1,199	5/6	3/0
7 Sept. 86	31 Dec. 85	22 Sept. 86	18			100	1,912	8/3	3/9
30 May 89	31 Dec. 85	1 June 89	36			100	2,400	9/7	6/1
Morocco									
25 Oct. 83	1 May 83	1 Sept. 83	16	y		85	1,152	7/3	3/9
17 Sept. 85	1 May 83	1 Sept. 85	18	y		90	1,124	8/3	3/9
6 Mar. 87	1 May 83	1 Mar. 87	16		y	100	1,008	9/3	4/9
26 Oct. 88	1 May 83	1 July 88	18		y	100	969	9/3	4/9
11 Sept. 90[c]	1 May 83	1 Jan. 90	15		y	100	1,390	19/5, 14/5	9/11, 7/11
27 Feb. 92[c]	1 May 83	1 Feb. 92	11	y	y	100	1,303	19/5, 14/7	9/11, 8/1

(Table continues on next page)

Table A3.2 Multilateral debt relief agreements with official creditors, January 1980–December 2001 (continued)

Country and date of agreement	Contract cutoff date	Consolidation period for current maturities		Consolidation includes		Share of debt consolidated (percent)	Amount consolidated (millions of dollars)	Repayment terms[a]	
		Start date	Length (months)	Arrears	Previously rescheduled debt			Maturity (years/months)	Grace (years/months)
Mozambique									
25 Oct. 84	1 Feb. 84	1 July 84	12	y		95	283	10/6	5/0
16 June 87	1 Feb. 84	1 June 87	19	y		100	361	19/3	9/9
14 June 90	1 Feb. 84	1 July 90	30	y	y	100	719	Menu	Menu
23 Mar. 93	1 Feb. 84	1 Jan. 94	24		y	100	440	Menu	Menu
21 Nov. 96	1 Feb. 84	1 Nov. 96	36	y	y	100	664	Menu	Menu
9 July 99	1 Feb. 84	1 July 99	Stock	y	y	100	1,860	Menu	Menu
15 Mar. 00	1 Feb. 84	Deferral	12	y	y	100	36	Menu	Menu
20 Nov. 00	1 Feb. 84	1 Sep 01	Stock	y	y	100	2,234	Menu	Menu
Nicaragua									
17 Dec. 91	1 Nov. 88	1 Jan. 92	15	y	y	100	722	Menu	Menu
21 Mar. 95	1 Nov. 88	1 Apr. 95	27	y	y	100	783	Menu	Menu
22 Apr. 98	1 Nov. 88	1 Mar. 98	36	y	y	100	214	Menu	Menu
Niger									
14 Nov. 83	1 July 83	1 Oct. 83	12			90	36	8/6	4/6
30 Nov. 84	1 July 83	1 Oct. 84	14			90	26	9/5	4/11
21 Nov. 85	1 July 83	1 Dec. 85	12			90	38	9/6	5/ 0
20 Nov. 86	1 July 83	3 Dec. 86	12			100	34	9/6	5/ 0
21 Apr. 88	1 July 83	5 Dec. 87	13			100	37	19/6	10/0
16 Dec. 88	1 July 83	1 Jan. 89	12			100	48	Menu	Menu
18 Sept. 90	1 July 83	1 Sept. 90	28	y	y	100	116	Menu	Menu
4 Mar. 94	1 July 83	1 Jan. 94	15	y	y	100	160	Menu	Menu
19 Mar. 96	1 July 83	1 Dec. 96	31	y	y	100	128	Menu	Menu
25 Jan. 01	1 July 83	1 Dec. 00	36	y	y	100	115	Menu	Menu
Nigeria									
16 Dec. 86	1 Oct. 85	1 Oct. 86	15	y		100	6,251	6/6	2/0
3 Mar. 89	1 Oct. 85	1 Jan. 89	16	y		100	5,600	9/4	4/10
18 Jan. 91[c]	1 Oct. 85	1 Jan. 91	15	y		100	3,300	19/5, 14/5	9/11, 7/11
12 Dec. 00	1 Oct. 85	1 Jan 00	12	y		100	23,100	19/5, 14/5	9/11, 7/11
Pakistan									
14 Jan. 81*	1 July 80	15 Jan. 81	18			90	263	Variable	Variable
30 Jan. 99	30 Sept. 97	1 Jan. 99	24	y	y	100	3,250	20/0, 18/0	10/0, 3/0
23 Jan. 01	30 Sept. 97	1 Dec. 00	10	y	y	100	3,250	20/0, 18/0	10/0, 3/0
14 Dec. 01	30 Sept. 97	30 Nov. 01	Stock	y	y	100	12,500	38/0, 23/0	15/0, 5/0
Panama									
19 Sept. 85	31 Dec. 84	15 Sept. 85	16			50	19	7/4	2/10
14 Nov. 90[e]	31 Dec. 84	1 Nov. 90	17	y	y	100	200	9/4	4/10
Peru									
26 July 83	1 Jan. 83	1 May 83	12			90	466	7/6	3/0
5 June 84	1 Jan. 83	1 May 84	15			90	704	8/5	4/11
17 Sept. 91[c]	1 Jan. 83	1 Oct. 91	15	y	y	100	5,910	19/5, 14/5	9/11, 7/11
4 May 93[c]	1 Jan. 83	1 Jan. 93	39		y	100	1,527	18/5, 13/5	8/11, 6/11
20 July 96	1 Jan. 83	30 Apr. 96	Stock				6,724	17/0, 19/3	0/6, 2/0
Philippines									
21 Dec. 84	1 Apr. 84	1 Jan. 85	18	y		100	757	9/3	4/9
22 Jan. 87	1 Apr. 84	1 Jan. 87	18			100	862	9/3	4/9
26 May 89	1 Apr. 84	1 June 89	25	y		100	1,850	9/0	5/6
20 June 91[c]	1 Apr. 84	1 July 91	14		y	100	1,096	19/5, 14/5	9/11, 7/11
19 July 94[d]	1 Apr. 84	1 Aug. 94	17	y	y	100	586	19/4, 14/4	9/10, 7/10

Table A3.2 Multilateral debt relief agreements with official creditors, January 1980–December 2001 (continued)

| Country and date of agreement | Contract cutoff date | Consolidation period for current maturities | | Consolidation includes | | Share of debt consolidated (percent) | Amount consolidated (millions of dollars) | Repayment terms[a] | |
		Start date	Length (months)	Arrears	Previously rescheduled debt			Maturity (years/ months)	Grace (years/ months)
Poland									
27 Apr. 81*	1 Jan. 80	1 May 81	8	y		90	2,110	7/6	4/0
15 July 85*	1 Jan. 84	1 Jan. 82	36	y		100	10,930	10/6	5/0
19 Nov. 85*	1 Jan. 84	1 Jan. 86	12			100	1,400	9/2	4/8
16 Dec. 87*	1 Jan. 84	1 Jan. 88	12	y	y	100	9,027	9/0	4/6
16 Feb. 90	1 Jan. 84	1 Jan. 90	15	y	y	100	10,400	13/9	8/3
21 Apr. 91	1 Jan. 84	Balances: 30 Mar. 91		y	y	100	29,871	Menu	Menu
Romania									
9 July 82	1 Jan. 82	1 Jan. 82	12	y		80	234	6/0	3/0
18 May 83	1 Jan. 82	1 Jan. 83	12			60	736	6/0	3/0
Russian Federation									
2 Apr. 93[f]	1 Jan. 91	1 Jan. 93	12	y		100	14,363	10/0	6/0
2 June 94	1 Jan. 91	1 Jan. 94	12			100	7,100	15/2	2/9
3 June 95	1 Jan. 91	1 Jan. 95	12			100	6,400	15/4	2/10
15 Apr. 96	1 Jan. 91	1 Jan. 96	Stock			100	40,200	21/5	2/11
1 Aug. 99	1 Jan. 91	1 July 99	18	y	y	100	8,040	Variable	Variable
Rwanda									
21 July 98	31 Dec. 94	1 July 98	35			100	64	Menu	Menu
São Tomé and Principe									
16 May 00	1 Apr. 99	31 Mar. 00	37	y		100	28	Menu	Menu
Senegal									
13 Oct. 81	1 July 81	1 July 81	12			85	75	8/6	4/0
29 Nov. 82	1 July 81	1 July 82	12			85	74	8/9	4/3
21 Dec. 83	1 Jan. 83	1 July 83	12			90	72	8/6	4/0
18 Jan. 85	1 Jan. 83	1 Jan. 85	18	y		95	122	8/3	3/9
21 Nov. 86	1 Jan. 83	1 July 86	16			100	65	9/4	4/10
17 Nov. 87	1 Jan. 83	1 Nov. 87	12			100	79	15/6	6/0
24 Jan. 89	1 Jan. 83	1 Nov. 88	14		y	100	143	Menu	Menu
12 Feb. 90	1 Jan. 83	1 Jan. 90	12	y	y	100	107	Menu	Menu
21 June 91	1 Jan. 83	1 July 91	12	y	y	100	114	Menu	Menu
3 Mar. 94	1 Jan. 83	1 Jan. 94	15	y	y	100	237	Menu	Menu
20 Apr. 95	1 Jan. 83	1 Apr. 95	29		y	100	169	Menu	Menu
17 June 98	1 Jan. 83	17 June 98	Stock	y	y	100	428	Menu	Menu
24 Oct. 00	1 Jan. 83	interim relief		y	y	100	21	Menu	Menu
Sierra Leone									
8 Nov. 80	1 July 79	1 July 79	30	y		90	37	9/6	4/0
8 Feb. 84	1 July 83	1 Jan. 84	12	y	y	90	25	10/0	5/0
19 Nov. 86	1 July 83	1 July 86	16	y	y	100	86	9/4	4/10
20 Nov. 92	1 July 83	1 Nov. 92	16	y	y	100	164	Menu	Menu
20 July 94	1 July 83	1 Aug. 94	17	Arrears	y	100	42	Menu	Menu
25 Apr. 96	1 July 83	1 Jan. 96	24	y	y	100	39	Menu	Menu
16 Oct. 01	1 July 83	1 Oct. 01	36	y	y	100	180	Menu	Menu
Somalia									
6 Mar. 85	1 Oct. 84	1 Jan. 85	12	y		95	127	9/6	5/0
22 July 87	1 Oct. 84	1 Jan. 87	24	y	y	100	153	19/0	9/6
Sudan									
18 Mar. 82	1 July 81	1 July 81	18	y	y	90	203	9/6	4/6
4 Feb. 83	1 Jan. 83	1 Jan. 83	12		y	100	518	15/0	5/6
2 May 84	1 Jan. 84	1 Jan. 84	12		y	100	249	15/6	6/0

(Table continues on next page)

Table A3.2 Multilateral debt relief agreements with official creditors, January 1980–December 2001 *(continued)*

| Country and date of agreement | Contract cutoff date | Consolidation period for current maturities | | Consolidation includes | | Share of debt consolidated *(percent)* | Amount consolidated *(millions of dollars)* | Repayment terms[a] | |
		Start date	Length *(months)*	Arrears	Previously rescheduled debt			Maturity *(years/ months)*	Grace *(years/ months)*
Tanzania									
18 Sept. 86	30 June 86	1 Oct. 86	12	y		100	1,046	9/6	5/0
13 Dec. 88	30 June 86	1 Jan. 89	6	y	y	100	377	Menu	Menu
16 Mar. 90	30 June 86	1 Jan. 90	12	y	y	100	199	Menu	Menu
21 Jan. 92	30 June 86	1 Jan. 92	30	y	y	100	691	Menu	Menu
21 Jan. 97	30 June 86	1 Dec. 96	36	y	y	100	1,608	Menu	Menu
14 Apr. 00	30 June 86	31 Mar. 00	36	y	y	100	714	Menu	Menu
Togo									
20 Feb. 81	1 July 80	1 Jan. 81	24			85	232	8/6	4/0
12 Apr. 83	1 Jan. 83	1 Jan. 83	12	y	y	90	300	9/6	5/0
6 June 84	1 Jan. 83	1 Jan. 84	16		y	95	75	9/4	4/10
24 June 85	1 Jan. 83	1 May 85	12			95	27	10/6	5/0
22 Mar. 88	1 Jan. 83	1 Jan. 88	15	y	y	100	139	15/5	7/11
20 June 89	1 Jan. 83	16 Apr. 89	14		y	100	76	Menu	Menu
9 July 90	1 Jan. 83	1 July 90	24		y	100	88	Menu	Menu
19 June 92[d]	1 Jan. 83	1 July 92	24		y	100	52	Menu	Menu
23 Feb. 95	1 Jan. 83	1 Feb. 95	33	y	y	100	237	Menu	Menu
Trinidad and Tobago									
25 Jan. 89	1 Sept. 88	1 Jan. 89	14	y		100	209	9/5	4/11
27 Apr. 90	1 Sept. 88	1 Mar. 90	13			100	110	8/4	3/10
Turkey									
23 July 80*	30 June 80	1 July 80	36	y	y	90	3,000	9/0	4/6
Uganda									
18 Nov. 81	1 July 81	1 July 81	12	y		90	30	9/0	4/6
1 Dec. 82	1 July 81	1 July 82	12			90	19	9/0	4/6
19 June 87	1 July 81	1 July 87	12	y	y	100	170	14/6	6/0
26 Jan. 89	1 July 81	1 Jan. 89	18	y	y	100	89	Menu	Menu
17 June 92	1 July 81	1 July 92	17	y	y	100	39	Menu	Menu
20 Feb. 95	1 July 81	1 Feb. 95	Stock	y	y	100	110	Menu	Menu
24 Apr. 98	1 July 81	1 Apr. 98	Stock		y	100	148	Menu	Menu
12 Sept. 00	1 July 81	1 Sept. 00	Stock		y	100	150	Menu	Menu
Ukraine									
13 July 01	31 Dec. 98	19 Dec. 00	22	y		100	580	12/0	3/0
Vietnam									
14 Dec. 93	1 Jan. 90	Arrears as of 31 Dec. 93		y		100	791	Menu	Menu
Yemen, Rep. of									
24 Sept. 96	1 Jan. 93	1 Sept. 96	10	y		100	113	Menu	Menu
20 Nov. 97	1 Jan. 93	1 Nov. 97	36	y		100	1,444	Menu	Menu
14 June 01	1 Jan. 93	31 Dec. 00	Stock	y		100	420	Menu	Menu
Yugoslavia, Fed. Rep. (Serbia/ Montenegro)									
22 May 84*	2 Dec. 82	1 Jan. 84	12			100	500	6/6	4/0
24 May 85*	2 Dec. 82	1 Jan. 85	16			90	812	8/4	3/10
13 May 86*	2 Dec. 82	16 May 86	23			85	901	8/6	4/0
13 July 88*	2 Dec. 82	1 Apr. 88	15		y	100	1,291	9/5	5/11
16 Nov. 01	1 Apr. 88	20 Dec. 00	Stock		y	100	4,500	Menu	Menu

Table A3.2 Multilateral debt relief agreements with official creditors, January 1980–December 2001 *(continued)*

Country and date of agreement	Contract cutoff date	Consolidation period for current maturities		Consolidation includes		Share of debt consolidated *(percent)*	Amount consolidated *(millions of dollars)*	Repayment terms[a]	
		Start date	Length *(months)*	Arrears	Previously rescheduled debt			Maturity *(years/ months)*	Grace *(years/ months)*
Zambia									
16 May 83	1 Jan. 83	1 Jan. 83	12	y		90	375	9/6	5/0
20 July 84	1 Jan. 83	1 Jan. 84	12	y	y	100	253	9/6	5/0
4 Mar. 86	1 Jan. 83	1 Jan. 86	12	y	y	100	371	9/6	5/0
12 July 90	1 Jan. 83	1 July 90	18	y	y	100	963	Menu	Menu
23 July 92	1 Jan. 83	1 July 92	33	y	y	100	917	Menu	Menu
27 Feb. 96	1 Jan. 83	1 Jan. 96	36	y	y	100	566	Menu	Menu
16 Apr. 99	1 Jan. 83	1 Apr. 99	36	y	y	100	1,060	Menu	Menu

.. Not applicable.

* The rescheduling was concluded outside of formal Paris Club auspices.

"Menu" terms refer to the options agreed to at the 1988 Toronto economic summit meeting.

Note: The figures in this table are commitment values (amounts of agreed-on debt relief). They correspond to the disbursement figures (minus debt forgiveness, when applicable) for debt restructuring shown in the *Global Development Finance: Country Tables*. All agreements shown in this table, except those indicated with an asterisk, were negotiated through the Paris Club.

a. Maturity is measured here from the end of the consolidation period to the date of the final amortization payment; the grace period is the time between the end of the consolidation period and the date of the first amortization payment. The secretariat of the Paris Club measures grace and maturity from the midpoint of the consolidation period.

b. The agreement signed in March 1995 covered a 36-month period, but a new agreement was signed in December 1995 covering the stock of debt, starting 12 months after the beginning of the consolidation period of the previous agreement.

c. Agreement with a Paris Club–designated lower-middle-income country with heavy official debt. These agreements also allow for debt conversions, subject to the limit for each creditor country (for non-ODA debt) of US$10 million or 10 percent of the debt outstanding as of the beginning of the consolidation period, whichever is higher. Where two sets of figures for repayment terms (maturity and grace) are given, the first set represents ODA debt and the second non-ODA debt.

d. The agreement was canceled.

e. The agreement was implemented in 1991 because of the agreement's conditionality on an IMF program that took place in 1991.

f. Agreement follows the deferral signed in January 1992 by the former Soviet republics.

Sources: World Bank DRS; IMF; Paris Club Secretariat.

Appendix 4
Regional Economic Developments and Prospects

East Asia and Pacific

Europe and Central Asia

Latin America and the Caribbean

Middle East and North Africa

South Asia

Sub-Saharan Africa

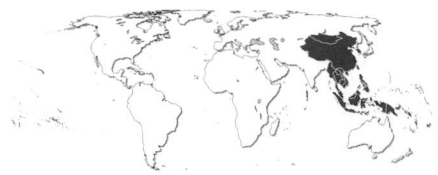

East Asia and Pacific

GNI per capita, 2000: $1,060

GDP growth in East Asia, 1999–2001

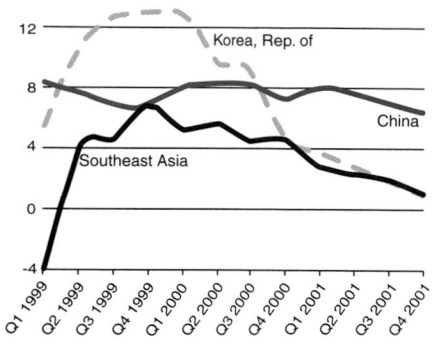

Year-over-year percentage change

Source: World Bank.

Industrial production in East Asia, 1999–2002

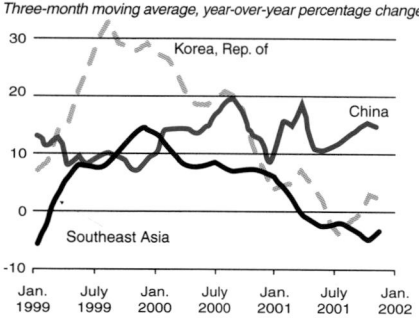

Three-month moving average, year-over-year percentage change

Source: Datastream and World Bank staff estimates.

Export in dollars, growth for East Asia, 1999–2001

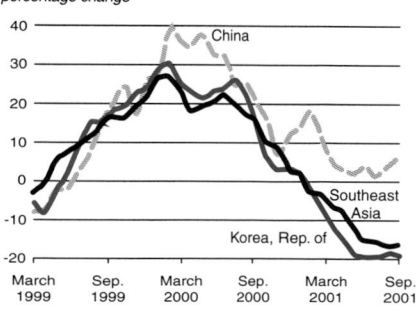

Three-month moving average, year-over-year percentage change

Source: Datastream.

Recent developments

Growth in the East Asia and Pacific region slowed sharply in 2001, from 7.4 percent in 2000 to 4.6 percent. Excluding China, growth slowed more, from 7 percent in 2000 to 2.3 percent in 2001. The downturn in growth was concentrated in the high-tech exporting countries, which suffered disproportionately from the global recession in high-tech sectors.[1] Chinese growth was maintained at rates above 7 percent through substantial fiscal stimulus. And Vietnam grew by 5.5 percent by further increasing its share in export markets. But, partly related to its export success, the country suffered significant terms-of-trade losses.

Regional merchandise export volumes showed little to no growth in 2001, following an advance of 23 percent in 2000. And dollar export revenues fell (3.7 percent) for the first time since 1998. Moreover, loss of tourism revenue was significant in the wake of September 11, especially for Thailand and the Philippines. Worker remittances in the latter country were down sharply, a direct effect of the slowdown in world trade and tourism, because a significant portion of remittances come from Philippine seamen on cargo and cruise vessels.

Many countries in the region were able to use countercyclical monetary and fiscal policies to limit the adverse effects on growth caused by worsening external conditions. Rapidly falling international interest rates facilitated domestic interest rate declines in several countries. Over the course of 2001, policy rates fell 140 basis points in the Republic of Korea and 550 basis points in the Philippines. In both countries unemployment stabilized in the first half of 2001 and decreased in the second half of the year.

Across the region fiscal balances deteriorated, but the impact of this stimulus on domestic inflation and exchange rate levels was limited. For Thailand, Korea, and the Philippines, currency depreciation vis-à-vis the dollar ranged between 2 and 6.5 percent during 2001. The 9 percent depreciation of the rupiah, despite a 400 basis point increase in policy interest rates, made Indonesia an exception in the region.

Despite a decisive reduction in current account surpluses, the region saw a $50 billion increase in reserves during the year. The improved external positions since the East Asian crisis made an increase in reserves possible despite a fall in export revenues and domestic stimulus, and a decline in capital flows. Indonesia, struggling with a difficult political and social environment, was one of the few countries where reserves declined.

Capital market flows decline

Gross flows from the international capital markets fell dramatically during 2001. The aggregate of bond and equity issuance and bank lending dropped by $25.8 billion in the year (almost 40 percent) to reach a level of $40.9 billion—only moderately above the outturns of 1998, at the peak of the East Asian crisis. In contrast with conditions at that time—large-scale withdrawal of short-term banking debt—the 2001 downturn in flows reflects in part a decrease in demand for funds in the region, as well as limited investor supply of capital for high-tech ventures. The falloff in flows to East Asia amounted to one-half of the decline in flows to all emerging markets for the year.

Banking flows, which traditionally account for about 50 percent of market-based financing for the region, dropped by $10.7 billion, or 36 percent, with the decline in international bank credit broadly based across countries. This development likely reflects the confluence of several factors: increasing availability of preferred long-term capital through the international bond markets; decreasing demand for funds from a balance of payments perspective, against the background of continued (albeit diminishing) current account surpluses and record high reserve levels; and falling requirements for working capital and trade finance, with steep recession in high-tech manufacturing sectors across developing East Asia.

International equity placement fell from a record $23 billion in 2000 to $7.2 billion. China, which is the premier source of equity issuance among emerging markets ($21.9 billion placed in 2000, or 62 percent of total equity during that year), found international market conditions unfavorable for issuing larger share volumes (particularly for high-tech firms). And investor appetite for emerging market exposure was diminished during most of the year. Despite the less opportune environment, Korea and Thailand stepped up international placements, the former more substantially, from $1 billion in 2000 to $3.7 billion in 2001.

The shift from bank-sourced financing to the bond markets was of note during the year. Although bond issuance in East Asia advanced by about $1 billion over 2000 levels to $14.7 billion, a number of countries began to participate more fully in the market. China increased issuance by more than $1 billion to $2.5 billion, Malaysia by $750 million to $2.2 billion, and Thailand to $280 million. In contrast, Indonesia and the Philippines, under the weight of structural economic difficulties at present, were limited in their ability to expand use of

the market, and issuance dropped by $200 million in the former and $625 million in the latter country during the year.

Bond market conditions were variable over the course of 2001. Spreads on East Asian secondary market debt increased moderately from an average 295 basis points in 2000 to 350 basis points in 2001—but these figures tend to mask the dynamics of financial market developments in the year. A narrowing of the regional spread by 50 basis points over the first half of 2001 was reversed by October as concerns regarding the Argentine situation and the health of the global economy mounted. By early January 2002, however, spreads fell quickly by 100 basis points, with the Philippines, a focus of some market concern, experiencing an easing of more than 200 basis points.

Foreign direct investment

Net inflows of foreign direct investment (FDI) to the region were $48.5 billion in 2001, a decline of $3.6 billion, or 6.9 percent, from 2000. At first glance, this amount must be considered a robust outturn in the context of global and East Asian regional recessions. Once more, such aggregates tend to mask a shifting distribution of investment flows across countries of the region.

The bulk of FDI flows continues to be directed to China, at $44 billion in 2001, a sharp $6 billion advance over the $38 billion recorded in 2000, returning flows to the record levels of 1997. But, with the exception of Vietnam, FDI flows into other large East Asian countries declined—in some cases precipitously—during the year. As an extreme case, for the fourth year in succession, FDI flowed out of Indonesia at an accelerated pace of $6 billion in 2001.[2] FDI dropped by $6

Export and import volume growth in East Asia, 1998–2001

Three-month moving average, year-over-year percentage change

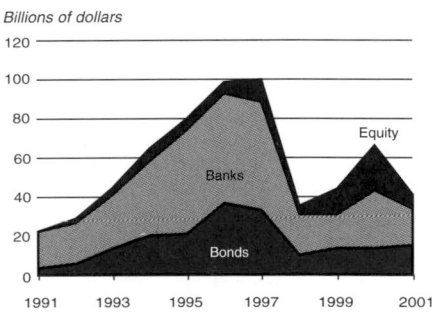

Note: EA-5 comprises Indonesia, the Republic of Korea, Malaysia, the Philippines, and Thailand.
Source: World Bank Economic Policy and Prospects Group.

Gross capital market flows to East Asia, 1991–2001

Billions of dollars

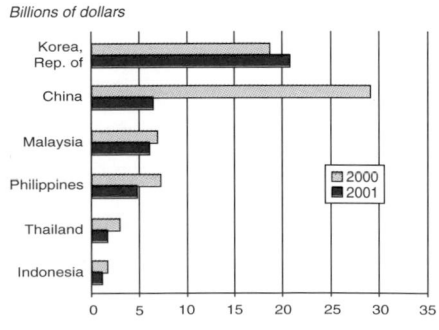

Source: Euromoney.

Capital market flows by country, 2000 and 2001

Billions of dollars

Source: World Bank Economic Policy and Prospects Group.

167

East Asian bond spreads, 2001

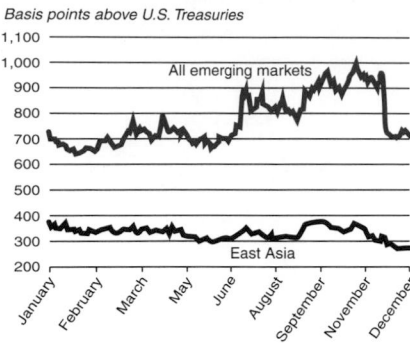

Basis points above U.S. Treasuries

Source: J.P. Morgan Chase through Bloomberg.

Selected East Asian bond spreads, 2001

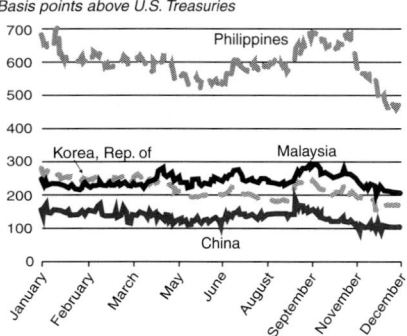

Basis points above U.S. Treasuries

billion, or two-thirds, in Korea; by $660 million, or 40 percent, in Malaysia; by 32 percent in Thailand; and by 20 percent in the Philippines.

The decline in FDI flows to these countries likely has its roots in the current downturn in the semiconductor and computer markets, where for several years overseas investment in new capacity had been buoyant. FDI flows to East Asia, excluding China, accumulated to $50 billion from 1998 to 2000, a good proportion of the accumulation occurring in the technology sectors.

Prospects and risks

Buoyed by the anticipated rebound in global high-tech markets (signs of which are now emerging in the United States), East Asia is expected to lead recovery in the developing world. During the fourth quarter of 2001, industrial production in high-tech East Asia, (Korea and Malaysia among middle-income countries, Singapore and Taiwan [China] among the newly industrialized economies) has turned the corner decisively, in line with an upturn in Asian semiconductor sales. However, recovery in GDP growth is likely to appear muted in annual figures for 2002, as regional output is expected to register 5.2 percent growth in the year, up from 4.6 percent in 2001. But in the absence of ad-

verse surprises, the momentum underlying the current upswing could produce regional growth near 7 percent by 2003, growth similar to the robust outturns of 2000.

As most countries in the region have generally kept real exchange rate levels below their precrisis averages, they are expected to benefit fully from the turnaround in global trade, with export growth of nearly 10 percent in 2003 and 2004.

Yet, downside risks to this more encouraging view remain large. The recovery in global high-tech sectors may not be as robust as has been the case in past cycles. In particular, the unprecedented bursting of the high-tech bubble in financial markets may exert a larger drag on the availability of funds for high-tech firms than is assumed in the baseline. In broader scope, near-term revival of world demand continues to hinge on the spending behavior of the U.S. consumer. And abrupt changes in consumer confidence could serve to delay or protract recovery for some time.

Within East Asia, the economic and political situation in Indonesia remains difficult, potentially dampening the recovery foreseen in the baseline. And the "war on terrorism" has increased global uncertainty, with several countries in the region potentially directly affected in future.

Foreign direct investment, 1991–2001

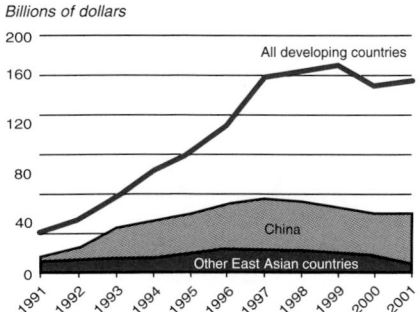

Billions of dollars

Source: World Bank.

Notes

1. The most adversely affected were Korea and the newly industrialized economies (NIEs)—Hong Kong (China), Singapore, and Taiwan (China), which are not included in the aggregate for developing East Asia.

2. Negative net FDI in Indonesia is the result of repayments of intrafirm loans from foreign subsidiaries to their parents abroad.

Foreign direct investment by country, 2000 and 2001

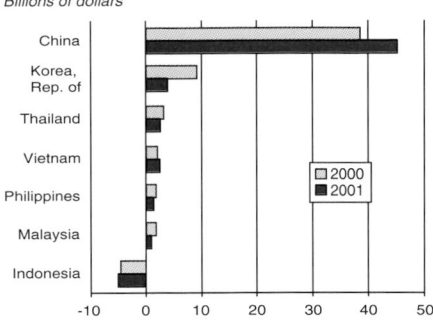

Billions of dollars

Source: World Bank Economic Policy and Prospects Group.

East Asia and Pacific forecast summary

(percent per year)

Growth rates/ratios	1991–2000	1999	2000	Estimate 2001	Baseline forecast 2002	2003	2004
Real GDP growth	7.2	7.0	7.4	4.6	5.2	6.9	6.5
Consumption per capita	5.4	6.3	6.4	4.9	5.5	5.6	5.9
GDP per capita	6.0	5.9	6.4	3.7	4.2	6.0	5.6
Population	1.2	1.1	1.0	0.9	0.9	0.9	0.8
Gross domestic investment/GDP[a]	30.3	28.9	29.9	30.8	31.4	31.2	31.0
Inflation[b]	5.4	0.1	3.4	4.2	6.8	6.4	6.3
Central government budget balance/GDP	-1.1	-2.5	-2.7	-2.9	-2.9	-2.9	-2.5
Export market growth[c]	8.3	7.3	14.2	-0.3	2.6	7.8	7.6
Export volume[d]	12.7	7.5	22.0	2.6	7.1	9.4	10.7
Terms of trade/GDP[e]	-0.3	0.1	-0.9	-1.2	0.2	-0.5	-0.3
Current account/GDP	0.5	4.6	3.5	1.9	2.3	1.8	1.2
Memo items							
GDP growth: East Asia excluding China	5.3	6.9	7.0	2.3	3.5	5.9	5.5

a. Fixed investment, measured in real terms
b. Local currency GDP deflator, median.
c. Weighted average growth of import demand in export markets.
d. Goods and nonfactor services
e. Change in terms of trade, measured as a proportion of GDP (percent).
Source: World Bank baseline forecast, February 2002.

Real effective exchange rates, 1997–2002

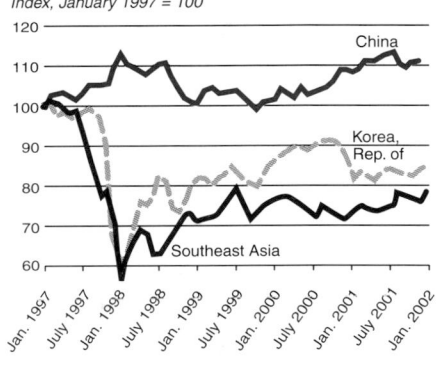

Index, January 1997 = 100

Source: J.P. Morgan Chase.

High-tech emerging Asia:[a] Semiconductor dollar sales and industrial production, 1997–2001

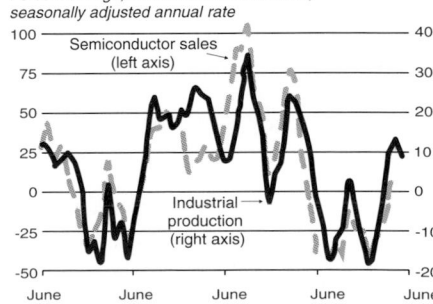

Percent change, three-month/three-month, seasonally adjusted annual rate

Note: Through November 2001.
a. Republic of Korea, Malaysia, Singapore, and Taiwan (China).
Source: Datastream; World Bank staff estimates.

Europe and Central Asia

GNI per capita, 2000: $2,010

GDP growth rates, 1970–2001

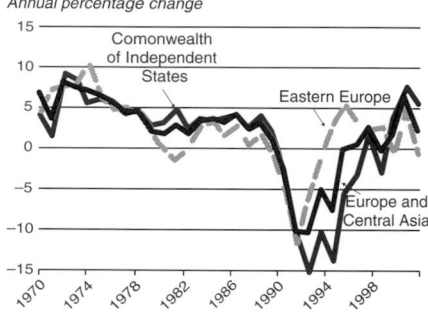

Source: World Bank.

Industrial production, 1997–2001

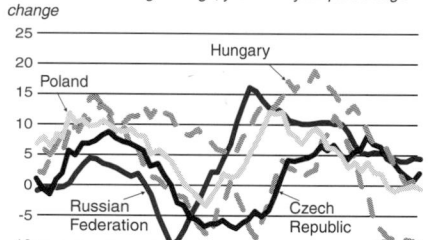

Source: Datastream.

Russian imports and partner exports, 1997–2001

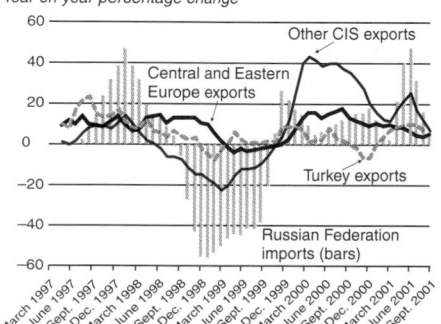

Source: International Monetary Fund, *International Finance Statistics*; and World Bank.

Recent developments

Output growth in Europe and Central Asia slowed markedly to an estimated 2.2 percent in 2001 from 6.4 percent in 2000. A sharp deceleration in export markets contributed to this slowdown, but domestic factors were more significant—with a particularly pronounced downturn in Turkey and a notable deceleration of growth in Poland. While performance varied across countries, the general trend was an easing of growth during 2001. Most European and Central Asian countries experienced declining inflation—particularly in the Commonwealth of Independent States (CIS), where the median rate fell from 17.3 percent in 2000 to 8.8 percent in 2001—and falling interest rates, reflecting a drop in import prices and international interest rates. At the same time, a number of European and Central Asian countries (the Czech Republic, Kazakhstan, Poland, Ukraine, and Uzbekistan, among others) witnessed some deterioration in fiscal balances, generally because of the adoption of more expansionary fiscal policies.

The Central and Eastern European countries (including the Baltics and Turkey) experienced a contraction in output of 0.8 percent in 2001, following a robust 5 percent expansion in 2000. Pulling down the outturn for this group, the severe banking and currency crises in Turkey in February 2001 ushered in a sharp contraction of its economy over the year. Growth in the Central and Eastern Europe, excluding Turkey, declined to 2.9 percent in 2001 from 3.8 percent in 2000. This moderate deceleration reflected a slowdown in domestic demand in a few countries, especially in Poland, which had pursued a tight monetary

policy through much of 2001; the former Yugoslav Republic of Macedonia, where civil war disrupted economic activity; and Slovenia, which witnessed a contraction in investment that was due in part to an increase in interest rates. Declining exports to Western Europe contributed to softening growth, given the Central and Eastern European economies' high exposure to Euro Area import demand. For example, Hungary, Poland, and the Slovak Republic's export volume growth decelerated markedly in 2001. However, import compression in a number of Central and Eastern European countries, including Turkey and Poland, mitigated weaker export performance from a balance of payments perspective.

The countries seeking accession to the European Union (EU) received a boost in November 2001, when the European Commission released its regular annual reports on the 10 European and Central Asian candidates— all Central and Eastern European countries.[1] The commission reported that all candidates made substantial progress in adopting the *aqcuis communautaire* (body of European Community law) over the year and that most of the countries (excluding Bulgaria and Romania) are expected to be ready to join in the near term. Some hurdles remain, as EU members have yet to formalize agreements in a number of important areas, mainly pertaining to agriculture and budgetary issues.

The CIS achieved strong 5.5 percent growth in 2001, though this is a significant moderation from the exceptionally robust 7.9 percent output advance of 2000. The slowdown mainly reflected easing energy prices from the highs witnessed in 2000. In

Russia, some of the Caucasus countries, and Central Asia, firm energy prices funded increased fiscal outlays and investment. Further, domestic demand in Russia continued to benefit, albeit moderately, from ongoing import substitution spurred by the 1998 devaluation, as the ruble remains below precrisis levels. However, the 7 percent appreciation of the real effective exchange rate in 2001—culminating in the ruble losing roughly half of the competitive advantage it had gained because of the 1998 devaluation—is eroding this impetus. Firm growth in Russia, the CIS's largest economy, has also been key to generating strong external demand for other countries in Europe and Central Asia, especially those of the CIS and the Baltics.

Contagion from the financial crisis in Turkey was not notably apparent in the rest of Europe and Central Asia. For the region, excluding Turkey, spreads on secondary market debt instruments declined from an average of 1,020 basis points during 2000 to an average of 854 points during 2001. For example, spreads declined significantly in Russia from just below 1,340 basis points in 2000 to 955 for 2001, and in Croatia, from 380 basis points to 225. In Turkey, the average spread increased sharply from just over 530 basis points in 2000 to over 900 in 2001, and stabilized in the beginning of 2002 near 650 points.

Aside from rating downgrades for Turkish debt early in the year because of concerns about fiscal policy and the banking sector, (to B− from B+, according to Standard and Poor's [S&P]), credit ratings elsewhere in the region were upgraded. The Slovak Republic's rating was raised to investment grade by S&P, tied to progress in EU accession negotiations and the restructuring of state banks. A number of other European and Central Asian sovereigns were upgraded during 2001, including Bulgaria, Estonia, Kazakhstan, Romania, and Russia. The shifts in credit quality were attributed to various factors, including improvements in economic structure (Bulgaria, Estonia, and Russia), in the banking sector (Romania), or in external liquidity (Kazakhstan and Romania).

Gross capital market flows and foreign direct investment

Capital market commitments (bonds, bank lending, and portfolio equity) to Europe and Central Asia experienced a massive 34 percent decline during 2001 to $28.2 billion from a total $43 billion in 2000. The sharp drop-off is a reflection of the currency and banking sector crisis in Turkey, where flows fell by nearly $15 billion in the year, while gross capital market commitments to the rest of the region were flat at $21 billion. The largest decline for the region in aggregate was posted in banking flows, down from over $25 billion in 2000 to about $17 billion in 2001. Again, the decline in flows to Turkey of $6.5 billion accounts for the bulk of the reduction, though Poland and Russia experienced a moderate decline in banking flows.

Bond and equity flows to the region also fell sharply, both posting a drop-off of close to $3 billion. A large $6.3 billion decline in bond flows to Turkey was partially offset by substantial upswings in bond issuance by Hungary, Poland, Romania, and Russia. And a fall of $3 billion in equity placement from the region is almost wholly attributable to declines in flows to Turkey.

Foreign direct investment (FDI) flows remained much more resilient, totaling $28.5 in 2001, the same level

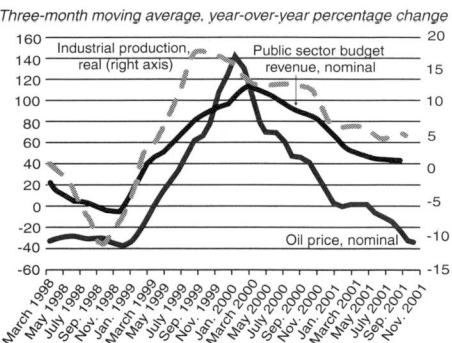

Russian Federation: Oil prices, fiscal linkage, and growth, 1998–2001

Three-month moving average, year-over-year percentage change

Source: World Bank.

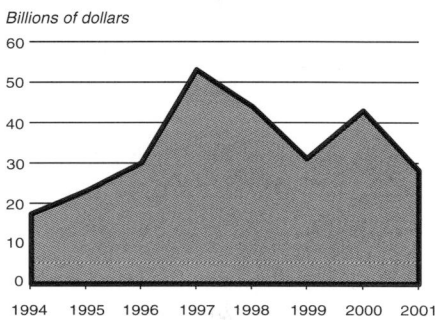

Gross capital market commitments, 1994–2001

Billions of dollars

Source: World Bank.

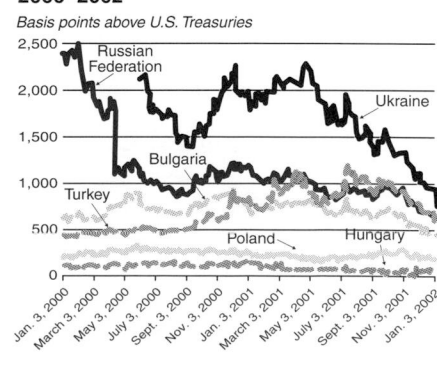

Secondary market spreads for selected European and Central Asia countries, 2000–2002

Basis points above U.S. Treasuries

Source: J.P. Morgan Chase

Composition of gross capital market commitments, 1996 and 2001

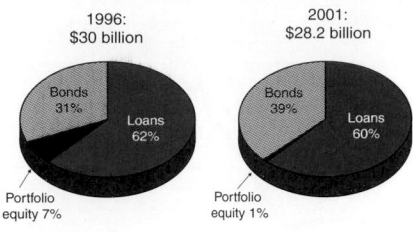

1996:
$30 billion

2001:
$28.2 billion

Source: World Bank.

Gross capital market commitments, 2001

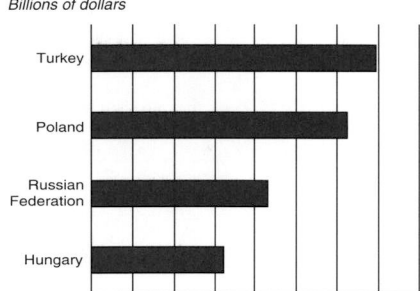

Billions of dollars

Source: World Bank.

Net foreign direct investment, 1994–2001

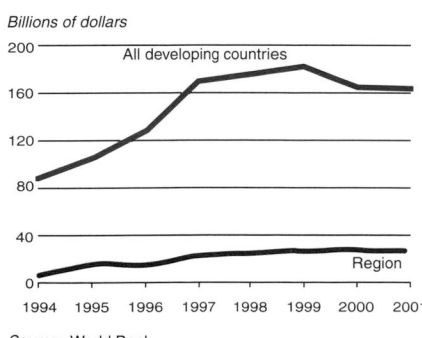

Billions of dollars

Source: World Bank.

as posted in 2000. However, a majority of countries in Europe and Central Asia witnessed a decline in FDI from year-earlier levels. Poland experienced the largest falloff—nearly $3 billion in 2001 to $6.5 billion—followed by the Slovak Republic with a $1 billion decline, half the 2000 level. A $2.5 billion increase to $3.5 billion in FDI flows to Turkey and an increase of $1.3 billion to Kazakhstan (to $2.5 billion) served to offset the decline in flows to Poland and the Slovak Republic.

Debt negotiations

Georgia, Ukraine, and the Federal Republic of Yugoslavia concluded external debt-restructuring agreements with Paris Club creditors during 2001. These agreements are expected to reduce 2000 debt service to Paris Club creditors from $88 million to $33 million for Georgia, and from an initial amount of $800 million in 2001 to $285 million for Ukraine in 2002. For the Federal Republic of Yugoslavia, the debt-restructuring agreement is expected to restrict debt service to below $100 million per year through 2005. Russia was unsuccessful in its bid early in 2001 to restructure its external debt with Paris Club creditors, and has been paying its commitments in full under the existing agreement. In June 2001, the Turkish Treasury conducted a domestic swap auction to extend the maturity profile of domestic borrowing and reduce the financing requirement for 2001. And the Kyrgyz Republic is expected to begin negotiations for debt restructuring with the Paris Club creditors in March 2002.

Prospects and risks

Growth in the region is expected to firm moderately to about 3.2 percent in 2002 and to strengthen to 4.3 percent in 2003. An assumption of stabi-

lization and recovery to positive growth in Turkey, together with firming external demand for the region, should provide the foundation for reacceleration of growth. And monetary easing in a number of countries following a period of policy tightening (for example, as pursued in Poland since late 2001) is expected to boost growth over the period. But for hydrocarbon exporters, growth is anticipated to slow moderately in 2002, reflecting lower oil prices and a concomitant slowdown in government spending and investment.

Aggregate growth in Europe and Central Asia is forecast to decelerate marginally to 4 percent in 2004, in part due to an expected moderation of external demand. For countries seeking accession to the EU (almost all of Central and Eastern Europe), deepening reforms, continued significant inflows of FDI, as well as steady external demand should provide continued strong impetus to growth. Growth for the Central and Eastern European countries is forecast to average 4.7 percent by 2004. The main threats to the forecast for Central and Eastern Europe emanate from fiscal and external deficits. There is also a modest risk that the EU accession process might be delayed, should remaining negotiations (such as on agricultural and budgetary issues) run into difficulties.

The outlook is more clouded for the CIS, with threats to the forecast on both the up- and downsides. These reflect the uncertainty in global oil markets and political factors. Growth in the CIS is projected to slow to close to 3 percent by 2004. One adverse factor is lower oil prices in real terms through 2004, down from the high levels witnessed in 2000 and 2001. The hydrocarbon-exporting countries of the CIS will need to manage commodity price volatility if they are to see stable growth. And in a number of CIS countries, large public sectors, overextended social security systems, and significant off-budget expenditures remain important challenges to achieving fiscal balance, which is essential for sustained growth. On the upside, the recent cooperation of a number of Central Asian countries with the U.S.-led intervention in Afghanistan is expected to lead to increased foreign assistance.

Note

1. The 10 countries are Bulgaria, the Czech Republic, Estonia, Hungary, Latvia, Lithuania, Poland, Romania, the Slovak Republic, and Slovenia. Turkey is also seeking EU membership.

Net foreign direct investment by country, 2001

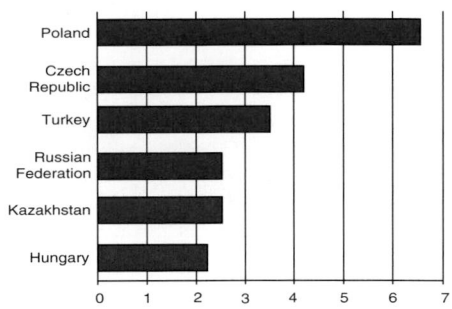

Source: World Bank.

Europe and Central Asia forecast summary

(percent per year)

Growth rates/ratios	1991–2000	1999	2000	Estimate 2001	Baseline forecast 2002	2003	2004
Real GDP growth	−2.3	1.6	6.4	2.2	3.2	4.3	4.0
Consumption per capita	−2.7	−1.9	5.0	0.8	3.2	3.6	3.5
GDP per capita	−2.5	1.5	6.2	2.1	3.1	4.2	3.9
Population	0.2	0.2	0.1	0.1	0.1	0.1	0.1
Gross domestic investment/GDP[a]	22.0	20.9	21.4	20.5	21.0	21.4	21.6
Inflation[b]	347.7	7.6	7.4	5.9	6.1	6.3	6.9
Central government budget balance/GDP	−4.8	−4.5	−2.5	−1.7	−2.8	−3.0	−3.1
Export market growth[c]	5.3	−0.8	11.7	6.1	3.4	7.6	7.2
Export volume[d]	0.6	−0.7	12.0	9.8	7.0	10.8	9.8
Terms of trade/GDP[e]	−0.3	0.2	−1.3	0.2	−2.0	−0.5	−0.1
Current account/GDP	−0.4	0.2	2.2	2.2	−0.4	−0.8	−0.9
Memo items							
GDP growth:							
transition countries	−3.2	3.3	6.2	4.4	3.4	4.0	4.0
Central and Eastern Europe	1.6	−0.6	5.0	−0.8	2.6	4.8	4.7
Central and Eastern Europe[f]	0.7	2.1	3.8	2.9	2.8	4.1	4.9
CIS	−5.2	4.3	7.9	5.5	3.8	3.9	3.3

a. Fixed investment, measured in real terms.
b. Local currency GDP deflator, median.
c. Weighted average growth of import demand in export markets.
d. Goods and nonfactor services.
e. Change in terms of trade, measured as a proportion of GDP (percent).
f. Excluding Turkey.
Source: World Bank baseline forecast, February 2002.

GNI per capita, 2000: $3,670

GDP growth in selected Latin America and the Caribbean countries, 1999–2001

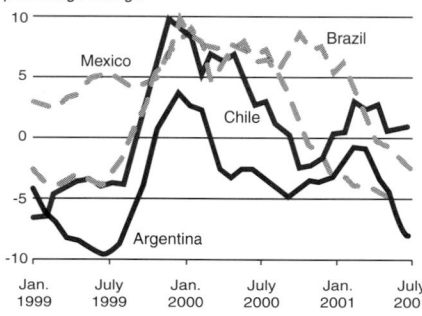

Percent, year-over-year

Source: World Bank.

Industrial production in selected Latin America and the Caribbean countries, 1999–2001

Three-month moving average, year-over-year percentage change

Source: Datastream.

Export in dollars, growth for selected Latin America and the Caribbean countries, 1999–2002

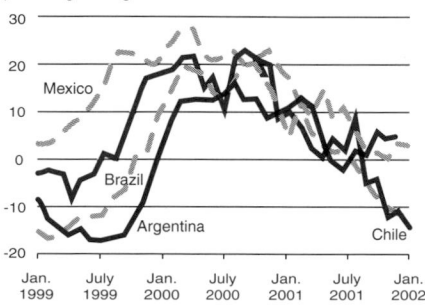

Three-month moving average, year-over-year percentage change

Source: Datastream.

Latin America and the Caribbean

Recent developments

Regional gross domestic product (GDP) grew 0.6 percent in 2001, about 0.3 percentage points lower than the forecast in *Global Economic Prospects 2002*, and a substantial slowdown from the 3.8 percent growth recorded in 2000. Weak external conditions, a progressive worsening of the political and economic situation in Argentina, and weather-related adversity in Brazil and Central America were the main contributors to the growth slowdown in the region. GDP in the region (excluding Argentina) grew only 1.3 percent, while output growth in Central America was below 1 percent for the first time in a decade.

A sharp fall in world trade growth and steep declines in dollar prices of key commodities exported by the region reduced export revenues. Export volumes are estimated to have grown a paltry 1.4 percent in 2001 after growing by 9 percent in 2000, mirroring the collapse in import demand in export markets. Moreover, falling commodity prices caused aggregate exports, in U.S. dollars, to decline by 1.4 percent, a sea change from the 19 percent rise in 2000. Export revenues fell at a more rapid pace after September 11 as security tightened along the Mexican-U.S. border, commodity prices fell further, and tourism revenues collapsed. Weak exports and limited access to private capital markets slowed output growth, resulting in the region's dollar imports falling by 0.8 percent. Oil exporters saw their trade surpluses diminish while most others had an improvement in their trade balances. The net result was a widening of the region's trade surplus by about $17 billion. The regional current account deficit widened by $5 billion, reflecting the larger trade surplus being offset by lower receipts

from tourism and remittances. The current account deficit (2.7 percent of GDP) was financed by drawing down reserves by about $1.2 billion, and by an increase in inflows from official creditors.

Only Chile and the República Bolivariana de Venezuela had the flexibility to embark on expansionary macroeconomic policies to mitigate the growth slowdown. High public debt loads and large external financing requirements prevented most countries from adopting countercyclical policies. However, interest rates were reduced significantly in several countries with floating exchange rates (for example, Colombia, Mexico, and Peru). Argentina benefited little from the fall in international interest rates as domestic interest rates remained high because of heightened exchange and credit risks. Instead, fiscal policy was progressively tightened in the course of the year, further depressing growth. Brazil raised interest rates and fiscal revenues, while Mexico cut spending in order to limit the rise in the fiscal deficit caused by slowing growth and declining oil tax revenues. The result was a general increase in regional unemployment, falling inflation rates in most countries, and little change in real interest rates or in fiscal balances.

The economic and political situation in Argentina deteriorated throughout the year, culminating in a full-blown financial and currency crisis in December. With high debt service payments and limited access to international capital markets, the authorities pursued a "zero" fiscal deficit policy to seek debt relief from creditors. A successful swap for domestic debt was concluded in August, and a similar swap for external debt was planned for the fourth quarter. However, turmoil in international capital markets in the wake of September

11, as well as mounting civil and political resistance to the tight fiscal policy, proved too great for the government to overcome. Spreads on Argentina's international debt rose to more than 5,000 basis points, production collapsed, and tax revenues fell, causing the economy to enter a downward spiral. GDP declined for a third consecutive year, by 3.8 percent. In December, the de la Rua government fell, and the currency peg was eventually discarded in January.

Brazil suffered mild contagion from deteriorating conditions in Argentina—on top of a drought-induced energy crisis and a sharp decline in foreign direct investment (FDI) inflows. The Brazilian *real* depreciated by 30 percent between January and mid-October, and spreads rose by 570 basis points over the period. However, sharply tightening fiscal and monetary policies and a robust upturn in FDI during the fourth quarter reversed these trends and confirmed a decoupling from events in Argentina by year end. Output growth was about 2 percent in 2001. The smaller Mercosur partners were much more adversely affected by the Argentine situation and saw their GDP either fall (Paraguay and Uruguay) or grow tepidly (Bolivia). In Mexico, GDP was flat as slowing U.S. growth took its toll on exports, while the authorities followed the U.S. lead in lowering interest rates.

The Andean countries fared somewhat better. Growth was about 2.5 percent in the República Bolivariana de Venezuela as the government continued to expand fiscal policy even as oil revenues began to shrink. The economy weakened in the second half of the year as capital flight intensified, resulting in the level of reserves falling sharply and little new investment. Relations between the government, the private sector, and labor unions deteriorated over the course of the year, raising risks of a political crisis. In

Ecuador, construction of an oil pipeline boosted growth to more than 5 percent and, along with falling oil prices, caused the current account to move from a sizable surplus in 2000 to deficit. Colombian growth slowed from income losses tied to lower coffee prices and falling oil revenues, and the current account deficit widened. Peru had a successful political transition in mid-year, and the investment climate improved thereafter, allowing growth to begin a modest recovery in the second half of the year.

Central America and the Caribbean experienced a particularly difficult year. Drought in some Central American countries adversely affected agricultural production at the same time as coffee prices collapsed. This created famine conditions and raised the incidence of poverty sharply. Weakening labor markets in North America contributed to a falloff in remittances to the region, while Caribbean tourism revenues fell steeply in the fourth quarter, tied to generalized risk aversion on the part of travelers in the wake of September 11. Costa Rica, in addition to suffering from low coffee prices and weakened tourism revenues, was also negatively affected by the global slowdown in high-tech sectors.

Capital market flows fell

Capital market commitments to Latin America totaled about $75 billion in 2001, 17 percent below 2000 levels. The decline was due to sharp falloffs in commercial bank lending and international equity placement, while bond financing remained at 2000 levels. Were Argentina to be excluded from the year's outturns, bond volumes would have risen by 38 percent and bank lending and equity issues would have declined moderately, leading to a fall in total capital market commitments of just 4 percent.

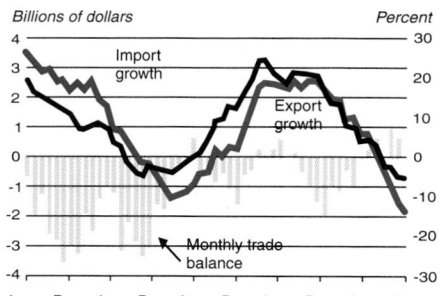

Merchandise trade growth in Latin America and the Caribbean countries, 1997–2001

Three-month moving average, year-over-year percentage change

Note: Excluding the República Bolivariana de Venezuela. Monthly trade balance on left axis. Import and export growth calculated as a three-month moving average in current U.S. dollars. *Source:* Datastream.

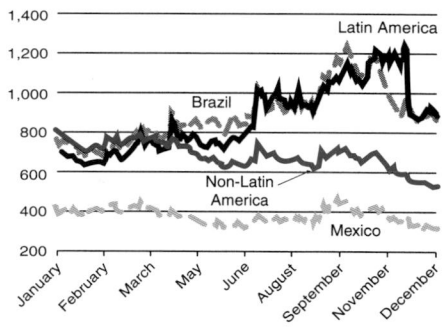

Latin American spreads, 2001

Basis points above U.S. Treasuries

Source: J.P. Morgan Chase through Bloomberg.

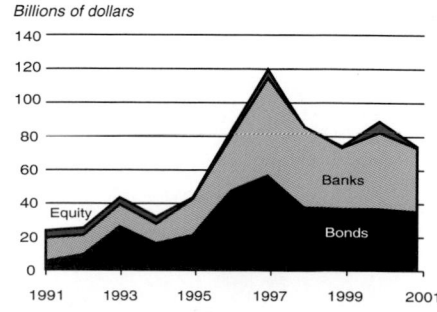

Gross capital market flows to Latin America and the Caribbean countries, 1991–2001

Billions of dollars

Source: Euromoney.

Foreign direct investment, 1991–2001

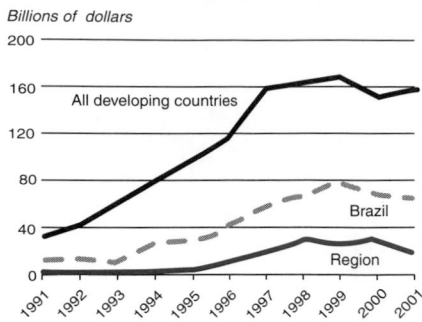

Billions of dollars

Source: World Bank.

Foreign direct investment by country, 2001

Billions of dollars

Source: World Bank.

Access to international bond markets in 2001 was good for most countries but intermittent. Spreads on secondary market debt—one indicator of investor risk perception regarding emerging markets—were fairly steady in the first half of the year, with those for investment-grade countries (such as Chile and Mexico), as well as for Colombia, compressing. As the Argentine situation began to deteriorate in July, spreads rose for most Latin countries (Colombia and Peru are exceptions) even while those for countries outside the region continued to narrow. Immediately after September 11, spreads for all emerging markets rose, but this trend was short-lived. Brazilian spreads followed Argentine spreads for most of the year, but the market made a decisive break in mid-October, with Brazilian spreads falling by 250 basis points by December. Bond volumes followed the pattern of spreads, with little issuance in September and October (after subdued flows in July and August). However, the bond market flourished in the last two months of the year. Many countries in the region raised more from bond issuance in 2001 than in 2000. Argentina was the exception, as bond issuance collapsed from over $12 billion in 2000 to about $1.5 billion in 2001.

Bank lending to Latin America fell by 18 percent in 2001, fairly uniformly across countries. This reflects the weaker international environment—smaller trade flows and fewer cross-border mergers and acquisitions—but the fall was less than the 25 percent decline in developing-country bank flows. International equity issuance was down more than 80 percent, also in line with the fall experienced by all emerging markets.

FDI flows held up

FDI flows to the region reached about $71 billion, 6 percent below the $75 billion registered in 2000. FDI to Argentina and Brazil (to a lesser extent) fell, but this was made up by increases in virtually all other countries. Mexico, with flows of approximately $25 billion, surpassed Brazil as the favored destination of investors in Latin America, and was second only to China among developing countries.

FDI has become the most important source of financing for the current account in many countries. More important, the size of last year's FDI inflow is a sign of improvement in macroeconomic management within the region and improved investor confidence, as large-scale privatization programs have begun to abate.

Prospects and risks

Prospects for 2002 have dimmed considerably in light of the weakening of the global environment after September 11 and the Argentine crisis. Growth rates in a number of countries softened into the fourth quarter of 2001, with negative carryover effects running into early 2002. The region's GDP is likely to grow by about 0.5 percent in the year.

While most countries could achieve somewhat faster growth this year than in 2001, Argentina and the República Bolivariana de Venezuela face difficult challenges. In Argentina, the combination of default, devaluation, and the freeze on deposits (instituted to stem a run on banks and capital flight) at the start of the year, and in the context of a fragile social situation, could result in protracted output reduction and instability. One risk is exchange rate "overshooting," causing inflation to rise significantly and output to decline sharply. Whether this scenario continues into 2003 depends on how quickly a credible program can be put into place. In the República Bolivariana de Venezuela, the political situation is deteriorating and capital flight is continuing while oil prices are softening, limiting the authorities' ability to continue pursuing expansionary policies.

Expected regional growth for both 2003 and 2004 is 3.8 percent, reflecting a much improved external environment as well as different timing in the acceleration of growth across countries (particularly in Argentina). The baseline forecast is predicated on the assumption that countries will maintain macroeconomic stability, that the Argentine situation will stabilize and economic growth will resume during the course of 2003.

However, downside risks remain significant. Public sector debt remains high (above 50 percent of GDP) in a number of countries, and significant policy slippage could place public debt dynamics on an unsustainable path.

Markets perceive that this risk is higher for countries facing presidential elections (Bolivia, Brazil, Colombia, and Ecuador) this year—although Brazil has implemented sound macroeconomic policies in recent years. Many countries in the region remain highly indebted and require debt rollovers on a continuing basis. And international interest rates are likely to rise in 2003 and 2004, raising debt-servicing costs. While the adoption of more flexible exchange rate regimes in recent years has improved export growth potential for many countries, for smaller countries in Central America and the Caribbean, export markets continue to be more narrowly based. Developing the institutional capability to break into global markets is still critical for many.

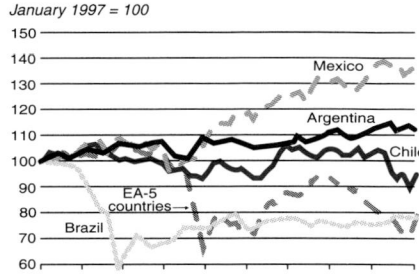

Real effective exchange rates, 1997–2001

January 1997 = 100

Note: EA-5 countries comprise Indonesia, the Republic of Korea, Malaysia, the Philippines, and Thailand.
Source: J.P. Morgan Chase.

Latin America and the Caribbean forecast summary

(percent per year)

Growth rates/ratios	1991–2000	1999	2000	Estimate 2001	Baseline forecast		
					2002	2003	2004
Real GDP growth	3.3	0.0	3.8	0.6	0.5	3.8	3.8
Consumption per capita	1.2	−1.9	2.1	−0.5	−1.3	1.8	2.1
GDP per capita	1.6	−1.6	2.2	−1.0	−1.0	2.3	2.4
Population	1.7	1.6	1.6	1.6	1.5	1.4	1.4
Gross domestic investment/GDP[a]	19.5	19.6	20.2	19.9	19.8	20.0	20.5
Inflation[b]	12.7	4.8	8.6	5.5	4.3	4.1	4.0
Central government budget balance/GDP	−3.5	−4.4	−2.7	−2.6	−2.8	−2.6	−2.2
Export market growth[c]	9.0	5.1	12.0	−0.4	1.6	7.7	7.3
Export volume[d]	8.5	6.9	9.1	1.4	5.3	11.5	8.9
Terms of Trade/GDP[e]	0.1	0.3	0.6	0.9	−0.4	0.0	0.1
Current account/GDP	−2.8	−3.2	−2.4	−2.7	−2.7	−2.8	−3.0
Memo items							
GDP growth:							
excluding Brazil	3.8	−0.4	3.4	−0.4	−0.7	3.6	3.9
Central America	4.4	4.4	2.7	0.7	1.6	3.6	3.8
Caribbean	3.5	5.0	5.3	1.4	3.0	3.7	3.8

a. Fixed investment, measured in real terms.
b. Local currency GDP deflator, median.
c. Weighted average growth of import demand in export markets.
d. Goods and nonfactor services.
e. Change in terms of trade, measured as a proportion of GDP (percent).
Source: World Bank baseline forecast, February 2002.

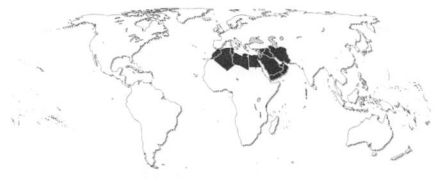

GNI per capita, 2000: $2,090

Middle East and North Africa

Gross domestic product growth, 1991–2004

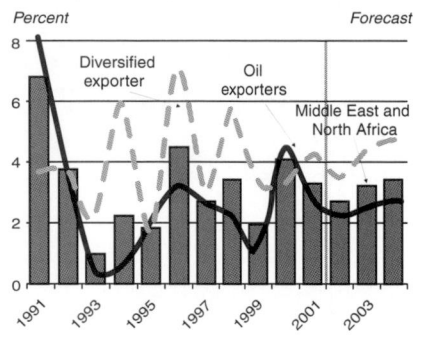

Source: World Bank Economic Policy and Prospects Group.

Export volume growth vis-à-vis export market growth, 1991–2004

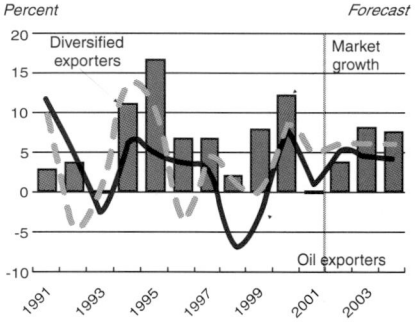

Source: World Bank Economic Policy and Prospects Group.

World oil price and Middle East and North Africa oil producer exports, 1990–2004

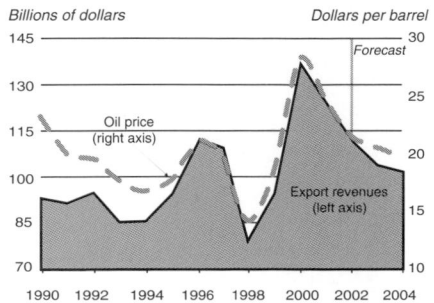

Source: World Bank Economic Policy and Prospects Group.

Recent developments

Growth in the Middle East and North Africa (MENA) region slowed to 3.1 percent in 2001, following a 4.2 percent advance in 2000, which reflected high oil prices and booming global growth and trade. Oil prices and external demand for oil moderated sharply over the course of 2001, resulting in lower output growth, narrowing current account surpluses, and higher budget deficits among the oil-dominant economies of the region. At the same time, progressive weakening of economic activity in continental Europe—the dominant export market for countries of the Maghreb and several of the Mashreq—exacted a heavy toll on export performance. And these adverse trends were exacerbated for several countries by declines in tourism receipts and worker remittances because of heightened security concerns after September 11. This trend was most acute for the Arab Republic of Egypt, but it was also important for Morocco and Tunisia.

Oil exporters faced much less favorable terms of trade in 2001, as the world oil price fell to $24.40 per barrel from $28.20 in 2000 (a decline of 14 percent).[1] Several cutbacks in Organization for Petroleum Exporting Countries (OPEC) quotas were imposed to establish a floor under prices, especially later in the year as global activity fell sharply. In the real sector, hydrocarbons production and export volumes declined, leading to gross domestic product (GDP) outturns of 2.5 percent, down from 3.6 percent growth in 2000. The growth of incomes also moderated, and current account surpluses and fiscal balances—the latter of which eased recently with oil prices near $30 per barrel—were squeezed by the fall in oil-related revenues.

Despite the fall in oil prices and global demand, financial positions among the middle-income exporters of the region remained positive in 2001. Public debt was retired, foreign reserves rose, and public expenditures were relatively restrained. Algeria and the Islamic Republic of Iran have both channeled surplus oil revenues into oil stabilization funds. By the end of July 2001, Algeria had accumulated around $7 billion. The Islamic Republic of Iran accumulated around $6 billion by March 31, and this is expected to grow by a further $3.9 billion by March 2002. These surpluses will be used to smooth consumption if oil prices fall below a predetermined level, and in the case of the Islamic Republic of Iran, a portion will also be set aside for domestic lending.

In a broader perspective, current account balances for all major oil exporters of the region (including the high-income producers Kuwait and the United Arab Emirates) remained positive at $40 billion, albeit lower than the $59 billion surplus of 2000. Government deficits, which had shrunk to zero or gone into surplus in many countries, also deteriorated slightly, but with few financing problems. In the case of Saudi Arabia, despite public sector wage restraint, the 2002 budget foresees a deficit of some $6 to $7 billion, contrasted with a surplus of similar magnitude in 2000. A potential medium-term concern for oil exporters is appreciation of real exchange rates, which would tend to diminish the competitiveness of the nonhydrocarbon sectors and, for example, in the Islamic Republic of Iran, make the transition to a unified exchange rate more difficult.

Growth in the *diversified exporters*[2] in 2001, at 3.6 percent, was similar to 2000 outturns (3.7 percent), despite booming agricultural output in Morocco, following several years of severe drought, and stable growth in Jordan. Growth for this group, excluding Jordan and Morocco, registered deceleration of some 0.4 percentage points, as activity in most countries fell below trend rates of the 1990s. A substantial portion of the lower growth outturns can be accounted for by the deterioration of external factors such as export market growth, tourism, services receipts, and transfers. The dramatic slowing of economic activity in the Euro Area was exacerbated by the abrupt loss of confidence and rise of uncertainty in the industrial countries as well as the Middle Eastern and South Asian regions following September 11. This continues to affect aviation-passenger and freight-related insurance costs, tourism, and near-term prospects for privatization of aviation-related parastatals in the MENA region. These factors have contributed to a doubling of the current account deficit for the diversified exporters to more than $2 billion in 2001.

Internal difficulties, many of which were present in these countries prior to the downturn in global activity, were also responsible for the poorer growth performance in 2001 in several countries. Egypt is still dealing with the consequences of twin deficits in its fiscal and current accounts, with the current account deficit reaching 1.6 percent of GDP in 2000 and the fiscal deficit growing to more than 5 percent of GDP in 2001. An adverse investment climate, high real interest rates, and some uncertainty about the direction of the exchange rate have slowed GDP growth to under 3 percent in 2001. Similar adverse fiscal trends are affecting countries such as Morocco and Tunisia, and may broaden across the diversified exporters as external revenue shortfalls become more acute in the near term.

But some countercyclical policy action has been possible. Recent improved inflation performance in Egypt has allowed a full percentage point reduction in the central bank discount rate; and exchange rates have been falling relative to the dollar as well as the euro over the second half of 2001, in Egypt, Morocco, Tunisia, and the Republic of Yemen. These measures may help to mitigate the effects of the global slowdown to a modest degree; but given the importance of the European Union as an export market and principal source of remittance and tourism income, recovery there will be necessary for a return of more buoyant external conditions.

Gross capital flows from international capital markets and FDI

Gross capital flows from international markets (bonds, bank lending, and equity placement) to the Middle East and North Africa rose during 2001, by $2.7 billion (an increase of 26 percent), fully offsetting the drop-off in flows that occurred in 2000. Commercial bank financing continues to dominate flows to the region and increased by some $165 million in the year to reach $7.7 billion. The increase, in a year that bank financing to other developing regions was falling, reflects the unique characteristics of oil-exporting economies. Egypt, the Islamic Republic of Iran, Oman, and Saudi Arabia remain the principal recipients of bank financing. Bond issuance jumped by $2.9 billion in the year to $5.3 billion, as those countries with access to the markets at present—Egypt, Lebanon, Morocco, and Tunisia—stepped up issuance as opportunities arose. Lebanon garnered some $3.1 billion in Eurobond issues, Egypt some $1.5 billion, and Tunisia $460 million in the year. Although tensions regarding the war on terrorism led to an increase in mar-

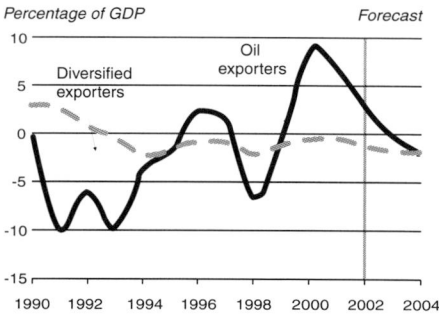

Current account balances, 1990–2004

Percentage of GDP   *Forecast*

Source: World Bank Economic Policy and Prospects Group.

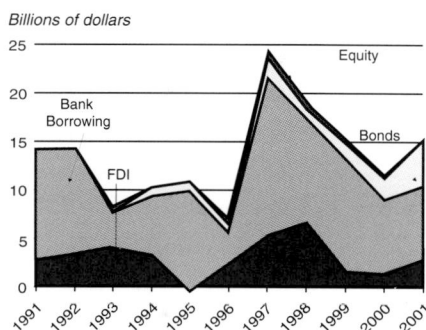

Composition of gross market flows plus foreign direct investment, 1991–2001

Billions of dollars

Source: World Bank Economic Policy and Prospects Group.

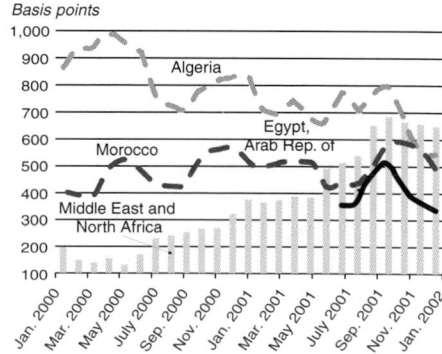

Emerging market bond spreads in the Middle East and North Africa region and selected countries, 2000–02

Basis points

Note: Regional spread is dominated by weight of Lebanon in terms of outstanding international bond issuance.
Source: J.P. Morgan/Chase.

Gross capital market flow commitments to the Middle East and North Africa region, 1999–2001

Billions of dollars

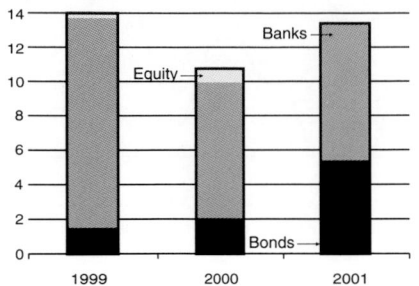

Source: Euromoney and the World Bank Economic Policy and Prospects Group.

Principal capital market participants, 2000 and 2001

Millions of dollars

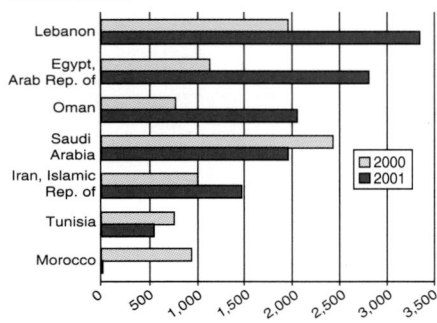

Source: World Bank Economic Policy and Prospects Group.

Principal foreign direct investment recipients, 2000 and 2001

Millions of dollars

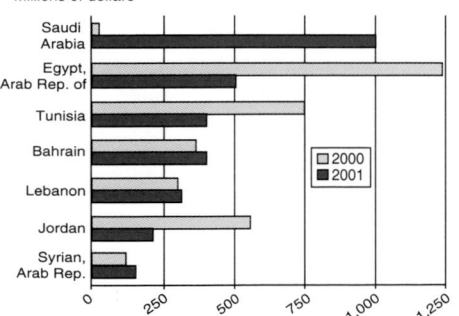

Source: World Bank Economic Policy and Prospects Group.

ket spreads toward 700 basis points, the situation eased somewhat in late 2001 and early 2002, and spreads for the region showed some improvement, falling by 250 basis points for Algeria, 150 points for Egypt, and 90 points for Morocco. However, spreads for Lebanon remain high as public debt continued to increase to very high levels. A general easing of investor risk aversion may be a welcome development moving into 2002, as signs of recovery in economic activity in the United States and East Asia have become clearer, and availability of finance is improving (liquidity in the industrial countries has risen substantially in a lower interest rate environment).

Portfolio equity issuance, traditionally small in the region, was virtually nil in 2001, as it fell to $7 million from $375 million in 2000, and from a recent peak of $720 million in 1997. This was in- line with the large decline in equity placement worldwide, which fell 75 percent in 2001, as stock markets around the world responded to declines in earnings and profitability. On balance, market-based flows to the region proved fairly resilient in the face of deteriorating global (and local) conditions.

FDI flows into the region increased, particularly to oil-exporting countries. FDI rose from $1.2 billion in 2000 to $2.6 billion in 2001. For the first time in three years, Saudi Arabia experienced net positive inflows of $1 billion, as limited foreign participation in hydrocarbon projects was approved. But many of the diversified exporters, such as Egypt and Jordan, experienced considerable falloffs in FDI, as current global conditions suggest that the prospects for privatization-related FDI, particularly in telecommunications and aviation, will be considerably dampened through the medium term, remaining well below 1997–98 levels.

Prospects

Given difficult conditions in the external environment, near-term prospects appear muted: growth recovery in the European Union is likely to lag behind that of North America and East Asia; underlying demand for hydrocarbons will require some time to reach 1999–2000 levels, and uncertainty associated with the war on terrorism will likely remain a dampening factor for regional dynamism. GDP growth is anticipated to fall to 2.7 percent in 2002, while recovery over the 2003–04 period may be protracted relative to other developing regions, rising to an average of 3.3 percent.

The slowdown in external demand will continue to affect the Middle East and North Africa well into 2002. Average oil prices have fallen below $20 per barrel early in the year, eroding the large current account surpluses and oil revenue boosts seen recently by governments in oil-exporting countries. Cuts in oil production quotas in OPEC countries will also reduce GDP growth prospects for some oil-exporting countries, although this will be balanced in countries such as the Islamic Republic of Iran and Algeria, which have large investment programs in the hydrocarbons sector. As a result, GDP growth among the oil exporters is likely to soften in 2002 to 2.2 percent, while the aggregate current account surplus may fall from $40 billion in 2001 (9.9 percent of GDP) to $6 billion (1.5 percent).

Lower export volumes, services income, and tourism receipts will continue to constrain growth in the diversified exporters, and current account deficits are likely to worsen in 2002. GDP growth in the year is anticipated to weaken to 3.1 percent, as Moroccan growth falls from post-drought highs in 2001. Tunisia and Jordan will benefit from the expected upturn in global activity in late 2002 and as the impacts of September 11 on tourism fade, although the intifada in the West Bank and Gaza may persist and cause more acute concerns for tourism in the Levant. The weak economic situation in Egypt has led the government to consider a range of policies to improve the business climate, including capital market reforms and independence for the central bank. Tax reforms, to ease the corporate tax burden and encourage compliance, are also being considered.

The rebound of the global economy in late 2002 into 2003 should help to stabilize growth in the region. There may be some upside potential for oil prices, but this will most likely be negated by higher non-OPEC supply, potentially implying a further deterioration of fiscal deficits and current account balances of oil exporters from the positive balances seen in recent years. However, given the recovery of foreign exchange reserves, the

resources available to countries such as the Islamic Republic of Iran and Algeria in their oil stabilization funds, as well as the lower levels of foreign debt achieved in recent years, oil exporters should have little problem in financing deficits. Improvement in external conditions should also be a boost to the diversified exporters, particularly Jordan and Tunisia, where export volumes have exceeded export market growth in 2001. Conditions in Egypt point to continued domestic weakness into 2003, as the government is likely to lower the fiscal deficit while the economy is growing much more slowly than during the late 1990s. Moroccan growth is heavily reliant on weather conditions but will also be affected by low prices for its commodity exports, and Morocco faces the challenge of increasing the competitiveness of its manufacturing sector as it implements the next stages of its European Union Association Agreement.

Foreign direct investment, 1991–2001

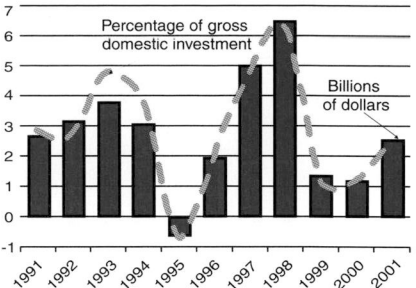

Source: World Bank Economic Policy and Prospects Group.

GDP growth, 2001–2004

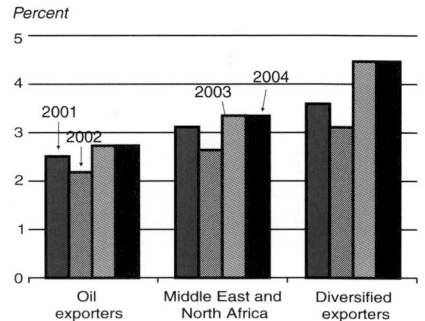

Source: World Bank Economic Policy and Prospects Group.

Middle East and North Africa forecast summary

(percent per year)

Growth rates/ratios	1991–2000	1999	2000	Estimate 2001	Baseline forecast 2002	2003	2004
Real GDP growth	3.2	2.0	4.2	3.1	2.7	3.3	3.3
Consumption per capita	0.4	0.5	1.7	1.4	1.0	0.8	0.9
GDP per capita	1.0	0.1	2.2	1.2	0.7	1.4	1.3
Population	2.2	1.9	2.0	1.9	1.9	1.9	1.9
Gross domestic investment/GDP[a]	21.2	21.5	21.7	22.1	22.4	22.6	22.8
Inflation[b]	5.3	5.7	3.8	3.8	3.4	3.3	3.1
Central government budget balance/GDP	–1.2	–1.2	–1.0	–0.5	–0.9	–1.1	–1.4
Export market growth[c]	7.2	8.2	12.9	0.1	2.2	7.9	7.4
Export volume[d]	4.9	4.0	7.4	2.1	3.0	5.2	4.7
Terms of trade/GDP[e]	0.5	5.3	8.8	–2.5	–3.7	0.1	–1.7
Current account/GDP	–1.7	1.4	7.6	5.5	0.7	0.9	–0.9
Memo items							
GDP growth: oil exporters	2.5	0.2	3.6	2.5	2.2	2.8	2.8
Diversified exporters	4.0	3.6	3.7	3.6	3.1	4.4	4.4

a. Fixed investment, measured in real terms.
b. Local currency GDP deflator, median.
c. Weighted average growth of import demand in export markets.
d. Goods and nonfactor services.
e. Change in terms of trade, measured as a proportion of GDP (percent).
Source: World Bank baseline forecast, February 2002.

On balance, growth for the diversified exporters during 2003–04 is projected to pick up to 4.4 percent; that for the oil-dominant economies to 2.8 percent, yielding an overall regional growth rate of 3.3 percent. Against a background of continued rapid population growth, this implies per capita income growth of about 1.5 percent over the period, suggesting continued difficulties in mitigating unemployment among the region's increasing, and increasingly youthful, work force.

Notes

1. Low- and middle-income oil-dominant countries in the MENA region reported here, supported by available data, are Bahrain, the Islamic Republic of Iran, Oman, Saudi Arabia, and the Republic of Yemen. High-income oil exporters include Kuwait and the United Arab Emirates; insufficient data are available for Qatar.

2. The group of diversified exporters of the region comprises Egypt, Jordan, Morocco, the Syrian Arab Republic, and Tunisia.

South Asia

GNI per capita, 2000: $440

Recent developments

Gross domestic product (GDP) in the South Asia region increased by 4.3 percent in 2001, up from 4 percent growth recorded in 2000, yet well below the 5.8 percent growth of 1999. The slowdown in world trade and the regional tensions after September 11 slowed merchandise exports from the region to merely 1.1 percent growth in 2001 compared to a robust 12.3 percent posted in 2000. There was also a sharp fall in growth rates of industrial production.

Importantly for growth, the agricultural sector recovered in the second half of 2001, after drought-induced stagnant output in the first half of 2001, with a bumper cotton crop in Pakistan and a good harvest in the Indian kharif season. Bangladesh showed around 6 percent growth in gross agricultural output (about the same growth as in recent years), reflecting government policies of encouraging the cultivation of high-yield crops. The service sector in India (50 percent of the Indian economy and about 35 percent of regional GDP), increased by almost 7 percent in 2001. Software exports from India grew 25 percent, despite the malaise in the global high-tech markets.

The external positions of major countries remained comfortable. Declines in key commodity prices (cotton prices fell by 20 percent) were balanced by the fall in oil prices, and the regional current account deficit deteriorated only marginally, to –1.3 percent of GDP compared with –0.8 percent in 2000. Pakistan, as a frontline state against terrorism, will receive ample financial support from the international community. Pakistan's reserve position improved significantly during 2001 to about three months of import coverage from a low of one

month import coverage in September 2000. Also, India has substantial foreign reserves, and with the relatively closed nature of its capital market, it is unlikely to face a financing problem in the near term.

Chronically high fiscal deficits are the Achilles heel of the region and they increased across the region in 2001. There was a steep decline in tax collections as a result of lower imports and stagnant corporate incomes in the manufacturing sectors. In Pakistan, overall tax collection was more than 3 percent below target in the third quarter of 2001, while collections from customs were 12 percent below target. In India, both import duties—more than 25 percent of total tax revenues—and corporate tax revenues are projected to be 8 percent below target in 2001. It is unlikely that the Indian central government will meet its deficit target of 4.7 percent of GDP for fiscal 2001–02, as it had already reached 50 percent of the deficit target by the first quarter of the fiscal year. The consolidated public sector deficit in India remained unchanged at 10.6 percent of GDP.

Inflation, as measured by the consumer price index, averaged 3.4 percent for the region. As in earlier years, government subsidies through the public distribution system cushioned the impact of poor crop production and higher oil prices (in the first part of the year) on consumer prices—which in turn is being reflected in a low rate of consumer inflation and growing fiscal and current account deficits. Responding to the slowdown in the economy and helped by global monetary easing and subdued domestic inflation, the Reserve Bank of India lowered the bank rate to 6.5 percent, the lowest rate since 1973. By contrast, interest rates in other countries

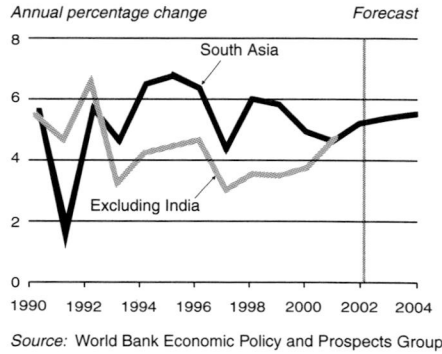

Gross domestic product growth rates, 1990–2004

Annual percentage change / Forecast

Source: World Bank Economic Policy and Prospects Group.

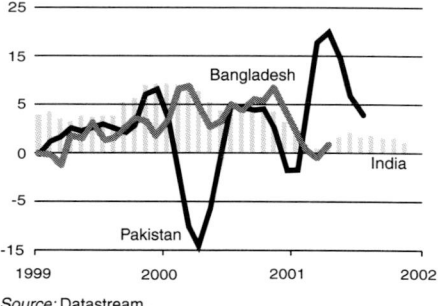

Industrial production index, 1999–2002

Three-month moving average, year-over-year percentage change

Source: Datastream.

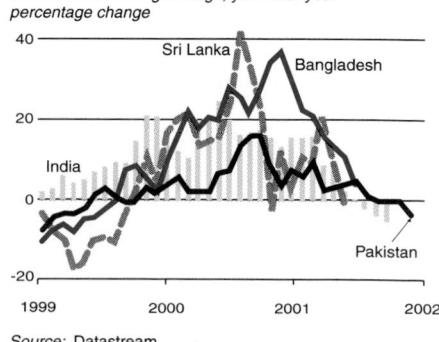

Merchandise exports, 1999–2002

Three-month moving average, year-over-year percentage change

Source: Datastream

International reserves, 1999–2001

Months of import coverage

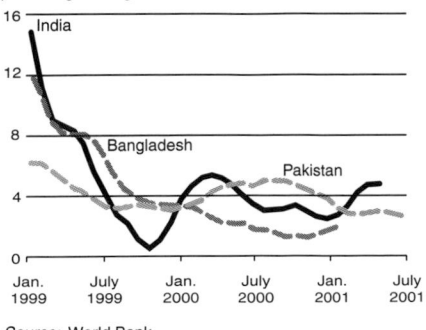

Source: World Bank.

Gross capital market flows, 1991–2001

Billions of dollars

Source: Euromoney.

Consumer price index, 1999–2001

Three-month moving average, year-over-year percentage change

Source: World Bank.

in the region were stable or slightly rising (for example in Pakistan.)

Capital flows

FDI to South Asia rose to $4.2 billion in 2001, a 35 percent increase from the previous year. Nevertheless, FDI to the region remains small, only 0.5 percent of GDP. South Asia produces 9 percent of developing countries' GDP but attracts only 2 percent of FDI flows to developing countries. The relatively small FDI flows into the region in part reflect little progress in privatization, glacial industrial regulations, and slow reforms in the labor market. Notwithstanding the recent successful sale of two highly profitable public enterprises in India, Videsh Sanchar Nigam Limited and IBP, privatization of other, often money losing, public companies remains a huge challenge. Nonetheless, FDI in India increased by a full $1 billion in the year, to reach $3.3 billion. But in Pakistan, privatization of the Pakistan Telecommunications Company and the United Bank has been delayed. The distribution of FDI flows within the region is more or less proportional to GDP, with 75 percent going to India and roughly 10 percent going to Pakistan and Bangladesh. This amount represents an impressive increase for Pakistan, which attracted only 0.5 percent of regional FDI inflows in 1996.

Lending by foreign banks, which accounts for the bulk of external private capital market commitments to the region, declined by more than $1 billion in 2001. Equity placement, which was hit hard due to heightened uncertainty created by the global economic slowdown and the September 11 events, declined by almost 50 percent. However, because these flows are relatively small and official aid increased, the decline in equity placement did not prevent a general improvement of reserves in the region,

despite the slight deterioration in the current account.

Prospects and risks

The region is expected to recover modestly in 2002, with an average growth rate of 4.9 percent, and thereafter remain at a rate around 5.3 percent. Domestic factors will be the immediate impetus to an up-tick in growth during the first half of 2002, while a recovery in the developed economies in the second half of 2002 will further accelerate growth. Agricultural output is expected to improve in the first half of 2002. This improvement should have a stimulating effect on the industrial sector, particularly the durable goods sector, because traditionally farmers tend to buy big ticket items (such as furniture, motorcycles, and bicycles) during periods of good harvest and consequently increased incomes. The war-related aid for Pakistan, especially to the export sector, is expected to quicken the recovery of its economy.

Assuming that the countries in the region follow their declared policies, the average fiscal deficit is expected to decline from 10.3 percent of GDP[1] in 2001 to 9.2 percent in 2004. In Pakistan, the International Monetary Fund–supported program is expected to result in a significant fall in the fiscal deficit and in the public debt burden. Following the Eleventh Finance Commission and Expenditure Reform Commission reports, the Indian central government has proposed medium-term fiscal policy reforms[2] that aim to cut the revenue deficit to zero by fiscal 2005–06, mainly by reforming the tax system, rationalizing expenditure, and reducing the number of central government employees by 10 percent. Realization of this program will be an imposing challenge, however. In India, efforts to reduce subsidies and spur privatization of public industries have had mixed success. In addition, the recent increase in regional tensions may put pressure on the budgets of the region.

The current account deficit is expected to improve marginally to 1 percent of GDP in 2002 and continue to decline steadily thereafter. In the early part of 2002, export growth is likely to be slow given sluggish growth in the region's major export markets (the United States and Europe). Recovery of the export sector should begin in earnest during the second half of 2002. Removal of sanctions by the United States and Japan on India and Pakistan will benefit the two countries in the medium term. However, continuation of military activity in the region is likely to have a depressing impact on exports due to an increased risk perception by Organisation for Economic Co-operation and Development–area importers. A major source of gains in the medium term will be exports of services, especially software, data, and business services, from India. The region is not expected to cut import tariffs in the near term and, therefore, import growth is expected to remain slow.

This forecast faces significant downside risks. As of the time of this writing, tensions between India and Pakistan remained at high levels. Even if recent moves toward peace bear fruit, the potential for additonal terrorist attacks cannot be ruled out. The war in Afghanistan appears to be drawing to a close, but that country may still be a source of regional instability. Over the longer term, the success of efforts to restrain fiscal deficits while continuing to achieve high growth rates remains uncertain. And the entry of China into the World Trade Organization creates a major competitive challenge for the manufacturing industries of the region.

Notes

1. For India we have used the consolidated public sector deficit.

2. As of the writing of this report, the proposed Fiscal Responsibility and Budget Management Bill is yet to be ratified by the Indian Parliament.

South Asia forecast summary

(percent per year)

Growth rates/ratios	1991–2000	1999	2000	Estimate 2001	Baseline forecast		
					2002	2003	2004
Real GDP growth	5.2	5.8	4.0	4.3	4.9	5.3	5.2
Consumption per capita	2.6	6.1	1.2	2.2	1.8	2.0	1.9
GDP per capita	3.2	3.9	2.1	2.6	3.2	3.6	3.6
Population	1.9	1.9	1.9	1.7	1.7	1.6	1.6
Gross domestic investment/GDP[a]	21.9	22.6	24.0	24.7	25.4	25.8	26.4
Inflation[b]	8.1	4.6	5.8	6.1	5.0	5.1	5.1
General government budget balance/GDP	–10.3	–9.8	–9.7	–10.3	–10.3	–9.7	–9.2
Export market growth[c]	7.3	7.2	12.7	1.1	2.6	7.3	6.9
Export volume[d]	9.3	1.8	7.7	3.8	5.3	10.0	8.1
Terms of trade/GDP[e]	–0.1	–0.5	–0.7	0.4	–0.1	0.2	0.1
Current account/GDP	–1.5	–0.9	–0.8	–1.3	–1.1	–0.8	–0.4
Memo items							
GDP growth: excluding India	4.3	3.6	4.2	3.8	3.9	4.8	5.2

a. Fixed investment, measured in real terms.
b. Local currency GDP deflator, median.
c. Weighted average growth of import demand in export markets.
d. Goods and nonfactor services.
e. Change in terms of trade, measured as a proportion of GDP (percent).
Source: World Bank baseline forecast, February 2002.

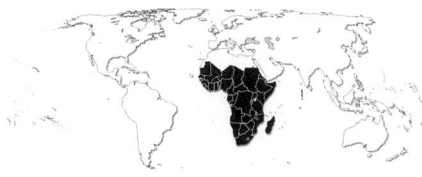

GNI per capita, 2000: $470

Sub-Saharan Africa

Recent developments

Growth slowed across much of Sub-Saharan Africa in 2001, reaching only 2.6 percent for the year, down from 3.1 percent in 2000. The slowdown was not evenly distributed. In a number of countries performance even improved while in others poor outcomes were attributable to a variety of factors, not least of which were civil strife and poor governance. Nevertheless, a common factor across the region was a marked deterioration in external sector performance. The global slowdown depressed import demand in Sub-Saharan Africa's main trading partners and held real merchandise export growth to just 2.1 percent compared to 7.5 percent in 2000. At the same time, export prices denominated in dollars fell by an average of 6.3 percent and the dollar value of export earnings fell 4.3 percent. The terms of trade deteriorated by 2.9 percent, which was equivalent to a further reduction in real income of 0.8 percent of gross domestic product (GDP).

Despite an increase in debt relief under the Heavily Indebted Poor Countries (HIPC) Initiative, official aid flows declined slightly while at the same time commercial flows remained limited. As a result the weak export performance served to compress imports. This compression was achieved with the help of weak income growth and currency depreciation and was reflected in a narrowing of the real trade deficit.

September 11 reinforced global and domestic factors that triggered the slowdown. Commodity prices fell sharply in the immediate aftermath, though except for oil, they largely reverted to trend over the next two months. Security concerns and the disruption to international air travel compounded local factors (crime and political instability in southern Africa)

contributing to a disappointing year-end tourist season. But a weak performance in 2001 was already in the cards by the time of the attacks: 50 to 90 percent of the drop in commodity prices for the year had already occurred by August, as had much of the exchange rate depreciation. In South Africa, quarterly national accounts data showed a clear weakening in the first three quarters of the year after a strong finish to 2000.

Several positive factors helped to mitigate the impact of the trade slowdown. First, generally better weather conditions led to a substantial recovery of agricultural production throughout the Horn of Africa, eastern and southern Africa, the great lakes region, and the Sahel. Though scattered drought conditions persisted in these regions, major failures of food and export crop production were largely avoided (Somalia was an exception). Meanwhile, in West Africa and the Sahel good rains contributed to bumper harvests.[1]

Second, there was a major expansion of debt relief under the HIPC Initiative. Ten Sub-Saharan African countries reached decision points in December 2000 and two more during the course of 2001, which more than doubled the number of countries in the region receiving debt service reduction, while two more countries reached completion points.[2] The timing was fortuitous insofar as it helped to relieve some of the pressure on current accounts.

Third, exchange rates fell across the region by an average of 15 percent in nominal terms or 8 percent in real terms,[3] reinforcing the adverse terms-of-trade shock, but boosting export competitiveness and helping to offset some of the impacts of commodity price weakness on commodity exporters. The real devaluation also implied a redistribution of income from

Gross domestic product growth, 1990–2001

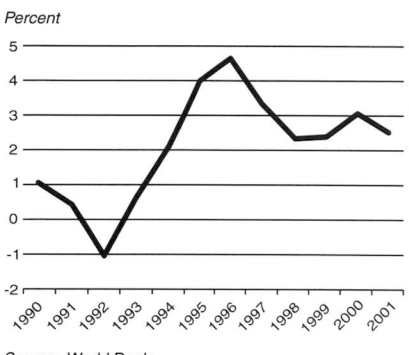

Percent

Source: World Bank.

Macro performance: oil exporters

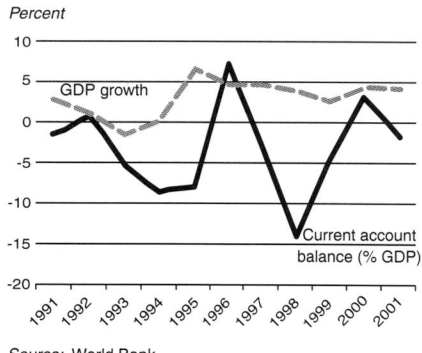

Percent

Source: World Bank.

Macro performance: non-oil exporters

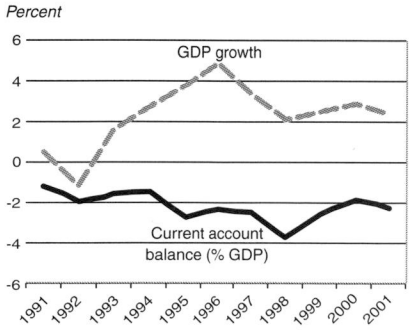

Percent

Source: World Bank.

importers to exporters. In the medium term the devaluations may prove inflationary, but at least for the time being a combination of lower food prices, depressed economic conditions, and tighter monetary management helped to contain inflation. Indeed, the median inflation rate fell from 6.1 percent to 5.4 percent in the year.

Finally, it is worth noting that although the slowdown was widespread, nearly a third of Sub-Saharan African countries achieved stronger growth. The best performer by a wide margin was Mozambique, where growth picked up from 2.1 percent in 2000 to 8.3 percent in 2001 as a result of agriculture's recovery from devastating floods in 2000 and a sharp rise in aluminum and electricity exports. But a number of other countries also showed gains, including Ethiopia and Uganda, where weather improved; Angola, Chad, and Cameroon, where there were major investments in energy sectors; Madagascar, which achieved strong export performance in textiles and tourism; and Sierra Leone, which enjoyed a down payment on a peace dividend.

Savings behavior and adjustment to the commodity cycle

External developments negatively affected both oil and non-oil commodity exporters in 2001, though circumstances were very different for the two groups. For oil exporters, terms of trade deteriorated by 8.9 percent in 2001, but that gave back only a small portion of a massive 80 percent rise over the previous two years, and conditions remained relatively buoyant. Growth eased from 4.4 percent in 2000 to 4 percent in 2001 but remained strong, particularly in the nontraditional oil exporters, Equatorial Guinea and Sudan. Terms-of-trade

gains of the magnitudes experienced over the past few years would be expected to give rise to substantial savings. This was the case as savings rates of the oil exporters tripled from 8.7 percent of GDP in 1998 to 27.2 percent in 2000 before falling marginally in 2001.[4] Roughly two-thirds of the savings increase took the form of a net accumulation of foreign assets, the rest took the form of a sharp rise in domestic investment, particularly in offshore oil and gas development. Oil rents accrued initially to the public sector before being transferred in large part to the private sector through subsidies and higher public spending.[5] Though data are not available to distinguish public and private savings, fiscal deficits narrowed from 8 percent of GDP in 1998 to 2.4 percent in 2000. Though oil prices remained relatively high in 2001, deficits again widened. Windfall savings, properly managed, afford a cushion against likely price reversals. But long experience and recent observation caution against fiscal expenditure booms followed by painful adjustment. The risk is particularly high for Nigeria in the run-up to elections in early 2003.

In contrast to oil producers, terms of trade for non-oil commodity exporters were little changed as falling oil prices on the import side offset some of the declines in export prices. Depressed commodity prices imposed severe hardship in many cases and pushed some countries to intervene by subsidizing farm prices, which had implications for budgetary spending. But overall macroeconomic adjustment was relatively limited. Terms of trade have fallen steadily since 1996, suggesting that there is little room for further dissaving.

Financial flows

Official aid remained the main source of foreign resource inflows in 2001,

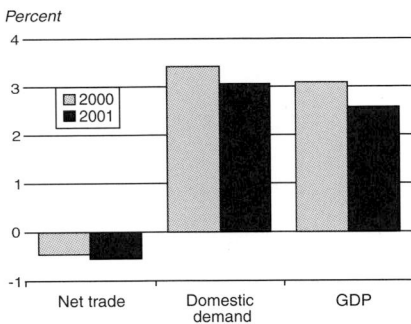

Contributions to growth, 2000 and 2001

Percent

Source: Datastream and DECPG staff estimates.

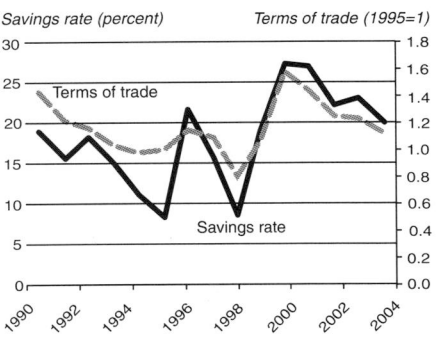

Terms of trade and savings rate in Sub-Saharan Africa oil exporters, 1990–2004

Source: World Bank Economic Policy and Prospects Group.

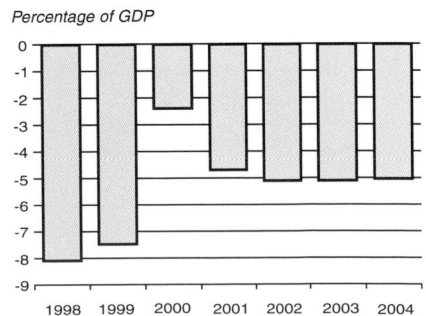

Oil exporters' fiscal balance, 1998–2004

Percentage of GDP

Source: World Bank Economic Policy and Prospects Group.

Rate of change in terms of trade for oil and non-oil exporters, 1998–2004

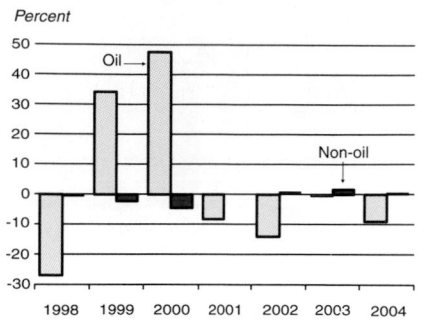

Percent

Source: World Bank Economic Policy and Prospects Group.

Gross domestic product growth of oil and non-oil exporters, 1998–2004

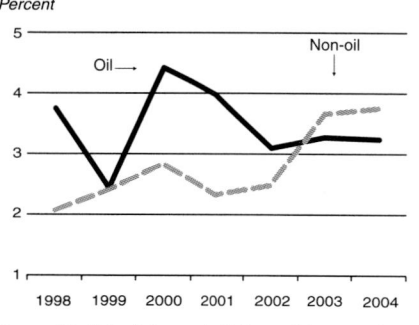

Percent

Source: World Bank Economic Policy and Prospects Group.

but worldwide, total official development assistance (ODA) declined from $39.5 billion to $37.5 billion and provisional estimates indicate that official flows to Sub-Saharan Africa declined proportionately. As noted, HIPC debt relief offered substantial benefits to some countries. For oil exporters, relatively strong current account positions helped to mitigate overall financing needs.

Foreign direct investment (FDI) appeared to jump sharply in 2001, nearly doubling to $13.7 billion from $6.8 billion in 2000. But almost all of the increase was to South Africa and reflected, in essence, a financial restructuring—the purchase of De Beers by Anglo-American—which shifted ownership of assets from South Africa to London without generating substantial new investment. Excluding the De Beers purchase, the figures show a decline from $6.6 billion in 2000 to $6.2 billion in 2001. Roughly 60 percent of this amount went to oil exporters, the largest recipient being Angola, which accounted for nearly 30 percent. Overall, a downward trend is evident, with energy-related FDI in particular expected to decline fairly sharply over the forecast period in light of lower prices.

Prospects and risks

The deep slowdown in the world economy and delayed recovery in industrial-country import demand will continue to depress commodity markets over the next 12 months. For Sub-Saharan Africa, the negative impact on exports and investment is expected to hold GDP growth to only 2.6 percent in 2002. In domestic economies, fixed capital formation will bear the brunt of the slow growth in expenditure—particularly in energy sectors, which will face weaker prices—while private and public consumption maintain a steadier pace. Near-term prospects are

especially bleak in southern Africa because of political uncertainty in Zimbabwe, though it is hoped that the situation there will move toward resolution with the presidential election in March. In the outer years of the forecast, exports are expected to accelerate with the recovery in the world economy, raising GDP growth across the region to 3.6 percent.

External performance will be the prime driver of the regional economy over the forecast period. Overall, the forecast anticipates that merchandise exports will grow by just 2 percent in real terms in 2002. In value terms, large price declines are expected for oil exporters, more than offsetting small gains for the rest; as a result export earnings will fall by 2 percent. Demands for tourism and other services exports are also likely to remain subdued, reflecting security concerns and the weak outlook for the European economy. As the world recovery accelerates in the second half of 2002, exports should begin to pick up, setting the stage for more robust growth of around 6 percent in 2003–04. Though trade prices in general should strengthen as the world economy gains pace, the impact on commodity markets is likely to be more muted, which will keep Sub-Saharan Africa's terms of trade from recovering strongly before the end of the forecast period.

The situation for oil exporters will be most challenging. Because oil prices will not return to the recent high levels, terms of trade are likely to trend lower and the opportunity to compensate by increasing real exports will be limited. Thus, major adjustments will be required to keep current account deficits at sustainable levels, and these adjustments will depress domestic demand, especially investment and public expenditure. Growth in oil exporters is expected to average around 3.2 percent over the forecast period. For non-oil producers, commodity export prices are expected to stabilize or even become slightly firmer in the outer years of the forecast, though a return even to the levels of the mid-1990s, let alone earlier times, seems unlikely. As the terms of trade stabilize or recover modestly, GDP growth should accelerate to near 4 percent, while current account deficits narrow slightly. While lower world commodity prices can only strengthen the impetus to diversify exports, African commodity producers should be competitive at the new, lower level of prices, especially with cheaper oil as an offset.

For the region's largest economy, South Africa, the slowdown is compounding the frustration with the slow pace of results from the government's promarket policy stance, though there is no credible alternative. Nigeria faces more severe challenges because of upcoming elections (in early 2003), lower social cohesion, and a deteriorating external environment. Nevertheless, for Nigeria, as for the region as a whole, policymakers will likely continue to be constrained by a growing acceptance of the need to improve macroeconomic management and maintain better relations with the International Monetary Fund. In Nigeria's case, that is especially true as debt relief on nearly $30 billion of external debt hangs in the balance.

Notes

1. Food and Agriculture Organization. 2001. "Food supply situation and crop prospects in Sub-Saharan Africa.".

2. Prior to December 2000, eight countries were at decision points: Benin, Burkina Faso, Cameroon, Mali, Mauritania, Mozambique, Senegal, and Tanzania; and Uganda was at a completion point. By December 2001, 17 countries were at decision points: Benin, Burkina Faso, Cameroon, Chad, Ethiopia, The

Current account balance of oil and non-oil exporters, 1998–2004

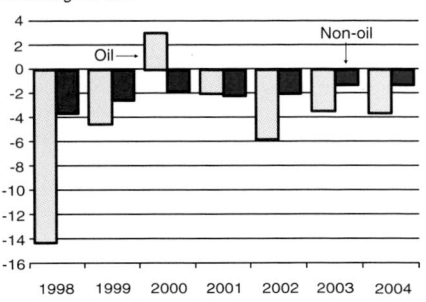

Percentage of GDP

Source: World Bank Economic Policy and Prospects Group.

Sub-Saharan Africa forecast summary

(percent per year)

Growth rates/ratios	1991–2000	1999	2000	Estimate 2001	Baseline forecast 2002	2003	2004
Real GDP growth	2.2	2.4	3.1	2.6	2.6	3.6	3.6
Consumption per capita	−0.2	0.1	0.6	0.3	0.5	1.4	1.2
GDP per capita	−0.4	0.0	0.6	0.1	0.2	1.3	1.3
Population	2.6	2.4	2.5	2.4	2.4	2.3	2.3
Gross domestic investment/GDP[a]	16.8	17.5	18.0	18.5	18.4	18.1	17.9
Inflation[b]	9.7	5.2	6.1	5.4	4.5	4.2	4.1
Central government budget balance/GDP	−5.0	−3.0	−3.1	−3.6	−3.7	−3.4	−3.2
Export market growth[c]	7.0	6.4	10.8	1.1	2.2	7.3	6.8
Export volume[d]	4.3	3.5	5.6	1.8	2.2	5.5	5.8
Terms of trade/GDP[e]	0.0	1.4	2.3	−1.0	−1.2	0.5	−0.7
Current account/GDP	−2.2	−2.2	−0.6	−1.8	−2.4	−1.4	−1.4
Memo items							
GDP growth: excluding							
South Africa	2.7	2.8	3.1	3.0	2.9	4.0	4.0
Oil exporters	2.8	2.4	4.4	4.0	3.1	3.3	3.2
CFA countries	2.5	2.1	2.7	2.4	2.5	4.0	3.7

a. Fixed investment, measured in real terms.
b. Local currency GDP deflator, median.
c. Weighted average growth of import demand in export markets.
d. Goods and nonfactor services.
e. Change in terms of trade, measured as a proportion of GDP (percent).
Source: World Bank baseline forecast, February 2002.

Gambia, Guinea, Guinea-Bissau, Madagascar, Malawi, Mali, Mauritania, Niger, Rwanda, São Tomé and Principe, Senegal, and Zambia; and three were at completion points: Uganda, Mozambique, and Tanzania.

3. Averages described in the remainder of this paragraph are calculated using GDP weights for 43 countries with data available. Note that median inflation (6 percent in 2001, see table) is substantially below mean inflation (13.5 percent in 2001) because of a few countries with very high inflation.

4. A rational response is to save transitory income fluctuations, and it is hard to imagine such a windfall would not be recognized as transitory. Both cross-country and case studies find typically 50 to 80 percent or more of major commodity windfalls are saved, at least initially. See, for example, Deaton and Miller 1996 and Collier and Gunning 2000.

5. Such as the 25 percent pay raise for Nigerian civil servants, announced for 2001, then temporarily delayed until 2002.

Appendix 5

Global Commodity Price Prospects

The broad declines in commodity prices in 2001 were another reminder of the key role played by the global industrial cycle in shaping commodity prices. In dollar terms, crude oil prices were down 13.7 percent, metals and minerals prices were down 9.6 percent, and agricultural prices were down 9 percent (figure A5.1).[1] Price declines were already well entrenched in the markets for metals and minerals and agricultural commodities by midyear. But the main decline in crude oil prices in 2001 occurred after the terrorist attacks on September 11, as OPEC (Organization of Petroleum Exporting Countries) producers kept the market well supplied, and now find it difficult to push prices higher because of the weakening in the global economy.

The projected rebound in global activity is the key reason to expect a change in the trend of commodity prices in the quarters ahead. The relatively tame nature of this rebound and the fact that current prices are generally below their 2001 average, however, means that the year-on-year recovery in prices in 2002 will be quite modest. Metals and minerals prices are projected to be up only 0.5 percent, and agricultural prices up by only 1.7 percent. Moreover, oil prices are not likely to move much from their current level, averaging about $20 per barrel in 2002 (which would be below the 2001 average of $24.35 per barrel). More upward momentum in prices should be evident in 2003, however. Metals and minerals prices should rise by 6.7 percent, agricultural prices by 7.6 percent and crude oil prices by 5 percent.

The demand for crude oil and metals and minerals is more responsive to changes in global economic and industrial activity than is the demand for agricultural commodities. Global strength in 2000 thus contributed to higher prices in those commodities, while it had little effect on agricultural prices. In addition, crude oil and metals and minerals production is more concentrated among fewer producers than is agricultural production. This facilitates supply cutbacks, as witnessed when OPEC producers quickly cut production and exports of crude in response to falling oil prices in 1998. Metals and minerals producers made similar but less effective cuts, which also led to price increases.

By contrast, agricultural producers are mostly small and dispersed, and coordinated supply cuts are difficult. As a result, agricultural production has continued to exceed demand in recent years, even though prices have been falling. In view of these adverse supply-demand conditions facing agriculture and the large decline in prices since 1997, the projection of an upturn in agricultural prices over the next three years is all the more striking. Price declines in agricultural commodities have now been large enough, however, that even dispersed producers are cutting production, and prices are indeed showing early signs of recovery.

Supply conditions also drive another key projection—that for crude oil. Following a muted recovery over the next 18 months or so, prices are forecast to decline anew, to average $19 a barrel in 2004, as OPEC and non-OPEC supplies increase faster than demand. Metals and minerals prices are projected to increase 0.5, 6.7, and 5.1 percent, respectively, during 2002–04 as economic activity recovers and producers slowly increase output. Agricultural prices are expected to rise by 1.7, 7.6, and 7.1 percent, respectively, during 2002–04 because

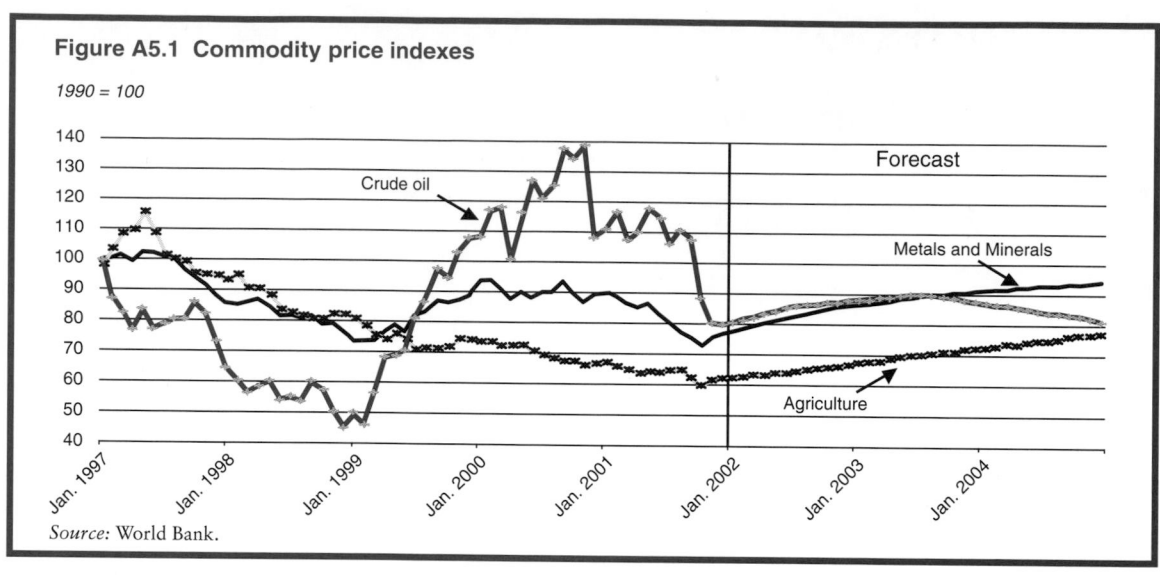

Figure A5.1 Commodity price indexes

1990 = 100

Forecast

Crude oil

Metals and Minerals

Agriculture

Jan. 1997 Jan. 1998 Jan. 1999 Jan. 2000 Jan. 2001 Jan. 2002 Jan. 2003 Jan. 2004

Source: World Bank.

of reduced production in response to current low prices and the modest demand increases that accompany a global economic recovery.

Commodity prices are inherently volatile, and efforts to reduce price volatility have generally been unsuccessful. The last of the United Nations (U.N.)–backed international commodity agreements (rubber) was suspended in 1999. The effort by the Association of Coffee Producing Countries to curtail exports and prevent sharp price declines has not been effective. The attempt by OPEC to keep prices in the $22–$28-per-barrel band was suspended after the terrorist attacks on September 11. Consequently, it seems unlikely that commodity price volatility will decline. This is a concern for developing countries that rely on commodity exports for a large share of export earnings or are large importers of key commodities such as food or oil.

The remainder of this appendix focuses on the outlook for individual commodities during the period 2002–04. Longer term price forecasts to 2015 are given in the appendix tables, but are not extensively discussed. Appendix table A5.9 presents nominal price forecasts for individual commodities and indexes, while tables A5.10 and A5.11 present real price forecasts for individual commodities and indexes.

Agriculture

The extreme weakness of agricultural prices is due to the combination of large increases in productivity and slow demand growth over the past decade. For example, global consumption of coffee, cotton, and grains each grew by less than 1 percent per year during the 1990s—less than population growth. In addition, yields of most crops increased, and this caused production to rise and prices to fall. It does not appear that this surplus of production capacity will dissipate soon or that demand will increase significantly, and because of that, future price increases are expected to be modest.

That said, agricultural prices are expected to recover beginning in 2002, because of reduced supplies, which follow from low prices, and slightly higher demand, which follows from the global economic recovery. Stocks of some commodities have been declining for several years (grains stocks are down 17 percent from the 1998 highs, and sugar stocks are expected to decline 14 percent by mid-2002), although stocks of other commodities (such as coffee, cotton, rubber, and soybeans) remain high. The outlook for individual commodities varies because of different demand, supply, and stock conditions.

Beverages

Beverage prices were mixed in 2001. Coffee prices fell 29 percent as Vietnam and Brazil increased production despite stagnant export growth (table A5.1). Tea prices fell 14 percent because of weak demand and a recovery of production in major exporters. Cocoa rose 18 percent on strong demand and an expected poor harvest in Côte d'Ivoire. Bev-

Table A5.1 Coffee Production (million bags)

	1997–88	1998–99	1999–2000	2000–01	2001–02
Brazil	22.8	35.6	30.8	34.10	33.7
Vietnam	6.9	7.5	11.0	15.0	13.3
Colombia	12.2	10.9	9.5	10.5	11.0
Indonesia	7.8	7.0	6.5	6.5	6.3
Mexico	5.1	5.0	6.2	5.3	5.5
Côte d'Ivoire	3.7	2.2	5.7	4.3	4.2
World	96.4	108.4	113.6	117.4	115.8

Source: U.S. Department of Agriculture.

erage prices are expected to recover slightly during 2002–04 (figure A5.2).

Since the price peak in 1997, cocoa prices went down 34 percent, coffee prices went down 67 percent, and tea prices went down 22 percent. We expect cocoa prices to increase 12 percent in 2002, and a further 8 percent in 2003 as cocoa grindings increase along with the expected recovery of the global economy, and production returns to about the 2.8 million tons level of the past several years (table A5.2). We also expect increased volatility in cocoa prices because of the uncertainty surrounding the new producer-led cocoa body in Côte d'Ivoire and continued political uncertainty.

The coffee market is expected to remain depressed for at least another season, with arabica prices expected to remain unchanged during 2002 and robusta prices making minor gains as Vietnam curtails production by 1 to 2 million bags. A recov-

ery is expected in 2003, with arabica and robusta prices each up 11 percent. However, this recovery could be delayed (especially for arabica) if Brazil increases coffee production to 40 million bags, as many analysts now expect. Nevertheless, the price levels experienced during the early 1990s are unlikely to be repeated, in the absence of adverse weather conditions, because of the supply increases.

Tea prices are expected to decline an additional 4.3 percent in 2002 as production continues to increase. Then prices are projected to make a gradual recovery, up 2.6 percent in 2003 and 3.2 percent in 2004. There is a risk that tea prices could continue to fall rather than recover in the next several years because of increased exports from Sri Lanka, Kenya, and India—the three largest tea exporters.

Food

Food prices increased about 2 percent in 2001, after reaching a 17-year low in 2000. Prices are expected to increase by 12 percent during 2002–04 because of reduced supplies and modest increases in demand that will accompany the expected global economic recovery (figure A5.3).

Fats and oils prices fell 7.5 percent in 2001, following a decline of 8.4 percent in 2000. Since 1997, vegetable oil prices (in dollars) have declined 40 percent because of large supplies and currency devaluations of major exporters such as Malaysia (which accounted for nearly 70 percent of palm oil

Table A5.2 Beverages global balance

	1970	1980	1990	1999	2000	2001	Annual growth rates (percent)		
							1970–80	1980–90	1990–2000
Coffee (*thousand bags*)									
Production	64,161	86,174	88,849	113,588	117,447	115,756	2.11	1.36	1.20
Consumption	71,536	79,100	96,300	110,400	111,100	110,000	1.01	1.97	0.22
Exports	54,186	60,996	76,163	92,338	89,642	92,956	0.78	2.41	1.06
	1970	1980	1990	1998	1999	2000			
Cocoa (*thousand tons*)									
Production	1,554	1,695	2,506	2,808	3,073	2,812	0.46	4.62	1.82
Grindings	1,418	1,556	2,335	2,762	2,967	3,014	0.16	4.48	2.38
Stocks	497	675	1,791	1,266	1,341	1,111	2.38	13.89	-3.95
Tea (*thousand tons*)									
Production	1,286	1,848	2,526	2,963	2,847	2,895	4.09	2.87	1.24
Exports	752	859	1,099	1,296	1,272	1,309	2.35	2.39	1.62

Note: Time references for coffee and cocoa are based on the crop year shown under the year that production begins: October to September for cocoa and April to March for coffee. For tea, data are in calendar years.
Sources: International Coffee Organization, International Cocoa Organization, International Tea Committee, Food and Agriculture Organization, U.S. Department of Agriculture, and World Bank.

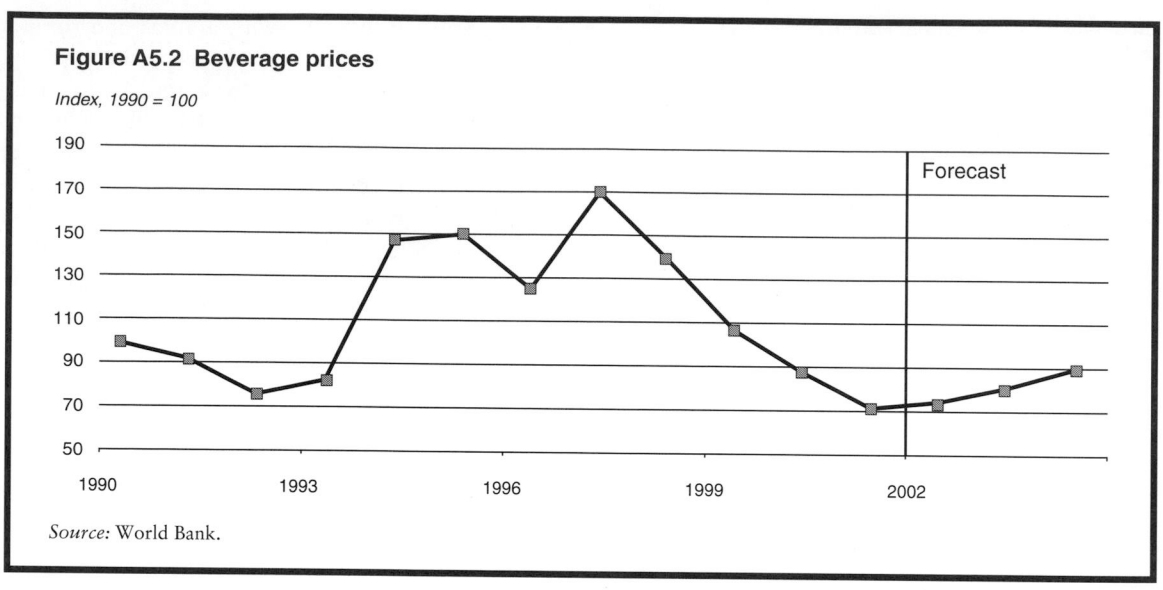

Figure A5.2 Beverage prices

Index, 1990 = 100

Forecast

Source: World Bank.

exports) and Brazil (which accounted for 30 percent of soybean oil exports).[2]

Prices of most fats and oils are expected to begin a substantial recovery during 2002. The prices of palm and soybean oils, the two dominant oils accounting for 19 and 21 percent of total fats and oils, are expected to increase by 17 and 12 percent, respectively. Lesser increases are expected during 2003. The overall index is expected to increase by 1.3 percent in 2002 and 2.9 percent in 2003. Demand should strengthen, especially because of the relaxing of import restrictions by China following

its joining the World Trade Organization, while palm oil supplies are expected to grow only 1 percent this season compared to the long-term average of 9 percent.

The index of grains prices fell 1.6 percent in 2001 and is expected to increase about 6 percent in 2002, as stocks fall to a projected 23 percent of total use—the lowest since 1995 (table A5.3).

Wheat production has declined for four consecutive years, and year-end stocks are expected to decline for the third consecutive year in 2001–02. This has caused wheat prices to increase 12 percent in

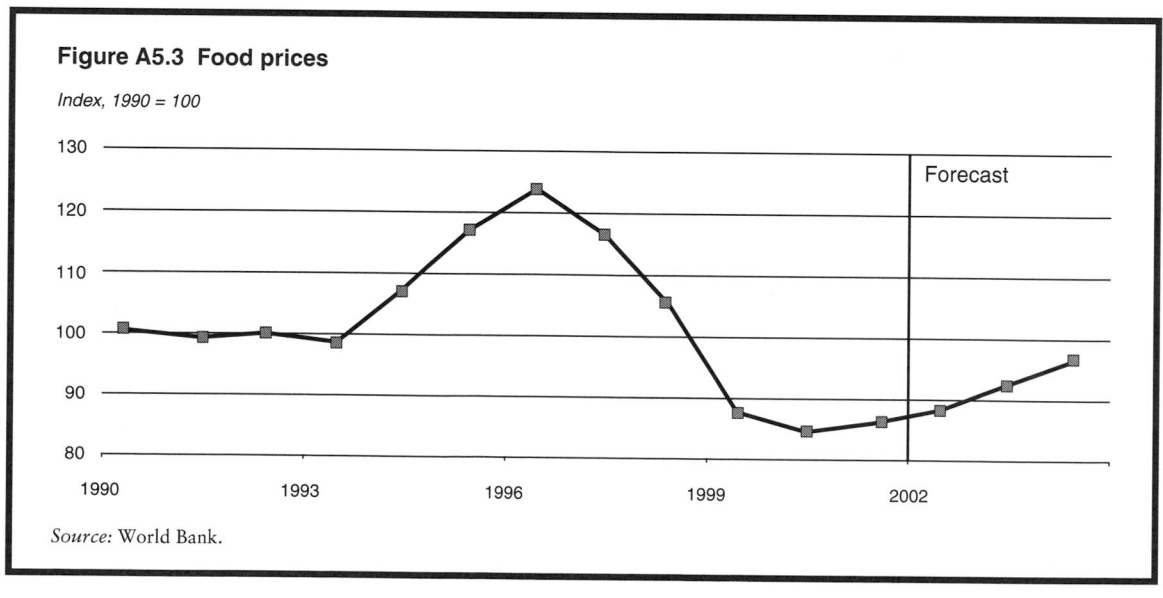

Figure A5.3 Food prices

Index, 1990 = 100

Forecast

Source: World Bank.

Table A5.3 Foods global balance

	1970	1980	1990	1999	2000	2001	Annual growth rates (percent) 1970–80	1980–90	1990–2000
Fats and oils			*Million tons*						
Production	39.78	58.09	80.84	113.50	117.09	119.10	3.68	3.54	3.70
Consumption	39.82	56.80	80.87	112.06	116.87	120.59	3.55	3.69	3.64
Exports	8.83	17.76	26.89	35.45	37.88	38.73	7.05	4.19	3.39
Stocks	5.18	9.25	12.15	14.22	14.46	12.94	7.09	2.44	0.69
Grains			*Million tons*						
Production	1,079	1,430	1,769	1,871	1,836	1,843	2.88	1.55	1.04
Consumption	1,114	1,450	1,717	1,872	1,872	1,894	2.58	1.78	1.02
Exports	119	229	232	282	268	266	6.35	0.13	0.94
Stocks	193	309	490	523	487	436	7.24	3.83	−0.56
Soybeans			*Thousand tons*						
Production	44,269	80,873	104,093	159,854	173,384	182,446	6.84	1.87	5.08
Consumption	47,988	84,017	103,643	159,758	173,000	180,744	6.53	2.04	4.99
Exports	12,572	24,514	24,488	47,254	54,880	56,694	5.24	0.80	2.88
Stocks	3,599	11,538	12,992	14,593	14,959	17,476	13.83	−0.66	0.20
Sugar			*Thousand tons (raw equivalent)*						
Production	70,272	88,488	114,178	143,220	136,111	128,184	2.80	1.59	3.26
Consumption	67,730	90,547	110,598	133,104	134,712	132,064	3.30	1.40	3.00
Exports	21,578	28,346	34,069	42,015	38,495	34,944	3.26	0.83	3.12
Stocks	17,639	17,253	21,260	35,939	35,474	30,451	3.96	−0.77	4.52

Note: Time references for grains, soybeans, and sugar are based on marketing years, shown under the year in which production begin, and vary by country; for fats and oils, crop years begin in September.
Source: U.S. Department of Agriculture; Oil World.

2001 from the 1999 lows. Prices are still 15 percent below the 1994 levels, when stocks were at comparable lows. Prices are projected to increase 4 percent in 2002 and an additional 4.5 percent in 2003. The risk to the forecast is on the upside if prices return to their historical relationship relative to stocks. A drought also threatens the Canadian and U.S. wheat crops and could lead to higher prices.

Maize prices in 2001 were only slightly above their lows in 1999 and 2000 despite the decline in maize stocks in 2000–01 and a projected further decline in stocks in 2001–02. If stocks fall as expected, they would about equal the levels in 1995, which preceded sharp maize price increases in 1995 and 1996. One of the factors that have kept maize prices low is the large supply of soybean meal, which substitutes for maize as livestock and poultry feed. However, the low maize stocks and the fall in production in major exporting countries in 2001–02 should cause maize prices to rise about 6 percent in 2002 and an additional 9 percent in 2003.

Rice prices fell 14.6 percent in 2001, to the lowest nominal price since 1972 and the lowest price relative to wheat since at least 1960. The extreme weakness in rice prices is due, at least in part,

to the currency devaluation in Thailand, the largest exporter of rice. Global rice production and stocks declined in 2000–01 and are projected to decline in 2001–02. Rice prices began to rise in late 2001 and are expected to increase by 10 percent in 2002 and an additional 10 percent in 2003.

Soybean prices fell 7.6 percent in 2001, down 36 percent from their 1996 highs. The stock situation for soybeans is very different from that of most other crops. Soybean production has increased at an unprecedented 5 percent per year rate since 1990, sending soybean carryover stocks to near-record levels and prices to the lowest nominal levels since 1972. Ninety-five percent of the increase in global production was in the three main exporting countries (Argentina, Brazil, and the United States), which account for nearly 90 percent of world exports and about 80 percent of world production. The production increases in Argentina and Brazil were driven by improved yields and new varieties that can be grown in previously unfavorable climatic conditions. This allowed soybean production to expand farther north in Brazil and contributed to the more than doubling of Brazilian production from 1990 to 2001. The increase in U.S. production

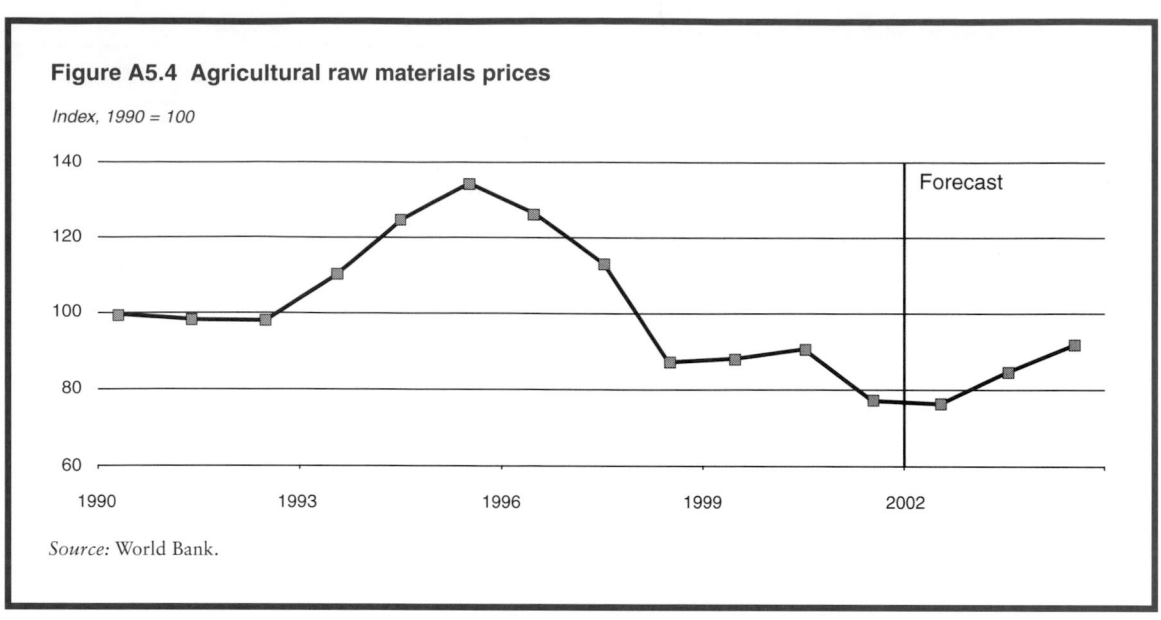

Figure A5.4 Agricultural raw materials prices

Index, 1990 = 100

Source: World Bank.

was due to policy changes that allowed producers to shift away from maize and also to improved varieties that allowed soybeans to displace wheat in some areas. Soybean prices are projected to increase modestly—by 5 percent in 2002 and by 7 percent in 2003. This would leave nominal prices nearly 30 percent below the price peak of 1996.

Sugar prices were up 6.6 percent in 2001 following the 31 percent increase in 2000 from the lows in 1999. Sugar prices are expected to rise about 4 percent in 2002 and an additional 2 percent in 2003, as global production is expected to fall about 6 percent and year-end stocks are expected to fall about 14 percent in 2002. Brazil, the largest exporter, is expected to have slightly higher production in 2002 than in 2001, but production is expected to remain below the peak level of 2000. Other major exporters, such as Australia and Thailand, are also expected to have slightly larger production in 2001, but production will likely remain well below recent peaks. Russia, the largest importer in recent years, with as much as 15 percent of world imports, is expected to reduce imports.

Raw materials

The index of agricultural raw materials prices (comprising cotton, natural rubber, and tropical hardwoods) declined 15 percent in 2001, and 43 percent since the peak in 1995 (figure A5.4). The declines have been due to weak currencies of major ex-

porters, such as Malaysia, large production increases (cotton), and weak demand (timber).

Cotton prices (according to the Cotlook A Index) fell 23 percent in 2001 compared with 2000 mainly in response to an 8 percent surge in global production (table A5.4). More than 80 percent of the increase came from China and the United States, which account for a combined 45 percent of global production. Cotton demand has been weak, and is expected to decline slightly in 2001–02. Ending stocks are expected to increase nearly 15 percent, pushing the stocks-to-use ratio to a record high of 53 percent. The International Cotton Advisory Committee expects production to fall by about 4 percent in 2002–03, but the stocks-to-use ratio is still expected to remain high. Prices are projected to fall 5.6 percent in 2002 and then increase in 2003 but remain well below the 2000 level.

Natural rubber prices fell 13 percent in 2001, mostly because of weak demand for tires—the largest use of natural rubber. Car tire demand declined 10 percent in the United States, 4 percent in France, and 1 percent in Japan during the first half of 2001 compared to 2000. Major exporters (Indonesia, Malaysia, and Thailand) announced plans to cut production in 2002. However, past such efforts have been largely unsuccessful. Natural rubber prices are expected to decline 5 percent in 2002 and increase 14 percent in 2003 as the global economy recovers.

Table A5.4 Raw materials global balance

							Annual growth rates (percent)		
	1970	1980	1990	1999	2000	2001	1970–80	1980–90	1990–2000
Cotton			*Thousand tons*						
Production	11,740	13,832	18,970	19,067	19,261	20,856	1.22	3.09	0.84
Consumption	12,173	14,215	18,576	19,803	19,651	19,590	1.11	3.10	0.21
Exports	3,875	4,414	5,081	6,150	5,739	6,167	0.93	2.79	0.49
Stocks	4,605	4,895	6,645	9,038	8,630	9,896	1.71	2.83	1.38
	1970	1980	1990	1998	1999	2000			
Natural rubber			*Thousand tons*						
Production	3,140	3,820	5,080	6,820	6,810	6,830	1.78	3.17	3.08
Consumption	3,090	3,770	5,190	6,540	6,670	7,320	1.58	3.16	3.25
Net exports	2,820	3,280	3,950	4,690	4,660	5,000	1.26	2.07	1.84
Stocks	1,440	1,480	1,500	2,300	2,530	2,150	0.60	0.23	3.71
	1970	1980	1990	1997	1998	1999	1970–80	1980–90	1990–99
Tropical timber			*Thousand cubic meters*						
Logs, produced	210	262	300	311	289	299	1.47	1.71	0.45
Logs, imported	36.1	42.2	25.1	17.9	14.6	18.9	0.18	–5.10	–5.36
Sawnwood, produced	98.5	115.8	131.8	115.0	108.3	108.2	1.17	1.74	–1.99
Sawnwood, imported	7.1	13.2	16.1	21.2	19.5	21.6	4.95	2.57	3.33
Plywood, produced	33.4	39.4	48.2	56.1	47.6	52.0	1.17	2.02	0.46
Plywood, imported	4.9	6.0	14.9	19.5	18.3	18.3	0.69	9.10	3.60

Note: Year references for cotton are based on the crop year shown under the production year beginning in August; for rubber and tropical timber, the year refers to the calendar year.
Sources: International Cotton Advisory Committee, International Rubber Study Group, Food and Agriculture Organization, and World Bank.

Tropical timber prices fell 18.8 percent in 2001, and are down 35 percent from their 1995 highs, because of weak import demand—especially in the European Union and Japan. The strength of the dollar versus the yen and European currencies contributed to lower dollar prices. Malaysian sawnwood export volumes fell by about 12 percent in the first half of 2001. China has continued to increase log imports for processing and re-export. African timber export prices have remained stronger than Asian prices because of the shift of imports from Asia to Africa by European importers. Tropical timber prices are expected to remain about unchanged in 2002 before increasing by a total of 24 percent in 2003 and 2004.

Fertilizers

Fertilizer prices were broadly lower in 2001, as slow demand growth continued the trends of the 1990s (table A5.5), and surplus production capacity remained large for all major products. The recovery in

Table A5.5 Fertilizer global balance

							Annual growth rates (percent)		
	1970	1980	1990	1997	1998	1999	1970–80	1980–90	1990–99
Nitrogen			*Million tons*						
Production	33.30	62.78	82.26	87.60	88.48	90.85	6.53	3.12	1.11
Consumption	31.76	60.78	77.14	80.12	82.62	85.53	6.86	2.60	1.15
Exports	6.77	13.15	19.48	23.24	23.95	24.58	7.23	5.10	2.62
Phosphate			*Million tons*						
Production	22.04	34.51	39.35	32.81	32.99	32.65	3.72	1.70	–2.05
Consumption	21.12	31.70	35.90	33.34	33.17	33.15	3.85	1.39	–0.88
Exports	2.92	7.51	10.50	12.24	12.54	12.90	8.37	5.01	2.31
Potash			*Million tons*						
Production	17.59	27.46	26.82	26.16	24.98	25.42	3.97	–0.03	–0.59
Consumption	16.43	24.24	24.68	22.63	22.36	22.68	3.93	0.05	–0.94
Exports	9.45	16.72	19.82	22.52	22.13	22.63	4.89	0.73	1.48

Note: All data are in marketing years.
Source: Food and Agriculture Organization.

grain prices is expected to support higher fertilizer prices in 2002, since an estimated 55 percent of total fertilizer use is for grains.

Nitrogen (urea) prices were down 6 percent in 2001 after increasing 44 percent in 2000 from extremely depressed levels. The Food and Agriculture Organization (FAO)/Industry Working Group estimates that global nitrogen fertilizer capacity exceeded current consumption by 11 percent in 2001–02 and that demand will increase fast enough to reduce surplus capacity to 8 percent within four years. We expect urea prices to rise 23 percent by 2004 because of increased grain prices and the reduction in surplus production capacity.

Phosphate prices were marginally lower in 2001 after falling sharply in 2000. Diammonium phosphate (DAP) prices fell 4.2 percent and triple-super phosphate (TSP) prices fell 3.6 percent in 2001 compared to 2000. Prices are expected to increase 18 and 14 percent, respectively, for DAP and TSP by 2004 as surplus capacity declines and agricultural commodity prices rise.

Potash prices declined 3.6 percent in 2001 compared with 2000 after increasing slowly in each of the three previous years. Although surplus capacity remains large (it is estimated at 28 percent), prices have been kept relatively stable by industry cuts in production. Prices are expected to increase slowly because of tight supply management and steady increases in demand. By 2004, nominal prices are projected to rise 4 percent from 2001 levels.

Metals and minerals

The index of metals and minerals prices fell 9.6 percent in 2001 because of rising inventories and weak demand as a result of slowing economic activity (table A5.6). Low prices led to a number of production cutbacks, notably in copper and aluminum, which helped stem the price declines. Prices began to recover late in the year on expectations that an economic recovery would lead to higher demand for metals. Inventories remain high for many metals—the exceptions being lead and nickel—but the global balance for most metals is expected to move into deficit during the year.

Metals prices are expected to continue to rebound moderately in 2002 and record stronger increases in 2003–04. Real prices are expected to decline in the longer term, as production costs continue to fall because of technological innovation and improved managerial practices.

Aluminum prices fell 6.8 percent in 2001 as a result of weak demand and a sharp run-up in inventories (figures A5.5 and A5.6). Prices have been partly supported by reductions of more than 2 million tons of annual production capacity, mainly in the United States and Brazil because of power shortages. About 1.6 million tons of smelting capacity in the U.S. Pacific Northwest was idled following the electricity crisis on the West Coast, while at least 0.3 million tons were taken off-line in Brazil under mandatory rationing because of hydroelectric shortages in the region.

Table A5.6 Metals and minerals global balance

	1970	1980	1990	1999	2000	2001	Annual growth rates (percent)		
							1970–80	1980–90	1990–2000
Aluminum			*Thousand tons*						
Production	10,257	16,027	19,362	23,705	24,642	24,360	3.2	1.9	2.2
Consumption	9,996	14,771	19,244	23,456	24,994	24,200	3.2	1.8	2.2
LME ending stocks		68	311	775	322	821	n.a.	–0.3	0.4
Copper			*Thousand tons*						
Production	7,583	9,242	10,809	14,455	14,834	15,400	1.9	1.1	3.5
Consumption	7,294	9,400	10,780	14,095	15,160	14,720	2.5	1.0	3.3
LME ending stocks	72	123	179	790	357	799	7.4	–5.6	15.7
Nickel			*Thousand tons*						
Production	0	717	842	1,028	1,105	1,138	n.a.	1.6	3.1
Consumption	0	742	858	1,076	1,152	1,125	n.a.	1.5	2.6
LME ending stocks	2	5	4	47	10	20	n.a.	–0.5	8.3

n.a. Not available.
Sources: World Bureau of Metal Statistics, the London Metal Exchange (LME), and World Bank.

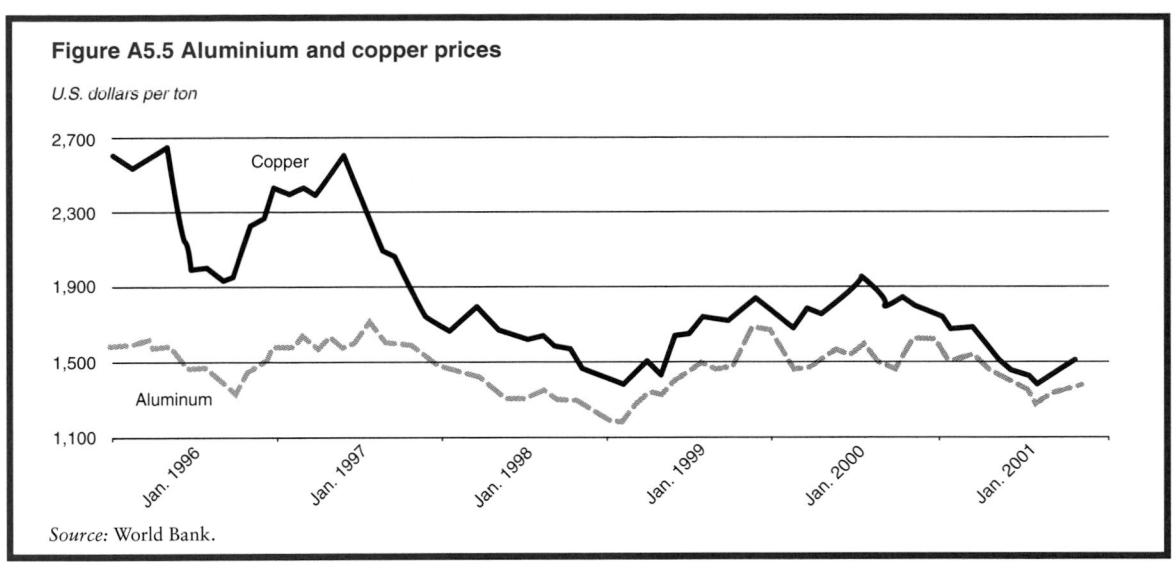

Figure A5.5 Aluminium and copper prices

U.S. dollars per ton

Source: World Bank.

It is uncertain when the idled capacity may be reactivated, but with such large amounts of capacity overhanging the market, the potential restarts could serve to cap prices in 2002. While prices could begin to recover in the second half of 2002, annual prices are expected to remain fairly flat.

In 2003, inventories are expected to decline because of rising demand, and prices are expected to move higher and continue to rise in the medium term, as demand increases keep the market in deficit. However, over the longer term, new low-cost capacity is expected to come on-stream and real prices are expected to continue their declines.

Copper prices declined 13 percent in 2001, as world consumption fell 3 percent while production increased about 4 percent. London Metal Exchange (LME) stocks rose to 800,000 tons (figure A5.6). Low prices prompted a number of announced production cutbacks late in the year, which totaled about 500,000 tons per year (tpy) at year's end.

The production cuts are expected to contribute to a net decline in global output of about 1 percent in 2002. A recovery in demand of 3 percent is expected to lead to a 3 percent rise in prices. This gain is moderate because of the high level of inventories and uncertainty about the extent of recovery in de-

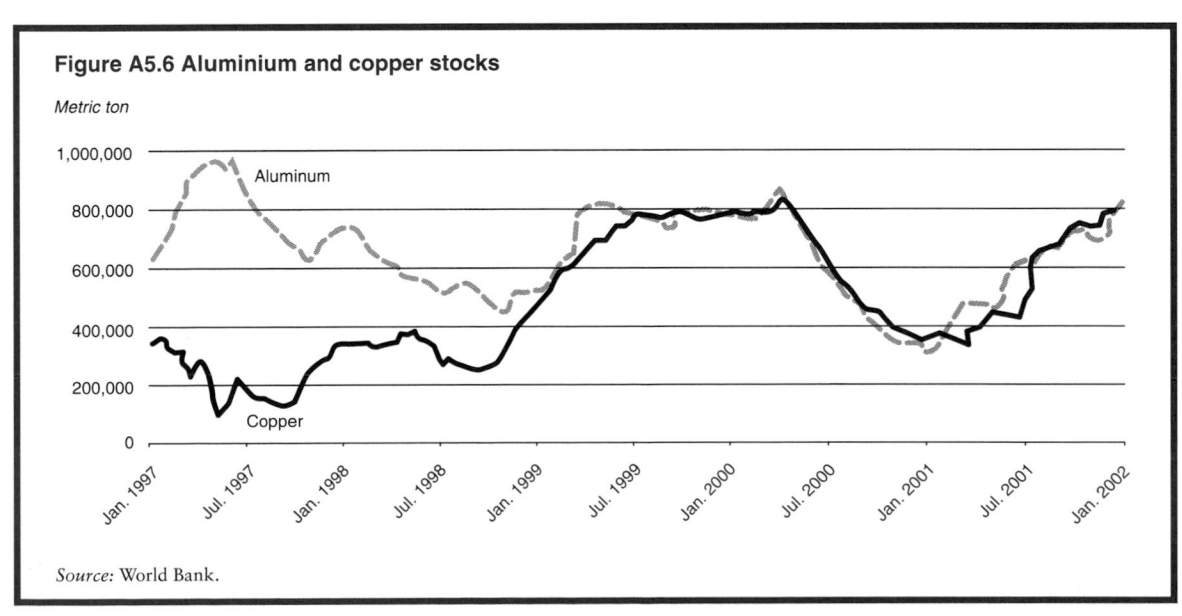

Figure A5.6 Aluminium and copper stocks

Metric ton

Source: World Bank.

Table A5.7 Gold global balance

	Tons								Percent per year
	1991	1994	1995	1996	1997	1998	1999	2000	1991–00
Jewelry	2,359	2,619	2,792	2,851	3,349	3,156	3,149	3,175	3.4
Other fabrication	517	456	502	484	560	569	595	563	1.0
Bar hoarding	252	231	306	182	325	173	240	198	−2.6
Other						208	170	10	n.a.
Total demand	3,129	3,305	3,600	3,518	4,234	4,106	4,154	3,946	4.0
Mine production	2,162	2,282	2,276	2,361	2,479	2,538	2,568	2,573	2.0
Net official sales	100	130	167	279	326	374	464	471	18.8
Old gold scrap	482	617	624	640	628	1,097	616	611	2.7
Net hedging	66	105	475	142	504	97	506		n.a.
Other	319	171	57	95	297			291	−1.0
Total supply	3,129	3,305	3,600	3,518	4,234	4,106	4,154	3,946	2.6

n.a. Not available.
Sources: Gold Field Minerals Service and World Bank.

mand. Price increases are expected to accelerate to 8 percent and 6 percent, respectively, during 2003 and 2004 as demand continues to outstrip increases in production. Over the longer term, increases in new low-cost capacity are expected, and real prices are expected to decline.

Nickel prices fell 32 percent last year, but the decline was from unusually high levels in 2000 when exceptionally strong demand and low inventories resulted in a very tight market. In 2001, consumption fell more than 2 percent from weak demand for stainless steel, while production is estimated to have increased more than 3 percent. This led to a doubling of LME inventories, although stocks are low compared with levels during the 1990s.

The market balance is expected to remain in surplus in 2002, as production again outstrips projected demand growth of some 4 to 5 percent. With relatively low inventories, expectations of increasingly tighter markets are expected to result in higher prices this year. A shortage of nickel production is likely beyond 2002, as there appears to be a lack of new development projects during 2003–05, partly because of disappointments with new pressurized acid leach technology. Consequently, prices could spike sharply higher during this period if demand growth rose quickly.

Gold prices declined 3 percent in 2001 to $271 per troy ounce (toz), because of weak demand and ample supplies (table A5.7). Demand in major markets fell nearly 2 percent during the first nine months of 2001, in part because of the strong U.S. dollar. The price decline was kept modest mainly

because of a rally following September 11, which took prices towards $300 toz, as some investors turned to gold as a refuge after the terrorist attacks in the United States. Prices returned to the $275 toz level in November and December, as underlying market fundamentals remained weak. Central bank sales continue, with the U.K. government completing a series of auctions totaling 395 tons in early 2002.

Gold prices are projected to average $275 toz over the 2002-04 period, and remain at or below $300 toz over the longer term. Prices above this level will likely stimulate new supplies, encourage producer sales, and lessen demand, while prices dropping toward $250 toz will reduce investment and encourage consumption. Mine production is expected to continue to increase moderately, as new low-cost operations come onstream. An important determinant of prices will be the decision by central banks whether to further stem official gold sales when the Washington Agreement expires in 2004.

Petroleum

Crude oil prices averaged $24.4 per barrel in 2001—down 13.7 percent from 2000—and ended the year below $19 per barrel. The price decline was due to falling demand, rising non-OPEC production, higher inventories, and speculative selling (table A5.8). Oil demand had been weakening prior to the terrorist attacks in the United States on September 11 because of slowing economic growth, but slumped further following the attacks, partly because of significantly reduced air travel and mild weather, and also expectations of lower economic

Table A5.8 Petroleum global balance

	1970	1980	1990	2000	2001	2002	Annual growth rates (percent)		
							1970–80	1980–90	1990–2000
OECD	34.0	41.5	41.5	47.8	47.7	47.5	2.0	0.0	1.4
former Soviet Union	5.0	8.9	8.4	3.6	3.7	3.7	5.9	−0.6	−8.1
Other non-OECD	6.8	12.3	16.1	24.4	24.6	24.8	6.1	2.7	4.3
Total consumption	**45.7**	**62.6**	**66.0**	**75.9**	**76.0**	**76.0**	**3.2**	**0.5**	**1.4**
OPEC	23.5	27.2	24.5	30.8	30.2	28.7	1.5	−1.0	2.3
former Soviet Union	7.1	12.1	11.5	7.9	8.6	9.0	5.4	−0.5	−3.6
Other non-OPEC	17.4	24.6	30.9	38.0	38.1	38.6	3.5	2.3	2.1
Total production	**48.0**	**63.9**	**66.9**	**76.7**	**76.8**	**76.3**	**2.9**	**0.5**	**1.4**
Stock change, miscellaneous	2.3	1.3	0.9	0.8	0.8	0.3			

Sources: BP, the International Energy Agency, and World Bank.

growth. OPEC also committed to keep the market well supplied, and inventories rose to more comfortable levels, compared to the very low levels of early 2000 (figure A5.7).

The 10 OPEC countries (excluding Iraq, which remains outside the quota system because of U.N. sanctions) reduced production four times in the past year by a combined total of 5 million barrels per day (mb/d) (figure A5.8), in an attempt to maintain prices within its targeted price range of $22 to $28 a barrel. OPEC's latest cut of 1.5 mb/d, effective January 2002, was made only after five non-OPEC producers agreed to contribute nearly 0.5 mb/d of

cuts to help stabilize prices. OPEC also decided to suspend its price band for six months.

All of the cuts are for six months, except for Russia, which only committed to reduce crude oil exports for three months. Russia did not agree to reduce crude production or limit product exports. As a result, actual reductions in non-OPEC production from these five countries may be limited to only 0.1 mb/d. Compliance within OPEC countries is expected to be less than in 2001, as some countries face difficulties reducing output.

In 2002, the requirements for OPEC oil are projected to be lower than in 2001, because of min-

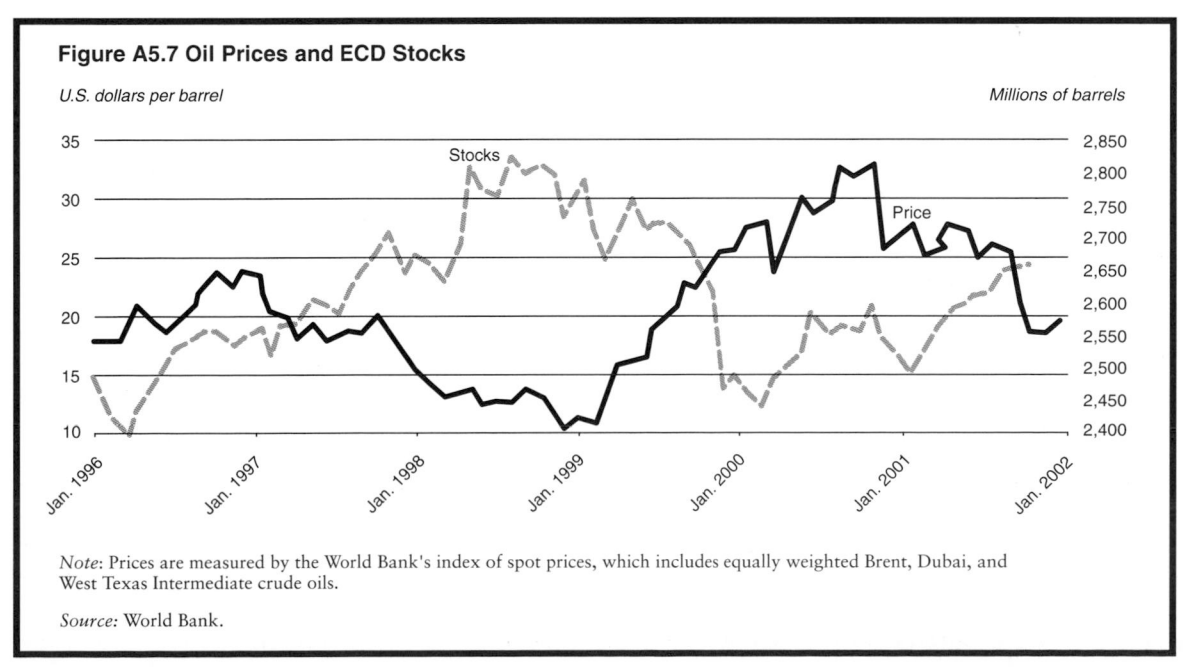

Figure A5.7 Oil Prices and ECD Stocks

U.S. dollars per barrel   *Millions of barrels*

Note: Prices are measured by the World Bank's index of spot prices, which includes equally weighted Brent, Dubai, and West Texas Intermediate crude oils.

Source: World Bank.

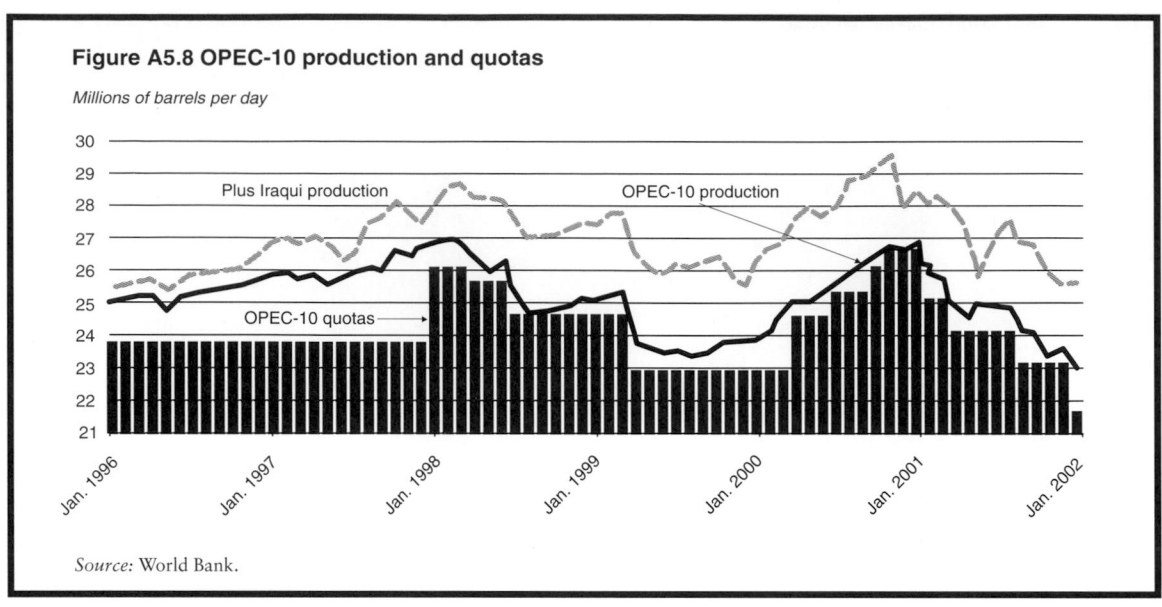

Figure A5.8 OPEC-10 production and quotas

Millions of barrels per day

Source: World Bank.

imal growth in global oil demand and a continued rise in non-OPEC supplies. Consequently OPEC will need to produce an estimated 1.5 mb/d less oil than in 2001 to stabilize prices. Oil demand is expected to show little growth this year, even with a moderate economic recovery in the second half of this year. Non-OPEC supplies are expected to increase by 1 mb/d, notably in Russia, despite the recent commitments.

Supporting prices may prove difficult in the first half of this year, especially if demand deteriorates, and deteriorating demand may pressure OPEC to cut production further. However, as demand recovers, compliance should become easier and inventories should converge on last year's levels, providing further support to prices.

A major upside threat to prices is a potential supply disruption from further actions to combat global terrorism. Should there be a significant supply disruption, oil prices could rise sharply. However, surplus production capacity in OPEC has widened to well over 6 mb/d, and this could compensate for some loss in exports because of disruptions caused by the war on terrorism.

In the medium term, OPEC is expected to continue its policy of adjusting output to keep inventories lean and maintain prices around $25 per barrel. This requires OPEC to micromanage the market and take preemptive actions, which can prove difficult given the uncertainties of future levels of de-

mand and competing supplies. Although demand is expected to grow moderately, significant production is expected to come onstream by mid-decade, especially from West Africa and the former Soviet Union. Rising capacity is also expected within OPEC. While OPEC will be required to raise production in 2003, non-OPEC producers are expected to capture much of the growth in demand in the 2004–05 period.

Oil prices are expected to average $20 per barrel 2002, rising to $21 in 2003, but falling below $20 a barrel by mid-decade, because of rising supply competition. A threat to the near-term forecast is that OPEC could take strong, concerted action on production levels over the next few years to keep prices at or above $25 per barrel. If successful, such action would reduce world demand and increase competing supplies, and prices would still be expected to fall below $20 a barrel by mid-decade.

Notes

1. Oil prices are measured by the World Bank's index of spot prices, which includes equally weighted Brent, Dubai, and West Texas Intermediate crude oils. Percentage changes in this appendix refer to year-to-year changes unless noted otherwise.

2. Currency devaluations of major exporters can lead to declines in individual commodity prices in dollar terms (see box 1.1 on p. 20 of *Global Development Finance 2001*.

Table A5.9   Commodity prices and price projections in current dollars

		Actual					Projections				
Commodity	Unit	1970	1980	1990	2000	2001	2002	2003	2005	2010	2015
Energy											
Coal, U.S.	$/mt	n.a.	43.10	41.67	33.06	44.86	38.00	36.00	34.00	35.00	36.00
Crude oil, average	$/bbl	1.21	36.87	22.88	28.23	24.35	20.00	21.00	18.00	19.00	21.00
Natural gas, Europe	$/mmbtu	n.a.	3.40	2.55	3.86	4.06	3.30	3.10	2.75	2.75	3.00
Natural gas, U.S.	$/mmbtu	0.17	1.55	1.70	4.31	3.96	2.50	2.60	2.75	3.00	3.25
Non-energy commodities											
Agriculture											
Beverages											
Cocoa	c/kg	67.5	260.4	126.7	90.6	106.9	120.0	130.0	140.0	157.0	168.0
Coffee, other milds	c/kg	114.7	346.6	197.2	192.0	137.3	138.9	154.3	209.4	265.0	280.0
Coffee, robusta	c/kg	91.4	324.3	118.2	91.3	60.7	63.9	70.6	88.2	132.0	142.6
Tea, auctions (3) average	c/kg	83.5	165.9	205.8	187.6	159.8	153.0	157.0	170.0	182.0	184.0
Food											
Fats and oils											
Coconut oil	$/mt	397.2	673.8	336.5	450.3	318.1	375.0	450.0	600.0	645.0	670.0
Copra	$/mt	224.8	452.7	230.7	304.8	202.1	350.0	400.0	450.0	480.0	500.0
Groundnut oil	$/mt	378.6	858.8	963.7	713.7	680.3	725.0	775.0	820.0	850.0	875.0
Palm oil	$/mt	260.1	583.7	289.8	310.3	285.7	330.0	360.0	400.0	450.0	475.0
Soybean meal	$/mt	102.6	262.4	200.2	189.2	181.0	183.0	192.0	215.0	225.0	235.0
Soybean oil	$/mt	286.3	597.6	447.3	338.1	354.0	390.0	405.0	425.0	460.0	505.0
Soybeans	$/mt	116.9	296.2	246.8	211.8	195.8	205.0	220.0	240.0	250.0	260.0
Grains											
Maize	$/mt	58.4	125.3	109.3	88.5	89.6	96.0	105.0	122.0	125.0	130.0
Rice, Thai, 5%	$/mt	126.3	410.7	270.9	202.4	172.8	190.0	210.0	235.0	260.0	265.0
Sorghum	$/mt	51.8	128.9	103.9	88.0	95.2	91.8	100.4	116.6	119.5	123.5
Wheat, US, HRW	$/mt	54.9	172.7	135.5	114.1	126.8	131.0	138.0	155.0	160.0	165.0
Other food											
Bananas, US, new series	$/mt	166.1	377.3	540.9	424.0	583.3	540.1	523.6	529.1	568.0	590.0
Beef, US	c/kg	130.4	276.0	256.3	193.2	212.9	211.6	213.8	213.8	220.5	230.0
Oranges	$/mt	168.0	400.2	531.1	363.2	609.2	575.0	550.0	500.0	525.0	550.0
Shrimp, Mexican	c/kg	n.a.	1,152	1,069	1,513	1,517	1,350	1,500	1,650	1,700	1,720
Sugar, world	c/kg	8.2	63.16	27.67	18.04	19.04	18.50	19.20	22.00	23.00	24.00
Agricultural raw materials											
Timber											
Logs, Cameroon	$/cum	43.0	251.7	343.5	275.4	266.1	265.0	275.0	300.0	338.0	385.0
Logs, Malaysia	$/cum	43.1	195.5	177.2	190.0	159.1	155.0	170.0	215.0	260.0	295.0
Sawnwood, Malaysia	$/cum	175.0	396.0	533.0	594.7	481.4	485.0	550.0	625.0	720.0	820.0
Other raw materials											
Cotton	c/kg	67.6	206.2	181.9	130.2	105.8	101.4	114.6	132.3	149.9	160.0
Rubber, RSS1, Malaysia	c/kg	40.7	142.5	86.5	69.1	60.0	57.3	63.9	77.2	87.7	95.1
Tobacco	$/mt	1,076	2,276	3,392	2,976	3,012	3,080	3,150	3,250	3,275	3,300
Fertilizers											
DAP	$/mt	54.0	222.2	171.4	154.2	147.7	155.0	160.0	170.0	175.0	180.0
Phosphate rock	$/mt	11.00	46.71	40.50	43.75	41.77	41.50	42.00	43.00	45.00	46.00
Potassium chloride	$/mt	32.0	115.7	98.1	122.5	118.1	120.0	121.5	125.0	127.0	130.0
TSP	$/mt	43.0	180.3	131.8	137.7	126.9	130.0	135.0	145.0	150.0	155.0
Urea, E. Europe, bagged	$/mt	n.a.	n.a.	119.3	101.1	95.3	99.6	108.6	126.7	131.3	135.8
Metals and minerals											
Aluminum	$/mt	556	1,456	1,639	1,549	1,444	1,450	1,550	1,700	1,800	1,850
Copper	$/mt	1,416	2,182	2,661	1,813	1,578	1,625	1,800	2,000	2,050	2,100
Gold	$/toz	35.9	607.9	383.5	279.0	271.0	275.0	275.0	275.0	300.0	300.0
Iron ore, Carajas	c/dmtu	9.84	28.09	32.50	28.79	30.03	29.50	30.00	32.00	33.00	33.00
Lead	c/kg	30.3	90.6	81.1	45.4	47.6	52.5	55.0	60.0	64.0	64.5
Nickel	$/mt	2,846	6,519	8,864	8,638	5,945	6,000	6,300	6,500	6,700	6,800
Silver	c/toz	177.0	2,064	482.0	499.9	438.6	475.0	500.0	520.0	550.0	550.0
Tin	c/kg	367.3	1,677	608.5	543.6	448.4	440.0	475.0	525.0	540.0	550.0
Zinc	c/kg	29.6	76.1	151.4	112.8	88.6	85.0	92.5	100.0	110.0	120.0

$/mt, dollars per metric ton; $/bbl, dollars per barrel; $/mmbtu, dollars per million British thermal units; c/kg, cents per kilogram, $/cum, dollars per cubic meter; $/toz, dollars per troy ounce; c/dmtu, cents per dry metric ton unit.
n.a. Not available.
Note: Projections as of February 27, 2002.
Source: World Bank Economic Policy and Prospects Group.

Table A5.10   Commodity prices and price projections in constant 1990 dollars

Commodity	Unit	Actual					Projections				
		1970	1980	1990	2000	2001	2002	2003	2005	2010	2015
Energy											
Coal, U.S.	$/mt	n.a.	54.71	41.67	33.97	46.77	39.82	36.42	32.04	30.46	29.26
Crude oil, average	$/bbl	4.31	46.80	22.88	29.01	25.39	20.96	21.24	16.96	16.54	17.07
Natural gas, Europe	$/mmbtu	n.a.	4.32	2.55	3.96	4.23	3.04	3.03	2.59	2.39	2.44
Natural gas, US	$/mmbtu	0.61	1.97	1.70	4.43	4.12	2.62	2.78	2.69	2.61	2.64
Non-Energy Commodities											
Agriculture											
Beverages											
Cocoa	c/kg	240.6	330.5	126.7	93.1	111.4	125.7	131.5	131.9	136.6	136.5
Coffee, other milds	c/kg	408.8	440.0	197.2	197.3	143.2	145.5	156.1	197.3	230.6	227.6
Coffee, robusta	c/kg	325.7	411.7	118.2	93.8	63.3	67.0	71.4	83.1	114.9	115.9
Tea, auctions (3) average	c/kg	297.7	210.6	205.8	192.8	166.6	160.3	158.8	160.2	158.4	149.5
Food											
Fats and oils											
Coconut oil	$/mt	1416.0	855.3	336.5	462.7	331.6	392.9	455.2	565.3	561.4	544.5
Copra	$/mt	801.6	574.7	230.7	313.1	210.7	366.7	404.6	424.0	417.8	406.3
Groundnut oil	$/mt	1349.5	1090.1	963.7	733.3	709.2	759.6	783.9	772.6	739.8	711.1
Palm oil	$/mt	927.1	740.9	289.8	318.8	297.8	345.8	364.2	376.9	391.6	386.0
Soybean meal	$/mt	365.7	333.1	200.2	194.4	188.7	191.7	194.2	202.6	195.8	191.0
Soybean oil	$/mt	1020.8	758.6	447.3	347.4	369.1	408.6	409.7	400.5	400.4	410.4
Soybeans	$/mt	416.8	376.0	246.8	217.7	204.2	214.8	222.5	226.1	217.6	211.3
Grains											
Maize	$/mt	208.2	159.0	109.3	91.0	93.5	100.6	106.2	115.0	108.8	105.7
Rice, Thai, 5%	$/mt	450.3	521.4	270.9	208.0	180.2	199.1	212.4	221.4	226.3	215.4
Sorghum	$/mt	184.7	163.6	103.9	90.4	99.3	96.2	101.6	109.9	104.0	100.4
Wheat, US, HRW	$/mt	195.7	219.3	135.5	117.2	132.2	137.3	139.6	146.1	139.3	134.1
Other food											
Bananas	$/mt	592.1	478.9	540.9	435.7	608.1	565.9	529.6	498.6	494.3	479.5
Beef, US	c/kg	465.0	350.3	256.3	198.5	222.0	221.7	216.3	201.5	191.9	186.9
Oranges	$/mt	599.1	508.0	531.1	373.2	635.1	602.5	556.3	471.1	456.9	447.0
Shrimp, Mexican	c/kg	n.a.	1,462	1,069	1,554	1,582	1,415	1,517	1,555	1,480	1,398
Sugar, world	c/kg	29.32	80.17	27.67	18.5	19.9	19.4	19.4	20.7	20.0	19
Agricultural raw materials											
Timber											
Logs, Cameroon	$/cum	153.3	319.5	343.5	283.0	277.4	277.7	278.2	282.7	294.2	312.9
Logs, Malaysia	$/cum	153.8	248.2	177.2	195.2	165.8	162.4	172.0	202.6	226.3	239.7
Sawnwood, Malaysia	$/cum	623.9	502.7	533.0	611.1	501.8	508.2	556.3	588.9	626.6	666.4
Other raw materials											
Cotton	c/kg	241.1	261.7	181.9	133.8	110.3	106.3	116.0	124.6	130.5	130.0
Rubber, RSS1, Malaysia	c/kg	145.2	180.8	86.5	71.0	62.6	60.1	64.7	72.7	76.4	77.3
Tobacco	$/mt	3,836	2,889	3,392	3,058	3,140	3,227	3,186	3,062	2,850	2,682
Fertilizers											
DAP	$/mt	192.5	282.1	171.4	158.5	154.0	162.4	161.9	160.2	152.3	146.3
Phosphate rock	$/mt	39.2	59.3	40.5	45.0	43.5	43.5	42.5	40.5	39.2	37.4
Potassium chloride	$/m.t	114.1	146.9	98.1	125.9	123.1	125.7	122.9	117.8	110.5	105.7
TSP $/mt153.3	228.8	131.8	141.5	132.3		136.2	136.6	136.6	130.6	126.0	
Urea, E. Europe, bulk	$/mt	n.a.	n.a.	119.3	103.9	99.4	104.3	109.9	119.4	114.2	110.4
Metals and minerals											
Aluminum	$/mt	1,982	1,848	1,639	1,592	1,505	1,519	1,568	1,602	1,567	1,503
Copper	$/mt	5,047	2,770	2,661	1,863	1,645	1,703	1,821	1,884	1,784	1,707
Gold	$/toz	128.1	771.6	383.5	286.7	282.5	288.1	278.2	259.1	261.1	243.8
Iron ore	c/dmtu	35.1	35.7	32.5	29.6	31.3	30.9	30.4	30.2	28.7	26.8
Lead	c/kg	108.0	115.0	81.1	46.6	49.6	55.0	55.6	56.5	55.7	52.4
Nickel	$/mt	10,147	8,275	8,864	8,876	6,198	6,287	6,373	6,125	5,831	5,526
Silver	c/toz	631.0	2619.4	482.0	513.7	457.3	497.7	505.8	490.0	478.7	447.0
Tin	c/kg	1309.6	2129.3	608.5	558.5	467.5	461.0	480.5	494.7	470.0	447.0
Zinc	c/kg	105.5	96.6	151.4	115.9	92.3	89.1	93.6	94.2	95.7	97.5

$/mt, dollars per metric ton; $/bbl, dollars per barrel; $/mmbtu, dollars per million British thermal units; c/kg, cents per kilogram, $/cum, dollars per cubic meter; $/toz, dollars per troy ounce; c/dmtu, cents per dry metric ton unit.

n.a. Not available.

Note: Projections as of February 27, 2002.

Source: World Bank Economic Policy and Prospects Group.

Table A5.11 Weighted indexes of commodity prices and inflation

Index	Actual					Projections[a]				
	1970	1980	1990	2000	2001	2002	2003	2005	2010	2015
Current dollars										
Petroleum	5.3	161.2	100.0	123.4	106.4	87.4	91.8	78.7	83.0	91.8
Nonenergy commodities[b]	43.8	125.5	100.0	86.9	79.0	80.0	85.9	96.6	106.1	111.6
Agriculture	45.8	138.1	100.0	87.7	79.8	81.1	87.4	99.7	111.9	118.9
Beverages	56.9	181.4	100.0	88.4	72.1	74.8	81.6	100.7	123.6	130.8
Food	46.7	139.3	100.0	84.5	86.1	88.4	92.5	100.9	106.4	110.4
Fats and oils	64.4	148.7	100.0	96.2	89.0	95.5	102.7	115.5	123.8	129.9
Grains	46.7	134.3	100.0	79.5	78.2	83.0	90.0	102.0	107.7	110.9
Other food	32.2	134.3	100.0	77.7	88.1	85.6	85.6	88.3	91.4	94.1
Raw materials	36.4	104.6	100.0	91.4	77.4	76.5	85.0	97.4	110.2	121.2
Timber	31.8	79.0	100.0	111.0	90.2	90.5	102.2	117.8	136.6	155.5
Other raw materials	39.6	122.0	100.0	78.0	68.6	66.9	73.2	83.5	92.2	97.8
Fertilizers	30.4	128.9	100.0	105.8	98.8	100.0	102.9	108.6	112.8	116.1
Metals and minerals	40.4	94.2	100.0	83.0	75.1	75.4	80.5	87.7	91.3	93.3
Constant 1990 dollars[c]										
Petroleum	18.9	204.6	100.0	126.8	111.0	91.6	92.8	74.1	72.3	74.6
Nonenergy commodities	156.3	159.3	100.0	89.3	82.3	83.9	86.8	91.0	92.3	90.7
Agriculture	163.3	175.3	100.0	90.1	83.2	85.0	88.4	93.9	97.4	96.7
Beverages	202.8	230.3	100.0	90.8	75.1	78.4	82.6	94.9	107.6	106.3
Food	166.5	176.8	100.0	86.8	89.7	92.6	93.6	95.1	92.6	89.7
Fats and oils	229.5	188.7	100.0	98.9	92.8	100.0	103.9	108.8	107.7	105.6
Grains	166.6	170.5	100.0	81.7	81.5	86.9	91.0	96.1	93.8	90.1
Other food	114.9	170.5	100.0	79.9	91.8	89.7	86.6	83.2	79.6	76.5
Raw materials	129.8	132.7	100.0	93.9	80.7	80.1	86.0	91.8	95.9	98.5
Timber	113.3	100.3	100.0	114.0	94.1	94.9	103.4	111.0	118.9	126.3
Other raw materials	141.1	154.9	100.0	80.1	71.5	70.1	74.0	78.7	80.2	79.5
Fertilizers	108.3	163.6	100.0	108.7	103.0	104.8	104.1	102.3	98.2	94.4
Metals and minerals	143.9	119.6	100.0	85.3	78.3	79.0	81.4	82.6	79.5	75.8
Inflation indixes, 1990 = 100[d]										
MUV index[e]	28.05	78.78	100.00	97.32	95.92	95.44	98.86	106.13	114.90	123.05
% change per year		10.88	2.41	-0.27	-1.44	-0.50	3.59	3.61	1.60	1.38
US GDP deflator	33.59	65.93	100.00	123.73	126.45	128.10	130.15	135.80	151.41	168.82
% change per year		6.98	4.25	2.15	2.20	1.30	1.60	2.15	2.20	2.20

a. Commodity price projections as of January 18, 2002.

b. The World Bank primary commodity price indexes are computed based on 1987–89 export values in U.S. dollars for low- and middle-income economies, rebased to 1990. Weights for the subgroup indexes expressed as ratios to the non-energy index are as follows in percent: agriculture 69.1; fertilizers 2.7; metals and minerals 28.2; beverages 16.9; food 29.4; raw materials 22.8; fats and oils 10.1; grains 6.9; other food 12.4; timber 9.3; and other raw materials 13.6.

c. Computed from unrounded data and deflated by the manufacturing unit value (MUV) index.

d. Inflation indexes for 2001–10 are projections as of November 12, 2001. MUV for 2000 is an estimate. Growth rates for years 1980, 1990, 2000, 2005, 2010, and 2015, refer to compound annual rate of change between adjacent endpoint years; all others are annual growth rates from the previous year.

e. Unit value index in U.S. dollar terms of manufactures exported from the G-5 countries (France, Germany, Japan, United Kingdom, and the United States) weighted proportionally to the countries' exports to the developing countries.

Source: World Bank Development Prospects Group. Historical U.S. GDP deflator: U.S. Department of Commerce. January 18, 2002.

Summary tables

Methodology

The World Bank is the sole repository for statistics on the external debt of developing countries on a loan-by-loan basis. The Debtor Reporting System (DRS), set up in 1951 to monitor these statistics, is maintained by the staff of the Financial Data Team (FIN), part of the Development Data Group of Development Economics.

Methodology for aggregating data

Using the DRS data, in combination with information obtained from creditors through the debt data collection systems of other agencies such as the Bank for International Settlements (BIS) and the Organisation for Economic Co-operation and Development (OECD), the staff of the Financial Data Team estimate the total external indebtedness of developing countries. The data are also supplemented by estimates made by country economists of the World Bank and desk officers of the International Monetary Fund (IMF).

Converting to a common currency

Since debt data are normally reported to the World Bank in the currency of repayment, they have to be converted into a common currency (usually U.S. dollars) to produce summary tables. Stock figures (such as the amount of debt outstanding) are converted using end-period exchange rates, as published in the IMF's *International Financial Statistics* (line ae). Flow figures are converted at annual average exchange rates (line rf). Projected debt service is converted using end-period exchange rates. Debt repayable in multiple currencies, goods, or services and debt with a provision for maintenance of value of the currency of repayment are shown at book value. Because flow data are converted at annual average exchange rates and stock data at year-end exchange rates, year-to-year changes in debt outstanding and disbursed are sometimes not equal to net flows (disbursements less principal

repayments); similarly, changes in debt outstanding including undisbursed debt differ from commitments less repayments. Discrepancies are particularly significant when exchange rates have moved sharply during the year; cancellations and reschedulings of other liabilities into long-term public debt also contribute to the differences.

Public and publicly guaranteed debt

All data related to public and publicly guaranteed debt are from debtors except for lending by some multilateral agencies, in which case data are taken from the creditors' records. These creditors include the African Development Bank, the Asian Development Bank, the IMF, the Inter-American Development Bank, and the International Bank for Reconstruction and Development (IBRD) and the International Development Association (IDA). (The IBRD and IDA are components of the World Bank.)

Starting with the 1988–89 edition of *World Debt Tables* (as this book was previously titled), all data pertaining to World Bank loans from 1985 onward are recorded at their current market value. Starting with the 1991–92 edition, all data pertaining to Asian Development Bank loans from 1989 onward are recorded at their current market value. Starting with the 1998 edition, all data pertaining to African Development Bank and African Development Fund loans from 1997 onward are recorded at their current market value as well.

Private nonguaranteed debt

The DRS was expanded in 1970 to incorporate private nonguaranteed long-term debt. Reports, submitted annually, contain aggregate data for disbursed and outstanding debt, disbursements, principal repayments, interest payments, principal and interest rescheduled for the reporting year, and projected payments of principal and interest. Data are usually presented in dollars and currency conversion is not necessary. A few reporting countries choose to provide data on their private nonguaranteed debt in the loan-by-loan format used for reporting public and publicly guaranteed debt. In those cases the currency conversion and projection methodology just described is used.

Although the reporting countries fully recognize the importance of collecting data on private nonguaranteed debt when it constitutes a significant portion of total external debt, detailed data are available only in countries that have registration requirements covering private debt, most commonly in connection with exchange controls. Where formal registration of foreign borrowing is not mandatory, compilers must rely on balance of payments data and financial surveys.

This edition includes data on private nonguaranteed debt, either as reported or as estimated, for 79 countries for which this type of debt is known to be significant.

For private nonguaranteed debt that is not reported, the standard estimation approach starts from a calculation of the stock of debt outstanding, using data available from creditors. Figures on guaranteed export credits, obtained from the OECD's Creditor Reporting System (CRS), are supplemented by loan-by-loan information on official lending to private borrowers and by information on noninsured commercial bank lending to the private sector.

Disbursements and debt service payments for private nonguaranteed debt are more difficult to estimate. Amortization is estimated by making an assumption regarding the proportion of debt repaid each year and then applying these ratios to generate a first approximation of annual principal repayments. Disbursements are then estimated as a residual between net flows (equal to the change in the stock of debt) and estimated amortization. Interest payments are estimated by applying an assumed average interest rate to the stock of debt outstanding.

Data on the balance of payments flows provide useful guidelines in the process of building a time series because private nonguaranteed debt can be treated as a residual between total net long-term borrowing and net long-term borrowing recorded in the DRS for public and publicly guaranteed debt.

Short-term debt

The World Bank regards the individual reporting country as the authoritative source of information on its own external liabilities. But for short-term debt, defined as debt with an original maturity of one year or less, accurate information is not widely available from debtors. By its nature, short-term debt is difficult to monitor; loan-by-loan registration is normally impractical, and most reporting arrangements involve periodic returns to a country's central bank from its banking sector. Since 1982 the quality of such reporting has improved, but only a few developing countries have figures available for short-term debt.

Where information from debtors is not available, data from creditors can indicate the magnitude of a country's short-term debt. The most important source is the BIS's semiannual series showing the maturity distribution of commercial banks' claims on developing countries. Those data are reported residually. However, an estimate of short-term liabilities by original maturity can be calculated by deducting from claims due in one year those that had a maturity of between one and two years 12 months earlier.

There are several problems with this method. Valuation adjustments caused by exchange rate movements will affect the calculations, as will prepayment and refinancing of long-term maturities falling due. Moreover, not all countries' commercial banks report in a way that allows the full maturity distribution to be determined, and the BIS data include liabilities only to banks within the reporting area. Nevertheless, combining these estimates with data on officially guaranteed short-term suppliers' credits compiled by the OECD gives what may be thought of as a lower-bound estimate of a country's short-term debt. Even on this basis, however, the results need to be interpreted with caution. Where short-term debt has been rescheduled, the effect of lags in reporting and differences in the treatment of the rescheduled debt by debtors and creditors may result in double counting if short-term debt derived from creditor sources is added to long-term debt reported by the country to obtain total external liabilities.

Some of the short-term debt estimates published are drawn from debtor and creditor sources, but most are from creditor sources. Only for a few countries can the data be regarded as authoritative, but they offer a guide to the size of a country's short-term (and, hence, its total) external debt. The quality of these data is likely to improve.

Use of IMF credit

Data related to the operations of the IMF come from the IMF Treasurer's Department and are converted from special drawing rights (SDRs) into dollars using end-of-period exchange rates for stocks and average over the period exchange rates for converting flows, as described earlier. IMF trust fund loans and operations under the structural adjustment and enhanced structural adjustment facilities are presented together with all of the Fund's special facilities (the buffer stock, compensatory financing, extended fund, and oil facilities).

Treatment of arrears

The DRS collects information on arrears in both principal and interest. Principal in arrears is included and identified in the amount of long-term debt outstanding. Interest in arrears of long-term debt and the use of IMF credit is included and identified in the amount of short-term debt outstanding. If and when interest in arrears is capitalized under a debt reorganization agreement, the amount of interest capitalized will be added to the amount of long-term debt outstanding and the corresponding deduction made from the amount of short-term debt outstanding.

Treatment of debt restructurings

The DRS attempts to capture accurately the effects of the different kinds of restructurings on both debt stocks and debt flows, consistent with the circumstances under which the restructuring takes place. Whether a flow has taken place is sometimes difficult to determine.

In compiling and presenting the debt data, a distinction is made between cash flows and imputed flows. Based on this criterion, rescheduled service payments and the shift in liabilities from one financial instrument to another as a result of rescheduling are considered to be imputed flows.

The imputed flows are recorded separately in the World Bank External Debt (WBXD) system, but these debt restructuring transactions are not evident in the main body of the debt data—only the resulting effect of these transactions is reflected.

Changes in creditor and debtor status that can result from debt restructuring are also reflected. For example, when insured commercial credits are rescheduled, the creditor classification shifts from private sources to official sources (bilateral). This reflects the assumption of the assets by the official credit insurance agencies of the creditor countries. The debts to the original creditors are reduced by the amounts rescheduled, and a new obligation to the official creditor agencies is created. This shift also applies to private nonguaranteed debt that is reduced by the amounts rescheduled, which in turn are included in the public and publicly guaranteed debt owed to official creditors. On the debtor side, when a government accepts responsibility for the payment of rescheduled debt previously owed by private enterprises, the DRS registers a change in debtor categories in the DRS. Similarly, when short-term debt is included in a restructuring agreement, the rescheduled amount is shifted from short-term to long-term debt.

Methodology for projecting data

An important feature of the WBXD system of the DRS is its ability to project future disbursements of unutilized commitments and future debt service payments.

Undisbursed debt

Projections of disbursements help underpin future capital requirements in the implementation of externally financed projects. In addition, they help determine the interest portion of projected debt service. Future interest payments are based on projected debt outstanding that is itself determined by projected disbursements and repayments. The underlying assumptions of these projections are that loan commitments will be fully utilized and that the debtor country will repay all sums due. Future disbursements and debt service refer only to existing debt and do not reflect any assumptions on future borrowing.

Disbursement projections use two methods:
- *Specific schedules.* Debtor countries are requested to submit a calendar of future disbursements, if available, at the time individual loans are first reported. Country authorities are in a better position to provide estimated disbursement schedules when there is a solid public sector investment program in place.
- *Standard schedules.* In the absence of specific schedules, the WBXD system projects disbursements by applying a set of profiles to the last actual undisbursed balance of individual loans. The profiles are

derived under the assumption that specific sources of funds have some common characteristics that cause them to disburse, in the aggregate, in some observable pattern. Accordingly, some thirty profiles have been derived that roughly correspond to creditor type. Profiles exist for concessional and nonconcessional loans from official creditors. For bilateral lending, profiles have been developed for the Development Assistance Committee, the Organization of Petroleum Exporting Countries (OPEC), and other creditor groupings. For multilateral lending, specific profiles are available for major international organizations. An estimating equation for each profile is derived by applying regression analysis techniques to a body of data that contains actual disbursement information for more than 100,000 loans. Although these standard profiles are reestimated from time to time, under the best scenario they can only approximate the disbursement pattern of any single loan.

Future debt service payments

Most projections of future debt service payments generated by the WBXD system are based on the repayment terms of the loans. Principal repayments (amortization) are based on the amount of loan commitments, and the amortization profile of most loans follows a set pattern. Using the first and final payment dates and the frequency of the payments, the system calculates the stream of principal payments due. If future payments are irregular, the WBXD system requires a schedule.

Projected future interest payments are calculated similarly. Interest is based on the amount of debt disbursed and outstanding at the beginning of the period. Again, using the first and final interest payment dates and the frequency of payments, the system calculates the stream of interest payments due. If interest payments are irregular, the WBXD system requires a schedule.

The published figures for projected debt service obligations are converted into U.S. dollars using the end-December 2000 exchange rates. Likewise the projection routine for variable interest rate debt, such as commercial bank debt based on the London interbank offer rate (LIBOR), assumes that the rate prevailing at the end of December 2000 will be effective throughout.

Sources and definitions

The edition of *Global Development Finance* presents reported or estimated data on the total external debt of all low- and middle-income countries.

Format

The *Country Tables* volume of *Global Development Finance* has been expanded to include summary tables along with the standard country tables for the 136 individual countries that report to the World Bank's Debtor Reporting System (DRS). Summary tables present selected debt and resource flow statistics for the individual reporting countries and external debt data for regional and income groups. Regional and income group totals in the summary tables include estimates for the 12 low- and middle-income countries that do not report to the DRS. Because these estimates are not shown separately in the tables, most group totals are larger than the sum of the DRS figures shown. The format of the regional and income group tables draws on the individual country table format and includes graphic presentations.

For the 136 individual countries that report to the World Bank's DRS, tables are presented in a four-page layout containing 10 sections.

Section 1 summarizes the external debt of the country.

Total external debt stocks (EDT) consist of public and publicly guaranteed long-term debt, private nonguaranteed long-term debt (whether reported or estimated by the staff of the World Bank), the use of IMF credit, and estimated short-term debt. Interest in arrears on long-term debt and the use of IMF credit are added to the short-term debt estimates and are shown as separate lines. Arrears of principal and of interest have been disaggregated to show the arrears owed to official creditors and the arrears owed to private creditors. Export credits and principal in arrears on long-term debt are shown as memorandum items.

Total debt flows are consolidated data on disbursements, principal repayments, and interest payments for total long-term debt and transactions with the IMF.

Net flows on debt are disbursements on long-term debt and IMF purchases minus principal repayments on long-term debt and IMF repurchases up to 1984. Beginning in 1985 this line includes the change in stock of short-term debt (including interest arrears for long-term debt). Thus if the change in stock is positive, a disbursement is assumed to have taken place; if negative, a repayment is assumed to have taken place.

Total debt service (TDS) shows the debt service payments on total long-term debt (public and publicly guaranteed and private nonguaranteed), use of IMF credit, and interest on short-term debt.

Section 2 provides data series for aggregate net resource flows and net transfers (long term).

Net resource flows (long term) are the sum of net resource flows on long-term debt (excluding IMF credit) plus net foreign direct investment, portfolio equity flows, and official grants (excluding technical cooperation). Grants for technical cooperation are shown as a memorandum item. Also shown as memorandum items are official net resource flows and private net resource flows. Official net resource flows are the sum of net flows on long-term debt to official creditors (excluding the IMF) plus official grants (excluding technical cooperation). Private net resource flows are the sum of net flows on debt to private creditors plus net foreign direct investment and portfolio equity flows. Official net transfers and private net transfers are shown as memorandum items as well.

Net transfers (long term) are equal to net long-term resource flows minus interest payments on long-term loans and foreign direct investment profits.

Section 3 provides data series for major economic aggregates. The gross national income (GNI) series uses yearly average exchange rates in converting GNI from local currency into U.S. dollars. The economic aggregates are prepared for the convenience of users; the usual caution should be exercised in using them for economic analysis.

SECTION 4 provides debt indicators: ratios of debt and debt service to some of the economic aggregates.

SECTION 5 provides detailed information on stocks and flows of long-term debt and its various components. Data on bonds issued by private entities without public guarantee, compiled for major borrowers, are included in private nonguaranteed debt. IBRD loans and IDA credits are shown as memorandum items.

SECTION 6 provides information on the currency composition of long-term debt. The six major currencies in which the external debt of low- and middle-income countries is contracted are separately identified, as is debt denominated in special drawing rights and debt repayable in multiple currencies.

SECTION 7 provides information on restructurings of long-term debt starting in 1985. It shows both the stock and flows rescheduled each year. In addition, the amount of debt forgiven (interest forgiven is shown as a memorandum item) and the amount of debt stock reduction (including debt buyback) are also shown separately. (See the Methodology section for a detailed explanation of restructuring data.)

SECTION 8 reconciles the stock and flow data on total external debt for each year, beginning with 1989. This section is designed to illustrate the changes in stock that have taken place due to five factors: the net flow on debt, the net change in interest arrears, the capitalization of interest, the reduction in debt resulting from debt forgiveness or other debt reduction mechanisms, and the cross-currency valuation effects. The residual difference—the change in stock not explained by any of the factors identified above—is also presented. The residual is calculated as the sum of identified accounts minus the change in stock. Where the residual is large it can, in some cases, serve as an illustration of the inconsistencies in the reported data. More often, however, it can be explained by specific borrowing phenomena in individual countries. These are explained in the Country Notes section.

SECTION 9 provides information on the average terms of new commitments on public and publicly guaranteed debt and information on the level of commitments from official and private sources.

SECTION 10 provides anticipated disbursements and contractual obligations on long-term debt contracted up to December 2000.

Sources

The principal sources of information for the tables in these two volumes are reports to the World Bank through the DRS from member countries that have received either IBRD loans or IDA credits. Additional information has been drawn from the files of the World Bank and the IMF.

Reporting countries submit detailed (loan-by-loan) reports through the DRS on the annual status, transactions, and terms of the long-term external debt of public agencies and that of private ones guaranteed by a public agency in the debtor country. This information forms the basis for the tables in these volumes.

Aggregate data on private debt without public guarantee are compiled and published as reliable reported and estimated information becomes available. This edition includes data on private nonguaranteed debt, either as reported or as estimated, for 79 countries.

The short-term debt data are as reported by the debtor countries or are estimates derived from creditor sources. The principal creditor sources are the semiannual series of commercial banks' claims on developing countries, published by the Bank for International Settlements (BIS), and data on officially guaranteed suppliers' credits compiled by the Organisation for Economic Co-operation and Development (OECD). For some countries, estimates were prepared by pooling creditor and debtor information.

Interest in arrears on long-term debt and the use of IMF credit are added to the short-term debt estimates and shown as separate lines in section 1. Arrears of interest and of principal owed to official and to private creditors are identified separately.

Export credits are shown as a memorandum item in section 1. Data prior to 1998 include official export credits, and suppliers' credits and bank credits officially guaranteed or insured by an export credit agency. Both long-term and short-term exports credits are included. For 1998 to 2000 export credits include all export credits extended, guaranteed, insured, or rescheduled by the official sector of OECD countries. The source for this information is the Creditor Reporting System (CRS) of the OECD.

Data on long-term debt reported by member countries are checked against, and supplemented by, data from several other sources. Among these are the statements and reports of several regional development banks and government lending agencies, as well as the reports received by the World Bank under the CRS from the members of the Development Assistance Committee (DAC) of the OECD.

Every effort has been made to ensure the accuracy and completeness of the debt statistics. Nevertheless, quality and coverage vary among debtors and may also vary for the same debtor from year to year. Coverage has been improved through the efforts of the reporting agencies and the work of World Bank missions, which visit member countries to gather data and to provide technical assistance on debt issues.

Definitions

For all regional, income, and individual country tables, data definitions are presented below or footnoted where appropriate. Data definitions for other summary tables are, likewise, consistent with those below.

Summary debt data

TOTAL DEBT STOCKS are defined as the sum of public and publicly guaranteed long-term debt, private nonguaranteed long-term debt, the use of IMF credit, and short-term debt. The relation between total debt stock and its components is illustrated on page xx.

Long-term external debt is defined as debt that has an original or extended maturity of more than one year and that is owed to nonresidents and repayable in foreign currency, goods, or services. Long-term debt has three components:

• *Public debt,* which is an external obligation of a public debtor, including the national government, a political subdivision (or an agency of either), and autonomous public bodies.

• *Publicly guaranteed debt,* which is an external obligation of a private debtor that is guaranteed for repayment by a public entity.

• *Private nonguaranteed external debt,* which is an external obligation of a private debtor that is not guaranteed for repayment by a public entity.

In the tables, public and publicly guaranteed long-term debt are aggregated.

Short-term external debt is defined as debt that has an original maturity of one year or less. Available data permit no distinction between public and private nonguaranteed short-term debt.

Interest in arrears on long-term debt is defined as interest payment due but not paid, on a cumulative basis.

Principal in arrears on long-term debt is defined as principal repayment due but not paid, on a cumulative basis.

The memorandum item *export credits* includes official export credits, suppliers' credits, the official non-ODA lending, and bank credits officially guaranteed or insured by an export credit agency. Both long-term and short-term credits are included here.

Use of IMF credit denotes repurchase obligations to the IMF with respect to all uses of IMF resources (excluding those resulting from drawings in the reserve tranche) shown for the end of the year specified. Use of IMF credit comprises purchases outstanding under the credit tranches, including enlarged access resources and all special facilities (the buffer stock, compensatory financing, extended fund, and oil facilities), trust fund loans, and operations under the structural adjustment and enhanced structural adjustment facilities. Data are from the Treasurer's Department of the IMF.

• *IMF purchases* are total drawings on the general resources account of the IMF during the year specified, excluding drawings in the reserve tranche.

• *IMF repurchases* are total repayments of outstanding drawings from the general resources account during the year specified, excluding repayments due in the reserve tranche.

To maintain comparability between data on transactions with the IMF and data on long-term debt, use of IMF credit outstanding at year end (stock) is converted to dollars at the SDR exchange rate in effect at the end of the year. Purchases and repurchases (flows) are converted at the average SDR exchange rate for the year in which transactions take place.

Net purchases will usually not reconcile changes in the use of IMF credit from year to year. Valuation effects from the use of different exchange rates frequently explain much of the difference, but not all. Other factors are increases in quotas (which expand a country's reserve tranche and can thereby lower the use of IMF credit as defined here), approved purchases of a country's currency by another member country drawing on the general resources account, and various administrative uses of a country's currency by the IMF.

TOTAL DEBT FLOWS include disbursements, principal repayments, net flows and transfers on debt, and interest payments.

Disbursements are drawings on loan commitments during the year specified.

Principal repayments are the amounts of principal (amortization) paid in foreign currency, goods, or services in the year specified.

Net flows on debts (or net lending or net disbursements) are disbursements minus principal repayments.

Interest payments are the amounts of interest paid in foreign currency, goods, or services in the year specified.

Net transfers on debt are net flows minus interest payments (or disbursements minus total debt service payments).

The concepts of net flows on debt, net transfers on debt, and aggregate net flows and net transfers are illustrated on pages xxi and xxii.

Total debt service paid (TDS) is debt service payments on total long-term debt (public and publicly guaranteed and private nonguaranteed), use of IMF credit, and interest on short-term debt.

Aggregate net resource flows and transfers

NET RESOURCE FLOWS (LONG TERM) are the sum of net resource flows on long-term debt (excluding IMF) plus non–debt-creating flows.

NON–DEBT-CREATING FLOWS are net foreign direct investment, portfolio equity flows, and official grants (excluding technical cooperation). Net foreign direct investment and portfolio equity flows are treated as private source flows. Grants for technical cooperation are shown as a memorandum item.

Foreign direct investment (FDI) is defined as investment that is made to acquire a lasting management interest (usually 10 percent of voting stock) in an enterprise operating in a country other than that of the investor (defined according to residency), the investor's purpose being an effective voice in the management of the enterprise. It is the sum of equity capital, reinvestment of earnings, other long-term capital, and short-term capital as shown in the balance of payments.

Portfolio equity flows are the sum of country funds, depository receipts (American or global), and direct purchases of shares by foreign investors.

Grants are defined as legally binding commitments that obligate a specific value of funds available for disbursement for which there is no repayment requirement.

The memorandum item *technical cooperation grants* includes free-standing technical cooperation grants, which are intended to finance the transfer of technical and managerial skills or of technology for the purpose of building up general national capacity without reference to any specific investment projects; and investment-related technical cooperation grants, which are provided to strengthen the capacity to execute specific investment projects.

Profit remittances on foreign direct investment are the sum of reinvested earnings on direct investment and other direct investment income and are part of net transfers.

Major economic aggregates

Five economic aggregates are provided for the reporting economies.

Gross national income, or GNI (Gross national product, or GNP, in previous editions) is the sum of value added by all resident producers plus any product taxes (less subsidies) not included in the valuation of output plus net receipts of primary income (compensation of employees and property income) from abroad. The national accounts data for most developing countries are collected from national statistical organizations and central banks by visiting and resident World Bank missions. Data on GNI are from the Macroeconomic Data Team of the Development Economics Development Data Group of the World Bank.

Exports of goods and services (XGS) are the total value of goods and services exported as well as income and worker remittances received.

Imports of goods and services (MGS) are the total value of goods and services imported and income paid.

International reserves (RES) are the sum of a country's monetary authority's holdings of special drawing rights (SDRs), its reserve position in the IMF, its holdings of foreign exchange, and its holdings of gold (valued at year-end London prices).

Current account balance is the sum of the credits less the debits arising from international transactions in goods, services, income, and current transfers. It represents the transactions that add to or subtract from an economy's stock of foreign financial items.

Data on exports and imports (on a balance of payments basis), international reserves, and current account balances are drawn mainly from the files of the IMF, supplemented by World Bank staff estimates. Balance of payments data are presented according to the fifth edition of the IMF's *Balance of Payments Manual*, which made several adjustments to its presentation of trade statistics. Coverage of goods was expanded to include in imports the value of goods received for processing and repair (on a gross basis). Their subsequent re-export is recorded in exports (also on a gross basis). This approach will cause a country's imports and exports to increase without affecting the balance of goods. In addition, all capital transfers, which were included with current transfers in the fourth edition of the *Balance of Payments Manual*, are now shown in a separate capital (as opposed to financial) account, and so do not contribute to the current account balance.

Debt indicators

The macroeconomic aggregates and debt data provided in the tables are used to generate ratios that analysts use to assess the external situations of developing countries. Different analysts give different weights to these indicators, but no single indicator or set of indicators can substitute for a thorough analysis of the overall situation of an economy. The advantage of the indicators in *Global Development Finance* is that they are calculated from standardized data series that are compiled on a consistent basis by the World Bank and the IMF. The ratios offer various measures of the cost of, or capacity for, servicing debt in terms of the foreign exchange or output forgone. The following ratios are provided based on total external debt:

EDT/XGS is total external debt to exports of goods and services (including workers' remittances).

EDT/GNI is total external debt to gross national income.

TDS/XGS, also called the debt service ratio, is total debt service to exports of goods and services (including workers' remittances).

INT/XGS, also called the interest service ratio, is total interest payments to exports of goods and services (including workers' remittances).

INT/GNI is total interest payments to gross national income.

RES/EDT is international reserves to total external debt.

RES/MGS is international reserves to imports of goods and services.

Short-term/EDT is short-term debt to total external debt.

Concessional/EDT is concessional debt to total external debt.

Multilateral/EDT is multilateral debt to total external debt.

Long-term debt

Data on long-term debt include eight main elements:

DEBT OUTSTANDING AND DISBURSED is the total outstanding debt at year end.

DISBURSEMENTS are drawings on loan commitments by the borrower during the year.

PRINCIPAL REPAYMENTS are amounts paid by the borrower during the year.

NET FLOWS received by the borrower during the year are disbursements minus principal repayments.

INTEREST PAYMENTS are amounts paid by the borrower during the year.

NET TRANSFERS are net flows minus interest payments during the year; negative transfers show net transfers made by the borrower to the creditor during the year.

DEBT SERVICE (LTDS) is the sum of principal repayments and interest payments actually made.

UNDISBURSED DEBT is total debt undrawn at year end; data for private nonguaranteed debt are not available.

Data from individual reporters are aggregated by type of creditor. *Official creditors* includes multilateral and bilateral debt.

• *Loans from multilateral organizations* are loans and credits from the World Bank, regional development banks, and other multilateral and intergovernmental agencies. Excluded are loans from funds administered by an international organization on behalf of a single donor government; these are classified as loans from governments.

• *Bilateral loans* are loans from governments and their agencies (including central banks), loans from autonomous bodies, and direct loans from official export credit agencies.

Private creditors include bonds, commercial banks, and other private creditors. Commercial banks and other private creditors comprise bank and trade-related lending.

• *Bonds* include publicly issued or privately placed bonds.

- *Commercial banks* are loans from private banks and other private financial institutions.
- *Other private* includes credits from manufacturers, exporters, and other suppliers of goods, and bank credits covered by a guarantee of an export credit agency.

Four characteristics of a country's debt are given as memorandum items for long-term debt outstanding and disbursed (LDOD).

Concessional LDOD conveys information about the borrower's receipt of aid from official lenders at concessional terms as defined by the DAC, that is, loans with an original grant element of 25 percent or more. Loans from major regional development banks—African Development Bank, Asian Development ment Bank, and the Inter-American Development Bank—and from the World Bank are classified as concessional according to each institution's classification and not according to the DAC definition, as was the practice in earlier reports.

Variable interest rate LDOD is long-term debt with interest rates that float with movements in a key market rate such as the London interbank offer rate (LIBOR) or the U.S. prime rate. This item conveys information about the borrower's exposure to changes in international interest rates.

Public sector LDOD and private sector LDOD convey information about the distribution of long-term debt for DRS countries by type of debtor (central government, state and local government, central bank; private bank, private debt).

Currency composition of long-term debt

The six major currencies in which the external debt of low- and middle-income countries is contracted are separately identified, as is debt denominated in special drawing rights and debt repayable in multiple currencies.

Debt restructurings

Debt restructurings include restructurings in the context of the Paris Club, commercial banks, debt-equity swaps, buybacks, and bond exchanges. Debt restructuring data capture the noncash or inferred flows associated with rescheduling and restructuring. These are presented to complement the cash-basis transactions recorded in the main body of the data.

Debt stock rescheduled is the amount of debt outstanding rescheduled in any given year.

Principal rescheduled is the amount of principal due or in arrears that was rescheduled in any given year.

Interest rescheduled is the amount of interest due or in arrears that was rescheduled in any given year.

Debt forgiven is the amount of principal due or in arrears that was written off or forgiven in any given year.

Interest forgiven is the amount of interest due or in arrears that was written off or forgiven in any given year.

Debt stock reduction is the amount that has been netted out of the stock of debt using debt conversion schemes such as buybacks and equity swaps or the discounted value of long-term bonds that were issued in exchange for outstanding debt.

Debt stock-flow reconciliation

Stock and flow data on total external debt are reconciled for each year, beginning with 1989. The data show the changes in stock that have taken place due to the net flow on debt, the net change in interest arrears, the capitalization of interest, the reduction in debt resulting from debt forgiveness or other debt reduction mechanisms, and the cross-currency valuation effects. The residual difference—the change in stock not explained by any of these factors—is also presented, calculated as the sum of identified accounts minus the change in stock.

Average terms of new commitments

The average terms of borrowing on public and publicly guaranteed debt are given for all new loans contracted during the year and separately for loans from official and private creditors. To obtain averages, the interest rates, maturities, and grace periods in each category have been weighted by the amounts of the loans. The grant equivalent of a loan is its commitment (present) value, less the discounted present value of its contractual debt service; conventionally, future service payments are discounted at 10 percent. The grant element of a loan is the grant equivalent expressed as a percentage of the amount committed. It is used as a measure of the overall cost of borrowing. Loans with an original grant element of 25 percent or more are defined as concessional. The average grant element has been weighted by the amounts of the loans.

Commitments cover the total amount of loans for which contracts were signed in the year specified; data for private nonguaranteed debt are not available.

Projections on existing pipeline

Projected *debt service* payments are estimates of payments due on existing debt outstanding, including undisbursed. They do not include service payments that may become due as a result of new loans contracted in subsequent years. Nor do they allow for effects on service payments of changes in repayment patterns owing to prepayment of loans or to rescheduling or refinancing, including repayment of outstanding arrears, that occurred after the last year of reported data.

Projected *disbursements* are estimates of drawings of unutilized balances. The projections do not take into account future borrowing by the debtor country. (See the Methodology section for a detailed explanation of how undisbursed balances are projected.)

Exchange rates

Data received by the World Bank from its members are expressed in the currencies in which the debts are repayable or in which the transactions took place. For aggregation, the Bank converts these amounts to U.S. dollars using the IMF par values or central rates, or the current market rates where appropriate. Service payments, commitments, and disbursements (flows) are converted to U.S. dollars at the average rate for the year. Debt outstanding and disbursed at the end of a given year (a stock) is converted at the rate in effect at the end of that year. Projected debt service, however, is converted to U.S. dollars at rates in effect at end-December 2000. Debt repayable in multiple currencies, goods, or services and debt with a provision for maintenance of value of the currency of repayment are shown at book value.

Adjustments

Year-to-year changes in debt outstanding and disbursed are sometimes not equal to net flows; similarly, changes in debt outstanding, including undisbursed, differ from commitments less repayments. The reasons for these differences are cancellations, adjustments caused by the use of different exchange rates, and the rescheduling of other liabilities into long-term public debt.

Symbols

The following symbols have been used throughout:
- 0.0 indicates that a datum exists, but is negligible, or is a true zero.
- .. indicates that a datum is not available.
- Dollars are current U.S. dollars unless otherwise specified.

Country groups

Regional groups

East Asia and the Pacific

Cambodia (P)
China (E)
Fiji (A)
Indonesia (P)
Korea, Rep. (A)
Lao PDR (P)
Malaysia (E)
Mongolia (E)
Myanmar (E)
Papua New Guinea (A)
Philippines (A)
Samoa (A)
Solomon Islands (A)
Thailand (P)
Tonga (E)
Vanuatu (E)
Vietnam (P)
Kiribati
Korea, Dem. Rep.

Europe and Central Asia

Albania (A)
Armenia (A)
Azerbaijan (A)
Belarus (A)
Bosnia and Herzegovina[a] (P)
Bulgaria (A)
Croatia (A)
Czech Republic (P)
Estonia (E)
Georgia (A)
Hungary (A)
Kazakhstan (A)
Kyrgyz Republic (A)
Latvia (A)
Lithuania (A)
Macedonia, FYR (A)
Moldova (A)
Poland (A)

Romania (A)
Russian Federation[b] (E)
Slovak Republic (A)
Tajikistan (A)
Turkey (A)
Turkmenistan (E)
Ukraine (A)
Uzbekistan (A)
Yugoslavia, Fed. Rep.[a] (E)
Gibraltar

Latin America and the Caribbean

Argentina (A)
Belize (A)
Bolivia (A)
Brazil (P)
Chile (A)
Colombia (A)
Costa Rica (A)
Dominica (A)
Dominican Republic (A)
Ecuador (E)
El Salvador (A)
Grenada (A)
Guatemala (A)
Guyana (A)
Haiti (P)
Honduras (A)
Jamaica (A)
Mexico (A)
Nicaragua (A)
Panama (A)
Paraguay (A)
Peru (A)
St. Kitts and Nevis (A)
St. Lucia (A)
St. Vincent and the Grenadines (A)
Trinidad and Tobago (E)
Uruguay (A)
Venezuela, R.B. de (P)
Antigua and Barbuda

Cuba
Suriname

Middle East and North Africa

Algeria (A)
Djibouti (P)
Egypt, Arab Rep. (A)
Iran, Islamic Rep. (E)
Jordan (P)
Lebanon (P)
Morocco (A)
Oman (A)
Syrian Arab Republic (E)
Tunisia (A)
Yemen, Rep. (P)
Bahrain
Iraq
Libya
Saudi Arabia

South Asia

Bangladesh (A)
Bhutan (A)
India (P)
Maldives (A)
Nepal (A)
Pakistan (P)
Sri Lanka (A)
Afghanistan

Sub-Saharan Africa

Angola (P)
Benin (A)
Botswana (A)
Burkina Faso (A)
Burundi (E)
Cameroon (P)
Cape Verde (A)
Central African Republic (E)

Chad (P)
Comoros (P)
Congo, Dem. Rep. (A)
Congo, Rep. (E)
Côte d'Ivoire (E)
Equatorial Guinea (E)
Eritrea (A)
Ethiopia (P)
Gabon (A)
Gambia, The (A)
Ghana (E)
Guinea (E)
Guinea-Bissau (E)
Kenya (A)
Lesotho (P)
Liberia (E)
Madagascar (P)
Malawi (E)
Mali (P)
Mauritania (A)
Mauritius (A)
Mozambique (P)
Niger (P)
Nigeria (E)
Rwanda (E)
São Tomé and Principe (P)
Senegal (P)
Seychelles (E)
Sierra Leone (A)
Somalia (E)
South Africa (E)
Sudan (E)
Swaziland (E)
Tanzania (P)
Togo (P)
Uganda (P)
Zambia (P)
Zimbabwe (P)
Namibia

Note: Countries printed in normal type are reporters to the Debtor Reporting System (DRS); those printed in italics do not report to the DRS but are included in aggregate tables. Letters in parenthesis indicate DRS reporters' status: (A) as reported, (P) preliminary, and (E) estimated. The status "as reported" indicates that the country was fully current in its reporting under the DRS and that World Bank staff are satisfied that the reported data give an adequate and fair representation of the country's total public debt. "Preliminary" data are based on reported or collected information but, because of incompleteness or other reasons, include an element of staff estimation. "Estimated" data indicate that countries are not current in their reporting and that a significant element of staff estimation has been necessary in producing the data tables.
a. For Bosnia and Herzegovina total debt before 1999, excluding IBRD and IMF obligations and short-term debt, is included under Yugoslavia, Fed. Rep.
b. Includes the debt of the former Soviet Union on the assumption that 100 percent of all outstanding external debt as of December 1991 has become a liability of the Russian Federation.

Income groups

Low-income countries

Angola
Armenia
Azerbaijan
Bangladesh
Benin
Bhutan
Burkina Faso
Burundi
Cambodia
Cameroon
Central African Republic
Chad
Comoros
Congo, Dem. Rep.
Congo, Rep.
Côte d'Ivoire
Eritrea
Ethiopia
Gambia, The
Georgia
Ghana
Guinea
Guinea-Bissau
Haiti
India
Indonesia
Kenya
Kyrgyz Republic
Lao PDR
Lesotho
Liberia
Madagascar
Malawi
Mali
Mauritania
Moldova
Mongolia
Mozambique
Myanmar
Nepal
Nicaragua
Niger
Nigeria
Pakistan

Rwanda
São Tomé and Principe
Senegal
Sierra Leone
Solomon Islands
Somalia
Sudan
Tajikistan
Tanzania
Togo
Uganda
Ukraine
Uzbekistan
Vietnam
Yemen, Rep.
Zambia
Zimbabwe
Afghanistan
Korea, Dem. Rep.

Middle-income countries

Albania
Algeria
Argentina
Belarus
Belize
Bolivia
Bosnia and Herzegovina
Botswana
Brazil
Bulgaria
Cape Verde
Chile
China
Colombia
Costa Rica
Croatia
Czech Republic
Djibouti
Dominica
Dominican Republic
Ecuador
Egypt, Arab Rep.
El Salvador
Equatorial Guinea
Estonia
Fiji
Gabon
Grenada
Guatemala
Guyana
Honduras
Hungary
Iran, Islamic Rep.
Jamaica
Jordan
Kazakhstan
Korea, Rep.
Latvia
Lebanon
Lithuania
Macedonia, FYR
Malaysia
Maldives
Mauritius

Mexico
Morocco
Oman
Panama
Papua New Guinea
Paraguay
Peru
Philippines
Poland
Romania
Russian Federation
Samoa
Seychelles
Slovak Republic
South Africa
Sri Lanka
St. Kitts and Nevis
St. Lucia
St. Vincent and the Grenadines
Swaziland
Syrian Arab Republic
Thailand
Tonga
Trinidad and Tobago
Tunisia
Turkey
Turkmenistan
Uruguay
Vanuatu
Venezuela, R.B. de
Yugoslavia, Fed. Rep.
Antigua and Barbuda
Bahrain
Cuba
Gibraltar
Iraq
Kiribati
Libya
Namibia
Saudi Arabia
Suriname

Note: Countries printed in normal type are reporters to the Debtor Reporting System (DRS); those printed in italics do not report to the DRS but are included in aggregate tables. Low-income countries are those in which 2000 GNI per capita (calculated using the *World Bank Atlas* method) was no more than $755; middle-income countries are those in which GNI per capita was between $756 and $9,265.

ALL DEVELOPING COUNTRIES

(US$ billion)

	1970	1980	1990	2000	2001
SUMMARY DEBT DATA					
TOTAL DEBT STOCKS (EDT)	**72.8**	**609.4**	**1,458.4**	**2,492.0**	**2,442.1**
Long-term debt (LDOD)	**62.6**	**451.6**	**1,179.3**	**2,047.7**	**1,998.7**
Public and publicly guaranteed	47.3	381.1	1,113.8	1,490.4	1,467.6
Private nonguaranteed	15.4	70.6	65.5	557.3	531.1
Use of IMF credit	**0.8**	**12.2**	**34.7**	**64.3**	**74.8**
Short-term debt	**9.4**	**145.6**	**244.4**	**380.0**	**368.6**
of which interest arrears on LDOD	0.0	2.5	52.7	33.3	30.8
Memo:					
IBRD	4.4	22.2	95.5	120.2	120.1
IDA	1.8	11.9	45.1	88.9	88.8
TOTAL FLOWS ON DEBT					
Disbursements	**13.4**	**113.8**	**136.6**	**274.8**	**253.0**
Long-term debt	13.1	107.8	128.4	264.7	222.6
Public and publicly guaranteed	9.0	86.4	109.6	143.6	143.5
Private nonguaranteed	4.2	21.5	18.9	121.1	79.1
IMF purchases	**0.3**	**6.0**	**8.2**	**10.1**	**30.5**
Memo:					
IBRD	0.7	4.5	13.6	13.4	12.2
IDA	0.2	1.6	4.3	5.2	5.9
Principal repayments	**6.8**	**44.5**	**93.5**	**272.1**	**259.7**
Long-term debt	6.1	42.5	85.3	251.1	242.1
Public and publicly guaranteed	3.6	30.8	75.9	141.1	143.4
Private nonguaranteed	2.5	11.8	9.4	109.9	98.6
IMF repurchases	**0.7**	**2.0**	**8.2**	**21.1**	**17.7**
Memo:					
IBRD	0.2	1.1	8.5	10.1	10.0
IDA	0.0	0.0	0.3	1.0	1.2
Net flows on debt	**6.7**	**102.4**	**59.7**	**-0.8**	**-15.7**
of which short-term debt	0.1	33.1	16.5	-3.5	-9.0
Interest payments (INT)	**2.4**	**48.9**	**70.3**	**126.7**	**122.2**
Long-term debt	2.4	32.8	54.5	104.1	101.9
Net transfers on debt	**4.3**	**53.6**	**-10.7**	**-127.5**	**-137.9**
Total debt service (TDS)	**9.2**	**93.4**	**163.8**	**398.9**	**381.9**
AGGREGATE NET RESOURCE FLOWS AND NET TRANSFERS (LONG-TERM)					
NET RESOURCE FLOWS	**11.2**	**82.8**	**99.1**	**261.1**	**196.5**
Net flow of long-term debt (ex. IMF)	7.0	65.3	43.1	13.6	-19.5
Foreign direct investment (net)	2.2	4.4	24.1	166.7	168.2
Portfolio equity flows	0.0	0.0	3.7	50.9	18.5
Grants (excluding technical coop.)	1.9	13.1	28.2	29.9	29.2
NET TRANSFERS	**3.5**	**27.3**	**27.0**	**111.5**	**39.3**
Interest on long-term debt	2.4	32.8	54.5	104.1	101.9
Profit remittances on FDI	5.3	22.7	17.6	45.4	55.3
MAJOR ECONOMIC INDICATORS					
Gross national income (GNI)	669.0	2,901.2	4,273.9	6,376.1	6,388.8
Exports of goods & services (XGS)	..	692.5	906.1	2,198.8	2,175.7
of which workers' remittances	..	14.0	25.4	52.4	53.4
Imports of goods & services (MGS)	..	680.4	935.7	2,158.8	2,165.9
International reserves (RES)	..	212.1	223.2	830.7	1,137.9
Current account balance	..	-7.8	-25.0	48.9	1.5
DEBT INDICATORS					
EDT / XGS (%)	..	88.0	161.0	113.3	112.2
EDT / GNI (%)	10.9	21.0	34.1	39.1	38.2
TDS / XGS (%)	..	13.5	18.1	18.1	17.6
INT / XGS (%)	..	7.1	7.8	5.8	5.6
INT / GNI (%)	0.4	1.7	1.7	2.0	1.9
RES / MGS (months)	..	3.7	2.9	4.6	6.3
Short-term / EDT (%)	12.9	23.9	16.8	15.3	15.1
Concessional / EDT (%)	34.0	18.2	21.5	15.4	15.4
Multilateral / EDT (%)	10.1	8.0	14.2	13.9	14.2

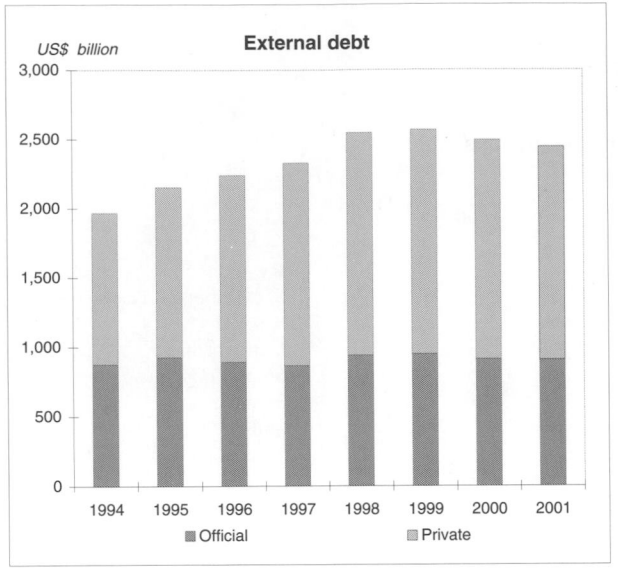

External debt

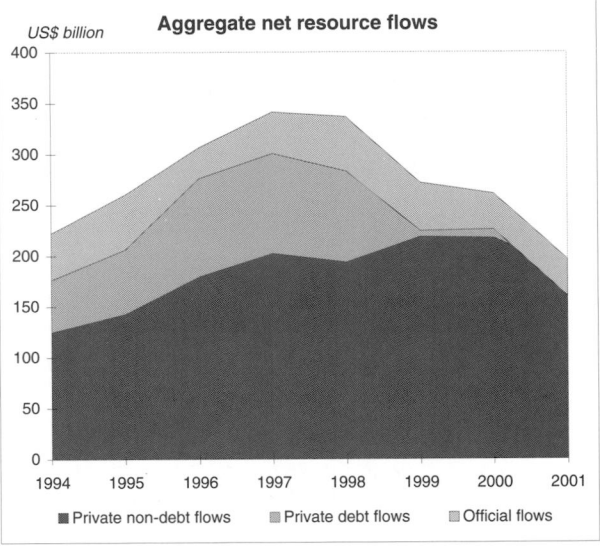

Aggregate net resource flows

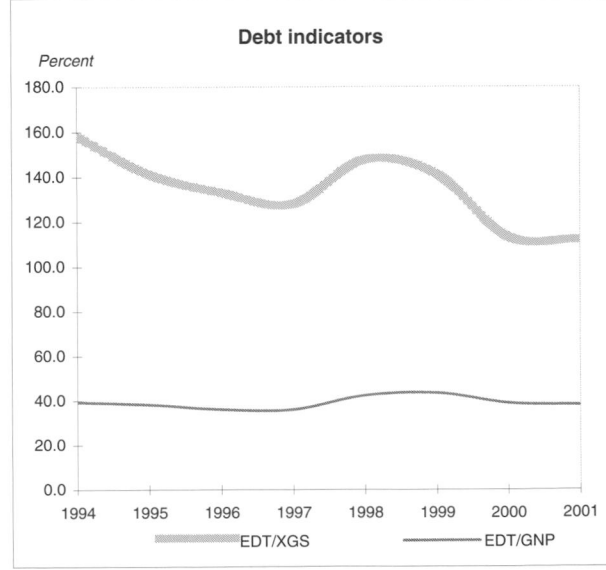

Debt indicators

ALL DEVELOPING COUNTRIES

(US$ billion)

	1970	1980	1990	2000	2001
LONG-TERM DEBT					
DEBT OUTSTANDING (LDOD)	**62.6**	**451.6**	**1,179.3**	**2,047.7**	**1,998.7**
Public and publicly guaranteed	**47.3**	**381.1**	**1,113.8**	**1,490.4**	**1,467.6**
Official creditors	33.6	178.2	604.2	843.8	827.8
Multilateral	7.3	48.8	207.4	346.6	346.8
Bilateral	26.3	129.4	396.8	497.3	481.0
Private creditors	13.6	202.8	509.6	646.6	639.8
Bonds	1.8	13.1	107.3	392.4	408.8
Private nonguaranteed	**15.4**	**70.6**	**65.5**	**557.3**	**531.1**
Bonds	0.0	0.0	0.8	124.5	123.5
DISBURSEMENTS	**13.1**	**107.8**	**128.4**	**264.7**	**222.6**
Public and publicly guaranteed	**9.0**	**86.4**	**109.6**	**143.6**	**143.5**
Official creditors	5.0	29.1	52.9	54.2	53.3
Multilateral	1.2	9.3	27.5	33.6	30.8
Bilateral	3.8	19.8	25.4	20.5	22.6
Private creditors	4.0	57.2	56.6	89.4	90.2
Bonds	0.1	1.7	6.1	55.4	54.0
Private nonguaranteed	**4.2**	**21.5**	**18.9**	**121.1**	**79.1**
Bonds	0.0	0.0	0.7	19.4	13.7
PRINCIPAL REPAYMENTS	**6.1**	**42.5**	**85.3**	**251.1**	**242.1**
Public and publicly guaranteed	**3.6**	**30.8**	**75.9**	**141.1**	**143.4**
Official creditors	1.6	7.3	25.5	48.8	46.0
Multilateral	0.4	1.7	12.5	23.1	19.2
Bilateral	1.2	5.6	13.0	25.7	26.8
Private creditors	2.1	23.5	50.4	92.3	97.4
Bonds	0.1	0.5	5.6	40.8	43.5
Private nonguaranteed	**2.5**	**11.8**	**9.4**	**109.9**	**98.6**
Bonds	0.0	0.0	0.0	17.2	14.7
NET FLOWS ON DEBT	**7.0**	**65.3**	**43.1**	**13.6**	**-19.5**
Public and publicly guaranteed	**5.3**	**55.6**	**33.6**	**2.5**	**0.1**
Official creditors	3.4	21.9	27.4	5.3	7.3
Multilateral	0.8	7.7	15.0	10.5	11.6
Bilateral	2.6	14.2	12.4	-5.2	-4.3
Private creditors	1.9	33.7	6.2	-2.9	-7.2
Bonds	0.0	1.2	0.5	14.6	10.5
Private nonguaranteed	**1.7**	**9.7**	**9.5**	**11.2**	**-19.6**
Bonds	0.0	0.0	0.7	2.2	-1.0
CURRENCY COMPOSITION OF LONG-TERM DEBT (PERCENT)					
Deutsche mark	8.5	6.6	8.6	5.3	..
French franc	5.2	5.5	5.7	2.7	..
Japanese yen	2.3	6.9	10.5	11.3	..
Pound sterling	10.9	3.4	2.2	0.9	..
U.S. dollars	47.4	49.7	41.2	60.0	..
Multiple currency	11.5	10.9	14.7	7.1	..
All other currencies	13.2	8.5	9.8	6.8	..
DEBT STOCK-FLOW RECONCILIATION					
Total change in debt stocks	..	..	103.4	-73.8	..
Net flows on debt	6.7	102.4	59.7	-0.8	-15.7
Net change in interest arrears	..	..	15.5	-6.9	..
Interest capitalized	..	..	5.8	14.0	..
Debt forgiveness or reduction	..	..	-34.4	-25.3	..
Cross-currency valuation	..	..	47.4	-50.9	..
Residual	..	..	9.4	-3.9	..
AVERAGE TERMS OF NEW COMMITMENTS					
ALL CREDITORS					
Interest (%)	5.0	9.2	7.0	7.4	..
Maturity (years)	21.0	16.3	17.7	13.6	..
Grant element (%)	32.1	7.7	19.4	13.3	..
Official creditors					
Interest (%)	3.6	5.5	5.5	5.2	..
Maturity (years)	28.3	25.1	23.6	21.7	..
Grant element (%)	45.2	29.5	31.3	33.8	..
Private creditors					
Interest (%)	7.2	12.0	8.5	8.3	..
Maturity (years)	9.8	9.8	11.5	10.2	..
Grant element (%)	12.0	-8.5	6.9	4.8	..
Memo:					
Commitments	12.1	98.6	123.5	124.9	..
Official creditors	7.3	41.8	63.2	36.6	..
Private creditors	4.8	56.7	60.3	88.3	..

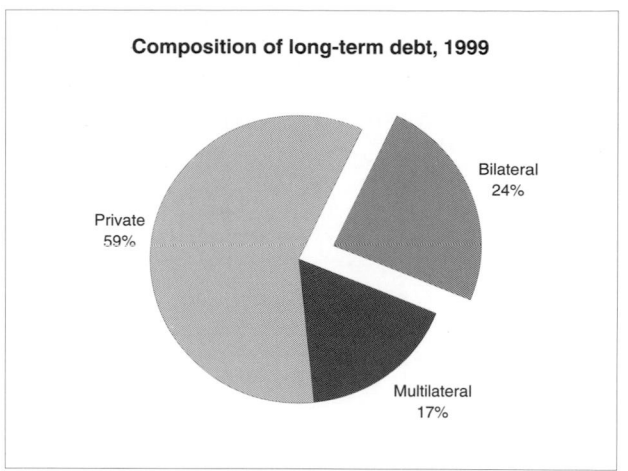

Composition of long-term debt, 1999

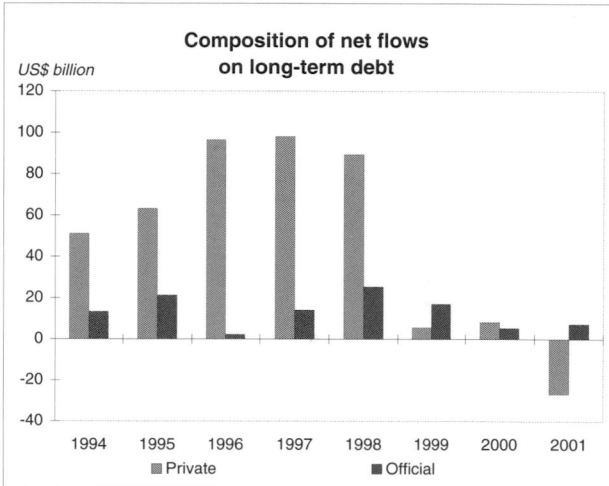

Composition of net flows on long-term debt

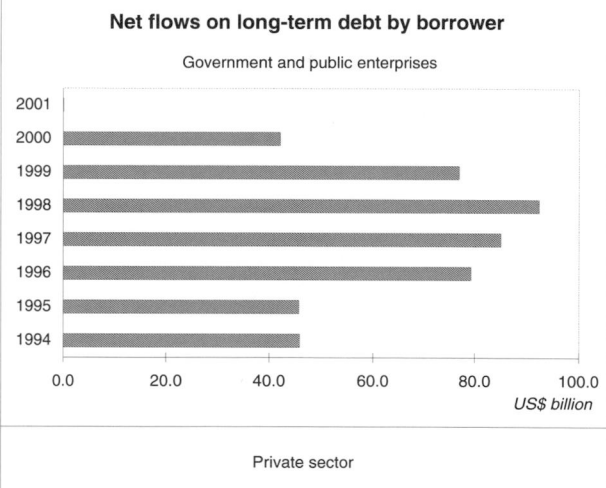

Net flows on long-term debt by borrower

Government and public enterprises

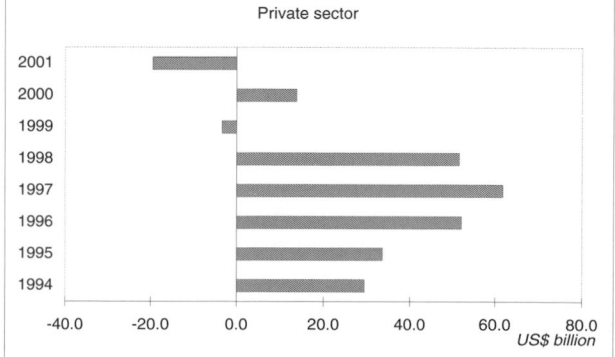

Private sector

EAST ASIA AND PACIFIC

(US$ billion)

	1970	*1980*	*1990*	*2000*	*2001*
SUMMARY DEBT DATA					
TOTAL DEBT STOCKS (EDT)	**11.2**	**94.1**	**274.0**	**633.0**	**604.3**
Long-term debt (LDOD)	**9.1**	**66.7**	**222.7**	**502.2**	**483.7**
Public and publicly guaranteed	6.9	55.6	195.7	333.9	326.8
Private nonguaranteed	2.2	11.1	27.0	168.4	156.9
Use of IMF credit	**0.2**	**2.2**	**2.1**	**22.3**	**13.4**
Short-term debt	**1.9**	**25.2**	**49.2**	**108.4**	**107.3**
of which interest arrears on LDOD	0.0	0.0	1.9	5.2	5.2
Memo:					
IBRD	0.4	5.0	23.4	38.5	38.1
IDA	0.0	1.0	5.2	12.7	12.8
TOTAL FLOWS ON DEBT					
Disbursements	**2.1**	**17.4**	**35.5**	**50.0**	**44.1**
Long-term debt	2.0	16.3	35.4	48.5	43.5
Public and publicly guaranteed	1.2	12.8	24.0	30.8	32.4
Private nonguaranteed	0.8	3.5	11.4	17.7	11.1
IMF purchases	**0.1**	**1.1**	**0.1**	**1.5**	**0.6**
Memo:					
IBRD	0.1	1.0	2.7	3.3	2.7
IDA	0.0	0.1	0.6	0.7	0.7
Principal repayments	**0.8**	**5.9**	**24.5**	**61.2**	**64.2**
Long-term debt	0.8	5.6	23.2	60.9	55.5
Public and publicly guaranteed	0.4	3.7	18.6	38.1	32.9
Private nonguaranteed	0.4	1.9	4.7	22.8	22.6
IMF repurchases	**0.0**	**0.2**	**1.3**	**0.3**	**8.7**
Memo:					
IBRD	0.0	0.2	2.0	2.2	2.5
IDA	0.0	0.0	0.0	0.1	0.1
Net flows on debt	**1.2**	**18.3**	**20.0**	**-14.1**	**-21.3**
of which short-term debt	0.0	6.8	9.0	-2.9	-1.2
Interest payments (INT)	**0.2**	**7.7**	**15.2**	**31.6**	**29.6**
Long-term debt	0.2	4.6	11.9	25.2	24.0
Net transfers on debt	**1.0**	**10.6**	**4.8**	**-45.6**	**-50.9**
Total debt service (TDS)	**1.1**	**13.5**	**39.8**	**92.7**	**93.8**

AGGREGATE NET RESOURCE FLOWS AND NET TRANSFERS (LONG-TERM)					
NET RESOURCE FLOWS	**2.1**	**13.1**	**27.7**	**74.6**	**52.2**
Net flow of long-term debt (ex. IMF)	1.2	10.6	12.2	-12.4	-12.0
Foreign direct investment (net)	0.3	1.3	11.1	52.1	48.5
Portfolio equity flows	0.0	0.0	2.3	32.3	13.4
Grants (excluding technical coop.)	0.7	1.2	2.1	2.5	2.3
NET TRANSFERS	**1.6**	**3.5**	**10.7**	**34.3**	**11.0**
Interest on long-term debt	0.2	4.6	11.9	25.2	24.0
Profit remittances on FDI	0.4	5.0	5.1	15.1	17.3

MAJOR ECONOMIC INDICATORS					
Gross national income (GNI)	133.5	445.4	920.9	2,025.5	2,053.9
Exports of goods & services (XGS)	..	..	252.8	854.9	814.8
of which workers' remittances	..	0.3	1.1	2.0	2.0
Imports of goods & services (MGS)	..	..	261.3	800.3	783.0
International reserves (RES)	..	..	86.3	380.4	433.7
Current account balance	..	-10.2	-5.6	58.2	30.8

DEBT INDICATORS					
EDT / XGS (%)	..	..	108.4	74.0	74.2
EDT / GNI (%)	8.4	21.1	29.8	31.3	29.4
TDS / XGS (%)	..	..	15.7	10.9	11.5
INT / XGS (%)	..	..	6.0	3.7	3.6
INT / GNI (%)	0.2	1.7	1.7	1.6	1.4
RES / MGS (months)	..	..	4.0	5.7	6.7
Short-term / EDT (%)	16.6	26.8	18.0	17.1	17.8
Concessional / EDT (%)	32.9	18.4	28.1	15.9	16.9
Multilateral / EDT (%)	4.5	8.3	14.2	12.4	13.1

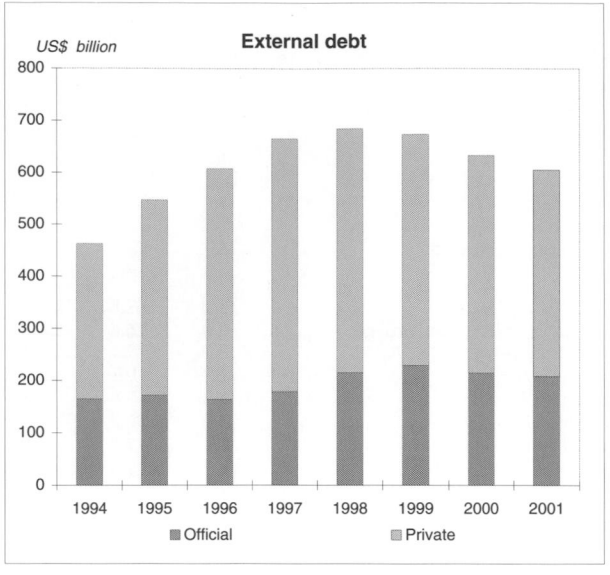

External debt

US$ billion

Official / Private (1994–2001)

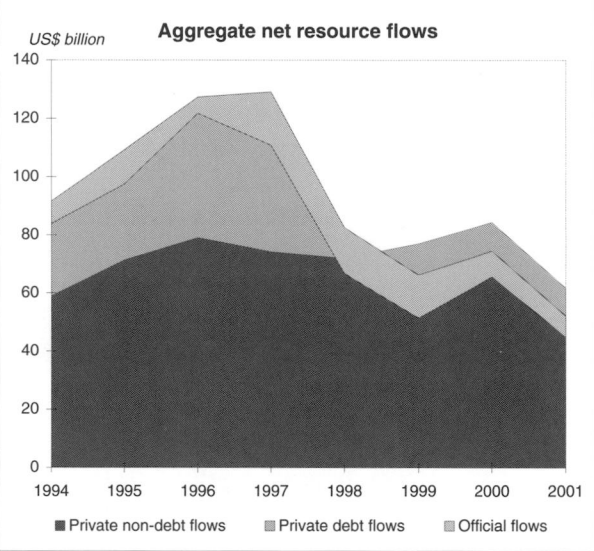

Aggregate net resource flows

US$ billion

Private non-debt flows / Private debt flows / Official flows (1994–2001)

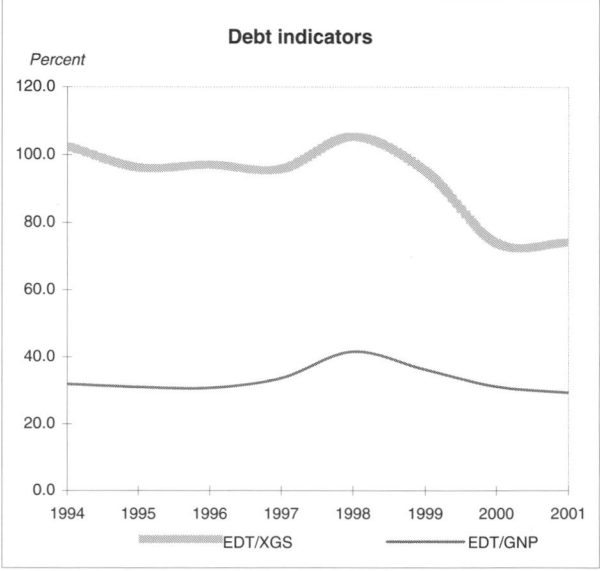

Debt indicators

Percent

EDT/XGS / EDT/GNP (1994–2001)

EAST ASIA AND PACIFIC

(US$ billion)

	1970	1980	1990	2000	2001
LONG-TERM DEBT					
DEBT OUTSTANDING (LDOD)	**9.1**	**66.7**	**222.7**	**502.2**	**483.7**
Public and publicly guaranteed	**6.9**	**55.6**	**195.7**	**333.9**	**326.8**
Official creditors	4.7	27.3	117.6	191.6	194.3
Multilateral	0.5	7.8	38.8	78.3	79.4
Bilateral	4.2	19.5	78.8	113.3	114.8
Private creditors	2.2	28.3	78.1	142.3	132.5
Bonds	0.1	1.9	14.4	59.2	61.7
Private nonguaranteed	**2.2**	**11.1**	**27.0**	**168.4**	**156.9**
Bonds	0.0	0.0	0.6	46.9	46.0
DISBURSEMENTS	**2.0**	**16.3**	**35.4**	**48.5**	**43.5**
Public and publicly guaranteed	**1.2**	**12.8**	**24.0**	**30.8**	**32.4**
Official creditors	0.7	4.0	11.7	16.6	15.5
Multilateral	0.1	1.6	4.9	5.9	5.3
Bilateral	0.6	2.4	6.8	10.7	10.2
Private creditors	0.5	8.8	12.3	14.2	16.9
Bonds	0.0	0.3	1.8	4.2	9.4
Private nonguaranteed	**0.8**	**3.5**	**11.4**	**17.7**	**11.1**
Bonds	0.0	0.0	0.5	4.5	5.0
PRINCIPAL REPAYMENTS	**0.8**	**5.6**	**23.2**	**60.9**	**55.5**
Public and publicly guaranteed	**0.4**	**3.7**	**18.6**	**38.1**	**32.9**
Official creditors	0.1	0.9	5.5	10.3	10.6
Multilateral	0.0	0.3	2.7	3.7	3.5
Bilateral	0.1	0.7	2.8	6.5	7.1
Private creditors	0.3	2.7	13.1	27.9	22.3
Bonds	0.0	0.0	3.1	6.2	6.7
Private nonguaranteed	**0.4**	**1.9**	**4.7**	**22.8**	**22.6**
Bonds	0.0	0.0	0.0	5.5	5.9
NET FLOWS ON DEBT	**1.2**	**10.6**	**12.2**	**-12.4**	**-12.0**
Public and publicly guaranteed	**0.8**	**9.1**	**5.5**	**-7.3**	**-0.5**
Official creditors	0.6	3.0	6.2	6.3	4.9
Multilateral	0.1	1.3	2.3	2.2	1.8
Bilateral	0.6	1.7	4.0	4.1	3.1
Private creditors	0.2	6.1	-0.7	-13.6	-5.4
Bonds	0.0	0.2	-1.3	-2.1	2.7
Private nonguaranteed	**0.4**	**1.5**	**6.7**	**-5.1**	**-11.5**
Bonds	0.0	0.0	0.5	-1.0	-0.9
CURRENCY COMPOSITION OF LONG-TERM DEBT (PERCENT)					
Deutsche mark	7.7	5.0	3.7	1.8	..
French franc	3.5	3.2	2.3	1.2	..
Japanese yen	6.1	18.0	28.8	25.9	..
Pound sterling	4.3	1.7	0.9	0.4	..
U.S. dollars	53.5	40.8	24.0	58.4	..
Multiple currency	6.7	16.6	22.0	6.6	..
All other currencies	17.6	7.6	15.3	3.3	..
DEBT STOCK-FLOW RECONCILIATION					
Total change in debt stocks	..	..	32.8	-40.4	..
Net flows on debt	1.2	18.3	20.0	-14.1	-21.3
Net change in interest arrears	..	..	0.5	-0.5	..
Interest capitalized	..	..	0.2	0.0	..
Debt forgiveness or reduction	..	..	-1.1	-8.8	..
Cross-currency valuation	..	..	11.2	-15.7	..
Residual	..	..	1.9	-1.4	..
AVERAGE TERMS OF NEW COMMITMENTS					
ALL CREDITORS					
Interest (%)	5.0	9.7	6.7	5.9	..
Maturity (years)	23.0	16.3	19.2	13.7	..
Grant element (%)	35.4	6.6	22.7	22.1	..
Official creditors					
Interest (%)	4.1	6.0	5.0	5.0	..
Maturity (years)	28.6	22.9	24.5	23.1	..
Grant element (%)	45.7	29.2	37.5	35.9	..
Private creditors					
Interest (%)	6.8	13.0	8.4	6.6	..
Maturity (years)	12.2	10.3	13.7	7.2	..
Grant element (%)	15.8	-13.8	7.4	12.6	..
Memo:					
Commitments	1.7	19.5	26.9	26.9	..
Official creditors	1.1	9.2	13.6	10.9	..
Private creditors	0.6	10.2	13.3	15.9	..

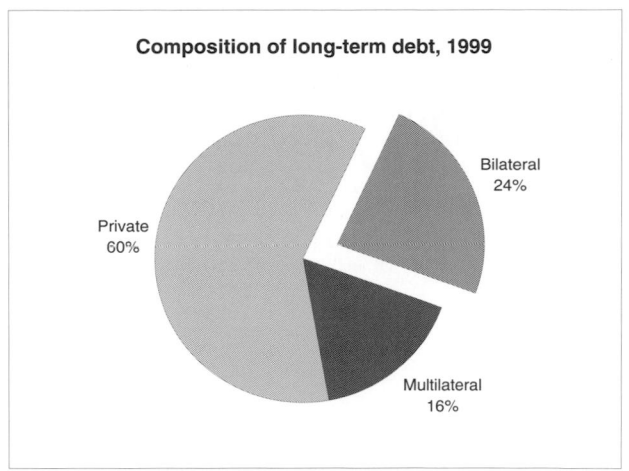

Composition of long-term debt, 1999

Bilateral 24%
Private 60%
Multilateral 16%

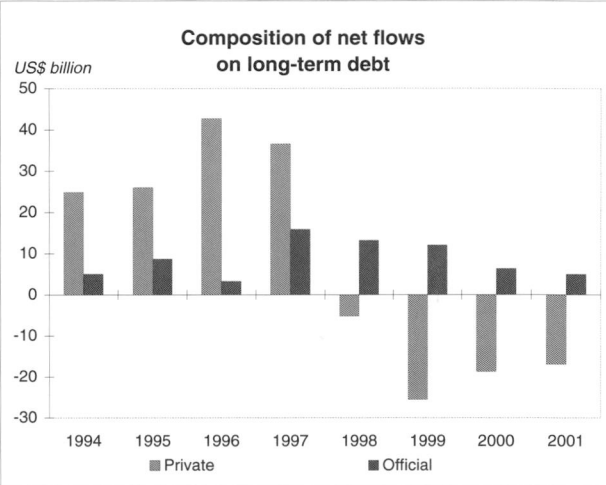

Composition of net flows on long-term debt

US$ billion

■ Private ■ Official

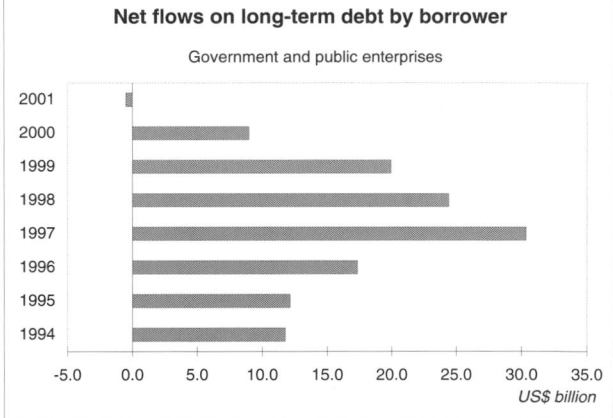

Net flows on long-term debt by borrower

Government and public enterprises

US$ billion

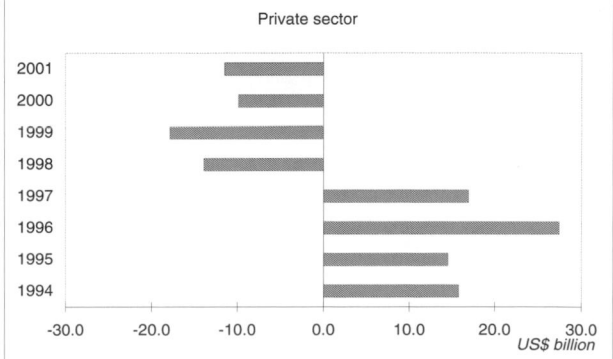

Private sector

US$ billion

EUROPE AND CENTRAL ASIA

(US$ billion)

	1970	1980	1990	2000	2001
SUMMARY DEBT DATA					
TOTAL DEBT STOCKS (EDT)	**5.0**	**75.6**	**219.9**	**499.3**	**485.9**
Long-term debt (LDOD)	**4.0**	**56.4**	**177.7**	**396.4**	**384.3**
Public and publicly guaranteed	3.1	44.9	172.8	284.4	284.4
Private nonguaranteed	0.9	11.5	4.9	112.1	99.9
Use of IMF credit	**0.1**	**2.1**	**1.3**	**22.0**	**27.2**
Short-term debt	**1.0**	**17.1**	**40.9**	**81.0**	**74.5**
of which interest arrears on LDOD	0.0	0.3	13.0	9.3	6.8
Memo:					
IBRD	0.3	3.3	10.3	22.8	24.0
IDA	0.1	0.2	0.2	2.7	2.9
TOTAL FLOWS ON DEBT					
Disbursements	**1.1**	**21.3**	**30.0**	**62.6**	**54.3**
Long-term debt	1.0	20.1	29.3	58.2	42.3
Public and publicly guaranteed	0.5	16.8	27.5	25.6	26.7
Private nonguaranteed	0.5	3.3	1.8	32.6	15.6
IMF purchases	**0.1**	**1.2**	**0.7**	**4.4**	**12.0**
Memo:					
IBRD	0.1	0.8	1.2	3.1	3.2
IDA	0.0	0.0	0.0	0.4	0.3
Principal repayments	**0.6**	**7.2**	**19.8**	**51.7**	**56.8**
Long-term debt	0.5	6.9	19.0	46.6	50.8
Public and publicly guaranteed	0.3	4.8	17.5	21.1	25.8
Private nonguaranteed	0.2	2.0	1.5	25.5	25.0
IMF repurchases	**0.1**	**0.3**	**0.7**	**5.1**	**6.0**
Memo:					
IBRD	0.0	0.1	1.1	1.4	1.4
IDA	0.0	0.0	0.0	0.0	0.0
Net flows on debt	**0.5**	**13.5**	**3.1**	**20.3**	**-6.6**
of which short-term debt	0.0	-0.6	-7.1	9.4	-4.1
Interest payments (INT)	**0.1**	**5.4**	**12.3**	**23.2**	**22.6**
Long-term debt	0.1	3.4	9.6	18.2	18.2
Net transfers on debt	**0.3**	**8.1**	**-9.2**	**-2.9**	**-29.2**
Total debt service (TDS)	**0.7**	**12.6**	**32.1**	**74.9**	**79.4**
AGGREGATE NET RESOURCE FLOWS AND NET TRANSFERS (LONG-TERM)					
NET RESOURCE FLOWS	**0.6**	**13.5**	**12.5**	**54.0**	**29.9**
Net flow of long-term debt (ex. IMF)	0.5	13.2	10.2	11.6	-8.5
Foreign direct investment (net)	0.1	0.0	1.1	28.5	28.5
Portfolio equity flows	0.0	0.0	0.2	5.4	1.3
Grants (excluding technical coop.)	0.1	0.3	1.0	8.5	8.6
NET TRANSFERS	**0.4**	**10.1**	**2.7**	**32.7**	**7.6**
Interest on long-term debt	0.1	3.4	9.6	18.2	18.2
Profit remittances on FDI	0.0	0.0	0.2	3.1	4.1
MAJOR ECONOMIC INDICATORS					
Gross national income (GNI)	..	..	1,236.3	926.7	986.9
Exports of goods & services (XGS)	..	..	..	414.3	431.7
of which workers' remittances	..	..	..	6.7	6.7
Imports of goods & services (MGS)	..	..	..	409.1	421.1
International reserves (RES)	..	..	..	129.5	134.7
Current account balance	..	..	..	14.6	19.5
DEBT INDICATORS					
EDT / XGS (%)	..	..	..	120.5	112.6
EDT / GNI (%)	..	..	17.8	53.9	49.2
TDS / XGS (%)	..	..	..	18.1	18.4
INT / XGS (%)	..	..	..	5.6	5.2
INT / GNI (%)	..	..	1.0	2.5	2.3
RES / MGS (months)	..	..	..	3.8	3.8
Short-term / EDT (%)	19.7	22.6	18.6	16.2	15.3
Concessional / EDT (%)	36.8	9.2	5.8	4.7	4.9
Multilateral / EDT (%)	12.6	5.8	7.6	6.9	6.9

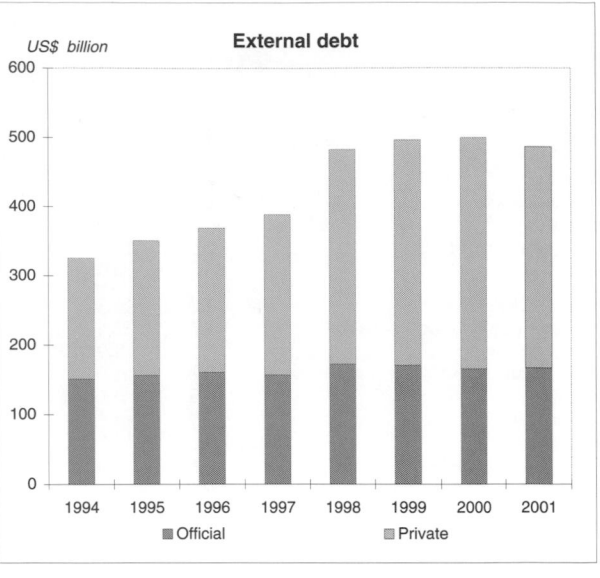

External debt

US$ billion

Official · Private

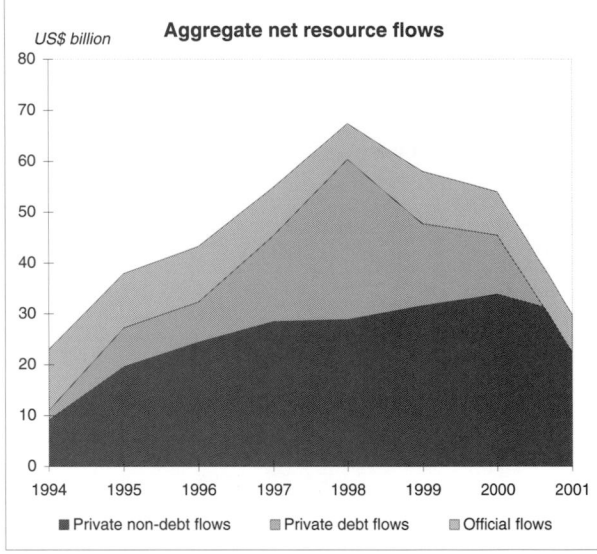

Aggregate net resource flows

US$ billion

Private non-debt flows · Private debt flows · Official flows

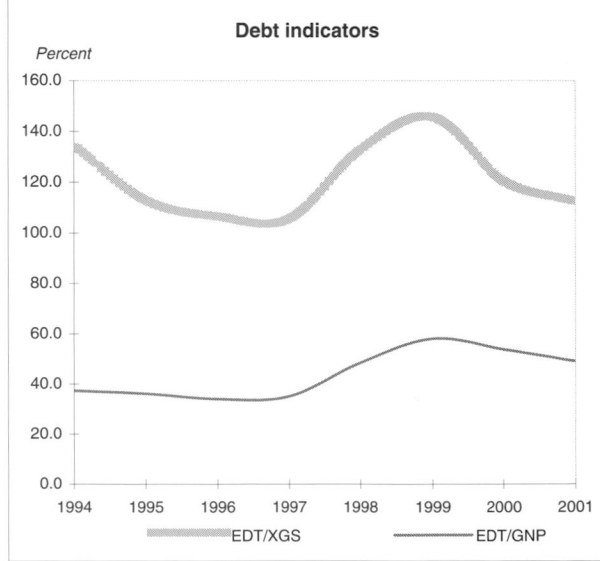

Debt indicators

Percent

EDT/XGS · EDT/GNP

EUROPE AND CENTRAL ASIA

(US$ billion)

	1970	1980	1990	2000	2001
LONG-TERM DEBT					
DEBT OUTSTANDING (LDOD)	**4.0**	**56.4**	**177.7**	**396.4**	**384.3**
Public and publicly guaranteed	**3.1**	**44.9**	**172.8**	**284.4**	**284.4**
Official creditors	2.6	18.6	64.3	143.1	139.0
Multilateral	0.6	4.4	16.6	34.5	33.4
Bilateral	2.0	14.2	47.7	108.5	105.5
Private creditors	0.4	26.3	108.4	141.3	145.4
Bonds	0.0	0.2	11.9	91.7	97.5
Private nonguaranteed	0.9	11.5	4.9	112.1	99.9
Bonds	0.0	0.0	0.0	18.7	16.9
DISBURSEMENTS	**1.0**	**20.1**	**29.3**	**58.2**	**42.3**
Public and publicly guaranteed	**0.5**	**16.8**	**27.5**	**25.6**	**26.7**
Official creditors	0.5	5.1	7.0	7.4	8.5
Multilateral	0.2	1.0	2.3	4.8	4.3
Bilateral	0.3	4.0	4.7	2.5	4.2
Private creditors	0.1	11.7	20.5	18.2	18.2
Bonds	0.0	0.1	2.0	11.3	9.0
Private nonguaranteed	**0.5**	**3.3**	**1.8**	**32.6**	**15.6**
Bonds	0.0	0.0	0.0	5.8	0.7
PRINCIPAL REPAYMENTS	**0.5**	**6.9**	**19.0**	**46.6**	**50.8**
Public and publicly guaranteed	**0.3**	**4.8**	**17.5**	**21.1**	**25.8**
Official creditors	0.2	1.7	3.1	7.3	9.7
Multilateral	0.1	0.2	1.5	2.8	2.5
Bilateral	0.1	1.5	1.7	4.5	7.2
Private creditors	0.1	3.1	14.4	13.7	16.1
Bonds	0.0	0.0	0.1	5.8	4.8
Private nonguaranteed	**0.2**	**2.0**	**1.5**	**25.5**	**25.0**
Bonds	0.0	0.0	0.0	2.7	2.5
NET FLOWS ON DEBT	**0.5**	**13.2**	**10.2**	**11.6**	**-8.5**
Public and publicly guaranteed	**0.2**	**11.9**	**10.0**	**4.5**	**0.9**
Official creditors	0.3	3.3	3.8	0.0	-1.2
Multilateral	0.1	0.9	0.8	2.0	1.8
Bilateral	0.2	2.5	3.0	-2.0	-3.0
Private creditors	-0.1	8.6	6.1	4.5	2.1
Bonds	0.0	0.1	1.9	5.5	4.2
Private nonguaranteed	**0.3**	**1.3**	**0.3**	**7.1**	**-9.4**
Bonds	0.0	0.0	0.0	3.1	-1.8
CURRENCY COMPOSITION OF LONG-TERM DEBT (PERCENT)					
Deutsche mark	16.0	11.0	25.1	15.1	..
French franc	2.7	9.3	5.0	2.0	..
Japanese yen	0.1	2.4	7.5	5.9	..
Pound sterling	5.0	2.6	1.8	0.6	..
U.S. dollars	44.7	41.8	32.2	58.8	..
Multiple currency	15.2	21.5	10.6	7.1	..
All other currencies	14.9	6.8	11.0	7.4	..
DEBT STOCK-FLOW RECONCILIATION					
Total change in debt stocks	..	..	21.2	2.9	..
Net flows on debt	0.5	13.5	3.1	20.3	-6.6
Net change in interest arrears	..	..	5.2	-1.0	..
Interest capitalized	..	..	2.2	4.4	..
Debt forgiveness or reduction	..	..	-1.1	-11.6	..
Cross-currency valuation	..	..	10.1	-9.8	..
Residual	..	..	1.7	0.8	..
AVERAGE TERMS OF NEW COMMITMENTS					
ALL CREDITORS					
Interest (%)	4.2	10.2	8.4	7.5	..
Maturity (years)	19.2	12.5	11.9	11.0	..
Grant element (%)	37.3	2.1	8.7	10.9	..
Official creditors					
Interest (%)	3.8	7.5	7.9	6.2	..
Maturity (years)	20.1	16.7	13.6	17.1	..
Grant element (%)	40.3	19.6	12.0	23.8	..
Private creditors					
Interest (%)	6.3	11.2	8.6	7.8	..
Maturity (years)	13.4	10.9	11.1	9.2	..
Grant element (%)	18.2	-4.4	7.2	7.1	..
Memo:					
Commitments	0.8	12.7	30.3	24.4	..
Official creditors	0.7	3.4	9.4	5.6	..
Private creditors	0.1	9.3	20.9	18.8	..

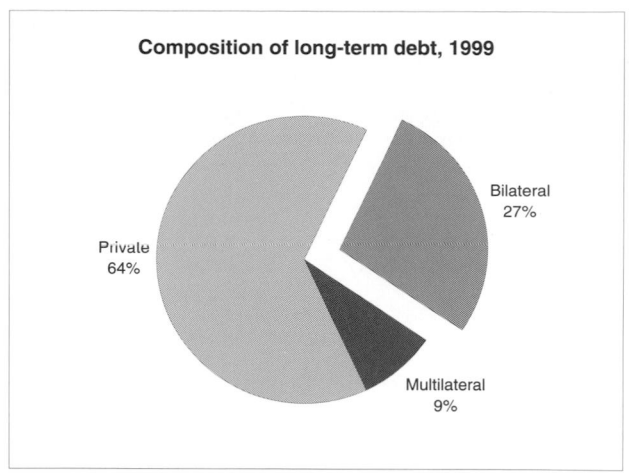

Composition of long-term debt, 1999

Bilateral 27%
Private 64%
Multilateral 9%

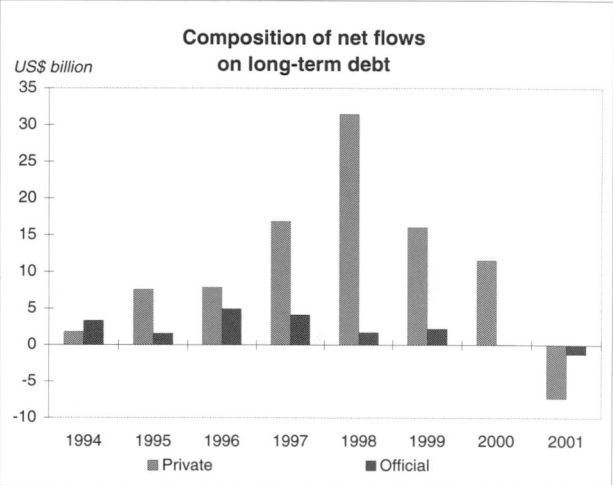

Composition of net flows on long-term debt

US$ billion

■ Private ■ Official

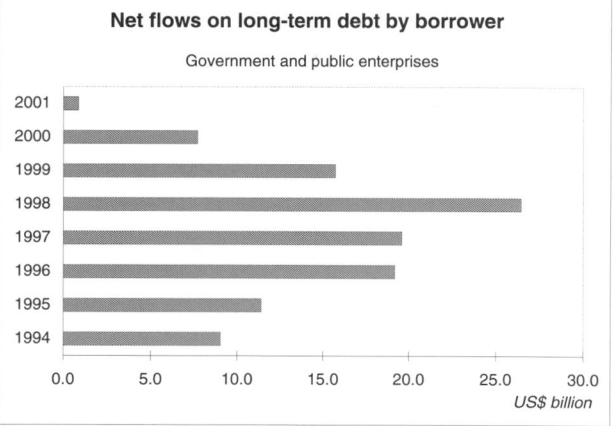

Net flows on long-term debt by borrower

Government and public enterprises

US$ billion

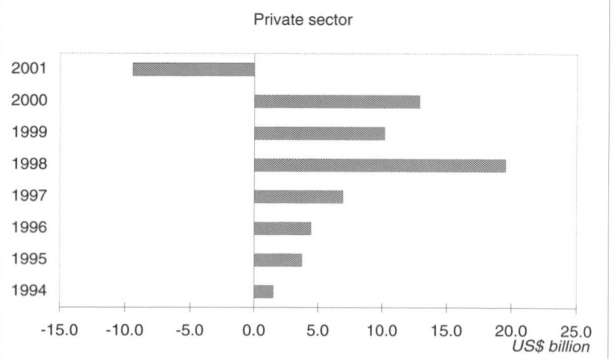

Private sector

US$ billion

LATIN AMERICA AND CARIBBEAN

(US$ billion)

	1970	*1980*	*1990*	*2000*	*2001*
SUMMARY DEBT DATA					
TOTAL DEBT STOCKS (EDT)	**32.5**	**257.2**	**474.7**	**774.4**	**787.1**
Long-term debt (LDOD)	27.6	187.3	379.2	661.7	659.7
Public and publicly guaranteed	15.8	144.8	354.2	415.1	415.7
Private nonguaranteed	11.9	42.5	25.1	246.7	244.0
Use of IMF credit	**0.1**	**1.4**	**18.3**	**8.8**	**23.9**
Short-term debt	**4.8**	**68.5**	**77.2**	**103.8**	**103.5**
of which interest arrears on LDOD	0.0	0.1	25.6	1.7	1.7
Memo:					
IBRD	2.1	7.7	34.7	37.5	38.2
IDA	0.1	0.4	1.1	3.4	3.5
TOTAL FLOWS ON DEBT					
Disbursements	**6.6**	**44.8**	**34.0**	**127.5**	**119.4**
Long-term debt	6.5	44.3	29.2	124.0	102.4
Public and publicly guaranteed	3.7	31.4	24.5	55.9	53.8
Private nonguaranteed	2.8	13.0	4.7	68.0	48.6
IMF purchases	**0.1**	**0.4**	**4.8**	**3.5**	**17.0**
Memo:					
IBRD	0.4	1.6	6.1	5.6	4.9
IDA	0.0	0.1	0.1	0.2	0.3
Principal repayments	**3.8**	**21.7**	**22.7**	**125.9**	**105.6**
Long-term debt	3.5	21.2	19.1	111.7	104.0
Public and publicly guaranteed	1.7	14.2	16.8	53.4	56.3
Private nonguaranteed	1.8	7.0	2.2	58.2	47.7
IMF repurchases	**0.3**	**0.5**	**3.7**	**14.3**	**1.6**
Memo:					
IBRD	0.1	0.4	3.3	3.8	3.9
IDA	0.0	0.0	0.0	0.0	0.0
Net flows on debt	**2.8**	**46.1**	**20.4**	**-3.3**	**13.4**
of which short-term debt	0.0	23.0	9.1	-4.9	-0.3
Interest payments (INT)	**1.4**	**24.6**	**22.7**	**53.3**	**51.1**
Long-term debt	1.4	17.6	18.7	46.1	44.2
Net transfers on debt	**1.4**	**21.5**	**-2.3**	**-56.6**	**-37.7**
Total debt service (TDS)	**5.1**	**46.3**	**45.4**	**179.2**	**156.8**
AGGREGATE NET RESOURCE FLOWS AND NET TRANSFERS (LONG-TERM)					
NET RESOURCE FLOWS	**4.2**	**29.9**	**21.8**	**99.3**	**73.8**
Net flow of long-term debt (ex. IMF)	3.0	23.1	10.1	12.3	-1.6
Foreign direct investment (net)	1.1	6.1	8.2	75.1	70.8
Portfolio equity flows	0.0	0.0	1.1	9.4	2.2
Grants (excluding technical coop.)	0.2	0.6	2.3	2.5	2.4
NET TRANSFERS	**0.8**	**7.4**	**-3.3**	**32.5**	**5.2**
Interest on long-term debt	1.4	17.6	18.7	46.1	44.2
Profit remittances on FDI	2.0	4.9	6.3	20.7	24.3
MAJOR ECONOMIC INDICATORS					
Gross national income (GNI)	160.6	745.6	1,064.7	1,891.3	1,819.5
Exports of goods & services (XGS)	..	127.4	185.9	463.1	471.3
of which workers' remittances	..	1.2	4.8	17.4	17.2
Imports of goods & services (MGS)	..	159.8	194.0	518.4	517.3
International reserves (RES)	5.5	57.3	58.6	159.6	158.4
Current account balance	..	-30.2	-1.0	-46.7	-51.4
DEBT INDICATORS					
EDT / XGS (%)	..	201.9	255.4	167.2	167.0
EDT / GNI (%)	20.3	34.5	44.6	41.0	43.3
TDS / XGS (%)	..	36.3	24.5	38.7	33.3
INT / XGS (%)	..	19.3	12.2	11.5	10.9
INT / GNI (%)	0.9	3.3	2.1	2.8	2.8
RES / MGS (months)	..	4.3	3.6	3.7	3.7
Short-term / EDT (%)	14.7	26.7	16.3	13.4	13.2
Concessional / EDT (%)	13.0	9.3	10.2	4.0	4.0
Multilateral / EDT (%)	9.1	5.5	12.6	12.0	12.4

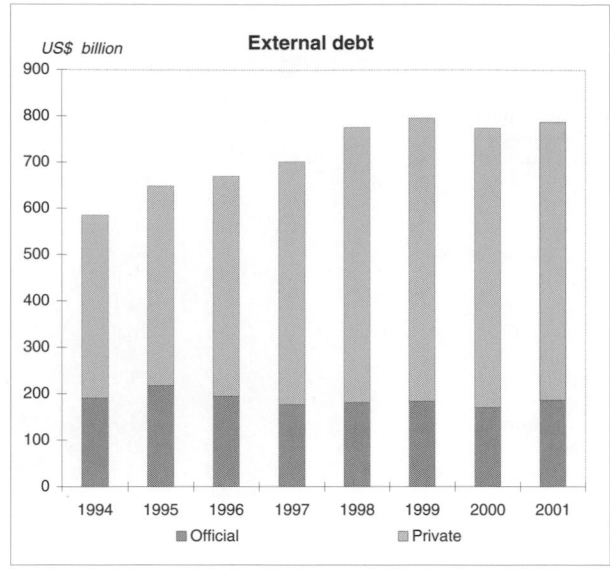

External debt

US$ billion

Official / Private (1994–2001)

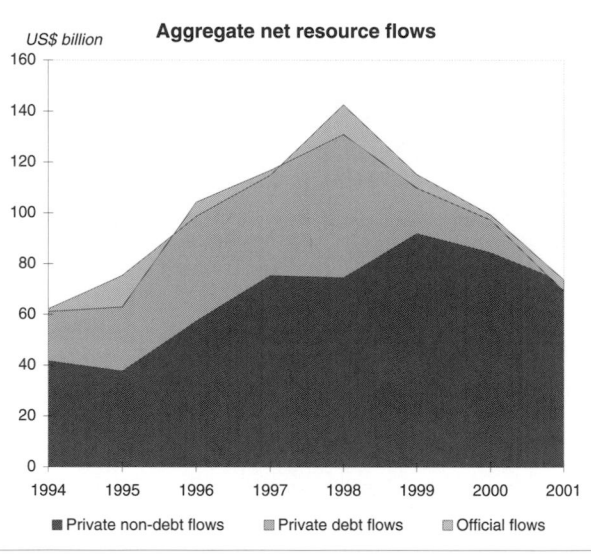

Aggregate net resource flows

US$ billion

Private non-debt flows / Private debt flows / Official flows (1994–2001)

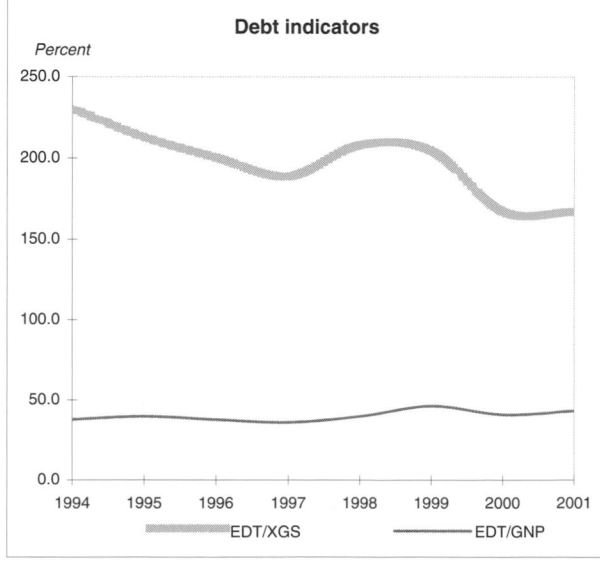

Debt indicators

Percent

EDT/XGS / EDT/GNP (1994–2001)

LATIN AMERICA AND CARIBBEAN

(US$ billion)

	1970	*1980*	*1990*	*2000*	*2001*
LONG-TERM DEBT					
DEBT OUTSTANDING (LDOD)	**27.6**	**187.3**	**379.2**	**661.7**	**659.7**
Public and publicly guaranteed	**15.8**	**144.8**	**354.2**	**415.1**	**415.7**
Official creditors	8.1	45.0	146.0	160.7	161.0
Multilateral	2.9	14.1	59.9	92.9	97.4
Bilateral	5.2	30.9	86.1	67.8	63.6
Private creditors	7.6	99.8	208.1	254.3	254.7
Bonds	1.2	9.6	75.9	213.0	217.3
Private nonguaranteed	**11.9**	**42.5**	**25.1**	**246.7**	**244.0**
Bonds	0.0	0.0	0.2	53.3	54.0
DISBURSEMENTS	**6.5**	**44.3**	**29.2**	**124.0**	**102.4**
Public and publicly guaranteed	**3.7**	**31.4**	**24.5**	**55.9**	**53.8**
Official creditors	1.3	6.8	13.8	16.5	14.7
Multilateral	0.6	3.0	9.0	13.7	11.3
Bilateral	0.8	3.9	4.8	2.9	3.4
Private creditors	2.4	24.6	10.7	39.4	39.1
Bonds	0.1	1.2	1.9	32.3	29.9
Private nonguaranteed	**2.8**	**13.0**	**4.7**	**68.0**	**48.6**
Bonds	0.0	0.0	0.2	8.3	6.5
PRINCIPAL REPAYMENTS	**3.5**	**21.2**	**19.1**	**111.7**	**104.0**
Public and publicly guaranteed	**1.7**	**14.2**	**16.8**	**53.4**	**56.3**
Official creditors	0.5	2.1	7.0	17.1	12.7
Multilateral	0.2	0.7	4.7	9.9	6.7
Bilateral	0.3	1.4	2.2	7.1	6.0
Private creditors	1.2	12.1	9.9	36.4	43.6
Bonds	0.1	0.4	2.0	26.8	30.2
Private nonguaranteed	**1.8**	**7.0**	**2.2**	**58.2**	**47.7**
Bonds	0.0	0.0	0.0	8.8	5.7
NET FLOWS ON DEBT	**3.0**	**23.1**	**10.1**	**12.3**	**-1.6**
Public and publicly guaranteed	**2.0**	**17.1**	**7.7**	**2.5**	**-2.5**
Official creditors	0.8	4.7	6.8	-0.5	2.0
Multilateral	0.4	2.2	4.2	3.7	4.6
Bilateral	0.4	2.4	2.6	-4.3	-2.7
Private creditors	1.2	12.4	0.9	3.0	-4.5
Bonds	0.1	0.8	0.0	5.5	-0.3
Private nonguaranteed	**1.0**	**6.0**	**2.5**	**9.8**	**0.9**
Bonds	0.0	0.0	0.2	-0.5	0.8
CURRENCY COMPOSITION OF LONG-TERM DEBT (PERCENT)					
Deutsche mark	7.8	5.5	5.9	3.7	..
French franc	2.3	1.8	3.6	1.0	..
Japanese yen	0.1	4.4	5.7	6.1	..
Pound sterling	4.5	1.3	1.4	0.7	..
U.S. dollars	63.0	63.1	55.0	70.5	..
Multiple currency	16.9	9.4	17.4	5.9	..
All other currencies	3.5	3.3	2.5	6.6	..
DEBT STOCK-FLOW RECONCILIATION					
Total change in debt stocks	..	..	22.3	-21.8	..
Net flows on debt	2.8	46.1	20.4	-3.3	13.4
Net change in interest arrears	..	..	9.1	-0.3	..
Interest capitalized	..	..	1.5	0.2	..
Debt forgiveness or reduction	..	..	-18.7	-4.0	..
Cross-currency valuation	..	..	11.5	-9.1	..
Residual	..	..	-1.5	-5.3	..
AVERAGE TERMS OF NEW COMMITMENTS					
ALL CREDITORS					
Interest (%)	7.0	11.5	7.9	9.0	..
Maturity (years)	14.4	12.5	15.0	13.8	..
Grant element (%)	16.7	-5.9	12.3	3.0	..
Official creditors					
Interest (%)	6.0	7.8	7.0	6.6	..
Maturity (years)	23.4	21.2	18.0	16.9	..
Grant element (%)	27.4	14.7	18.8	20.6	..
Private creditors					
Interest (%)	7.7	13.0	9.1	9.5	..
Maturity (years)	8.9	9.0	11.0	13.0	..
Grant element (%)	10.1	-14.2	3.8	-1.1	..
Memo:					
Commitments	4.4	33.2	26.0	50.0	..
Official creditors	1.6	9.6	14.8	9.5	..
Private creditors	2.7	23.6	11.1	40.4	..

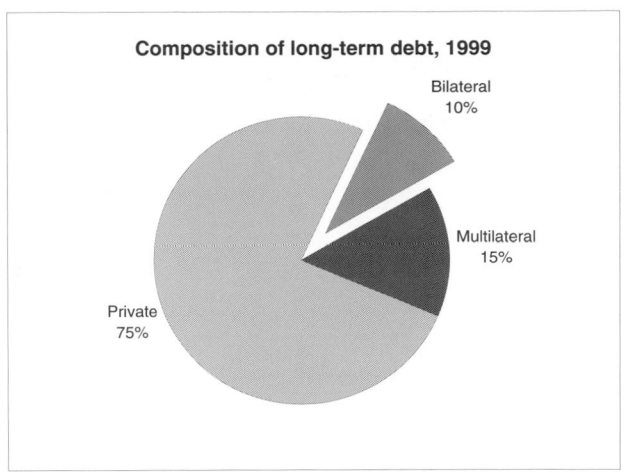

Composition of long-term debt, 1999

Bilateral 10%
Multilateral 15%
Private 75%

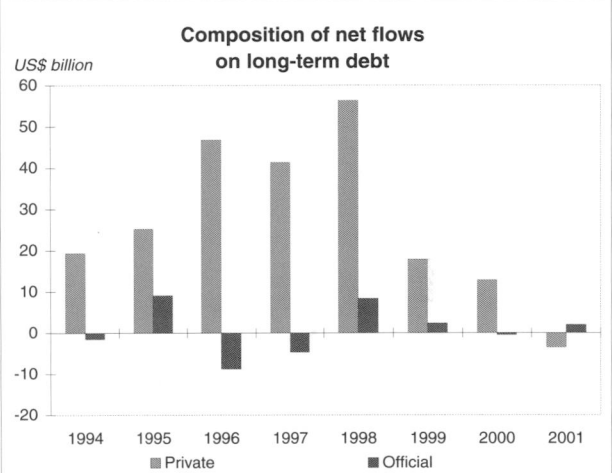

Composition of net flows on long-term debt

US$ billion

■ Private ■ Official

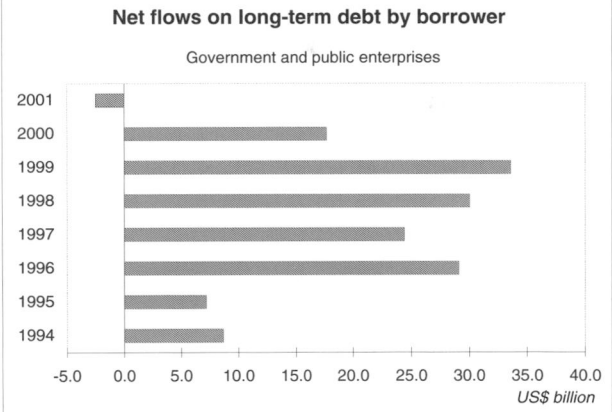

Net flows on long-term debt by borrower

Government and public enterprises

US$ billion

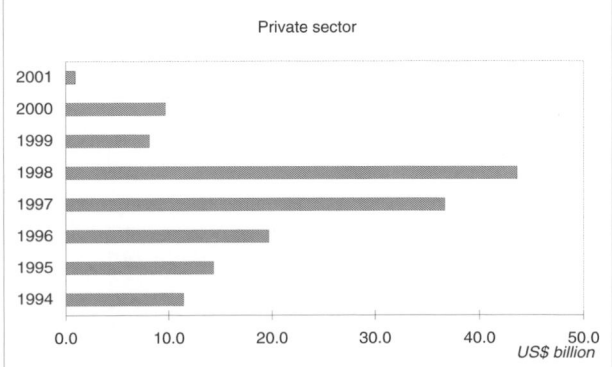

Private sector

US$ billion

MIDDLE EAST AND NORTH AFRICA

(US$ billion)

	1970	*1980*	*1990*	*2000*	*2001*
SUMMARY DEBT DATA					
TOTAL DEBT STOCKS (EDT)	**4.8**	**83.8**	**183.5**	**203.8**	**196.6**
Long-term debt (LDOD)	**4.2**	**61.8**	**137.8**	**153.8**	**150.3**
Public and publicly guaranteed	4.2	61.2	136.3	147.0	143.7
Private nonguaranteed	0.0	0.6	1.5	6.8	6.6
Use of IMF credit	**0.1**	**0.9**	**1.8**	**2.5**	**2.3**
Short-term debt	**0.6**	**21.1**	**43.9**	**47.4**	**43.9**
of which interest arrears on LDOD	0.0	0.4	2.9	2.7	2.7
Memo:					
IBRD	0.1	2.4	8.3	7.7	7.3
IDA	0.0	0.7	1.8	2.7	2.7
TOTAL FLOWS ON DEBT					
Disbursements	**0.9**	**12.3**	**14.6**	**11.7**	**15.0**
Long-term debt	0.9	12.0	14.5	11.6	14.8
Public and publicly guaranteed	0.8	11.7	14.4	10.2	13.8
Private nonguaranteed	0.0	0.3	0.1	1.4	1.0
IMF purchases	**0.0**	**0.4**	**0.1**	**0.0**	**0.2**
Memo:					
IBRD	0.0	0.4	1.2	0.5	0.7
IDA	0.0	0.1	0.0	0.1	0.1
Principal repayments	**0.4**	**5.1**	**15.6**	**16.2**	**15.2**
Long-term debt	0.4	4.8	15.2	16.0	14.9
Public and publicly guaranteed	0.4	4.7	15.1	14.6	13.8
Private nonguaranteed	0.0	0.1	0.2	1.3	1.1
IMF repurchases	**0.0**	**0.2**	**0.4**	**0.2**	**0.3**
Memo:					
IBRD	0.0	0.1	0.8	0.9	0.8
IDA	0.0	0.0	0.0	0.0	0.1
Net flows on debt	**0.5**	**8.7**	**0.6**	**-7.5**	**-3.7**
of which short-term debt	0.0	1.4	1.7	-3.0	-3.5
Interest payments (INT)	**0.1**	**6.5**	**8.6**	**8.7**	**8.3**
Long-term debt	0.1	3.9	5.2	6.5	6.3
Net transfers on debt	**0.4**	**2.2**	**-7.9**	**-16.2**	**-12.1**
Total debt service (TDS)	**0.5**	**11.5**	**24.2**	**24.9**	**23.6**
AGGREGATE NET RESOURCE FLOWS AND NET TRANSFERS (LONG-TERM)					
NET RESOURCE FLOWS	**1.1**	**8.5**	**10.1**	**1.5**	**6.2**
Net flow of long-term debt (ex. IMF)	0.5	7.1	-0.7	-4.3	-0.1
Foreign direct investment (net)	0.3	-3.3	2.5	1.2	2.6
Portfolio equity flows	0.0	0.0	0.0	0.8	0.0
Grants (excluding technical coop.)	0.4	4.7	8.3	3.8	3.6
NET TRANSFERS	**-1.1**	**-5.2**	**3.6**	**-6.3**	**-3.0**
Interest on long-term debt	0.1	3.9	5.2	6.5	6.3
Profit remittances on FDI	2.1	9.9	1.3	1.3	2.8
MAJOR ECONOMIC INDICATORS					
Gross national income (GNI)	39.1	380.3	401.3	643.7	598.7
Exports of goods & services (XGS)	..	206.1	161.1	238.5	230.1
of which workers' remittances	..	5.1	10.5	9.7	10.1
Imports of goods & services (MGS)	..	147.5	147.5	185.3	194.0
International reserves (RES)	4.5	76.2	39.2	87.8	94.9
Current account balance	..	47.0	1.9	28.1	19.3
DEBT INDICATORS					
EDT / XGS (%)	..	40.7	113.9	85.5	85.4
EDT / GNI (%)	12.3	22.0	45.7	31.7	32.8
TDS / XGS (%)	..	5.6	15.0	10.5	10.2
INT / XGS (%)	..	3.1	5.3	3.7	3.6
INT / GNI (%)	0.3	1.7	2.1	1.4	1.4
RES / MGS (months)	..	6.2	3.2	5.7	5.9
Short-term / EDT (%)	11.5	25.2	23.9	23.3	22.4
Concessional / EDT (%)	51.8	21.5	24.2	27.9	28.0
Multilateral / EDT (%)	3.6	6.7	8.6	11.4	11.2

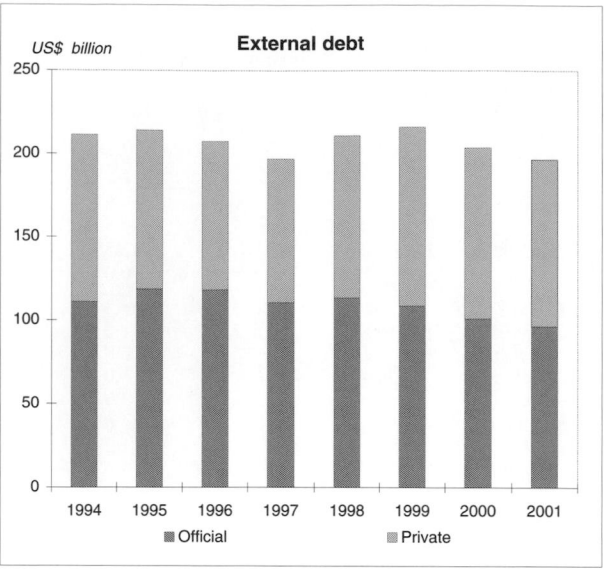

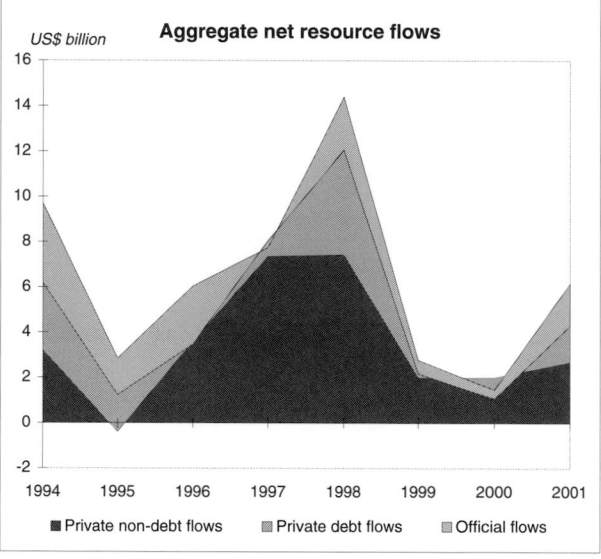

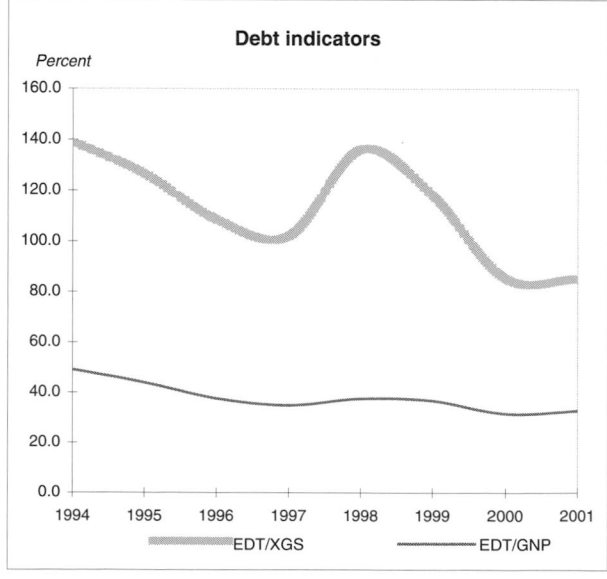

MIDDLE EAST AND NORTH AFRICA

(US$ billion)

	1970	1980	1990	2000	2001
LONG-TERM DEBT					
DEBT OUTSTANDING (LDOD)	**4.2**	**61.8**	**137.8**	**153.8**	**150.3**
Public and publicly guaranteed	**4.2**	**61.2**	**136.3**	**147.0**	**143.7**
Official creditors	3.0	31.5	81.0	98.3	93.7
Multilateral	0.2	5.6	15.8	23.3	21.9
Bilateral	2.9	25.9	65.2	75.0	71.8
Private creditors	1.1	29.7	55.3	48.7	50.0
Bonds	0.0	0.7	2.2	8.0	12.3
Private nonguaranteed	0.0	0.6	1.5	6.8	6.6
Bonds	0.0	0.0	0.0	0.8	0.9
DISBURSEMENTS	**0.9**	**12.0**	**14.5**	**11.6**	**14.8**
Public and publicly guaranteed	**0.8**	**11.7**	**14.4**	**10.2**	**13.8**
Official creditors	0.4	5.8	6.3	2.7	3.4
Multilateral	0.0	0.7	2.4	1.8	2.1
Bilateral	0.4	5.1	4.0	1.0	1.3
Private creditors	0.4	5.9	8.1	7.5	10.5
Bonds	0.0	0.1	0.0	1.4	4.8
Private nonguaranteed	**0.0**	**0.3**	**0.1**	**1.4**	**1.0**
Bonds	0.0	0.0	0.0	0.1	0.2
PRINCIPAL REPAYMENTS	**0.4**	**4.8**	**15.2**	**16.0**	**14.9**
Public and publicly guaranteed	**0.4**	**4.7**	**15.1**	**14.6**	**13.8**
Official creditors	0.2	0.9	5.0	6.1	5.1
Multilateral	0.0	0.2	1.3	2.1	2.3
Bilateral	0.2	0.7	3.7	4.0	2.8
Private creditors	0.2	3.8	10.1	8.5	8.7
Bonds	0.0	0.0	0.1	0.9	0.5
Private nonguaranteed	**0.0**	**0.1**	**0.2**	**1.3**	**1.1**
Bonds	0.0	0.0	0.0	0.1	0.1
NET FLOWS ON DEBT	**0.5**	**7.1**	**-0.7**	**-4.3**	**-0.1**
Public and publicly guaranteed	**0.5**	**7.0**	**-0.7**	**-4.4**	**0.0**
Official creditors	0.2	4.9	1.4	-3.4	-1.7
Multilateral	0.0	0.5	1.1	-0.3	-0.2
Bilateral	0.2	4.4	0.3	-3.1	-1.5
Private creditors	0.3	2.1	-2.0	-1.0	1.7
Bonds	0.0	0.0	-0.1	0.5	4.3
Private nonguaranteed	**0.0**	**0.1**	**0.0**	**0.1**	**-0.1**
Bonds	0.0	0.0	0.0	0.1	0.1
CURRENCY COMPOSITION OF LONG-TERM DEBT (PERCENT)					
Deutsche mark	7.7	6.4	6.6	4.1	..
French franc	18.6	9.3	11.1	8.3	..
Japanese yen	0.0	5.7	6.3	8.1	..
Pound sterling	4.1	1.3	1.4	0.8	..
U.S. dollars	33.0	46.4	38.2	38.8	..
Multiple currency	3.1	4.7	7.5	3.4	..
All other currencies	32.5	12.4	12.5	12.4	..
DEBT STOCK-FLOW RECONCILIATION					
Total change in debt stocks	..	..	-5.7	-12.4	..
Net flows on debt	0.5	8.7	0.6	-7.5	-3.7
Net change in interest arrears	..	..	-1.5	0.1	..
Interest capitalized	..	..	0.2	0.1	..
Debt forgiveness or reduction	..	..	-10.6	-0.2	..
Cross-currency valuation	..	..	5.3	-4.0	..
Residual	..	..	0.2	-0.9	..
AVERAGE TERMS OF NEW COMMITMENTS					
ALL CREDITORS					
Interest (%)	4.6	6.4	7.4	5.8	..
Maturity (years)	18.6	18.1	13.5	11.9	..
Grant element (%)	33.5	24.1	15.8	20.1	..
Official creditors					
Interest (%)	3.7	4.7	5.5	4.2	..
Maturity (years)	23.6	24.1	21.4	19.6	..
Grant element (%)	43.6	38.8	32.4	38.4	..
Private creditors					
Interest (%)	6.3	8.6	8.8	6.7	..
Maturity (years)	9.4	10.7	7.6	8.0	..
Grant element (%)	14.7	5.7	3.4	10.5	..
Memo:					
Commitments	1.2	11.5	15.3	7.0	..
Official creditors	0.8	6.4	6.6	2.4	..
Private creditors	0.4	5.1	8.8	4.6	..

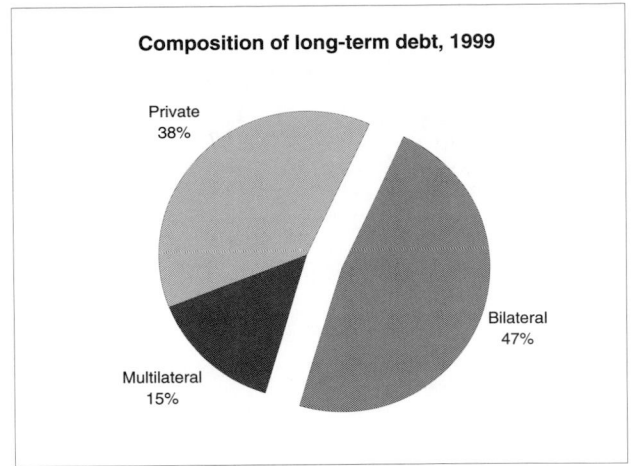

Composition of long-term debt, 1999

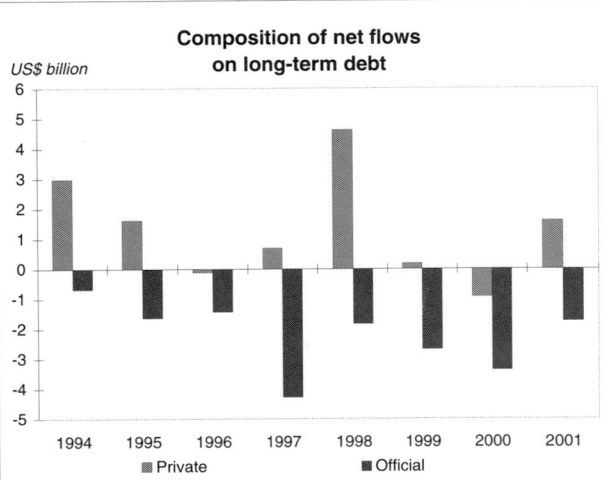

Composition of net flows on long-term debt

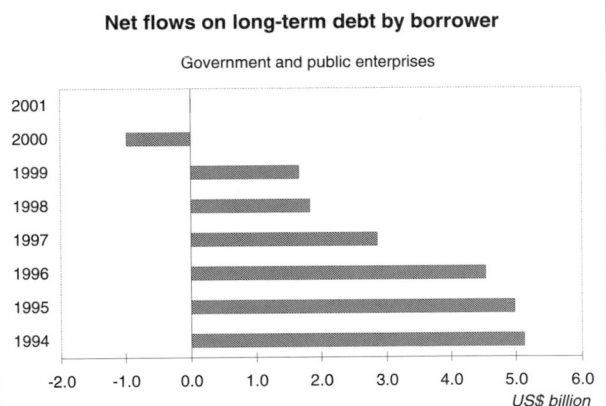

Net flows on long-term debt by borrower — Government and public enterprises

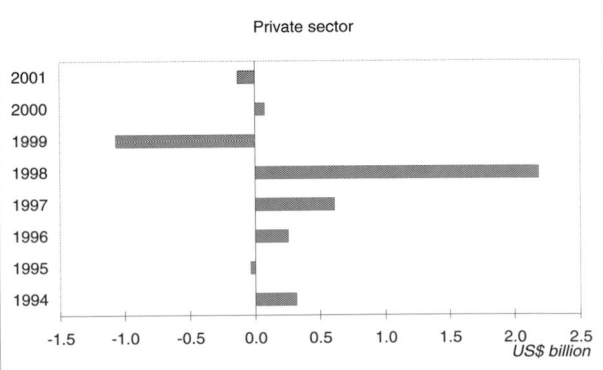

Private sector

SOUTH ASIA

(US$ billion)

	1970	1980	1990	2000	2001
SUMMARY DEBT DATA					
TOTAL DEBT STOCKS (EDT)	**12.3**	**37.8**	**129.5**	**165.7**	**159.3**
Long-term debt (LDOD)	**11.7**	**32.9**	**112.6**	**157.7**	**151.9**
Public and publicly guaranteed	11.6	32.5	110.8	146.4	140.6
Private nonguaranteed	0.1	0.4	1.7	11.4	11.4
Use of IMF credit	**0.1**	**2.5**	**4.5**	**1.9**	**1.7**
Short-term debt	**0.4**	**2.5**	**12.4**	**6.0**	**5.6**
of which interest arrears on LDOD	0.0	0.0	0.0	0.1	0.1
Memo:					
IBRD	0.9	1.2	9.6	10.2	9.6
IDA	1.3	7.1	21.1	33.9	32.5
TOTAL FLOWS ON DEBT					
Disbursements	**1.6**	**6.3**	**12.1**	**14.4**	**9.4**
Long-term debt	1.6	4.6	10.3	14.2	9.2
Public and publicly guaranteed	1.5	4.3	10.0	13.7	8.3
Private nonguaranteed	0.0	0.3	0.3	0.5	0.9
IMF purchases	**0.0**	**1.6**	**1.9**	**0.2**	**0.1**
Memo:					
IBRD	0.1	0.2	1.6	0.8	0.7
IDA	0.1	0.9	1.6	1.7	2.0
Principal repayments	**0.8**	**1.5**	**5.3**	**9.1**	**8.1**
Long-term debt	0.5	1.2	4.1	8.4	7.8
Public and publicly guaranteed	0.5	1.1	3.8	7.7	6.9
Private nonguaranteed	0.0	0.1	0.4	0.7	0.9
IMF repurchases	**0.3**	**0.3**	**1.2**	**0.7**	**0.3**
Memo:					
IBRD	0.1	0.1	0.6	1.2	0.9
IDA	0.0	0.0	0.2	0.6	0.6
Net flows on debt	**0.8**	**5.8**	**8.4**	**4.3**	**0.9**
of which short-term debt	0.0	1.0	1.6	-1.0	-0.4
Interest payments (INT)	**0.3**	**1.2**	**6.2**	**5.6**	**5.7**
Long-term debt	0.3	0.9	4.7	5.3	5.4
Net transfers on debt	**0.5**	**4.6**	**2.3**	**-1.3**	**-4.9**
Total debt service (TDS)	**1.1**	**2.8**	**11.4**	**14.7**	**13.8**
AGGREGATE NET RESOURCE FLOWS AND NET TRANSFERS (LONG-TERM)					
NET RESOURCE FLOWS	**1.4**	**6.4**	**9.1**	**13.3**	**8.9**
Net flow of long-term debt (ex. IMF)	1.0	3.4	6.1	5.8	1.4
Foreign direct investment (net)	0.1	0.2	0.5	3.1	4.2
Portfolio equity flows	0.0	0.0	0.1	2.1	0.9
Grants (excluding technical coop.)	0.3	2.8	2.4	2.2	2.4
NET TRANSFERS	**1.1**	**5.5**	**4.3**	**7.7**	**2.6**
Interest on long-term debt	0.3	0.9	4.7	5.3	5.4
Profit remittances on FDI	0.0	0.0	0.1	0.3	0.9
MAJOR ECONOMIC INDICATORS					
Gross national income (GNI)	82.1	234.0	399.7	608.4	651.0
Exports of goods & services (XGS)	4.3	23.0	39.9	106.9	112.6
of which workers' remittances	..	4.6	5.0	15.8	16.2
Imports of goods & services (MGS)	6.1	30.4	54.7	116.4	121.7
International reserves (RES)	..	15.4	8.9	47.3	55.1
Current account balance	..	-6.3	-14.2	-6.6	-9.9
DEBT INDICATORS					
EDT / XGS (%)	287.5	164.4	324.7	154.9	141.5
EDT / GNI (%)	15.0	16.2	32.4	27.2	24.5
TDS / XGS (%)	25.2	12.0	28.7	13.8	12.3
INT / XGS (%)	6.8	5.3	15.5	5.3	5.1
INT / GNI (%)	0.4	0.5	1.5	0.9	0.9
RES / MGS (months)	..	6.1	2.0	4.9	5.4
Short-term / EDT (%)	3.5	6.5	9.6	3.6	3.5
Concessional / EDT (%)	75.5	74.1	56.3	52.4	52.4
Multilateral / EDT (%)	18.0	24.7	29.5	38.1	38.4

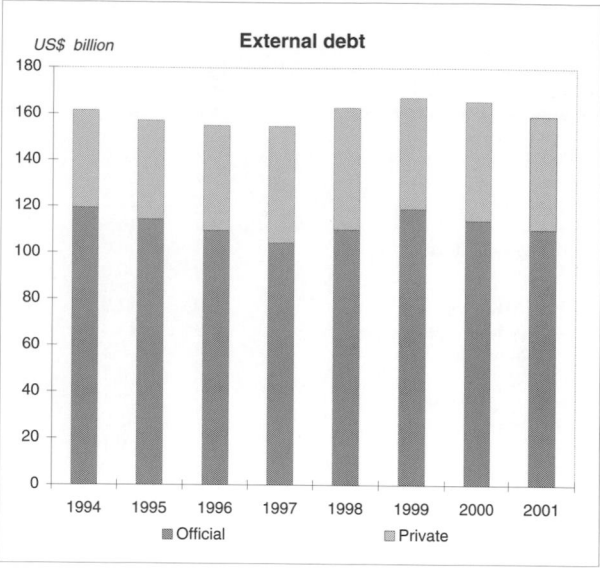

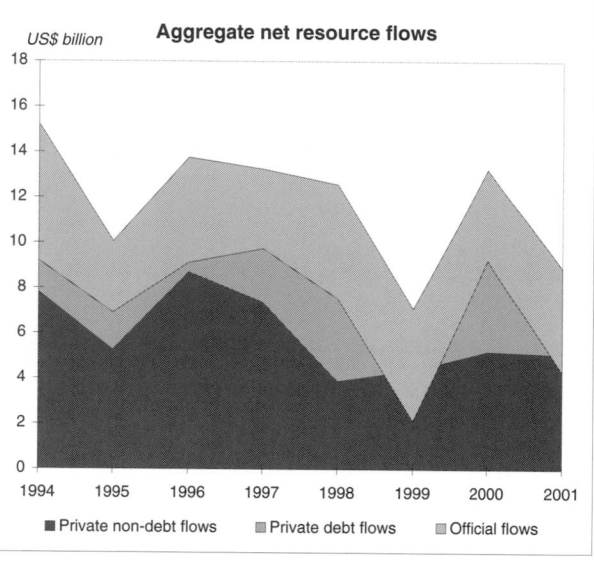

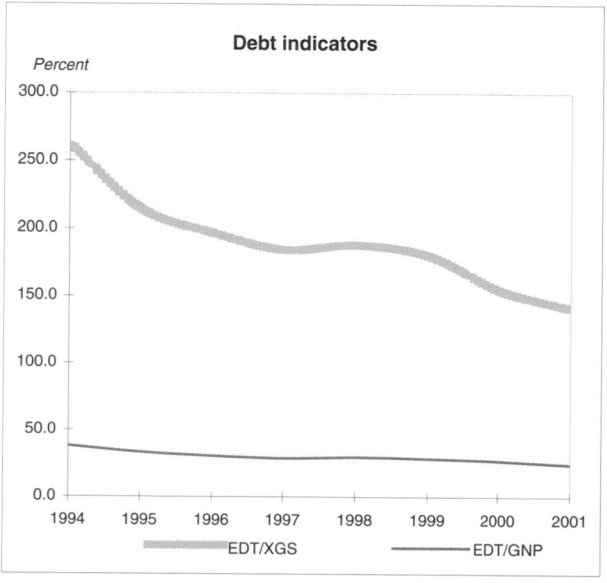

SOUTH ASIA

(US$ billion)

	1970	1980	1990	2000	2001
LONG-TERM DEBT					
DEBT OUTSTANDING (LDOD)	**11.7**	**32.9**	**112.6**	**157.7**	**151.9**
Public and publicly guaranteed	**11.6**	**32.5**	**110.8**	**146.4**	**140.6**
Official creditors	10.9	30.1	86.5	112.2	108.3
Multilateral	2.2	9.3	38.2	63.0	61.2
Bilateral	8.7	20.8	48.3	49.1	47.1
Private creditors	0.7	2.4	24.3	34.2	32.2
Bonds	0.0	0.0	2.6	11.3	11.0
Private nonguaranteed	0.1	0.4	1.7	11.4	11.4
Bonds	0.0	0.0	0.0	2.9	2.5
DISBURSEMENTS	**1.6**	**4.6**	**10.3**	**14.2**	**9.2**
Public and publicly guaranteed	**1.5**	**4.3**	**10.0**	**13.7**	**8.3**
Official creditors	1.4	3.3	6.9	7.1	6.7
Multilateral	0.2	1.4	4.4	4.3	4.1
Bilateral	1.2	1.9	2.5	2.8	2.6
Private creditors	0.1	1.0	3.1	6.5	1.6
Bonds	0.0	0.0	0.4	5.5	0.0
Private nonguaranteed	**0.0**	**0.3**	**0.3**	**0.5**	**0.9**
Bonds	0.0	0.0	0.0	0.0	0.1
PRINCIPAL REPAYMENTS	**0.5**	**1.2**	**4.1**	**8.4**	**7.8**
Public and publicly guaranteed	**0.5**	**1.1**	**3.8**	**7.7**	**6.9**
Official creditors	0.4	0.9	2.4	5.4	4.5
Multilateral	0.1	0.1	1.0	2.9	2.4
Bilateral	0.3	0.8	1.4	2.5	2.1
Private creditors	0.1	0.2	1.4	2.3	2.4
Bonds	0.0	0.0	0.3	0.6	0.3
Private nonguaranteed	**0.0**	**0.1**	**0.4**	**0.7**	**0.9**
Bonds	0.0	0.0	0.0	0.0	0.4
NET FLOWS ON DEBT	**1.0**	**3.4**	**6.1**	**5.8**	**1.4**
Public and publicly guaranteed	**1.0**	**3.2**	**6.2**	**6.0**	**1.4**
Official creditors	1.0	2.3	4.5	1.8	2.2
Multilateral	0.1	1.3	3.4	1.5	1.8
Bilateral	0.9	1.1	1.2	0.3	0.4
Private creditors	0.0	0.9	1.7	4.2	-0.8
Bonds	0.0	0.0	0.1	4.9	-0.3
Private nonguaranteed	**0.0**	**0.2**	**-0.1**	**-0.2**	**0.0**
Bonds	0.0	0.0	0.0	0.0	-0.3
CURRENCY COMPOSITION OF LONG-TERM DEBT (PERCENT)					
Deutsche mark	9.3	8.4	5.9	3.7	..
French franc	1.4	2.3	1.6	1.3	..
Japanese yen	5.3	8.9	11.9	14.9	..
Pound sterling	21.7	17.8	4.8	2.5	..
U.S. dollars	41.1	41.3	51.6	55.4	..
Multiple currency	9.2	7.4	13.7	15.0	..
All other currencies	11.5	10.0	4.5	2.0	..
DEBT STOCK-FLOW RECONCILIATION					
Total change in debt stocks	..	..	13.1	-1.6	..
Net flows on debt	0.8	5.8	8.4	4.3	0.9
Net change in interest arrears	..	..	0.0	0.0	..
Interest capitalized	..	..	0.0	0.2	..
Debt forgiveness or reduction	..	..	0.0	0.0	..
Cross-currency valuation	..	..	1.6	-5.7	..
Residual	..	..	3.1	-0.5	..
AVERAGE TERMS OF NEW COMMITMENTS					
ALL CREDITORS					
Interest (%)	2.5	4.7	4.6	6.6	..
Maturity (years)	32.6	32.6	24.7	13.6	..
Grant element (%)	45.1	27.1	34.2	20.6	..
Official creditors					
Interest (%)	2.2	2.2	3.6	5.2	..
Maturity (years)	34.9	39.2	29.0	23.1	..
Grant element (%)	48.7	34.5	40.8	35.0	..
Private creditors					
Interest (%)	5.9	12.8	6.7	7.7	..
Maturity (years)	11.7	10.9	15.3	5.4	..
Grant element (%)	12.5	2.6	19.7	8.2	..
Memo:					
Commitments	2.1	8.4	13.5	10.8	..
Official creditors	1.9	6.5	9.3	5.0	..
Private creditors	0.2	2.0	4.2	5.8	..

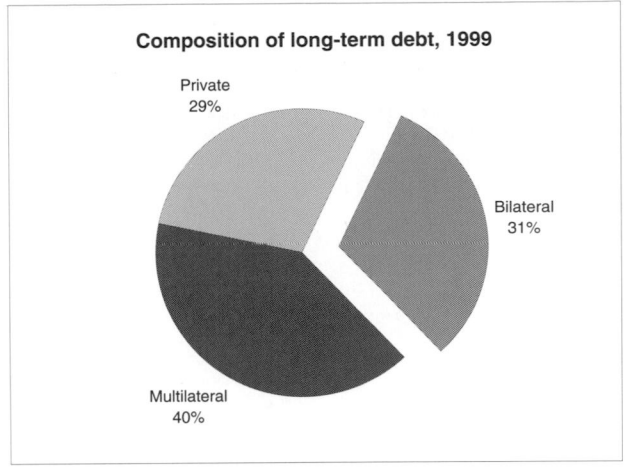

Composition of long-term debt, 1999

Private 29%
Bilateral 31%
Multilateral 40%

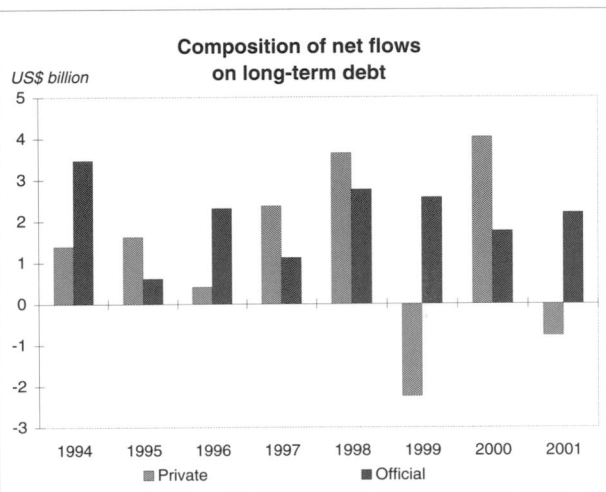

Composition of net flows on long-term debt

■ Private ■ Official

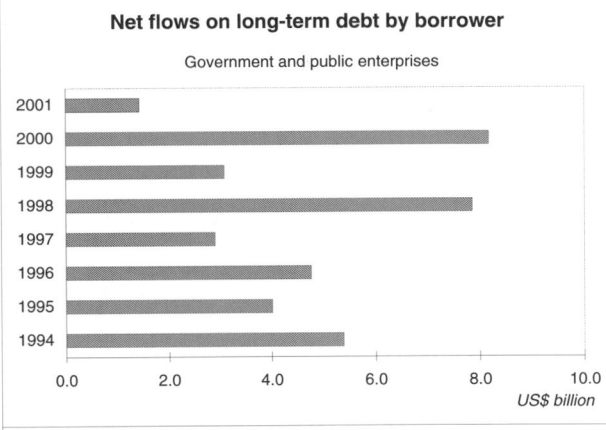

Net flows on long-term debt by borrower

Government and public enterprises

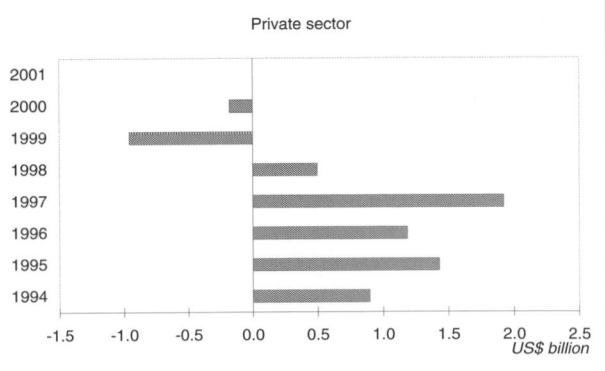

Private sector

SUB-SAHARAN AFRICA

(US$ billion)

	1970	1980	1990	2000	2001
SUMMARY DEBT DATA					
TOTAL DEBT STOCKS (EDT)	**6.9**	**60.9**	**176.9**	**215.8**	**208.9**
Long-term debt (LDOD)	**6.1**	**46.7**	**149.4**	**175.8**	**168.7**
Public and publicly guaranteed	5.8	42.1	144.1	163.8	156.5
Private nonguaranteed	0.3	4.6	5.3	12.0	12.3
Use of IMF credit	**0.1**	**3.0**	**6.6**	**6.7**	**6.3**
Short-term debt	**0.8**	**11.2**	**20.9**	**33.3**	**33.8**
of which interest arrears on LDOD	0.0	1.7	9.3	14.3	14.2
Memo:					
IBRD	0.6	2.5	9.2	3.5	2.9
IDA	0.2	2.6	15.8	33.6	34.5
TOTAL FLOWS ON DEBT					
Disbursements	**1.3**	**11.8**	**10.4**	**8.7**	**10.9**
Long-term debt	1.2	10.6	9.7	8.2	10.4
Public and publicly guaranteed	1.1	9.4	9.1	7.3	8.4
Private nonguaranteed	0.1	1.2	0.6	0.8	1.9
IMF purchases	**0.0**	**1.2**	**0.7**	**0.5**	**0.6**
Memo:					
IBRD	0.1	0.4	0.8	0.1	0.1
IDA	0.1	0.4	2.0	2.2	2.4
Principal repayments	**0.5**	**3.2**	**5.6**	**8.1**	**9.8**
Long-term debt	0.4	2.8	4.6	7.5	9.0
Public and publicly guaranteed	0.3	2.2	4.2	6.2	7.6
Private nonguaranteed	0.1	0.6	0.5	1.4	1.4
IMF repurchases	**0.1**	**0.4**	**1.0**	**0.5**	**0.8**
Memo:					
IBRD	0.0	0.1	0.7	0.6	0.5
IDA	0.0	0.0	0.1	0.3	0.3
Net flows on debt	**0.9**	**10.1**	**7.1**	**-0.5**	**1.7**
of which short-term debt	0.1	1.5	2.3	-1.1	0.5
Interest payments (INT)	**0.2**	**3.5**	**5.3**	**4.3**	**4.7**
Long-term debt	0.2	2.4	4.4	3.1	3.8
Net transfers on debt	**0.7**	**6.6**	**1.7**	**-4.8**	**-3.1**
Total debt service (TDS)	**0.6**	**6.7**	**10.9**	**12.3**	**14.5**
AGGREGATE NET RESOURCE FLOWS AND NET TRANSFERS (LONG-TERM)					
NET RESOURCE FLOWS	**1.7**	**11.4**	**17.9**	**18.5**	**25.5**
Net flow of long-term debt (ex. IMF)	0.9	7.8	5.1	0.6	1.3
Foreign direct investment (net)	0.4	0.0	0.8	6.7	13.6
Portfolio equity flows	0.0	0.0	0.0	0.9	0.7
Grants (excluding technical coop.)	0.4	3.6	12.0	10.3	9.9
NET TRANSFERS	**0.7**	**6.1**	**11.8**	**10.6**	**15.8**
Interest on long-term debt	0.2	2.4	4.4	3.1	3.8
Profit remittances on FDI	0.7	2.9	1.7	4.8	5.9
MAJOR ECONOMIC INDICATORS					
Gross national income (GNI)	60.6	258.8	280.9	302.6	294.4
Exports of goods & services (XGS)	..	92.7	84.9	121.3	116.8
of which workers' remittances	..	0.8	0.8	0.7	1.1
Imports of goods & services (MGS)	..	93.5	91.7	127.8	128.8
International reserves (RES)	3.1	22.9	15.4	26.3	26.6
Current account balance	..	0.1	-1.8	1.4	-0.6
DEBT INDICATORS					
EDT / XGS (%)	..	65.7	208.3	177.9	178.8
EDT / GNI (%)	11.4	23.5	63.0	71.3	70.9
TDS / XGS (%)	..	7.2	12.8	10.2	12.4
INT / XGS (%)	..	3.8	6.3	3.5	4.1
INT / GNI (%)	0.3	1.4	1.9	1.4	1.6
RES / MGS (months)	..	3.0	2.0	2.5	2.5
Short-term / EDT (%)	10.9	18.4	11.8	15.4	16.2
Concessional / EDT (%)	46.3	27.0	33.1	38.7	38.8
Multilateral / EDT (%)	12.6	12.5	21.6	25.3	25.5

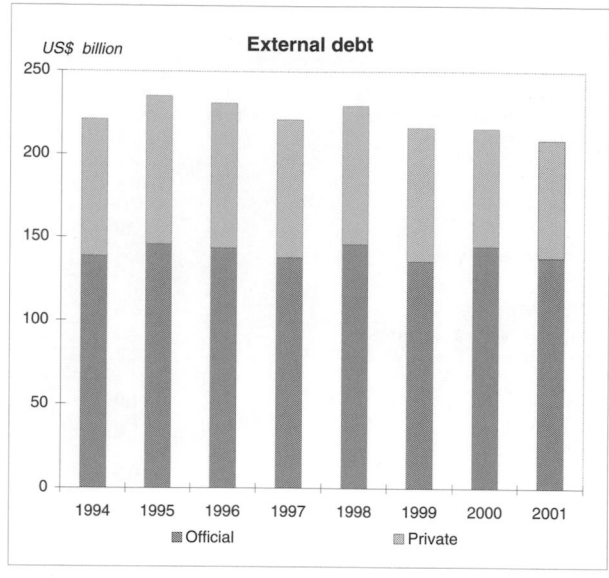

External debt

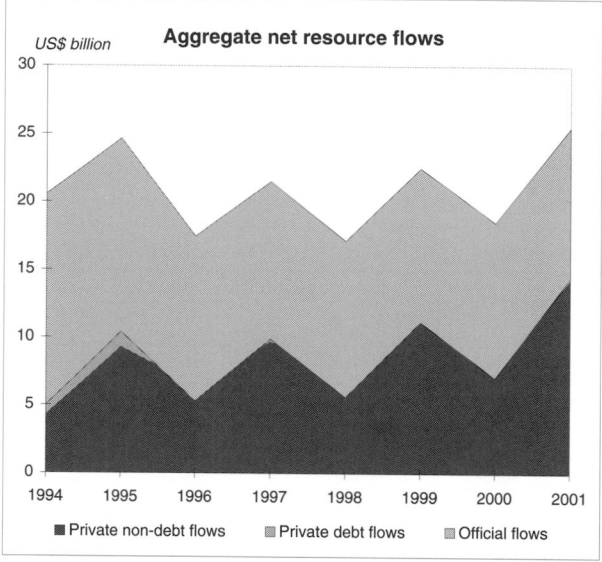

Aggregate net resource flows

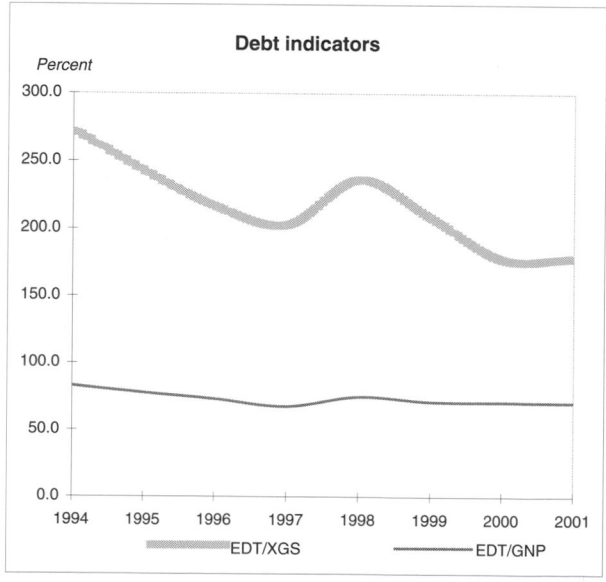

Debt indicators

SUB-SAHARAN AFRICA

(US$ billion)

	1970	1980	1990	2000	2001
LONG-TERM DEBT					
DEBT OUTSTANDING (LDOD)	**6.1**	**46.7**	**149.4**	**175.8**	**168.7**
Public and publicly guaranteed	**5.8**	**42.1**	**144.1**	**163.8**	**156.5**
Official creditors	4.2	25.7	108.7	138.0	131.5
Multilateral	0.9	7.6	38.2	54.5	53.3
Bilateral	3.3	18.1	70.6	83.5	78.2
Private creditors	1.6	16.3	35.4	25.8	24.9
Bonds	0.4	0.6	0.3	9.1	9.1
Private nonguaranteed	0.3	4.6	5.3	12.0	12.3
Bonds	0.0	0.0	0.0	2.0	3.2
DISBURSEMENTS	**1.2**	**10.6**	**9.7**	**8.2**	**10.4**
Public and publicly guaranteed	**1.1**	**9.4**	**9.1**	**7.3**	**8.4**
Official creditors	0.7	4.2	7.2	3.8	4.6
Multilateral	0.2	1.7	4.5	3.1	3.7
Bilateral	0.5	2.6	2.6	0.7	0.9
Private creditors	0.5	5.1	1.9	3.5	3.9
Bonds	0.0	0.1	0.0	0.8	0.9
Private nonguaranteed	**0.1**	**1.2**	**0.6**	**0.8**	**1.9**
Bonds	0.0	0.0	0.0	0.7	1.3
PRINCIPAL REPAYMENTS	**0.4**	**2.8**	**4.6**	**7.5**	**9.0**
Public and publicly guaranteed	**0.3**	**2.2**	**4.2**	**6.2**	**7.6**
Official creditors	0.2	0.7	2.6	2.7	3.4
Multilateral	0.0	0.2	1.3	1.7	1.9
Bilateral	0.1	0.5	1.2	1.0	1.5
Private creditors	0.2	1.5	1.6	3.5	4.2
Bonds	0.0	0.0	0.0	0.5	1.0
Private nonguaranteed	**0.1**	**0.6**	**0.5**	**1.4**	**1.4**
Bonds	0.0	0.0	0.0	0.0	0.0
NET FLOWS ON DEBT	**0.9**	**7.8**	**5.1**	**0.6**	**1.3**
Public and publicly guaranteed	**0.8**	**7.2**	**4.9**	**1.1**	**0.8**
Official creditors	0.5	3.6	4.6	1.1	1.2
Multilateral	0.1	1.5	3.2	1.4	1.8
Bilateral	0.4	2.1	1.4	-0.3	-0.6
Private creditors	0.3	3.6	0.3	0.0	-0.4
Bonds	0.0	0.0	0.0	0.3	-0.1
Private nonguaranteed	**0.0**	**0.6**	**0.2**	**-0.5**	**0.6**
Bonds	0.0	0.0	0.0	0.7	1.2
CURRENCY COMPOSITION OF LONG-TERM DEBT (PERCENT)					
Deutsche mark	6.6	7.0	6.4	2.6	..
French franc	14.4	13.8	14.1	7.6	..
Japanese yen	0.1	5.4	4.0	4.2	..
Pound sterling	22.5	5.7	5.4	2.0	..
U.S. dollars	21.4	35.4	36.5	61.6	..
Multiple currency	11.2	8.8	10.4	7.0	..
All other currencies	23.4	22.2	20.5	12.5	..
DEBT STOCK-FLOW RECONCILIATION					
Total change in debt stocks	..	..	19.8	-0.5	..
Net flows on debt	0.9	10.1	7.1	-0.5	1.7
Net change in interest arrears	..	..	2.2	-5.3	..
Interest capitalized	..	..	1.7	9.0	..
Debt forgiveness or reduction	..	..	-2.9	-0.7	..
Cross-currency valuation	..	..	7.7	-6.6	..
Residual	..	..	3.9	3.5	..
AVERAGE TERMS OF NEW COMMITMENTS					
ALL CREDITORS					
Interest (%)	3.7	7.0	4.3	3.2	..
Maturity (years)	23.9	17.3	32.6	24.8	..
Grant element (%)	47.5	21.8	43.5	48.7	..
Official creditors					
Interest (%)	2.0	4.1	3.5	0.9	..
Maturity (years)	32.0	25.1	37.1	39.1	..
Grant element (%)	67.4	42.8	51.2	77.5	..
Private creditors					
Interest (%)	6.6	10.0	8.1	5.9	..
Maturity (years)	10.2	9.4	11.7	8.1	..
Grant element (%)	13.3	0.2	7.7	15.0	..
Memo:					
Commitments	1.9	13.3	11.5	6.0	..
Official creditors	1.2	6.7	9.5	3.2	..
Private creditors	0.7	6.6	2.0	2.8	..

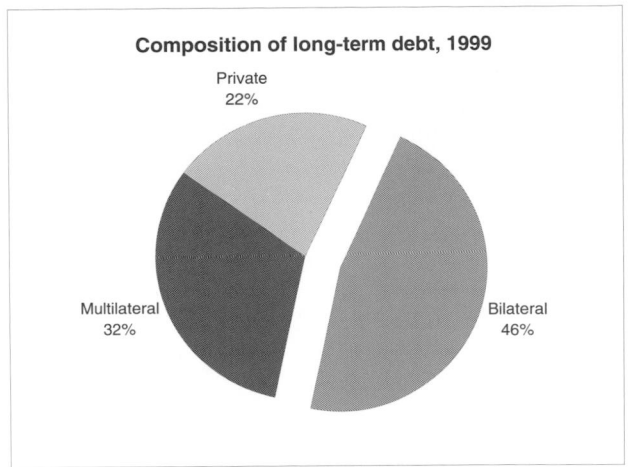

Composition of long-term debt, 1999

- Private 22%
- Multilateral 32%
- Bilateral 46%

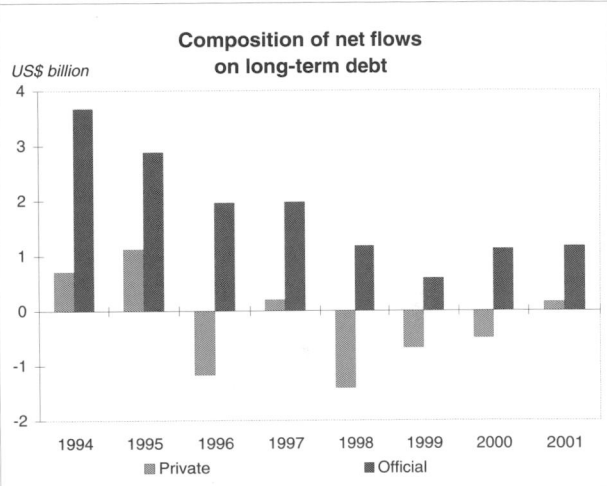

Composition of net flows on long-term debt

■ Private ■ Official

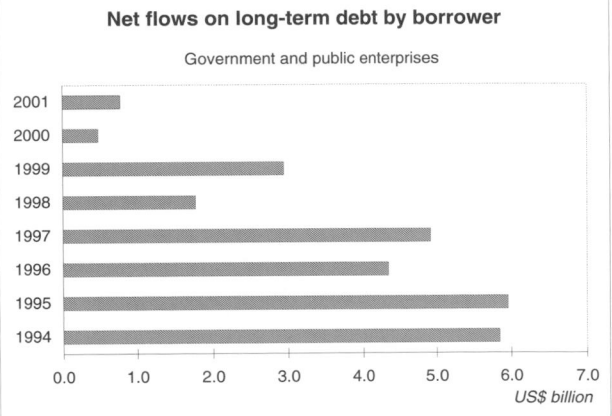

Net flows on long-term debt by borrower

Government and public enterprises

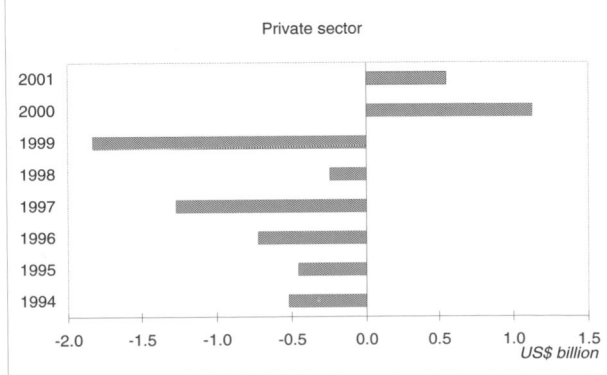

Private sector

SEVERELY INDEBTED LOW-INCOME COUNTRIES

(US$ billion)

	1970	1980	1990	1999	2000
SUMMARY DEBT DATA					
TOTAL DEBT STOCKS (EDT)	**13.1**	**84.3**	**252.9**	**353.1**	**342.6**
Long-term debt (LDOD)	**11.7**	**67.8**	**213.2**	**286.6**	**279.7**
Public and publicly guaranteed	11.0	60.5	198.8	233.5	235.1
Private nonguaranteed	0.6	7.2	14.3	53.1	44.7
Use of IMF credit	**0.3**	**3.0**	**5.7**	**17.4**	**17.6**
Short-term debt	**1.2**	**13.5**	**34.0**	**49.0**	**45.2**
of which interest arrears on LDOD	0.0	1.7	10.6	23.9	19.5
Memo:					
IBRD	0.8	3.4	18.8	18.1	17.6
IDA	0.4	3.4	13.6	27.4	27.7
TOTAL FLOWS ON DEBT					
Disbursements	**2.3**	**14.7**	**19.5**	**16.5**	**12.7**
Long-term debt	2.3	13.5	19.3	14.1	11.0
Public and publicly guaranteed	2.0	11.7	13.9	11.5	8.2
Private nonguaranteed	0.3	1.8	5.4	2.6	2.9
IMF purchases	**0.1**	**1.2**	**0.3**	**2.4**	**1.7**
Memo:					
IBRD	0.1	0.7	2.1	2.0	1.2
IDA	0.1	0.4	1.3	1.6	1.7
Principal repayments	**0.7**	**4.5**	**10.9**	**17.5**	**16.8**
Long-term debt	0.6	4.0	10.1	17.0	16.3
Public and publicly guaranteed	0.5	2.8	8.5	9.6	7.9
Private nonguaranteed	0.1	1.2	1.6	7.4	8.3
IMF repurchases	**0.1**	**0.5**	**0.8**	**0.5**	**0.6**
Memo:					
IBRD	0.0	0.1	1.1	1.5	1.4
IDA	0.0	0.0	0.1	0.2	0.3
Net flows on debt	**1.7**	**12.9**	**13.8**	**-3.0**	**-3.5**
of which short-term debt	0.1	2.7	5.2	-2.0	0.6
Interest payments (INT)	**0.3**	**4.8**	**9.1**	**9.9**	**10.9**
Long-term debt	0.3	3.5	7.6	7.9	8.7
Net transfers on debt	**1.4**	**8.1**	**4.7**	**-12.8**	**-14.4**
Total debt service (TDS)	**1.0**	**9.3**	**20.0**	**27.3**	**27.7**
AGGREGATE NET RESOURCE FLOWS AND NET TRANSFERS (LONG-TERM)					
NET RESOURCE FLOWS	**2.3**	**12.8**	**19.7**	**9.4**	**2.9**
Net flow of long-term debt (ex. IMF)	1.7	9.5	9.2	-2.9	-5.2
Foreign direct investment (net)	0.1	0.0	2.0	3.4	0.4
Portfolio equity flows	0.0	0.0	0.3	1.3	0.4
Grants (excluding technical coop.)	0.5	3.4	8.2	7.7	7.3
NET TRANSFERS	**1.2**	**3.9**	**9.0**	**-3.5**	**-10.4**
Interest on long-term debt	0.3	3.5	7.6	7.9	8.7
Profit remittances on FDI	0.8	5.5	3.0	4.9	4.6
MAJOR ECONOMIC INDICATORS					
Gross national income (GNI)	59.0	261.8	287.2	319.4	341.5
Exports of goods & services (XGS)	..	..	76.4	114.2	144.0
of which workers' remittances	..	2.2	2.4	3.9	2.6
Imports of goods & services (MGS)	..	..	87.2	125.0	142.8
International reserves (RES)	2.0	22.5	16.9	35.3	38.3
Current account balance	..	-2.7	-7.4	-4.2	8.5
DEBT INDICATORS					
EDT / XGS (%)	..	..	331.0	309.2	237.9
EDT / GNI (%)	22.2	32.2	88.1	110.5	100.3
TDS / XGS (%)	..	..	26.2	23.9	19.3
INT / XGS (%)	..	..	11.9	8.6	7.6
INT / GNI (%)	0.5	1.8	3.2	3.1	3.2
RES / MGS (months)	..	..	2.3	3.4	3.2
Short-term / EDT (%)	8.9	16.0	13.5	13.9	13.2
Concessional / EDT (%)	57.1	36.1	34.3	33.8	33.7
Multilateral / EDT (%)	10.1	11.5	19.8	21.4	21.5

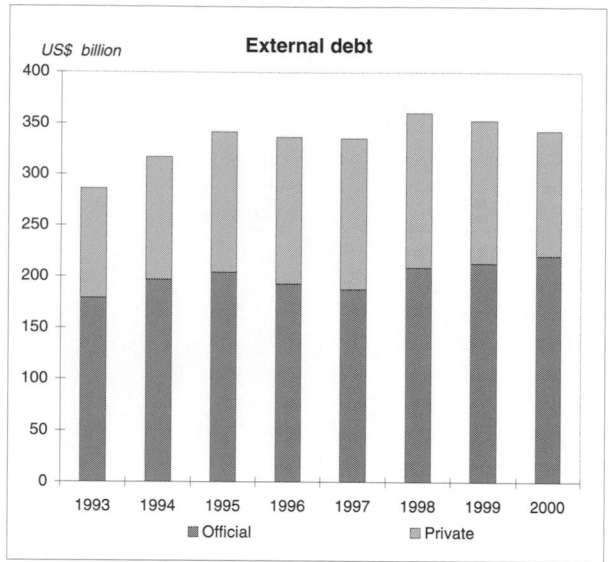

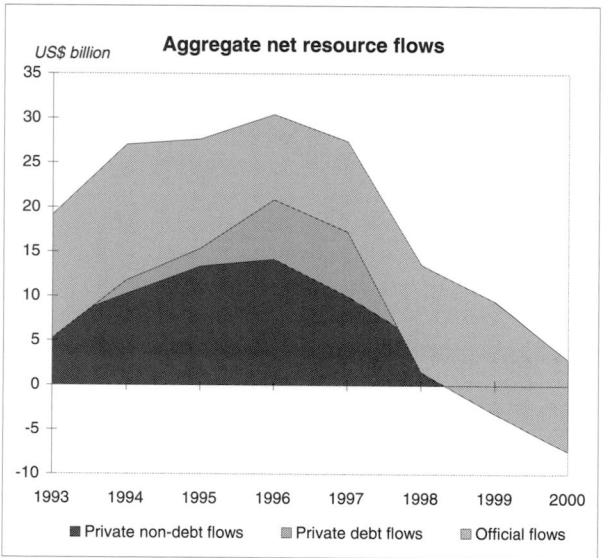

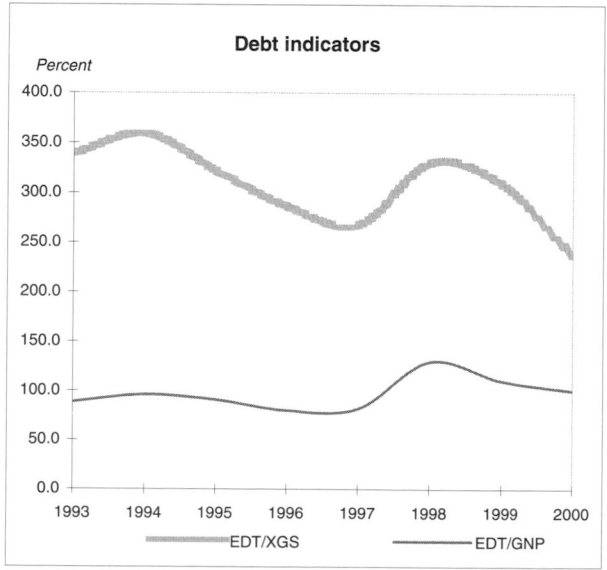

SEVERELY INDEBTED LOW-INCOME COUNTRIES

(US$ billion)

	1970	1980	1990	1999	2000
LONG-TERM DEBT					
DEBT OUTSTANDING (LDOD)	**11.7**	**67.8**	**213.2**	**286.6**	**279.7**
Public and publicly guaranteed	**11.0**	**60.5**	**198.8**	**233.5**	**235.1**
Official creditors	9.2	41.0	150.4	195.1	202.5
Multilateral	1.3	9.7	50.0	75.6	73.8
Bilateral	7.9	31.3	100.4	119.5	128.7
Private creditors	1.8	19.5	48.4	38.3	32.6
Bonds	0.1	0.2	0.7	6.0	6.0
Private nonguaranteed	**0.6**	**7.2**	**14.3**	**53.1**	**44.7**
Bonds	0.0	0.0	0.1	8.5	6.4
DISBURSEMENTS	**2.3**	**13.5**	**19.3**	**14.1**	**11.0**
Public and publicly guaranteed	**2.0**	**11.7**	**13.9**	**11.5**	**8.2**
Official creditors	1.4	5.7	11.3	10.2	7.3
Multilateral	0.2	1.9	6.0	6.1	4.9
Bilateral	1.2	3.8	5.3	4.1	2.4
Private creditors	0.6	6.0	2.6	1.3	0.8
Bonds	0.0	0.0	0.0	0.0	0.0
Private nonguaranteed	**0.3**	**1.8**	**5.4**	**2.6**	**2.9**
Bonds	0.0	0.0	0.1	0.0	0.4
PRINCIPAL REPAYMENTS	**0.6**	**4.0**	**10.1**	**17.0**	**16.3**
Public and publicly guaranteed	**0.5**	**2.8**	**8.5**	**9.6**	**7.9**
Official creditors	0.3	1.1	4.2	5.2	4.3
Multilateral	0.0	0.3	1.9	2.9	3.1
Bilateral	0.2	0.9	2.3	2.3	1.2
Private creditors	0.3	1.7	4.3	4.4	3.6
Bonds	0.0	0.0	0.1	0.3	0.0
Private nonguaranteed	**0.1**	**1.2**	**1.6**	**7.4**	**8.3**
Bonds	0.0	0.0	0.0	1.2	2.4
NET FLOWS ON DEBT	**1.7**	**9.5**	**9.2**	**-2.9**	**-5.2**
Public and publicly guaranteed	**1.5**	**8.9**	**5.4**	**1.9**	**0.2**
Official creditors	1.1	4.6	7.1	5.0	3.0
Multilateral	0.2	1.7	4.1	3.1	1.9
Bilateral	1.0	2.9	3.1	1.9	1.2
Private creditors	0.4	4.3	-1.8	-3.1	-2.8
Bonds	0.0	0.0	-0.1	-0.3	0.0
Private nonguaranteed	**0.2**	**0.6**	**3.8**	**-4.8**	**-5.5**
Bonds	0.0	0.0	0.1	-1.2	-2.1
CURRENCY COMPOSITION OF LONG-TERM DEBT (PERCENT)					
Deutsche mark	6.8	7.3	6.4	4.2	2.9
French franc	8.6	8.4	8.8	6.1	4.8
Japanese yen	4.3	10.7	13.0	17.7	14.5
Pound sterling	9.7	2.9	3.6	2.7	1.4
U.S. dollars	38.9	40.8	33.3	45.7	54.5
Multiple currency	9.8	8.4	14.9	9.5	8.8
All other currencies	21.5	18.6	15.4	9.7	8.8
DEBT STOCK-FLOW RECONCILIATION					
Total change in debt stocks	..	..	29.8	-7.2	-10.4
Net flows on debt	1.7	12.9	13.8	-3.0	-3.5
Net change in interest arrears	..	..	2.5	2.8	-4.4
Interest capitalized	..	..	1.5	1.1	9.1
Debt forgiveness or reduction	..	..	-1.4	-4.7	-0.5
Cross-currency valuation	..	..	11.0	-2.0	-11.3
Residual	..	..	2.3	-1.5	0.2
AVERAGE TERMS OF NEW COMMITMENTS					
ALL CREDITORS					
Interest (%)	3.3	7.2	5.3	3.6	3.2
Maturity (years)	27.4	18.6	22.4	19.8	25.1
Grant element (%)	52.3	22.0	34.5	42.1	50.9
Official creditors					
Interest (%)	2.2	4.2	4.7	3.2	2.5
Maturity (years)	33.5	26.7	24.5	21.4	30.2
Grant element (%)	66.0	44.3	39.7	45.9	61.0
Private creditors					
Interest (%)	6.5	10.5	8.0	7.1	5.9
Maturity (years)	10.1	9.8	12.8	6.1	6.8
Grant element (%)	13.9	-2.5	10.5	9.8	14.7
Memo:					
Commitments	3.3	16.8	18.0	9.1	5.5
Official creditors	2.4	8.8	14.8	8.2	4.3
Private creditors	0.9	8.0	3.2	1.0	1.2

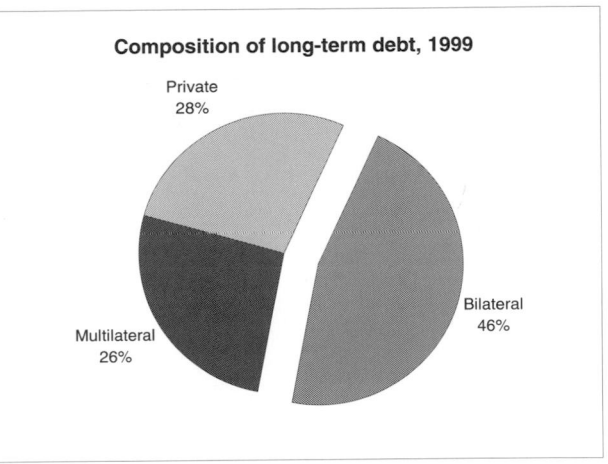

Composition of long-term debt, 1999

Private 28%
Multilateral 26%
Bilateral 46%

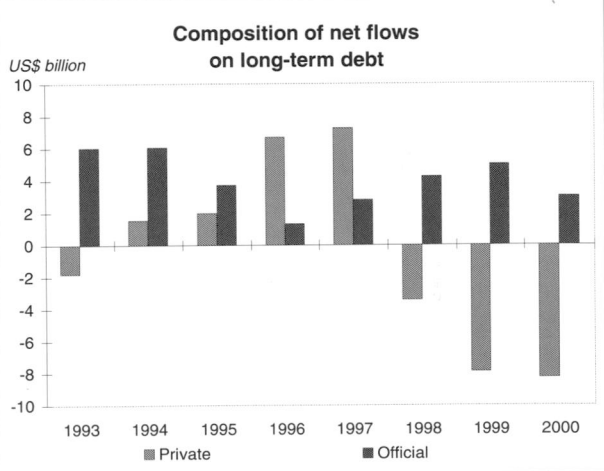

Composition of net flows on long-term debt

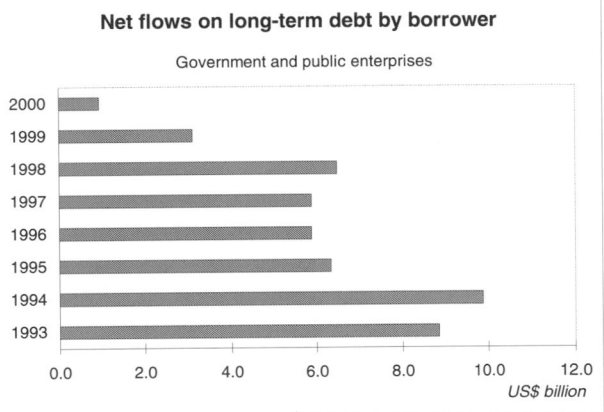

Net flows on long-term debt by borrower

Government and public enterprises

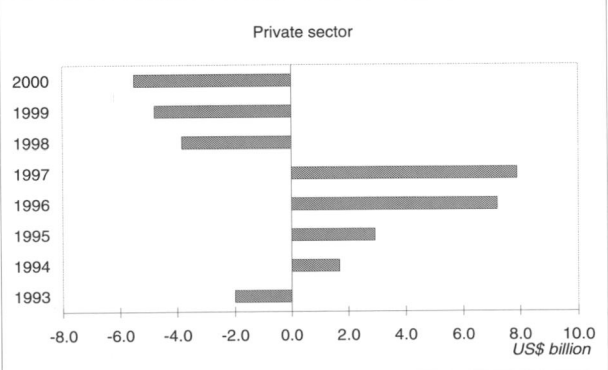

Private sector

SEVERELY INDEBTED MIDDLE-INCOME COUNTRIES

(US$ billion)

	1970	1980	1990	1999	2000
SUMMARY DEBT DATA					
TOTAL DEBT STOCKS (EDT)	**15.7**	**140.5**	**298.7**	**512.7**	**502.3**
Long-term debt (LDOD)	**13.6**	**109.6**	**234.8**	**412.8**	**411.7**
Public and publicly guaranteed	6.8	84.6	225.8	267.4	267.2
Private nonguaranteed	6.8	24.9	9.0	145.4	144.5
Use of IMF credit	**0.0**	**0.6**	**6.3**	**14.8**	**8.2**
Short-term debt	**2.1**	**30.4**	**57.7**	**85.1**	**82.5**
of which interest arrears on LDOD	0.0	0.0	22.4	3.1	3.0
Memo:					
IBRD	0.6	3.2	14.2	19.4	20.5
IDA	0.0	0.2	0.2	0.3	0.3
TOTAL FLOWS ON DEBT					
Disbursements	**3.3**	**21.6**	**9.8**	**75.6**	**74.0**
Long-term debt	3.2	21.4	9.2	69.4	71.7
Public and publicly guaranteed	1.7	16.0	8.3	32.9	34.1
Private nonguaranteed	1.6	5.4	0.9	36.5	37.6
IMF purchases	**0.0**	**0.2**	**0.6**	**6.2**	**2.3**
Memo:					
IBRD	0.1	0.7	1.4	3.7	3.1
IDA	0.0	0.0	0.1	0.0	0.0
Principal repayments	**1.7**	**11.1**	**14.4**	**73.7**	**68.1**
Long-term debt	1.6	10.9	12.7	70.6	59.9
Public and publicly guaranteed	0.8	6.9	11.6	27.1	29.0
Private nonguaranteed	0.9	4.0	1.1	43.4	30.9
IMF repurchases	**0.1**	**0.2**	**1.8**	**3.1**	**8.2**
Memo:					
IBRD	0.0	0.2	1.6	1.7	1.7
IDA	0.0	0.0	0.0	0.0	0.0
Net flows on debt	**1.5**	**20.4**	**-0.3**	**-1.1**	**4.2**
of which short-term debt	0.0	10.0	4.3	-3.0	-1.7
Interest payments (INT)	**0.7**	**12.7**	**8.0**	**29.6**	**30.6**
Long-term debt	0.7	9.4	6.2	24.9	26.3
Net transfers on debt	**0.8**	**7.8**	**-8.3**	**-30.7**	**-26.4**
Total debt service (TDS)	**2.5**	**23.8**	**22.5**	**103.3**	**98.6**

AGGREGATE NET RESOURCE FLOWS AND NET TRANSFERS (LONG-TERM)					
NET RESOURCE FLOWS	**2.2**	**16.6**	**1.8**	**58.5**	**65.7**
Net flow of long-term debt (ex. IMF)	1.6	10.5	-3.5	-1.2	11.8
Foreign direct investment (net)	0.5	2.8	3.2	55.8	46.7
Portfolio equity flows	0.0	0.0	0.0	2.7	5.7
Grants (excluding technical coop.)	0.1	3.4	2.1	1.3	1.5
NET TRANSFERS	**0.4**	**5.0**	**-7.1**	**26.1**	**30.2**
Interest on long-term debt	0.7	9.4	6.2	24.9	26.3
Profit remittances on FDI	1.1	2.2	2.8	7.6	9.3

MAJOR ECONOMIC INDICATORS					
Gross national income (GNI)	85.6	393.5	675.1	923.2	985.9
Exports of goods & services (XGS)	..	50.5	73.0	124.5	141.8
of which workers' remittances	..	0.7	1.2	4.6	5.0
Imports of goods & services (MGS)	..	72.2	76.3	167.5	180.2
International reserves (RES)	3.1	22.9	19.8	75.9	72.0
Current account balance	..	-17.6	0.5	-37.4	-33.7

DEBT INDICATORS					
EDT / XGS (%)	..	278.4	409.3	412.0	354.3
EDT / GNI (%)	18.3	35.7	44.3	55.5	51.0
TDS / XGS (%)	..	47.2	30.8	83.0	69.6
INT / XGS (%)	..	25.1	11.0	23.8	21.6
INT / GNI (%)	0.9	3.2	1.2	3.2	3.1
RES / MGS (months)	..	3.8	3.1	5.4	4.8
Short-term / EDT (%)	13.1	21.6	19.3	16.6	16.4
Concessional / EDT (%)	12.1	14.8	16.2	6.5	6.2
Multilateral / EDT (%)	5.7	4.1	7.8	9.0	9.4

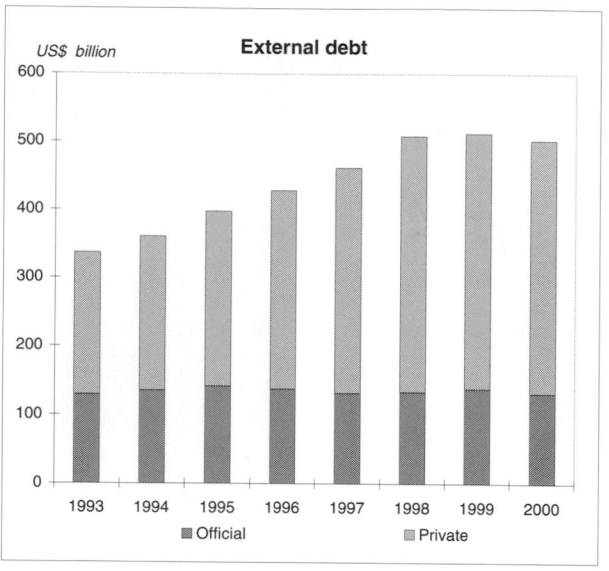

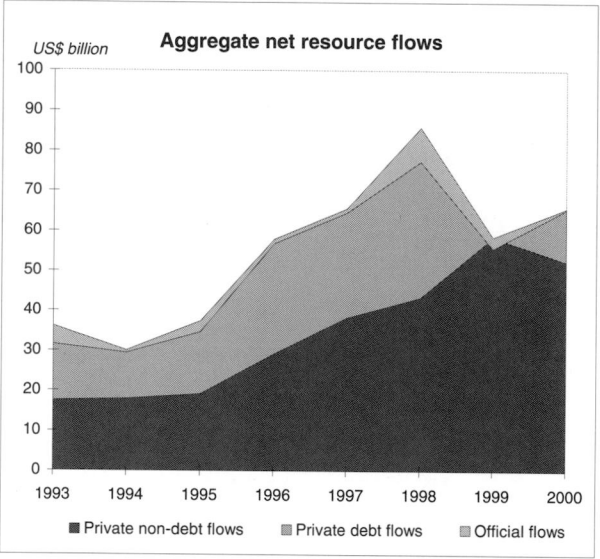

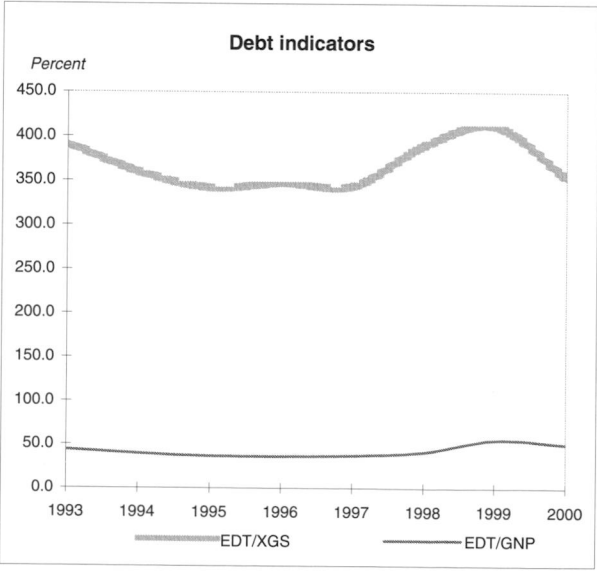

SEVERELY INDEBTED MIDDLE-INCOME COUNTRIES

(US$ billion)

	1970	1980	1990	1999	2000
LONG-TERM DEBT					
DEBT OUTSTANDING (LDOD)	**13.6**	**109.6**	**234.8**	**412.8**	**411.7**
Public and publicly guaranteed	**6.8**	**84.6**	**225.8**	**267.4**	**267.2**
Official creditors	3.2	34.0	104.3	122.8	122.9
Multilateral	0.9	5.7	23.4	46.2	47.0
Bilateral	2.3	28.3	80.9	76.6	76.0
Private creditors	3.5	50.6	121.5	144.6	144.3
Bonds	0.4	4.1	14.1	125.6	125.5
Private nonguaranteed	**6.8**	**24.9**	**9.0**	**145.4**	**144.5**
Bonds	0.0	0.0	0.0	29.1	28.1
DISBURSEMENTS	**3.2**	**21.4**	**9.2**	**69.4**	**71.7**
Public and publicly guaranteed	**1.7**	**16.0**	**8.3**	**32.9**	**34.1**
Official creditors	0.5	4.6	4.5	10.7	9.5
Multilateral	0.2	1.2	2.4	9.1	7.8
Bilateral	0.3	3.4	2.1	1.6	1.6
Private creditors	1.1	11.4	3.8	22.2	24.7
Bonds	0.1	0.5	0.2	21.1	21.1
Private nonguaranteed	**1.6**	**5.4**	**0.9**	**36.5**	**37.6**
Bonds	0.0	0.0	0.0	2.7	4.3
PRINCIPAL REPAYMENTS	**1.6**	**10.9**	**12.7**	**70.6**	**59.9**
Public and publicly guaranteed	**0.8**	**6.9**	**11.6**	**27.1**	**29.0**
Official creditors	0.2	1.3	4.9	9.0	10.8
Multilateral	0.1	0.3	2.3	4.1	6.2
Bilateral	0.2	1.0	2.6	4.9	4.6
Private creditors	0.5	5.6	6.7	18.1	18.2
Bonds	0.0	0.2	0.9	9.7	15.4
Private nonguaranteed	**0.9**	**4.0**	**1.1**	**43.4**	**30.9**
Bonds	0.0	0.0	0.0	3.5	5.1
NET FLOWS ON DEBT	**1.6**	**10.5**	**-3.5**	**-1.2**	**11.8**
Public and publicly guaranteed	**0.9**	**9.0**	**-3.3**	**5.7**	**5.1**
Official creditors	0.3	3.2	-0.3	1.7	-1.3
Multilateral	0.1	0.9	0.1	5.0	1.7
Bilateral	0.2	2.4	-0.4	-3.3	-3.0
Private creditors	0.6	5.8	-3.0	4.1	6.5
Bonds	0.1	0.3	-0.7	11.4	5.7
Private nonguaranteed	**0.7**	**1.4**	**-0.2**	**-6.9**	**6.7**
Bonds	0.0	0.0	0.0	-0.8	-0.8
CURRENCY COMPOSITION OF LONG-TERM DEBT (PERCENT)					
Deutsche mark	10.1	6.0	6.6	4.7	4.6
French franc	1.6	2.4	4.4	2.0	1.7
Japanese yen	0.1	5.8	5.3	6.5	6.5
Pound sterling	6.2	1.9	1.5	1.0	0.9
U.S. dollars	60.1	51.2	47.9	61.6	60.8
Multiple currency	12.8	6.8	11.9	4.9	4.3
All other currencies	7.4	4.3	3.5	7.9	9.8
DEBT STOCK-FLOW RECONCILIATION					
Total change in debt stocks	..	..	8.8	4.4	-10.4
Net flows on debt	1.5	20.4	-0.3	-1.1	4.2
Net change in interest arrears	..	..	8.8	-1.1	-0.1
Interest capitalized	..	..	0.9	0.1	0.5
Debt forgiveness or reduction	..	..	-6.5	-1.6	-3.4
Cross-currency valuation	..	..	6.0	-4.2	-6.4
Residual	..	..	-0.1	12.3	-5.2
AVERAGE TERMS OF NEW COMMITMENTS					
ALL CREDITORS					
Interest (%)	6.9	11.2	6.7	8.7	9.5
Maturity (years)	13.9	11.8	15.9	9.2	15.1
Grant element (%)	16.8	-4.1	21.0	5.0	0.2
Official creditors					
Interest (%)	6.0	7.4	5.7	5.9	6.3
Maturity (years)	22.6	17.0	19.8	12.2	16.6
Grant element (%)	26.0	17.8	29.5	20.6	21.7
Private creditors					
Interest (%)	7.4	12.9	8.7	10.2	10.1
Maturity (years)	9.7	9.6	8.0	7.4	14.8
Grant element (%)	12.3	-13.4	3.8	-3.9	-3.9
Memo:					
Commitments	2.2	18.1	5.8	35.0	31.6
Official creditors	0.7	5.4	3.9	12.7	5.0
Private creditors	1.5	12.7	1.9	22.4	26.6

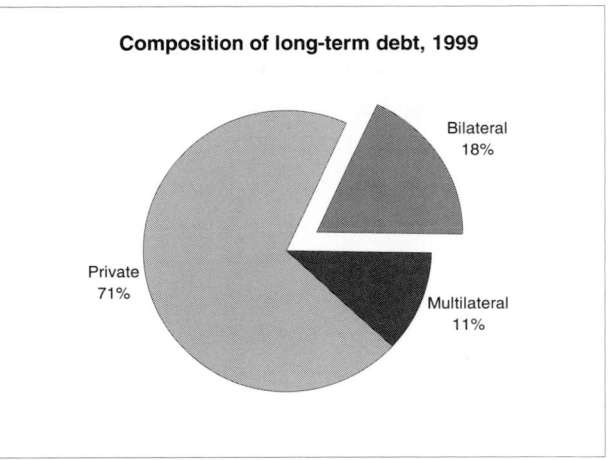

Composition of long-term debt, 1999

Bilateral 18%
Multilateral 11%
Private 71%

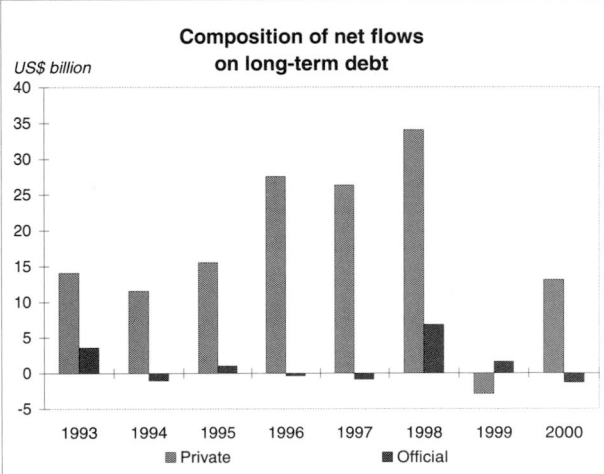

Composition of net flows on long-term debt

US$ billion

■ Private ■ Official

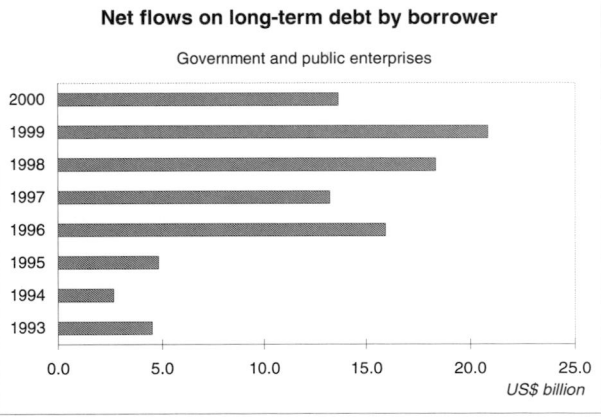

Net flows on long-term debt by borrower

Government and public enterprises

US$ billion

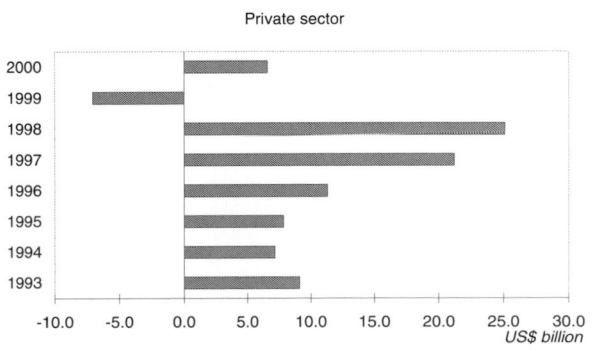

Private sector

US$ billion

MODERATELY INDEBTED LOW-INCOME COUNTRIES

(US$ billion)

	1970	1980	1990	1999	2000
SUMMARY DEBT DATA					
TOTAL DEBT STOCKS (EDT)	**2.0**	**12.1**	**39.2**	**54.3**	**52.6**
Long-term debt (LDOD)	**1.8**	**9.8**	**32.6**	**46.5**	**45.6**
Public and publicly guaranteed	1.7	9.4	31.4	43.5	42.6
Private nonguaranteed	0.1	0.5	1.2	3.0	3.0
Use of IMF credit	**0.1**	**0.8**	**2.2**	**3.0**	**2.6**
Short-term debt	**0.1**	**1.5**	**4.5**	**4.8**	**4.4**
of which interest arrears on LDOD	0.0	0.0	0.8	0.5	0.8
Memo:					
IBRD	0.1	0.5	1.5	1.0	0.9
IDA	0.1	0.9	6.7	14.5	14.5
TOTAL FLOWS ON DEBT					
Disbursements	**0.2**	**2.7**	**3.4**	**4.3**	**3.0**
Long-term debt	0.2	2.3	3.0	3.9	2.8
Public and publicly guaranteed	0.2	2.2	2.7	3.5	2.6
Private nonguaranteed	0.0	0.1	0.2	0.4	0.2
IMF purchases	**0.0**	**0.4**	**0.4**	**0.4**	**0.2**
Memo:					
IBRD	0.0	0.1	0.0	0.1	0.1
IDA	0.0	0.2	1.0	1.0	1.0
Principal repayments	**0.1**	**0.7**	**1.6**	**2.5**	**2.3**
Long-term debt	0.1	0.6	1.2	2.0	1.8
Public and publicly guaranteed	0.1	0.5	1.1	1.8	1.6
Private nonguaranteed	0.0	0.1	0.1	0.2	0.3
IMF repurchases	**0.0**	**0.1**	**0.4**	**0.5**	**0.5**
Memo:					
IBRD	0.0	0.0	0.2	0.1	0.1
IDA	0.0	0.0	0.0	0.1	0.1
Net flows on debt	**0.1**	**2.2**	**2.7**	**2.8**	**0.0**
of which short-term debt	0.0	0.2	0.9	1.0	-0.7
Interest payments (INT)	**0.0**	**0.5**	**1.1**	**1.2**	**1.1**
Long-term debt	0.0	0.3	0.7	0.9	0.9
Net transfers on debt	**0.1**	**1.7**	**1.6**	**1.6**	**-1.1**
Total debt service (TDS)	**0.1**	**1.2**	**2.6**	**3.7**	**3.5**
AGGREGATE NET RESOURCE FLOWS AND NET TRANSFERS (LONG-TERM)					
NET RESOURCE FLOWS	**0.3**	**3.4**	**6.6**	**8.0**	**6.8**
Net flow of long-term debt (ex. IMF)	0.1	1.7	1.8	1.9	0.9
Foreign direct investment (net)	0.1	0.2	0.0	1.1	1.1
Portfolio equity flows	0.0	0.0	0.0	0.0	0.0
Grants (excluding technical coop.)	0.1	1.5	4.8	4.9	4.8
NET TRANSFERS	**0.2**	**2.8**	**5.6**	**6.7**	**5.6**
Interest on long-term debt	0.0	0.3	0.7	0.9	0.9
Profit remittances on FDI	0.1	0.3	0.3	0.4	0.4
MAJOR ECONOMIC INDICATORS					
Gross national income (GNI)	..	47.3	79.1	69.0	66.8
Exports of goods & services (XGS)	..	..	18.9	25.5	28.1
of which workers' remittances	..	0.4	1.9	1.6	1.6
Imports of goods & services (MGS)	..	..	22.5	30.7	31.7
International reserves (RES)	..	..	2.5	8.2	8.4
Current account balance	..	-2.3	-2.4	-1.9	0.2
DEBT INDICATORS					
EDT / XGS (%)	..	..	208.1	213.2	187.0
EDT / GNI (%)	..	25.7	49.6	78.7	78.8
TDS / XGS (%)	..	..	14.0	14.4	12.3
INT / XGS (%)	..	..	5.7	4.6	4.1
INT / GNI (%)	..	1.1	1.4	1.7	1.7
RES / MGS (months)	..	..	1.3	3.2	3.2
Short-term / EDT (%)	4.3	12.7	11.4	8.9	8.4
Concessional / EDT (%)	50.6	40.2	51.8	62.4	63.7
Multilateral / EDT (%)	8.8	17.7	30.1	40.9	41.5

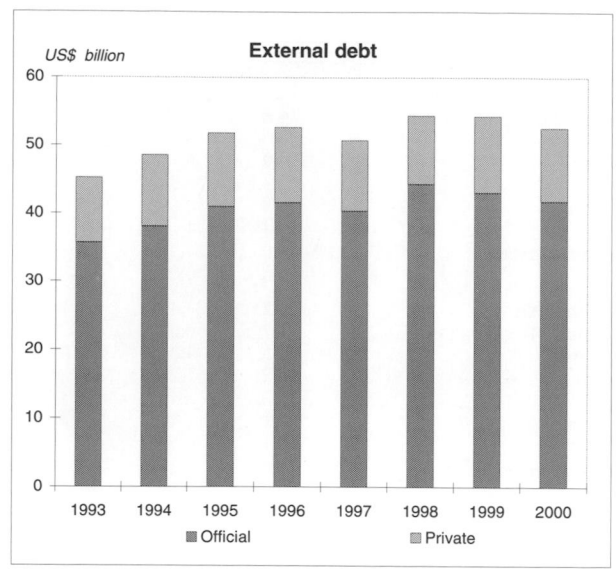

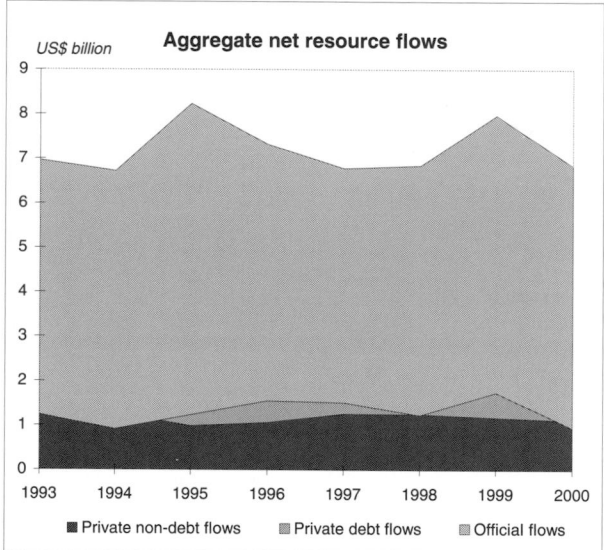

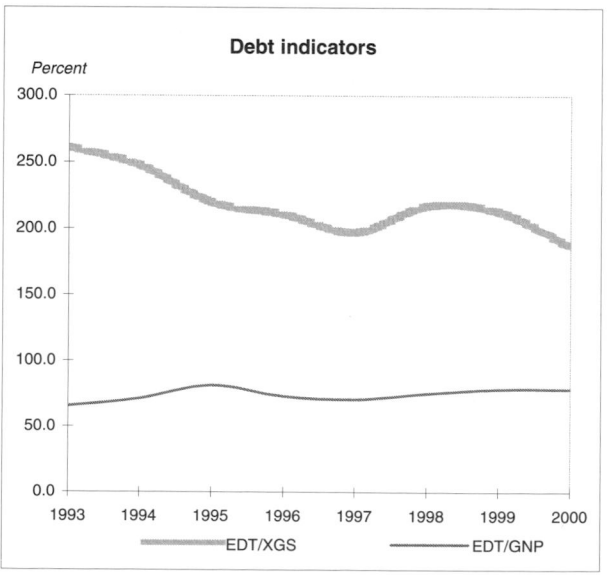

MODERATELY INDEBTED LOW-INCOME COUNTRIES

(US$ billion)

	1970	1980	1990	1999	2000
LONG-TERM DEBT					
DEBT OUTSTANDING (LDOD)	**1.8**	**9.8**	**32.6**	**46.5**	**45.6**
Public and publicly guaranteed	**1.7**	**9.4**	**31.4**	**43.5**	**42.6**
Official creditors	1.2	6.4	26.2	40.1	39.2
Multilateral	0.2	2.1	11.8	22.2	21.8
Bilateral	1.1	4.2	14.4	17.9	17.3
Private creditors	0.5	3.0	5.2	3.4	3.5
Bonds	0.2	0.6	0.3	0.1	0.1
Private nonguaranteed	**0.1**	**0.5**	**1.2**	**3.0**	**3.0**
Bonds	0.0	0.0	0.0	0.3	0.3
DISBURSEMENTS	**0.2**	**2.3**	**3.0**	**3.9**	**2.8**
Public and publicly guaranteed	**0.2**	**2.2**	**2.7**	**3.5**	**2.6**
Official creditors	0.1	1.5	2.1	2.5	2.2
Multilateral	0.0	0.5	1.4	1.6	1.5
Bilateral	0.1	1.0	0.7	0.8	0.7
Private creditors	0.0	0.7	0.6	1.0	0.4
Bonds	0.0	0.1	0.0	0.0	0.0
Private nonguaranteed	**0.0**	**0.1**	**0.2**	**0.4**	**0.2**
Bonds	0.0	0.0	0.0	0.0	0.0
PRINCIPAL REPAYMENTS	**0.1**	**0.6**	**1.2**	**2.0**	**1.8**
Public and publicly guaranteed	**0.1**	**0.5**	**1.1**	**1.8**	**1.6**
Official creditors	0.0	0.2	0.7	1.2	1.1
Multilateral	0.0	0.0	0.4	0.6	0.6
Bilateral	0.0	0.1	0.3	0.6	0.5
Private creditors	0.0	0.3	0.4	0.6	0.5
Bonds	0.0	0.0	0.0	0.0	0.0
Private nonguaranteed	**0.0**	**0.1**	**0.1**	**0.2**	**0.3**
Bonds	0.0	0.0	0.0	0.0	0.0
NET FLOWS ON DEBT	**0.1**	**1.7**	**1.8**	**1.9**	**0.9**
Public and publicly guaranteed	**0.1**	**1.7**	**1.7**	**1.6**	**1.0**
Official creditors	0.1	1.3	1.5	1.3	1.1
Multilateral	0.0	0.5	1.0	1.0	1.0
Bilateral	0.1	0.9	0.4	0.2	0.1
Private creditors	0.0	0.4	0.2	0.4	-0.1
Bonds	0.0	0.0	0.0	0.0	0.0
Private nonguaranteed	**0.0**	**0.0**	**0.1**	**0.2**	**-0.1**
Bonds	0.0	0.0	0.0	0.0	0.0
CURRENCY COMPOSITION OF LONG-TERM DEBT (PERCENT)					
Deutsche mark	9.1	7.0	2.5	3.2	3.0
French franc	5.6	12.4	10.1	4.9	4.3
Japanese yen	0.1	1.2	3.4	9.3	8.9
Pound sterling	45.6	10.9	3.9	2.1	1.8
U.S. dollars	14.6	28.1	35.7	51.9	54.1
Multiple currency	6.0	11.3	11.4	9.9	9.4
All other currencies	18.3	26.1	30.6	5.7	6.1
DEBT STOCK-FLOW RECONCILIATION					
Total change in debt stocks	..	..	4.9	-0.1	-1.7
Net flows on debt	0.1	2.2	2.7	2.8	0.0
Net change in interest arrears	..	..	0.1	-0.1	0.3
Interest capitalized	..	..	0.2	0.1	0.0
Debt forgiveness or reduction	..	..	-1.5	-0.7	-0.3
Cross-currency valuation	..	..	1.3	-1.8	-2.3
Residual	..	..	2.1	-0.4	0.4
AVERAGE TERMS OF NEW COMMITMENTS					
ALL CREDITORS					
Interest (%)	1.8	4.2	3.0	2.4	1.5
Maturity (years)	28.4	24.2	51.9	27.8	36.2
Grant element (%)	63.7	42.8	54.9	56.9	70.5
Official creditors					
Interest (%)	1.4	3.5	2.5	1.5	1.3
Maturity (years)	30.2	27.8	57.7	33.1	37.4
Grant element (%)	68.3	49.9	61.1	68.4	73.0
Private creditors					
Interest (%)	6.1	6.7	6.9	5.2	7.2
Maturity (years)	7.8	11.5	10.9	11.1	5.3
Grant element (%)	12.0	18.0	10.8	20.8	6.9
Memo:					
Commitments	0.2	3.1	3.6	3.4	1.9
Official creditors	0.2	2.4	3.2	2.6	1.9
Private creditors	0.0	0.7	0.5	0.8	0.1

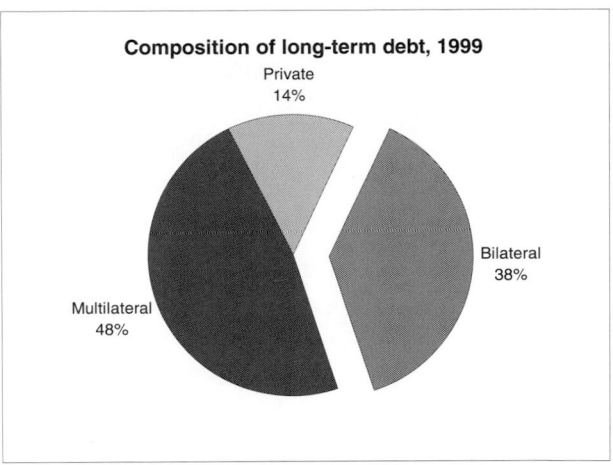

Composition of long-term debt, 1999

Private 14%; Bilateral 38%; Multilateral 48%

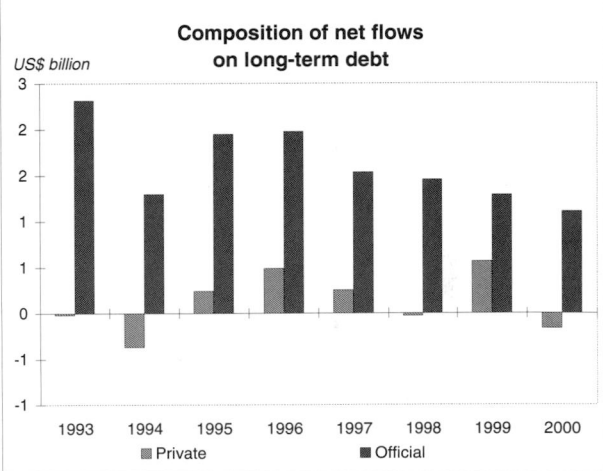

Composition of net flows on long-term debt

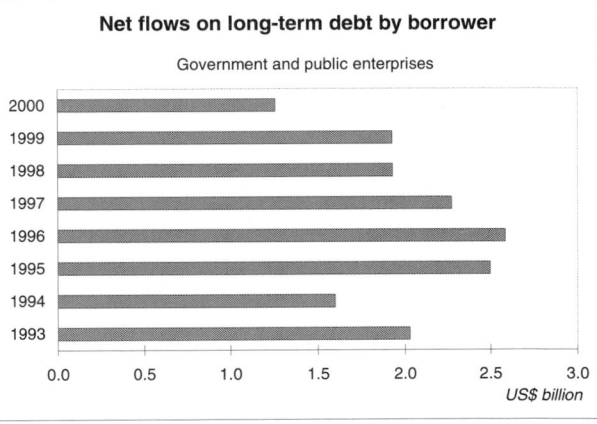

Net flows on long-term debt by borrower

Government and public enterprises

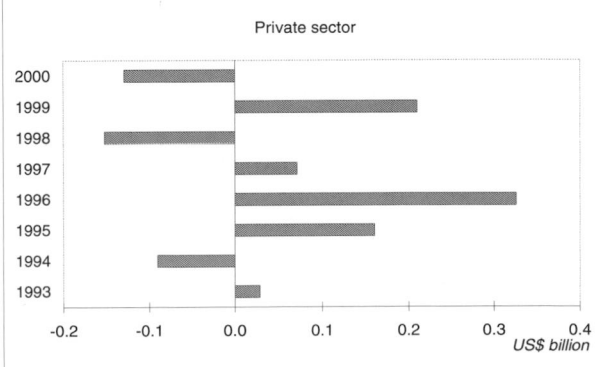

Private sector

MODERATELY INDEBTED MIDDLE-INCOME COUNTRIES

(US$ billion)

	1970	1980	1990	1999	2000
SUMMARY DEBT DATA					
TOTAL DEBT STOCKS (EDT)	**17.2**	**149.9**	**351.3**	**722.0**	**703.8**
Long-term debt (LDOD)	**13.6**	**104.7**	**288.5**	**595.5**	**583.4**
Public and publicly guaranteed	10.1	89.4	266.5	413.6	403.0
Private nonguaranteed	3.5	15.2	22.1	181.9	180.5
Use of IMF credit	**0.2**	**3.2**	**7.4**	**26.5**	**25.2**
Short-term debt	**3.4**	**42.1**	**55.3**	**99.9**	**95.1**
of which interest arrears on LDOD	0.0	0.0	6.0	7.0	4.8
Memo:					
IBRD	1.3	5.9	27.2	28.6	28.7
IDA	0.2	0.6	1.1	2.9	2.9
TOTAL FLOWS ON DEBT					
Disbursements	**3.5**	**30.3**	**53.1**	**82.4**	**74.7**
Long-term debt	3.3	28.9	50.9	79.6	70.6
Public and publicly guaranteed	2.2	21.8	43.8	46.9	41.9
Private nonguaranteed	1.1	7.2	7.1	32.7	28.6
IMF purchases	**0.2**	**1.3**	**2.2**	**2.8**	**4.2**
Memo:					
IBRD	0.2	1.3	3.8	3.4	3.5
IDA	0.0	0.0	0.1	0.4	0.2
Principal repayments	**1.6**	**11.9**	**38.3**	**61.8**	**65.4**
Long-term debt	1.4	11.5	36.6	56.1	61.3
Public and publicly guaranteed	0.8	8.3	34.1	29.3	32.5
Private nonguaranteed	0.6	3.2	2.5	26.7	28.8
IMF repurchases	**0.2**	**0.4**	**1.8**	**5.7**	**4.1**
Memo:					
IBRD	0.1	0.3	2.5	2.8	2.7
IDA	0.0	0.0	0.0	0.0	0.0
Net flows on debt	**1.9**	**25.6**	**10.3**	**8.0**	**7.7**
of which short-term debt	0.0	7.3	-4.5	-12.6	-1.6
Interest payments (INT)	**0.5**	**12.9**	**25.3**	**36.4**	**37.5**
Long-term debt	0.5	7.9	20.7	30.5	31.1
Net transfers on debt	**1.4**	**12.8**	**-15.0**	**-28.4**	**-29.8**
Total debt service (TDS)	**2.1**	**24.8**	**63.6**	**98.2**	**102.9**
AGGREGATE NET RESOURCE FLOWS AND NET TRANSFERS (LONG-TERM)					
NET RESOURCE FLOWS	**2.6**	**21.2**	**27.3**	**69.6**	**48.9**
Net flow of long-term debt (ex. IMF)	1.9	17.5	14.4	23.5	9.3
Foreign direct investment (net)	0.3	2.4	8.2	34.8	29.2
Portfolio equity flows	0.0	0.0	1.2	6.2	5.8
Grants (excluding technical coop.)	0.4	1.3	3.5	5.1	4.5
NET TRANSFERS	**0.8**	**10.0**	**1.7**	**25.9**	**2.9**
Interest on long-term debt	0.5	7.9	20.7	30.5	31.1
Profit remittances on FDI	1.3	3.3	4.9	13.2	14.9
MAJOR ECONOMIC INDICATORS					
Gross national income (GNI)	..	842.3	1,204.1	1,126.2	1,223.5
Exports of goods & services (XGS)	..	159.8	258.6	521.5	625.3
of which workers' remittances	..	3.1	7.0	9.3	9.1
Imports of goods & services (MGS)	..	164.5	266.6	481.1	561.1
International reserves (RES)	..	58.7	71.8	202.2	220.5
Current account balance	..	-6.2	-5.8	43.1	53.2
DEBT INDICATORS					
EDT / XGS (%)	..	93.8	135.8	138.5	112.5
EDT / GNI (%)	..	17.8	29.2	64.1	57.5
TDS / XGS (%)	..	15.5	24.6	18.8	16.5
INT / XGS (%)	..	8.0	9.8	7.0	6.0
INT / GNI (%)	..	1.5	2.1	3.2	3.1
RES / MGS (months)	..	4.3	3.2	5.0	4.7
Short-term / EDT (%)	19.8	28.1	15.8	13.8	13.5
Concessional / EDT (%)	25.6	8.8	9.0	7.0	6.9
Multilateral / EDT (%)	11.5	6.6	13.7	8.6	8.7

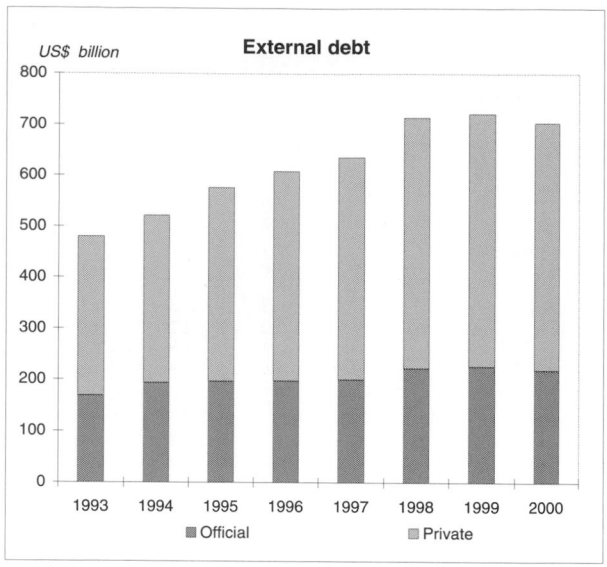

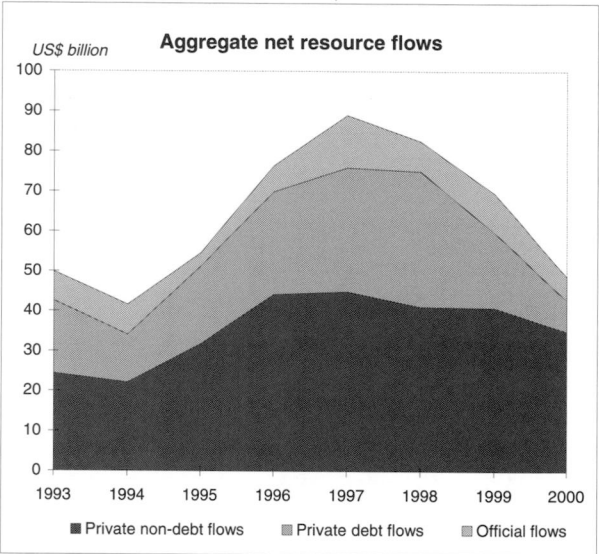

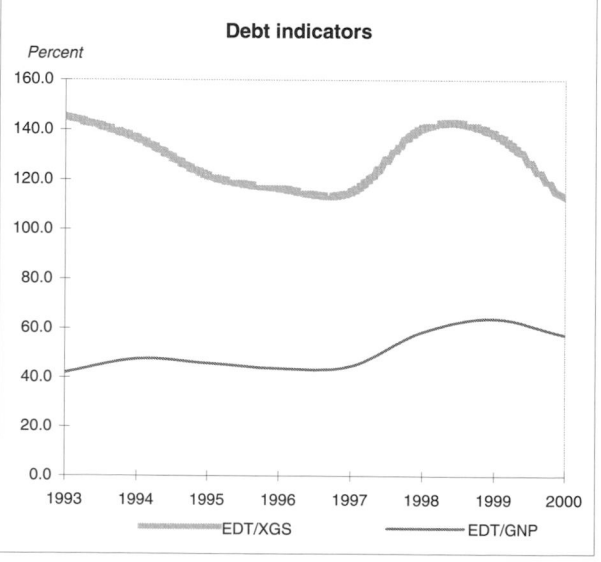

MODERATELY INDEBTED MIDDLE-INCOME COUNTRIES

(US$ billion)

	1970	*1980*	*1990*	*1999*	*2000*
LONG-TERM DEBT					
DEBT OUTSTANDING (LDOD)	**13.6**	**104.7**	**288.5**	**595.5**	**583.4**
Public and publicly guaranteed	**10.1**	**89.4**	**266.5**	**413.6**	**403.0**
Official creditors	6.8	30.5	96.9	198.9	193.3
Multilateral	2.0	9.9	48.1	62.3	61.4
Bilateral	4.9	20.7	48.8	136.6	131.9
Private creditors	3.2	58.9	169.5	214.8	209.7
Bonds	0.5	4.1	39.8	111.9	139.5
Private nonguaranteed	**3.5**	**15.2**	**22.1**	**181.9**	**180.5**
Bonds	0.0	0.0	0.1	35.7	34.0
DISBURSEMENTS	**3.3**	**28.9**	**50.9**	**79.6**	**70.6**
Public and publicly guaranteed	**2.2**	**21.8**	**43.8**	**46.9**	**41.9**
Official creditors	1.1	5.5	15.9	14.9	13.2
Multilateral	0.4	2.1	7.4	8.0	6.9
Bilateral	0.7	3.4	8.5	7.0	6.3
Private creditors	1.1	16.2	27.9	32.0	28.7
Bonds	0.0	0.5	3.3	18.2	17.2
Private nonguaranteed	**1.1**	**7.2**	**7.1**	**32.7**	**28.6**
Bonds	0.0	0.0	0.0	4.0	1.8
PRINCIPAL REPAYMENTS	**1.4**	**11.5**	**36.6**	**56.1**	**61.3**
Public and publicly guaranteed	**0.8**	**8.3**	**34.1**	**29.3**	**32.5**
Official creditors	0.3	1.6	7.3	10.3	11.8
Multilateral	0.2	0.4	3.8	5.0	5.7
Bilateral	0.2	1.1	3.5	5.3	6.1
Private creditors	0.4	6.7	26.7	19.0	20.6
Bonds	0.1	0.1	2.1	7.7	7.8
Private nonguaranteed	**0.6**	**3.2**	**2.5**	**26.7**	**28.8**
Bonds	0.0	0.0	0.0	1.4	3.3
NET FLOWS ON DEBT	**1.9**	**17.5**	**14.4**	**23.5**	**9.3**
Public and publicly guaranteed	**1.4**	**13.5**	**9.7**	**17.6**	**9.5**
Official creditors	0.7	4.0	8.6	4.6	1.4
Multilateral	0.2	1.7	3.6	3.0	1.2
Bilateral	0.5	2.3	5.0	1.7	0.2
Private creditors	0.7	9.5	1.2	13.0	8.1
Bonds	0.0	0.4	1.2	10.4	9.5
Private nonguaranteed	**0.4**	**4.0**	**4.6**	**6.0**	**-0.2**
Bonds	0.0	0.0	0.0	2.5	-1.5
CURRENCY COMPOSITION OF LONG-TERM DEBT (PERCENT)					
Deutsche mark	7.3	7.5	14.9	11.7	10.0
French franc	5.9	8.4	4.3	1.7	1.8
Japanese yen	0.5	8.0	13.6	13.8	13.0
Pound sterling	6.2	1.9	1.4	0.7	0.6
U.S. dollars	56.3	47.9	39.0	59.5	61.1
Multiple currency	15.7	16.4	15.8	6.9	6.4
All other currencies	6.9	7.4	7.4	4.2	5.7
DEBT STOCK-FLOW RECONCILIATION					
Total change in debt stocks	..	..	27.1	8.3	-18.3
Net flows on debt	1.9	25.6	10.3	8.0	7.7
Net change in interest arrears	..	..	4.5	1.6	-2.2
Interest capitalized	..	..	0.4	5.3	4.4
Debt forgiveness or reduction	..	..	-4.1	-0.5	-11.7
Cross-currency valuation	..	..	14.0	-6.0	-14.6
Residual	..	..	2.0	-0.2	-1.9
AVERAGE TERMS OF NEW COMMITMENTS					
ALL CREDITORS					
Interest (%)	5.7	9.7	7.9	6.0	7.1
Maturity (years)	16.8	15.5	13.4	14.4	12.1
Grant element (%)	25.0	3.5	12.2	23.1	13.7
Official creditors					
Interest (%)	4.7	7.0	6.9	3.9	5.8
Maturity (years)	22.9	23.7	17.6	19.9	19.1
Grant element (%)	35.3	21.1	21.0	39.2	27.8
Private creditors					
Interest (%)	6.9	11.4	8.6	7.6	7.6
Maturity (years)	9.5	10.5	10.7	10.3	9.1
Grant element (%)	12.7	-7.2	6.6	11.2	7.4
Memo:					
Commitments	2.6	25.1	49.0	48.7	45.0
Official creditors	1.4	9.5	19.1	20.8	13.7
Private creditors	1.2	15.6	29.9	27.9	31.2

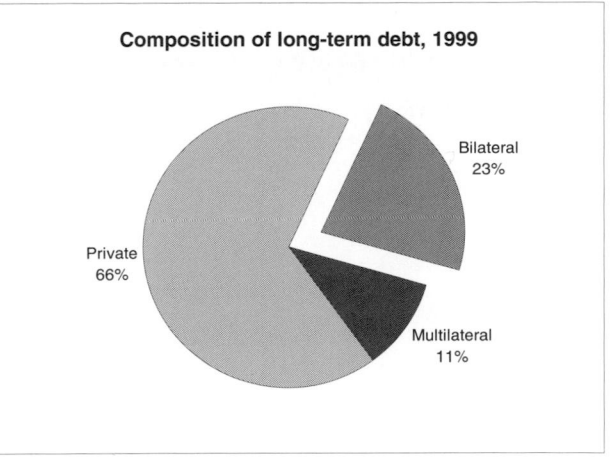

Composition of long-term debt, 1999

Private 66%
Bilateral 23%
Multilateral 11%

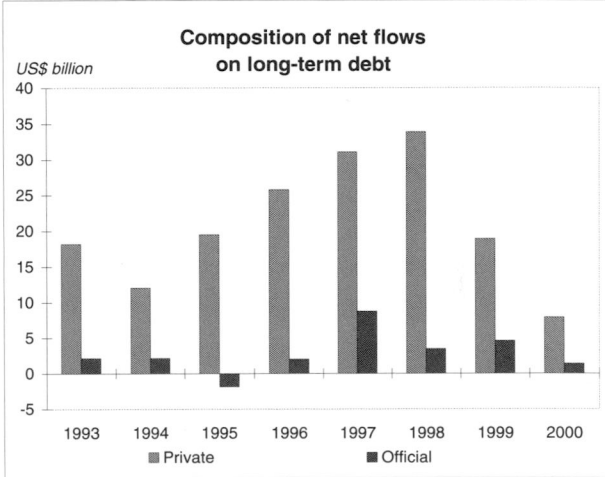

Composition of net flows on long-term debt

US$ billion

■ Private   ■ Official

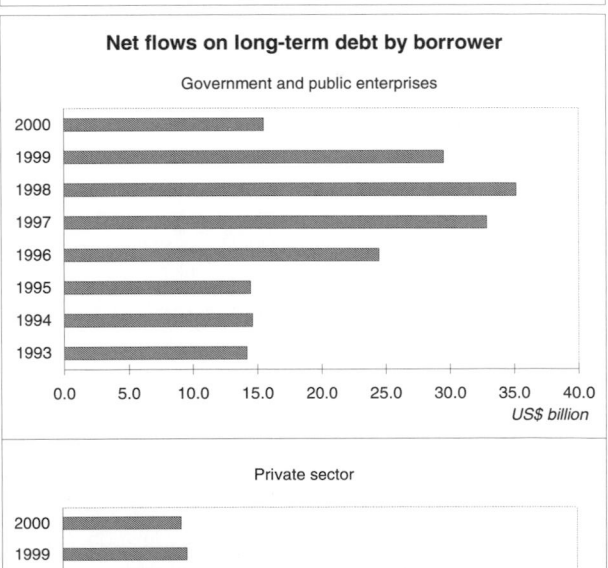

Net flows on long-term debt by borrower

Government and public enterprises

US$ billion

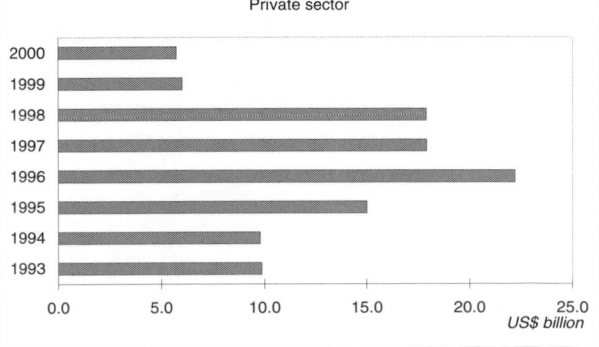

Private sector

US$ billion

OTHER DEVELOPING COUNTRIES

(US$ billion)

	1970	1980	1990	1999	2000
SUMMARY DEBT DATA					
TOTAL DEBT STOCKS (EDT)	**24.8**	**222.6**	**516.3**	**923.6**	**890.6**
Long-term debt (LDOD)	**21.9**	**159.8**	**410.2**	**751.5**	**727.3**
Public and publicly guaranteed	17.7	137.1	391.3	584.0	542.6
Private nonguaranteed	4.3	22.7	18.9	167.5	184.7
Use of IMF credit	**0.2**	**4.6**	**13.2**	**17.2**	**10.6**
Short-term debt	**2.7**	**58.1**	**92.9**	**154.9**	**152.8**
of which interest arrears on LDOD	0.0	0.7	12.9	5.8	5.2
Memo:					
IBRD	1.6	9.2	33.8	52.6	52.5
IDA	1.1	6.8	23.4	41.5	43.5
TOTAL FLOWS ON DEBT					
Disbursements	**4.2**	**44.6**	**50.8**	**107.3**	**110.3**
Long-term debt	4.1	41.6	46.0	104.4	108.6
Public and publicly guaranteed	2.9	34.7	40.9	62.1	56.7
Private nonguaranteed	1.2	7.0	5.2	42.4	51.9
IMF purchases	**0.0**	**3.0**	**4.8**	**2.8**	**1.7**
Memo:					
IBRD	0.2	1.8	6.2	5.9	5.5
IDA	0.1	0.9	2.0	2.4	2.4
Principal repayments	**2.7**	**16.3**	**28.2**	**120.4**	**119.5**
Long-term debt	2.4	15.5	24.8	102.9	111.8
Public and publicly guaranteed	1.5	12.2	20.7	64.8	70.1
Private nonguaranteed	0.8	3.3	4.1	38.2	41.6
IMF repurchases	**0.3**	**0.8**	**3.4**	**17.5**	**7.8**
Memo:					
IBRD	0.1	0.5	3.1	4.0	4.2
IDA	0.0	0.0	0.1	0.5	0.6
Net flows on debt	**1.4**	**41.2**	**33.3**	**-18.5**	**-9.2**
of which short-term debt	0.0	12.9	10.6	-5.4	0.0
Interest payments (INT)	**0.8**	**18.0**	**26.9**	**45.0**	**46.6**
Long-term debt	0.8	11.8	19.4	35.3	37.4
Net transfers on debt	**0.7**	**23.2**	**6.4**	**-63.4**	**-55.9**
Total debt service (TDS)	**3.5**	**34.3**	**55.1**	**165.4**	**166.2**
AGGREGATE NET RESOURCE FLOWS AND NET TRANSFERS (LONG-TERM)					
NET RESOURCE FLOWS	**3.8**	**28.8**	**42.7**	**126.3**	**136.8**
Net flow of long-term debt (ex. IMF)	1.7	26.2	21.2	1.5	-3.2
Foreign direct investment (net)	1.2	-1.0	10.8	89.2	89.2
Portfolio equity flows	0.0	0.0	1.2	24.3	39.0
Grants (excluding technical coop.)	0.8	3.6	9.5	11.2	11.8
NET TRANSFERS	**1.0**	**5.7**	**19.6**	**76.7**	**83.1**
Interest on long-term debt	0.8	11.8	19.4	35.3	37.4
Profit remittances on FDI	2.0	11.4	3.7	14.3	16.2
MAJOR ECONOMIC INDICATORS					
Gross national income (GNI)	324.4	1,346.6	2,014.2	3,424.0	3,744.9
Exports of goods & services (XGS)	..	380.4	480.0	1,031.5	1,260.7
of which workers' remittances	..	7.6	13.0	31.2	34.1
Imports of goods & services (MGS)	..	339.4	484.2	1,025.8	1,242.0
International reserves (RES)	..	..	112.2	442.3	491.6
Current account balance	..	20.9	-10.0	10.7	20.8
DEBT INDICATORS					
EDT / XGS (%)	..	58.5	107.6	89.5	70.7
EDT / GNI (%)	7.6	16.5	25.6	27.0	23.8
TDS / XGS (%)	..	9.0	11.5	16.0	13.2
INT / XGS (%)	..	4.7	5.6	4.4	3.7
INT / GNI (%)	0.2	1.3	1.3	1.3	1.2
RES / MGS (months)	..	..	2.8	5.2	4.8
Short-term / EDT (%)	10.8	26.1	18.0	16.8	17.2
Concessional / EDT (%)	40.1	18.6	24.5	17.5	17.3
Multilateral / EDT (%)	11.9	9.6	14.4	15.1	16.0

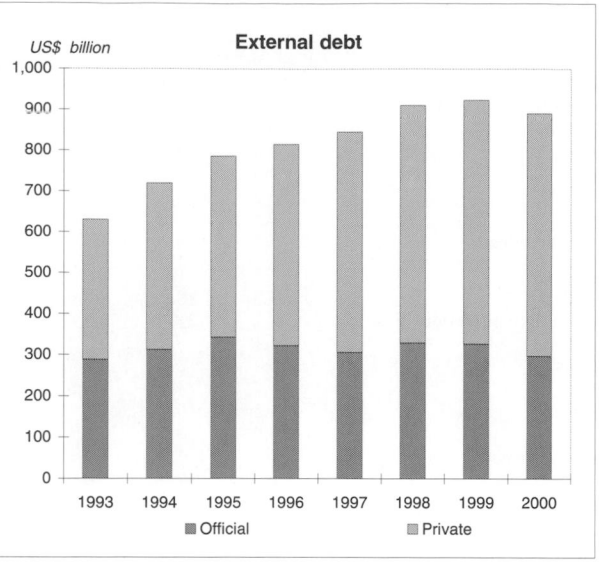

External debt

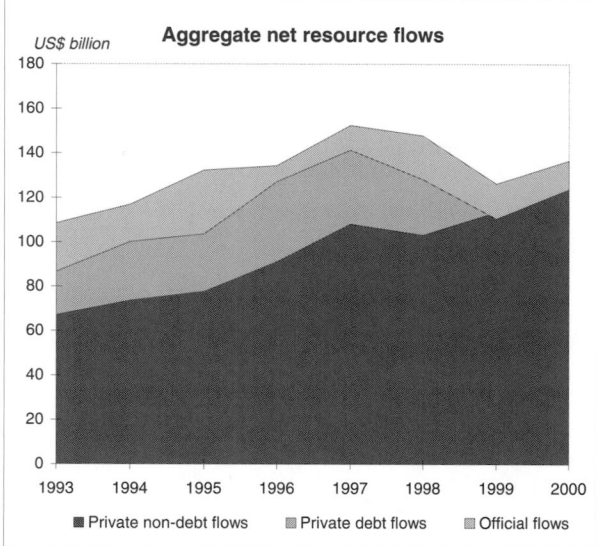

Aggregate net resource flows

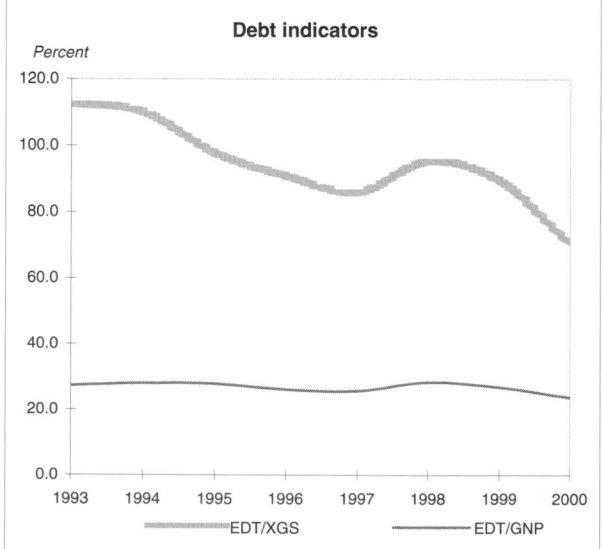

Debt indicators

OTHER DEVELOPING COUNTRIES

(US$ billion)

	1970	1980	1990	1999	2000
LONG-TERM DEBT					
DEBT OUTSTANDING (LDOD)	**21.9**	**159.8**	**410.2**	**751.5**	**727.3**
Public and publicly guaranteed	**17.7**	**137.1**	**391.3**	**584.0**	**542.6**
Official creditors	13.1	66.3	226.3	308.6	286.0
Multilateral	2.9	21.3	74.1	139.3	142.6
Bilateral	10.2	45.0	152.3	169.3	143.4
Private creditors	4.5	70.8	165.0	275.4	256.6
Bonds	0.5	4.1	52.4	123.4	121.3
Private nonguaranteed	**4.3**	**22.7**	**18.9**	**167.5**	**184.7**
Bonds	0.0	0.0	0.6	49.9	55.7
DISBURSEMENTS	**4.1**	**41.6**	**46.0**	**104.4**	**108.6**
Public and publicly guaranteed	**2.9**	**34.7**	**40.9**	**62.1**	**56.7**
Official creditors	1.9	11.8	19.0	24.4	21.9
Multilateral	0.4	3.6	10.4	13.3	12.4
Bilateral	1.5	8.3	8.6	11.1	9.5
Private creditors	1.0	22.8	21.8	37.7	34.8
Bonds	0.0	0.5	2.6	14.2	17.1
Private nonguaranteed	**1.2**	**7.0**	**5.2**	**42.4**	**51.9**
Bonds	0.0	0.0	0.6	8.5	13.0
PRINCIPAL REPAYMENTS	**2.4**	**15.5**	**24.8**	**102.9**	**111.8**
Public and publicly guaranteed	**1.5**	**12.2**	**20.7**	**64.8**	**70.1**
Official creditors	0.7	3.1	8.5	19.9	20.8
Multilateral	0.1	0.6	4.1	6.7	7.6
Bilateral	0.6	2.5	4.3	13.2	13.3
Private creditors	0.8	9.1	12.2	44.9	49.3
Bonds	0.0	0.2	2.5	7.9	17.6
Private nonguaranteed	**0.8**	**3.3**	**4.1**	**38.2**	**41.6**
Bonds	0.0	0.0	0.0	7.2	6.4
NET FLOWS ON DEBT	**1.7**	**26.2**	**21.2**	**1.5**	**-3.2**
Public and publicly guaranteed	**1.4**	**22.5**	**20.1**	**-2.7**	**-13.4**
Official creditors	1.2	8.8	10.6	4.5	1.1
Multilateral	0.3	2.9	6.3	6.6	4.9
Bilateral	0.9	5.8	4.3	-2.1	-3.7
Private creditors	0.2	13.7	9.6	-7.2	-14.5
Bonds	0.0	0.4	0.2	6.3	-0.5
Private nonguaranteed	**0.4**	**3.7**	**1.1**	**4.2**	**10.2**
Bonds	0.0	0.0	0.6	1.3	6.6
CURRENCY COMPOSITION OF LONG-TERM DEBT (PERCENT)					
Deutsche mark	9.7	6.1	7.1	4.1	3.5
French franc	4.0	3.6	5.4	3.0	2.8
Japanese yen	3.1	5.4	10.7	12.1	11.3
Pound sterling	12.8	5.1	2.4	1.1	1.0
U.S. dollars	45.8	55.5	43.4	57.9	61.6
Multiple currency	10.2	10.8	15.6	8.7	7.9
All other currencies	13.4	6.1	10.6	6.5	5.3
DEBT STOCK-FLOW RECONCILIATION					
Total change in debt stocks	..	..	32.9	13.4	-33.0
Net flows on debt	1.4	41.2	33.3	-18.5	-9.2
Net change in interest arrears	..	..	-0.5	0.9	-0.6
Interest capitalized	..	..	2.8	0.6	0.0
Debt forgiveness or reduction	..	..	-20.9	0.0	-9.4
Cross-currency valuation	..	..	15.2	-1.9	-16.4
Residual	..	..	3.1	32.3	2.6
AVERAGE TERMS OF NEW COMMITMENTS					
ALL CREDITORS					
Interest (%)	5.1	9.1	7.0	5.4	6.9
Maturity (years)	22.2	17.3	17.8	17.2	11.5
Grant element (%)	26.3	6.7	18.2	22.6	15.3
Official creditors					
Interest (%)	3.9	4.8	5.4	3.5	5.7
Maturity (years)	27.9	27.3	23.8	17.8	21.4
Grant element (%)	34.3	27.3	30.6	36.6	29.6
Private creditors					
Interest (%)	7.7	12.6	8.5	7.0	7.4
Maturity (years)	9.9	9.3	12.5	16.8	7.5
Grant element (%)	9.5	-9.7	7.0	10.8	9.5
Memo:					
Commitments	3.6	35.5	47.0	56.1	40.9
Official creditors	2.5	15.7	22.2	25.7	11.6
Private creditors	1.2	19.8	24.8	30.3	29.2

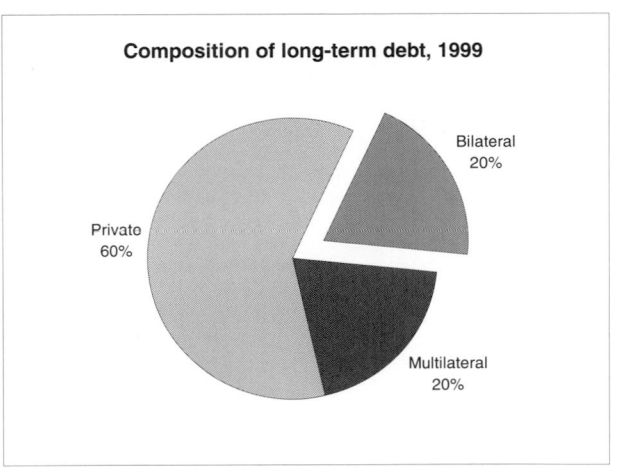

Composition of long-term debt, 1999

Bilateral 20%
Private 60%
Multilateral 20%

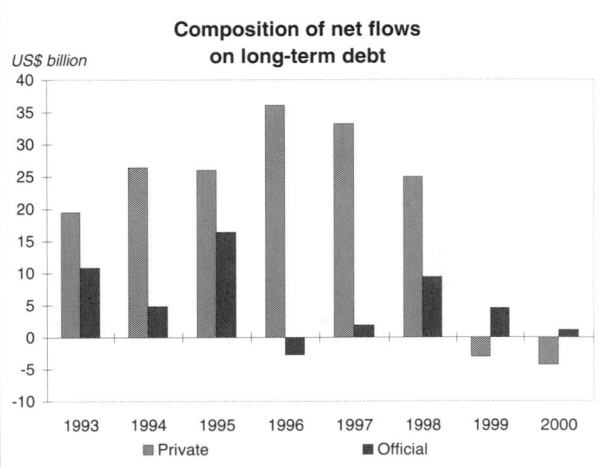

Composition of net flows on long-term debt

US$ billion

■ Private ■ Official

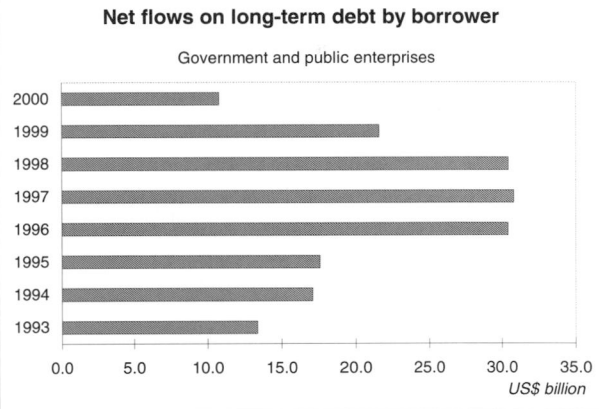

Net flows on long-term debt by borrower

Government and public enterprises

US$ billion

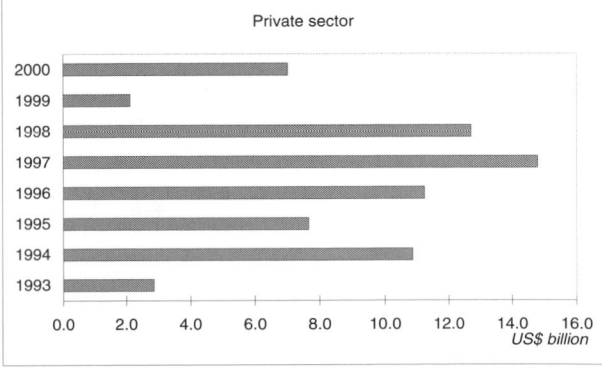

Private sector

US$ billion

LOW-INCOME COUNTRIES

(US$ billion)

	1970	1980	1990	1999	2000
SUMMARY DEBT DATA					
TOTAL DEBT STOCKS (EDT)	**23.5**	**125.2**	**418.6**	**574.0**	**550.5**
Long-term debt (LDOD)	**21.7**	**102.9**	**357.3**	**487.5**	**471.1**
Public and publicly guaranteed	20.8	94.9	340.3	422.4	412.8
Private nonguaranteed	0.9	8.0	17.0	65.2	58.2
Use of IMF credit	**0.3**	**5.3**	**11.3**	**24.8**	**23.6**
Short-term debt	**1.5**	**17.0**	**50.0**	**61.7**	**55.9**
of which interest arrears on LDOD	0.0	1.7	12.9	26.1	20.6
Memo:					
IBRD	1.4	4.8	28.1	28.9	27.6
IDA	1.6	10.5	38.6	70.5	72.9
TOTAL FLOWS ON DEBT					
Disbursements	**3.5**	**21.8**	**33.0**	**31.3**	**30.8**
Long-term debt	3.4	19.0	30.5	27.6	28.6
Public and publicly guaranteed	3.1	16.8	24.7	23.5	24.2
Private nonguaranteed	0.3	2.2	5.8	4.1	4.5
IMF purchases	**0.1**	**2.8**	**2.5**	**3.7**	**2.2**
Memo:					
IBRD	0.2	0.9	3.4	3.1	2.1
IDA	0.1	1.5	3.6	4.2	4.4
Principal repayments	**1.3**	**6.1**	**16.8**	**30.3**	**30.1**
Long-term debt	1.0	5.4	14.6	28.4	27.8
Public and publicly guaranteed	0.9	4.0	12.6	19.1	18.1
Private nonguaranteed	0.1	1.4	2.0	9.3	9.7
IMF repurchases	**0.3**	**0.7**	**2.2**	**2.0**	**2.3**
Memo:					
IBRD	0.1	0.2	1.8	2.5	2.5
IDA	0.0	0.0	0.2	0.8	0.9
Net flows on debt	**2.2**	**19.3**	**23.7**	**0.0**	**0.5**
of which short-term debt	0.1	3.6	7.5	-0.9	-0.3
Interest payments (INT)	**0.5**	**6.0**	**15.4**	**16.5**	**17.7**
Long-term debt	0.5	4.3	12.4	13.9	14.8
Net transfers on debt	**1.7**	**13.3**	**8.3**	**-16.5**	**-17.2**
Total debt service (TDS)	**1.9**	**12.1**	**32.2**	**46.9**	**47.8**
AGGREGATE NET RESOURCE FLOWS AND NET TRANSFERS (LONG-TERM)					
NET RESOURCE FLOWS	**3.7**	**21.0**	**33.5**	**26.9**	**25.2**
Net flow of long-term debt (ex. IMF)	2.4	13.6	15.9	-0.8	0.9
Foreign direct investment (net)	0.3	0.2	2.2	9.7	6.6
Portfolio equity flows	0.0	0.0	0.4	2.6	2.5
Grants (excluding technical coop.)	1.0	7.1	14.9	15.3	15.2
NET TRANSFERS	**2.3**	**10.8**	**17.7**	**7.1**	**4.9**
Interest on long-term debt	0.5	4.3	12.4	13.9	14.8
Profit remittances on FDI	0.9	5.8	3.4	5.7	5.5
MAJOR ECONOMIC INDICATORS					
Gross national income (GNI)	165.8	595.4	851.7	983.3	1,031.1
Exports of goods & services (XGS)	..	..	140.1	251.0	303.3
of which workers' remittances	..	5.3	7.0	18.5	18.2
Imports of goods & services (MGS)	..	..	172.3	278.2	315.7
International reserves (RES)	..	36.7	26.2	88.5	97.0
Current account balance	..	-9.5	-22.0	-10.7	6.3
DEBT INDICATORS					
EDT / XGS (%)	..	..	298.8	228.7	181.5
EDT / GNI (%)	14.2	21.0	49.2	58.4	53.4
TDS / XGS (%)	..	..	23.0	18.7	15.8
INT / XGS (%)	..	..	11.0	6.6	5.8
INT / GNI (%)	0.3	1.0	1.8	1.7	1.7
RES / MGS (months)	..	..	1.8	3.8	3.7
Short-term / EDT (%)	6.5	13.6	12.0	10.8	10.2
Concessional / EDT (%)	64.7	45.5	43.6	39.6	40.1
Multilateral / EDT (%)	13.0	15.5	21.9	25.9	26.8

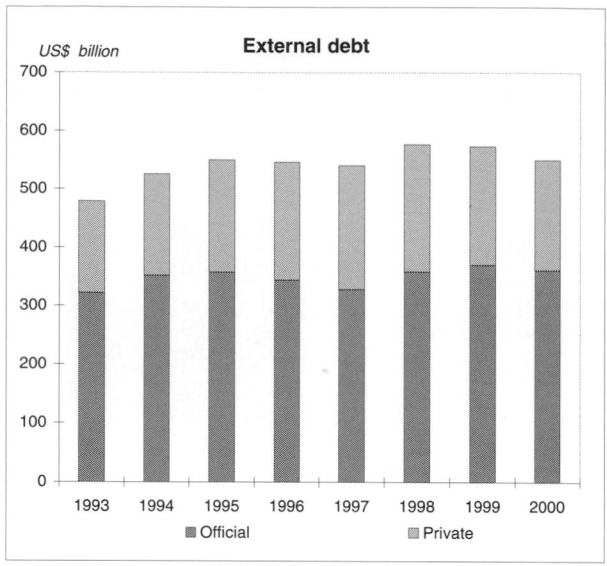

External debt

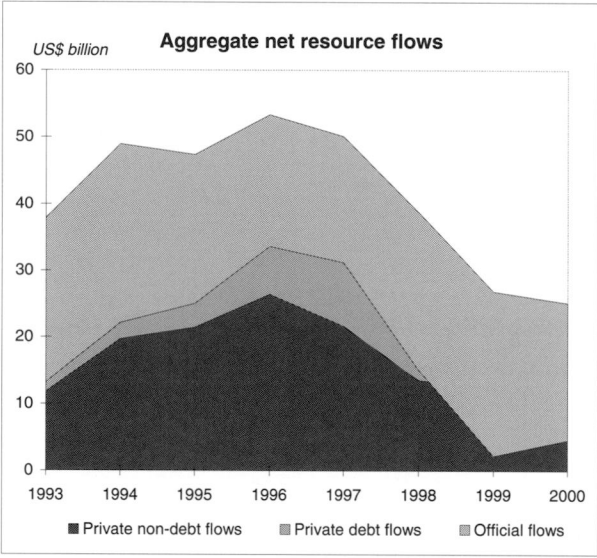

Aggregate net resource flows

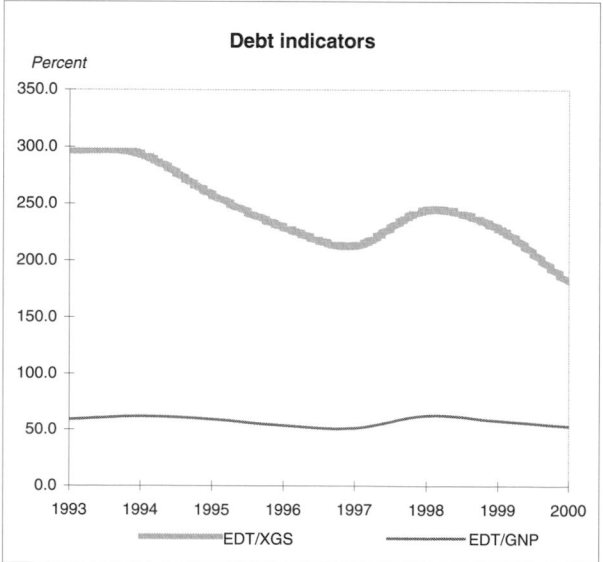

Debt indicators

LOW-INCOME COUNTRIES

(US$ billion)

	1970	1980	1990	1999	2000
LONG-TERM DEBT					
DEBT OUTSTANDING (LDOD)	**21.7**	**102.9**	**357.3**	**487.5**	**471.1**
Public and publicly guaranteed	**20.8**	**94.9**	**340.3**	**422.4**	**412.8**
Official creditors	18.2	70.2	262.1	344.8	337.2
Multilateral	3.1	19.4	91.8	148.8	147.7
Bilateral	15.1	50.8	170.3	196.0	189.5
Private creditors	2.6	24.7	78.2	77.6	75.7
Bonds	0.3	0.8	3.6	14.7	19.6
Private nonguaranteed	0.9	8.0	17.0	65.2	58.2
Bonds	0.0	0.0	0.1	11.6	9.5
DISBURSEMENTS	**3.4**	**19.0**	**30.5**	**27.6**	**28.6**
Public and publicly guaranteed	**3.1**	**16.8**	**24.7**	**23.5**	**24.2**
Official creditors	2.4	9.4	18.6	19.4	16.3
Multilateral	0.4	3.6	10.6	11.7	10.2
Bilateral	2.0	5.7	8.0	7.7	6.1
Private creditors	0.7	7.5	6.1	4.1	7.8
Bonds	0.0	0.1	0.4	0.0	5.5
Private nonguaranteed	**0.3**	**2.2**	**5.8**	**4.1**	**4.5**
Bonds	0.0	0.0	0.1	0.0	0.4
PRINCIPAL REPAYMENTS	**1.0**	**5.4**	**14.6**	**28.4**	**27.8**
Public and publicly guaranteed	**0.9**	**4.0**	**12.6**	**19.1**	**18.1**
Official creditors	0.6	1.9	6.7	10.0	10.9
Multilateral	0.1	0.4	3.0	5.2	5.7
Bilateral	0.5	1.5	3.7	4.8	5.2
Private creditors	0.3	2.1	5.9	9.1	7.2
Bonds	0.0	0.0	0.4	0.8	0.6
Private nonguaranteed	**0.1**	**1.4**	**2.0**	**9.3**	**9.7**
Bonds	0.0	0.0	0.0	2.0	2.4
NET FLOWS ON DEBT	**2.4**	**13.6**	**15.9**	**-0.8**	**0.9**
Public and publicly guaranteed	**2.2**	**12.8**	**12.1**	**4.3**	**6.1**
Official creditors	1.8	7.5	11.9	9.3	5.4
Multilateral	0.3	3.3	7.6	6.5	4.5
Bilateral	1.6	4.2	4.3	2.8	0.9
Private creditors	0.4	5.3	0.2	-5.0	0.7
Bonds	0.0	0.1	0.0	-0.8	4.9
Private nonguaranteed	**0.2**	**0.8**	**3.8**	**-5.1**	**-5.2**
Bonds	0.0	0.0	0.1	-2.0	-2.1
CURRENCY COMPOSITION OF LONG-TERM DEBT (PERCENT)					
Deutsche mark	8.0	7.2	5.4	4.0	3.1
French franc	5.5	7.0	6.5	4.3	3.6
Japanese yen	4.3	9.1	10.9	15.4	13.5
Pound sterling	18.2	8.7	4.0	2.6	1.8
U.S. dollars	37.4	37.7	37.7	48.1	55.5
Multiple currency	8.1	8.1	12.8	10.3	9.6
All other currencies	18.1	16.5	18.5	9.6	7.3
DEBT STOCK-FLOW RECONCILIATION					
Total change in debt stocks	..	..	47.7	-2.8	-23.5
Net flows on debt	2.2	19.3	23.7	0.0	0.5
Net change in interest arrears	..	..	3.0	2.9	-5.5
Interest capitalized	..	..	1.7	1.8	9.1
Debt forgiveness or reduction	..	..	-2.8	-5.2	-9.5
Cross-currency valuation	..	..	14.3	-2.4	-18.0
Residual	..	..	7.9	0.1	0.0
AVERAGE TERMS OF NEW COMMITMENTS					
ALL CREDITORS					
Interest (%)	3.0	6.3	4.8	3.1	4.8
Maturity (years)	28.9	22.9	26.5	23.8	20.2
Grant element (%)	47.7	24.2	35.8	49.3	37.0
Official creditors					
Interest (%)	2.1	3.5	4.0	2.7	3.2
Maturity (years)	33.8	30.9	30.5	26.0	29.7
Grant element (%)	56.9	39.4	42.4	53.9	54.8
Private creditors					
Interest (%)	6.4	10.8	7.2	5.6	7.4
Maturity (years)	10.3	10.0	14.1	9.4	5.5
Grant element (%)	12.9	-0.3	15.6	19.4	9.2
Memo:					
Commitments	4.5	26.5	31.5	17.4	17.6
Official creditors	3.6	16.4	23.7	15.0	10.7
Private creditors	0.9	10.1	7.8	2.3	6.9

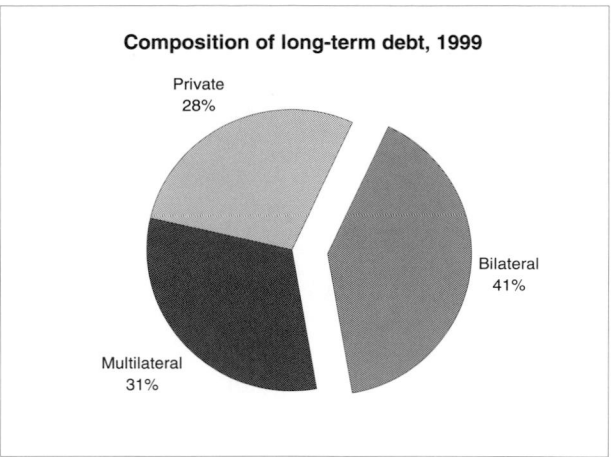

Composition of long-term debt, 1999

Private 28%

Bilateral 41%

Multilateral 31%

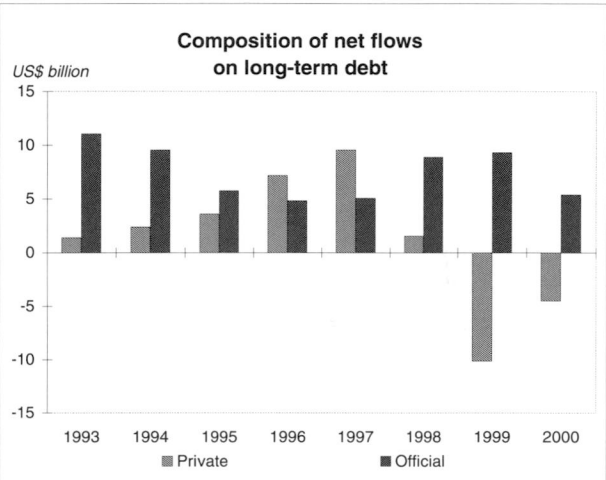

Composition of net flows on long-term debt

US$ billion

■ Private   ■ Official

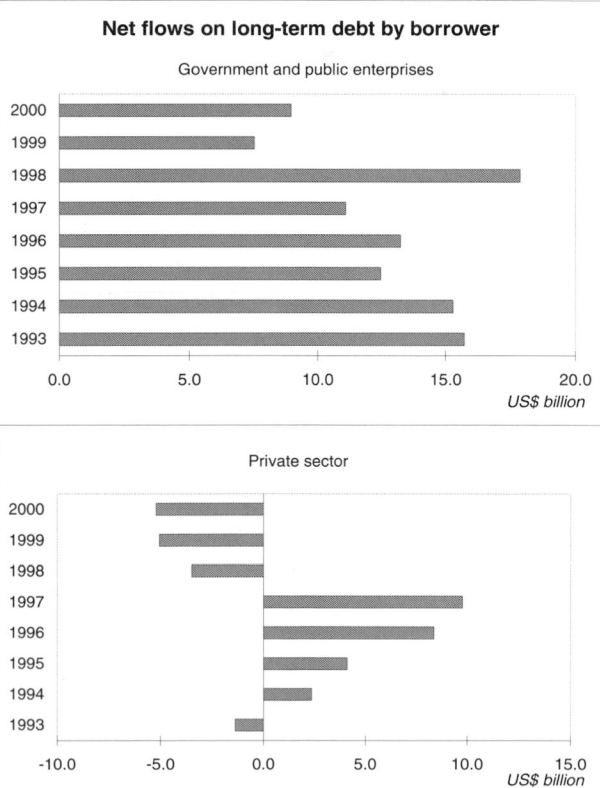

Net flows on long-term debt by borrower

Government and public enterprises

US$ billion

Private sector

US$ billion

MIDDLE-INCOME COUNTRIES

(US$ billion)

	1970	1980	1990	1999	2000
SUMMARY DEBT DATA					
TOTAL DEBT STOCKS (EDT)	**49.2**	**484.2**	**1,039.8**	**1,991.8**	**1,941.4**
Long-term debt (LDOD)	**41.0**	**348.7**	**822.0**	**1,605.5**	**1,576.6**
Public and publicly guaranteed	26.5	286.2	773.5	1,119.7	1,077.6
Private nonguaranteed	14.5	62.5	48.5	485.8	499.0
Use of IMF credit	**0.4**	**7.0**	**23.4**	**54.1**	**40.7**
Short-term debt	**7.8**	**128.5**	**194.4**	**332.2**	**324.1**
of which interest arrears on LDOD	0.0	0.8	39.8	14.1	12.7
Memo:					
IBRD	3.0	17.4	67.5	90.7	92.5
IDA	0.3	1.4	6.5	16.2	16.1
TOTAL FLOWS ON DEBT					
Disbursements	**10.0**	**92.0**	**103.6**	**254.8**	**244.0**
Long-term debt	9.7	88.8	97.9	243.8	236.0
Public and publicly guaranteed	5.9	69.5	84.8	133.4	119.4
Private nonguaranteed	3.8	19.3	13.0	110.4	116.6
IMF purchases	**0.3**	**3.2**	**5.8**	**11.0**	**8.0**
Memo:					
IBRD	0.5	3.6	10.2	12.0	11.3
IDA	0.0	0.1	0.8	1.2	0.8
Principal repayments	**5.5**	**38.4**	**76.7**	**245.5**	**242.1**
Long-term debt	5.0	37.1	70.7	220.2	223.3
Public and publicly guaranteed	2.7	26.7	63.4	113.5	123.0
Private nonguaranteed	2.3	10.4	7.3	106.7	100.3
IMF repurchases	**0.4**	**1.3**	**6.0**	**25.3**	**18.8**
Memo:					
IBRD	0.2	0.8	6.7	7.5	7.5
IDA	0.0	0.0	0.0	0.1	0.2
Net flows on debt	**4.5**	**83.1**	**36.0**	**-11.8**	**-1.3**
of which short-term debt	0.0	29.5	9.0	-21.1	-3.2
Interest payments (INT)	**1.8**	**42.8**	**54.9**	**105.5**	**109.0**
Long-term debt	1.8	28.5	42.1	85.7	89.5
Net transfers on debt	**2.6**	**40.3**	**-18.9**	**-117.3**	**-110.3**
Total debt service (TDS)	**7.3**	**81.2**	**131.6**	**351.0**	**351.1**
AGGREGATE NET RESOURCE FLOWS AND NET TRANSFERS (LONG-TERM)					
NET RESOURCE FLOWS	**7.5**	**61.9**	**64.7**	**245.0**	**236.0**
Net flow of long-term debt (ex. IMF)	4.6	51.7	27.2	23.6	12.7
Foreign direct investment (net)	1.9	4.2	21.9	174.6	160.1
Portfolio equity flows	0.0	0.0	2.3	31.8	48.3
Grants (excluding technical coop.)	0.9	6.0	13.2	14.9	14.7
NET TRANSFERS	**1.3**	**16.5**	**11.1**	**124.7**	**106.2**
Interest on long-term debt	1.8	28.5	42.1	85.7	89.5
Profit remittances on FDI	4.4	16.9	11.4	34.6	39.8
MAJOR ECONOMIC INDICATORS					
Gross national income (GNI)	504.3	2,316.3	3,428.3	4,892.6	5,346.2
Exports of goods & services (XGS)	..	566.8	766.9	1,565.3	1,895.9
of which workers' remittances	..	8.8	18.4	32.0	34.2
Imports of goods & services (MGS)	..	544.9	764.7	1,552.4	1,843.1
International reserves (RES)	..	175.4	196.9	675.5	733.7
Current account balance	..	1.6	-2.9	21.0	42.6
DEBT INDICATORS					
EDT / XGS (%)	..	85.4	135.6	127.3	102.4
EDT / GNI (%)	9.8	20.9	30.3	40.7	36.3
TDS / XGS (%)	..	14.3	17.2	22.4	18.5
INT / XGS (%)	..	7.6	7.2	6.7	5.8
INT / GNI (%)	0.4	1.9	1.6	2.2	2.0
RES / MGS (months)	..	3.9	3.1	5.2	4.8
Short-term / EDT (%)	15.9	26.6	18.7	16.7	16.7
Concessional / EDT (%)	19.3	11.1	12.6	8.6	8.3
Multilateral / EDT (%)	8.7	6.1	11.1	9.9	10.2

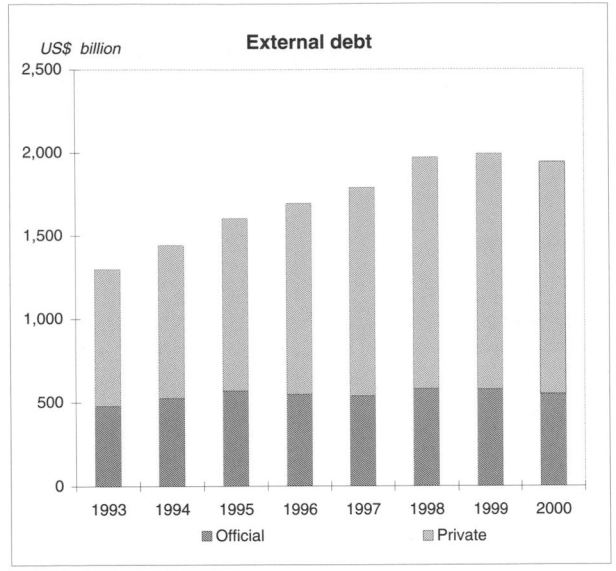

External debt

US$ billion

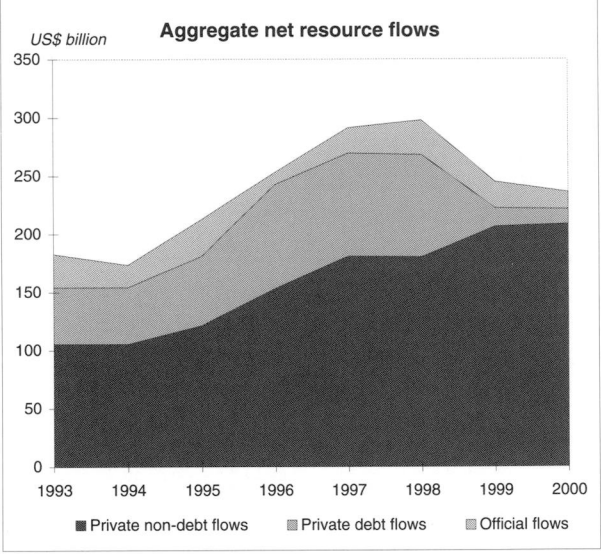

Aggregate net resource flows

US$ billion

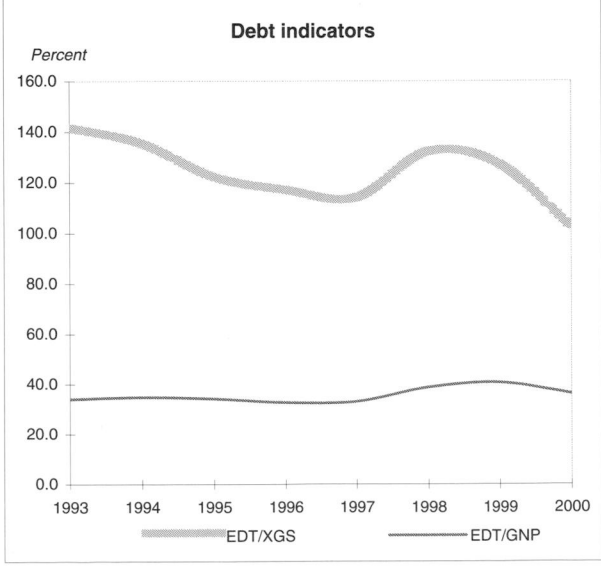

Debt indicators

Percent

MIDDLE-INCOME COUNTRIES

(US$ billion)

	1970	1980	1990	1999	2000
LONG-TERM DEBT					
DEBT OUTSTANDING (LDOD)	**41.0**	**348.7**	**822.0**	**1,605.5**	**1,576.6**
Public and publicly guaranteed	**26.5**	**286.2**	**773.5**	**1,119.7**	**1,077.6**
Official creditors	15.5	108.1	342.1	520.7	506.7
Multilateral	4.3	29.4	115.6	196.9	198.9
Bilateral	11.2	78.6	226.5	323.9	307.8
Private creditors	11.0	178.1	431.4	598.9	570.9
Bonds	1.5	12.3	103.7	352.2	372.8
Private nonguaranteed	14.5	62.5	48.5	485.8	499.0
Bonds	0.0	0.0	0.7	111.8	115.1
DISBURSEMENTS	**9.7**	**88.8**	**97.9**	**243.8**	**236.0**
Public and publicly guaranteed	**5.9**	**69.5**	**84.8**	**133.4**	**119.4**
Official creditors	2.6	19.8	34.3	43.3	37.8
Multilateral	0.9	5.7	16.9	26.3	23.4
Bilateral	1.7	14.1	17.4	17.0	14.5
Private creditors	3.3	49.8	50.5	90.1	81.6
Bonds	0.1	1.6	5.7	53.4	49.9
Private nonguaranteed	**3.8**	**19.3**	**13.0**	**110.4**	**116.6**
Bonds	0.0	0.0	0.6	15.1	19.1
PRINCIPAL REPAYMENTS	**5.0**	**37.1**	**70.7**	**220.2**	**223.3**
Public and publicly guaranteed	**2.7**	**26.7**	**63.4**	**113.5**	**123.0**
Official creditors	1.0	5.3	18.8	35.5	37.9
Multilateral	0.3	1.3	9.6	14.1	17.4
Bilateral	0.7	4.0	9.3	21.4	20.5
Private creditors	1.7	21.4	44.5	78.0	85.1
Bonds	0.1	0.5	5.2	24.9	40.2
Private nonguaranteed	**2.3**	**10.4**	**7.3**	**106.7**	**100.3**
Bonds	0.0	0.0	0.0	11.4	14.8
NET FLOWS ON DEBT	**4.6**	**51.7**	**27.2**	**23.6**	**12.7**
Public and publicly guaranteed	**3.1**	**42.8**	**21.5**	**19.9**	**-3.6**
Official creditors	1.6	14.4	15.5	7.8	-0.1
Multilateral	0.6	4.4	7.4	12.2	6.0
Bilateral	1.0	10.0	8.1	-4.4	-6.1
Private creditors	1.5	28.4	6.0	12.1	-3.6
Bonds	0.0	1.1	0.5	28.6	9.8
Private nonguaranteed	**1.5**	**8.9**	**5.7**	**3.7**	**16.3**
Bonds	0.0	0.0	0.6	3.7	4.3
CURRENCY COMPOSITION OF LONG-TERM DEBT (PERCENT)					
Deutsche mark	9.0	6.4	10.1	7.1	6.2
French franc	4.9	4.9	5.3	2.5	2.4
Japanese yen	0.7	6.1	10.3	11.2	10.5
Pound sterling	5.1	1.7	1.5	0.8	0.6
U.S. dollars	55.2	53.7	42.8	60.3	61.7
Multiple currency	14.2	11.8	15.5	6.7	6.1
All other currencies	9.4	5.8	6.0	5.5	6.6
DEBT STOCK-FLOW RECONCILIATION					
Total change in debt stocks	..	..	55.7	21.6	-50.3
Net flows on debt	4.5	83.1	36.0	-11.8	-1.3
Net change in interest arrears	..	..	12.5	1.2	-1.4
Interest capitalized	..	..	4.1	5.4	4.9
Debt forgiveness or reduction	..	..	-31.6	-2.2	-15.8
Cross-currency valuation	..	..	33.1	-13.5	-32.9
Residual	..	..	1.6	42.5	-3.9
AVERAGE TERMS OF NEW COMMITMENTS					
ALL CREDITORS					
Interest (%)	6.2	10.3	7.7	6.6	7.8
Maturity (years)	16.3	13.8	14.6	13.7	12.5
Grant element (%)	22.8	1.6	13.8	17.0	9.4
Official creditors					
Interest (%)	5.0	6.7	6.4	4.3	6.1
Maturity (years)	23.1	21.3	19.4	16.3	18.5
Grant element (%)	34.1	23.2	24.6	32.0	25.1
Private creditors					
Interest (%)	7.4	12.2	8.7	8.2	8.3
Maturity (years)	9.6	9.7	11.1	11.9	10.6
Grant element (%)	11.8	-10.3	5.7	6.6	4.5
Memo:					
Commitments	7.6	72.1	92.0	135.0	107.3
Official creditors	3.7	25.5	39.5	55.0	25.9
Private creditors	3.8	46.6	52.6	80.1	81.5

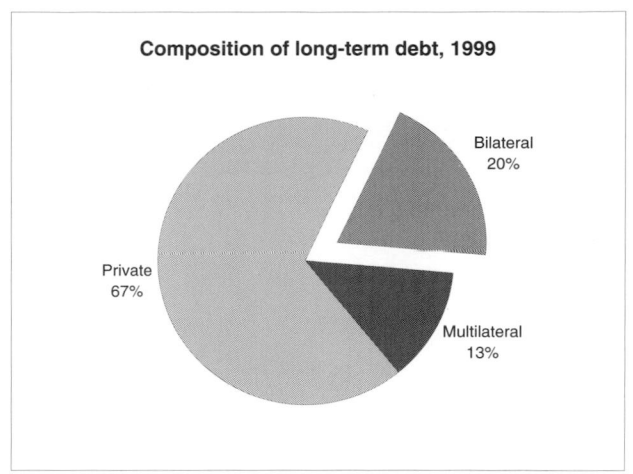

Composition of long-term debt, 1999

Bilateral 20%

Multilateral 13%

Private 67%

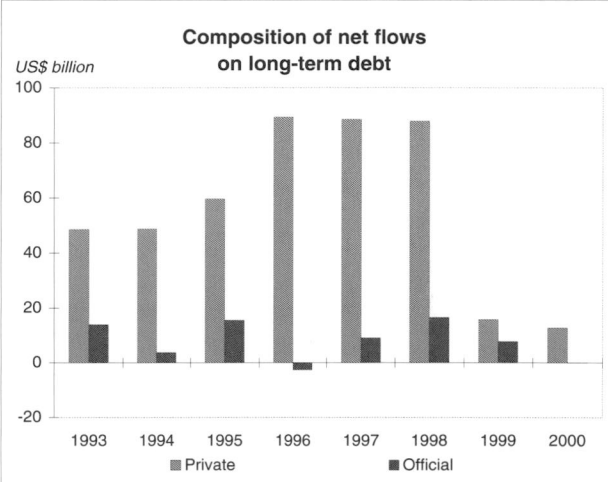

Composition of net flows on long-term debt

■ Private ■ Official

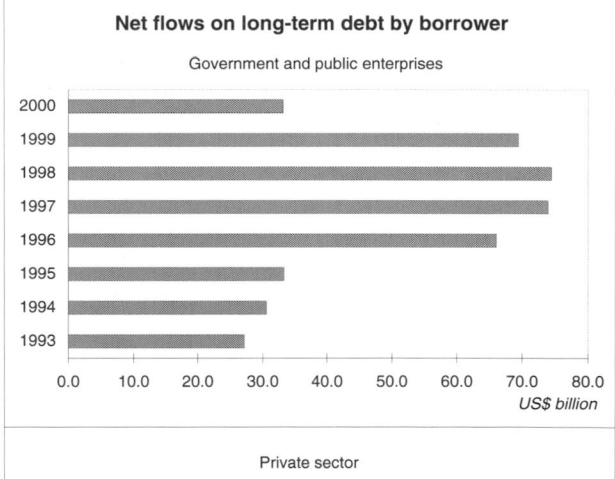

Net flows on long-term debt by borrower

Government and public enterprises

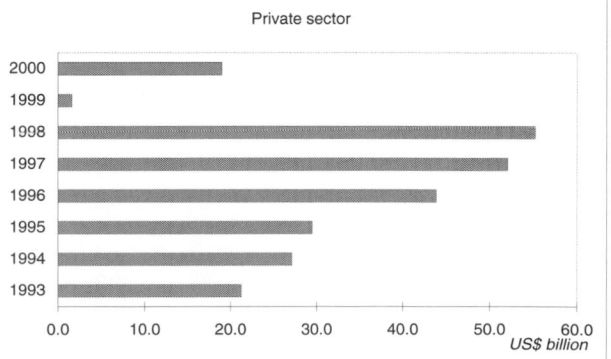

Private sector

SPECIAL PROGRAM OF ASSISTANCE

(US$ billion)

	1970	1980	1990	1999	2000
SUMMARY DEBT DATA					
TOTAL DEBT STOCKS (EDT)	**4.7**	**37.1**	**95.6**	**105.8**	**102.0**
Long-term debt (LDOD)	**4.2**	**29.0**	**79.8**	**91.4**	**88.5**
Public and publicly guaranteed	4.0	25.9	75.7	87.1	84.3
Private nonguaranteed	0.2	3.1	4.1	4.4	4.2
Use of IMF credit	**0.1**	**2.0**	**4.5**	**5.1**	**4.9**
Short-term debt	**0.4**	**6.1**	**11.4**	**9.3**	**8.6**
of which interest arrears on LDOD	0.0	1.6	3.3	2.8	3.1
Memo:					
IBRD	0.2	1.7	4.9	1.2	1.0
IDA	0.2	2.0	12.8	28.9	29.1
TOTAL FLOWS ON DEBT					
Disbursements	**1.0**	**7.7**	**7.1**	**3.9**	**3.9**
Long-term debt	1.0	6.9	6.5	3.4	3.4
Public and publicly guaranteed	1.0	6.3	6.0	3.2	3.4
Private nonguaranteed	0.1	0.6	0.4	0.2	0.0
IMF purchases	**0.0**	**0.7**	**0.6**	**0.5**	**0.5**
Memo:					
IBRD	0.0	0.3	0.3	0.0	0.0
IDA	0.1	0.3	1.8	1.8	2.1
Principal repayments	**0.3**	**2.1**	**3.4**	**3.5**	**2.6**
Long-term debt	0.2	1.9	2.7	3.0	2.2
Public and publicly guaranteed	0.2	1.5	2.3	2.5	2.0
Private nonguaranteed	0.0	0.4	0.4	0.5	0.3
IMF repurchases	**0.0**	**0.2**	**0.7**	**0.5**	**0.4**
Memo:					
IBRD	0.0	0.1	0.4	0.3	0.2
IDA	0.0	0.0	0.0	0.2	0.3
Net flows on debt	**0.8**	**6.1**	**5.2**	**0.5**	**0.2**
of which short-term debt	0.0	0.5	1.6	0.1	-1.1
Interest payments (INT)	**0.1**	**1.9**	**2.4**	**2.0**	**1.8**
Long-term debt	0.1	1.4	1.7	1.7	1.4
Net transfers on debt	**0.6**	**4.2**	**2.9**	**-1.5**	**-1.6**
Total debt service (TDS)	**0.4**	**4.0**	**5.8**	**5.5**	**4.4**
AGGREGATE NET RESOURCE FLOWS AND NET TRANSFERS (LONG-TERM)					
NET RESOURCE FLOWS	**0.9**	**7.8**	**13.2**	**11.1**	**11.4**
Net flow of long-term debt (ex. IMF)	0.8	5.0	3.7	0.4	1.2
Foreign direct investment (net)	-0.1	0.6	0.4	2.0	1.7
Portfolio equity flows	0.0	0.0	0.0	0.0	0.0
Grants (excluding technical coop.)	0.2	2.2	9.1	8.6	8.4
NET TRANSFERS	**0.5**	**5.7**	**11.0**	**8.9**	**9.4**
Interest on long-term debt	0.1	1.4	1.7	1.7	1.4
Profit remittances on FDI	0.3	0.7	0.5	0.5	0.5
MAJOR ECONOMIC INDICATORS					
Gross national income (GNI)	18.5	70.7	90.5	99.3	92.4
Exports of goods & services (XGS)	..	19.7	21.9	27.5	28.5
of which workers' remittances	..	0.4	0.5	0.5	0.6
Imports of goods & services (MGS)	..	28.3	32.6	39.2	38.8
International reserves (RES)	1.5	2.7	3.3	8.0	8.5
Current account balance	..	-7.2	-6.6	-5.8	-4.2
DEBT INDICATORS					
EDT / XGS (%)	..	188.3	436.3	384.5	357.5
EDT / GNI (%)	25.4	52.5	105.6	106.5	110.3
TDS / XGS (%)	..	20.4	26.5	20.1	15.6
INT / XGS (%)	..	9.6	10.8	7.4	6.3
INT / GNI (%)	0.7	2.7	2.6	2.1	1.9
RES / MGS (months)	..	1.2	1.2	2.4	2.6
Short-term / EDT (%)	8.0	16.5	11.9	8.8	8.4
Concessional / EDT (%)	51.7	32.9	46.5	62.7	63.8
Multilateral / EDT (%)	10.0	14.6	28.6	40.4	41.4

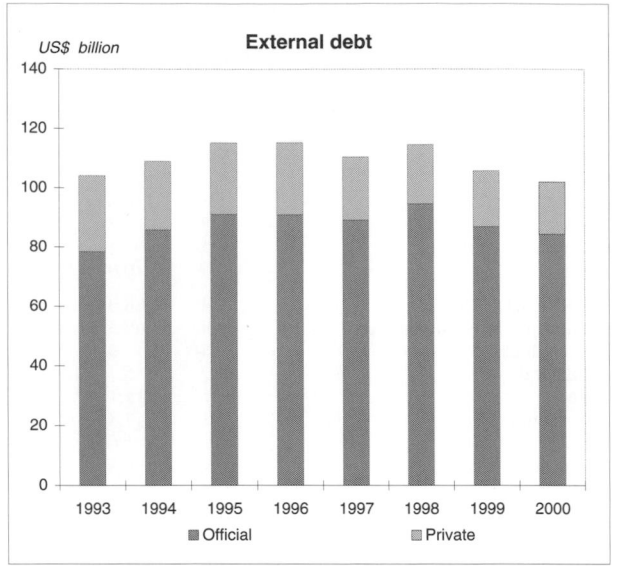

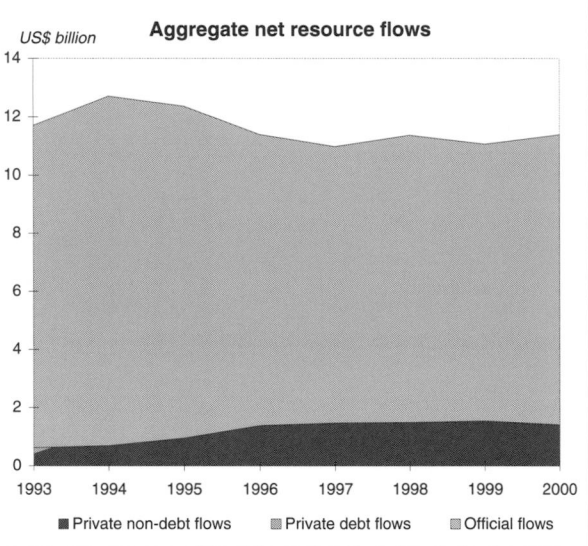

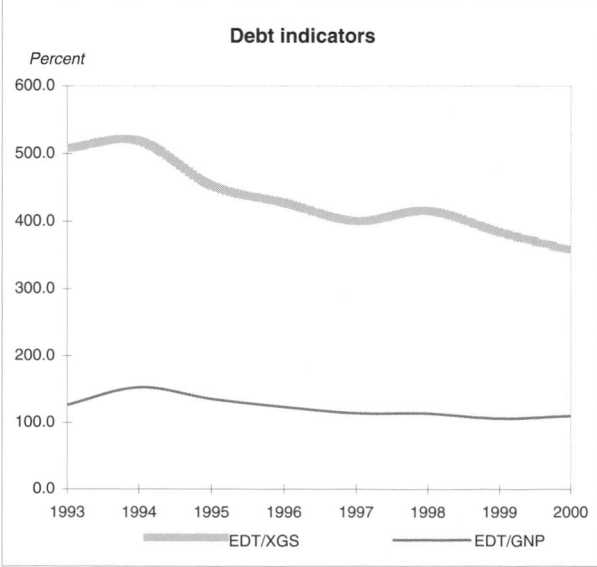

SPECIAL PROGRAM OF ASSISTANCE

(US$ billion)

	1970	1980	1990	1999	2000
LONG-TERM DEBT					
DEBT OUTSTANDING (LDOD)	**4.2**	**29.0**	**79.8**	**91.4**	**88.5**
Public and publicly guaranteed	**4.0**	**25.9**	**75.7**	**87.1**	**84.3**
Official creditors	2.9	16.9	65.3	81.8	79.3
Multilateral	0.5	5.4	27.3	42.7	42.2
Bilateral	2.5	11.5	38.0	39.0	37.1
Private creditors	1.1	9.0	10.4	5.3	5.1
Bonds	0.2	0.0	0.0	2.4	2.3
Private nonguaranteed	0.2	3.1	4.1	4.4	4.2
Bonds	0.0	0.0	0.0	0.3	0.3
DISBURSEMENTS	**1.0**	**6.9**	**6.5**	**3.4**	**3.4**
Public and publicly guaranteed	**1.0**	**6.3**	**6.0**	**3.2**	**3.4**
Official creditors	0.5	3.0	5.3	3.0	3.2
Multilateral	0.1	1.2	3.3	2.6	2.8
Bilateral	0.4	1.7	2.0	0.4	0.5
Private creditors	0.4	3.3	0.7	0.2	0.1
Bonds	0.0	0.0	0.0	0.0	0.0
Private nonguaranteed	**0.1**	**0.6**	**0.4**	**0.2**	**0.0**
Bonds	0.0	0.0	0.0	0.0	0.0
PRINCIPAL REPAYMENTS	**0.2**	**1.9**	**2.7**	**3.0**	**2.2**
Public and publicly guaranteed	**0.2**	**1.5**	**2.3**	**2.5**	**2.0**
Official creditors	0.1	0.4	1.4	2.1	1.7
Multilateral	0.0	0.1	0.9	1.1	1.0
Bilateral	0.1	0.3	0.5	1.0	0.7
Private creditors	0.1	1.1	0.9	0.4	0.3
Bonds	0.0	0.0	0.0	0.0	0.0
Private nonguaranteed	**0.0**	**0.4**	**0.4**	**0.5**	**0.3**
Bonds	0.0	0.0	0.0	0.0	0.0
NET FLOWS ON DEBT	**0.8**	**5.0**	**3.7**	**0.4**	**1.2**
Public and publicly guaranteed	**0.7**	**4.8**	**3.7**	**0.7**	**1.4**
Official creditors	0.4	2.5	3.9	0.9	1.5
Multilateral	0.1	1.1	2.4	1.5	1.8
Bilateral	0.3	1.5	1.5	-0.6	-0.2
Private creditors	0.3	2.2	-0.2	-0.2	-0.1
Bonds	0.0	0.0	0.0	0.0	0.0
Private nonguaranteed	**0.0**	**0.2**	**0.0**	**-0.3**	**-0.2**
Bonds	0.0	0.0	0.0	0.0	0.0
CURRENCY COMPOSITION OF LONG-TERM DEBT (PERCENT)					
Deutsche mark	6.8	5.9	3.9	3.3	3.1
French franc	19.3	17.7	17.4	11.5	10.7
Japanese yen	0.0	7.7	3.2	6.1	5.5
Pound sterling	21.6	5.4	3.7	2.6	2.3
U.S. dollars	21.3	28.4	30.4	50.1	52.3
Multiple currency	6.0	8.8	12.7	8.6	8.9
All other currencies	24.6	23.7	26.4	15.3	14.7
DEBT STOCK-FLOW RECONCILIATION					
Total change in debt stocks	..	..	11.1	-8.8	-3.8
Net flows on debt	0.8	6.1	5.2	0.5	0.2
Net change in interest arrears	..	..	0.2	-0.4	0.3
Interest capitalized	..	..	1.3	0.5	0.3
Debt forgiveness or reduction	..	..	-2.5	-5.0	-0.7
Cross-currency valuation	..	..	4.0	-4.3	-4.1
Residual	..	..	2.8	0.0	0.1
AVERAGE TERMS OF NEW COMMITMENTS					
ALL CREDITORS					
Interest (%)	3.3	6.5	3.3	1.4	0.9
Maturity (years)	27.1	18.4	39.4	35.7	39.4
Grant element (%)	53.2	25.0	52.7	71.4	77.7
Official creditors					
Interest (%)	1.8	3.7	2.7	1.3	0.9
Maturity (years)	34.6	26.9	42.8	37.1	39.6
Grant element (%)	71.0	47.2	58.6	74.0	78.0
Private creditors					
Interest (%)	6.5	9.4	8.5	3.1	3.5
Maturity (years)	10.3	9.6	12.0	19.0	20.6
Grant element (%)	13.0	2.2	5.1	40.6	42.7
Memo:					
Commitments	1.3	8.9	7.7	3.3	3.1
Official creditors	0.9	4.5	6.8	3.0	3.1
Private creditors	0.4	4.4	0.8	0.3	0.0

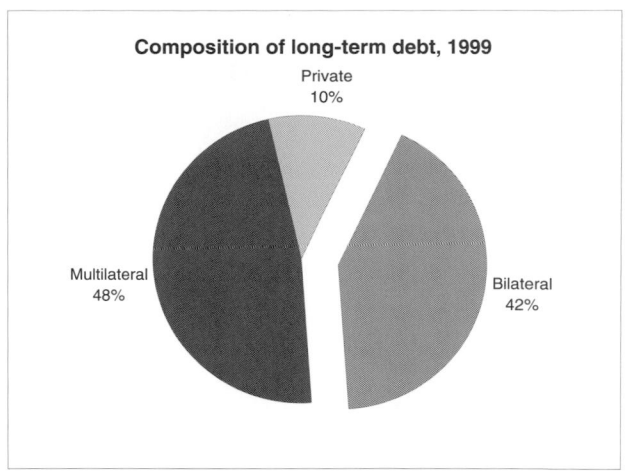

Composition of long-term debt, 1999

Private 10%
Multilateral 48%
Bilateral 42%

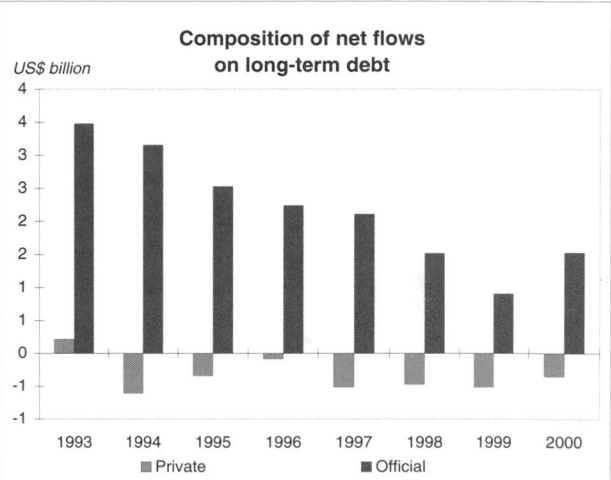

Composition of net flows on long-term debt

US$ billion

■ Private ■ Official

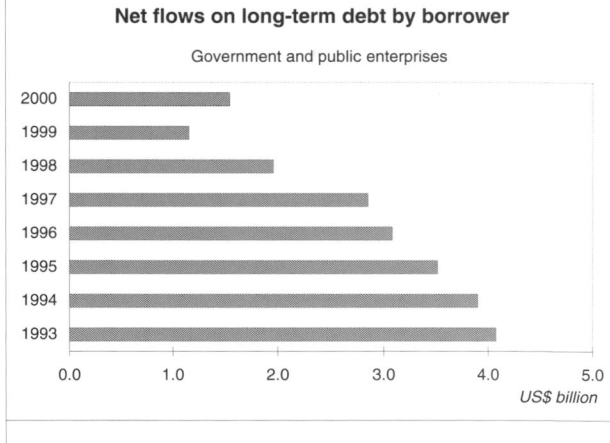

Net flows on long-term debt by borrower

Government and public enterprises

US$ billion

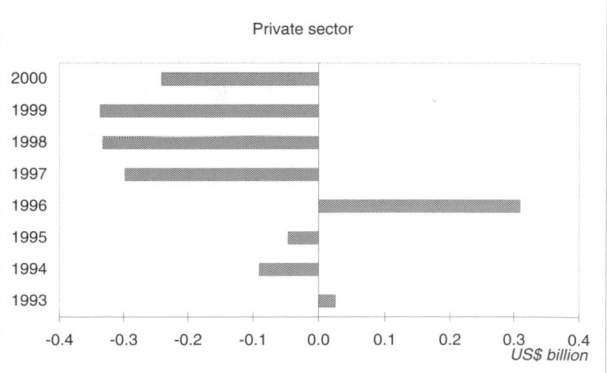

Private sector

US$ billion

POINT LOMA NAZARENE UNIVERSITY

RYAN LIBRARY